ISSUES IN RACE,
ETHNICITY,
GENDER, AND CLASS

SELECTIONS FROM CQ RESEARCHER

D1318345

Los Angeles | London | New Delhi
Singapore | Washington DC

For information:

Pine Forge Press
An Imprint of SAGE Publications, Inc.
2455 Teller Road
Thousand Oaks, California 91320
E-mail: order@sagepub.com

SAGE Publications Ltd.
1 Oliver's Yard
55 City Road
London EC1Y 1SP
United Kingdom

SAGE Publications India Pvt. Ltd.
B 1/I 1 Mohan Cooperative Industrial Area
Mathura Road, New Delhi 110 044
India

SAGE Publications Asia-Pacific Pte. Ltd.
33 Pekin Street #02-01
Far East Square
Singapore 048763

Printed in the United States of America

Library of Congress Cataloging-in-Publication Data

Issues in race, ethnicity, gender, and class : selections from CQ researcher.
    p. cm.
Includes bibliographical references.
ISBN 978-1-4129-7967-2 (pbk.)
    1. United States—Race relations. 2. United States—Ethnic relations. 3. Sexism—United States. 4. Social stratification—United States. I. CQ researcher.

E184.A1I8453 2010
305.800973—dc22   2009034082

This book is printed on acid-free paper.

09   10   11   12   13   10   9   8   7   6   5   4   3   2   1

Acquisitions Editor:	David Repetto
Editorial Assistant:	Nancy Scrofano
Production Editor:	Laureen Gleason
Typesetter:	C&M Digitals (P) Ltd.
Cover Designer:	Candice Harman
Marketing Manager:	Jennifer Reed Banando

Contents

ANNOTATED CONTENTS   vii

PREFACE   xi

CONTRIBUTORS   xiii

1. **Affirmative Action: Is It Time to End Racial Preferences?**   1
    Has affirmative action outlived
       its usefulness?   4
    Does race-based affirmative action
       still face powerful public opposition?   6
    Has affirmative action diverted attention
       from the poor quality of K–12
       education in low-income
       communities?   8
    Background   9
       Righting Wrongs   9
       Reversing Course   11
       Mending It   12
    Current Situation   15
       'Formal Equality'   15
       Over Their Heads?   18
    Outlook   19
       End of the Line?   19
    Notes   20
    Bibliography   22

2. **Human Trafficking and Slavery: Are the World's Nations Doing Enough to Stamp It Out?**   25
    Does buying slaves in order to free
       them solve the problem?   29
    Is the Trafficking Victims Protection
       Act tough enough?   31
    Should most forms of child labor be
       eliminated?   32
    Background   33
       Ancient Practice   33
       Slavery Goes Global   35
       Outlawing Slavery   38
    Current Situation   38
       Human Trafficking   38
       Slavery and Forced Labor   42
    Outlook   43
       Impact of Globalization   43
    Notes   43
    Bibliography   44

3. **Immigration Debate: Can Politicians Find a Way to Curb Illegal Immigration?**   47
    Should employers be penalized for
       hiring illegal immigrants?   50
    Can guest worker programs be fixed?   52

Should illegal immigrants be allowed to attend public colleges and universities? 54
Background 56
  Earlier Waves 56
  Mass Deportation 56
  Immigration Reform 58
  Changes in 1996 62
  Public Opinion 64
Current Situation 65
  Difficult Fix 65
  Federal Inaction 65
Outlook 66
  Tough Talk 66
Notes 67
Bibliography 68

4. Racial Diversity in Public Schools: Has the Supreme Court Dealt a Blow to Integration? 71
Should school systems promote racial diversity in individual schools? 75
Should school systems seek to promote socioeconomic integration in individual schools? 76
Is the focus on diversity interfering with efforts to improve education in all schools? 79
Background 80
  The 'Common School' 80
  'Elusive' Equality 84
  'Diversity' Challenged 86
Current Situation 88
  'Resegregation' Seen 88
  Legal Options Eyed 89
Outlook 90
  'Minimal Impact'? 90
Notes 91
Bibliography 92

5. Reparations Movement: Should Payments Be Made for Historical Wrongs? 95
Should the United States pay reparations to African-American descendants of slaves? 98
Have efforts to collect reparations for Holocaust victims gone too far? 100

Does putting a price tag on suffering diminish that suffering? 102
Background 103
  Ancient Notion 103
  Native Americans 103
  Restitution to "Comfort Women" 105
  Japanese-Americans 106
  The Holocaust 107
Current Situation 109
  Reparations for Slavery 109
Outlook 112
  Starting a Dialogue 112
Notes 112
Bibliography 113

6. American Indians: Are They Making Meaningful Progress at Last? 117
Is the federal government neglecting Native Americans? 120
Have casinos benefited Indians? 122
Would money alone solve American Indians' problems? 123
Background 124
  Conquered Homelands 124
  Forced Assimilation 126
  Termination 128
  Activism 129
  Self-Determination 129
Current Situation 130
  Self-Government 130
  Limits on Gambling 131
  Trust Settlement 134
  Supreme Court Ruling 135
Outlook 135
  Who Is an Indian? 135
Notes 136
Bibliography 139

7. America's Border Fence: Will It Stem the Flow of Illegal Immigrants? 141
Can a border fence stem the flow of illegal immigrants? 145
Would blocking all illegal immigrants hurt or benefit the U.S. economy? 146
Does the fence harm U.S relations with Mexico and other countries? 148

Background	150
Building Walls	150
Bracero Program	150
'Tortilla Curtain' Rises	153
Facing the Fence	155
Current Situation	156
Local Blowback	156
Legal Challenges	158
Straddling the Fence	159
Outlook	159
Demographic Solution	159
Notes	160
Bibliography	162

8. China in Africa: Is China Gaining Control of Africa's Resources? — **165**

Is China benefiting Africa's economy?	168
Do China's policies threaten human rights in Africa?	170
Are China and the West headed for a showdown over Africa's natural resources?	171
Background	174
Breaking Colonial Ties	174
Colonialism's Legacy	175
China's Return	176
Resource Envy	179
Current Situation	181
Communism to Capitalism	181
Africa Reacts	181
Competition Heats Up	182
Outlook	184
Belle of the Ball	184
Notes	185
Bibliography	189

9. Anti-Semitism in Europe: Are Israel's Policies Spurring a New Wave of Hate Crimes? — **191**

Is anti-Semitism on the rise in Europe?	196
Is anti-Zionism a cover-up for anti-Semitism?	198
Is anti-Semitism as severe as racial discrimination against other minorities in Europe?	205
Background	208
'Blood Libel' Slander	208

Restricting Jewish Refugees	209
Forged 'Protocols'	212
Holocaust Denial	214
Postwar Poland's Anti-Semitism	214
Facing the Holocaust	215
Anti-Semitism Re-emerges	216
International Action	216
Current Situation	217
Britain Reacts	217
French Anti-Semitism?	218
Outlook	219
Growing Discomfort	219
Notes	219
Bibliography	222

10. Anti-Americanism: Is Anger at the U.S. Growing? — **225**

Is the United States the primary force behind globalization policies that harm other countries?	228
Is the United States threatening other cultures?	231
Is the "American Century" over?	233
Background	235
The Ungrateful Son	235
Religious Differences	238
Foreign Affairs Bully?	238
American Exceptionalism	239
Current Situation	240
Missteps and Failures	240
Support for Israel	242
A Good Neighbor?	242
Missed Opportunities	243
Outlook	243
Lasting Damage?	243
Notes	244
Bibliography	246

11. Crisis in Darfur: Is There Any Hope for Peace? — **249**

Has genocide occurred in Darfur?	253
Would arresting Sudanese President Bashir do more harm than good?	255
Is China blocking peace in Darfur?	257
Background	259
Ostrich Feathers, Ivory and Slaves	259

Independence and Instability 261
Another Civil War 261
Darfur Erupts 264
Current Situation 265
Indicting Bashir 265
International Betrayal 266
Mission Impossible? 268
Outlook 270
Bleak Future 270
Notes 271
Bibliography 275

12. **The Obama Presidency: Can Barack
Obama Deliver the Change He Promises?** **277**
Is President Obama on the right
track in fixing the U.S. economy? 280
Is President Obama on the right track
in Iraq and Afghanistan? 281
Is President Obama on the right track
in winning support for his programs
in Congress? 287
Background 289
'A Mutt, Like Me' 289
Red, Blue and Purple 294
'Yes, We Can' 295
A Team of Centrists? 300
Current Situation 301
Moving Quickly 301
Working With Congress 304
Outlook 305
Peril and Promise 305
Notes 307
Bibliography 307

13. **Middle-Class Squeeze:
Is More Government Aid Needed?** **311**
Is a stable middle class a thing of the past? 314
Is overconsumption at the
root of the middle class' problems? 315
Are aggressive new government
programs needed to bolster the
middle class? 317
Background 318
Evolving Concept 318
Downward Slide 320
Impact of Globalization 323
Current Situation 326
Narrowing the Gap 326

Cash-Strapped States 328
Outlook 329
Silver Lining? 329
Notes 330
Bibliography 333

14. **Women's Rights: Are Violence and
Discrimination Against Women
Declining?** **335**
Has globalization been good for women? 340
Should governments impose electoral
quotas for women? 342
Do international treaties improve
women's rights? 346
Background 348
'Structural Defects' 348
Push for Protections 348
Women's 'Bill of Rights' 349
Beijing and Beyond 351
Current Situation 354
Rise of Fundamentalism 354
Evolving Gender Policies 355
Political Prospects 358
Impunity for Violence 358
Outlook 359
Economic Integration 359
Notes 361
Bibliography 366

15. **Gay Marriage Showdowns: Will Voters
Bar Marriage for Same-Sex Couples?** **369**
Should same-sex couples be allowed
to marry? 373
Should state constitutions prohibit
marriage for same-sex couples? 375
Should states recognize same-sex
marriages from other states? 376
Background 377
Coming Out 377
Debating Marriage 379
California Showdown 383
Current Situation 384
Gay Marriage Ban Trailing 384
Marriage Cases Waiting 387
Outlook 388
'It's About Marriage' 388
Notes 389
Bibliography 390

Annotated Contents

Affirmative Action:
Is It Time to End Racial Preferences?

Since the 1970s, affirmative action has played a key role in helping minorities get ahead. But many Americans say school and job candidates should be chosen on merit, not race. This November, ballot initiatives in Colorado and Nebraska would eliminate race as a selection criterion for job or school candidates but would allow preferences for those trying to struggle out of poverty, regardless of their race. It's an approach endorsed by foes of racial affirmative action. Big states, meanwhile, including California and Texas, are still struggling to reconcile restrictions on the use of race in college admissions designed to promote diversity. Progress toward that goal has been slowed by a major obstacle: Affirmative action hasn't lessened the stunning racial disparities in academic performance plaguing elementary and high school education. Still, the once open hostility to affirmative action of decades ago has faded. Even some race-preference critics don't want to eliminate it entirely but seek ways to keep diversity without eroding admission and hiring standards.

Human Trafficking and Slavery: Are the
World's Nations Doing Enough to Stamp It Out?

From the villages of Sudan to the factories, sweatshops and brothels of India and South Asia, slavery and human trafficking still flourish. Some 27 million people worldwide are held in some form of slavery, forced prostitution or bonded labor. Some humanitarian groups buy captives' freedom, but critics say that only encourages slave traders to seize more victims. Meanwhile, nearly a million people are forcibly trafficked across international borders annually and held in captivity. Even in the United States, thousands of women and children from overseas are forced to become sex workers. Congress recently strengthened the Trafficking Victims Protection Act, but critics say it is still not tough enough, and that certain U.S. allies that harbor traffickers are treated with "kid gloves" for political reasons.

Immigration Debate: Can Politicians Find a Way to Curb Illegal Immigration?

The number of illegal immigrants in the country has topped 12 million, making immigration once again a central topic of debate. Moreover, with undocumented workers spreading far beyond traditional "gatekeeper" states such as California and Texas, complaints about illegal immigrants have become a daily staple of talk radio. Enacting tougher enforcement policies has become a dominant theme in the 2008 presidential campaign, particularly on the Republican side. Just in the past year, states and localities have passed hundreds of bills to crack down on employers and illegal immigrants seeking public benefits. But Congress has been unable to act, despite a bipartisan deal brokered last year by the Bush administration. A new administration and the next Congress will likely face what has proved so far an impossible task — curbing the number of immigrants without causing labor shortages in key economic sectors such as agriculture and hospitality.

Racial Diversity in Public Schools: Has the Supreme Court Dealt a Blow to Integration?

Fifty years after the Supreme Court outlawed racial segregation in public schools, a new ruling has raised doubts about how far local school boards can go to integrate classrooms. The court's 5-4 ruling in cases from Seattle and Louisville bars school districts from using race as a factor in individual pupil assignments. Like many other school districts, the two school systems used racial classifications to promote diversity in the face of segregated housing patterns. But parents argued the plans improperly denied their children their school of choice because of race. Dissenting justices said the ruling was a setback for racial equality. In a pivotal concurrence, however, Justice Anthony M. Kennedy said schools still have some leeway to pursue racial diversity. Meanwhile, some experts argue that socioeconomic integration — bringing low-income and middle-class students together — is a more effective way to pursue educational equity.

Reparations Movement: Should Payments Be Made for Historical Wrongs?

After the Civil War, efforts to compensate former slaves were blocked. Now calls are getting louder for payments to the descendants of slaves to help the nation come to terms with the injustice of slavery. But opponents worry that reparations would only widen the divide between the races. Meanwhile, survivors of the Nazi Holocaust have had considerable success in obtaining restitution from governments and corporations linked to Hitler's "final solution." Seeking reparations is not about money, they say, but about winning justice for the victims. But some Jewish Americans argue that the reparations movement has turned a historical tragedy into a quest for money. Other mistreated groups recently have picked up the call for reparations, including World War II "comfort women" and Australian Aborigines.

American Indians: Are They Making Meaningful Progress at Last?

Winds of change are blowing through Indian Country, improving prospects for many of the nation's 4.4 million Native Americans. The number of tribes managing their own affairs has increased dramatically, and an urban Indian middle class is quietly taking root. The booming revenues of many Indian-owned casinos seem the ultimate proof that Indians are overcoming a history of mistreatment, poverty and exclusion. Yet most of the gambling houses don't rake in stratospheric revenues. And despite statistical upticks in socioeconomic indicators, American Indians are still poorer, more illness-prone and less likely to be employed than their fellow citizens. Meanwhile, tribal governments remain largely dependent on direct federal funding of basic services — funding that Indian leaders and congressional supporters decry as inadequate. But government officials say they are still providing essential services despite budget cuts.

America's Border Fence: Will It Stem the Flow of Illegal Immigrants?

America is rushing to build 670 miles of fencing along the U.S.-Mexican border by the end of the year. The fence — or wall, as critics along the border call it — is to include 370 miles of fencing intended to stop illegal immigrants on foot and 300 miles of vehicle barriers. To speed construction, the Bush administration is using unprecedented authority granted by Congress to waive environmental-, historic- and cultural-protection laws. No one claims that building physical barriers along roughly a third of America's 2,000-mile Southern border will stem illegal immigration by itself, but supporters believe it is an essential first step in "securing the border," providing a critical line of defense against illegal migration, drug smugglers and even terrorists. Opponents see it as a multibillion-dollar waste that will only shift illegal immigrants toward more dangerous and difficult routes into the country, while doing environmental, cultural and economic damage.

China in Africa: Is China Gaining Control of Africa's Resources?

China is expanding its presence and influence across Africa. Sino-African trade has jumped nearly six-fold in recent years, and some 800 Chinese businesses operate across the continent. After centuries of enslavement, colonization and failed economic policies imposed by the West, Africans are attracted by China's no-strings-attached model of aid and investment. But while China is helping to build new ports and roads, it also is inundating Africa with low-cost goods and labor, resulting in the loss of many African businesses and jobs. Moreover, China's ever-growing demand for oil and other natural resources has led it to invest in oil-rich countries like Sudan, which have been condemned by the West for genocidal practices or human-rights abuses. In response, the United States and other Western nations are playing catch-up in the race for African oil, while scrambling to hold onto their once-historic dominance over Africa's other resources and markets.

Anti-Semitism in Europe: Are Israel's Policies Spurring a New Wave of Hate Crimes?

A wave of anti-Jewish attacks on individuals and synagogues has beset Europe since 2000, when the second Palestinian uprising against Israel's occupation began. In France anti-Semitic youth gangs recently abducted and tortured two young Jewish men, one of whom was murdered. European soccer fans routinely taunt Jewish teams with Hitler salutes and chants, such as "Hamas, Hamas,

Jews to the gas!" And while anti-Semitic attacks overall dipped slightly in some countries, violent assaults on individuals spiked last year, reaching a record high in Britain. Some scholars worry that the "new anti-Semitism" incorporates anti-Zionist language, which has become increasingly acceptable — particularly among Palestinian sympathizers in academia and the media. But Israel's critics — some of whom are Jewish — warn that calling people anti-Semitic because they oppose Israel's treatment of the Palestinians confuses the public. If the charge is made too often, they suggest, people will become cynical and won't recognize genocidal evil when it occurs.

Anti-Americanism: Is Anger at the U.S. Growing?

"We are all Americans," a banner headline in Le Monde declared after the terrorist attacks on Sept. 11, 2001. But the warm embrace from France and the rest of the global community was short-lived. The U.S. invasion of Iraq has unleashed a torrent of anger at the United States. Often directed at President George W. Bush and his policies, it takes aim at everything from the abuses at Abu Ghraib prison to the mounting death toll in Iraq to U.S. policies on climate change. Before the war, anti-Americanism had seemed the province of leftists who demonized capitalism, or those who resented America's unrelenting cultural influence — what some call the McGlobalization of the world. Now, anti-Americanism seems epidemic, especially in the Muslim world but also in Europe, Asia and Latin America. In European intellectual circles it has even become a badge of honor. Ironically, while resentment of the U.S. simmers, people seeking economic opportunity continue to emigrate to the U.S.

Crisis in Darfur: Is There Any Hope for Peace?

More than two years after government and rebel fighters signed a peace agreement in Sudan, violence is still rampant in Darfur. At least 2.4 million people have been displaced and up to 400,000 have died since 2003. And observers say the situation is getting worse. Rebel groups have splintered into more than a dozen warring factions, bandits are attacking relief workers, and drought threatens to make next year among the deadliest in Darfur's history. Despite pressure from religious and human-rights groups, the international community seems unable — or unwilling — to find a lasting solution. A year after the

U.N. authorized the world's largest peacekeeping force in Darfur, only 37 percent of the authorized personnel have been deployed, and no military helicopters have been provided. The International Criminal Court is considering genocide charges against Sudanese President Omar Hassan al-Bashir, but some fear an indictment would trigger more violence than justice. Some say China, Sudan's largest trading partner and arms supplier, should pressure Sudan to end the violence.

The Obama Presidency: Can Barack Obama Deliver the Change He Promises?

As the 44th president of the United States, Barack Hussein Obama confronts a set of challenges more daunting perhaps than any chief executive has faced since the Great Depression and World War II. At home, the nation is in the second year of a recession that Obama warns may get worse before the economy starts to improve. Abroad, he faces the task of withdrawing U.S. forces from Iraq, reversing the deteriorating conditions in Afghanistan and trying to ease the Israeli-Palestinian conflict. Still, Obama begins his four years in office with the biggest winning percentage of any president in 20 years and a strong Democratic majority in both houses of Congress. In addition, as the first African-American president, Obama starts with a reservoir of goodwill from Americans and people and governments around the world. But he began encountering criticism and opposition from Republicans in his first days in office as he filled in the details of his campaign theme: "Change We Can Believe In."

Middle-Class Squeeze: Is More Government Aid Needed?

Millions of families who once enjoyed the American dream of home ownership and upward financial mobility are sliding down the economic ladder — some into poverty. Many have been forced to seek government help for the first time. The plunging fortunes of working families are pushing the U.S. economy deeper into recession as plummeting demand for goods and services creates a downward economic spiral. A consumption binge and growing consumer debt beginning in the 1990s contributed to the middle-class squeeze, but the bigger culprits were exploding prices for necessities such as housing, medical care and college tuition, cuts in employer-funded benefits and, some say, government policies that favored the wealthy. President Barack Obama has promised major aid for the middle class, and some economists are calling for new programs — most notably national health coverage — to assist working Americans.

Women's Rights: Are Violence and Discrimination Against Women Declining?

Women around the world have made significant gains in the past decade, but tens of millions still face significant and often appalling hardship. Most governments now have gender-equality commissions, electoral gender quotas and laws to protect women against violence. But progress has been mixed. A record number of women now serve in parliaments, but only 14 of the world's 193 countries currently have elected female leaders. Globalization has produced more jobs for women, but they still constitute 70 percent of the world's poorest inhabitants and 64 percent of the illiterate. Spousal abuse, female infanticide, genital mutilation, forced abortions, bride-burnings, acid attacks and sexual slavery remain pervasive in some countries, and rape and sexual mutilation have reached epic proportions in the war-torn Democratic Republic of the Congo. Experts say without greater economic, political and educational equality, the plight of women will not improve, and society will continue suffering the consequences.

Gay Marriage Showdowns: Will Voters Bar Marriage for Same-Sex Couples?

The California Supreme Court gave gay rights advocates a major victory in May, ruling the state's constitution guarantees same-sex couples the same marriage rights as opposite-sex pairs. Thousands of same-sex couples from California and around the country have already taken advantage of the decision to obtain legal recognition from California for their unions. Opponents, however, have placed on the state's Nov. 4 ballot a constitutional amendment that would deny marriage rights to same-sex couples by defining marriage as the union of one man and one woman. Similar proposals are on the ballot in Arizona and Florida. The ballot-box showdowns come as nationwide polls indicate support for some legal protection for same-sex couples, but not necessarily marriage equality. In California, one early poll showed support for the ballot measure, but more recently it has been trailing. Opposing groups expect to spend about $20 million each before the campaign ends.

Preface

Is it time to end racial preferences? Can politicians find a way to curb illegal immigration? Are Israel's policies spurring a new wave of hate crimes? Are violence and discrimination against women declining? Will voters bar marriage for same-sex couples? Can Barack Obama deliver the change he promises? These questions and many more are addressed in a unique selection of articles for debate focused on race, ethnicity, gender and class offered exclusively through *CQ Researcher*, CQ Press and SAGE. This collection aims to promote in-depth discussion, facilitate further research, and help students formulate their own positions on crucial issues.

This first edition includes fifteen up-to-date reports by *CQ Researcher*, an award-winning weekly policy brief that brings complicated issues down to earth. This book is intended to supplement core courses in the sociology curriculum focused on race, ethnicity, gender and class. The contents are modeled after our text by Joseph F. Healey titled *Race, Ethnicity, Gender, and Class, Fifth Edition (Election Update)*, and is similar to all of the mainstream texts in this area. This collection was carefully crafted to cover a range of issues, including affirmative action, immigration, hate crimes, women's rights, gay marriage, the Obama presidency and much more. This reader will help your students gain a deeper, more critical perspective of timely and important race, ethnicity, gender and class issues.

CQ RESEARCHER

CQ Researcher was founded in 1923 as *Editorial Research Reports* and was sold primarily to newspapers as a research tool. The magazine was renamed and redesigned in 1991 as *CQ Researcher*. Today, students are its primary audience. While still used by hundreds of journalists and newspapers, many of which reprint portions of the reports, the *Researcher's* main subscribers are now high school, college and public libraries. In 2002, *Researcher* won the American Bar Association's coveted Silver Gavel award for magazine excellence for a series of nine reports on civil liberties and other legal issues.

Researcher staff writers — all highly experienced journalists — sometimes compare the experience of writing a *Researcher* report to drafting a college term paper. Indeed, there are many similarities. Each report is as long as many term papers — about 11,000 words — and is written by one person without any significant outside help. One of the key differences is that writers interview leading experts, scholars and government officials for each issue.

Like students, staff writers begin the creative process by choosing a topic. Working with the *Researcher's* editors, the writer identifies a controversial subject that has important public policy implications. After a topic is selected, the writer embarks on one to two weeks of intense research. Newspaper and magazine articles are clipped or downloaded, books are ordered and information is gathered from a wide variety of sources, including interest groups, universities and the government. Once the writers are well informed, they develop a detailed outline, and begin the interview process. Each report requires a minimum of ten to fifteen interviews with academics, officials, lobbyists and people working in the field. Only after all interviews are completed does the writing begin.

CHAPTER FORMAT

Each issue of *CQ Researcher*, and therefore each selection in this book, is structured in the same way. Each begins with an overview, which briefly summarizes the areas that will be explored in greater detail in the rest of the chapter. The next section chronicles important and current debates on the topic under discussion and is structured around a number of key questions. These questions are usually the subject of much debate among practitioners and scholars in the field. Hence, the answers presented are never conclusive but detail the range of opinion on the topic.

Next, the "Background" section provides a history of the issue being examined. This retrospective covers important legislative measures, executive actions and court decisions that illustrate how current policy has evolved. Then the "Current Situation" section examines contemporary policy issues, legislation under consideration and legal action being taken. Each selection concludes with an "Outlook" section, which addresses possible regulation, court rulings and initiatives from Capitol Hill and the White House over the next five to ten years.

Each report contains features that augment the main text: two to three sidebars that examine issues related to the topic at hand, a pro versus con debate between two experts, a chronology of key dates and events and an annotated bibliography detailing major sources used by the writer.

ACKNOWLEDGMENTS

We wish to thank many people for helping to make this collection a reality. Tom Colin, managing editor of *CQ Researcher*, gave us his enthusiastic support and cooperation as we developed this edition. He and his talented staff of editors and writers have amassed a first-class library of *Researcher* reports, and we are fortunate to have access to that rich cache. We also wish to thank our colleagues at CQ Press, a division of SAGE and a leading publisher of books, directories, research publications and Web products on U.S. government, world affairs and communications. They have forged the way in making these readers a useful resource for instruction across a range of undergraduate and graduate courses.

Some readers may be learning about *CQ Researcher* for the first time. We expect that many readers will want regular access to this excellent weekly research tool. For subscription information or a no-obligation free trial of *CQ Researcher*, please contact CQ Press at www.cqpress .com or toll-free at 1-866-4CQ-PRESS (1-866-427-7737).

We hope that you will be pleased by this edition of *Issues in Race, Ethnicity, Gender, and Class: Selections From CQ Researcher*. We welcome your feedback and suggestions for future editions. Please direct comments to David Repetto, Sr. Acquisitions Editor, Pine Forge Press, an Imprint of SAGE Publications, 2455 Teller Road, Thousand Oaks, CA 91320, or david.repetto@sagepub .com.

—The Editors of SAGE

Contributors

Thomas J. Billitteri is a *CQ Researcher* staff writer based in Fairfield, Pennsylvania, who has more than 30 years' experience covering business, nonprofit institutions and public policy for newspapers and other publications. His recent *CQ Researcher* reports include "Campaign Finance," "Human Rights in China" and "Financial Bailout." He holds a BA in English and an MA in journalism from Indiana University.

Karen Foerstel is a freelance writer who has worked for the Congressional Quarterly *Weekly Report* and *Daily Monitor, The New York Post* and *Roll Call,* a Capitol Hill newspaper. She has published two books on women in Congress, *Climbing the Hill: Gender Conflict in Congress* and *The Biographical Dictionary of Women in Congress.* She currently lives and works in London. She has worked in Africa with ChildsLife International, a nonprofit that helps needy children around the world, and with Blue Ventures, a marine conservation organization that protects coral reefs in Madagascar.

Sarah Glazer, a London-based freelancer, is a regular contributor to *CQ Researcher.* Her articles on health, education and social-policy issues have appeared in *The New York Times, The Washington Post, The Public Interest* and *Gender and Work,* a book of essays. Her most recent *CQ Global Researcher* report was "Radical Islam in Europe." She graduated from the University of Chicago with a BA in American history.

Alan Greenblatt is a staff writer at *Governing* magazine. He previously covered elections, agriculture and military spending for

CQ Weekly, where he won the National Press Club's Sandy Hume Award for political journalism. He graduated from San Francisco State University in 1986 and received a master's degree in English literature from the University of Virginia in 1988. His recent *CQ Researcher* reports include "Sex Offenders" and "Pension Crisis."

Kenneth Jost graduated from Harvard College and Georgetown University Law Center. He is the author of the *Supreme Court Yearbook* and editor of *The Supreme Court from A to Z* (both CQ Press). He was a member of the *CQ Researcher* team that won the 2002 ABA Silver Gavel Award. His previous reports include "School Desegregation," "Black Colleges" and "Affirmative Action."

Reed Karaim, a freelance writer living in Tucson, Arizona, has written for *The Washington Post, U.S. News and World Report, Smithsonian, American Scholar, USA Weekend* and other publications. He is the author of the novel *If Men Were Angels,* which was selected for the Barnes & Noble Discover Great New Writers series. He is also the winner of the Robin Goldstein Award for Outstanding Regional Reporting and other journalism awards. Karaim is a graduate of North Dakota State University in Fargo, North Dakota.

Peter Katel is a *CQ Researcher* staff writer who previously reported on Haiti and Latin America for *Time* and *Newsweek* and covered the Southwest for newspapers in New Mexico. He has received several journalism awards, including the Bartolomé Mitre Award for coverage of drug trafficking, from the Inter-American Press Association. He holds an AB in university studies from the University of New Mexico. His recent reports include "Oil Jitters," "Race and Politics" and "Rise in Counterinsurgency."

Sam Loewenberg, now based in Berlin, is an award-winning freelance writer who has reported on global issues for *The New York Times, The Economist, The Washington Post,* and *Newsweek* among others. He covered the terrorist bombings in both Madrid and London as well as the anti-globalization movement in Brazil. He is a former Columbia University Knight-Bagehot Journalism Fellow.

David Masci specializes in science, religion and foreign policy issues. Before joining *The CQ Researcher* in 1996, he was a reporter at Congressional Quarterly's *Daily Monitor* and *CQ Weekly.* He holds a law degree from The George Washington University and a BA in medieval history from Syracuse University. His recent reports include "Rebuilding Iraq" and "Torture."

1

Affirmative Action

Is It Time to End Racial Preferences?

Peter Katel

Law student Jessica Peck Corry, executive director of the Colorado Civil Rights Initiative, supports Constitutional Amendment 46, which would prohibit all government entities in Colorado from discriminating for or against anyone because of race, ethnicity or gender. Attorney Melissa Hart counters that the amendment would end programs designed to reach minority groups.

JESSICA PECK CORRY
Colorado Civil Rights Initiative

MELISSA HART
Coloradans for Equal Opportunity

TV screenshot courtesy "DemocracyNow"

From *CQ Researcher*,
October 17, 2008.

No white politician could have gotten the question George Stephanopoulos of ABC News asked Sen. Barack Obama. "You said . . . that affluent African-Americans, like your daughters, should probably be treated as pretty advantaged when they apply to college," he began. "How specifically would you recommend changing affirmative action policies so that affluent African-Americans are not given advantages and poor, less affluent whites are?"[1]

The Democratic presidential nominee, speaking during a primary election debate in April, said his daughters' advantages should weigh more than their skin color. "You know, Malia and Sasha, they've had a pretty good deal."[2]

But a white applicant who has overcome big odds to pursue an education should have those circumstances taken into account, Obama said. "I still believe in affirmative action as a means of overcoming both historic and potentially current discrimination," Obama said, "but I think that it can't be a quota system and it can't be something that is simply applied without looking at the whole person, whether that person is black, or white or Hispanic, male or female."[3]

Supporting affirmative action on the one hand, objecting to quotas on the other — Obama seemed to know he was threading his way through a minefield. Decades after it began, affirmative action is seen by many whites as nothing but a fancy term for racial quotas designed to give minorities an unfair break. Majority black opinion remains strongly pro-affirmative action, on the grounds that the legacy of racial discrimination lives on. Whites and blacks are 30 percentage points apart on the issue, according to a 2007 national survey by the nonpartisan Pew Research Center.[4]

Americans Support Boost for Disadvantaged

A majority of Americans believe that individuals born into poverty can overcome their disadvantages and that society should be giving them special help (top poll). Fewer, however, endorse race-based affirmative action as the way to help (bottom).

	Agree	Disagree
We should help people who are working hard to overcome disadvantages and succeed in life.	93%	6
People who start out with little and work their way up are the real success stories.	91	7
Some people are born poor, and there's nothing we can do about that.	26	72
We shouldn't give special help at all, even to those who started out with more disadvantages than most.	16	81

If there is only one seat available, which student would you admit to college, the high-income student or the low-income student?	Percentage selecting:	
	Low-income student	High-income student
If both students get the same admissions test score?	63%	3%
If low-income student gets a slightly lower test score?	33	54
If the low-income student is also black, and the high-income student is white?	36	39
If the low-income student is also Hispanic, and the high-income student is not Hispanic?	33	45

Source: Anthony P. Carnevale and Stephen J. Rose, "Socioeconomic Status, Race/ Ethnicity, and Selective College Admissions," The Century Foundation, March 2003

Now, with the candidacy of Columbia University and Harvard Law School graduate Obama turning up the volume on the debate, voters in two states will be deciding in November whether preferences should remain in effect in state government hiring and state college admissions.

Originally, conflict over affirmative action focused on hiring. But during the past two decades, the debate has shifted to whether preference should be given in admissions to top-tier state schools, such as the University of California at Los Angeles (UCLA) based on race, gender or ethnic background. Graduating from such schools is seen as an affordable ticket to the good life, but there aren't enough places at these schools for all applicants, so many qualified applicants are rejected.

Resentment over the notion that some applicants got an advantage because of their ancestry led California voters in 1996 to ban affirmative action in college admissions. Four years later, the Florida legislature, at the urging of then-Gov. Jeb Bush, effectively eliminated using race as an admission standard for colleges and universities. And initiatives similar to the California referendum were later passed in Washington state and then in Michigan, in 2006.

Race is central to the affirmative action debate because the doctrine grew out of the civil rights movement and the Civil Rights Act of 1964, which outlawed discrimination based on race, ethnicity or gender. The loosely defined term generally is used as a synonym for advantages — "preferences" — that employers and schools extend to members of a particular race, national origin or gender.

"The time has come to pull the plug on race-based decision-making," says Ward Connerly, a Sacramento, Calif.-based businessman who is the lead organizer of the Colorado and Nebraska ballot initiative campaigns, as well as earlier ones elsewhere. "The Civil Rights Act of 1964 talks about treating people equally without regard to race, color or national origin. When you talk about civil rights, they don't just belong to black people."

Connerly, who is black, supports extending preferences of some kind to low-income applicants for jobs — as long as the beneficiaries aren't classified by race or gender.

But affirmative action supporters say that approach ignores reality. "If there are any preferences in operation in our society, they're preferences given to people with white skin and who are men and who have financial and other advantages that come with that," says Nicole Kief, New York-based state strategist for the American Civil

Liberties Union's racial justice program, which is opposing the Connerly-organized ballot initiative campaigns.

Yet, of the 38 million Americans classified as poor, whites make up the biggest share: 17 million people. Blacks account for slightly more than 9 million and Hispanics slightly less. Some 576,000 Native Americans are considered poor. Looking beyond the simple numbers, however, reveals that far greater percentages of African-Americans and Hispanics are likely to be poor: 25 percent of African-Americans and 20 percent of Hispanics live below the poverty line, but only 10 percent of whites are poor.[5]

In 2000, according to statistics compiled by *Chronicle of Higher Education* Deputy Editor Peter Schmidt, the average white elementary school student attended a school that was 78 percent white, 9 percent black, 8 percent Hispanic, 3 percent Asian and 30 percent poor. Black or Hispanic children attended a school in which 57 percent of the student body shared their race or ethnicity and about two-thirds of the students were poor.[6]

These conditions directly affect college admissions, according to The Century Foundation. The liberal think tank reported in 2003 that white students account for 77 percent of the students at high schools in which the greatest majority of students go on to college. Black students account for only 11 percent of the population at these schools, and Hispanics 7 percent.[7]

A comprehensive 2004 study by the Urban Institute, a nonpartisan think tank, found that only about half of black and Hispanic high school students graduate, compared to 75 and 77 percent, respectively, of whites and Asians.[8]

Politically conservative affirmative action critics cite these statistics to argue that focusing on college admissions and hiring practices rather than school reform was a big mistake. The critics get some support from liberals who want to keep affirmative action — as long as it's based on socioeconomic status instead of race. "Affirmative action based on race was always kind of a cheap and quick fix that bypassed the hard work of trying to develop the talents of low-income minority students generally," says Richard D. Kahlenberg, a senior fellow at The Century Foundation.

Basing affirmative action on class instead of race wouldn't exclude racial and ethnic minorities, Kahlenberg argues, because race and class are so closely intertwined.

President Lyndon B. Johnson noted that connection in a major speech that laid the philosophical foundations for affirmative action programs. These weren't set up for another five years, a reflection of how big a change they represented in traditional hiring and promotion practices, where affirmative action began. "You do not take a person who, for years, has been hobbled by chains and liberate him, bring him up to the starting line of a race and then say, 'You are free to compete with all the others,' and still justly believe that you have been completely fair," Johnson said in "To Fulfill These Rights," his 1965 commencement speech at Howard University in Washington, D.C., one of the country's top historically black institutions.[9]

Elite Schools Graduate Fewest Minorities

Among college-bound blacks and Hispanics, larger percentages graduated from "less advantaged" high schools than from the "most advantaged" schools.

Percentage of High School Seniors Going to Four-year Colleges, by Race

Attended More-Advantaged Schools

6% 11% 7% 77%
7% 17% 9% 76%
4% 13% 14% 68%
9% 13% 13% 65%

Attended Less-Advantaged Schools

Asian / Black / Hispanic / White

Source: Anthony P. Carnevale and Stephen J. Rose, "Socioeconomic Status, Race/Ethnicity, and Selective College Admissions," Century Foundation, March 2003

Liasion/Lara Joe Regan

Asian-American enrollment at the University of California at Berkeley rose dramatically after California voters in 1996 approved Proposition 209, a ballot initiative that banned affirmative action at all state institutions. Enrollment of African-American, Hispanic and Native American students, however, plunged.

By the late 1970s, a long string of U.S. Supreme Court decisions began setting boundaries on affirmative action, partly in response to white job and school applicants who sued over "reverse discrimination." The court's bottom line: Schools and employers could take race into account, but not as a sole criterion. Setting quotas based on race, ethnicity or gender was prohibited. (The prohibition of gender discrimination effectively ended the chances for passage of the proposed Equal Rights Amendment [ERA], which feminist organizations had been promoting since 1923. The Civil Rights Act, along with other legislation and court decisions, made many supporters of women's rights "lukewarm" about the proposed amendment, Roberta W. Francis, then chair of the National Council of Women's Organizations' ERA task force, wrote in 2001.)[10]

The high court's support for affirmative action has been weakening through the years. Since 1991 the court has included Justice Clarence Thomas, the lone black member and a bitter foe of affirmative action. In his 2007 autobiography, Thomas wrote that his Yale Law School degree set him up for rejection by major law firm interviewers. "Many asked pointed questions unsubtly suggesting that they doubted I was as smart as my grades indicated," he wrote. "Now I knew what a law degree from Yale was worth when it bore the taint of racial preference."[11]

Some of Thomas' black classmates dispute his view of a Yale diploma's worth. "Had he not gone to a school like Yale, he would not be sitting on the Supreme Court," said William Coleman III, a Philadelphia attorney who was general counsel to the U.S. Army in the Clinton administration.[12]

But that argument does not seem to impress Thomas, who was in a 5-4 minority in the high court's most recent affirmative action ruling, in which the justices upheld the use of race in law-school admissions at the University of Michigan. But even Justice Sandra Day O'Connor, who wrote the majority opinion, signaled unease with her position. In 25 years, she wrote, affirmative action would "no longer be necessary."[13]

Paradoxically, an Obama victory on Nov. 4 might be the most effective anti-affirmative action event of all.

"The primary rationale for affirmative action is that America is institutionally racist and institutionally sexist," Connerly, an Obama foe, told The Associated Press. "That rationale is undercut in a major way when you look at the success of Sen. [Hillary Rodham] Clinton and Sen. Obama."

Asked to respond to Connerly's remarks, Obama appeared to draw some limits of his own on affirmative action. "Affirmative action is not going to be the long-term solution to the problems of race in America," he told a July convention of minority journalists, "because, frankly, if you've got 50 percent of African-American or Latino kids dropping out of high school, it doesn't really matter what you do in terms of affirmative action; those kids are not getting into college."[14]

As critics and supporters discuss the future of affirmative action, here are some of the questions being debated:

Has affirmative action outlived its usefulness?

In the United States of the late 1960s and '70s, even some outright opponents of race-based affirmative action conceded that it represented an attempt to deal with the consequences of longstanding, systematic racial discrimination, which had legally ended only shortly before.

But ever since opposition to affirmative action began growing in the 1980s, its opponents themselves have invoked the very principles that the civil rights movement had embraced in its fight to end discrimination. Taking a job or school applicant's race or ethnicity into account is immoral, opponents argue, even for supposedly benign purposes. And a policy of racial/ethnic preferences, by definition, cannot lead to equality.

In today's United States, critics say, minority applicants don't face any danger that their skin color or ethnic heritage will hold them back. Instead, affirmative-action beneficiaries face continuing skepticism from others — and even from themselves, that they somehow were given an advantage that their academic work didn't entitle them to receive.

Meanwhile, opponents and supporters readily acknowledge that a disproportionate share of black and Latino students receive substandard educations, starting in and lasting through high school. Affirmative action hasn't eliminated the link between race/ethnicity and poverty and academic deprivation, they agree.

Few Poor Students Attend Top Schools

Nearly three-quarters of students entering tier 1 colleges and universities come from the wealthiest families, but only 3 percent of students from the bottom quartile enter top schools. Far more students from poorer backgrounds enroll in less prestigious schools, and even more in community colleges.

Socioeconomic Status of Entering College Classes

School prestige level	First quartile (lowest)	Second quartile	Third quartile	Fourth quartile (highest)
Tier 1	3%	6%	17%	74%
Tier 2	7	18	29	46
Tier 3	10	19	36	35
Tier 4	16	21	28	35
Community Colleges	21	30	27	22

Source: Anthony P. Carnevale and Stephen J. Rose, "Socioeconomic Status, Race/ Ethnicity, and Selective College Admissions," The Century Foundation, March 2003

Critics of race preferences, however, say they haven't narrowed the divide that helped to trigger affirmative action in the first place. Affirmative action advocates favor significantly reforming K-12 education while simultaneously giving a leg up to minorities who managed to overcome their odds at inadequate public schools.

And some supporters say affirmative action is important for other reasons, which transcend America's racial history. Affirmative action helps to ensure continuation of a democratic political culture, says James E. Coleman Jr., a professor at Duke University Law School.

"It's not just about discrimination or past discrimination," says Coleman, who attended all-black schools when growing up and then graduated from Harvard College and Columbia Law School in the early 1970s, during the early days of affirmative action. "It's in our self-interest. We want leaders of all different backgrounds, all different races; we ought to educate them together."

But Connerly, the California businessman behind anti-affirmative action ballot initiatives, says that race and gender preferences are the wrong tool with which to promote diversity, because they effectively erode

academic standards. "Excellence can be achieved by any group of people," says Connerly, a former member of the University of California Board of Regents. "So we will keep the standards where they ought to be, and we will expect people to meet those standards."

But legislators interested in a "quick fix" have found it simpler to mandate diversity than to devise ways to improve schools. "There are times when someone has to say, 'This isn't right. We're going to do something about it,' " Connerly says. "But in the legislative process, I can find no evidence of leadership anywhere."

Like others, Connerly also cites the extraordinary academic achievements of Asian-American students — who haven't benefited from affirmative action. Affirmative action supporters don't try to dispute that point. "At the University of California at Berkeley, 40 percent of the students are Asian," says Terry H. Anderson, a history professor at Texas A&M University in College Station. "What does that say about family structure? It makes a big statement. Family structure is so important, and it's something that affirmative action can't help at all."

But if encouraging minority-group enrollment at universities doesn't serve as a social and educational cure-all, says Anderson, who has written a history of affirmative

Few Poor Students Score High on SAT

Two-thirds of students who scored at least 1300 on the SAT came from families ranking in the highest quartile of socioeconomic status, compared with only 3 percent of students from the lowest-income group. Moreover, more than one-fifth of those scoring under 1000 — and 37 percent of non-test-takers — come from the poorest families.

SAT Scores by Family Socioeconomic Status*

Score	First Quartile (lowest)	Second Quartile	Third Quartile	Fourth Quartile (highest)
>1300	3%	10%	22%	66%
1200–1300	4	14	23	58
1100–1200	6	17	29	47
1000–1100	8	24	32	36
<1000	21	25	30	24
Non-taker	37	30	22	10

* The maximum score is 1600

Note: Percentages do not add to 100 due to rounding.

Source: Anthony P. Carnevale and Stephen J. Rose, "Socioeconomic Status, Race/ Ethnicity, and Selective College Admissions," The Century Foundation, March 2003

Does race-based affirmative action still face powerful public opposition?

At the state and federal level, affirmative action has generated enormous conflict over the decades, played out in a long chain of lawsuits and Supreme Court decisions, as well as the hard-fought ballot initiatives this year in Arizona, Missouri and Oklahoma — all three of which ended in defeat for race, ethnic and gender preferences.

But today's political agenda — dominated by the global financial crisis, the continuing downward slide of real estate prices, the continuing conflict in Iraq and escalated combat in Afghanistan — would seem to leave little space for a reignited affirmative action conflict.

Nevertheless, supporters and opponents of affirmative action fought hard in five states over proposed ballot initiatives, two of which will go before voters in November.

Nationally, the nonpartisan Pew Research Center reported last year that black and white Americans are divided by a considerable margin on whether minority group members should get preferential treatment. Among blacks, 57 answered yes, but only 27 percent of whites agreed. That gap was somewhat bigger in 1991, when 68 percent of blacks and only 17 percent of whites favored preferences.[15]

Obama's statement to ABC News' Stephanopoulos that his daughters shouldn't benefit from affirmative action reflected awareness of majority sentiment against race preference.[16]

Still, the exchange led to some predictions that it would resurface. "The issue of affirmative action is likely to dog Sen. Obama on the campaign trail as he seeks to win over white, blue-collar voters in battleground states like Michigan," The Wall Street Journal predicted in June.[17]

Just two and a half weeks before the election, that forecast hadn't come to pass. However, earlier in the year interest remained strong enough that campaigners for

action, the policy still serves a valuable purpose. "It's become part of our culture. On this campus, it's been 'out' to be racist for years and years. I'm looking at kids born in 1990; they just don't feel self-conscious about race or gender, they just expect to be treated equally."

Standing between the supporters and the enemies of affirmative action's racial/ethnic preferences are the affirmative action reformers. "I don't think it's time to completely abolish all forms of affirmative action," says the Century Foundation's Kahlenberg. "But it's clear there are strong legal, moral and political problems with relying solely on race."

And at the practical level, race isn't the only gauge of hardship that some students must overcome, even to be capable of competing for admission to a top-tier school. "There are students from low-income backgrounds," Kahlenberg says, "who aren't given the same opportunities as wealthier students are given, and they deserve a leg up in admissions. Someone's test scores and grades are a reflection not only of how hard they work and how talented they are, but what sorts of opportunities they've had."

state ballot initiatives were able to gather 136,589 signatures in Nebraska and about 130,000 in Colorado to require that the issue be put before voters in those states.

Meanwhile, the initiative efforts in Arizona, Missouri and Oklahoma were doomed after the validity of petition signatures was challenged in those states. Connerly, the chief organizer of the initiatives, blames opponents' tactics and, in Oklahoma, an unusually short, 90-day window during which signatures must be collected. But once initiatives get on ballots, he says, voters approve them. "There is something about the principle of fairness that most people understand."

Without congressional legislation prohibiting preferences, Connerly says, the initiatives are designed to force state governments "to abide by the moral principle that racial discrimination — whether against a white or black or Latino or Native American — is just wrong."

But reality can present immoral circumstances as well, affirmative action defenders argue. "Racial discrimination and gender discrimination continue to present obstacles to people of color and women," says the American Civil Liberties Union's (ACLU) Kief. "Affirmative action is a way to chip away at some of these obstacles."

Kief says the fact that Connerly has played a central role in all of the initiatives indicates that true grassroots opposition to affirmative action is weak in states where initiatives have passed or are about to be voted on.

However, The Century Foundation's Kahlenberg points out that pro-affirmative action forces work hard to block ballot initiatives, because when such initiatives have gone before voters they have been approved. And the most recent successful ballot initiative, in Michigan in 2006, passed by a slightly bigger margin — 57 percent to 43 percent — than its California counterpart in 1996, which was approved by 54-46.[18]

Further evidence that anti-affirmative action initiatives are hard to fight surfaced this year in Colorado, where the group Coloradans for Equal Opportunity failed to round up enough signatures to put a pro-affirmative action initiative on the ballot.

Kahlenberg acknowledges that affirmative action politics can be tricky. Despite abiding public opposition to preferences, support among blacks is so strong that Republican presidential campaigns tend to downplay affirmative action, for fear of triggering a huge turnout among black voters, who vote overwhelmingly Democratic. In 1999,

AFP/Getty Images/Emmanuel Dunand

Democratic presidential candidate Sen. Barack Obama, speaking in Philadelphia on Oct. 11, 2008, represents the new face of affirmative action in the demographically changing United States: His father was Kenyan and a half-sister is half-Indonesian.

then-Florida Gov. Jeb Bush kept a Connerly-sponsored initiative out of that state largely in order to lessen the chances of a major black Democratic mobilization in the 2000 presidential election, in which his brother would be running.[19]

"When you have an initiative on the ballot," Kahlenberg says, "some Republicans think that it increases minority turnout, so they're not sure whether these initiatives play to their party or not." Republican opposition to affirmative action goes back to the Reagan administration. Reagan, however, passed up a chance to ban affirmative action programs throughout the federal government, displaying a degree of GOP ambivalence. However, Connerly is an outspoken Republican.[20]

Nevertheless, an all-out Republican push against affirmative action during the past decade failed to catch on at the national level. In 1996, former Republican Senate Majority Leader Bob Dole of Kansas was running for president, and the affirmative action initiative was on the same ballot in California. "The initiative passed, but there was no trickle-down help for Bob Dole," says Daniel A. Smith, a political scientist at the University of Florida who has written on affirmative action politics.

This year, to be sure, anxieties growing out of the financial crisis and economic slowdown could rekindle passions over preferences. But Smith argues the economic environment makes finger-pointing at minorities less likely. "Whites are not losing jobs to African-Americans," he says. "Whites and African-Americans are losing jobs to the Asian subcontinent — they're going to

Bangalore. The global economy makes it more difficult to have a convenient domestic scapegoat for lost jobs."

Has affirmative action diverted attention from the poor quality of K-12 education in low-income communities?

If there's one point on which everyone involved in the affirmative action debate agrees, it's that public schools attended by most low-income students are worsening.

"The educational achievement gap between racial groups began growing again in the 1990s," Gary Orfield, a professor of education and social policy at Harvard University, wrote. "Our public schools are becoming increasingly segregated by race and income, and the segregated schools are, on average, strikingly inferior in many important ways, including the quality and experience of teachers and the level of competition from other students. . . . It is clear that students of different races do not receive an equal chance for college."[21]

The decline in education quality has occurred at the same time various race-preference policies have governed admission to the nation's best colleges and universities. The policies were designed to provide an incentive for schools and students alike to do their best, by ensuring that a college education remains a possibility for all students who perform well academically.

But the results have not been encouraging. In California alone, only 36 percent of all high school students in 2001 had taken all the courses required for admission to the state university system, according to a study by the Civil Rights Project at Harvard University. Among black students, only 26 percent had taken the prerequisites, and only 24 percent of Hispanics. Meanwhile, 41 percent of white students and 54 percent of Asians had taken the necessary courses.[22]

In large part as a result of deficient K-12 education, decades of race-preference affirmative action at top-tier colleges and universities have yielded only small percentages of black and Hispanic students. In 1995, according to an exhaustive 2003 study by The Century Foundation, these students accounted for 6 percent of admissions to the 146 top-tier institutions.[23]

Socioeconomically, the picture is even less diverse. Seventy-four percent of students came from families in the wealthiest quarter of the socioeconomic scale; 3 percent came from families in the bottom quarter.[24]

For race-preference opponents, the picture demonstrates that efforts at ensuring racial and ethnic diversity in higher education would have been better aimed at improving K-12 schools across the country.

"If you've tried to use race for 40-some years, and you still have this profound gap," Connerly says, "yet cling to the notion that you have given some affirmative action to black and Latino and American Indian students — though Asians, without it, are outstripping everybody — maybe the way we've been doing it wasn't the right way to do it."

Meanwhile, he says, making a point that echoes through black, conservative circles, "Historically black colleges and universities (HBCUs) — if you look at doctors and pharmacists across our nation, you'll find them coming from schools that are 90 percent black. These schools are not very diverse, but they put a premium on quality."

But not all HBCUs are in that class, affirmative action supporters point out. "A lot of people who come out with a degree in computer science from minority-serving institutions know absolutely no mathematics," says Richard Tapia, a mathematics professor at Rice University and director of the university's Center for Equity and Excellence in Education. "I once went to a historically black university and had lunch with a top student who was going to do graduate work at Purdue, but when I talked to her I realized that her knowledge of math was on a par with that of a Rice freshman. The gap is huge."

Tapia, who advocates better mentoring for promising minority students at top-flight institutions, argues that the effect of relegating minority students to a certain defined group of colleges and universities, including historically black institutions, limits their chances of advancement in society at large. "From the elite schools you're going to get leadership."

Still, a question remains as to whether focusing on preferential admissions has helped perpetuate the very conditions that give rise to preferences in the first place.

"At the K-12 level you could argue that affirmative action has led to stagnation," says Richard Sander, a professor of law at UCLA Law School. "There's very little forward movement, very little closing of the black-white gap of the past 20 to 30 years."

Coleman of Duke University agrees that public education for most low-income students needs help. But that issue has nothing to do with admissions to top-drawer universities and professional schools, he says. "Look at minority students who get into places like that," he says. "For the most part, they haven't gone to the weakest high schools; they've often gone to the best."

Yet the affirmative action conflict focuses on black students, who are assumed to be academically under-qualified, Coleman says, while white students' place at the best schools isn't questioned. The classroom reality differs, he says. "We have a whole range of students with different abilities. All of the weak students are not minority students; all of the strong students are not white students."

BACKGROUND

Righting Wrongs

The civil rights revolution of the 1950s and '60s forced a new look at the policies that had locked one set of Americans out of most higher-education institutions and higher-paying jobs.

As early as 1962, the Congress of Racial Equality (CORE), one of the most active civil-rights organizations, advocated hiring practices that would make up for discrimination against black applicants. "We are approaching employers with the proposition that they have effectively excluded Negroes from their work force a long time, and they now have a responsibility and obligation to make up for their past sins," the organization said in a statement from its New York headquarters.[25]

Facing CORE-organized boycotts, a handful of companies in New York, Denver, Detroit, Seattle and Baltimore changed their hiring procedures to favor black applicants.

In July 1964, President Lyndon B. Johnson pushed Congress to pass the landmark Civil Rights Act, which had been championed by President John F. Kennedy since his 1960 presidential election campaign.

The law's Title VII, which prohibits racial, religious or sexual discrimination in hiring, said judges enforcing the law could order "such affirmative action as may be appropriate" to correct violations.[26]

Title VII didn't specify what kind of affirmative action could be decreed. But racial preferences were openly discussed in the political arena as a tool to equalize opportunities. Official working definitions of affirmative action didn't emerge until the end of the 1960s, under President Richard M. Nixon.

In 1969, the administration approved the "Philadelphia Plan," which set numerical goals for black and other minority employment on federally financed construction jobs. One year later, the plan was expanded to cover all businesses with 50 or more employees and federal contracts of at least $50,000. The contracts were to set hiring goals and timetables designed to match up a firm's minority representation with the workforce demographics in its area. The specified minorities were: "Negro, Oriental, American Indian and Spanish Surnamed Americans."[27]

The sudden change in the workplace environment prompted a wave of lawsuits. In the lead, a legal challenge by 13 black electric utility workers in North Carolina led to one of the most influential U.S. Supreme Court decisions on affirmative action, the 1971 *Griggs v. Duke Power Co.* case.[28]

In a unanimous decision, the high court concluded that an aptitude test that was a condition of promotion for the workers violated the Civil Rights Act. Duke Power may not have intended the test to weed out black applicants, Chief Justice Warren E. Burger wrote in the decision. But, he added, "Congress directed the thrust of the Act to the consequences of employment practices, not simply the motivation."[29]

If the point of the Civil Rights Act was to ensure that the consequences of institutions' decisions yielded balanced workforces, then goals and timetables to lead to that outcome were consistent with the law as well. In other words, eliminating racial discrimination could mean paying attention to race in hiring and promotions.

That effort would produce a term that captured the frustration and anger among white males who were competing with minority-group members for jobs, promotions or school admissions: "reverse discrimination."

The issue went national with a challenge by Allan Bakke, a white, medical school applicant, to the University of California. He'd been rejected two years in a row while minority-group members — for whom 16 slots in the 100-member class had been set aside — were admitted with lower qualifying scores.

After the case reached the Supreme Court, the justices in a 5-4 decision in 1978 ordered Bakke admitted and prohibited the use of racial quotas. But they allowed race to be considered along with other criteria. Representing the University of California was former Solicitor General Archibald Cox, the Watergate special prosecutor who was

CHRONOLOGY

1960s *Enactment of civil rights law opens national debate on discrimination.*

1964 Civil Rights Act of 1964 bars discrimination in employment and at federally funded colleges.

1965 President Lyndon B. Johnson calls for a massive national effort to create social and economic equality.

1969 Nixon administration approves "Philadelphia Plan" setting numerical goals for minority employment on all federally financed building projects.

1970s-1980s *Affirmative action expands throughout the country, prompting legal challenges and growing voter discontent, leading to new federal policy.*

1971 The U.S. Supreme Court's landmark *Griggs v. Duke Power Co.* decision, growing out of a challenge by 13 black electric utility workers in North Carolina, is seen as authorizing companies and institutions to set out goals and timetables for minority hiring.

1978 Supreme Court's decision in *University of California Regents v. Bakke,* arising from a medical-school admission case, rules out racial quotas but allows race to be considered with other factors.

1980 Ronald W. Reagan is elected president with strong support from white males who see affirmative action as a threat.

1981-1983 Reagan administration reduces affirmative action enforcement.

1985 Attorney General Edwin Meese III drafts executive order outlawing affirmative action in federal government; Reagan never signs it.

1987 Supreme Court upholds job promotion of a woman whose advancement was challenged by a male colleague claiming higher qualifications.

1990s *Ballot initiatives banning race and gender preferences prompt President Bill Clinton to acknowledge faults in affirmative action.*

1994 White voter discontent energizes the "Republican revolution" that topples Democrats from control of Congress.

1995 Supreme Court rules in *Adarand Constructors v. Peña* that affirmative action programs must be "narrowly tailored" for cases of extreme discrimination. . . . Clinton concedes that affirmative action foes have some valid points but concludes, "Mend it, but don't end it." . . . Senate votes down anti-affirmative action bill.

1996 California voters pass nation's first ballot initiative outlawing racial, ethnic and gender preferences. . . . 5th U.S. Circuit Court of Appeals rules that universities can't take race into account in evaluating applicants.

1998 Washington state voters pass ballot initiative identical to California's.

2000s *Affirmative action in university admissions stays on national agenda, leading to major Supreme Court ruling; Sen. Barack Obama's presidential candidacy focuses more attention on the issue.*

2003 Supreme Court's *Gratz v. Bollinger* ruling rejects University of Michigan undergraduate admission system for awarding extra points to minority applicants, but simultaneous *Grutter v. Bollinger* decision upholds UM law school admissions policy, which includes race as one factor among many. . . . Justice Sandra Day O'Connor writes in 5-4 majority opinion in *Grutter* that affirmative action won't be necessary in 25 years. . . . Century Foundation study finds strong linkage between socioeconomic status, race and chances of going to college.

2006 Michigan passes nation's third ballot initiative outlawing racial, ethnic and gender preferences.

2008 Opponents of affirmative action in Arizona, Missouri and Oklahoma fail to place anti-affirmative action initiatives on ballot, but similar campaigns succeed in Colorado and Nebraska. . . . U.S. Civil Rights Commission opens study of minority students majoring in science and math. . . . Saying his daughters are affluent and shouldn't benefit from race preferences, Obama endorses affirmative action for struggling, white college applicants.

fired on orders of President Nixon in 1973. Cox's grand-daughter, Melissa Hart, helps lead the opposition to an anti-affirmative action ballot initiative in Colorado (*see p. 15*).[30]

In 1979 and 1980, the court upheld worker training and public contracting policies that included so-called set-asides for minority-group employees or minority-owned companies. But in the latter case, the deciding opinion specified that only companies that actually had suffered discrimination would be eligible for those contracts.[31]

Divisions within the Supreme Court reflected growing tensions in the country as a whole. A number of white people saw affirmative action as injuring the educational and career advancement of people who hadn't themselves caused the historical crimes that gave rise to affirmative action.

Reversing Course

President Ronald W. Reagan took office in 1981 with strong support from so-called "Reagan Democrats" — white, blue-collar workers who had turned against their former party on issues including affirmative action.[32]

Initially, Reagan seemed poised to fulfill the hopes of those who wanted him to ban all preferences based on race, ethnicity and gender. The latter category followed an upsurge of women fighting to abolish limits on their education and career possibilities.

Yet Reagan's appointees were divided on the issue, and the president himself never formalized his rejection of quotas and related measures. Because no law required the setting of goals and timetables, Reagan could have banned them by executive order. During Reagan's second term, Attorney General Edwin Meese III drafted such an order. But Reagan never signed it.

Nevertheless, the Reagan administration did systematically weaken enforcement of affirmative action. In Reagan's first term he cut the budgets of the Equal Employment Opportunity Commission and the Office of Federal Contract Compliance — the two front-line agencies on the issue — by 12 and 34 percent, respectively, between 1981 and 1983. As a result, the compliance office blocked only two contractors during Reagan's two terms, compared with 13 that were barred during President Jimmy Carter's term.

The Justice Department also began opposing some affirmative action plans. In 1983, Justice won a partial court reversal of an affirmative action plan for the New Orleans Police Department. In a police force nearly devoid of black supervisors, the plan was designed to expand the number — a move considered vital in a city whose population was nearly one-half black.

Affirmative action cases kept moving through the Supreme Court. In 1984-1986, the court overturned plans that would have required companies doing layoffs to disregard the customary "first hired, last fired" rule, because that custom endangered most black employees, given their typically short times on the job.

And in 1987, a 5-4 Supreme Court decision upheld an Alabama state police plan requiring that 50 percent of promotions go to black officers. The same year, the court upheld 6-3 the promotion of a woman employee of Santa Clara County, Calif., who got promoted over a male candidate who had scored slightly higher on an assessment. The decision marked the first court endorsement of affirmative action for women.

In the executive branch, divided views persisted in the administration of Reagan's Republican successor, George H. W. Bush. In 1990 Bush vetoed a pro-affirmative action bill designed to reverse recent Supreme Court rulings, one of which effectively eased the way for white men to sue for reverse discrimination.

The legislation would have required "quotas," Bush said, explaining his veto. But the following year, he signed a compromise, the Civil Rights Act of 1991.[33] Supported by the civil rights lobby, the bill wrote into law the *Griggs v. Duke Power* requirement that an employer prove that a job practice — a test, say — is required for the work in question. A practice that failed that test could be shown to result in discrimination, even if that hadn't been the intention.

Bush also reversed a directive by his White House counsel that would have outlawed all quotas, set-asides and related measures. The administration's ambivalence reflected divided views in American society. Local government and corporate officials had grown appreciative of affirmative action for calming racial tensions. In 1985, the white Republican mayor of Indianapolis refused a Justice Department request to end affirmative action in the police department. Mayor William Hudnut said that the "white majority has accepted the fact that we're making a special effort for minorities and women."[34]

Yet among white males, affirmative action remained a very hot-button issue. "When we hold focus groups," a Democratic pollster said in 1990, "if the issue of

'Percent Plans' Offer Alternative to Race-Based Preferences

But critics say approach fails to level playing field.

In recent years, voters and judges have blocked race and ethnicity preferences in university admissions in three big states with booming minority populations — California, Florida and Texas. Nonetheless, lawmakers devised a way to ensure that public universities remain open to black and Latino students.

The so-called "percent plans" promise guaranteed admission based on a student's high school class standing, not on skin tone. That, at least is the principle.

But the man who helped end racial affirmative action preferences in two of the states involved argues affirmative action is alive and well, simply under another name. Moreover, says Ward Connerly, a black businessman in Sacramento, Calif., who has been a leader in organizing anti-affirmative action referendums, the real issue — the decline in urban K-12 schools — is being ignored.

"Legislatures and college administrators lack the spine to say, 'Let's find the problem at its core,' " says Connerly, a former member of the University of California Board of Regents. "Instead, they go for a quick fix they believe will yield the same number of blacks and Latinos as before."

Even Connerly's opponents agree "percent plans" alone don't put high schools in inner cities and prosperous suburbs on an equal footing. "In some school districts in Texas, 50 percent of the graduates could make it here easily," says Terry H. Anderson, a history professor at Texas A&M University in College Station. "Some school districts are so awful that not one kid could graduate here, I don't care what race you're talking about."

All the plans — except at selective schools — ignore SAT or ACT scores (though students do have to present their scores). The policy troubles Richard D. Kahlenberg, a senior fellow at The Century Foundation, who champions "class-based" affirmation action. "The grade of A in one high school is very different from the grade of A in another," he says.

Texas lawmakers originated the percent plan concept after a 5th U.S. Circuit Court of Appeals decision in 1996 (*Hopwood v. Texas*) prohibited consideration of race in college admissions. Legislators proposed guaranteeing state university admissions to the top 10 percent of graduates of the state's public and private high schools. Then-Gov. George W. Bush signed the bill, which includes automatic admission to the flagship campuses, the University of Texas at Austin and Texas A&M.[1]

In California, the impetus was the 1996 voter approval of Proposition 209, which prohibited racial and ethnic preferences by all state entities. Borrowing the Texas idea, California lawmakers devised a system in which California high school students in the top 4 percent of their classes are eligible for the California system, but not necessarily to attend the two star institutions, UC Berkeley and UCLA. (Students in the top 4 percent-12.5 percent range are admitted to community colleges and can transfer to four-year institutions if they maintain 2.4 grade-point averages.)[2]

Connerly was active in the Proposition 209 campaign and was the key player — but involuntarily — in Florida's adoption of a percent plan. In 1999, Connerly was preparing to mount an anti-affirmative action initiative in Florida. Then-Gov. Jeb Bush worried it could hurt his party's standing with black voters — with possible repercussions on his brother

affirmative action comes up, you can forget the rest of the session. That's all . . . that's talked about."[35]

Mending It

From the early 1990s to 2003 race-based affirmative action suffered damage in the political arena and the courts.

In 1994, white male outrage at preferences for minority groups and women was a key factor in congressional elections that toppled Democrats from control of both houses. As soon as the Congress changed hands, its new leaders targeted affirmative action. "Sometimes the best-qualified person does not get the job because he or she

George's presidential campaign. Instead Gov. Bush launched "One Florida," a percent plan approved by the legislature.

In Florida, the top 20 percent of high school graduates are guaranteed admission to the state system. To attend the flagship University of Florida at Gainesville they must meet tougher standards. All three states also require students to have completed a set of required courses.

Percent plan states also have helped shape admissions policies by experimenting with ways to simultaneously keep academic standards high, while ensuring at least the possibility that promising students of all socioeconomic circumstances have a shot at college.

In Florida, the consequences of maintaining high admissions standards at UF were softened by another program, "Bright Futures," which offers tuition reductions of 75 percent — or completely free tuition — depending on completion of AP courses and on SAT or ACT scores.

The effect, says University of Florida political scientist Daniel A. Smith, is to ensure a plentiful supply of top students of all races and ethnicities. "We have really talented minorities — blacks, Latinos, Asian-Americans — because 'One Florida' in combination with 'Bright Futures' has kept a lot of our talented students in the state. We have students who turned down [partial] scholarships to Duke and Harvard because here they're going for free."

At UCLA, which also has maintained rigorous admission criteria, recruiters spread out to high schools in low-income areas in an effort to ensure that the school doesn't become an oasis of privilege. The realities of race and class

"The time has come to pull the plug on race-based decision-making," says Ward Connerly, a Sacramento, Calif., businessman who spearheaded anti-affirmative action ballot initiatives in Colorado, Nebraska and other states.

mean that some of that recruiting work takes place in mostly black or Latino high schools.

"It's the fallacy of [Proposition] 209 that you can immediately move to a system that doesn't take account of race and that treats everybody fairly," said Tom Lifka, a UCLA assistant vice chancellor in charge of admissions. He said the new system meets legal standards.[3]

Consciously or not, Lifka was echoing the conclusion of the most thorough analysis of the plans' operations in the three states. The 2003 study, sponsored by Harvard University's Civil Rights Project, concluded that the states had largely succeeded in maintaining racial and ethnic diversity on their campuses.

But the report added that aggressive recruitment, academic aid to high schools in low-income areas and similar measures played a major role.

"Without such support," wrote Catherine L. Horn, an education professor at the University of Houston, and Stella M. Flores, professor of public policy and higher education at Vanderbilt, "the plans are more like empty shells, appearing to promise eligibility, admission and enrollment for previously excluded groups but actually doing very little."[4]

---

[1] Catherine L. Horn and Stella M. Flores, "Percent Plans in College Admissions: A Comparative Analysis of Three States' Experiences," Civil Rights Project, Harvard University, 2003, pp. 20-23, www.civil rightsproject.ucla.edu/research/affirmativeaction/tristate.pdf.

[2] *Ibid.*

[3] Quoted in David Leonhardt, "The New Affirmative Action," *The New York Times Magazine*, Sept. 30, 2007, p. 76.

[4] Horn and Flores, *op. cit.*, pp. 59-60.

---

may be one color," Majority Leader Dole said in a television interview. "That may not be the way it should be in America."[36]

The following year, the U.S. Supreme Court imposed limits on the use of preferences, ruling on a white, male contractor's challenge to a federal program that encouraged general contractors to favor minority subcontractors. Justice O'Connor wrote in the 5-4 majority opinion in *Adarand Constructors v. Peña* that any racial or ethnic preferences had to be "narrowly tailored" to apply only to "pervasive, systematic and obstinate discriminatory conduct."[37]

Supporters of affirmative action in Lansing, Mich., rally against a proposed statewide anti-affirmative action ballot initiative in September 2006; voters approved the proposal that November. The initiative followed a 2003 U.S. Supreme Court ruling upholding the use of race in law-school admissions at the University of Michigan. Justice Sandra Day O'Connor, who wrote the majority 5-4 opinion, predicted, however, that in 25 years affirmative action would "no longer be necessary."

Some justices had wanted all preferences overturned. Though that position failed to win a majority, the clear unease that O'Connor expressed added to the pressure on politicians who supported affirmative action.

In that climate, President Bill Clinton gave a 1995 speech at the National Archives in Washington in which he acknowledged that critics had a point. He said he didn't favor "the unjustified preference of the unqualified over the qualified of any race or gender." But affirmative action was still needed because discrimination persisted, Clinton added. His bottom line: "Mend it, but don't end it."[38]

The slogan seemed to match national politicians' mood. One day after Clinton's speech, the Senate voted down a bill to abolish all preferences, with 19 Republicans siding with Democrats in a 61-36 vote.

But in California, one of the country's major affirmative action laboratories, the "end it" argument proved more popular. Racial/ethnic preferences had become a major issue in a state whose minority population was booming. California's higher-education system also included two of the nation's top public institutions: the University of California at Berkeley (UCB) and UCLA.

Among many white, Anglo Californians, affirmative action had come to be seen as a system under which black and Latino applicants were getting into those two schools at the expense of whites or Asians with higher grades and SAT scores.

By 1996, the statewide university system's majority-Republican Board of Regents voted to end all race, ethnic and gender preferences in admissions. The board did allow universities to take applicants' socioeconomic circumstances into account.

And in the same year, California voters approved Proposition 209, which outlawed all race, ethnicity and gender preferences by all state entities. Connerly helped organize that referendum and followed up with successful campaigns in Washington state in 1998 and in Michigan in 2003.

Meanwhile, the "reverse discrimination" issue that had been decided in the *Bakke* case flared up in Texas, where Cheryl Hopwood and two other white applicants to the University of Texas law school challenged their rejections, pointing to the admissions of minority students with lower grades and test scores. In 1996, the 5th U.S. Circuit Court of Appeals decided for the plaintiffs, ruling that universities couldn't take race into account when assessing applicants.

The appeals judges had overruled the *Bakke* decision, at least in their jurisdiction of Texas, Mississippi and Louisiana, yet the Supreme Court refused to consider the case.

But in 2003, the justices ruled on two separate cases, both centering on admissions to another top-ranked public higher education system: the University of Michigan. One case arose from admissions procedures for the undergraduate college, the other from the system for evaluating applicants to the university's law school.[39]

The Supreme Court decided against the undergraduate admissions policy because it automatically awarded 20 extra points on the university's 150-point evaluation scale to blacks, Latinos and American Indians. By contrast, the law school took race into account in what Justice O'Connor, in the majority opinion in the 5-4 decision, called a "highly individualized, holistic review" of each candidate aimed at producing a diverse student population.[40]

CURRENT SITUATION

'Formal Equality'

In the midst of war and the Wall Street meltdown, affirmative action may not generate as many headlines as it used to. But the issue still packs enough punch to have put anti-affirmative action legislation up for popular vote in Colorado and Nebraska this year.

"This is a progressive approach," said Jessica Peck Corry, executive director of the Colorado Civil Rights Initiative, which is campaigning for proposed Constitutional Amendment 46. The amendment would prohibit all state government entities from discriminating for or against anyone because of race, ethnicity or gender. "America is too diverse to put into stagnant race boxes," she says.

Melissa Hart, a co-chair of "No On 46," counters that the amendment would require "formal equality" that shouldn't be confused with the real thing. She likens the proposal to "a law that says both the beggar and the king may sleep under a bridge." In the real world, she says, only one of them will spend his nights in a bedroom.

Unlike California, Michigan and Washington — the states where voters have approved initiatives of this type over the past 12 years — the Colorado campaign doesn't follow a major controversy over competition for university admissions.

To be sure, Corry — a libertarian Republican law student, blogger and past failed candidate for state Senate — has publicly opposed affirmative action for several years.[41] But Corry, who is also a policy analyst at the Denver-based Independence Institute, a libertarian think tank, acknowledges that the referendum campaign in Colorado owes its start to Connerly. He began taking the ballot initiative route in the 1990s, after concluding that neither state legislatures nor Congress would ever touch the subject.

"They just seem to lack the stomach to do what I and the majority of Americans believe should be done," Connerly says. "Clearly, there's a disconnect between elected officials and the people themselves."

Connerly's confidence grows out of his success with the three previous initiatives. But this year, his attempts to get his proposal before voters in Arizona, Missouri and Oklahoma all failed because his campaign workers didn't gather enough valid signatures to get the initiatives on the ballot.

Connerly blames what he calls an overly restrictive initiative process in Oklahoma, as well as organized opposition by what he calls "blockers," who shadowed signature-gatherers and disputed their explanations of the amendments.

Opponents had a different name for themselves. "Our voter educators were simply that — voter educators," said Brandon Davis, political director of the Service Employees International Union in Missouri. "Ward Connerly should accept what Missourians said, and he should stop with the sore-loser talk."[42]

The opposition began deploying street activists to counter what they call the deliberately misleading wording of the proposed initiatives. In Colorado, Proposition 46 is officially described as a "prohibition against discrimination by the state" and goes on to ban "preferential treatment to any individual or group on the basis of race, sex, color, ethnicity or national origin."[43]

"We want an acknowledgement that disadvantage cannot be specifically determined based on looking at some race data or gender data," Corry says. But tutoring, counseling and other activities should be extended to all who need help because of their socioeconomic circumstances, she contends.

Likewise, a project to interest girls in science and math, for instance, would have to admit boys. "In a time when America is losing its scientific advantage by the second, why are you excluding potential Nobel prize winners because they're born with the wrong biology?" she asks rhetorically.

Hart says that many tutoring and similar programs tailored to low-income students in Colorado already welcome all comers, regardless of race or ethnicity. But she questions why a math and science program tailored for girls should have to change its orientation. Likewise, Denver's specialized public schools for American Indian students would have to change their orientation entirely. "Class-based equal opportunity programs are not substitutes for outreach, training and mentoring on the basis of race and gender," she says.

The issue of class comes up in personal terms as well. Corry portrays herself as the product of a troubled home who had to work her way through college and graduate school. Though her father was a lawyer, her mother abandoned the family and wound up living on the streets. And Corry depicts Hart as a member of the privileged

The Preference Program Nobody Talks About

How "legacies" get breaks at top colleges.

Many critics say race-based affirmative action gives minority college applicants an unfair advantage. But reporter Peter Schmidt found an even more favored population — rich, white kids who apply to top-tier schools.

"These institutions feel very dependent on these preferences," Schmidt writes in his 2007 book, *Color and Money: How Rich White Kids Are Winning the War Over College Affirmative Action.* "They throw up their hands and say, 'There's no other way we can raise the money we need.'"

Colleges admit these students — "legacies," in college-admission lingo — because their parents are donation-making graduates. Offspring of professors, administrators or (in the case of top state universities) politically influential figures get open-door treatment as well.

"Several public college lobbyists, working in both state capitals and with the federal government in and around Washington, have told me that they spend a significant portion of their time lobbying their own colleges' admissions offices to accept certain applicants at the behest of public officials," Schmidt writes.[1]

Especially in regard to legacies and the families' donations, Schmidt says, "There is a utilitarian argument that the money enables colleges to serve students in need. But there isn't a correlation between how much money they're bringing in and helping low-income students."

As deputy editor of the *Chronicle of Higher Education,* Schmidt has been covering affirmative action conflicts since his days as an Associated Press reporter writing about protests over racial tensions at the University of Michigan in the mid-1990s.

His book doesn't deal exclusively with applicants from privileged families — who, by the nature of American society, are almost all white and academically well-prepared. But Schmidt's examination of privileged applicants frames his reporting on the more familiar issues of preferences based on race, ethnicity and gender.

According to Schmidt, Harvard as of 2004 accepted about 40 percent of the legacies who applied, compared to about 11 percent of applicants overall. In the Ivy League in general, children of graduates made up 10-15 percent of the undergraduates.

Though the issue is sensitive for college administrators, Schmidt found some members of the higher-education establishment happy to see it aired.

"Admissions officers are the ones who are finding the promising kids — diamonds in the rough — and getting emotionally invested in getting them admitted, then sitting down with the development officer or the coach and finding that these kids are knocked out of the running," he says.

Some education experts dispute that conclusion. Abigail Thernstrom, a senior fellow at the conservative Manhattan Institute and vice-chair of the U.S. Commission on Civil Rights, opposes "class-based" affirmative action (as well as racial/ethnic preferences), calling it unnecessary. She says that when top-tier schools look at an applicant from a disadvantaged background "who is getting a poor education — a diamond in the rough but showing real academic progress — and compare that student to someone from Exeter born with a silver spoon in his mouth, there's no question that these schools are going to take that diamond in the rough, if they think he or she will be able to keep up."

But some of Schmidt's findings echo what affirmative action supporters have observed. James E. Coleman Jr., a law professor at Duke University, argues against the tendency to focus all affirmative action attention on blacks and Latinos. "The idea is that any white student who gets here deserves to be here. They're not questioned. This has always been true."

At the same time, Coleman, who is black, agrees with Schmidt that those who start out near the top of the socioeconomic ladder have access to first-class educations before they even get to college. Coleman himself, who graduated from Harvard and from Columbia Law School, says he never had a single white classmate in his Charlotte, N.C., schools until he got accepted to a post-high school preparatory program at Exeter, one of the nation's most prestigious prep schools. "I could tell that my educational background and preparation were woefully inadequate compared to students who had been there since ninth grade," he recalls. "I had to run faster."

Schmidt says the politics of affirmative action can give rise to tactical agreements between groups whose interests might seem to conflict. In one dispute, he says, "Civil rights groups and higher-education groups had a kind of uneasy alliance: The civil rights groups would not challenge the admissions process and go after legacies as long as affirmative action remained intact."

But, he adds, "There are people not at the table when a deal like that is struck. If you're not a beneficiary of one or the other side of preferences, you don't gain from that agreement."

---

[1] Peter Schmidt, *Color and Money: How Rich White Kids Are Winning the War Over College Affirmative Action* (2007), p. 32.

AT ISSUE

Would many black and Latino science and math majors be better off at lesser-ranked universities?

YES
Rogers Elliott
Professor Emeritus, Department of Psychology and Brain Sciences, Dartmouth College

From testimony before U.S. Civil Rights Commission, Sept. 12, 2008

Race preferences in admissions in the service of affirmative action are harming the aspirations, particularly, of blacks seeking to be scientists.

The most elite universities have very high levels in their admission standards, levels which minorities — especially blacks — don't come close to meeting.

[Thus], affirmative action in elite schools, which they pursue vigorously and successfully, leaves a huge gap, probably bigger than it would be for affirmative action at an average school. That is what constitutes the problem.

At elite schools, 90 percent of science majors [got] 650 or above on the SAT math score. About 80 percent of the white/Asian group are 650 or above, but only 25 percent of the black group have that score or better. The gaps that are illustrated in these data have not gotten any better. They have, in fact, gotten a little bit worse: The gap in the SAT scores between blacks and whites, which got to its smallest extent in about 1991 — 194 points — is back to 209.

The higher the standard at the institution, the more science they tend to do. But the [lower-ranking schools] still do science, and your chances of becoming a scientist are better. Now, obviously, there are differences. The higher institutions have eliteness going for them. They have prestige going for them, and maybe getting a degree from Dartmouth when you want to be a doctor will leave you better off in this world even though you're not doing the thing you started with as your aspiration.

Seventeen of the top 20 PhD-granting institutions for blacks in this country, are HBCUs [historically black colleges and universities].

Elite institutions are very performance-oriented. They deliberately take people at a very high level to begin with — with a few exceptions — and then they make them perform, and they do a pretty good job of it. If you're not ready for the first science course, you might as well forget it. Some of these minority students had mostly A's . . . enough to get to Dartmouth or Brown or Cornell or Yale. They take their first course, let's say, in chemistry; at least 90 percent of the students in that course are bright, motivated, often pre-med, highly competitive whites and Asians. And these [minority] kids aren't as well-prepared. They may get their first C- or D in a course like that because the grading standards are rigorous, and you have to start getting it from day one.

NO
Prof. Richard A. Tapia
Director, Center on Excellence and Equity, Rice University

From testimony before U.S. Civil Rights Commission, Sept. 12, 2008

The nation selects leaders from graduates and faculty of U.S. universities with world-class science, technology, engineering and math (STEM) research programs. If we, the underrepresented minorities, are to be an effective component in STEM leadership, then we must have an equitable presence as students and faculty at the very top-level research universities.

Pedigree, unfortunately, is an incredible issue. Top research universities choose faculty from PhDs produced at top research universities. PhDs produced at minority-serving schools or less-prestigious schools will not become faculty at top research universities. Indeed, it's unlikely they'll become faculty at minority-serving institutions. A student from a research school with a lesser transcript is stronger than a student from a minority-serving institution with all A's.

So are the students who come from these minority-serving institutions incompetent? No. There's a level of them that are incredibly good and will succeed wherever they go. And usually Stanford and Berkeley and Cornell will get those. Then there's a level below that you can work with. I produced many PhDs who came from minority-serving institutions. Is there a gap in training? Absolutely.

We do not know how to measure what we really value: Creativity. Underrepresented minorities can be quite creative. For example, the Carl Hayden High School Robotic Team — five Mexican-American students from West Phoenix — beat MIT in the final in underwater robotics. They were not star students, but they were incredibly creative.

Treating everyone the same is not good enough. Sink or swim has not worked and will not work. It pays heed to privilege, not to talent. Isolation, not academics, is often the problem. We must promote success and retention with support programs. We must combat isolation through community-building and mentoring.

Ten percent of the students in public education in Texas are accepted into the University of Texas, automatically — the top 10 percent. They could have said look, these students are not prepared well. They're dumped at our doorstep, let's leave them. They didn't. The Math Department at the University of Texas at Austin built support programs where minorities are retained and succeed. It took a realization that here they are, let's do something with them.

Race and ethnicity should not dictate educational destiny. Our current path will lead to a permanent underclass that follows racial and ethnic lines.

TV cameramen in Lincoln, Neb., shoot boxes of signed voter petitions that qualified a proposed initiative to be put on the ballot in Nebraska this coming November calling for a ban on most types of affirmative action.

AP Photo/Nati Harnik

class, a granddaughter of former Solicitor General Cox and a graduate of Harvard University and Harvard Law School. "People like Melissa, I believe, are well-intentioned but misguided," Corry says. "The worst thing you can do to someone without connections is to suggest that they can't make it without preferences."

Hart, rapping Corry for bringing up personal history rather than debating ideas, adds that her father and his part of the family are potato farmers from Idaho.

"I am proudly the granddaughter of Archibald Cox, proud of the fact that he argued the *Bakke* case for the University of California, and proud to be continuing a tradition of standing up for opportunity in this country," she says.

The Nebraska campaign, taking place in a smaller state with little history of racial or ethnic tension and a university where competition for admission isn't an issue, has generated somewhat less heat. But as in Colorado, college-preparation and other programs of various kinds that target young women and American Indians would be threatened by the amendment, says Laurel Marsh, executive director of the Nebraska ACLU.

Over Their Heads?

The U.S. Civil Rights Commission is examining one of the most explosive issues in the affirmative action debate: whether students admitted to top universities due to

racial preferences are up to the academic demands they face at those institutions.

Math and the hard sciences present the most obvious case, affirmative action critics — and some supporters — say. Those fields are at the center of the commission's inquiry because students from high schools in low-income areas — typically minority students — tend to do poorly in science and math, in part because they require considerable math preparation in elementary and high school.

Sander of UCLA, who has been studying the topic, testified to the commission that for students of all races who had scored under 660 on the math SAT, only 5 percent of blacks and 3.5 percent of whites obtained science degrees. But of students who scored 820 or above on the SAT, 44 percent of blacks graduated with science or engineering degrees. Among whites, 35 percent graduated with those degrees — illustrating Sander's point that that issue is one of academic preparation, not race.

Abigail Thernstrom, the commission's vice-chair, says that most graduates of run-of-the-mill urban schools labor under a major handicap in pursuing math or science degrees. "By the time they get to college they're in bad shape in a discipline like math, where all knowledge is cumulative," she says. "The colleges are inheriting a problem that, in effect, we sweep under the rug."

Thernstrom, a longtime affirmative action critic, bases her views both on her 11 years of service on the Massachusetts state Board of Education and on data assembled by academics, including Sander. "Test scores do predict a lot, high school grades predict a lot," Sander says in an interview, disputing critics of his work who say students from deficient high schools can make up in college what they missed earlier.

Testifying to the commission on Sept. 12, Sander presented data showing that black and Hispanic high school graduates tend to be more interested than their white counterparts in pursuing science and math careers, but less successful in holding on to majors in those fields in college. Lower high school grades and test scores seem to account for as much as 75 percent of the tendency to drop out of those fields, he says.

Sander added that a student's possibilities can't be predicted from skin color and that the key factor associated with inadequate academic preparation is socioeconomic status. "We ought to view that as good news, because that means there's no intrinsic or genetic gap," he testified.

Rogers Elliott, an emeritus psychology and brain sciences professor at Dartmouth College, told the commission that the best option for many black and Hispanic students who want to pursue science or math careers is to attend lower-rated universities. Among institutions that grant the most PhDs to blacks, 17 of the top 20 are HBCUs, Elliott said, "and none of them is a prestige university."

Richard Tapia, a Rice University mathematician, countered that consigning minority-group students who aren't stars to lower-ranking universities would be disastrous. Only top-tier universities, he argued, provide their graduates with the credibility that allows them to assert leadership. "Research universities must be responsible for providing programs that promote success," he said, "rather than be let off the hook by saying that minority students should go to minority-serving institutions or less prestigious schools."

Tapia directs such a program — one of a handful around the country — that he says has helped Rice students overcome their inadequate earlier schooling. But he accepts Sander's and Elliott's data and says students with combined SAT scores below 800 would not be capable of pursuing math or science majors at Rice.

Tapia, the son of Mexican immigrants who didn't attend college, worked at a muffler factory after graduating from a low-achieving Los Angeles high school. Pushed by a co-worker to continue his education, he enrolled in community college and went on to UCLA, where he earned a doctorate. He attributes his success to a big dose of self-confidence — something that many people from his background might not have but that mentors can nurture.

A commission member sounded another practical note. Ashley L. Taylor Jr., a Republican lawyer from Richmond, Va., who is black, argued that colleges have a moral obligation to tell applicants if their SAT scores fall within the range of students who have a shot of completing their studies. "If I'm outside that range, no additional support is going to help me," he said.

Sander agrees. "African-American students and any other minority ought to know going into college the ultimate outcomes for students at that college who have their profile."

Tapia agreed as well. "I had a student that I was recruiting in San Antonio who had a 940 SAT and was going to Princeton. I said, 'Do you know what the average at Princeton is?' He said, "Well, my teachers told me it was about 950.' I said, 'Well, I think you'd better check it out.' "

In fact, the average combined math and verbal SAT score of students admitted to Princeton is 1442.[44]

OUTLOOK

End of the Line?

Social programs don't come with an immortality guarantee. Some supporters as well as critics of affirmative action sense that affirmative action, as the term is generally understood, may be nearing the end of the line.

"I expect affirmative action to die," says Tapia. "People are tired of it. And if we had to depend on affirmative action forever, then there was something wrong. If you need a jump-start on your battery, and you get it jumped, fine. If you start needing it everywhere you go, you'd better get another battery."

Tapia's tone is not triumphant. He says the decline in public school quality is evidence that "it didn't work, and we didn't do a good job." But he adds that the disparities between the schooling for low-income and well-off students is what makes affirmative action necessary. "Sure, in an ideal world, you wouldn't have to do these things, but that's not the world we live in."

UCLA's Sander, who favors reorienting affirmative action — in part by determining an academic threshold below which students admitted by preference likely will fail — sees major change on the horizon. For one thing, he says, quantities of data are now accessible concerning admission standards, grades and other quantifiable effects of affirmative action programs.

In addition, he says, today's reconfigured Supreme Court likely would rule differently than it did on the 2003 University of Michigan cases that represent its most recent affirmative action rulings.

Justice O'Connor, who wrote the majority decision in the 5-4 ruling that upheld the use of race in law-school admissions, has retired, replaced by conservative Justice Samuel A. Alito. "The Supreme Court as it stands now has a majority that's probably ready to overrule" that decision, Sander says. A decision that turned on the newly available data "could lead to a major Supreme Court decision that could send shockwaves through the system."

For now, says Kahlenberg of The Century Foundation, affirmative action has already changed form in states that have restricted use of racial and ethnic preferences. "It's not as if universities and colleges have simply thrown up their hands," he says. "They now look more aggressively at economic disadvantages that students face. The bigger picture is that the American public likes the idea of diversity but doesn't want to use racial preferences to get there."

Anderson of Texas A&M agrees that a vocabulary development marks the shift. "We've been changing affirmative action and quotas to diversity," he says. "Diversity is seen as good, and has become part of our mainstream culture."

In effect, diversity has come to mean hiring and admissions policies that focus on bringing people of different races and cultures on board — people like Obama, for example. "Obama's talking about merit, and keeping the doors open for all Americans, and strengthening the middle class," Anderson says.

Obama, whose father was Kenyan and whose half-sister is half-Indonesian, also represents another facet of the changing face of affirmative action. "Our society is becoming a lot more demographically complicated," says Schmidt, of *The Chronicle of Higher Education* and author of a recent book on affirmative action in college admissions. "All of these racial groups that benefit from affirmative action as a result of immigration — they're not groups that have experienced oppression and discrimination in the United States. And people are marrying people of other races and ethnicities. How do you sort that out? Which parent counts the most?"

All in all, Schmidt says, the prospects for affirmative action look dim. "In the long term, the political trends are against it," he says. "I don't see a force out there that's going to force the pendulum to swing the other way."

At the same time, many intended beneficiaries — African-Americans whose history set affirmative action in motion — remain untouched by it because of the deficient schools they attend.

The catastrophic state of public schools in low-income America remains — and seems likely to remain — a point on which all sides agree. Whether anything will be done about it is another story.

Top schools will continue to seek diverse student bodies, says Coleman of Duke law school. But the public schools continue to deteriorate. "I haven't seen any effort by people who oppose affirmative action, or people who support it, to do anything to improve the public school system. We ought to improve the quality of education because it's in the national interest to do that."

NOTES

1. See "Transcript: Obama and Clinton Debate," ABC News, April 16, 2008, http://abcnews.go.com/Politics/DemocraticDebate/story?id=4670271&page=1.

2. *Ibid.*

3. *Ibid.*

4. See "Trends in Political Values and Core Attitudes: 1987-2007," Pew Research Center for People and the Press, March 22, 2007, pp. 40-41, http://people-press.org/reports/pdf/312.pdf.

5. See Alemayehu Bishaw and Jessica Semega, "Income, Earnings, and Poverty Data from the 2007 American Community Survey," U.S. Census Bureau, August 2008, p. 20, www.census.gov/prod/2008pubs/acs-09.pdf.

6. See Peter Schmidt, *Color and Money: How Rich White Kids Are Winning the War Over College Affirmative Action* (2007), p. 47.

7. See Anthony P. Carnevale and Stephen J. Rose, "Socioeconomic Status, Race/Ethnicity, and Selective College Admissions," The Century Foundation, March 2003, pp. 26, 79, www.tcf.org/Publications/Education/carnevale_rose.pdf.

8. See Christopher B. Swanson, "Who Graduates? Who Doesn't? A Statistical Portrait of High School Graduation, Class of 2001," The Urban Institute, 2004, pp. v-vi, www.urban.org/UploadedPDF/410934_WhoGraduates.pdf.

9. Quoted in Ira Katznelson, *When Affirmative Action Was White: An Untold History of Racial Inequality in Twentieth-Century America* (2005), p. 175.

10. See Roberta W. Francis, "Reconstituting the Equal Rights Amendment: Policy Implications for Sex Discrimination," 2001, www.equalrightsamendment.org/APSA2001.pdf.

11. See Clarence Thomas, *My Grandfather's Son: A Memoir* (2007), p. 126.

12. Quoted in "Justice Thomas Mocks Value of Yale Law Degree," The Associated Press, Oct. 22, 2007, www.foxnews.com/story/0,2933,303825,00.html. See also, Coleman profile in Berger&Montague, P.C., law firm Web site, www.bergermontague.com/attorneys.cfm?type=1.

13. See Linda Greenhouse, "Justices Back Affirmative Action by 5 to 4, But Wider Vote Bans a Racial Point System," *The New York Times*, June 24, 2003, p. A1.

14. "Barack Obama, July 27, 2008, Unity 08, High Def, Part II," www.youtube.com/watch?v=XIoRzNVTyH4&eurl=http://video.google.com/videosearch?q=obama%20UNITY&ie=UTF-8&oe=utf-8&rls=org.mozilla:enUS:official&c.UNITY is a coalition of the Asian-American Journalists Association, the National Association of Black Journalists, the National Association of Hispanic Journalists and the Native American Journalists Association, www.unityjournalists.org.

15. See "Trends in Political Values . . .," *op. cit.*, pp. 40-41.

16. See http://abcnews.go.com/Politics/Democratic Debate/story?id=4670271.

17. See Jonathan Kaufman, "Fair Enough?" *The Wall Street Journal*, June 14, 2008.

18. See Christine MacDonald, "Ban lost in college counties," *Detroit News*, Nov. 9, 2006, p. A16; and "1996 General Election Returns for Proposition 209," California Secretary of State, Dec. 18, 1996, http://vote96.sos.ca.gov/Vote96/html/vote/prop/prop-209.961218083528.html.

19. See Sue Anne Pressley, "Florida Plan Aims to End Race-Based Preferences," *The Washington Post*, Nov. 11, 1999, p. A15.

20. See Walter Alarkon, "Affirmative action emerges as wedge issue in election," *The Hill*, March 11, 2008, http://thehill.com/campaign-2008/affirmative-action-emerges-as-wedge-issue-in-election-2008-03-11.html.

21. *Ibid.*, p. viii.

22. Catherine L. Horn and Stella M. Flores, "Percent Plans in College Admissions: A Comparative Analysis of Three States' Experiences," The Civil Rights Project, Harvard University, February 2003, pp. 30-31, http://eric.ed.gov/ERICDocs/data/ericdocs2sql/content_storage_01/0000019b/80/1a/b7/9f.pdf.

23. See Carnevale and Rose, *op. cit.*, pp. 10-11.

24. *Ibid.*

25. Quoted in Terry H. Anderson, *The Pursuit of Fairness: A History of Affirmative Action* (2004), p. 76. Unless otherwise indicated, material in this subsection is drawn from this book.

26. For background, see the following *Editorial Research Reports:* Richard L. Worsnop, "Racism in America," May 13, 1964; Sandra Stencel, "Reverse Discrimination," Aug. 6, 1976; K. P. Maize and Sandra Stencel, "Affirmative Action Under Attack," March 30, 1979; and Marc Leepson, "Affirmative Action Reconsidered," July 31, 1981, all available in *CQ Researcher Plus Archive*.

27. Quoted in Anderson, *op. cit.*, p. 125. For more background, see Richard L. Worsnop, "Racial Discrimination in Craft Unions," *Editorial Research Reports*, Nov. 26, 1969, available in *CQ Researcher Plus Archive*.

28. *Griggs v. Duke Power*, 401 U.S. 424 (1971), http://caselaw.lp.findlaw.com/scripts/getcase.pl?court=US&vol=401&invol=424. For background, see Mary H. Cooper, "Racial Quotas," *CQ Researcher*, May 17, 1991, pp. 277-200; and Kenneth Jost, "Rethinking Affirmative Action," *CQ Researcher*, April 28, 1995, pp. 269-392.

29. *Ibid.*

30. See *University of California Regents v. Bakke*, 438 U.S. 265 (1978), http://caselaw.lp.findlaw.com/scripts/getcase.pl?court=US&vol=438&invol=265.

31. See *United Steelworkers of America, AFL-CIO-CLC v. Weber, et al.*, 443 U.S. 193 (1979), http://caselaw.lp.findlaw.com/scripts/getcase.pl?court=US&vol=443&invol=193; and *Fullilove v. Klutznick*, 448 U.S. 448 (1980), www.law.cornell.edu/supct/html/historics/USSC_CR_0448_0448_ZS.html.

32. Unless otherwise indicated, this subsection is drawn from Anderson, *op. cit;* and Jost, *op. cit.*

33. For background, see Cooper, *op. cit.*

34. Anderson, *op. cit.*, p. 186.

35. *Ibid.*, p. 206.

36. Quoted in *ibid.*, p. 233. Unless otherwise indicated this subsection is drawn from Anderson, *op. cit.*

37. *Ibid.*, p. 242.

38. *Ibid.*, p. 244.

39. For background, see Kenneth Jost, "Race in America," *CQ Researcher*, July 11, 2003, pp. 593-624.

40. Quoted in Greenhouse, *op. cit.*

41. "Controversial Bake Sale to Go On at CU, College Republicans Protesting Affirmative Action," 7 News, Feb. 10, 2004, www.thedenverchannel.com/news/2837956/detail.html.

42. Quoted in Kavita Kumar, "Affirmative action critic vows he'll try again," *St. Louis Post-Dispatch*, May 6, 2008, p. D1.

43. "Amendment 46: Formerly Proposed Initiative 2007-2008 #31," Colorado Secretary of State, undated, www.elections.colorado.gov/DDefault.aspx?tid=1036.

44. College data, undated, www.collegedata.com/cs/data/college/college_pg01_tmpl.jhtml? schoolId=111.

BIBLIOGRAPHY

Books

Anderson, Terry H., *The Pursuit of Fairness: A History of Affirmative Action*, Oxford University Press, 2004.
A Texas A&M historian tells the complicated story of affirmative action and the struggles surrounding it.

Kahlenberg, Richard D., ed., *America's Untapped Resource: Low-Income Students in Higher Education*, The Century Foundation Press, 2004.
A liberal scholar compiles detailed studies that add up to a case for replacing race- and ethnic-based affirmative action with a system based on students' socioeconomic status.

Katznelson, Ira, *When Affirmative Action Was White: An Untold History of Racial Inequality in Twentieth-Century America*, Norton, 2005.
A Columbia University historian and political scientist argues that affirmative action — favoring whites — evolved as a way of excluding Southern blacks from federal social benefits.

Schmidt, Peter, *Color and Money: How Rich White Kids are Winning the War Over College Affirmative Action*, Palgrave Macmillan, 2007.
An editor at *The Chronicle of Higher Education* explores the realities of race, class and college admissions.

Sowell, Thomas, *Affirmative Action Around the World: An Empirical Study*, Yale University Press, 2004.
A prominent black conservative and critic of affirmative action dissects the doctrine and practice and its similarities to initiatives in the developing world, of which few Americans are aware.

Articles

Babington, Charles, "Might Obama's success undercut affirmative action," *The Associated Press*, June 28, 2008, www.usatoday.com/news/politics/2008-06-28-3426171631_x.htm.
In a piece that prompted a debate question to presidential candidate Barack Obama, a reporter examines a possibly paradoxical consequence of the 2008 presidential campaign.

Jacobs, Tom, "Affirmative Action: Shifting Attitudes, Surprising Results," *Miller-McCune*, June 20, 2008, www.miller-mccune.com/article/447.
A new magazine specializing in social issues surveys the long-running debate over university admissions. (*Miller-McCune* is published by SAGE Publications, parent company of CQ Press.)

Leonhardt, David, "The New Affirmative Action," *New York Times Magazine*, Sept. 30, 2007, p. 76.
A journalist specializing in economic and social policy explores UCLA's efforts to retool its admissions procedures.

Liptak, Adam, "Lawyers Debate Why Blacks Lag At Major Firms," *The New York Times*, Nov. 29, 2006, p. A1.
A law correspondent airs a tough debate over affirmative action's success, or lack of it, at big law firms.

Matthews, Adam, "The Fixer," *Good Magazine*, Aug. 14, 2008, www.goodmagazine.com/section/Features/the_fixer.
A new Web-based publication for the hip and socially conscious examines the career of black businessman and affirmative-action critic Ward Connerly.

Mehta, Seema, "UCLA accused of illegal admissions practices," *Los Angeles Times*, Aug. 30, 2008, www.latimes.com/news/local/la-me-ucla30-2008aug30,0,6489043.story.

Mehta examines the latest conflict surrounding the top-tier university's retailored admissions procedures.

Reports and Studies

Coleman, James E. Jr. and Mitu Gulati, "A Response to Professor Sander: Is It Really All About the Grades?" *North Carolina Law Review*, 2006, pp. 1823-1829.

Two lawyers, one of them a black who was a partner at a major firm, criticize Sander's conclusions, arguing he overemphasizes academic deficiencies.

Horn, Catherine L. and Stella M. Flores, "Percent Plans in College Admissions: A Comparative Analysis of Three States' Experiences," The Civil Rights Project, Harvard University, February 2003.

Educational policy experts with a pro-affirmative action perspective dig into the details of three states' alternatives to traditional affirmative action.

Prager, Devah, "The Mark of a Criminal Record," *American Journal of Sociology*, March 2003, pp. 937-975.

White people with criminal records have a better chance at entry-level jobs than black applicants with clean records, an academic's field research finds.

Sander, Richard H., "The Racial Paradox of the Corporate Law Firm," *North Carolina Law Review*, 2006, pp. 1755-1822.

A much-discussed article shows that a disproportionate number of black lawyers from top schools leave major law firms before becoming partners.

Swanson, Christopher B., "Who Graduates? Who Doesn't? A Statistical Portrait of Public High School Graduation, Class of 2001," *The Urban Institute*, 2004, www.urban.org/publications/410934.html.

A centrist think tank reveals in devastating detail the disparity in high schools between races and classes.

For More Information

American Association for Affirmative Action, 888 16th St., N.W., Suite 800, Washington, DC 20006; (202) 349-9855; www.affirmativeaction.org. Represents human resources professionals in the field.

American Civil Liberties Union, 125 Broad St., 18th Floor, New York, NY 10004; www.aclu.org/racialjustice/aa/index.html. The organization's Racial Justice Program organizes legal and voter support for affirmative action programs.

American Civil Rights Institute, P.O. Box 188350, Sacramento, CA 95819; (916) 444-2279; www.acri.org/index.html. Organizes ballot initiatives to prohibit affirmative action programs based on race and ethnicity preferences.

Diversity Web, Association of American Colleges and Universities, 1818 R St., N.W., Washington, DC 20009; www.diversityweb.org. Publishes news and studies concerning affirmative action and related issues.

www.jessicacorry.com. A Web site featuring writings by Jessica Peck Corry, director of the Colorado campaign for a racial preferences ban.

Project SEAPHE (Scale and Effects of Admissions Preferences in Higher Education), UCLA School of Law, Box 951476, Los Angeles, CA 90095; (310) 206-7300; www.seaphe.org. Analyzes data on the effects of racial and other preferences.

U.S. Commission on Civil Rights, 624 Ninth St., N.W., Washington, DC 20425; (202) 376-7700; www.usccr.gov. Studies and reports on civil rights issues and implements civil rights laws.

Human Trafficking and Slavery

Are the World's Nations Doing Enough to Stamp It Out?

David Masci

Tearful Eastern European women comfort each other after being freed in 2000 from an American-owned hotel in Phnom Penh, Cambodia, where they were forced to have sex with businessmen and government officials. Traffickers in Eastern Europe often lure young women into bondage by advertising phony jobs abroad for nannies, models or actresses.

From *CQ Researcher*, March 26, 2004.

O ne morning in May, 7-year-old Francis Bok walked to the market in Nymlal, Sudan, to sell some eggs and peanuts. The farmer's son had made the same trip many times before.

"I was living a very good life with my family," he recalls today. "I was a happy child."

But his happy life ended that day in 1986. Arab raiders from northern Sudan swept into the village, sowing death and destruction. "They came on horses and camels and running on foot, firing machine guns and killing people everywhere," he says. His entire family — mother, father and two sisters — died in the attack.

The raiders grabbed Francis and several other children, lashed them to donkeys and carried them north for two days. Then the children were parceled out to their captors. Francis went to a man named Giema Abdullah.

For the next 10 years, the boy tended his "owner's" goats and cattle. He slept with the animals, never had a day off and was rarely fed properly.

"He treated me like an animal, he even called me an animal, and he beat me," Francis says. "There was no joy. Even when I remembered my happy life before, it only made me sad."

In 1996, Francis escaped to Sudan's capital, Khartoum; then he made his way to Cairo, Egypt, and eventually in 2000 to the United States, which admitted him as a refugee.

As all American students learn, the Civil War ended slavery in the United States in 1865. Internationally, the practice was banned by several agreements and treaties, beginning in

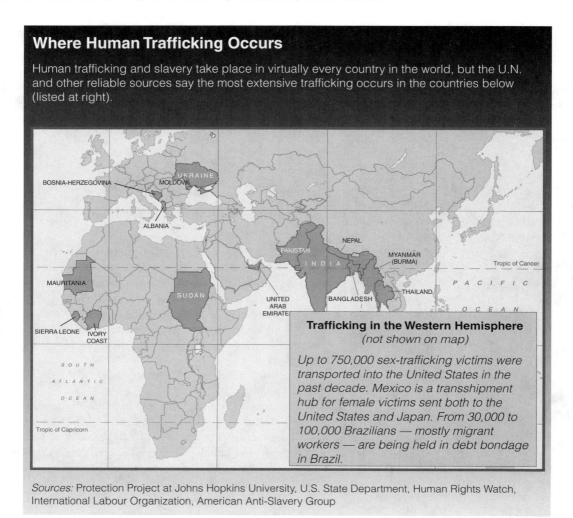

Where Human Trafficking Occurs

Human trafficking and slavery take place in virtually every country in the world, but the U.N. and other reliable sources say the most extensive trafficking occurs in the countries below (listed at right).

Trafficking in the Western Hemisphere
(not shown on map)

Up to 750,000 sex-trafficking victims were transported into the United States in the past decade. Mexico is a transshipment hub for female victims sent both to the United States and Japan. From 30,000 to 100,000 Brazilians — mostly migrant workers — are being held in debt bondage in Brazil.

Sources: Protection Project at Johns Hopkins University, U.S. State Department, Human Rights Watch, International Labour Organization, American Anti-Slavery Group

1926 with the Slavery Convention of the League of Nations. But for tens of millions of people around the world, including millions of children like Francis, slavery never ended. An estimated 27 million people currently are held in some form of bondage, according to anti-slavery groups like Free the Slaves.[1] From the villages of Sudan and Mauritania in Africa to the factories, sweatshops and brothels of South Asia, slavery in its rawest, cruelest form is very much alive in the 21st century.

Many of those in bondage were kidnapped, like Francis. Others go voluntarily to different countries, thinking they are heading for a better life, only to be forced into a nightmare of prostitution or hard labor. Many more work as bonded laborers, tied to lifetime servitude because their father or grandfather borrowed money they couldn't repay.

Trafficking people across international borders has become a $12-billion-a-year global industry that touches virtually every country. The U.S. government estimates that between 800,000 and 900,000 people are trafficked internationally every year, many of them women and children, transported as sex workers.[2] The total includes up to 20,000 people forcibly trafficked into the United

Europe	
Albania	Up to 90 percent of the girls in rural areas don't go to school for fear of being abducted and sold into sexual servitude.
Bosnia and Herzegovina	A quarter of the women working in nightclubs claim they were forced into prostitution. The U.N. police task force is suspected of covering up its involvement in the sex trade.
Moldova	Up to 80 percent of the women trafficked as prostitutes in Western Europe may be Moldovans.
Ukraine	Up to 400,000 Ukrainian women have been trafficked for sexual exploitation in the past decade, Ukraine says. Ukrainian sex slaves can fetch up to $25,000 in Israel.
Africa	
Ivory Coast	A girl can allegedly be bought as a slave in Abidjan for about $7; a shipment of 10 children from Mali for work on the cocoa plantations costs about $420.
Mauritania	Light-skinned Arab Berbers today are thought to exploit hundreds of thousands of black African slaves. Slave raids in the 13th century began systemic slavery in Mauritania.
Sudan	Muslim tribesmen from northern Sudan still stage slave raids on non-Muslim Dinka peoples in the south, taking thousands of women and children.
Asia	
Bangladesh	An estimated 25,000 women and children are trafficked annually from Bangladesh.
India	Parents have sold an estimated 15 million children into bonded labor in return for meager loans from moneylenders.
Myanmar	The ruling military junta coerces minorities into forced labor in factories that benefit the regime and foreign corporations.
Nepal	A major source of women trafficked into Indian brothels; in addition, an estimated 75,000 people are trapped as bonded laborers in Nepal.
Pakistan	Millions of Pakistanis, often members of religious minorities, are forced to work as brick makers or in the fields of feudal landowners.
Thailand	Children sold by their parents make up a significant percentage of prostitutes in Thailand, which is a prime destination for pedophile sex tourists.
United Arab Emirates	Many women trafficked from the former Soviet Union end up in the UAE.

States annually, according to the Central Intelligence Agency.[3] (*See sidebar, p. 36.*)

Lyudmilla's story is typical. Like many desperately poor young women, the single mother of three from the former Soviet republic of Moldova responded to an advertisement promising work in Italy. Instead she was taken to a brothel in Macedonia, where she spent two horrific years in sexual slavery before escaping in 2002.[4]

Venecija, a Bulgarian, also ended up in a Macedonian brothel. "We were so tired we couldn't get out of bed," she recalled. "But [we had to] put on makeup and meet customers," she said after escaping. Those who refused were beaten until they "changed their minds."[5]

John Eibner of Christian Solidarity International pays an Arab trader to free 132 slaves in Madhol, northern Sudan, in 1997. Critics of slave-redemption say it only encourages more slave-taking, but supporters say that not trying to free slaves would be unconscionable.

Traffickers control their victims through a variety of coercive means. In addition to rape and beatings, they keep their passports, leaving them with few options if they do manage to escape.

And the violence can follow those who do get away. Mercy, a young West African woman trafficked to Italy, escaped her tormentors only to see her sister killed in retribution after Mercy told human rights groups about her experience.[6]

The vast majority of slaves and victims of human trafficking come from the poorest parts of Africa, Asia, Latin America and Eastern Europe, where smooth-talking traffickers often easily deceive desperate victims or their parents into believing that they are being offered a "better life."

"Being poor doesn't make you a slave, but it does make you vulnerable to being a slave," says Peggy Callahan, a spokeswoman for Free the Slaves, based in Washington, D.C.

Some Christian groups and non-governmental organizations (NGOs) have tried to buy slaves out of bondage, particularly in Sudan, where two decades of civil war have stoked the slave trade. But many humanitarian groups argue that so-called slave redemption merely increases the demand for slaves.

International efforts to fight slavery and trafficking have increased dramatically over the last 10 years, with the United States playing a leading role. President Bush dramatized America's commitment in an address to the U.N. General Assembly on Sept. 23, 2003. The president had been expected to focus on security issues in the Middle East, but he devoted a substantial portion of his remarks to urging the international community to do more to fight trafficking.

"There is a special evil in the abuse and exploitation of the most innocent and vulnerable," Bush said. "Nearly two centuries after the abolition of the transatlantic slave trade, and more than a century after slavery was officially ended in its last strongholds, the trade in human beings for any purpose must not be allowed to thrive."[7]

The cornerstone of recent American anti-trafficking efforts is the 2000 Trafficking Victims Protection Act, which mandates the cutoff of most non-humanitarian U.S. aid for any nation deemed not trying hard enough to address the problem.

"The act breaks new ground because it actually tries to bring about changes in other countries," says Wendy Young, director of external relations for the Women's Commission for Refugee Women and Children in New York City.

"It's making a difference in countries all over the world," agrees Rep. Christopher H. Smith, R-N.J., one of the law's authors.

But critics contend the act is too weak to force real behavior changes. "It's very easy for countries to avoid sanctions just by taking a few largely meaningless actions," says Katherine Chon, co-director of the Polaris Project, an anti-trafficking advocacy group in Washington. She also accuses the administration of giving a pass to important allies, like Saudi Arabia, regardless of what they do to ameliorate their forced-labor practices.

All sides agree that many countries where trafficking occurs have a long way to go before they attain the level of economic, legal and political maturity needed to entirely eliminate the practice. "I don't think people realize just how desperately poor and chaotic many countries are today," says Linda Beher, a spokeswoman for the New York City-based United Methodist Committee On Relief, which assists trafficking victims.

A tragic consequence of this poverty is child labor, which many experts see as a cousin to slavery. In the developing world today, nearly 200 million children ages 5-14 are put to work to help support their families, according to the International Labour Organization

(ILO). Almost half are under age 12, and more than 20 million are engaged in highly hazardous work, such as tanning leather or weaving rugs, exposing them to unhealthy chemicals or airborne pollutants.[8]

Some humanitarian aid workers describe much child labor as inherently coercive, because young children often have no choice.

The ILO argues that eliminating child labor and sending children to school would ultimately benefit nations with child laborers by raising income levels. (*See graph, p. 30.*) But some economists counter that putting even a fraction of the working children in school would be prohibitively expensive.

As experts debate resolving what has been called one of the greatest humanitarian problems of the 21st century, here are some of the questions they are asking:

Does buying slaves in order to free them solve the problem?

In recent years, would-be Samaritans — from Christian missionaries to famous rock musicians — have worked to free slaves in Africa. Although slave trading occurs in many countries, the rescue efforts largely have focused on war-torn Sudan, where Muslim raiders from the north have enslaved hundreds of thousands of Christian and animist tribesmen in the south.

The Sudanese government has done virtually nothing to stop the practice and has even encouraged it as a means of prosecuting the war against the rebellious south, according to the U.S. State Department's 2003 "Trafficking in Persons Report."

Since 1995, Christian Solidarity International (CSI) and other slave-redemption groups operating in Sudan say they have purchased the freedom of more than 60,000 people by providing money for local Sudanese to buy slaves and then free them.[9]

Fighting the Traffickers

The 2000 Trafficking Victims Protection Act requires the State Department to report each year on global efforts to end human trafficking. Last year, 15 countries were placed in Tier 3, for those deemed to be doing little or nothing against trafficking. Countries in Tier 3 for three years in a row can lose all U.S. non-humanitarian aid. Tier 1 countries are considered to be actively fighting trafficking. Seventy-five countries are in Tier 2, indicating they are making some efforts against trafficking.

State Department Anti-Trafficking Ratings

Tier 1 — Actively Fighting Trafficking		
Austria	Hong Kong	Poland
Belgium	Italy	Portugal
Benin	South Korea	Spain
Colombia	Lithuania	Sweden
Czech Republic	Macedonia	Switzerland
Denmark	Mauritius	Taiwan
France	Morocco	United Arab Emirates
Germany	The Netherlands	United Kingdom
Ghana		

Tier 3 — Doing Little or Nothing		
Belize	Georgia	North Korea
Bosnia and Herzegovina	Greece	Sudan
Myanmar	Haiti	Suriname
Cuba	Kazakhstan	Turkey
Dominican Republic	Liberia	Uzbekistan

Source: "2003 Trafficking in Persons Report," Office to Monitor and Combat Trafficking in Persons, Department of State, June 2003

"Women and children are freed from the terrible abuse, the rape, the beatings, the forcible conversions [to Islam] — all of the horrors that are an inherent part of slavery in Sudan," said John Eibner, director of CSI's redemption program.[10]

Halfway around the world, *New York Times* columnist Nicholas D. Kristof had his own brush with slave redemption when he traveled to Cambodia and freed two female sex slaves. "I woke up her brothel's owner at dawn," he wrote of his efforts to purchase one of the prostitutes, "handed over $150, brushed off demands for interest on the debt and got a receipt for $150 for buying

Economic Benefits Cited for Ending Child Labor

Banning child labor and educating all children would raise the world's total income by 22 percent, or $4.3 trillion, over 20 years, according to the International Labour Organization (ILO). The principal benefit would be the economic boost that most countries would experience if all children were educated through lower secondary school, plus substantial but less dramatic health benefits. The ILO analysis assumes countries that banned child labor would pay poor parents for their children's lost wages, something critics say is unrealistically expensive.

Net Economic Benefits of Eliminating Child Labor
(as a percentage of annual gross national income)

Region	Percentage	Value
Asia	27.0%	($2.9 trillion)
Latin America	9.3%	($330.6 billion)
North Africa, Middle East	23.2%	($444.4 billion)
Sub-Saharan Africa	54.0%	($584.4 billion)
Transitional countries*	5.1%	($124.2 billion)
Global	22.2%	($4.3 trillion)

* Transitional countries — such as Taiwan, Singapore and Malaysia — are no longer considered "developing" but not yet classified as fully industrialized.

Source: "Investing in Every Child," International Programme on the Elimination of Child Labour, International Labour Office, December 2003

a girl's freedom. Then Srey Neth and I fled before the brothel's owner was even out of bed."[11]

While experts concede that slave redeemers are well-intentioned, many contend the practice actually does more harm than good. "When you have people running around buying up slaves, you help create market demand for more slaves," says Jim Jacobson, president of Christian Freedom International, a relief group in Front Royal, Va., that stopped its slave-repatriation efforts five years ago. "It's really just simple economics."

Kevin Bales, author of *Disposable People: New Slavery in the Global Economy* and president of Free the Slaves, agrees. "This is like paying a burglar to redeem the television set he just stole," says Bales, a noted expert on contemporary slavery. "It's better to find other ways to free people, like going to the police or taking them out of bondage by force."

Indeed, Jacobson says, redemption only puts more money in the pockets of unscrupulous and often violent slave traders. "These people end up taking the money and buying more guns and hiring more thugs to go out and take more slaves," he says.

In addition, the critics say, many "slaves" pretend to be in bondage to defraud Westerners. "If you talk to aid workers in these places, you'll find that [bogus slave traders] are literally picking up [already free] people from across town and 'selling' them an hour later," Free the Slaves' Callahan says.

"So much of it is a huge scam operation," agrees Jacobson. "A lot of these people aren't really slaves."

But supporters of redemption say it would be unconscionable not to attempt to free slaves, even if slavers will go out searching for new victims. "Slaves are treated so badly, especially the women and children, who have been beaten and raped," says William Saunders, human rights counsel for the Family Research Council, a conservative social-policy group, and co-founder of the Bishop Gassis Sudan Relief Fund, both in Washington. "How can you not try to free these people?"

Saunders and others also contend that slave buyers take steps to avoid creating a bigger market for slaves. "In the Sudan, they use the local currency, because a dollar or a [British] pound is the sort of powerful magnet that might give people incentives to take more slaves or present non-slaves," he says.

In addition, redemption supporters say, they usually cap what they will pay per person — typically $50. "There's a real effort to ensure that we don't inflate the value of slaves," says Tommy Ray Calvert, chief of external operations for the Boston-based American Anti-Slavery Group (AASG).

Calvert contends that the redemptions have helped decrease slave raids in Sudan. The redemptions "brought world attention to the issue and forced our government and others to start pressuring the Sudanese to stop this evil practice," he says.

Moreover, Saunders refutes the charge that redeemers simply set people free without trying to ensure that they are true slaves. "They try to repatriate these people directly to their villages," Saunders says. "They don't just buy their freedom and let them go."

But the critics remain dubious. "It's so hard to get anywhere in Sudan that there is no way that they could actually follow all of these people back to their home villages," Jacobson says. "It would take weeks or months."

Moreover, he says, "they don't have any idea whether the people they've freed have been coached or whether the village they're going to is really their village. It's simply impossible to know."

Is the Trafficking Victims Protection Act tough enough?

The $12 billion human-trafficking industry is now the world's third-largest illegal business, surpassing every other criminal enterprise except the drug and arms trades, according to the United Nations.[12]

In October 2000, the U.S. government zeroed in on the problem, enacting the Trafficking Victims Protection Act (TVPA), which targets the illegal trade both at home and abroad.[13] The law established the State Department's Office to Monitor and Combat Trafficking in Persons, which issues an annual report on what countries are doing to end trafficking.

The report uses a three-tiered system to rank countries — from states that actively fight trafficking (Tier 1) to those doing little (Tier 3). Countries classified as Tier 3 for three years in a row are subject to a cut-off of non-humanitarian U.S. aid. (*See sidebar, p. 36.*)

On the domestic side, the law allows U.S. authorities to charge alleged traffickers in the United States under the tough federal anti-racketeering law (RICO). According to the State Department, 111 persons have been charged with trafficking in the first three years since the law was enacted, a threefold increase over the three-year period before the TVPA went into effect.[14]

The law also makes it easier for trafficked victims to acquire refugee status in the United States and allows them to sue their victimizers for damages in civil court.

Rescuers return 14 children to their native Bangladesh after they were abducted to India. Children in poor countries sometimes are sold by their parents or kidnapped by traffickers and forced to work without pay, frequently in hazardous conditions.

President Bill Clinton signed the bill into law on Oct. 28, 2000, saying it would provide "important new tools and resources to combat the worldwide scourge of trafficking."

Today, however, critics argue that while the act is "a step in the right direction," it is ultimately not tough enough to shake up the industry, especially internationally. "Of course, it's good that we have it, but frankly we have an awfully long way to go," says the Polaris Project's Chon.

She especially criticizes provisions requiring countries to fight trafficking or face American penalties. "It's just not strong enough because it allows countries to avoid sanctions with just superficial acts," she says.

For example, she says, Japan responded to U.S. pressure to curtail sex trafficking by "giving Cambodia a few million dollars in anti-trafficking aid and holding a symposium on trafficking." But the Japanese did "not really do anything to substantially crack down on their own widespread problem."

Yet, she adds, the United States has said Japan has been tackling trafficking enough to avoid a Tier 3 classification and the prospect of sanctions. "Japan is an important ally," she says. "Need I say more?"

Other critics allege that certain countries are treated with "kid gloves" for political reasons. "States like Saudi

Arabia and countries from the former Soviet Union, which are important American allies, have been pushed up to Tier 2 because stopping slavery isn't the priority [in U.S. foreign relations] it should be," says Calvert of the AASG.

Calvert is especially incensed that the government failed to classify Mauritania, on Africa's northwestern coast, in Tier 3, calling it instead a "special case" because of insufficient information to make an accurate determination. "This is a country with literally hundreds of thousands of people in chattel slavery and everyone knows it, and yet it gets a pass," he says. "That is just unbelievable to me."

But supporters contend that the TVPA, while not perfect, helps move problem countries in the right direction. "It's important to have a tool we can use to push foreign governments to act against this terrible abuse of human dignity, and this law does that," says Beher, of the United Methodist Committee On Relief.

In Japan, for instance, the law has helped make the fight against trafficking more effective, raising public awareness of the problem dramatically as a result of the debate over its ranking in the TVPA, supporters add.

"When Japan was dropped from Tier 1 to Tier 2, it was very embarrassing for them, and all of a sudden you saw this real public debate about the trafficking issue — which is a huge problem there," says Diana Pinata, a spokeswoman for Vital Voices, a global woman's advocacy group in Washington. "If nothing else, the [annual State Department trafficking] report and the threat of sanctions keeps the issue in the spotlight in these countries, and that's very positive."

Besides Japan, several other countries, including Russia, Saudi Arabia and Indonesia, have dramatically improved their anti-trafficking efforts as a result of pressure brought to bear by the TVPA, says John Miller, director of the Office to Combat Trafficking. "We've seen real efforts all over the world," he says. "Some have been more substantial than others, but there already has been a lot of progress."

Moreover, Miller rejects the charge of political favoritism. "Look at the Tier 3 list, and you'll see that there are U.S. allies like Greece and Turkey there," he says. "These decisions aren't being made on the basis of politics."

Pinata agrees. "When we speak to NGO workers and others in the field working on this issue, we get the sense that the trafficking report's assessment of these countries is essentially correct," she says.

Should most forms of child labor be eliminated?

Zara Cigay, 12, and her two younger brothers don't go to school. Instead, they help their parents and extended family, migrant farm workers who pick cotton and other crops in southern Turkey.

"Wherever there is a job, we do it," said Huseyin Cigay, Zara's great-uncle. "The children work with us everywhere."[15]

More than 250 million children around the world between the ages of 5 and 17 are working, according to the ILO. Most are in developing countries in Africa and Asia, and nearly half work full time like Zara and her brothers.[16]

Many do strenuous farm labor. In cities, they do everything from retailing and domestic service to manufacturing and construction. In nations beset by civil wars, thousands of children have been forced to fight in rebel armies.[17]

A large portion of child labor is coerced, according to child-welfare experts. Children are often sold by their parents or kidnapped and forced to work virtually as slaves for no pay. In India, children are literally tied to weaving looms so that they cannot run away.

Labor experts uniformly condemn forced and bonded labor. But on the question of child labor in general, the experts are split over whether the practice should be condoned under certain circumstances.

Human rights advocates and others point to the ILO's 1999 Worst Forms of Child Labor Convention, which prohibits all full-time work and any work by children under 12 but sanctions part-time, non-hazardous labor for teenagers that does not interfere with their social development.[18]

"Under international law, children have a right to a basic education," says Karin Landgren, chief of child protection at the United Nations Children's Fund (UNICEF). "Work should never interfere with this."

In addition, Landgren says, "They need to have time to play and participate freely in their country's cultural and social life. This is vitally important if they are to develop into healthy adults."

A recent ILO report says that child labor negatively impacts all levels of society. "Child labor perpetuates poverty, because when children don't have an education and a real chance to develop to their fullest potential, they are mortgaging their future," says Frans Roselaers, director of the organization's international program on the elimination of child labor and author of the report.

Child labor also costs societies economically by producing uneducated adult workers, Roselaers says. "Countries with a lot of child workers are stunting their economic growth," he says, "because they will only end up producing an army of weak and tired workers with no skills."

But some economists counter that child labor, even full-time work, is often a necessity in developing countries. "In an ideal world, children would spend all of their time at school and at play, but poor people in poor countries don't have the kind of options that we in rich countries do," says Ian Vasquez, director of the Project on Global Economic Liberty at the Cato Institute, a libertarian think tank. "When you begin to restrict children's options for work, you can end up hurting children and their families."

Indeed, child labor often is the only thing that stands between survival and starvation, some experts say. "No parents want their child to work, but child labor helps families get by," says Deepak Lal, a professor of international-development studies at the University of California, Los Angeles. "When a country's per capita income rises to about $3,000 or $4,000, child labor usually fades away."

In addition, Lal says, working children often end up with a better education than those who don't work. "The public education system is a failure in many parts of the developing world and really doesn't offer much to the children who attend school," he says. "But if a child works and his family earns enough to send him or his siblings to private school, that can really pay off."

Finally, Vasquez argues that outlawing child labor would only drive the problem underground, where there is no government oversight, and abuses would increase. "In Bangladesh, girls were prevented from continuing to work in textile plants, so many ended up as prostitutes," he says. "People need to make money, and if you deny them one route, they'll take another."

But Roselaers counters that child workers would not be driven to more dangerous and demeaning jobs if the international community eased the transition from work to school. In the case of Bangladesh, he says, the threat of a consumer boycott by Western countries prompted textile factory owners to fire their child employees.

"The factory owners panicked and fired the kids, and so, yes, there were problems," he says. "But when groups like the ILO and UNICEF came in, we started offering the parents stipends to make up for the lost income and easing the children's transition from work to school."

Some 1 million children are now being helped to make the transition from work to school, according to a recent ILO report.[19] In India, for instance, the ILO and the U.S. Department of Labor are spending $40 million this year to target 80,000 children working in hazardous jobs.[20]

Nonetheless, Lal says, such a program could only make a small dent in the problem. "You can't give a stipend to each of the many millions of families that send their children to work," he says. "There isn't enough money to do this, so it's not a realistic solution, just a palliative that make Westerners feel good about themselves."

BACKGROUND

Ancient Practice

Slavery is as old as human civilization. All of the world's great founding cultures, including those in Mesopotamia, China, Egypt and India, accepted slavery as a fact of life.[21] The practice also was common in sub-Saharan Africa and the Americas.

Neither the Bible nor the great thinkers of Greece and Rome took firm positions against slavery. Some, like the Greek philosopher Aristotle, vigorously defended it.

It was not until Enlightenment philosophers like John Locke and Voltaire established new definitions of human freedom and dignity in the 17th and 18th centuries, that large numbers of people started questioning the morality of keeping another person in bondage.

Ancient societies typically acquired slaves from outside their borders, usually through war or territorial conquest. Captives and conquered people often served as agricultural workers or domestic servants.

Slavery probably reached its zenith in ancient Greece and then Rome, where human trafficking became a huge and profitable industry. In many Greek cities, including powerful Athens and Sparta, as many as half the residents

19th Century *After thousands of years, slavery is abolished in much of the world.*

1821 Congress enacts the Missouri Compromise, specifying which new U.S. states will allow slavery.

1833 England outlaws slavery throughout its empire.

1839 The world's first international abolitionist group, Anti-slavery International, is founded in England.

1848 Slavery abolished in French colonies.

1863 President Abraham Lincoln issues Emancipation Proclamation.

December 1865 The 13th Amendment abolishes slavery.

1873 Spain ends slavery in Puerto Rico.

1888 Brazil outlaws slavery.

1900-1990 *International treaties to halt slavery are adopted.*

1919 International Labour Organization (ILO) is founded.

1926 League of Nations outlaws slavery.

1945 United Nations is founded.

1946 U.N. Children's Fund is established.

1948 U.N.'s Universal Declaration of Human Rights prohibits slavery.

1951 International Organization for Migration is founded to help migrants.

1956 Supplementary Convention on the Abolition of Slavery, the Slave Trade, and Institutions and Practices Similar to Slavery outlaws debt bondage, serfdom and other forced-labor practices.

1978 Human Rights Watch is founded.

1983 Sudan's civil war begins, pitting the Muslim north against the Christian and animist south, leading to slave raids in the south.

1990s *The end of the Cold War and other geopolitical changes allow trafficking and slavery to expand.*

1991 Collapse of the Soviet Union leads to a dramatic rise in trafficking in Eastern Europe.

1994 American Anti-Slavery Group is founded.

1995 Christian and non-governmental organizations begin redeeming slaves in Sudan.

June 1, 1999 ILO adopts the Worst Forms of Child Labor Convention.

2000-Present *United States and other countries renew efforts to fight slavery and trafficking.*

March 2000 Free the Slaves is founded.

Oct. 28, 2000 President Bill Clinton signs the Trafficking Victims Protection Act.

Nov. 15, 2000 United Nations approves the Protocol to Prevent, Suppress and Punish the Trafficking in Persons.

Feb. 14, 2002 Polaris Project is founded to fight trafficking.

June 10, 2002 State Department's Office to Monitor and Combat Trafficking releases its first "Trafficking in Persons Report."

March 11, 2003 Brazilian President Luiz Inacio Lula da Silva unveils anti-slavery initiative.

Sept. 19, 2003 President Bush signs Trafficking Victims Protection Act Reauthorization.

Sept. 23, 2003 President Bush delivers a major anti-trafficking address at the U.N. General Assembly.

January 2004 U.N. launches year-long commemoration of anti-slavery movement.

Summer 2004 State Department's Fourth Annual "Trafficking in Persons Report" to be released.

were slaves. In Rome, slavery was so widespread that even common people could afford to have one or two.[22]

Slaves in the ancient world often did more than just menial tasks. Some, especially in the Roman Empire, became physicians and poets. Others achieved great influence, managing estates or assisting powerful generals or politicians.

Great Roman thinkers like Pliny the Younger and Cicero urged masters to treat their slaves with kindness and even to let them "share your conversations, your deliberations and your company," Cicero wrote.[23] Perhaps as a result, manumission, or the freeing of slaves by their masters, was commonplace, usually after many years of service.

Ultimately, however, Roman slavery was maintained by cruelty and violence, including the use of severe flogging and even crucifixion. Slave revolts, common in the first and second centuries B.C., were brutally suppressed.

The collapse of the western half of the Roman Empire in the 5th-century A.D. led to a new, more fragmented, power structure in Western Europe often centered around local warlords (knights) and the Catholic Church. The new order did not eliminate slavery, but in many areas slaves became serfs, or peasants tied to the local lord's land and could not leave without his permission.[24]

In the East, meanwhile, a new force — Islam — was on the rise. For the Arabs who swept into the Mediterranean basin and the Near East beginning in the 7th century, traditional slavery was a way of life, just as it had been for the Romans. In the ensuing centuries, the Arabs brought millions of sub-Saharan Africans, Asians and Europeans to the slave markets for sale throughout the Middle East.

Meanwhile, slavery remained commonplace elsewhere. In North America, Indians along the Eastern seaboard and in the Pacific Northwest often enslaved members of other tribes taken in war. The more advanced indigenous civilizations to the south, like the Aztec and Mayans in what is now Mexico, and the Inca of Peru, also relied upon slaves. And on the Indian subcontinent, the strict Hindu caste system held tens of millions in virtual bondage.

Slavery Goes Global

In the 15th century, European explorers and adventurers sailing to new territories in Asia, Africa and the Americas began a new chapter in the history of slavery.

By 1650, the Dutch, Spanish, Portuguese, French and English had established colonies throughout the world. The new territories, especially in the Americas, produced new crops such as sugar and tobacco, as well as gold and other minerals. Initially, enslaved indigenous peoples did the harvesting and mining in South America. But ill treatment and disease quickly decimated native populations, prompting the importation of slaves from Africa.

From the mid-1500s to the mid-1800s, almost 9 million Africans were shipped mostly to Latin America — particularly to today's Brazil, Haiti and Cuba — under the most inhumane conditions. About 5 percent — about 400,000 — of all the African slaves ended up in the United States.[25]

On the sugar plantations of the West Indies and South America, crushing work and brutal punishment were the norm. Although Spain and Portugal had relatively liberal laws concerning the treatment of slaves — they could marry, sue a cruel owner and even buy their freedom — they were rarely enforced.

In the British colonies and later in the United States, slaves enjoyed somewhat better working conditions and medical care. Nonetheless, life was harsh and in some ways more difficult. Since slaves in Latin America and the Caribbean usually outnumbered Europeans, they were able to retain more of their African customs. In British America, where by 1750 whites outnumbered slaves by more than four to one, Africans quickly lost many of their cultural underpinnings.

Most American slavery was tied to the great Southern plantations that grew tobacco, rice and other cash crops. Although slavery also was practiced in Northern states, it was never as widespread and had been largely abolished by 1800.

By the late 18th century, Southern slavery also appeared headed for extinction, as industrialization and other trends took hold, rendering the plantation system increasingly economically unfeasible. But Eli Whitney's invention of the cotton gin in 1793 gave American slavery a new lease on life. The gin made the labor-intensive process of separating the seeds from the cotton easy, enabling slaves to dramatically increase their output.[26]

Meanwhile, the rise of textile mills in England and elsewhere was creating a new demand for the fluffy, white fiber. By the early 19th century, many Southern plantations that had been unprofitably growing other crops

Fighting Trafficking in the United States

Seven men were sent to prison on Jan. 29, 2004, for holding several Latin American women against their will in South Texas, forcing them to work without pay and raping them repeatedly.

The case was the latest in a series of sex-trafficking cases prosecuted under the Trafficking Victims Protection Act (TVPA) of 2000, which established stiff penalties for human trafficking and provided mandatory restitution to victims.[1] In the last three years, the Justice Department has prosecuted 132 traffickers — three times the number charged in the three years before the law was enacted.[2]

Last year, Congress updated the law to make trafficking a racketeering offense and allow victims to sue their captors in U.S. courts.

"While we have made much progress in combating human trafficking . . . we have not yet eradicated modern-day slavery," reauthorization sponsor Rep. Christopher H. Smith, R-N.J., said during consideration of the bill by the House International Relations Committee on July 23, 2003.

The Central Intelligence Agency estimates that between 18,000 and 20,000 people are trafficked into the United States each year.[3] Many are women — kidnapped or lured here with promises of marriage or work as nannies, models, waitresses, factory workers and exotic dancers. Once they arrive, they are stripped of their passports and forced to work as sex slaves, laborers or domestic servants until their smuggling or travel "debts" are repaid. The average victim is 20 years old.[4]

"They tell them they'll make a lot of money, they'll be free, they'll have a beautiful life," says Marisa B. Ugarte, executive director of the Bilateral Safety Corridor Coalition, a San Diego organization that assists trafficking victims in Mexico and the United States. "But once they are here, everything changes."

Prior to passage of the TVPA, many of the victims were treated as criminals and subject to deportation. Today, they can apply to the Bureau of Citizen and Immigration Services for one of 5,000 "T" nonimmigrant visas available each year. The visas allow them to remain in the United States if they are assisting in the investigation or prosecution of traffickers. They may then apply for permanent residency if their removal would cause severe hardship.[5]

The Department of Homeland Security had received 721 T-status applications as of June 30, 2003: 301 were granted, 30 were denied and 390 are pending.[6]

Mohamed Mattar, co-director of the Protection Project, a human-rights research institute at Johns Hopkins University, said the visa program has been stymied by victims' reluctance to go to law enforcement authorities for help.

This fear is fed by the fact that many police officers remain unaware of the TVPA and are more likely to arrest the victims than the perpetrators, says Donna M. Hughes, an authority on sex trafficking at the University of Rhode Island.

"We need to start treating [Johns] like the perpetrators they are, and not like lonely guys," Hughes adds. "We need a renewal of ideas at the state and local level."

Under the TVPA, alien trafficking victims who do come forward can receive federal benefits normally available to refugees.

Historically, most trafficked victims have come from Latin America and Southeast Asia, smuggled across the porous Mexican border by "coyotes" or escorted by "jockeys" pretending to be a boyfriend or cousin.[7] Since the early 1990s, however, there has been an influx of women from the former Soviet Union and Central and Eastern Europe,

were now making plenty of money using slaves to pick and process cotton.

Around the same time, however, a movement to abolish slavery began to gather steam in the Northern states. For decades, Americans had debated the morality of slavery. During deliberations over independence in 1776, many delegates to the Second Continental Congress — including John Adams, Benjamin Franklin and Virginia slaveholder Thomas Jefferson — had pushed to make the elimination of slavery part of the movement for America's independence. But resistance from the South and the need for colonial unity against the British doomed the proposal.

The debate over slavery, however, did not go away. The issue complicated the new country's efforts to form

where trafficking rings recruit women with newspaper ads and billboards beckoning them to prosperous futures in the United States.

Undocumented migrant workers are also vulnerable to traffickers. On March 2, 2004, a federal district judge sentenced Florida labor contractor Ramiro Ramos to 15 years in prison for holding migrant workers in servitude and forcing them to work in citrus groves until they had paid off their transportation debts.[8]

In some instances, diplomats and international civil servants bring domestic workers — often illiterate women from Africa, Asia and Latin America — into the United States legally, but then force them to work long hours for almost no pay. In one case, an Ethiopian maid for an International Monetary Fund staffer says she worked eight years for seven days a week, 15 hours a day for less than 3 cents an hour.[9]

Although the employer claimed the maid was his guest, he disappeared before a lawsuit filed by the maid, Yeshehareg Teferra, could be prosecuted. "I was not their guest," Teferra told a reporter. "I was their slave "[10]

Foreign diplomats bring 3,800 domestic servants into the United States each year under special temporary work visas, which allow them only to work for the employer who sponsored them. The employer promises to abide by U.S. labor laws, but there is almost no oversight of the program, so the abuse of servants remains under law enforcement's radar screen, human rights advocates say.[11]

But foreign nationals are not the only victims of domestic trafficking. Homeless and runaway American children also are preyed upon by pimps, who troll malls and clubs in search of teenagers they can "turn." Typically, the pimps befriend the girls, ply them with drugs and then use their addiction to turn them into prostitutes.[12]

There are between 100,000 and 300,000 such citizen victims in the United States, though they're more often overlooked by police, says Derek Ellerman, co-founder of the Polaris Project, a grass-roots anti-trafficking organization. "There is a glaring bias in enforcement" of the Mann Act, which bans the transport of children and adults across state lines for prostitution, Ellerman says. "U.S. kids who are being targeted [by traffickers] just are not being protected."

For the traffickers — many of them members of gangs or loosely linked criminal networks — trafficking is much more lucrative than smuggling contraband items, because human slaves can provide a source of long-term income through prostitution and forced labor. "There's a market for cheap labor, and there's a market for cheap sex, and traffickers know they can make money in it," Michele Clark, co-director of the Protection Project, says.

— Kelly Field

---

[1] Department of Justice press release, Jan. 29, 2004.

[2] Department of Justice press release, March 2, 2004.

[3] Department of Justice, "Assessment of U.S. Activities to Combat Trafficking in Persons," August 2003, p. 3.

[4] Amy O'Neill Richard, "International Trafficking in Women to the United States: A Contemporary Manifestation of Slavery and Organized Crime," DCI Exceptional Intelligence Analyst Program, pp. 3-5.

[5] John R. Miller, "The United States' Effort to Combat Trafficking in Persons," *International Information Program Electronic Journal*, U.S. State Department, June 2003.

[6] Department of Justice, *op. cit.*, August 2003, p. 9.

[7] Peter Landesman, "The Girls Next Door," *The New York Times Magazine*, Jan. 25, 2004.

[8] Justice Department, *op. cit.*, March 2, 2004.

[9] William Branigin, "A Life of Exhaustion, Beatings, and Isolation," *The Washington Post*, Jan. 5, 1999, p. A6.

[10] Quoted in *ibid.*

11 Richard, *op. cit.*, p. 28,

[12] Janice G. Raymond and Donna M. Hughes, "Sex Trafficking of Women in the United States, International and Domestic Trends," Coalition Against Trafficking in Women, March 2001, p. 52.

---

its governing institutions and to expand westward, forcing increasingly abolitionist Northerners and slaveholding Southerners to craft tortured compromises to keep the nation together.

In 1789, delegates to the Constitutional Convention hammered out the infamous Three-fifths Compromise, permitting each slave to be counted as three-fifths of a person for purposes of apportioning the number of representatives each state had in the new Congress.[27] And in 1821, Congress passed the Missouri Compromise, drawing a line westward along the 36.30 parallel. The new Western states above the line would be admitted to the Union as "free" states, while those below the boundary would be so-called slave states.

Nearly 200 Million Young Kids Must Work

Nearly a fifth of the world's young children have to work, including 110 million in Asia and fully a quarter of all the children in sub-Saharan Africa.

Working Children, Ages 5 to 14, By Region
(in millions)

Region	Total Working	Percentage of children in region
Asia	110.4	18.7%
Latin America	16.5	17.0
North Africa, Middle East	9.0	10.2
Sub-Saharan Africa	37.9	25.3
Transitional countries*	8.3	14.6
Total	**182.1**	**18.5%**

* Transitional countries — such as Taiwan, Singapore and Malaysia — are no longer considered "developing" but not yet classified as fully industrialized.

Source: "Investing in Every Child," International Programme on the Elimination of Child Labour, International Labour Office, December 2003

Outlawing Slavery

Much of the rest of the world, however, was abolishing slavery. In the early 1800s, many of the newly independent nations of Spanish America won their independence and immediately outlawed human bondage. Simón Bolívar, who liberated much of Latin America, was a staunch abolitionist, calling slavery "the daughter of darkness."[28]

In Europe, the tide also was turning. Largely due to the efforts of abolitionist William Wilberforce, the British Empire outlawed the practice in 1833, although de facto slavery continued in India and some other colonies. In 1848, France also freed the slaves in its colonies.

However, in the United States, peaceful efforts at compromise over slavery failed, and the issue finally helped trigger the Civil War in 1861. In 1863, during the height of the conflict, President Abraham Lincoln issued the "Emancipation Proclamation," freeing all slaves in the Southern, or Confederate, states. Soon after the war ended with Union victory in 1865, the 13th Amendment to the Constitution abolished slavery altogether.[29]

After the Civil War, the worldwide abolition of slavery continued. Spain outlawed the practice in Puerto Rico in 1873 and in Cuba in 1886. More important, Brazil began dismantling its huge slave infrastructure in 1888.

Today, slavery is illegal in every country in the world and is outlawed by several treaties. "In international law, the outlawing of slavery has become what is called *jus cogens*, which means that it's completely accepted and doesn't need to be written into new treaties and conventions," says Bales of Free the Slaves.

The foundation of this complete acceptance rests on several groundbreaking international agreements, beginning with the 1926 Slavery Convention of the League of Nations, which required signatory countries to work to abolish every aspect of the practice.[30]

Slavery also is banned by the 1948 Universal Declaration of Human Rights, which holds that "no one shall be held in slavery or servitude; slavery and the slave trade shall be prohibited in all their forms."[31]

Other conventions prohibiting the practice include the 1930 ILO Convention on Forced Labor and a 1956 Supplementary Convention on the Abolition of Slavery, the Slave Trade, and Institutions and Practices Similar to Slavery.

More recently, the United Nations in 2001 approved a Protocol to Prevent, Suppress and Punish the Trafficking in Persons as part of a major convention on fighting organized crime. The protocol requires signatories to take action to fight trafficking and protect its victims. It has been signed by 117 countries and ratified by 45.[32] While the United States has not yet ratified the document, it has the support of the White House and is expected to win Senate approval in the near future.

CURRENT SITUATION

Human Trafficking

The poorest and most chaotic parts of the developing world supply most trafficking victims — often women and children destined for the sex trade.

In South Asia, young women and children routinely are abducted or lured from Nepal, Pakistan, India, Bangladesh, Cambodia and Myanmar (Burma) to work in brothels in India's large cities, notably Bombay, and the Persian Gulf states. Thousands also end up in Bangkok, Thailand's capital and an infamous sex-tourism mecca.

In Asia, the victims' own families often sell them to traffickers. "In Nepal, entire villages have been emptied of girls," says Pinata of Vital Voices. "Obviously, this could not have happened without the complicity between traffickers and the victims' families."

Parents sell their children for a variety of reasons — virtually all linked to poverty, Pinata says. "Some think the child will have a better life or that their daughter will be able to send money home," she says. "For some, it's just one less mouth to feed."

"Even when they have a sense of what their children will be doing, many parents feel they don't have a choice," adds UNICEF's Landgren. "They feel that literally anything is better than what they have now."

In Eastern Europe, traffickers often lure women into bondage by advertising in local newspapers for nanny positions in the United States or Western Europe. For instance, Tetiana, a Ukrainian woman, was offered 10 times her salary to be an au pair in Italy. Instead she was forced into prostitution in Istanbul, Turkey.[33]

Others are promised work as models or actresses. In some cases, the victims even put up their own money for their travel expenses, only to find themselves prisoners in a European brothel or in Mexico, awaiting transport across the border to the United States.[34]

Even those who understand at the outset that they are going to be prostitutes are not prepared for the brutality they face. "They're unaware of how much abuse, rape, psychological manipulation and coercion is involved," says the Polaris Project's Chon.

Eastern Europe is particularly fertile ground for sex traffickers, she says. The collapse of communism more than a decade ago has left many parts of the region, especially Ukraine, Moldova and Belarus, economically and politically stunted. "These countries are just full of desperate people who will do anything for a chance at a better life," she says.

To make matters worse, brothel owners prize the region's many light-skinned, blonde women. "Lighter women are very popular in places like the United States,

Six-year-old Ratan Das breaks rocks at a construction site in Agartala, India, where he earns about 40 cents a day to supplement his widowed mother's 60-cents-per-day income. India has more child laborers than any other country — about 120 million — followed by Pakistan, Bangladesh, Indonesia and Brazil.

Europe and Asia," Chon says. "So these women are in demand."

In Africa, more people are trafficked for forced labor than as sex slaves. "In Africa, you have a lot of people being taken and sent to pick cotton and cocoa and other forms of agricultural labor," says Vital Voices' Pinata.

Regardless of their origin, once victims are lured into a trafficking ring, they quickly lose control over their destiny. "If they have a passport, it's usually taken from them and they're abused, physically and psychologically, in order to make them easier to control," says the United Methodist Committee On Relief's Beher.

When victims of trafficking reach their final destination, they rarely have freedom of any kind. "A 16-year-old girl who had been trafficked into Kosovo to be a prostitute told me that when she wasn't working in the bar, she was literally locked into her room and not allowed out," Beher says. "That's the sort of thing we see all the time."

Organized crime plays a key role in most human trafficking. "Most of what you are dealing with here is criminal networks," says Miller of the Office to Combat Trafficking. "You can't take someone out of the Czech Republic and drive her to the Netherlands and hand her over to another trafficker and then to a brothel without real cooperation."

A 16-year-old Cambodian girl rescued from a brothel peers from her hiding place in Phnom Penh. An estimated 300,000 women are trapped in slave-like conditions in the Southeast Asian sex trade. Cambodia recently agreed to join the first U.N. program aimed at halting the trafficking of women in the region.

Indeed, smuggling rings often team up with criminal groups in other countries or maintain "branch offices" there. And most traffickers are involved in other criminal activities, such as drugs and weapons smuggling. "Many drug gangs in Southeast Asia are spinning off into trafficking because it's very low risk and very lucrative," says the Women's Commission's Young, who adds that unlike a shipment of drugs, human cargo can earn traffickers money for years.

These crime networks, especially in Eastern Europe and Asia, operate freely, in large part because they have corrupted many local officials. "So many people are being moved across borders that it's impossible to believe that government officials aren't cooperating," Young says. "Like drugs and other illegal activities, this is very corrupting, especially in poor countries where the police are poorly paid."

In addition to stepping up law enforcement, countries can do many things to fight trafficking, UNICEF's Landgren says. "For example, the United Kingdom has a new system that keeps tabs on children entering the country," she says. "By keeping track of children that come in from abroad, we can better protect them."

And in Brazil, where landowners often lure peasants to their farms with promises of work only to put them in debt bondage, President Luiz Ignacio Lula da Silva has stepped up efforts to free forced laborers. Lula, as the president is called, also has called for a change in the constitution to allow the confiscation of land for those convicted of enslaving workers.

Even countries that have long allowed trafficking are beginning to address the issue. Moldova, for instance, has begun prosecuting traffickers and has created a database of employment agencies that help people find legitimate work abroad.[35]

NGOs have also taken steps to help. For instance, some groups run safe houses where trafficking victims who escape can find shelter and security. "We provide them with medical and psychological care," says Beher, whose group operates a house in Kosovo's capital, Pristina. "We allow them to stay until they recover and then help them to get home, which is usually somewhere else in Eastern Europe, like Romania or Moldova."

The Polaris Project maintains three 24-hour hotlines (in English, Thai and Korean) in the United States to allow both victims and third parties to report trafficking activity. Polaris also has a trafficking database to help law enforcement and other officials gather information about potential cases.

But international organizations and NGOs can only do so much, says Beher, because impoverished, poorly governed countries will always be breeding grounds for trafficking. "Until the causes disappear, all we in the international aid community can do is fight the symptoms," she says.

"In order to really get rid of this problem," Beher continues, "you need political stability and a strong civil society, which in turn leads to the rule of law and stronger law enforcement. You know, there's a reason why there aren't a lot of Finnish people being trafficked."

But Calvert of the American Anti-Slavery Group says governments and international organizations could virtually shut down the trade in human beings if they wanted to. "The international community is in a state of denial and lacks the commitment to fight this," he says. "Look at Britain: They had whole fleets of ships devoted to stopping the slave trade on the high seas, and it worked."

Calvert says the United Nations and other international groups should be more aggressive and

Is the Trafficking Victims Protection Act tough enough?

YES
Rep. Christopher H. Smith, R-N.J.
Chairman, U.S. Helsinki Commission

Written for *The CQ Researcher,* March 15, 2004

Each year, nearly a million people worldwide are bought and sold into the commercial sex industry, sweatshops, domestic servitude and other dehumanizing situations.

In October 2000, President Clinton signed into law the Trafficking Victims Protection Act (TVPA), which I authored. It provided a multifaceted approach to halting human trafficking through law enforcement, prevention and aid to victims. It also represented two major policy changes: up to life in prison for those who traffic in humans and treatment of the people trafficked — largely women, children, and teenagers — as victims rather than as criminals. In 2003, the law was expanded and strengthened.

As President Bush noted in his historic speech at the United Nations in September 2003, the global community must do more to eradicate human slavery. But significant progress has been made in just a few years, thanks largely to the law's three-tier system and annual "Trafficking in Persons Report" mandated by the law.

When the first report came out, the State Department listed 23 nations in Tier 3 as the worst offenders. It pulled no punches and did not hesitate to name offending nations, including our allies, if they were not making "serious and sustained" efforts to fight trafficking. Naming names was a measure I fought hard to include in the law, even though it was initially opposed by the previous administration.

Thanks to the report and the threat of sanctions, most nations have improved their record on trafficking. Only 15 countries were in Tier 3 during the most recent 2003 report, and most of them made enough progress in the ensuing months to avoid economic sanctions. The State Department is continually improving the scope of the report so it will present the most accurate and thorough picture of the worldwide trafficking problem.

The message from the United States is loud and clear: If you are committed to the fight against human slavery, we welcome you as an ally. But if you continue to look askance when it comes to this horrible crime and pretend you don't have a trafficking problem, we're going to aggressively push you to make reforms, and we'll use economic sanctions as a means to that end.

NO
Tommy Calvert, Jr.
*Chief of External Operations,
American Anti-Slavery Group*

Written for *The CQ Researcher,* March 15, 2004

Most anti-slavery experts would agree the TVPA is a good law, but that slavery can be defeated in our lifetime only if we give the law priority in attention and funding — and apply it equally to friends and foes alike.

The "Trafficking in Person's Report" (TIPS) required by the law does not reveal the full story on global slavery, but only a snapshot. The criteria used to determine progress in the fight against slavery — by focusing on government action rather than on total slavery within a nation's borders — skew our view of realities on the ground.

South Korea, for example, has a serious problem with trafficking — an estimated 15,000 people trafficked per year — but it is ranked in Tier 1, the best ranking a government can receive. Nations can create many seemingly tough laws and programs to fight slavery. However, organized crime may still run thriving trafficking operations in the face of such policies, which may in reality be weak or ineffectual.

Last year marked the first time that countries designated by the "Trafficking In Persons Report" as the worst offenders — Tier 3 — would automatically be subject to U.S. sanctions, which can only be waived by the president.

The State Department gave wide latitude to the standards for Tier 2, perhaps to keep strategic allies from being hit with sanctions. Both Brazil and Saudi Arabia, for instance, received Tier 2 designations. But Brazil's president has launched one of the world's most ambitious plans to end slavery, while Saudi Arabia has no laws outlawing human trafficking and has prosecuted no offenders. Thus, the report's rankings equate a major national initiative to end slavery with royal lip service.

Some Middle Eastern and North African countries may have advanced in the rankings because they are being courted by the administration to support the war on terror and our plans for change in the region. But there is evidence these countries have not really progressed in the fight against human bondage.

The long-term effect of such discrepancies is to reduce the credibility of the report and lengthen the time it takes to eradicate slavery.

Pakistani Minister for Education Zobaida Jalal and Deputy Labor Under Secretary for International Labor Affairs Thomas Moorhead sign an agreement in Islamabad on Jan. 23, 2002, calling for the U.S. to provide $5 million to help educate working children in Pakistan.

uncompromising in combating slavery. "They had weapons inspectors didn't they?" he asks. "Well that's what we need to fight this. We need that kind of action."

Slavery and Forced Labor

Slavery today bears little resemblance to earlier forms of bondage. For instance, 150 years ago in the American South, a healthy slave was a valuable piece of property, worth up to $40,000 in today's dollars, according to Free the Slaves.[36] By contrast, slaves today are often worth less than $100, giving slaveholders little incentive to care for them.

Although slavery exists nearly everywhere, it is most prevalent in the poorer parts of South Asia, where an estimated 15 million to 20 million people are in bonded labor in India, Pakistan, Bangladesh and Nepal.

Bonded labor usually begins when someone borrows money from someone else and agrees to work for that person until the debt is paid. In most cases, the debt is never paid and the borrower and his immediate family become virtual slaves, working in exchange for basic amenities like food and shelter.

"Often you see a whole family in bondage for three or four generations because once someone borrows a small amount of money you're trapped," says Callahan of Free the Slaves. "You don't pay off the principal of the loan, you just keep paying off the interest."

Bonded laborers work at jobs ranging from making bricks in Pakistan to farming, cigarette rolling and carpet making in India. In the western Indian state of Gujarat, some 30,000 bonded families harvest salt in the marshes. The glare from the salt makes them color-blind. When they die, the laborers cannot even be cremated, according to Hindu custom, because their bodies have absorbed too much salt to burn properly.[37]

Slavery is also widespread in sub-Saharan Africa, where the Anti-Slavery Group estimates that at least 200,000 people are in bondage. Besides Sudan, the largest concentration of African slaves is in Mauritania. For hundreds of years, Mauritania's lighter-skinned ruling elite kept their darker compatriots in a system of chattel slavery, with generations being born into servitude. Although the country formally outlawed slavery in 1980, the practice is thought to still be widespread.

"For the thousands of slaves who were legally freed in 1980, life did not change at all," Bales writes. "No one bothered to tell the slaves about it. Some have never learned of their legal freedom, some did so years later, and for most legal freedom was never translated into actual freedom." Today, slaves are still "everywhere" in Mauritania "doing every job that is hard, onerous and dirty."[38]

Slaves also pick cotton in Egypt and Benin, harvest cocoa and other crops in Ivory Coast and mine diamonds in Sierra Leone.

In addition, hundreds of youngsters are abducted each year and forced to become soldiers for rebel fighters in war zones like Uganda and Congo.

Child soldiers often are made to do horrible things. A girl in Uganda who was kidnapped at 13 was forced to kill and abduct other children during her five years in captivity.[39]

But slavery also flourishes beyond the developing world. Although the problem is not as widespread, forced labor and servitude also occur in Europe and the United States — in brothels, farms and sweatshops. "It's amazing, but there are slaves in the United States doing all kinds of things," says Miller of the Office to Combat Trafficking. "Recently authorities found a group of Mexican [agricultural workers] who had been trafficked to work for no pay in Florida. It's unbelievable."

Moreover, slavery is not confined to just seedy brothels or plantations. In upscale American neighborhoods too, people, usually from other countries, have been enslaved, often as domestics. Last year, for instance, a suburban Maryland couple was convicted of forced labor for coercing an illegal alien from Ghana to work seven days a week as a domestic servant without pay. And from time to time, foreign diplomats are found to be harboring unpaid domestic workers from their home countries who cannot leave to work for someone else because the diplomats hold their visas.[40]

OUTLOOK

Impact of Globalization

The increasing ease of travel and communication brought about by globalization has helped many industries, including illegal ones like trafficking and slavery.

"Globalization has certainly made trafficking and slavery easier, but it is a double-edged sword," says Jacobson of Christian Freedom International. "It has also helped us to more quickly and effectively shine a spotlight on the evil thugs who are doing these bad things."

Moreover, Jacobson says, as globalization improves the general standard of living in the developing world, it becomes harder for traffickers to prey on innocents. "When the boats are rising for everyone, poverty and despair are alleviated," he says. "When someone gets a job and education and health care, they are much less susceptible to being abused."

The Polaris Project's Chon is also optimistic, although for different reasons. "I'm very upbeat about all of this, because tackling these problems is a matter of political will, and I think the world is slowly beginning to pay more attention to these issues," she says. "I feel as though we're at the same point as the [American] abolitionist movement at the beginning of the 19th century, in that things are slowly beginning to move in the right direction."

Rep. Smith agrees. "There's a fever all over the world to enact new, tough policies to deal with this," he says. "Because the U.S. is out front on this, a lot of countries are beginning to follow suit."

Moreover, the optimists note, victims themselves are increasingly fighting for their rights. "There is a silent revolution going on right now, in places like India, where people are literally freeing themselves from slavery," says Callahan of Free the Slaves, referring to thousands of quarry slaves in northern India who recently have left

their bondage and begun new lives. "If this kind of thing keeps up, in a few decades these problems will be blips on the radar screen compared to what they are today."

But Beher of the United Methodist Committee on Relief sees little change ahead because of continuing poverty and societal dysfunction. "The problems that lead to trafficking and slavery are very complicated, and there are no easy fixes," she says. "We need to build up the economies and the civil society of the places where these things happen in order to get rid of this once and for all. And I'm afraid that that is going to take many decades."

Indeed, "Things could get a lot worse before they get better," warns Young of the Women's Commission for Refugee Women and Children, comparing trafficking to the drug trade.

"It's so profitable, and there is so little risk in getting caught that it seems like there will be plenty of this kind of thing going on for the foreseeable future."

NOTES

1. See www.freetheslaves.net/slavery_today/index.html.
2. Figure cited in "2003 Trafficking in Persons Report," U.S. Department of State, p. 7.
3. Frank Trejo, "Event Underscores Scope, Toll of Human Trafficking," *Dallas Morning News*, March 4, 2003, p. 3B.
4. Richard Mertens, "Smuggler's Prey: Poor Women of Eastern Europe," *The Christian Science Monitor*, Sept. 22, 2002, p. A7.
5. Quoted in *ibid*.
6. "Trafficking in Persons Report," *op. cit.*, p. 6.
7. The entire text of President Bush's speech can be found at www.whitehouse.gov/news/releases/2003/09/20030923-4.html.
8. "IPEC Action Against Child Labour: 2002-2003," International Labour Organization, January 2004, p. 15; see also ILO, "Investing in Every Child," December 2003, p. 32.
9. Figure cited in Davan Maharaj, "Panel Frowns on Efforts to Buy Sudan Slaves' Freedom," *Los Angeles Times*, May 28, 2002, p. A3.
10. Quoted from "60 Minutes II," May 15, 2002.

11. Nicholas D. Kristof, "Bargaining For Freedom," *The New York Times*, Jan 21, 2004, p. A27.

12. Figure cited at "UNICEF Oral Report on the Global Challenge of Child Trafficking," January 2004, at: www.unicef.org/about/TraffickingOralreport.pdf.

13. Full text of the law is at: www.state.gov/documents/organization/10492.pdf. The law was reauthorized in December 2003.

14. Figures cited at www.state.gov/g/tip/rls/fs/28548.htm.

15. Richard Mertens, "In Turkey, Childhoods Vanish in Weary Harvests," *The Christian Science Monitor*, May 8, 2003, p. 7.

16. ILO, *op. cit.*

17. See Brian Hansen, "Children in Crisis," *The CQ Researcher*, Aug. 31, 2001, p. 657.

18. See: www.ilo.org/public/english/standards/ipec/ratify_govern.pdf.

19. ILO, *op. cit.*, January 2004, p. 37.

20. "With a Little U.S. Help, ILO Targets Child Labour," *Indian Express*, March 3, 2004.

21. Hugh Thomas, *World History: The Story of Mankind from Prehistory to the Present* (1996), pp. 54-55.

22. *Ibid.*, pp. 105-107.

23. Quoted in Michael Grant, *The World of Rome* (1960), p. 116.

24. Thomas, *op. cit.*, pp. 107-110.

25. Figures cited in *ibid.*, p. 279.

26. John Hope Franklin and Alfred A Moss, Jr., *From Slavery to Freedom: A History of African-Americans* (2000), p. 100.

27. *Ibid.*, p. 94.

28. From a speech before the Congress of Angostura in 1819. See http://www.fordham.edu/halsall/mod/1819bolivar.html.

29. Franklin and Moss, *op. cit.*, p. 244.

30. The full text of the convention can be found at www.unicri.it/1926%20slavery%20convention.pdf.

31. Quoted at www.un.org/Overview/rights.html.

32. A complete list of those countries that have signed and ratified the protocol are at www.unodc.org/unodc/en/crime_cicp_signatures_trafficking.html.

33. Sylvie Briand, "Sold into Slavery: Ukrainian Girls Tricked into Sex Trade," Agence France Presse, Jan. 28, 2004.

34. Peter Landesman, "The Girls Next Door, *The New York Times Magazine*, Jan. 25, 2004, p. 30.

35. "Trafficking in Person's Report," *op. cit.*, p. 107.

36. See www.freetheslaves.net/slavery_today/index.html.

37. Christopher Kremmer, "With a Handful of Salt," *The Boston Globe*, Nov. 28, 1999.

38. Kevin Bales, *Disposable People: The New Slavery in the Global Economy* (1999), p. 81.

39. Thomas Wagner, "Study Documents Trauma of Child Soldiers," Associated Press Online, March 11, 2004.

40. Ruben Castaneda, "Couple Enslaved Woman," *The Washington Post*, June 10, 2003, p. B1.

BIBLIOGRAPHY

Books

Bales, Kevin, *Disposable People: New Slavery in the Global Economy*, University of California Press, 1999.
The president of Free the Slaves and a leading expert on slavery offers strategies to end the practice.

Bok, Francis, *Escape From Slavery: The True Story of My Ten Years In Captivity and My Journey to Freedom in America*, St. Martin's Press, 2003.
A former slave in Sudan tells the gripping story of his ordeal and eventual journey to the United States.

Franklin, John Hope, and, Alfred Moss Jr., *From Slavery to Freedom: A History of African Americans*, McGraw-Hill, 2000.
Franklin, a renowned professor emeritus of history at Duke University and Moss, an associate professor at the University of Maryland, discuss the slave trade and slavery in the United States up to the Civil War.

Articles

"A Cargo of Exploitable Souls," *The Economist*, June 1, 2002.
The article examines human trafficking of prostitutes and forced laborers into the United States.

Bales, Kevin, "The Social Psychology of Modern Slavery," *Scientific American*, **April 2002, p. 68.**
A leading expert on slavery examines the psychological underpinnings that may drive both traffickers and slaveholders as well as their victims.

Cockburn, Andrew, "Hidden in Plain Sight: The World's 27 Million Slaves," *National Geographic*, **Sept. 2003, p. 2.**
A correspondent for London's *Independent* takes a hard look at slavery; includes chilling photographs of victims.

Hansen, Brian, "Children in Crisis," *The CQ Researcher*, **Aug. 31, 2001, pp. 657-688.**
Hansen examines the exploitation of children around the world, including sexual slaves and forced laborers.

Kristof, Nicolas D., "Bargaining For Freedom," *The New York Times*, **Jan. 21, 2004, p. A27.**
The veteran columnist describes how he "bought" and freed two sex slaves in Cambodia. The article is part of Kristof's series on his experiences in Southeast Asia.

Landesman, Peter, "The Girls Next Door," *The New York Times Magazine*, **Jan. 25, 2004, p. 30.**
Landesman's detailed exposé of trafficking focuses on the importation of young girls into the U.S. for prostitution.

Maharaj, Davan, "Panel Frowns on Efforts to Buy Sudan Slaves Freedom," *Los Angeles Times*, **May 28, 2002, p. 3.**
The article details the controversy surrounding the practice of slave redemption in Sudan.

Mertens, Richard, "Smugglers' Prey: Poor Women of Eastern Europe," *The Christian Science Monitor*, **Sept. 25, 2002, p. 7.**
The article examines the plight of Eastern European women trafficked into sexual slavery who manage to escape.

Miller, John, R., "Slavery in 2004," *The Washington Post*, **Jan. 1, 2004, p. A25.**
The director of the State Department's Office to Monitor and Combat Trafficking in Persons argues that the Trafficking Victims Protection Act has prodded other countries to act.

Power, Carla, *et al.*, **"Preying on Children,"** *Newsweek*, **Nov. 17, 2003, p. 34.**
The number of children being trafficked into Western Europe is rising, helped by more porous borders and the demand for young prostitutes.

Vaknin, Sam, "The Morality of Child Labor," *United Press International*, **Oct. 4, 2002.**
UPI's senior business correspondent argues that organizations opposed to most forms of child labor impose unrealistic, rich-world standards on the poorest countries.

Reports

"Investing in Every Child: An Economic Study of the Costs and Benefits of Eliminating Child Labor," *International Labour Organization*, **December 2003.**
The ILO contends that ending child labor would improve economic growth in the developing world.

"IPEC Action Against Child Labor: 2002-2003," *International Labour Organization*, **January 2004.**
The report charts the progress made by the ILO's International Program on the Elimination of Child Labor (IPEC), which funds anti-child labor initiatives around the world.

"Trafficking in Persons Report," *U.S. Department of State*, **June 2003.**
The annual report required by the Trafficking Victims Protection Act assesses global anti-trafficking efforts.

For More Information

American Anti-Slavery Group, 198 Tremont St., Suite 421, Boston, MA 02116; (800) 884-0719; www.iabolish.org.

Casa Alianza, 346 West 17th St., New York, N.Y. 10011; (212) 727-4000; www.casa-alianza.org. A San Jose, Costa Rica, group that aids street children in Latin America.

Christian Children's Fund, 2821 Emerywood Parkway, Richmond, VA 23294; (800) 776-6767; www.christian childrensfund.org. CCF works in 28 countries on critical children's issues.

Christian Freedom International, P.O. Box 535, Front Royal, VA 22630; (800) 323-CARE (2273); (540) 636-8907; www.christianfreedom.org. An interdenominational human rights organization that combines advocacy with human itarian assistance for persecuted Christians.

Christian Solidarity International, Zelglistrasse 64, CH-8122 Binz, Zurich, Switzerland; www.csi-int.ch/index .html. Works to redeem slaves in Sudan.

Defence for Children International, P.O. Box 88, CH 1211, Geneva 20, Switzerland; (+41 22) 734-0558; www .defence-for-children.org. Investigates sexual exploitation of children and other abuses.

Free the Children, 1750 Steeles Ave. West, Suite 218, Concord, Ontario, Canada L4K 2L7; (905) 760-9382; www .freethechildren.org. This group encourages youth to help exploited children.

Free the Slaves, 1326 14th St., N.W., Washington, DC 20005; (202) 588-1865; www.freetheslaves.net.

Human Rights Watch, 350 Fifth Ave., New York, NY 10118; (212) 290-4700; www.hrw.org. Investigates abuses worldwide.

International Labour Organization, 4, route des Morillons, CH-1211, Geneva 22, Switzerland; www.ilo.org. Sets and enforces worldwide labor standards.

Polaris Project, P.O. Box 77892, Washington, DC 20013; (202) 547-7990; www.polarisproject.org. Grass-roots organization fighting trafficking.

United Methodist Committee On Relief, 475 Riverside Dr., New York, NY 10115; (800) 554-8583; gbgm-umc .org. Worldwide humanitarian group.

United Nations Children's Fund (UNICEF), 3 United Nations Plaza, New York, NY 10017; (212) 326-7000; www .unicef.org. Helps poor children in 160 countries.

Women's Commission on Refugee Women and Children, 122 East 42nd St., 12th Floor, New York, NY 10168-1289; (212) 551-3088; www.womenscommission.org. Aids trafficking victims in the developing world.

World Vision International, 800 West Chestnut Ave., Monrovia, Calif. 91016; (626) 303-8811; www.wvi.org. A Christian relief and development organization established in 1950.

3

Immigration Debate

*Can Politicians Find a Way
to Curb Illegal Immigration?*

Alan Greenblatt

A Mexican farmworker harvests broccoli near Yuma, Ariz. With the number of illegal immigrants in the U.S. now over 12 million — including at least half of the nation's 1.6 million farmworkers — tougher enforcement has become a dominant theme in the 2008 presidential campaign. Meanwhile, with Congress unable to act, states and localities have passed hundreds of bills cracking down on employers and illegal immigrants seeking public benefits.

From *CQ Researcher*,
February 1, 2008.

Getty Images/David McNew

John McCain, the senior senator from Arizona and the leading Republican candidate for president, has been hurt politically by the immigration issue.

McCain would allow illegal immigrants to find a way eventually to become citizens. The approach is seen by many Republican politicians and voters (and not a few Democrats) as akin to "amnesty," in effect rewarding those who broke the law to get into this country. Legislation that he helped craft with Sen. Edward M. Kennedy, D-Mass., and the White House went down to defeat in both 2006 and 2007.

McCain rejects the approach taken by House Republicans during a vote in 2005 and favored by several of his rivals in the presidential race — namely, classifying the 12 million illegal immigrants already in this country as felons and seeking to deport them. This wouldn't be realistic, he says, noting not only the economic demands that have brought the foreign-born here in the first place but also the human cost such a widespread crackdown would entail.

On the stump, McCain talks about an 80-year-old woman who has lived illegally in the United States for 70 years and has a son and grandson serving in Iraq. When challenged at Clemson University last November by a student who said he wanted to see all illegal immigrants punished, McCain said, "If you're prepared to send an 80-year-old grandmother who's been here 70 years back to some other country, then frankly you're not quite as compassionate as I am."[1]

As the issue of illegal immigrants reaches the boiling point, however, and as he gains in the polls, even McCain sounds not

47

California Has Most Foreign-Born Residents

California's nearly 10 million foreign-born residents represented about one-quarter of the national total in 2006 and more than twice as many as New York.

Foreign-Born Individuals by State, 2006*

Over 1 million
500,000-999,999
200,000-499,999
100,000-199,999
0-99,999

* Includes legal and illegal immigrants

Source: Migration Policy Institute

Complaints about illegal immigrants breaking the law or draining public resources have become a daily staple of talk radio programs, as well as CNN's "Lou Dobbs Tonight."

In a high-profile speech in August 2007, Newt Gingrich, a former Republican House Speaker, railed about two suspects in a triple murder in New Jersey who turned out to be illegal immigrants. He argued that President Bush should call Congress into special session to address the matter, calling himself "sickened" by Congress being in recess "while young Americans are being massacred by people who shouldn't be here."

Gingrich said Bush should be more serious about "winning the war here at home, which is more violent and more dangerous to Americans than Iraq or Iran."[4]

Concerns about terrorism have also stoked fears about porous borders and unwanted intruders entering the country.

quite so compassionate as before. In response to political pressures, McCain now shares the point of view of hard-liners who say stronger border security must come before allowing additional work permits or the "path to citizenship" that were envisioned by his legislation.

"You've got to do what's right, OK?" McCain told *The New Yorker* magazine recently. "But, if you want to succeed, you have to adjust to the American people's desires and priorities."[2]

Immigration has become a central concern for a significant share of the American public. Immigrants, both legal and illegal, are now 12.6 percent of the population — more than at any time since the 1920s.

Not only is the number of both legal and illegal immigrants — now a record 37.9 million — climbing rapidly but the foreign-born are dispersing well beyond traditional "gatekeeper" states such as California, New York and Texas, creating social tensions in places with fast-growing immigrant populations such as Georgia, Arkansas and Iowa.[3]

"Whenever I'm out with a [presidential] candidate at a town hall meeting, it's the exception when they do not get a question about immigration — whether it's a Democratic event or a Republican event," says Dan Balz, a veteran political reporter at *The Washington Post.*

With no resolution in sight to the immigration debate in Congress, the number of immigrant-related bills introduced in state legislatures tripled last year, to more than 1,500. Local communities are also crafting their own immigration policies. (*See sidebar, p. 58.*)

In contrast to the type of policies pursued just a few years ago, when states were extending benefits such as in-state tuition to illegal immigrants, the vast majority of current state and local legislation seeks to limit illegal immigrants' access to public services and to crack down on employers who hire them.

"For a long time, the American public has wanted immigration enforcement," says Ira Mehlman, media director of the Federation for American Immigration Reform (FAIR), which lobbies for stricter immigration limits.

"Is there a rhetorical consensus for the need for immigration control? The answer is clearly yes," Mehlman says. "When even John McCain is saying border security and enforcement have to come first before the amnesty he really wants, then there is really a consensus."

While most of the Republican presidential candidates are talking tougher on immigration today than two or three years ago, Democrats also are espousing the need for border security and stricter enforcement of current laws. But not everyone is convinced a majority of the public supports the "enforcement-only" approach that treats all illegal immigrants — and the people that hire them — as criminals.

"All through the fall, even with the campaign going on, the polls consistently showed that 60 to 70 percent of the public supports a path to citizenship," says Tamar Jacoby, a senior fellow at the Manhattan Institute who has written in favor of immigrant absorption into U.S. society.

There's a core of only about 20 to 25 percent of Americans who favor wholesale deportation, Jacoby says. "What the candidates are doing is playing on the scare 'em territory."

But over the last couple of years, in the congressional and state-level elections where the immigration issue has featured most prominently, the candidates who sought to portray themselves as the toughest mostly lost.

Some analysts believe that, despite the amount of media attention the issue has attracted, anti-immigrant hard-liners may have overplayed their hand, ignoring the importance of immigrant labor to a shifting U.S. economy.

"To be energized we need new workers, younger workers, who are going to be a part of the whole economy. We don't have them here in the United States," Sen. Kennedy told National Public Radio in 2006.

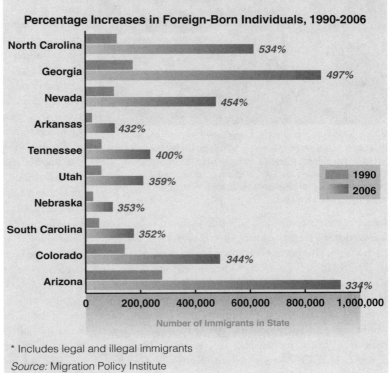

Fastest-Growing Foreign-Born Populations

Foreign populations at least tripled in 10 states since 1990. In North Carolina foreign-born residents increased by a record 534 percent.

Percentage Increases in Foreign-Born Individuals, 1990-2006

State	%
North Carolina	534%
Georgia	497%
Nevada	454%
Arkansas	432%
Tennessee	400%
Utah	359%
Nebraska	353%
South Carolina	352%
Colorado	344%
Arizona	334%

1990
2006

Number of Immigrants in State

* Includes legal and illegal immigrants

Source: Migration Policy Institute

"We need to have the skills of all of these people," he continued. "The fact is, this country, with each new wave of immigrants, has been energized and advanced, quite frankly, in terms of its economic, social, cultural and political life. I don't think we ought to fear it, we ought to welcome it."[5]

Polls have made it clear that the Republican Party, which is seen as generally tougher on the issue, is losing support among Hispanics — the fastest-growing segment of the population.

"The Bush strategy — enlightened on race, smart on immigration — developed in Texas and Florida with Jeb Bush — has been replaced by the Tancredo-Romney strategy, which is demonizing and scapegoating immigrants," said Simon Rosenberg, a Democratic strategist, "and that is a catastrophic event for the Republican Party."[6] Jeb Bush, the president's brother, served two

A prospective employer in Las Vegas holds up two fingers indicating how many day laborers he needs. One of the few pieces of immigration legislation still considered to have a chance in Congress this year is the SAVE Act, which would require all employers to use an electronic verification system to check the legal status of all workers.

terms as governor of Florida, while Colorado Rep. Tom Tancredo and former Massachusetts Gov. Mitt Romney each sought this year's GOP presidential nomination.*

There is a well-known precedent backing up Rosenberg's argument. In 1994, Pete Wilson, California's Republican governor, pushed hard for Proposition 187, designed to block illegal immigrants from receiving most public services. The proposition passed and Wilson won reelection, but it turned Hispanic voters in California against the GOP — a shift widely believed to have turned the state solidly Democratic.

"While there might be some initial appeal to trying to beat up on immigrants in all different ways, it ultimately isn't getting to the question of what you do with 12 million people," says Angela Kelley, director of the Immigration Policy Center at the American Immigration Law Foundation, which advocates for immigrants' legal rights. "It isn't a problem we can enforce our way out of."

But it's not a problem politicians can afford to ignore. There will be enormous pressure on the next president and Congress to come up with a package that imposes practical limits on the flow of illegal immigrants into the United States. Doing so while balancing the economic interests that immigrant labor supports will remain no less of a challenge, however.

---

* Tancredo dropped out in December, and Romney has been trailing McCain in the primaries.

That's in part because the immigration debate doesn't fall neatly along partisan lines. Pro-GOP business groups, for example, continue to seek a free flow of labor, while unions and other parts of the Democratic coalition fear just that.

"The Democrats tend to like immigrants, but are suspicious of immigration, while the Republicans tend to like immigration but are suspicious of immigrants," says Frank Sharry, executive director of the National Immigration Forum, a pro-immigration lobby group.

"Republicans want to deport 12 million people while starting a guest worker program," he says. "With Democrats, it's the reverse."

During a Republican debate in Florida last December, presidential candidate and former Massachusetts Gov. Mitt Romney took a less draconian position, moving away from his earlier calls to deport all illegals. "Those who have come illegally, in my view, should be given the opportunity to get in line with everybody else," he said. "But there should be no special pathway for those that have come here illegally to jump ahead of the line or to become permanent residents or citizens."[7]

One of the loudest anti-immigration voices belongs to Republican Oklahoma state Rep. Randy Terrill, author of one of the nation's toughest anti-immigration laws, which went into effect in December 2007. "For too long, our nation and our state have looked the other way and ignored a growing illegal immigration crisis," he said. "Oklahoma's working families should not be forced to subsidize illegal immigration. With passage of House bill 1804, we will end that burden on our citizens."[8] Among other things, the law gives state and local law enforcement officials the power to enforce federal immigration law.

As the immigration debate rages on, here are some of the specific issues that policy makers are arguing about:

Should employers be penalized for hiring illegal immigrants?

For more than 20 years, federal policy has used employers as a checkpoint in determining the legal status of workers. It's against the law for companies to knowingly hire illegal immigrants, but enforcement of this law has been lax, at best.

Partly as a result — but also because of the growing attention paid to illegal immigrants and the opportunities that may attract them to this country — the role of business in enforcing immigration policy has become a major concern.

"I blame 90 percent on employers," says Georgia state Sen. Chip Rogers. "They're the ones that are profiting by breaking the law."

The Immigration and Customs Enforcement agency has pledged to step up its efforts to punish employers who knowingly hire undocumented workers. In response, an Electrolux factory in Springfield, Tenn., fired more than 150 immigrant workers in December after Immigration and Customs Enforcement (ICE) agents arrested a handful of its employees.

Last year, ICE levied $30 million in fines and forfeitures against employers, but arrested fewer than 100 executives or hiring managers, compared with 4,100 unauthorized workers.[9]

One of the few pieces of immigration legislation still considered to have a chance in Congress this year is the SAVE Act (Secure America With Verification Enforcement), which would require all employers to use an electronic verification system to check the legal status of all workers. The House version of the bill boasts more than 130 cosponsors.

Employers are also being heavily targeted by state and local lawmakers. More than 300 employment-related laws addressing illegal immigrants have been recently passed by various levels of government, according to the U.S. Chamber of Commerce.

"There is still this general consensus that although the current employer-sanctions regime hasn't worked, the point of hire is the correct place to ensure that the employee before you is legally here," says Kelley, of the American Immigration Law Foundation.

But for all the efforts to ensure that businesses check the legal status of their workers — and to impose stiffer penalties on those who knowingly hire illegal immigrants — there is still considerable debate about whether such measures will ultimately resolve the problem.

Critics contend there is no easy way for employers to determine legal status. For one thing, documents often are faked. Dan Pilcher, spokesman for the Colorado Association of Commerce and Industry, notes that during a high-profile ICE raid on the Swift meatpacking plant in Greeley in December 2006, many of the arrests were for identity theft, not immigration violations, since

so many illegal immigrants were using Social Security numbers that belonged to other people.

"Even when those numbers are run through the system, the computers didn't pick up anything," Pilcher says. "Until that system [of verification] is bulletproof, it doesn't work to try to mandate that businesses be the front line of enforcement."

Concerns about the verification systems in place are shared across the ideological spectrum. "We're now 21 years after the enactment of employer sanctions, and we still haven't come up with a system that allows for instant verification," says Mehlman, at the Federation for American Immigration Reform. "If Visa and MasterCard can verify literally millions of transactions a day, there's no reason we can't have businesses verify the legal status of their employees."

"When you look to employers to be the ones that are going to have damages imposed for hiring someone who is not properly documented, the first thing you have to do is give me a program so I can make sure the person is legal for me to hire," says Bryan R. Tolar, director of marketing, education and environmental programs for the Georgia Agribusiness Council.

So far, though, there is no such system. The Department of Homeland Security's E-Verify system, which grew out of a pilot program, is the new checking point of choice. In fact, federal contractors will soon be required to check the residency status of employees using E-Verify. As of Jan. 1, a new state law requires all employers in Arizona to use the E-Verify system.

But such requirements have drawn lawsuits from both business groups and labor unions, who complain that E-Verify is based on unreliable databases. Tom Clark, executive vice president of the Denver Metro Chamber of Commerce, complains that E-Verify is not accurate and worries therefore that the employer sanctions contained in the Arizona law could lead to serious and unfair consequences.

Under the law, companies found guilty of hiring an illegal worker can lose their business licenses for 10 days; for second offenses they are at risk of forfeiting their licenses entirely. "Do you know the [power] that gives you to take out your competitors?" Clark asks.

Supporters of tougher employer sanctions say the databases are getting better all the time. Mark Krikorian, executive director of the Center for Immigration

Immigration Is on the Rise

The number of foreign-born people in the United States has nearly quadrupled since 1970, largely because of changes in immigration laws and increasing illegal immigration (top). The increase has pushed the foreign-born percentage of the population to more than 12 percent (bottom).

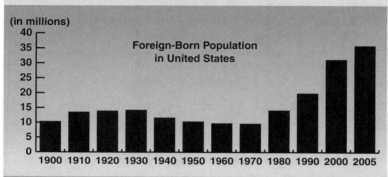

Number and Percentage of Foreign-Born Individuals in the U.S., 1900-2005

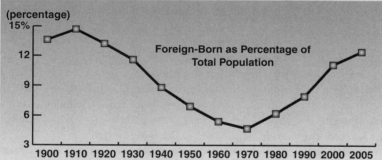

Source: Audrey Singer, "Twenty-first Century Gateways: Immigrant Incorporation in Suburban America," Metropolitan Policy Program, Brookings Institution, April 2007

Studies, says E-Verify needs to be made into a requirement for all American employers. Once they are handed a working tool, he says, all businesses need to follow the same rules.

"Legal status is a labor standard that needs to be enforced just like other labor standards," he says. "Holding business accountable to basic labor standards is hardly revolutionary."

The National Immigration Forum's Sharry agrees that employers "need to be held to account for who they hire." But he warns that imposing stiff penalties against them at a juncture when verification methods remain in doubt could create greater problems.

"Until you create an effective verification system, employer sanctions will drive the problem further underground and advantage the least scrupulous employers," Sherry says.

Can guest worker programs be fixed?

The United States has several different programs allowing foreigners to come into the country for a limited time, usually to work for specific "sponsoring" employers, generally in agriculture. But most of these programs have been criticized for being ineffective — both in filling labor demands and ensuring that temporary workers do not become permanent, illegal residents.

The best-known guest worker program, the H-2A visa program for visiting agricultural workers, has been derided by farmers as cumbersome and time-consuming, preventing them from timing their hiring of workers to growing and harvesting seasons. Farmers use H-2A visas only to cover an estimated 2 percent of farmworkers.

Instead, growers turn to the black market for undocumented workers. At least half of the nation's 1.6 million farmworkers — and as many as 70 percent by some estimates — are immigrants lacking documentation.[10]

Still, growers' groups have complained about labor shortages as border security and regulation of employers are tightening. Some growers in the Northwest last fall let cherries and apples rot because of a shortage of workers, and some in North Carolina did not plant cucumbers because of a fear they wouldn't find the workers to harvest them.[11]

Three federal agencies — Homeland Security, State and Labor — have been working in recent months to craft regulations to speed the H-2A visa process. But farmworker advocates worry that the sort of changes the administration has been contemplating could weaken labor protections for workers. Some critics of lax immigration policy complain, meanwhile, that the H-2A changes would allow employers to skirt a process designed to limit the flow of immigrant workers.

Changes adopted by or expected from the administration could weaken housing and wage standards that have traditionally been a part of temporary-worker programs, which date back to World War II, according to Bruce Goldstein, executive director of Farmworker Justice, a group that provides legal support to migrant workers.

Those changes would make a bad situation for farmworkers worse, Goldstein contends. "The government has failed to adopt policies that adequately protect workers from abuses and has failed to enforce the labor protections that are on the books," Goldstein says.

The Federation for American Immigration Reform's Mehlman criticizes the proposed changes for "trying to tip the balance in favor of employers.

"There's no evidence that we have a labor shortage in this country," Mehlman says. "You have businesses that have decided they don't want to pay the kind of wages American workers want in order to do these kinds of jobs."

Whether there is an overall labor shortage or not, clearly the numbers don't add up in agriculture. Officials with several immigration-policy groups note that the number of people coming to work in this country outnumber the visas available to new, full-time workers by hundreds of thousands per year.

"The only way we can provide for the labor needs of a growing and very diverse agriculture industry is to

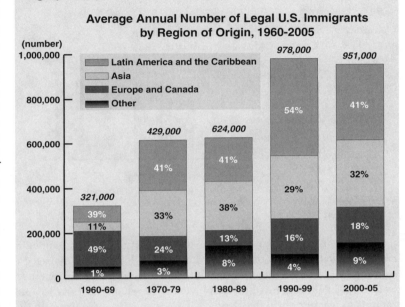

Legal Immigration Has Steadily Increased

The number of legal immigrants has risen steadily since the 1960s, from about 320,000 yearly to nearly 1 million. The largest group was from Latin America and the Caribbean. (In addition to legal entrants, more than a half-million immigrants arrive or remain in the U.S. illegally each year.)

Average Annual Number of Legal U.S. Immigrants by Region of Origin, 1960-2005

Legend:
- Latin America and the Caribbean
- Asia
- Europe and Canada
- Other

Period	1960-69	1970-79	1980-89	1990-99	2000-05
Total	321,000	429,000	624,000	978,000	951,000
Latin America and the Caribbean	39%	41%	41%	54%	41%
Asia	11%	33%	38%	29%	32%
Europe and Canada	49%	24%	13%	16%	18%
Other	1%	3%	8%	4%	9%

* Percentages may not total 100 due to rounding.

Source: "Economic Mobility of Immigrants in the United States," Economic Mobility Project, Pew Charitable Trusts, 2007

make sure there's an ample workforce to do it," says Tolar, at the Georgia Agribusiness Council. "Americans have proven that they're not willing to provide the work that needs doing at a wage agriculture can support."

Five years ago, a bipartisan group of congressmen, working with farmworkers, growers and church groups, proposed a piece of legislation known as the AgJobs bill. The attempt at a compromise between the most directly interested players has been a part of the guest worker and immigration debates ever since.

The bill would allow some 800,000 undocumented workers who have lived and worked in the U.S. for several years to register, pay a fine and qualify for green cards (proof of legal residency) by working in agriculture for three to five more years. It would also streamline the H-2A visa application process.

More Immigrants Moving to Suburbs

The gap between the number of immigrants who live in inner cities and suburbs widened significantly from 1980-2005. By 2005 more than 15 million foreign-born people were in suburbs, or three times as many in 1980. The number in cities doubled during the same period. Demographers attribute the popularity of the suburbs to their relative lack of crime, lower cost and better schools.

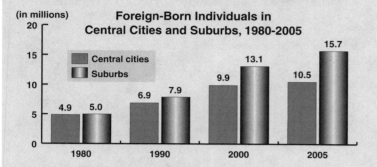

(in millions)
Foreign-Born Individuals in Central Cities and Suburbs, 1980-2005

- Central cities
- Suburbs

Year	Central cities	Suburbs
1980	4.9	5.0
1990	6.9	7.9
2000	9.9	13.1
2005	10.5	15.7

Source: Audrey Singer, "Twenty-first Century Gateways: Immigrant Incorporation in Suburban America," Metropolitan Policy Program, Brookings Institution, April 2007

Although it won Senate passage as part of a larger immigration bill in 2006, the current version of AgJobs has not gained traction due to complaints that it would reward illegal immigrants and employers with what amounts to "get out of jail free" cards.

In November 2007, Sen. Dianne Feinstein, D-Calif., announced that she would not seek to attach AgJobs as an amendment to a larger farm bill, due to strong opposition to legislation seen as helping illegal immigrants. "We know that we can win this," Feinstein said in a statement. But, she conceded, "When we took a clear-eyed assessment of the politics . . . it became clear that our support could not sustain these competing forces."

Feinstein vows to try again this year. But Krikorian, of the Center for Immigration Studies, which favors reduced immigration, counters that guest worker programs in any form are not the right solution. "They still imagine there's a way of admitting low-wage illegals and not have immigration consequences," he says. "It's a fantasy.

"Guest worker programs don't work anyway," he adds. "There's nothing as permanent as a temporary worker."

The American Immigration Law Foundation's Kelley speaks for many on the other side of the debate who argue that it's not enough to conclude that guest worker programs are problematic. Workers from other countries are going to continue to come into this country, she notes.

"We need somehow to replace what is an illegal flow with a legal flow," Kelley says. "We have a guest worker program now — it's called illegal immigration."

Should illegal immigrants be allowed to attend public colleges and universities?

Miami college students Juan Gomez, 18, and his brother Alex, 20, spent a week in jail in Fort Lauderdale last summer. They were both students at Miami Dade College but faced deportation as illegal immigrants. They had come to the United States from Colombia when they were toddlers.

In handcuffs while riding to the detention center, Juan managed to type out a text message to a friend on his cell phone. The friend set up a Facebook group that in turn led 3,000 people to sign petitions lobbying Congress on the brothers' behalf.

In response, Rep. Lincoln Diaz-Balart, R-Fla., and Sen. Christopher Dodd, D-Conn., introduced legislation to prevent their deportation. As a courtesy to Congress, immigration officials delayed their deportation for two more years.[12]

But the brothers may still face deportation, because Congress failed to pass the DREAM (Development, Relief and Education for Alien Minors) Act. The bill would protect students from deportation and allow young adults (up to age 30) to qualify for permanent legal status if they completed high school and at least two years of college or military service.

On Oct. 24, 2007, the Senate voted 52-48 to end debate and move to a vote on final passage — eight votes short of the 60 needed under Senate rules to end a filibuster. Opponents of the measure claimed it was an unfair plan to grant amnesty to illegal immigrants.

The debate over illegal immigration has regularly and heatedly intersected with questions about education for illegal immigrants: Do young people deserve a break even if their parents skirted the law in bringing them to this country? Should illegal immigrants be barred from publicly supported colleges?

The courts have made it clear that states must provide elementary and secondary educations to all comers, including illegal immigrants. But higher education is another matter entirely.

Ten states have passed legislation in recent years granting in-state tuition to children of illegal immigrants. Most passed their laws during the early years of this decade, before immigration had become such a heated political topic.

Similar proposals in other states have died recently, with critics charging that it would be wrong to reward people who are in the country illegally with one of American society's dearest prizes.

"It is totally unfair if you're going to grant in-state tuition to illegal aliens in Georgia and charge out-of-state tuition to someone from Pennsylvania," says Phil Kent, national spokesman for Americans for Immigration Control.

Katherine "Kay" Albiani, president of the California Community Colleges board, stepped down last month along with two other board members in response to criticism from Republican legislators. The board had voted unanimously last year to support legislation that would have allowed illegal immigrants to qualify for student financial aid and community-college fee waivers.

"We have the best benefit package of any state for illegal immigrants, so they come here," complained California Senate GOP leader Dick Ackerman.[13]

Some argue that illegal immigrants should be barred not only from receiving tuition breaks but also from attending public colleges and universities altogether. Public institutions of higher education, after all, are subsidized by taxpayers, and therefore all students — including illegal immigrants — receive an indirect form of aid from state or local governments.

"Every college student is subsidized to the tune of thousands of dollars a year," says Krikorian, of the Center for Immigration Studies. "They are taking slots and huge amounts of public subsidies that would otherwise go to Americans or legal immigrants."

"Our view is that they shouldn't be there in the first place, and they certainly shouldn't be subsidized by taxpayers," says Mehlman of FAIR. "The typical illegal

After living in Clarion, Iowa, for nine years, undocumented Mexican immigrant Patricia Castillo, right, and her family were deported for entering the country illegally. Townspeople like Doris Holmes and her daughter Kelli threw a fund-raiser to help the Castillos pay their legal bills.

AP Photo/The Messenger/Cynthia Kaneshiro

immigrant isn't coming to the U.S. for higher education. But once you're here, if the state says we'll subsidize your college education, that's a pretty good incentive to stay here."

Others argue that banning students because their parents chose to break the law would be a mistake. "We are a better country than to punish children for what their parents did," former Arkansas Gov. Mike Huckabee said during the Nov. 28 CNN/YouTube GOP presidential debate. Huckabee says he opposes the congressional DREAM Act, but his opponents in the primary campaign have pointed out his former support as governor for in-state tuition for longtime illegal residents.

Beyond the question of whether it's fair to punish students for decisions their parents made, some argue it would be a mistake to deprive illegal immigrants of educational opportunities. A college education may be an extra inducement for them to stay in this country, but the vast majority are likely to remain in this country anyway.

"If these are people who are going to live here for the rest of their lives, we want them to be as educated as possible," says the Manhattan Institute's Jacoby.

The American Immigration Law Foundation's Kelley agrees. She describes the DREAM Act as a reasonable compromise, saying it would protect students but wouldn't give illegal immigrants access to scholarships or grants. She argues that states that do offer in-state tuition rates to illegal immigrant students have not seen "a huge influx" of them.

"Saying to students who have been raised here and by all accounts are American and are graduating in high numbers and are doing well — 'You can't advance and go any further' — doesn't make sense," Kelley says. "It would be helpful to our economy to have these kids get college degrees."

BACKGROUND

Earlier Waves

The United States was created as a nation of immigrants who left Europe for political, religious and economic reasons. After independence, the new nation maintained an open-door immigration policy for 100 years. Two great waves of immigrants — in the mid-1800s and the late-19th and early-20th centuries — drove the nation's westward expansion and built its cities and industrial base.[14]

But while the inscription on the Statue of Liberty says America accepts the world's "tired . . . poor . . . huddled masses," Americans themselves vacillate between welcoming immigrants and resenting them — even those who arrive legally. For both legal and illegal immigrants, America's actions have been inconsistent and often racist.

In the 19th century, thousands of Chinese laborers were brought here to build the railroads and then were excluded — via the Chinese Exclusion Act of 1882 — in a wave of anti-Chinese hysteria. Other Asian groups were restricted when legislation in 1917 created "barred zones" for Asian immigrants.[15]

The racist undertones of U.S. immigration policy were by no means reserved for Asians. Describing Italian and Irish immigrants as "wretched beings," *The New York Times* on May 15, 1880, editorialized: "There is a limit to our powers of assimilation, and when it is exceeded the country suffers from something very like indigestion."

Nevertheless, from 1880 to 1920, the country admitted more than 23 million immigrants — first from Northern and then from Southern and Eastern Europe. In 1890, Census Bureau Director Francis Walker said the country was being overrun by "less desirable" newcomers from Southern and Eastern Europe, whom he called "beaten men from beaten races."

In the 1920s, public concern about the nation's changing ethnic makeup prompted Congress to establish a national-origins quota system. Laws in 1921, 1924 and 1929 capped overall immigration and limited influxes from certain areas based on the share of the U.S. population with similar ancestry, effectively excluding Asians and Southern and Eastern Europeans, such as Greeks, Poles and Russians.[16]

But the quotas only swelled the ranks of illegal immigrants — particularly Mexicans, who needed only to wade across the Rio Grande River. To stem the flow, the United States in 1924 created the U.S. Border Patrol to guard the 6,000 miles of U.S. land bordering Canada and Mexico.

After World War II, Congress decided to codify the scores of immigration laws that had evolved over the years. The landmark Immigration and Nationality Act of 1952 retained a basic quota system that favored immigrants from Northern Europe — especially the skilled workers and relatives of U.S. citizens among them. At the same time, it exempted immigrants from the Western Hemisphere from the quota system — except for the black residents of European colonies in the Caribbean.

Mass Deportation

The 1952 law also attempted to address — in the era's racist terms — the newly acknowledged reality of Mexican workers who crossed the border illegally. Border Patrol agents were given more power to search for illegal immigrants and a bigger territory in which to operate.

"Before 1944, the illegal traffic on the Mexican border . . . was never overwhelming," the President's Commission on Migratory Labor noted in 1951, but in the past seven years, "the wetback traffic has reached entirely new levels. . . . [I]t is virtually an invasion."[17]

In a desperate attempt to reverse the tide, the Border Patrol in 1954 launched "Operation Wetback," transferring nearly 500 Immigration and Naturalization Service (INS) officers from the Canadian perimeter and U.S. cities to join the 250 agents policing the U.S.-Mexican border and adjacent factories and farms. More than 1 million undocumented Mexican migrants were deported.

CHRONOLOGY

1920s *Hard economic times and public concern about the nation's changing ethnic makeup prompt Congress to limit immigration.*

1921-1929 Congress establishes immigration quota system, excluding Asians and Southern and Eastern Europeans.

1924 U.S. Border Patrol is created to block illegal immigrants, primarily Mexicans.

1940s-1950s *Expansion of U.S. economy during World War II attracts Mexican laborers. U.S. overhauls immigration laws, accepts war survivors and refugees from communist countries.*

1942 Controversial Bracero guest worker program allows Mexicans to work on American farms.

1952 Landmark Immigration and Nationality Act codifies existing quota system favoring Northern Europeans but permitting Mexican farmworkers in Texas.

1960s-1970s *Civil Rights Movement spurs U.S. to admit more Asians and Latin Americans.*

1965 Congress scraps national quotas, gives preference to relatives of immigrants.

1980s *Rising illegal immigration sparks crackdown.*

1986 Apprehension of a record 1.7 million illegal Mexican immigrants prompts lawmakers to legalize undocumented workers and for the first time impose sanctions on employers.

1990s-2000s *Congress again overhauls immigration laws amid national-security concerns.*

1993 Middle Eastern terrorists bomb World Trade Center; two had green cards.

1994 California voters pass Proposition 187, blocking illegal immigrants from receiving most public services; three years later it is largely declared unconstitutional.

1996 Number of illegal immigrants in U.S. reaches 5 million.

Sept. 11, 2001 Attacks on World Trade Center and Pentagon focus new attention on porous U.S. borders.

2004 The 9/11 Commission points to "systemic weaknesses" in border-control and immigration systems.

2005 Congress passes Real ID Act, requiring proof of identity for driver's licenses. . . . President Bush calls for a "temporary worker" program excluding "amnesty" for illegal immigrants. . . . House passes bill to classify illegal immigrants as felons and deport them.

2006 On April 20, Homeland Security Secretary Michael Chertoff announces a federal crackdown on employers who hire illegal aliens. . . . On May 1, hundreds of thousands of immigrants demonstrate across the country to call for legal status. . . . On Nov. 7, 69 percent of Hispanic voters support Democrats in congressional races, according to exit polls.

2007 On May 9, churches in coastal cities provide "sanctuaries" for undocumented families. . . . On May 17, President Bush and a bipartisan group of senators announce agreement on a comprehensive bill to strengthen border protection and allow illegal immigrants eventual access to citizenship. . . . On Aug. 10, the administration calls for more aggressive law enforcement, screening of new employees by federal contractors and firing of workers whose Social Security numbers don't match government databases. . . . On Oct. 24, the Senate fails to end debate on a proposal to protect illegal immigrants who are attending college from deportation. . . . On Dec. 26, Bush signs spending bill calling for 700 miles of "reinforced fencing" along U.S.-Mexico border.

Jan. 1, 2008 Arizona law holding employers responsible for checking legal status of workers is the most recent of hundreds of punitive, new state immigration laws. . . . On Jan. 22, Michigan stops issuing driver's licenses to illegal immigrants. . . . Implementation of Real ID Act, slated to go into effect in May, is postponed.

States Racing to Pass Restrictive Immigration Laws

Arizona, Georgia and Oklahoma seek to outdo Colorado.

Andrew Romanoff, the speaker of the Colorado House, offers a simple explanation for why his state enacted a sweeping immigration law in 2006.

"The immigration system is, by all accounts, broken," he says, "and the federal government has shown very little appetite for either enforcing the law or reforming the law."

In the absence of federal action on immigration, in 2007 every state in the nation considered legislation to address the issue, according to the National Conference of State Legislatures (NCSL). It released a study in November showing that states considered "no fewer than 1,562 pieces of legislation related to immigrants and immigration," with 244 passed into law in 46 states.[1] Both the number of bills and the number of new laws were three times higher than the totals in 2006.

When Colorado's law was enacted in 2006, it was considered perhaps the toughest in the country. It requires anyone older than 18 who is seeking state benefits to show identification proving legal status and requires employers to verify the legal status of workers. But it provides exemptions for certain types of medical care and was designed to hold harmless the children of illegal immigrants.

Colorado's approach has since been superseded by states such as Arizona, Georgia and Oklahoma, which have taken an even harder line. In fact, if there's one clear trend in state and local legislation, it's toward a stricter approach.

In Hazelton, Pa., a controversial set of laws has been held up by the courts. The ordinances would require businesses to turn employee information over to the city, which would then verify documents with the federal government. Prospective tenants would have to acquire a permit to rent by proving their legal right to be in the country.

"It used to be that state and local activity was all over the map," says Mark Krikorian, executive director of the Center for immigration Studies, which advocates reduced immigration. "Those that are loosening the rules now are the exception."

Georgia's law touches on every facet of state policy that relates to illegal immigrants. Under its provisions, state and local government agencies have to verify the legal residency of benefit recipients. Many employers will have to do the same whenever they make a hiring decision. And law enforcement agencies are given authority to crack down on human trafficking and fake documents.

Thousands of immigrants, both legal and illegal, have left Oklahoma following the November enactment of a law (HB 1804) that makes it a felony to knowingly transport illegal immigrants and requires employers to verify the immigration status of workers. It also limits some government benefits to those who can produce proof of citizenship.

Employers in numerous sectors, including hotels, restaurants and agriculture, have complained about labor shortages. But Republican state Rep. Randy Terrill, who wrote the law, says it will save the state money due to the abolition of public subsidies for illegal immigrants. "There's

Although the action enjoyed popular support and bolstered the prestige — and budget — of the INS, it exposed an inherent contradiction in U.S. immigration policy. The 1952 law contained a gaping loophole — the Texas Proviso — a blatant concession to Texas agricultural interests that relied on cheap labor from Mexico.

"The Texas Proviso said companies or farms could knowingly hire illegal immigrants, but they couldn't harbor them," said Lawrence Fuchs, former executive director of the U.S. Select Commission on Immigration and Refugee

Policy. "It was a duplicitous policy. We never really intended to prevent illegals from coming."

Immigration Reform

The foundation of today's immigration system dates back to 1965, when Congress overhauled the immigration rules, scrapping national-origin quotas in favor of immigration limits for major regions of the world and giving preference to immigrants with close relatives living in the United States. By giving priority to family reunification as a basis

significant evidence that HB 1804 is achieving its intended purpose," he said.[2]

States just a few years ago were debating the expansion of benefits for illegal immigrants, such as in-state tuition rates for college. But now politicians in most locales who appear to be aiding illegal immigrants in any way are widely castigated.

New York Gov. Eliot Spitzer, a Democrat, proposed in fall 2007 that illegal immigrants should be eligible for driver's licenses, arguing that would make them more likely to buy insurance. But the idea touched off a political firestorm not only in his state but also within the Democratic presidential campaign and he quickly backed down.

Early this year, Maryland Democratic Gov. Martin O'Malley called for his state to stop issuing driver's licenses to undocumented immigrants. (It's one of seven that currently do so.) "When you've got a New York governor getting clubbed over the head for trying to institute what Maryland has . . . you realize we are out of sync with the rest of the nation," said state House Republican leader Anthony J. O'Connell.[3]

Legislatures in at least a dozen states are already considering bills modeled on the get-tough approaches taken

A demonstrator in Tucson supports Proposition 200 on Dec. 22, 2004. The voter-approved Arizona law denies some public benefits to illegal immigrants.

elsewhere. Legislators in states neighboring Oklahoma, for instance, say that they feel pressure to introduce restrictive legislation, particularly from constituents in areas where immigrants who had lived in Oklahoma have relocated.

The fact that there's a sort of legislative arms race going on, with states trying to outdo each other on the immigration issue, has many people worried. A patchwork approach, with tough laws in scattered places driving some immigrants toward more lenient jurisdictions, is clearly not the way to resolve a national or even international issue such as immigration.

"Obviously, 50 different state immigration policies is ultimately unworkable," says Romanoff. "All of us much prefer a federal solution.

"The question is, how long should we wait? In Colorado we decided we could wait no longer."

[1] "2007 Enacted State Legislation Related to Immigrants and Immigration," National Conference of State Legislatures, Nov. 29, 2007, www.ncsl.org/print/immig/2007Immigrationfinal.pdf.

[2] Emily Bazar, "Strict Immigration Law Rattles Okla. Businesses," *USA Today*, Jan. 10, 2008, p. 1A.

[3] Lisa Rein, "Immigrant Driver ID Rejected by O'Malley," *The Washington Post*, Jan. 16, 2008, p. B1.

for admission, the amendments repaired "a deep and painful flaw in the fabric of American justice," President Lyndon B. Johnson declared at the time.

However, the law also dramatically changed the immigration landscape. Most newcomers now hailed from the developing world — about half from Latin America. While nearly 70 percent of immigrants had come from Europe or Canada in the 1950s, by the 1980s that figure had dropped to about 14 percent. Meanwhile, the percentage coming from Asia, Central America and the

Caribbean jumped from about 30 percent in the 1950s to 75 percent during the '70s.

In 1978, the select commission concluded that illegal immigration was the most pressing problem facing immigration authorities, a perception shared by the general public.[18] The number of border apprehensions peaked in 1986 at 1.7 million, driven in part by a deepening economic crisis in Mexico. Some felt the decade-long increase in illegal immigration was particularly unfair to the tens of thousands of legal petitioners waiting for years to obtain entry visas.

Are Voters Ignoring Immigration?

Iraq War, other issues, may resonate more.

Immigration has emerged as a pervasive political issue, a part of seemingly every state and local campaign and presidential debate. "No issue has dominated the Republican presidential nomination fight the way illegal immigration has," *The Washington Post* reported in January.[1]

A poll conducted by the *Post* and ABC News in December found that more Republican voters in Iowa picked immigration as the first or second most important issue to them — 30 percent — than any other issue. Only 6 percent of Iowa Democrats rated the issue so highly.[2]

Yet illegal immigration has also emerged as a key concern in the Democratic contest. After Sen. Hillary Rodham Clinton, D-N.Y., gave conflicting answers during an October debate about her opinion of Democratic New York Gov. Eliot Spitzer's abortive plan to issue driver's licenses to illegal immigrants, her opponents attacked her. That moment has been widely characterized as opening up the first crack in the façade of her "inevitability" as the Democratic nominee.

"This is a real wedge issue that Democrats need to get right," wrote Stan Greenberg and James Carville, two prominent Democratic Party strategists.[3]

Despite the attention that the issue gets from both candidates and the media, however, there's as yet scant evidence that illegal immigration resonates as strongly with voters as other issues such as the economy, health care or the war in Iraq. "The bottom line is, to most people it's not a pocketbook issue," says Arizona pollster Jim Haynes, "and the pocketbook tends to be seminal in determining how somebody's going to end up voting."

In 2006, several House incumbents and candidates who made tough stances against illegal immigration the centerpiece of their campaigns went down to defeat, including Reps. J.D. Hayworth, R-Ariz., and Jim Ryun, R-Kan.

The track record for gubernatorial candidates who focused their campaigns on immigration was no better that year. Len Munsil in Arizona, Ernest Istook in Oklahoma and Jim Barnett in Kansas all ran against Democratic incumbents and tried to take advantage of their opponents' seeming vulnerability on the immigration issue. None won more than 41 percent of the vote.

Rep. Tom Tancredo, R-Colo., based his presidential campaign on his strong support for tougher immigration measures, but never broke out of the low single digits in polls before dropping out of the race in December.

It was also difficult for candidates to make immigration decisive at the ballot box during the off-year elections of 2007. Even in contests where the issue played a prominent role, it didn't have the influence many observers had predicted. In local contests in New York, for example, Democrats did not pay the predicted price for Spitzer's idea of issuing driver's licenses to illegal immigrants. Instead, they fared better.

In Virginia, Republicans made tough talk on immigration central to their plans for holding on to their threatened majority in the state Senate this past November. They ended up losing control of that body after a decade in power. Local Virginia elections told much the same story.

In Loudoun County, where arguments about illegal newcomers have been intense for several years, Sheriff Stephen Simpson lost a primary bid for renomination but came back to win as an independent against an opponent who had accused him of being soft on immigration. "I think it was hyped up quite a bit in the election, not just in my race but in the area," Simpson says.

In numerous other local contests in Virginia, the injection of immigration as a central concern not only failed to change the outcome but barely shifted the winner's share of the vote from previous elections.

"The simple truth is that we've lost control of our own borders," declared President Ronald Reagan, "and no nation can do that and survive."[19]

In the mid-1980s, a movement emerged to fix the illegal-immigration problem. Interestingly, the debate on Capitol Hill was marked by bipartisan alliances described by Sen. Alan K. Simpson, R-Wyo., as "the goofiest ideological-bedfellow activity I've ever seen."[20] Conservative, anti-immigration think tanks teamed up with liberal labor unions and environmentalists favoring tighter restrictions

There were some races where opposition to illegal immigration was an effective political tactic. Tom Selders, the mayor of Greeley, Colo., lost after expressing sympathy for illegal immigrants snared in a federal raid on a local meatpacking plant. By showcasing immigration concerns, Republican Jim Ogonowski ran a surprisingly close race in an October special election in a Massachusetts congressional district that has long favored Democrats, although ultimately he lost.

"This issue has real implications for the country. It captures all the American people's anger and frustration not only with immigration but with the economy," said Rep. Rahm Emanuel of Illinois, chairman of the House Democratic Caucus and chief strategist for his party's congressional candidates in 2006. "It's self-evident. This is a big problem."[4]

But it has become surprisingly hard to outflank most candidates on this contentious subject. Last November's challenger to Charles Colgan, a Democratic state senator in Virginia, tried to paint him as soft, going so far as to distribute cartoons depicting Colgan helping people over the wall at the border. But Colgan countered by pointing out his votes in opposition to extending various benefits to illegal immigrants. "The first thing this nation must do is seal the border," he says. "We cannot let this influx continue." Colgan won reelection easily.

Why hasn't immigration, which is getting so much attention, proved to be a central concern when voters cast

Rep. Tom Tancredo, R-Colo., based his presidential campaign on his strong support for tougher immigration measures but got little traction and dropped out of the race in December 2007.

their ballots? For one thing, not everyone agrees on every proposal to make life tougher for illegal immigrants. And the GOP's hard line on immigration threatens to push Hispanic voters over to the Democratic Party.

But illegal immigration may be failing to take off as a voting issue not because of opposition to the hard-line proposals but because something like a consensus in favor of them has already emerged. It's a simple matter for any candidate to communicate a belief that border security should be tightened and that current laws should be more strictly enforced.

The emergence of that kind of consensus suggests that hardliners have in fact won a good portion of their argument. In his statement announcing he was leaving the presidential race, Tancredo said, "Just last week *Newsweek* declared that 'anti-immigrant zealot' [Tancredo] had already won. 'Now even Dems dance to his no mas salsa tune.' "

---

[1] Jonathan Weisman, "For Republicans, Contest's Hallmark Is Immigration," *The Washington Post*, Jan. 2, 2008, p. A1.

[2] "What Iowans Care About," *The Washington Post*, Jan. 3, 2008, p. A11.

[3] Perry Bacon Jr. and Anne E. Kornblut, "Issue of Illegal Immigration Is Quandary for Democrats," *The Washington Post*, Nov. 2, 2007, p. A2.

[4] Jonathan Weisman, "GOP Finds Hot Button in Illegal Immigration," *The Washington Post*, Oct. 23, 2007, p. A7.

on immigration. Pro-growth and business groups joined forces with longtime adversaries in the Hispanic and civil rights communities to oppose the legislation.

After several false starts, Congress passed the Immigration Reform and Control Act (IRCA) in October 1986 — the most sweeping revision of U.S. immigration policy in more than two decades. Using a carrot-and-stick approach, IRCA granted a general amnesty to all undocumented aliens who were in the United States before 1982 and imposed monetary sanctions — or

NBC NewsWire via AP Photo/Paul Drinkwater

A pro-immigrant rally in Atlanta draws a crowd on May 1, 2006. The nation's rapidly rising foreign-born population is dispersing well beyond "gatekeeper" states such as California and Texas to non-traditional destinations like Georgia, Arkansas and Iowa.

even prison — against employers who knowingly hired undocumented workers for the first time.

Changes in 1996

In the 1990s nearly 10 million newcomers — the largest influx ever — arrived on U.S. shores, with most still coming from Latin America and Asia.

Bill Clinton realized early in his presidency that the so-called amnesty program enacted in 1986 had not solved the illegal-immigration problem. And in the Border States, concern was growing that undocumented immigrants were costing U.S. taxpayers too much in social, health and educational services. On Nov. 8, 1994, California voters approved Proposition 187, denying

illegal immigrants public education or non-essential public-health services. Immigrants'-rights organizations immediately challenged the law, which a court later ruled was mostly unconstitutional. But the proposition's passage had alerted politicians to the intensity of anti-illegal immigrant sentiment.[21]

House Republicans immediately included a proposal to bar welfare benefits for legal immigrants in their "Contract with America," and in 1995, after the GOP had won control of the House, Congress took another stab at reforming the rules for both legal and illegal immigration. But business groups blocked efforts to reduce legal immigration, so the new law primarily focused on curbing illegal immigration.

The final legislation, which cleared Congress on Sept. 30, 1996, nearly doubled the size of the Border Patrol and provided 600 new INS investigators. It appropriated $12 million for new border-control devices, including motion sensors, set tougher standards for applying for political asylum and made it easier to expel foreigners with fake documents or none at all.[22] The law also severely limited — and in many cases completely eliminated — non-citizens' ability to challenge INS decisions in court.[23]

But the new law did not force authorities to crack down on businesses that employed illegal immigrants, even though there was wide agreement that such a crackdown was vital. As the Commission on Immigration Reform had said in 1994, the centerpiece of any effort to stop illegal entrants should be to "turn off the jobs magnet that attracts them."

By 1999, however, amid an economic boom and low unemployment, the INS had stopped raiding work sites to round up illegal immigrant workers and was focusing on foreign criminals, immigrant-smugglers and document fraud. As for cracking down on employers, an agency district director told *The Washington Post*, "We're out of that business." The idea that employers could be persuaded not to hire illegal workers "is a fairy tale."[24]

Legal immigration, however, has been diminished by the government response to the terrorist attacks of Sept. 11, 2001. In fiscal 2002-2003, the number of people granted legal permanent residence (green cards) fell by 34 percent; 28,000 people were granted political asylum, 59 percent fewer than were granted asylum in fiscal 2000-2001.[25] But the growth of illegal immigration under way

Would tighter border security curb illegal immigration?

YES Mark Krikorian
Executive Director, Center for Immigration Studies

Written for *CQ Researcher*, Jan. 23, 2008

Border security is one piece of the very large controlling-immigration puzzle. But policing borders, including the use of physical barriers where necessary, has been integral to the preservation of national sovereignty for centuries. In our country, some two-thirds of the illegal population has snuck across the border with Mexico; the rest entered legally — as tourists, students, etc. — and never left.

As part of the development of a modern, national immigration system, Congress in 1924 created the U.S. Border Patrol. As illegal immigration grew to massive proportions in the late 1970s, the Border Patrol's work became something of a charade, with a handful of officers returning whatever Mexican border-jumpers they could nab and then watching them immediately turn around and try again.

The first step in closing that revolving door came in 1993 and 1994, when new strategies were implemented in San Diego and El Paso, where most illegal immigration occurred, to deter crossings altogether rather than simply chase after people through streets and alleys after they'd already crossed.

Over the past decade-and-a-half, the enforcement infrastructure at the border has grown immensely, but it is still laughably inadequate. Although the number of agents at the Southern border has tripled, to some 12,000, that still represents an average of no more than two agents per mile per shift.

Expanded fencing has also been part of this build-up. In the past, when the region on both sides of our Southern border was essentially empty, the limited fencing in place was intended simply to keep cattle from wandering off. Now, with huge metropolises on the Mexican side, serious fencing is being built — first in San Diego, where illegal crossings have plummeted as a result, and now along more than 800 additional miles of the border, though this is still a work in progress. In addition to these physical barriers, we have had for years additional security measures (deceptively labeled "virtual fencing"), such as motion sensors, stadium lighting and remote-controlled cameras.

But while border enforcement is a necessary element of immigration control, it is not sufficient. There are three layers of immigration security — our visa-issuing consulates abroad, the border (including legal entry points) and the interior of the country. Improvements at the border are essential, and many are already under way. The weakest link today is the interior, where efforts to deny illegal immigrants jobs, driver's licenses, bank accounts, etc., are being fought at every turn by the business and ethnic lobbyists who benefit from open borders.

NO Douglas S. Massey
Professor of Sociology, Princeton University

From testimony before House Judiciary Subcommittee on Immigration, April 20, 2007

As envisioned under [the North American Free Trade Agreement], the economies of the U.S. and Mexico are integrating, and the rising cross-border movement of goods and services has been accompanied by migration of all sorts of people. Since 1986, the number of exchange visitors from Mexico has tripled, the number of business visitors has quadrupled and the number of intracompany transferees has grown 5.5 times.

Within this rapidly integrating economy, however, U.S. policy makers have somehow sought to prevent the cross-border movement of workers. We have adopted an increasingly restrictive set of immigration and border-enforcement policies. First, the Immigration Reform and Control Act of 1986 granted $400 million to expand the size of the Border Patrol. Then the 1990 Immigration Act authorized hiring another 1,000 officers. In 1993, these new personnel were deployed as part of an all-out effort to stop unauthorized border crossing in El Paso, a strategy that was extended to San Diego in 1994. Finally, the 1996 Illegal Immigration Reform and Immigrant Responsibility Act provided funds to hire an additional 1,000 Border Patrol officers per year through 2001.

In essence, the U.S. militarized the border with its closest neighbor, a nation to which it was committed by treaty to an ongoing process of economic integration. Rather than slowing the flow of immigrants into the U.S., however, this policy yielded an array of unintended and very negative consequences.

The most immediate effect was to transform the geography of border crossing. Whereas undocumented border crossing during the 1980s focused on San Diego and El Paso, the selective hardening of these sectors after 1993 diverted the flows to new and remote crossings. Undocumented Mexican migration was thus nationalized. The migrants got wise and simply went around built-up sectors. As a result, the probability of apprehension plummeted to record low levels. American taxpayers were spending billions more to catch fewer migrants.

And, rather than returning home possibly to face the gauntlet at the border again, Mexicans without documents remained longer in the U.S. The ultimate effect of restrictive border policies was to double the net rate of undocumented population growth, making Hispanics the nation's largest minority years before Census Bureau demographers had projected.

At this point, pouring more money into border enforcement will not help the situation, and in my opinion constitutes a waste of taxpayer money. We must realize that the solution to the current crisis does not lie in further militarizing the border with a friendly trading nation that poses no conceivable threat.

President George W. Bush announces the bipartisan compromise immigration deal he struck with Congress on May 17, 2007. The agreement would have granted temporary legal status to virtually all illegal immigrants. Despite the backing of most Democrats and several conservative Republicans, the package was defeated. Bush is flanked by Homeland Security Secretary Michael Chertoff, left, and Commerce Secretary Carlos Gutierrez.

before 9/11 continued, with 57 percent of the illegal immigrants coming from Mexico.[26]

Due to the family-reunification provision in immigration law, Mexico is also the leading country of origin for legal immigrants — with 116,000 of the 705,827 legal immigrants in fiscal 2002-2003 coming from Mexico.[27] No Middle Eastern or predominantly Muslim countries have high numbers of legal immigrants, although Pakistan was 13th among the top 15 countries of origin for legal immigrants in 1998.[28]

Public Opinion

The combination of concerns about terrorism and the growing number of illegal immigrants — and their movement into parts of the country unused to dealing with foreign newcomers — made illegal immigration a top-tier issue.

In 2005, Congress passed the Real ID Act, which grew out of the 9/11 Commission investigations into how Arab terrorists burrowed into American society to carry out the Sept. 11, 2001. Of the 19 hijackers, 13 had obtained legitimate driver's licenses, said Rep. F. James Sensenbrenner Jr., R-Wis., author of the legislation. The commission called for national standards for the basic American identification documents: birth certificates, Social Security cards and driver's licenses. In states that adopt the strict

requirements of the law — which begins to go into effect in May 2008 — license applicants will have to present ironclad proof of identity, which will be checked against federal and state databases.[29]

After the House in 2005 passed a punitive bill that would have classified illegal immigrants as felons, demonstrations in cities across the country drew hundreds of thousands of marchers during the spring of 2006. On May 1, hundreds of thousands more participated in what some billed as "the Great American Boycott of 2006." The idea was for immigrants, legal and illegal, to demonstrate their economic contribution to the country by staying away from their jobs on May Day.

In terms of numbers alone, the demonstrations of April and May were impressive. But they may also have spurred a backlash among some sectors of the public. "The size and magnitude of the demonstrations had some kind of backfire effect," John McLaughlin, a Republican pollster, told reporters after the first round of marches. "The Republicans that are tough on immigration are doing well right now."[30]

That turned out not to be the case come election-time, however. Some prominent critics of current immigration policy, including Republican Reps. Jim Ryun of Kansas and J.D. Hayworth of Arizona, went down to defeat in November 2006. Republicans in general paid a clear price among Hispanics for their tough stand. Exit polling in 2006 suggested that 30 percent of Hispanics voted for Republicans in congressional races that year, while Democrats garnered 69 percent. President Bush had taken 40 percent of the Hispanic vote in his reelection race two years earlier.[31] "I don't think we did ourselves any favors when we engaged the public in a major topic and didn't pass the legislation to deal with it," said Sen. Sam Brownback, R-Kan., who dropped out of the GOP presidential primary in October 2007.[32]

Perhaps partly in response, Republicans just after the 2006 elections selected as their new national chairman Florida Sen. Mel Martinez, a prominent Cuban-American who had served in the Bush Cabinet. The Federation for American Immigration Reform's Mehlman, then the outgoing party chairman, told reporters that he was concerned about where the party stood with Hispanics. "Hispanics are not single-issue voters, but GOP officials said the tone of the immigration debate hurt the party's standing with the fastest-growing minority group," *The Washington Post* reported.[33]

CURRENT SITUATION

Difficult Fix

Currently, immigration is the subject of countless legislative proposals at all levels of government. Congress under the new Democratic majority ushered in with the 2006 elections has generally considered more lenient legislation, but any proposal that seems to offer any sort of aid to illegal immigrants has failed to gain traction. In states and in many localities, meanwhile, hundreds of punitive bills have passed into law.

Amid much fanfare, President Bush and a bipartisan group of 10 senators announced an agreement on May 17, 2007, on a comprehensive compromise plan to tighten border security and address the fate of the nation's 12 million illegal immigrants. "The agreement reached today is one that will help enforce our borders," Bush said. "But equally importantly, it will treat people with respect. This is a bill where people who live here in our country will be treated without amnesty, but without animosity."[34]

The 380-page plan was worked out just in time to meet a deadline for the beginning of Senate debate on the issue. "The plan isn't perfect, but only a bipartisan bill will become law," said Sen. Kennedy.[35]

But immigration is the rare issue that cuts across partisan lines. Despite the backing of most Democrats, the Bush administration and conservative Republicans such as Kennedy's negotiating partner, Sen. Jon Kyl, R-Ariz., the package went down to defeat. Supporters were unable to muster the support of 60 senators necessary even to bring it to a vote in the face of determined opposition.

The agreement would have granted temporary legal status to virtually all illegal immigrants, allowing them to apply for residence visas and citizenship through a lengthy process. They would have to wait for eight years before applying for permanent resident status and pay fines of up to $5,000; in addition, heads of households would be forced to leave the country and reenter legally.

But the process could not begin for any illegal aliens — and a new guest worker program would also be put on hold — until after a tough border crackdown had gone into effect. The deal called for the deployment of 18,000 new Border Patrol agents and extensive new physical barriers, including 200 miles of vehicle barriers, 370 miles of fencing and 70 ground-based camera and radar towers. In addition, funding would be provided for the detention of 27,500 illegal immigrants, and new identification tools would be developed to help screen out illegal job applicants.

Conservative opponents of the package in the Senate — as well as most of the 2008 GOP presidential hopefuls — derided it as an "amnesty" bill, giving an unfair citizenship advantage to people who had come into the country illegally.

But liberals and immigration advocacy groups also questioned the terms of the Senate proposal, particularly a change in visa applications. In contrast to the current system, which stresses family ties, a new, complex, point system would favor skilled, educated workers. About 50 percent of the points would be based on employment criteria, with just 10 percent based on family connections.

Even if the Senate had passed the bill, its prospects in the House would have been dim. Despite the change in partisan control of Congress, there was still less sentiment in the House than in the Senate for any bill that was perceived as giving a break to illegal aliens. "Unless the White House produces 60 or 70 Republican votes in the House, it will be difficult to pass an immigration bill similar to the Senate proposal," Rep. Rahm Emanuel, D-Ill., chairman of the House Democratic Caucus, said in May 2007.[36]

Those votes would have been tough to get. Some staunch critics of immigration policy were defeated in the 2006 elections, but for the most part they were replaced by newcomers who also took a hard line against illegal immigration. "This proposal would do lasting damage to the country, American workers and the rule of law," said Lamar Smith of Texas, ranking Republican on the House Judiciary Committee, in response to the deal between senators and the White House. "Just because somebody is in the country illegally doesn't mean we have to give them citizenship."[37] The House did not vote at all on comprehensive immigration legislation in 2007.

Federal Inaction

Not long after the Senate's comprehensive bill failed, the attempt to extend legal status to immigrants attending college also failed. The DREAM Act would have protected students from deportation and allowed young adults (up to age 30) to qualify for permanent legal status if they completed high school and at least two years of college or military service.

On Oct. 24, Senate supporters fell eight votes short of the 60 needed to end debate on the bill and bring it to a final vote. The following month, supporters of legislation to address the issue of temporary guest workers — the AgJobs bill — announced that the political climate had turned against them, and they would drop their efforts at least until 2008.

"Amnesty for illegal immigrants is dead for this Congress," says Krikorian of the Center for Immigration Studies. "When the pro-amnesty side couldn't even pass small measures like the DREAM Act and the AgJobs bill, there's little doubt that legalizing illegal immigrants is dead in the water at least until 2009."

Given the pressure on Congress to do something to address the topic, those lobbying for tougher restrictions remain optimistic that this year could see passage of the Secure America With Verification Enforcement Act. The SAVE Act would require all employers to use an electronic verification system to check the legal status of all workers.

In the absence of successful congressional action thus far, the Bush administration last August unveiled a package designed to break the stalemate. The strategy includes stepped-up work-site raids and arrests of fugitive illegal immigrants. The administration also created a new requirement for federal contractors to use the E-Verify system for screening the legal status of new employees.

In October, a federal judge issued a temporary injunction blocking a part of the Homeland Security package that would have required employers to fire workers whose Social Security numbers do not match information in government databases.

The Immigrations and Customs Enforcement agency in January announced a plan to speed the deportation of foreign-born criminals. Under current law, immigrants convicted of crimes are only deported after serving their sentences. ICE intends to work with states to create parole programs that would allow for the early release of non-violent offenders if they agreed to immediate deportation. The program would place a strain on federal detention centers but provide fiscal relief and bed space to state and local governments housing such prisoners. Last year, ICE sent 276,912 people back to their home countries, including many who were not arrested for crimes but had violated civil immigration statutes.[38]

OUTLOOK
Tough Talk

Immigration will clearly remain an important part of the political conversation in this country. The factors that have made it so prominent — the record number of immigrants, both legal and illegal, and their dispersal into parts of the country that had not seen large influxes of immigrants in living memory — show little sign of abating.

The course that any policy changes will take will depend on who wins the presidency. Attempts at addressing the issue in a comprehensive way in Congress failed, due to concerted opposition to the compromise package brokered between the Bush White House and a bipartisan group of senators. Since that time, more modest bills have not been able to advance.

That means the issue will not be resolved as a policy matter until 2009, at the earliest. Instead, it will remain a major theme of the presidential campaign. Immigration has become, perhaps, the dominant issue among the Republican candidates, as well as one that Democrats have had to address in several particulars.

In a December interview with *The Boston Globe*, Illinois Sen. Barack Obama, one of the Democratic front-runners, predicted that any Republican candidate, save for McCain, would center his race on two things — fear of terrorism and fear of immigration.[39]

But the immigration issue has not broken along strictly partisan lines. Krikorian of the Center for Immigration Studies predicts that even if the election results in a Democratic president and Congress, the broad policy trajectory will be toward further tightening of immigration policy.

"I don't care whether it's a new Democratic or a new Republican president, they're going to have to address it," says Kent, of Americans for Immigration Control. "The new president will have to toughen up the border."

Politicians of all stripes indeed now pay homage to the idea that border security must be tightened and that current laws need more rigorous enforcement. But debate is still hot over questions of how much to penalize illegal immigrants and employers — and whether efforts to do just that may ultimately prove counterproductive.

Mehlman of the Federation for American Immigration Reform says "the forces that have been trying to promote amnesty and lots of guest workers are not going to go away." Mehlman says that even if current campaign rhetoric generally supports the tough approach his organization favors, the dynamic of actually changing policies in 2009 and after may not change that much.

"It wouldn't be the first time a politician said one thing during the campaign and acted differently once in office," he says.

He notes that the business groups that encourage immigration have deep pockets, but he believes that "this is an issue that the American public is making a stand on."

The National Immigration Forum's Sharry counters that the policy debate has been hijacked by heated political rhetoric and that it's become difficult to discuss what would be the best solutions without accusations being hurled if a proposal sounds at all "soft" on illegal immigrants.

Nevertheless, he notes, most people do not support the toughest proposals that would treat illegal immigrants as felons and seek their mass deportation. "I suspect it's going to take one or perhaps two election cycles to figure out who does it help and who does it hurt," Sharry says. "My prediction is that the Republican embrace of the extreme anti-immigrant groups will be seen in retrospect as an act of slow-motion suicide."

Douglas S. Massey, a Princeton University sociologist, agrees that the politics of this issue may play out poorly over the long term for those proposing a serious crackdown. He notes that there have been many occasions in American history when "beating on immigrants" has been an expedient strategy, but he argues it's never played well successfully as a sustained national issue.

"It's not a long-term strategy for political success, if you look at the future composition of America," Massey says, alluding in particular to the growth in foreign-born populations.

The political debate clearly will have a profound influence on the policy decisions made on immigration in the coming years. But the underlying demographic trends are likely to continue regardless. "With the baby boomers retiring, we will need barely skilled workers more than ever," says Jacoby, of the Manhattan Institute, referring in part to health-care aides.

She argues that growth in immigration is simply an aspect of globalization. Although people are uncomfortable with change and tend to see its downsides first, she believes that people will eventually realize large-scale migration is an inevitable part of the American future.

"We're in a bad time, and our politics are close to broken," she says, "but eventually American pragmatism will come to the surface."

NOTES

1. Quoted in Ryan Lizza, "Return of the Nativist," *The New Yorker*, Dec. 17, 2007, p. 46. For more on immigrant families that face being split up, see Pamela Constable, "Divided by Deportation: Unexpected Orders to Return to Countries Leave Families in Anguish During Holidays," *The Washington Post*, Dec. 24, 2007, p. B1.

2. Quoted in Lizza, *op. cit.*

3. Ellis Cose, "The Rise of a New American Underclass," *Newsweek*, Jan. 7, 2008, p. 74.

4. William Neikirk, "Gingrich Rips Bush on Immigration," *Chicago Tribune*, Aug. 15, 2007, p. 3.

5. Jennifer Ludden, "Q&A: Sen. Kennedy on Immigration, Then & Now," May 9, 2006, NPR.org, www.npr.org/templates/story/story.php?storyId=5393857.

6. Lizza, *op. cit.*

7. "GOP Hopefuls Debate Immigration on Univision," www.msnbc.msn.com/id/22173520/.

8. David Harper, "Terrill Leads Way on Issue," *Tulsa World*, Oct. 30, 2007, www.TulsaWorld.com.

9. Julia Preston, "U.S. to Speed Deportation of Criminals Behind Bars," *The New York Times*, Jan. 15, 2008, p. A12.

10. "Rot in the Fields," *The Washington Post*, Dec. 3, 2007, p. A16.

11. Steven Greenhouse, "U.S. Seeks Rules to Allow Increase in Guest Workers," *The New York Times*, Oct. 10, 2007, p. A16.

12. Kathy Kiely, "Children Caught in the Immigration Crossfire," *USA Today*, Oct. 8, 2007, p. 1A.

13. Patrick McGreevy, "Gov's Party Blocks His College Board Choice," *Los Angeles Times*, Jan. 15, 2008, p. B3.

14. Unless otherwise noted, material in the background section comes from Rodman D. Griffin, "Illegal Immigration," April 24, 1992, pp. 361-384; Kenneth Jost, "Cracking Down on Immigration," Feb. 3, 1995, pp. 97-120; David Masci, "Debate Over Immigration," July 14, 2000, pp. 569-592; and Peter Katel, "Illegal Immigration," May 6, 2005, pp. 393-420, all in *CQ Researcher*.

15. For background, see Richard L. Worsnop, "Asian Americans," *CQ Researcher*, Dec. 13, 1991, pp. 945-968.

16. For background, see "Quota Control and the National-Origin System," Nov. 1, 1926; "The National-Origin Immigration Plan," March 12, 1929; and "Immigration and Deportation," April 18, 1939, all in *Editorial Research Reports*, available from *CQ Researcher Plus Archive*, http://cqpress.com.

17. Quoted in Ellis Cose, *A Nation of Strangers: Prejudice, Politics and the Populating of America* (1992), p. 191.

18. Cited in Michael Fix, ed., *The Paper Curtain: Employer Sanctions' Implementation, Impact, and Reform* (1991), p. 2.

19. Quoted in Tom Morganthau, *et al.*, "Closing the Door," *Newsweek*, June 25, 1984.

20. Quoted in Dick Kirschten, "Come In! Keep Out!" *National Journal*, May 19, 1990, p. 1206.

21. Ann Chih Lin, ed., *Immigration*, CQ Press (2002), pp. 60-61.

22. William Branigin, "Congress Finishes Major Legislation; Immigration; Focus is Borders, Not Benefits," *The Washington Post*, Oct. 1, 1996, p. A1.

23. David Johnston, "Government is Quickly Using Power of New Immigration Law," *The New York Times*, Oct. 22, 1996, p. A20.

24. William Branigin, "INS Shifts 'Interior' Strategy to Target Criminal Aliens," *The Washington Post*, March 15, 1999, p. A3.

25. Deborah Meyers and Jennifer Yau, "US Immigration Statistics in 2003," Migration Policy Institute, Nov. 1, 2004, www.migrationinformation.org/USfocus/display.cfm?id=263; and Homeland Security Department, "2003 Yearbook of Immigration Statistics," http://uscis.gov/graphics/shared/statistics/yearbook/index.htm.

26. Jeffrey S. Passel, "Estimates of the Size and Characteristics of the Undocumented Population," Pew Hispanic Center, March 21, 2005, p. 8.

27. Meyers and Yau, *op. cit.*

28. Lin, *op. cit.*, p. 20.

29. For background, see Peter Katel, "Real ID," *CQ Researcher*, May 4, 2007, pp. 385-408.

30. David D. Kirkpatrick, "Demonstrations on Immigration are Hardening a Divide," *The New York Times*, April 17, 2006, p. 16.

31. Arian Campo-Flores, "A Latino 'Spanking,'" *Newsweek*, Dec. 4, 2006, p. 40.

32. Rick Montgomery and Scott Cannon, "Party Shift Won't End Immigration Debate," *The Washington Post*, Dec. 17, 2006, p. A11.

33. Jim VandeHei, "Florida Senator Will Be a Top RNC Officer," *The Washington Post*, Nov. 14, 2006, p. A4.

34. Karoun Demirjian, "Bipartisan Immigration Deal Reached," *Chicago Tribune*, May 18, 2007, p. 1.

35. *Ibid.*

36. Robert Pear and Jim Rutenberg, "Senators in Bipartisan Deal on Broad Immigration Bill," *The New York Times*, May 18, 2007, p. A1.

37. Demirjian, *op. cit.*

38. Julia Preston, "U.S. to Speed Deportation of Criminals Behind Bars," *The New York Times*, Jan. 15, 2008, p. A12.

39. Foon Rhee, "Obama Says He Wants a Mandate for Change," www.boston.com/news/politics/political intelligence/2007/12/obama_says_he_w.html.

BIBLIOGRAPHY

Books

Massey, Douglas S., ed., *New Faces in New Places: The Changing Geography of American Immigration, Russell Sage Foundation*, 2008.
A collection of academic pieces shows how the waves of recent immigrants have been dispersed across America

by shifts in various economic sectors and how their presence in areas outside traditional "gateways" has led to social tension.

Myers, Dowell, *Immigrants and Boomers: Forging a New Social Contract for the Future of America, Russell Sage Foundation*, 2007.
A demographer suggests that rates of immigration already may have peaked and argues that rather than being stigmatized immigrants need to be embraced as a replacement workforce for an aging Anglo population.

Portes, Alejandro, and Ruben G. Rumbaut, *Immigrant America: A Portrait*, 3rd ed., *University of California Press*, 2006.
This updated survey by two sociologists offers a broad look at where immigrants settle, what sort of work they do and how well they assimilate.

Articles

Bacon, Perry Jr., and Anne E. Kornblut, "Issue of Illegal Immigration Is Quandary for Democrats," *The Washington Post*, Nov. 2, 2007, p. A4.
Immigration is a wedge issue that can work against Democratic presidential candidates and is perhaps the strongest card in the GOP's deck.

Bazar, Emily, "Strict Immigration Law Rattles Okla. Businesses," *USA Today*, Jan. 10, 2008, p. 1A.
Numerous business sectors in Oklahoma are complaining about worker shortages in the wake of a new state law that makes transporting or sheltering illegal immigrants a felony.

Goodman, Josh, "Crackdown," *Governing*, July 2007, p. 28.
States are reacting to immigration pressures largely by enacting new restrictions on illegal immigrants and the employers who hire them.

Greenhouse, Steven, "U.S. Seeks Rules to Allow Increase in Guest Workers," *The New York Times*, Oct. 10, 2007, p. A16.
Bush administration officials say they will allow farmers to bring in more foreign labor.

Kiely, Kathy, "Children Caught in the Immigration Crossfire," *USA Today*, Oct. 8, 2007, p. 1A.

A million young, illegal immigrants in the United States face potential deportation since the failure of a bill designed to grant permanent legal status to those who finish high school and at least two years of higher education.

Lizza, Ryan, "Return of the Nativist," *The New Yorker*, Dec. 17, 2007, p. 46.
How a hard line on immigration became central to the GOP Republican debate, taken even by candidates who had previously favored a more conciliatory approach.

Preston, Julia, "U.S. to Speed Deportation of Criminals Behind Bars," *The New York Times*, Jan. 15, 2008, p. A12.
A federal agency pledges to step up arrests of employers who knowingly hire illegal immigrants, while speeding deportation of immigrants who have committed crimes.

Sandler, Michael, "Immigration: From the Capitol to the Courts," *CQ Weekly*, Dec. 10, 2007, p. 3644.
The lack of action on Capitol Hill has encouraged scores of state and local jurisdictions to step in with immigrant-related legislation.

Weisman, Jonathan, "For Republicans, Contest's Hallmark Is Immigration," *The Washington Post*, Jan. 2, 2008, p. A1.
Illegal immigration has been a dominant issue in the GOP presidential primary contests.

Reports and Studies

"2006 Yearbook of Immigration Statistics," *Department of Homeland Security*, Sept. 2007, www .dhs.gov/xlibrary/assets/statistics/yearbook/2006/ OIS_2006_Yearbook.pdf.
A wealth of statistical information about immigrant populations is presented, as well as enforcement actions.

"2007 Enacted State Legislation Related to Immigrants and Immigration," *National Conference of State Legislatures*, Nov. 29, 2007, www.ncsl.org/ print/immig/2007Immigrationfinal.pdf.
Last year, every state considered legislation related to immigration, with more than 1,500 bills introduced and 244 enacted into law. The amount of activity "in the continued absence of a comprehensive federal

reform" was unprecedented and represented a threefold increase in legislation introduced and enacted since 2006.

"2007 National Survey of Latinos: As Illegal Immigration Issue Heats Up, Latinos Feel a Chill," *Pew Hispanic Center*, **Dec. 19, 2007; available at http://pewhispanic.org/files/reports/84.pdf.**

The poll finds that the prominence of the illegal-immigration issue has Hispanics more concerned about deportation and discrimination but generally content with their place in U.S. society.

For More Information

American Immigration Law Foundation, 918 F St., N.W., 6th Floor, Washington, DC 20004; (202) 742-5600; www .ailf.org. Seeks to increase public understanding of immigration law and policy, emphasizing the value of immigration to American society.

Center for Comparative Immigration Studies, University of California, San Diego, La Jolla, CA 92093-0548; (858) 822-4447; www.ccis-ucsd.org. Compares U.S. immigration trends with patterns in Europe and Asia.

Center for Immigration Studies, 1522 K St., N.W., Suite 820, Washington, DC 20005-1202; (202) 466-8185; www .cis.org. The nation's only think tank exclusively devoted to immigration-related issues advocates reduced immigration.

Federation for American Immigration Reform, 25 Massachusetts Ave., NW, Suite 330, Washington, DC 20001; (202) 328-7004; http://fairus.org. A leading advocate for cracking down on illegal immigration and reducing legal immigration.

Metropolitan Policy Program, The Brookings Institution, 1775 Massachusetts Ave., N.W., Washington, DC 20036; (202) 797-6000; www.brookings.edu/metro.aspx. The think tank produces numerous reports on both immigration and broader demographics, including geographical mobility.

Migration Dialogue, University of California, Davis, 1 Shields Ave., Davis, CA 95616; (530) 752-1011; http:// migration.ucdavis.edu/index.php. A research center that focuses on immigration from rural Mexico and publishes two Web bulletins.

Migration Policy Institute, 1400 16th St., N.W., Suite 300, Washington, DC 20036; (202) 266-1940; www.migration policy.org. Analyzes global immigration trends and advocates fairer, more humane conditions for immigrants.

National Immigration Forum; 50 F St., N.W., Suite 300, Washington, DC 20001; (202) 347-0040; www.immigration forum.org. A leading advocacy group in support of immigrants' rights.

Racial Diversity in Public Schools

*Has the Supreme Court Dealt
a Blow to Integration?*

Kenneth Jost

White enrollment at Seattle's Ballard High School is above previous guidelines five years after a racial-diversity plan was suspended because of a legal challenge. The Supreme Court's June 28 decision invalidating racial-balance plans in Seattle and Louisville, Ky., bars school districts from using race for student-placement decisions but may permit some race-conscious policies to promote diversity.

From *CQ Researcher*,
September 14, 2007.

Hannah MacNeal's parents were glad to learn of an opening at the popular magnet elementary school near their upscale neighborhood in eastern Louisville, Ky. When they applied in mid-August for Hannah to enroll as a fourth-grader at Greathouse/Shryock Elementary, however, school system officials said she could not be admitted.

The reason: Hannah is white.

Only six weeks earlier, the U.S. Supreme Court had ruled that Jefferson County Public Schools (JCPS) — which includes Louisville — was violating the Constitution by assigning students to schools on the basis of their race.

Hannah's stepmother, Dana MacNeal, was surprised and upset when she learned Hannah would have been admitted to the school if she had been black. And she was all the more upset when JCPS Student Placement Director Pat Todd insisted on Aug. 14 that the Supreme Court ruling allowed the school system to continue maintaining separate attendance zones for black and white students for Greathouse/Shryock and two of the system's other three magnet elementary schools.

The school system's lawyers were surprised as well to learn of the policy. After the MacNeals decided to fight the decision keeping Hannah in her regular elementary school, officials agreed to enroll her at Greathouse/Shryock and scrap the racially separate boundary zones beginning in 2008.[1]

"Of course, they backed off from the position, knowing they were wrong," says Louisville attorney Ted Gordon, who represented

School Racial-Balance Plans in Louisville and Seattle

The Supreme Court's June 28, 2007, ruling on the school racial-diversity plans in Seattle and Jefferson County (Louisville) bars the use of racial classifications in individual pupil assignments but appears to permit some "race-neutral" policies aimed at racial diversity.

Jefferson County (Louisville) (98,000 students; 35 percent African-American)

History: County was racially segregated before *Brown v. Board of Education* ruling; court-ordered desegregation plan in 1975 called for crosstown busing between predominantly African-American West End and mainly white neighborhoods in eastern suburbs; court order dissolved in 2000; school board adopts pupil-assignment plan with use of racial classifications to promote diversity; assignment plan still in effect after Supreme Court decision, pending new plan expected for 2009-2010 academic year.

Details: Plan classifies students as "black" or "white" (including Asians, Hispanics and others); guidelines call for each elementary, middle or high school to have between 15 percent and 50 percent African-American enrollment; residence-based system assigns students to school within residential "cluster"; most West End neighborhoods assigned to schools outside area; student applications for transfer from assigned school evaluated on basis of several factors, including effect on racial makeup; under Supreme Court decision, individual transfer requests will no longer be denied on basis of race.

Seattle (45,000 students: 58 percent "non-white")

History: No history of mandatory segregation, but racially identifiable neighborhoods: predominantly black south of downtown, predominantly white to the north; racial-balance plan with crosstown busing voluntarily adopted in 1978; school choice introduced in 1990s, with race as one "tiebreaker" to distribute students among oversubscribed schools; school board suspended the plan in 2002 because of legal challenge; Supreme Court ruling held plan invalid.

Details: Ninth-graders permitted to apply to up to three of district's 10 high schools; tiebreakers used for applications to oversubscribed schools; sibling preference was most important factor, race second; race used if school's enrollment deviated by specified percentage from overall racial demographics: 40 percent white, 60 percent non-white.

the MacNeals in the latest round in his long-running battle to overturn Jefferson County's school racial-diversity policies. "They have to follow the law."

The Supreme Court's fractured ruling struck down pupil-assignment policies adopted in 2000 limiting African-American enrollment at any individual school in Jefferson County to between 15 percent and 50 percent of the student body. The ruling also rejected the Seattle school system's use of race as a "tiebreaker" for assigning students to high schools; the plan had been suspended in 2002 because of the litigation.[2] (*See box, above.*)

In response to the MacNeals' case, Todd's office drew up new boundary zones for the four magnet elementary schools that were approved by the school board on Sept. 10. For the longer term, officials are trying to find ways to maintain a measure of racial balance in the 98,000-student school system under the Supreme Court decision, which bars the use of racial classifications in individual pupil assignments but appears to permit some "race-neutral" policies aimed at racial diversity. (*See box, p. 72.*)

"We are going to do our best to achieve it," says JCPS Superintendent Sheldon Berman. "We are deeply committed to retaining the qualities of an integrated environment."

The court's June 28 decision dealt a blow to hundreds of school systems around the country that have adopted voluntary race-mixing plans after court-ordered desegregation plans lapsed in recent years.

Five of the justices — led by Chief Justice John G. Roberts Jr. — said using racial classifications in pupil assignments violated the Equal Protection Clause of the 14th Amendment. That is the same provision the court cited a half-century earlier in the famous *Brown v. Board of Education* (1954) ruling that found racial segregation in public schools unconstitutional.[3]

In a strong dissent, the court's four liberal justices — led by Stephen G. Breyer — said the ruling contradicted previous decisions upholding race-based pupil assignments and would hamper local school boards' efforts to prevent "resegregation" in individual schools. But one of the justices in the majority — Anthony M. Kennedy — joined the liberal minority in endorsing racial diversity as a legitimate goal. Kennedy listed several "race-neutral" policies, such as drawing attendance zones or building new schools to include students from different racial neighborhoods, that schools could adopt to pursue the goal.

The ruling drew sharp criticism from traditional civil rights advocates. "It's preposterous to think the 14th Amendment was designed to permit individual white parents to strike down a plan to help minority students have better access to schools and to prevent school districts from having integrated schools that are supported by a majority of the community," says Gary Orfield, a longtime civil rights advocate and director of the Civil Rights Project at UCLA's Graduate School of Education and Information Sciences.

Ted Shaw, president of the NAACP Legal Defense Fund, said the ruling blocks school boards from using "one of the few tools that are available" to create racially diverse schools. "The court has taken a significant step away from the promise of *Brown*," says Shaw. "And this comes on top of the reality that many school districts are highly segregated by race already."

Conservative critics of race-based school policies, however, applauded the ruling. "I don't think school districts should be drawing attendance zones or building

Racial Classifications Barred But Diversity Backed

The Supreme Court's June 28 decision in *Parents Involved in Community Schools v. Seattle School District No. 1* invalidating pupil-assignment plans in Seattle and Louisville bars school systems from assigning individual students to schools based on their race. In a partial concurrence, however, Justice Anthony M. Kennedy joined with the four dissenters in finding racial diversity to be a legitimate government interest and in permitting some race-conscious policies to achieve that goal.

Roberts (plurality opinion)

Scalia   Thomas   Alito

"Racial balancing is not transformed from 'patently unconstitutional' to a compelling state interest simply by relabeling it 'racial diversity.' "

Kennedy (concurring in part)

". . . [A] district may consider it a compelling interest to achieve a diverse student body. Race may be one component of that diversity. . . . What the government is not permitted to do . . . is to classify every student on the basis of race and to assign each of them to schools based on that classification."

Breyer (dissenting)

Stevens   Souter   Ginsburg

"The plurality . . . undermines [*Brown v. Board of Education's*] promise of integrated primary and secondary education that local communities have sought to make a reality. This cannot be justified in the name of the Equal Protection Clause."

Credits: AFP/Getty Images/Paul J. Richards (Alito, Kennedy, Roberts, Souter, Scalia, Thomas); Getty Images/Mark Wilson (Ginsburg, Stevens); AFP/Getty Images/ Brendan Smialowski (Breyer)

Southern Schools Least Segregated, But Slipping

Schools in the South were the least segregated in the nation in the 1970s and '80s, a distinction they maintained in the 2005 school year. But Southern schools have been resegregating steadily since 1988.

Change in Black Segregation in Southern Schools, 1954-2005

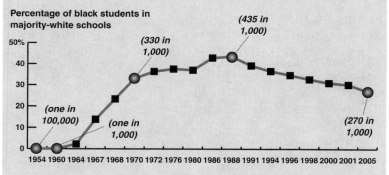

Source: Gary Orfield and Chungmei Lee, "Historic Reversals, Accelerating Resegregation, and the Need for New Integration Strategies," Civil Rights Project, UCLA, August 2007

diversity, we've already had some significant slippage at some selected schools," he says.[4]

Nationally, a new report by the UCLA Civil Rights Project concludes that African-American and Latino students are increasingly isolated from white students in public schools. Overall, nearly three-fourths of African-American students and slightly over three-fourths of Latino students attend predominantly minority schools. Both figures have been increasing since 1980, the report says.[5] (*See graphs, p. 75.*)

Critics of race-based pupil assignments are unfazed by the trends. "We're past guidelines, we're past quotas and we need to move on," says Gordon of the Louisville statistics. He calls instead for an array of reforms focused on schools with high concentrations of low-income students.

"All other things being equal, I like racially diverse schools," says Abigail Thernstrom, a senior fellow at the conservative Manhattan Institute and a former member of the Massachusetts Board of Education. "But I do not think it works from any angle to have government entities — whether they are federal courts or local school boards — try to engineer diversity."

Supporters of racial-balance plans argue that diversity in the classroom helps boost academic achievement for minority students without adversely affecting achievement for white students. Opponents dispute those claims. (*See sidebar, p. 85.*)

The debate over diversity also highlights a secondary dispute over the widespread practice of "tracking" — the offering of separate courses for students based on ability or previous achievement. Supporters say the practice matches curriculum to students' needs and abilities, but critics say it results in consigning already disadvantaged students — including a disproportionate number of African-Americans — to poor-quality education. (*See sidebar, p. 82.*)

Meanwhile, some experts and advocates are calling for shifting the focus away from race and instead trying

schools for the purpose of achieving a politically correct racial mix," says Roger Clegg, president of the Center for Equal Opportunity, which joined in a friend-of-the-court brief supporting the white families that challenged the Seattle and Louisville school policies.

"A lot of parents out there don't like it when their students are treated differently because of race or ethnicity," Clegg adds. "After these decisions, the odds favor those parents and those organizations that oppose school boards that practice racial or ethnic discrimination."

School officials in Louisville and Seattle and around the country are generally promising to continue race-mixing policies within the limits of the court's decision. "School boards are going to have to do the hard work to find more tailored ways of approaching diversity in their schools," says Francisco Negrón, general counsel of the National School Boards Association.

The evidence in Louisville and nationally suggests, however, that the goal will be hard to achieve. In Louisville, nine schools are now outside the district's 15/50 guidelines, with several having more than 55 percent African-American enrollment, according to Todd. "If the board wants to continue to maintain

White Students Are Racially Isolated

Segregation remained high in 2005-06 for all racial groups except Asians. White students remained the most racially isolated, although they attended schools with slightly more minority students than in the past. The average white student attended schools in which 77 percent of their peers were white. Meanwhile, more than half of black and Latino students' peers were black or Latino, and fewer than one-third of their classmates were white.

Racial Composition of Schools Attended by the Average . . .

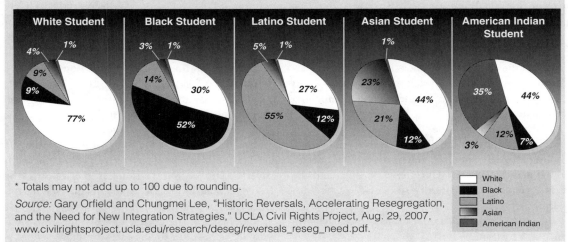

White Student
4%, 1%, 9%, 9%, 77%

Black Student
3%, 1%, 14%, 30%, 52%

Latino Student
5%, 1%, 27%, 55%, 12%

Asian Student
1%, 23%, 44%, 21%, 12%

American Indian Student
35%, 44%, 3%, 12%, 7%

Legend: White, Black, Latino, Asian, American Indian

* Totals may not add up to 100 due to rounding.

Source: Gary Orfield and Chungmei Lee, "Historic Reversals, Accelerating Resegregation, and the Need for New Integration Strategies," UCLA Civil Rights Project, Aug. 29, 2007, www.civilrightsproject.ucla.edu/research/deseg/reversals_reseg_need.pdf.

to promote socioeconomic integration — mixing low-income and middle- and upper-class students. Richard Kahlenberg, a senior fellow with the left-of-center Century Foundation who is most closely associated with the movement, says policies aimed at preventing high concentrations of low-income students will produce academic gains along with likely gains in racial and ethnic diversity.

"Providing all students with the chance to attend mixed-income schools can raise overall levels of achievement," Kahlenberg writes in a report released on the day of the Supreme Court decision.[6]

As the debate over diversity in public-school classrooms continues, here are the major questions being considered:

Should school systems promote racial diversity in individual schools?

School officials in Lynn, Mass., a former mill town 10 miles northeast of Boston, take pride in a pupil-assignment system that has helped maintain racial balance in most schools even as the town's Hispanic population has steadily increased over the past decade. "We work very hard to promote integration and cultural diversity so that our children are able to get along with each other," says Jan Birchenough, the administrator in charge of compliance with the state's racial-balance law.

But attorney Chester Darling says Lynn's policy of denying any transfer requests that would increase racial imbalance at an individual school "falls squarely within" the kinds of plans prohibited by the Supreme Court decision in the Louisville and Seattle cases. "It can't be race-neutral if you use the word race," says Darling, who is asking a federal judge in Boston to reopen a previously unsuccessful suit filed by parents challenging the policy.[7]

Critics of race-based assignment plans hope the Supreme Court decision will persuade or force school districts like Lynn's to drop any use of racial classifications in pupil placement. "Most school districts will look at the decision's bottom line, will consider that the Louisville and Seattle plans were not sloppily done, and yet at the end of the day were declared unconstitutional," says Clegg of the Center for Equal Opportunity. "This cost the school boards a lot of time and money, and they're going to have to pay the other side's lawyer."

But school board officials say the court's fractured ruling leaves room for local systems to consider race in trying to create racial and ethnic mixing in individual schools. "Race is still not out of the question," says Negrón of the school boards' association. "A plurality of the court said certain things that are not the law of the land. What the majority has done is invalidate these particular programs, but certainly left the door wide open to the use of race — which continues to be a compelling government interest."

Apart from the legal issue, supporters and opponents of racial-diversity plans also disagree on their educational and other effects. "There's a consensus in the academic world that there are clear educational benefits, and the benefits aren't just for minority students," says UCLA Professor Orfield.

Conversely, "racial isolation leads to reduced achievement," says Negrón.

Critics of racial-diversity policies, however, say those benefits are unproven and the logic of the claimed cause-effect relationship unconvincing. "There is very little empirical evidence," says Thernstrom, the Manhattan Institute fellow.

"I don't think how well you learn or what you learn depends on the color of the skin of the person sitting next to you," says Clegg. "Students in overwhelmingly white schoolrooms in Idaho and in overwhelmingly African-American classrooms in Washington, D.C., can each learn."

Critics cite as one concrete disadvantage the time spent on buses when students are transported out of their neighborhoods for the sake of racial balance. "There's no educational benefit there, and it's a waste of their very precious time," says Thernstrom. The travel burdens also hamper student participation in extracurricular activities and parental involvement, the critics say.

In traditional desegregation plans, those burdens typically fell for the most part on African-American students, who were transported out of their neighborhoods to schools in predominantly white areas. Busing was "usually a one-way street" for African-Americans, says James Anderson, head of the department of educational-policy studies at the University of Illinois, Champaign-Urbana.

In recent years, however, school-choice policies in some communities have meant increased busing for whites as well as minority students. Negrón cites the example of Pinellas County (Clearwater), Fla., which has a universal-choice program allowing students to enroll in any school in the county and providing transportation if requested. "It is a cost," Negrón says. "But school districts are finding that it depends on the facts and circumstances."

Civil rights advocates counter that racial isolation imposes much more serious costs for minority students. "The consequences of segregation of African-American students in public schools — and it is increasingly true for Latino students — have been concentration of poverty, deprivation of resources and a host of other problems that do impact on the quality of education," says the Legal Defense Fund's Shaw.

Like many of the critics, Thernstrom stops short of absolute opposition to any race-conscious school policies. "I don't mind" redrawing attendance zones for racial mixing, she says, "but I don't think we should be starry-eyed about what it's going to achieve."

Michael Rosman, president of the Center for Individual Rights, says schools should try to prevent "racial isolation" in individual schools "if it is shown to have deleterious educational effects."

But Illinois Professor Anderson says school boards should take affirmative steps to "take advantage" of diversity. "We could build wonderful, intellectually rich environments where kids really do have an exchange of ideas and an exchange of cultures and come out of that with a cosmopolitan sense of culture that is unique," he says. "How can you be global," he adds, "yet at the same time so parochial?"

Should school systems seek to promote socioeconomic integration in individual schools?

The consolidated school system in Wake County, N.C. — encompassing the rapidly growing Research Triangle Park area (near Raleigh and Durham) — made nationwide news in 2000 by dropping the use of racial guidelines in favor of socioeconomic-integration policies. The "Healthy School" assignment guidelines call for limiting individual schools to no more than 40 percent enrollment of students receiving free or reduced-price lunches or 25 percent enrollment of students performing below grade level.

Seven years later, the policies are a bragging point for the school system and exhibit No. 1 for advocates of socioeconomic integration. "Classrooms that are balanced from a diversity point of view are important to maintaining academic performance," says Michael Evans, the school system's communications director, citing the district's declining achievement gap for African-American, Hispanic and low-income students.

Some Wake County parents are not sold, however. Dave Duncan, the one-time president of the now largely inactive advocacy group Assignment by Choice, discounts the claimed academic gains by pointing to the relatively small percentage of students assigned under the guidelines and the comparable academic gains statewide. The school system "used the diversity issue as a smoke screen when there is criticism or opposition to the way they do the student-assignment process," Duncan says.

As the most prominent advocate of socioeconomic integration, the Century Foundation's Kahlenberg acknowledges varied results in districts with such policies. But he strongly argues that the policy of mixing students by socioeconomic background offers educational benefits in its own right and practical advantages for districts trying to promote racial diversity without running afoul of the Supreme Court's new limits on race-based assignments.

Non-Racial Approaches to Integration

Some 40 school districts around the country are seeking to diversify enrollment in individual schools through socioeconomic integration—typically, by setting guidelines for the percentage of students eligible for free or reduced-price lunch. Here are some of the districts taking such approaches, as drawn from a report by the Century Foundation's Richard Kahlenberg, a strong advocate of the policies.

School District *Enrollment: Percentage of whites (W), African-Americans (B), Hispanics (H), Asian-Americans (A)*

Berkeley, Calif. (*9,000: 31% W, 29% B, 17% H, 8% A*)

Socioeconomic and racial diversity guidelines were adopted in 2004 to replace a voluntary racial-integration plan; plan being phased-in one grade at a time; in 2005-06, eight of 11 elementary schools were within 15% of the districtwide average of 40% of students receiving subsidized lunches; most parents (71%) still receive first choice of schools.

Brandywine, Del. (*11,000: 54% W, 39% B, 3% H, 4% A*)

The district — comprising parts of Wilmington and surrounding suburbs — was granted an exception in 2001 by state Board of Education to law mandating neighborhood schools; plan limits subsidized-lunch enrollment to between 16% and 73%; plan credited with maintaining racial diversity; some evidence of academic gains in higher grades.

Cambridge, Mass. (*6,000: 37% B, 35% W, 15% H, 11% A*)

Plan adopted in 2001 to replace race-conscious "controlled choice" system says individual schools should be within 15 percentage points of districtwide percentage of free/reduced lunch students; race remains a potential factor in assignments; racial diversity maintained, socioeconomic diversity increased; limited evidence finds academic gains for low-income students, no negative effect on middle-income students.

Charlotte-Mecklenburg, N.C. (*129,000: 42% B, 36% W, 14% H, 4% A*)

School board dropped racial-desegregation effort, adopted public school choice plan after school system was declared "unitary" in 2001, or no longer a dual system based on race; plan gives some priority to low-income students in schools with concentrated poverty, but transfers to higher-performing schools are permitted only if seats are available; plan seen as unsuccessful in creating racial or socioeconomic integration.

La Crosse, Wis. (*7,000: 20% minority*)

Was first district to adopt socioeconomic integration policy in 1991-92 in response to influx of Hmong refugees; plan used redrawn attendance zones and busing to spread low-income students among elementary schools and two high schools; plan largely survived political battle in 1992-93 that included recall of several school board members; plan touted as success, but enrollments at most elementary schools have been and still are outside guidelines.

(Continued)

"There's a wide body of research that the single, best thing you can do for low-income kids is to give them the opportunity to attend a middle-class school," says

(Continued)

School District *Enrollment: Percentage of whites (W), African-Americans (B), Hispanics (H), Asian-Americans (A)*

Manatee County, Fla. (*42,000: 60% W, 20% H, 15% B, 4% other*)
District south of Tampa Bay has had limited success with a plan adopted in 2002 admitting students to schools based on maintaining socioeconomic balance: Only 10 elementary schools were within guidelines in 2005-06; among 14 schools with above-average low-income enrollment, only four showed adequate academic gains.

McKinney, Tex. (*20,000: 64% W, 21% H, 11% B, 3% other*)
Dallas suburb adopted socioeconomic-balance policy in 1995 by redrawing attendance zones; low-income students perform better on statewide tests than low-income students statewide; some opposition to longer bus rides, but plan said to have broad support.

Minneapolis, Minn. (*36,000: 41% B, 28% W, 16% H, 10% A*)
Desegregation suit settled in state court in 2000 with agreement to adopt four-year experiment to encourage socioeconomic integration; plan provides transportation for low-income students to suburban schools; also requires wealthier magnet schools in Minneapolis to set aside seats for low-income students; 2,000 low-income students attended suburban schools over four-year period; legislature voted to extend program after end of experiment.

Omaha, Neb. (*47,000: 44% W, 32% B, 21% H*)
School board adopted plan aimed at socioeconomic integration after system was declared unitary in 1999; low-income students given preference in weighted lottery for admission to magnet schools; 2006 proposal to expand plan to recently annexed neighborhoods prompted backlash in state legislature, but education groups won passage of 2007 bill to establish goal of socioeconomic diversity throughout metropolitan area.

Rochester, N.Y. (*33,000: 64% B, 22% H, 13% W*)
Managed-choice plan adopted in city in 2002 includes socioeconomic-fairness guidelines; vast majority of elementary school students (83%) are economically disadvantaged; plan seen as likely to have limited effect unless interdistrict choice program is established between city and suburbs.

San Francisco (*55,000: 32% Asian, 22% H, 13% B, 9% W*)
Student-assignment plan adopted in 2001 replaced racial-desegregation scheme with plan aimed at socioeconomic diversity; seven-part definition includes SES (socioeconomic status), academic achievement, language, other factors; plan seen as fairly successful in balancing schools by SES, less so in producing racial diversity; district is consistently top-performing urban district in state.

Wake County (Raleigh), N.C. (*136,000: 54% W, 27% B, 10% H, 5% A*)
Guidelines adopted in 2000 replacing racial guidelines limit schools to 40% free/reduced lunch, 25% reading below grade level; policies credited with maintaining racial diversity; role in academic gains questioned; school-zone changes due to growth draw criticism from some families.
Sources: Richard D. Kahlenberg, Century Foundation, "Rescuing Brown v. Board of Education: Profiles of Twelve School Districts Pursuing Socioeconomic School Integration," Century Foundation, June 28, 2007, www.tcf.org; news accounts.

higher academic achievement for low-income students and no adverse effect on others as long as there is "a strong core of students with middle-class background."

Kahlenberg says socioeconomic integration is also likely to produce some racial and ethnic mixing since the poverty rate among African-Americans and Latinos is higher than among whites. In educational terms, however, he says socioeconomic diversity is more valuable than racial diversity because the academic gains of mixing by class and income appear to be well established, while the claimed gains of race mixing are in dispute.

Traditional civil rights advocates like the Legal Defense Fund's Shaw do not quarrel with socioeconomic integration but insist that it is "not an adequate substitute for racial integration."

Orfield agrees that socioeconomic integration is "a good idea" but quickly adds, "You can't achieve racial integration very well by using social and economic integration."

"If you talk to districts that have relied solely on that, it doesn't reach all of the students that they need to reach," says Negrón at the school boards association.

For their part, conservatives raise fewer objections to mixing students by socioeconomic background than by race, but they worry the practice may merely be a pretext for racial classifications. "It has fewer constitutional problems," says Thernstrom. "It is less politically controversial."

"It's better than race-based student assignments," says Clegg at the Center for Equal Opportunity. "But if you're using socioeconomic status simply as a proxy for race, many of the same policy and legal problems remain."

Kahlenberg. Despite some well-publicized exceptions, schools with "concentrated levels of poverty" tend to have more student-discipline problems, lower caliber teachers and principals and less parental involvement than predominantly middle- or upper-class schools, he explains. Socioeconomic integration, he says, results in

Thernstrom is unconvinced, however, of the claimed academic benefits. "There are no proven results from it," she says. She scoffs at what she calls "the notion that if you sit next to somebody, differences [in values] are going to somehow melt away."

In any event, Clegg says he opposes either racial or socioeconomic mixing if it requires assigning students to schools distant from their homes. "Neighborhood schools are the preferable means of assignment," he says, "because you're not having to pay for busing and you're not having to put children on long bus rides, which keep them from engaging in extracurricular activities."

Kahlenberg disagrees. "I haven't heard anyone make a convincing case that from an educational perspective the best way to assign students is the place where their parents can afford to live," he says. "That's the way we do it, but there's no argument that's the best way to educate kids in our society."

From opposite perspectives, however, both Orfield and Thernstrom agree that socioeconomic integration engenders some of the same kinds of opposition that racial integration does. "You do have a lot of middle-class flight as a result," Thernstrom says. "It's not really more popular than racial integration," Orfield says.

Despite the resistance, Kahlenberg believes the policy would fulfill a fundamental goal of public education in the United States. "Most people believe at least in theory that education is the way for kids of any background to do well," he says. "As long as we have economically segregated schools, that promise is broken."

Is the focus on diversity interfering with efforts to improve education in all schools?

As he wrapped up his legal challenge to the Louisville pupil-assignment plan before the Supreme Court, attorney Gordon depicted the case as a choice between "diversity" and "educational outcome."

"For me," Gordon told the justices during the Dec. 4 arguments, "I would use all these millions of dollars. I would reduce teacher-student ratio. I would give incentive pay to the better teachers. I would [build] more magnet schools, more traditional schools."

"We presuppose that we're going to have bad schools and good schools in this country," he continued. "I don't think we can no [sic] longer accept that."

Gordon describes himself as a civil rights liberal, but his argument parallels the views of conservatives like Clegg. "School districts should be worrying less about the racial and ethnic mix than about improving the education that's offered at all schools," Clegg says.

"If you're just focusing on racial diversity, as it's called, for its own sake without trying to assess whether you're improving the educational outcomes," says Rosman, "then you're detracting from the overall goal of achieving educational excellence. In some instances, that's happened."

"The solution is to reduce the gap, the racial gap, the ethnic gap, the socioeconomic gap," says Thernstrom. "Then kids will be looked at as just kids without any kind of assumptions made about, you know, are they like me?"

Traditional civil rights groups and advocates insist that diversity and educational reform complement rather than conflict with each other. In any event, they say, the push for diversity is neither so strong nor so extensive as the critics contend.

"We haven't had any federal policy of promoting diversity since 1981," says Orfield, referring to the first year of Ronald Reagan's presidency. "We haven't had any new lawsuits to integrate schools for a long time. Ever since 1980, most desegregation plans have had voluntary choice and magnet schools, and almost all of them are part and parcel of educational reform plans."

John Trasviña, president and general counsel of the Mexican American Legal Defense and Educational Fund (MALDEF), calls the claimed conflict between diversity and educational quality "a diversion." Referring to educational reform, he says, "We aren't doing that either. It's always easy to say let's address some other issue. When it comes to do that, it's not done."

Diversity advocates dispute critics' suggestion that racial or economic integration has been pursued solely for its own sake with no attention to improving educational quality. "I don't think anybody ever thought that school integration by itself was a sufficient policy," Orfield says.

"The whole reason for economic integration is to promote academic achievement and raise the quality of schooling," says Kahlenberg. "No one has figured out how to make separate schools for rich and poor work well, certainly not for poor kids."

Orfield and Kahlenberg also dismiss concerns that the transportation costs entailed in some diversity plans take scarce dollars from other, more promising school-improvement initiatives. "We've spent billions and billions of dollars on low-income schools, which hasn't produced a lot of results," Kahlenberg says.

Orfield is even blunter about recent efforts to reduce the racial gap. "It's been a failure," he says. Desegregation and anti-poverty programs of the 1960s and '70s did narrow the racial-achievement gap, Orfield writes in the recent UCLA Civil Rights Project report. But he says "most studies" find that President Bush's No Child Left Behind law — which specifically calls for narrowing the achievement gap between white and minority pupils — has had "no impact" on the disparities so far.[8]

From opposite perspectives, Thernstrom and Trasviña lay out demanding agendas for schools to try to close the racial gap. "I want more learning going on," says Thernstrom. "You need really good schools. The day should be longer, the teachers should be better, the principals should have more authority.

"Our kids aren't learning enough in school," she continues. "That will level the playing field."

"We clearly need to improve the quality of our schools," says Trasviña. He calls for steps to reduce the dropout rate and to channel more students into so-called STEM courses (science, technology, engineering and math). But diversity helps, not hurts reform efforts, he says.

"While it is true that simply putting children of different backgrounds in seats in the same classroom does not necessarily improve the classroom experience by itself, [diversity] adds to it," Trasviña says. "And it adds to the political will to make sure that people understand that these are our schools."

BACKGROUND

The 'Common School'

The idea of free, universal public education has been espoused in the United States since the Revolutionary Era and still holds a central place in American thought as a tool for personal development and social cohesion. But the ideal of equal educational opportunity for all has never been obtained in practice. Even as education became more nearly universal in the 20th century, African-Americans and other racial and ethnic minorities faced blatant discrimination that was only partly alleviated by landmark court rulings outlawing legally mandated segregation.[9]

George Washington and Thomas Jefferson were among the nation's early leaders to call in general terms for mass public education, but the educational "system" of the early 19th century consisted of private academies, rural district schools and a handful of "charity" schools in cities. Horace Mann, the so-called father of American public education, used his appointment as Massachusetts' first commissioner of education in 1837 to advocate the "common school" — publicly supported and open to all. As University of Wisconsin educational historian William Reese explains, Mann saw education as a way to restore social harmony at a time of social tensions between rich and poor and between native-born and immigrants. Others saw the same connection. His fellow New Englander Alpheus Packard wrote in the 1840s of the "sons of wealth and poverty" gaining mutual respect by sitting side by side in a public school.[10]

Abolitionist Mann's vision had no practical meaning, however, for African-American slaves before the Civil War and only limited significance for their descendants for decades after slavery was abolished. Both before and after the Civil War, the vast majority of African-Americans "lived in states that were openly and explicitly opposed to their education," according to the University of Illinois' Anderson.

After emancipation slaves who had learned to read and write became teachers in rudimentary schools, aided by Northern missionaries and philanthropists and some sympathetic white Southerners. With the end of Reconstruction, however, Southern leaders "pushed back the gains that had been made," Anderson says. In a racially segregated system in the early 20th century, per capita spending for black pupils in the South amounted to one-fourth to one-half of the amount spent on whites.[11]

Education was becoming nearly universal for white Americans, even as racial segregation became entrenched for African-Americans and, in many places, for Mexican- and Asian-Americans.[12] Elementary school attendance was nearly universal by the 1920s. High schools — once viewed as fairly selective institutions — began doubling

C H R O N O L O G Y

Before 1950 *Free, universal public education is enshrined as American ideal and advances in practice, but African-Americans, Hispanics and Asian-Americans are consigned to separate and unequal schools in much of the country.*

1950s-1960s *Racial segregation in public schools is ruled unconstitutional, but desegregation is slow.*

1954, 1955 Supreme Court's unanimous decision in *Brown v. Board of Education* (1954) outlaws mandatory racial segregation in public schools; a year later court says school districts must dismantle dual systems "with all deliberate speed" (*Brown II*). "Massive resistance" in South stalls integration.

1964, 1965 Civil Rights Act of 1964 authorizes Justice Department to file school-desegregation suits; Title I of Elementary and Secondary Education Act provides targeted aid to school districts for low-income students.

1968 Supreme Court tells school districts to develop plans to dismantle dual systems "now."

1970s-1980s *Busing upheld as desegregation tool but draws strong protests in North and West as well as South; Supreme Court, Justice Department withdraw from desegregation cases.*

1971 Supreme Court unanimously upholds federal courts' power to order crosstown busing to desegregate schools.

1973 Supreme Court rejects federal constitutional right to equal school funding; one month later, New Jersey supreme court is first to sustain funding-equity suit under state constitution.

1974 U.S. Supreme Court, 5-4, bars court-ordered desegregation between inner cities and suburbs; decision is first in series of closely divided rulings that limit desegregation remedies.

1983 U.S. Department of Education report "A Nation at Risk" paints critical picture of rising mediocrity in U.S. schools, shifts agenda away from equity issues.

1990s *Racial isolation increases for African-Americans, Latinos; "reverse discrimination" suits by white students backed in some federal courts, fail in others.*

1991 La Crosse, Wis., becomes first school district to aim to balance enrollment by students' income status: "socioeconomic integration."

1995 Supreme Court signals federal courts to wrap up desegregation cases; lower courts respond by generally granting "unitary" status to school systems seeking to be freed from desegregation orders.

1998, 1999 Federal appeals courts in Boston, Richmond, Va., bar racial preferences in public school admission.

2000-Present *Socioeconomic integration advances; Latinos become largest ethnic minority; Supreme Court ruling bars racial classifications in pupil assignments.*

2000 Wake County (Raleigh), N.C., becomes largest school district to try socioeconomic integration.

2001 President George W. Bush wins congressional approval of No Child Left Behind Act, requiring school districts to meet achievement benchmarks, including closing racial gap.

2001-2005 White families challenge racial-diversity plans in Seattle and Louisville, Ky; federal courts back school districts, ruling plans are "narrowly tailored" to achieve "compelling" interest in diversity.

2005, 2006 Bush nominates John G. Roberts Jr. and Samuel A. Alito Jr. to Supreme Court; both win Senate confirmation, strengthening conservative majority on court.

2007 Supreme Court ruling in Louisville and Seattle cases limits use of race in pupil assignments, but five justices say race-neutral measures can be used to promote compelling interest in diversity; school boards vow to try to maintain racial diversity; advocates push socioeconomic integration on legal, political grounds.

'Tracking' Leads to Racial Separation in Classes

But grouping students by ability has wide support.

Ballard High School sits on a spacious campus in an overwhelmingly white suburban neighborhood in the eastern end of Jefferson County, Ky. As part of Jefferson County Public Schools' racial balance policies, however, Ballard's attendance zone includes neighborhoods on the opposite side of the county in Louisville's predominantly African-American West End section.

By drawing students from the West End, the school achieved around 25 percent black enrollment in the 2006-07 academic year. But despite the measure of racial balance in overall enrollment, Ballard students say blacks and whites are less than fully integrated inside. "Kids naturally separate," remarks Ben Gravel, a white 12th-grader, as he arrives at school on Aug. 13 for the opening of a new school year.

At Ballard — and in schools around the country — the racial separation is especially pronounced in the classroom itself. African-American students are disproportionately enrolled in less challenging, "low-track" classes and underrepresented in higher-track classes, such as advanced placement (AP) courses and international baccalaureate (IB) programs. In 2006, for example, African-Americans comprised about 13 percent of graduating high school seniors but only 6 percent of the total number of students who took advanced placement exams administered by the College Board.[1]

The widespread practice of tracking — or "ability grouping" as supporters prefer to call it — has been a contentious issue within education circles for more than two decades. "Detracking" advocates have had occasional success in pushing reforms, but the practice has persisted — in part because of strong resistance from parents of students enrolled in higher-track courses.[2]

Supporters say the practice matches curricular offerings to students' abilities and achievement level. "It doesn't make sense to the average person that you would put a non-reader in the same English classroom as some kid who's reading Proust," says Tom Loveless, director of the Brown Center on Educational Policy at the Brookings Institution in Washington.

Critics say the practice simply keeps already-disadvantaged students on a path to lower academic achievement. "If you have classes that are structured to give kids less of a challenge, those kids tend to fall farther behind," says Kevin Welner, an associate professor at the University of Colorado's School of Education in Boulder.

Civil rights advocates say the enrollment patterns reflect what they call "segregation by tracking." In her critique of the practice, Jeannie Oakes, director of urban schooling at UCLA's Graduate School of Education and Information Studies, cited research evidence indicating that African-American and Latino students were more likely to be assigned to low-track courses than white students even when they had comparable abilities or test scores.[3]

in enrollment each decade after 1890 thanks to a declining market for child labor and the growing enforcement of new compulsory education laws. Secondary school enrollment increased from 50 percent of 14-17-year-olds in 1920 to nearly 95 percent of that age group by the mid-1970s. Meanwhile, the average school year was also increasing — from 144 days in 1900 to 178 days in 1950. And per capita investment in education rose during the same period from 1.2 percent of national income to 2 percent.

The Supreme Court's 1954 decision in *Brown* outlawing racial segregation in public schools capped a half-century-long campaign by the NAACP to gain a measure of equal educational opportunity for African-Americans.[13] The legal campaign — directed by the future Supreme Court justice, Thurgood Marshall — was waged at a deliberate pace even as many black students and families were agitating for better schools at the local level. The eventual decision seemed far from inevitable beforehand. Only after 1950 did the NAACP decide to ask the court to abolish segregation rather than try to equalize the separate school systems. And the justices were closely divided after the first round of arguments in 1952; they joined in the unanimous ruling

"I wouldn't use the phrase 'segregation by tracking.' A lot of it is self-tracking," counters Abigail Thernstrom, a senior fellow at the conservative Manhattan Institute and co-author of a book on the educational gap between white and minority students. "Is it terrible that we have so few Latino and black students who are prepared to take the most educationally rigorous courses?" she adds. "Of course, it's terrible."

Welner acknowledges minority students often choose low-track courses, but faults school systems instead of the students. Minority parents and students often lack the information needed to understand the different course offerings, he says. And students "sometimes don't want to be the only minority in the high-track class," he says.

Loveless acknowledges the critics' complaints about low-track classes, but says the solution is to reform not to abolish them. "Let's fix the low-track classes," he says. Despite the critics' doubts, he says many private, charter and parochial schools have developed low-track curricula that more effectively challenge students than those often found in public schools.

"If we know how to create a high-track class, why would we then create a separate set of classes that don't have those opportunities?" Welner asks. "Why would we let students opt for a lesser education?"

Sixth-graders study science as part of the international baccalaureate curriculum at Harbour Pointe Middle School in Mukilteo, Wash.

Loveless says under a random-assignment system, high-achieving students "would lose quite a bit," middle-range students "would lose a bit" and lowest-achieving students "would probably benefit a little bit" — mainly by reducing the concentration of students with behavioral issues in low-track classes.

Welner disagrees that high-achieving students are necessarily harmed by reforms. "Good detracking doesn't take anything away from these kids," he says. "The high achievers are not only holding their own but are doing better after the reform."

Despite the recurrent clashes at the local level, Loveless predicts that tracking will continue to be a widespread practice. "Polls are very clear," he says. "Parents, teachers and students favor ability grouping. Those are three important constituency groups."

---

[1] College Board, "Advanced Placement: Report to the Nation 2006," p. 11 (www.collegeboard.com). For background, see Marcia Clemmitt, "AP and IB Programs," *CQ Researcher*, March 3, 2006, pp. 193-216.

[2] For opposing views, see Tom Loveless, *The Tracking Wars: State Reform Meets School Policy* (1999); Jeannie Oakes, *Keeping Track: How Schools Structure Inequality* (2d ed.), 2005.

[3] *Ibid.*, pp. 230-231.

---

in 1954 only after a second round of arguments and shrewd management of the case by the new chief justice, Earl Warren.*

The high court's "remedial" decision one year later in *Brown II* directed school districts to desegregate "with all deliberate speed." Many Southern politicians

---

* California, home to the nation's largest concentration of Asian-Americans and the second-largest concentration of Mexican-Americans after Texas, had abolished racial segregation in schools by law in 1947.

---

lent support to a campaign of "massive resistance" to the ruling by diehard segregationists. A decade after *Brown*, fewer than 5 percent of black students in the South were attending majority-white schools; more than three-fourths were attending schools with 90 percent minority enrollment.[14] In 1968, an evidently impatient Supreme Court declared that school districts had to develop plans to dismantle dual systems that promised "realistically" to work — and to work "now." Three years later, a new chief justice, Warren E. Burger, led a unanimous court in upholding the authority of local federal courts to order school districts to use

More Blacks and Latinos Attend Poorest Schools

The vast majority (79 percent) of white students attend schools where less than half the student body is poor, compared with 37 percent of black students and 36 percent of Hispanics. For schools where at least 91 percent of the students are poor, whites made up just 1 percent of the student body compared with 13 and 15 percent, respectively, for blacks and Hispanics.

Distribution of Students in Public Schools by Percentage Who Are Poor, 2005-2006

Percent Poor	Percentage of each race				
	White	Black	Latino	Asian	American Indian
0-10%	20	5	7	23	17
11-20%	17	5	5	14	6
21-30%	16	7	7	12	8
31-40%	14	9	8	11	9
41-50%	12	11	9	9	11
51-60%	9	11	10	8	11
61-70%	6	12	11	6	11
71-80%	3	13	12	6	10
81-90%	2	14	14	6	8
91-100%	1	13	15	4	9

* Totals may not add up to 100 due to rounding.

Source: Gary Orfield and Chungmei Lee, "Historic Reversals, Accelerating Resegregation, and the Need for New Integration Strategies," Civil Rights Project, UCLA, August 2007

Total number of students (in millions)	
White	28
Black	8
Latino	10
Asian	2
American Indian	1

cross-neighborhood busing as part of a desegregation plan.[15]

'Elusive' Equality

The campaign to desegregate schools stimulated broader efforts in the late 20th century to equalize educational opportunity at national, state and local levels. Initially, desegregation advanced in the South and to a lesser extent in other regions. But integration eventually stalled in the face of white opposition to busing, ambivalence among blacks and Supreme Court decisions easing pressure on local school districts to take affirmative steps to mix white and black students. School funding reform efforts produced some results, but as the 21st century began educational equality remained — in Professor Reese's word — "elusive."[16]

The Supreme Court's unanimity in school race cases broke down in the 1970s, and a continuing succession of closely divided decisions reduced districts' obligations to develop effective integration plans. In one of the most important rulings, the justices in 1974 divided 5-4 in a case from Detroit to bar court-ordered desegregation between predominantly black inner cities and predominantly white suburban districts. Three years later, the court essentially freed school districts from any obligation to prevent resegregation after adopting a racially neutral assignment plan. The decisions coincided with widespread opposition to busing for racial balance among white families in many communities, most dramatically in Boston in the 1970s, where police escorts were needed for buses taking pupils from predominantly black Roxbury to predominantly white South Boston.

African-American students and families, meanwhile, had mixed reactions to desegregation generally and busing in particular, according to Professor Anderson. In many districts, desegregation meant the closing or transformation of historically black schools that had provided a good education for many students. In the South, desegregation also often meant the loss of black principals and teachers. And busing was a "one-way street" for African-Americans: most plans entailed the transportation of black students away from their neighborhoods to a mixed reception at best in predominantly white communities.

From the start, the NAACP and other civil rights groups had viewed desegregation not only as a goal in its own right but also — and perhaps more importantly — as an instrument to equalize educational opportunities for black and white pupils. In the heady

Do Racial Policies Affect Academic Achievement?

Most studies find beneficial effects from integration.

When the Supreme Court outlawed racial segregation in schools in 1954, it relied heavily on research by the African-American psychologist Kenneth Clark purporting to show that attending all-black schools hurt black students' self-esteem. Over time, the court's reliance on Clark's study drew many critics, who questioned both the research and its prominent use in a legal ruling.

A half-century later, as they considered challenges to racial-diversity plans in Seattle and Louisville, Ky., the justices were deluged with sometimes conflicting research studies on the effects of racial policies on educational achievement. Among 64 friend-of-the-court briefs, nearly half — 27 — cited social science research. Most found beneficial effects from racial integration, but a minority questioned those claims.

The National Academy of Education, a select group of education scholars, created a seven-member committee to evaluate the various studies cited in the various briefs. Here are the committee's major conclusions from the research, released on June 29 — one day after the court found the school districts' plans unconstitutional:

Academic achievement. White students are not hurt by desegregation efforts or adjustments in racial composition of schools. African-American student achievement is enhanced by less segregated schooling, although the magnitude of the influence is quite variable. The positive effects for African-American students tend to be larger in the earlier grades.

Near-term intergroup relations. Racially diverse schools and classrooms will not guarantee improved intergroup relations, but are likely to be constructive. The research identifies conditions that need to be present in order for diversity to have a positive effect and suggests steps schools can take to realize the potential for improvement.

Long-term effects of school desegregation. Experience in desegregated schools increases the likelihood over time of greater tolerance and better intergroup relations among adults of different racial groups.

The critical-mass question. Racial diversity can avoid or mitigate harms caused by racial isolation, such as tokenism and stereotyping, particularly when accompanied by an otherwise beneficial school environment. Some briefs suggest a minimum African-American enrollment of 15 percent to 30 percent to avoid these harms, but the research does not support specifying any particular percentage.

Race-neutral alternatives. No race-neutral policy is as effective as race-conscious policies for achieving racial diversity. Socioeconomic integration is likely to marginally reduce racial isolation and may have other benefits. School choice generally and magnet schools in particular have some potential to reduce racial isolation, but could also increase segregation.

Source: Robert L. Linn and Kevin G. Welner (eds.), "Race-Conscious Policies for Assigning Students to Schools: Social Science Research and the Supreme Court Cases," National Academy of Education, June 29, 2007 (www.naeducation.org/Meredith_Report.pdf).

days of the civil rights era, Congress had put educational equality on the national agenda in 1965 by passing a law as part of President Lyndon B. Johnson's "war on poverty" to provide federal aid targeted to poor children.[17] By the end of the century, however, Title I of the Elementary and Secondary Education Act was seen as having produced mixed results at best — in part because allocation formulas shaped by the realities of congressional politics directed much of the money to relatively well-to-do suburban districts.

Meanwhile, advocates of educational equity had turned to the courts to try to reduce funding disparities between school districts — with mixed results.[18] The Supreme Court ruled in 1973 that funding disparities between

districts did not violate the federal Constitution. One month later, however, the New Jersey Supreme Court became the first state tribunal to find differential school funding to run afoul of a state constitutional provision. Over the next three decades, school funding suits resulted in court rulings in at least 19 states finding constitutional violations and ordering reforms. But funding disparities persisted. In a wide-ranging survey in 1998, *Education Week* gave 16 states a grade of C- or below on educational equity between school districts.[19]

At the same time, school policymakers were focusing on clamorous calls to improve educational quality stimulated by the publication in 1983 of a report by the Reagan administration's Department of Education sharply

Minnijean Brown, 15, one of the Little Rock Nine, arrives at Central High School on Sept. 25, 1957, guarded by soldiers sent by President Dwight. D. Eisenhower. Brown and eight other African-American students desegregated the Arkansas school three years after the Supreme Court's landmark *Brown v. Board of Education* ruling.

criticizing what was depicted as rising mediocrity in U.S. schools. The debate generated by "A Nation at Risk" brought forth all manner of proposals for imposing educational standards, revising curricula or introducing competition within public school systems or between public and private schools. The debate diverted policymakers' attention to some extent from diversity issues and led many white parents to worry more about their own children's education than about educational equity or diversity.[20]

By the end of the 1990s, federal courts were all but out of the desegregation business, and racial isolation — "resegregation" to civil rights advocates — was on the rise. In a trio of cases in 1991, 1993 and 1995, the Supreme Court gave federal courts unmistakable signals to withdraw from superintending desegregation plans. School districts that sought to be declared "unitary" — or no longer dual in nature — and freed from desegregation decrees, like Jefferson County, invariably succeeded. By 2001, at least two-thirds of black students and at least half of Latino students nationwide were enrolled in predominantly minority schools. And after narrowing in the 1980s, the educational-testing gaps between white and black students began to widen again in the 1990s. In 2000, the typical black student scored below about 75 percent of white students on most standardized tests.[21]

'Diversity' Challenged

Even as courts reduced the pressure on school districts to desegregate, hundreds of school systems adopted voluntary measures aimed at mixing students of different racial and ethnic backgrounds. Some plans that made explicit use of race in pupil assignments drew legal challenges from white families as "reverse discrimination." Meanwhile, several dozen school systems were adopting — and achieving some success with — diversity plans tied to socioeconomic status instead of race. Support for socioeconomic integration appeared to increase after the Supreme Court's June 28 decision in the Seattle and Louisville cases restricting the use of race in pupil assignments but permitting race-neutral policies to achieve diversity in the classroom.

School boards that voluntarily sought to achieve racial and ethnic mixing claimed that the policies generally improved education for all students while benefiting disadvantaged minorities and promoting broad political support for the schools. Many plans — like those in Seattle and Louisville — explicitly considered race in some pupil assignments, and several drew legal challenges. In November 1998 the federal appeals court in Boston struck down the use of racial preferences for blacks and Hispanics for admission to the prestigious Boston Latin School. Then in fall 1999, the federal appeals court in Richmond, Va., ruled in favor of white families challenging race-based policies in two districts in the Washington, D.C., suburbs. The rulings struck down a weighted lottery that advantaged blacks and Hispanics in Arlington County, Va., and a transfer policy in Montgomery County, Md., that limited students from changing schools in order to maintain racial balance.[22]

The idea of socioeconomic integration first gained national attention when the midsized town of La Crosse, Wis., redrew attendance zones in the early 1990s to shift students from an overcrowded, predominantly affluent high school to the town's second high school in the blue-collar section with a growing Hmong population. In Kahlenberg's account, the plan survived concerted political opposition, produced measurable educational progress and now enjoys widespread support. Cambridge, Mass., substituted socioeconomic integration policies for racial busing in 1999 after the federal appeals court ruling in the Boston Latin case. Wake County, N.C., similarly dropped its racial balancing plan in 2000 in favor of an assignment plan

Is racial diversity in the classroom essential to a good education?

YES
Janet W. Schofield
Professor of Psychology,
University of Pittsburgh

Written for *CQ Researcher*, September 2007

Education in a democratic society serves three basic purposes. It provides students with workforce skills, prepares them to function as thoughtful and informed citizens in a cohesive country and enriches their lives by awakening them to new knowledge, perspectives and possibilities. Racial diversity in schools and classrooms enhances the attainment of each of these goals.

The ability to work effectively with individuals from diverse backgrounds is a fundamental workplace skill, as the well-known report "What Work Requires of Schools," issued by President George H.W. Bush's administration, points out. Yet, many students never develop this skill because our country's neighborhoods, social institutions and religious organizations are often highly segregated. Racially diverse schools provide a milieu essential to the development of this crucial skill.

Racially diverse schools also have a vital role to play in developing fair-minded citizens and in promoting social cohesion. Research demonstrates that in-school contact with individuals from different backgrounds typically reduces prejudice, a fundamentally important outcome in our increasingly diverse society. In addition, students who attend diverse schools are more likely than others to choose diverse work and residential settings as adults, thus promoting social cohesion.

Racially diverse schools also enrich students' understanding and expand their perspectives by placing them in contact with others whose views and life experiences may be very different. Just as visiting a foreign country is a much richer and more powerful experience than reading about it, interacting with students from different backgrounds brings their perspectives and experiences alive in a way not otherwise possible.

Even individuals who discount the arguments above must acknowledge that heavily segregated minority schools disadvantage the very students most in need of an excellent educational environment. Such schools typically have relatively impoverished curricular offerings, great difficulty recruiting experienced teachers and high teacher-turnover rates, all of which may help to explain why research suggests that attending such schools typically undermines students' achievement relative to similar peers in more diverse schools.

Racial diversity in and of itself does not guarantee a good education, but as a recent report by the National Academy of Education suggests, it creates preconditions conducive to it. In our increasingly diverse democracy, the educational cost of segregated schools is too high for majority and minority students alike.

NO
Abigail Thernstrom
Senior Fellow, Manhattan Institute
Co-author, No Excuses: Closing the
Racial Gap in Learning

Written for *CQ Researcher*, September 2007

Racially diverse classrooms are desirable — of course. But are they essential to a good education? Absolutely not. If they were, big-city school districts would be stuck providing lousy educations for America's most disadvantaged children into the indefinite future. A large majority of students in 26 out of the 27 central-city districts with a public school population of at least 60,000 are non-white. The white proportion in these districts averages 16 percent. Thus, big-city schools will not be racially "diverse" unless we start flying white kids from Utah into, say, Detroit.

Or rather, they will not be racially "diverse" according to the Seattle school board's definition in the racial balancing plan the Supreme Court condemned last term. Seattle had divided students into only two racial groups: white and non-white. If schools were half-Asian, half-white, that was fine; if they were 30 percent white with the rest Asian, they weren't sufficiently "diverse," and educational quality would be somehow lacking.

What racial stereotyping! Do all non-white students express the same non-white views — with all white students having a "white" outlook? In fact, why is racial diversity the only kind that counts for those concerned about the group clustering in certain schools? What about a social class or religious mix?

And on the subject of racial stereotyping, do we really want to embrace the ugly assumption that black kids are incapable of learning unless they're hanging around some white magic? Good inner-city schools across the country are teaching the children who walk through the door. In excellent schools, if every one of the students is black — reflecting the demography of the neighborhood — the expectations for educational excellence do not change. And happily, there are no compelling studies showing enormous positive gains for black students when they attend schools with large numbers of whites.

Good education is not confined to academic learning. But there is no evidence that schools engaging in coercive racial mixing build a lifelong desire to "socialize with people of different races," as Seattle assumed. Visit a school lunchroom! Racial and ethnic clustering will be very much in evidence.

Those who insist school districts should turn themselves inside out to engineer racial diversity haven't a clue as to the limits of social policy. And they demean the capacity of non-Asian minority kids to learn, whatever the color of the kid in the seat next to them.

tied to free or reduced-lunch status to comply with the rulings by the Richmond-based appeals court in the Arlington and Montgomery County cases. By 2003, Kahlenberg claimed some 500,000 students nationwide were enrolled in school systems that used economic status as a factor in pupil assignments.[23]

However, the main school districts that had adopted racial balancing plans stuck with them despite legal challenges. Seattle adopted its "open choice" plan in 1998 — some two decades after it had become the largest school district in the nation to voluntarily adopt a racial busing plan. The ad hoc group Parents Involved in Community Schools filed its suit challenging the use of race as a "tiebreaker" in pupil assignments in July 2000. That same year, Jefferson County Public Schools adopted its controlled choice plan after a federal judge freed the system from a desegregation decree dating to 1975. Parent Crystal Meredith challenged the race-based assignments in April 2003. Federal district judges upheld the plans — in April 2001 in the Seattle case and in June 2004 in the Jefferson County case. The 4th U.S. Circuit Court of Appeals in Cincinnati then upheld the Jefferson County plan in July 2005. The Seattle case followed a more complicated appellate route. The school district suspended the plan after an initial setback in 2002, but eventually the 9th U.S. Circuit Court of Appeals in San Francisco upheld the plan in October 2005.

The Supreme Court's decision to hear the two cases immediately raised fears among civil rights advocates that the conservative majority fortified by President George W. Bush's appointments of Chief Justice Roberts and Justice Samuel A. Alito Jr. would strike down the plans. Questions by Roberts and Alito during arguments on Dec. 4, 2006, left little doubt about their positions. The high-drama announcement of the decision on June 28 lasted nearly 45 minutes with Roberts, Kennedy and Breyer each delivering lengthy summaries of his opinion from the bench.

"The way to stop discrimination on the basis of race," Roberts declared as he neared his conclusion, "is to stop discriminating on the basis of race."

Breyer was equally forceful in his dissent. "This is a decision that the court and this nation will come to regret," he said.

Almost immediately, however, Kennedy's pivotal concurrence began to draw the closest scrutiny as advocates and observers tried to discern what alternatives remained for school boards to use in engineering racial diversity. The National School Boards Association urged local boards to continue seeking diversity through "careful race-conscious policies." Administrators in Seattle and Louisville said they planned to do just that.

But Clegg of the Center for Equal Opportunity said school systems would be better off to drop racial classifications. "At the end of the day, these two plans didn't pass muster," he said. "And the impact will be to persuade other school districts that this is not a good idea."[24]

CURRENT SITUATION
'Resegregation' Seen

The Louisville and Seattle school systems are in the opening weeks of a new academic year, with few immediate effects from the Supreme Court decision invalidating their previous pupil-assignment plans. Officials in both districts are working on new pupil-assignment plans to put into effect starting in fall 2009, with racial diversity still a goal but race- or ethnic-based placements no longer permitted.

Both school systems, however, are reporting what civil rights advocates call "resegregation" — higher percentages of African-American students in predominantly minority schools. Critics of racial-diversity policies object to the term, arguing that segregation refers only to legally enforced separation of the races. Whatever term is used, a new report documents a national trend of "steadily increasing separation" in public schools between whites and the country's two largest minority groups: Latinos and African-Americans.

The report by the UCLA Civil Rights Project shows, for example, that the percentage of black students in majority-white schools rose from virtually zero in 1954 to a peak of 43.5 percent in 1988 before beginning a steady decline. In 2005 — the most recent year available — 27 percent of black students attended majority-white schools.

Meanwhile, the proportion of African-Americans attending majority-minority schools has been slowly increasing over the past two decades — reversing gains in integration in the 1960s and '70s — while the percentage of Latino students in majority-minority schools has grown steadily since the 1960s. In 2005, 73 percent of black students were in majority-minority schools, and more than one-third — 38 percent — were in "intensely segregated" schools with 90 to 100 percent minority enrollment. For Latinos, 78 percent of students were in majority-minority schools.

By contrast, Asian-Americans are described in the report as "the most integrated" ethnic group in public schools. In 2005, the average Asian student attended a school with 44 percent white enrollment — compared to 30 percent white enrollment for the average black student and 27 percent white enrollment for the average Latino. The report attributed the higher integration for Asians to greater residential integration and relatively small numbers outside the West.

Seattle was already experiencing increasing racial isolation after suspending its previous placement plan, which included race as one "tiebreaker" in pupil assignments. "There has been a decline in racial diversity since suspension of the plan," says Seattle Public Schools spokeswoman Patti Spencer.

In Louisville, nine schools now have African-American enrollment above the previous guideline limit of 50 percent — most of them in predominantly black neighborhoods in Louisville's West End or the heavily black areas in southwestern Jefferson County. Black enrollment in some schools in the predominantly white East End has declined, though not below the minimum figure of 15 percent in the previous guidelines.

The 15/50 guidelines remain "a goal," according to Student Placement Director Todd. "We're trying to prevent as much slippage as possible."

In Seattle, outgoing Superintendent Raj Manhas told reporters after the Supreme Court ruling that the school district would look at "all options available to us" to try to preserve racial diversity in the schools.[25] The new superintendent, Maria Goodloe-Johnson, is an African-American who was sharply critical of racial policies in her previous position as superintendent in Charleston, S.C. Since taking office in Seattle in July, however, Goodloe-Johnson has not addressed racial balance, according to Spencer.[26]

Opponents of the race-based policies say school districts should refocus their efforts. "Where school districts should focus is on education standards, not creating a specific racial mix of students," says Sharon Browne, a staff attorney with the Pacific Legal Foundation, the conservative public interest law firm that supported the legal challenges in Louisville and Seattle.

"The guidelines are gone," says attorney Gordon in Louisville. "They're past tense."

In Seattle, Kathleen Brose, the longtime school activist who founded Parents Involved in Community Schools to challenge the use of race for high school placements, says diversity is "important," but parental choice is more important. "The school district has been so focused on race," she adds, "that, frankly, I think they forgot about academics."

Legal Options Eyed

School boards around the country are re-examining their legal options for promoting diversity. At the same time, they are bracing for new legal challenges to their diversity plans that, so far, have not materialized.

The National School Boards Association plans to provide local boards with advisories on what policies can be used under the Supreme Court's decision to promote racial balance. But General Counsel Negrón expects few changes as a result of the ruling.

"School districts are not going to be changing their policies drastically to the extent that they will be abandoning their choices of diversity or integration as their goal, if that's what they've chosen to do," Negrón says. "School districts are going to comply with the law as they understand it. And there's a lot of room in Justice Kennedy's concurrence for school districts to be creative and innovative."

Barring any consideration of race, Negrón adds, "was just not what the decision stood for."

Pacific Legal Foundation attorney Browne, however, worries that school districts are not complying with the ruling. "We are very disappointed that there are school districts who are ignoring the decision by the U.S. Supreme Court and continuing to use race [in pupil assignments]," she says.

Browne says school districts should have begun developing contingency plans for assigning students on a non-racial basis after the oral arguments in the Seattle and Louisville cases in December indicated the court would find both plans unconstitutional.

The Louisville and Seattle cases themselves are still pending in lower federal courts, with winning lawyers in both cases asking the courts to order the school boards to pay attorneys' fees.

In Seattle, the firm of Davis Wright Tremaine is seeking $1.8 million in attorneys' fees despite having previously said that it was handling the parents' case pro bono — for free. "Congress specifically and explicitly wrote into the law that if the government is found to have violated citizens' civil rights, then the prevailing party should seek fee recovery," explained Mark Usellis, a spokesman for the firm. The school system reported spending $434,000 in legal fees on the case.[27]

Louisville solo practitioner Gordon is asking to be paid $200 per hour for the "hundreds of hours" he devoted to the case plus a bonus for the national impact of the case. Without specifying a figure, he also wants to be reimbursed for spending his own money on expenses and court costs. Meanwhile, plaintiff Crystal Meredith is asking for $125,000 in damages, which she attributes to lost wages, invasion of privacy and emotional distress.[28]

Gordon says he received several complaints from parents whose applications for transfers for their children had been denied on the basis of limited capacity at the school they had chosen. Gordon says he suspected school officials were actually denying the transfers on racial grounds, but the MacNeals' case was the only "smoking gun" he found.

The Pacific Legal Foundation is following up on "many inquiries" received from parents since the Supreme Court ruling, according to Browne, but no new cases have been filed. She declined to say where the complaints originated. The foundation has suits pending in California courts against the Los Angeles and Berkeley school districts over race-based policies.

If any new legal challenges are filed, Negrón expects federal courts will defer to local school boards' decisions, for the most part. "The [Supreme Court] didn't tell us exactly what to do," he explains. "School districts will be trying their best to come up with something that meets the requirements of the law and at the same time meets their educational interest in regard to diversity."

OUTLOOK

'Minimal Impact'?

In striking down the Seattle and Jefferson County racial-balance plans, Chief Justice Roberts cited figures from the two school districts showing that the policies actually affected relatively few students — only 52 pupils in Seattle and no more than 3 percent of the pupil assignments in Jefferson County. The "minimal impact," he wrote, "casts doubt on the necessity of using racial classifications."

Writing for the dissenters, however, Justice Breyer cast the stakes in broader terms by citing the growing percentage of black students in majority non-white schools nationwide. The Louisville and Seattle school boards, Breyer said, were asking to be able to continue using tools "to rid their schools of racial segregation." The plurality opinion, he concluded, was "wrong" to deny the school boards' "modest request."

Two months after the ruling, civil rights advocates are continuing to voice grave concerns that the decision will hasten what they call the resegregation of public schools nationwide. "We're going to have a further increase in segregation of American schools," says UCLA's Orfield. "School districts are going to have to jump through a whole series of hoops if they want to have some modest degree of integration."

Legal Defense Fund President Shaw fears new challenges not only to pupil-assignment plans but also to mentoring and scholarship programs specifically targeting racial minorities. "Our adversaries are not going to go away," says Shaw. "They're going to continue to attack race-conscious efforts to address racial inequality."

Opponents of racial-balance plans either discount the fears of increased racial isolation or minimize the harms of the trend if it materializes.

"I don't think there will be dramatic consequences from these decisions," says Rosman of the Center for Individual Rights. School systems with an interest in racial diversity "will find a way to do that legally," he says. "For schools that use race explicitly, it will still be a contentious matter."

"There's going to be less and less focus on achieving politically correct racial and ethnic balance and more focus on improving education," says the Center for Equal Opportunity's Clegg. "That's where the law's headed, and that's where policy's headed. We ought to be worrying less about integration anyhow."

For his part, the Century Foundation's Kahlenberg stresses that the number of school districts with race-conscious policies — guesstimated at around 1,000 — is a small fraction of the nationwide total of 15,000 school systems. Many of the districts that have been seeking racial balance will likely shift to socioeconomic integration, he says, "because that's a clearly legal way to raise academic achievement for kids and create some racial integration indirectly."

In Louisville, the county school board did vote on Sept. 10 to broaden its diversity criteria to include socio-economic status. "Race will still be a factor," Superintendent Berman said, "but it will not be the only factor."[29] Meanwhile, Student Placement Director Todd says Jefferson County's use of non-contiguous school-attendance zones to mix students from different racially identifiable neigh-borhoods is likely to be continued.

In his concurring opinion, Justice Kennedy suggested "strategic site selection" as another permissible policy to promote racial diversity — placing new schools so they draw students from different racial neighborhoods. The suggestion may prove impractical in many school districts. Jefferson County opened one new school this fall — in the rapidly growing and predominantly white eastern end, far removed from the African-American neighborhoods in the West End. As Breyer noted in his opinion, many urban school systems are unlikely to be building new schools because they are losing not gaining enrollment.

Changing demographics and changing social attitudes are inevitably bringing about changes in the schools. Within a decade or so, demographers expect white students will no longer comprise a majority of public school enroll-ment. And, as Abigail Thernstrom notes, young people have different attitudes toward race than their parents or grandparents.

"In terms of racial attitudes, we're on a fast track," Thernstrom says. "Young kids are dating across racial and ethnic lines. America is changing in very terrific ways and has been for some time. I expect that change to continue."

But University of Wisconsin educational historian Reese cautions against expecting racial issues to disappear. "It's like a never-never land to imagine that racial issues can somehow disappear," he says. "It's a nice thing to say that we should live in a kind of perfect world, but we don't. I can't imagine that it will disappear. It couldn't have disappeared in the past, and it won't disappear in the future."

NOTES

1. For coverage, see Chris Kenning, "Separate atten-dance zones voided," *The* [Louisville] *Courier-Journal*, Aug. 29, 2007, p. 1A.

2. The decision is *Parents Involved in Community Schools v. Seattle School District No. 1*, 552 U.S. _ _ _ (2007); the companion case was *Meredith v. Jefferson County Public Schools*. For a detailed chronicle of the cases, see Kenneth Jost, "Court Limits Use of Race in Pupil Assignments," in *The Supreme Court Yearbook 2006-2007*, http://library.cqpress.com/scyb/.

3. For background, see Kenneth Jost, "School Dese-gregation," *CQ Researcher*, April 23, 2004, pp. 345-372.

4. See Chris Kenning, "JCPS sees change in racial makeup," *The* [Louisville] *Courier-Journal*, Sept. 2, 2007, p. 1A.

5. Gary Orfield and Chungmei Lee, "Historic Reversals, Accelerating Resegregation, and the Need for New Integration Strategies," UCLA Civil Rights Project (formerly based at Harvard University), August 2007, pp. 29, 35.

6. Richard D. Kahlenberg, "Rescuing *Brown v. Board of Education*: Profiles of Twelve School Districts Pursuing Socioeconomic School Integration," June 28, 2007, p. 3.

7. For coverage, see Peter Schworm, "AG Urges Court to Uphold Lynn Plan," *The Boston Globe*, July 18, 2005, p. B4.

8. Orfield and Lee, *op. cit.*, pp. 7-8. For background, see Barbara Mantel, "No Child Left Behind," *CQ Researcher*, May 27, 2005, pp. 469-492.

9. Background drawn in part from William J. Reese, *America's Public Schools: From the Common School to "No Child Left Behind"* (2005); R. Freeman Butts, *Public Education in the United States: From Revolution to Reform* (1978).

10. Reese, *op. cit.*, pp. 10-11, 25-26.

11. For background, see James Anderson, *The Education of Blacks in the South, 1860-1935* (1988). See also Heather Andrea Williams, *Self-Taught: African American Education in Slavery and Freedom* (2003).

12. For background, see "School Desegregation," *op. cit.*, p. 350 (Latinos), pp. 356-357 (Asian-Americans), and sources cited therein.

13. Some background drawn from James T. Patterson, Brown v. Board of Education: *A Civil Rights Milestone and Its Troubled Legacy* (2001).

14. For data, see *ibid.*, pp. 228-230.

15. The decisions are *Green v. County School Board of New Kent County*, 391 U.S. 430 (1968), and *Swann v. Charlotte-Mecklenburg County Board of Education*, 402 U.S. 1 (1971).

16. Reese, *op. cit.*, p. 246. For background on later school desegregation cases, see Patterson, *op. cit.*

17. For background, see H. B. Shaffer, "Status of the War on Poverty," in *Editorial Research Reports*, Jan. 25, 1967, available at *CQ Researcher Plus Archive*, http://library.cqpress.com.

18. Background drawn from Kathy Koch, "Reforming School Funding," *CQ Researcher*, Dec. 10, 1999, pp. 1041-1064.

19. The decisions are *San Antonio Independent School District v. Rodriguez*, 411 U.S. 1 (1973), and *Robinson v. Cahill*, 62 A.2d 273 (N.J. 1973).

20. For background, see Charles S. Clark, "Attack on Public Schools," *CQ Researcher*, July 26, 1996, pp. 649-672.

21. See Patterson, *op. cit.*, p. 214 n.19, p. 234.

22. The decisions are *Wessmann v. Gittens*, 160 F.3d 790 (1st Cir. 1998); *Tuttle v. Arlington County School Board*, 195 F.3d 698 (4th Cir. 1999), *Eisenberg v. Montgomery County Public Schools*, 197 F.3d 123 (4th Cir. 1999). For coverage, see Beth Daley, "Court Strikes Down Latin School Race Admission Policy," *The Boston Globe*, Nov. 20, 1998, p. A1; Jay Mathews, "School Lottery Loses on Appeal," *The Washington Post*, Sept. 26, 1999, p. C1 (Arlington County); Brigid Schulte, "School Diversity Policy Is Overruled," *ibid.*, Oct. 7, 1999, p. A1 (Montgomery County).

23. See Richard D. Kahlenberg, *All Together Now* (2003 ed.)., p. xiii.

24. Quoted in Andrew Wolfson, "Desegregation Decision: Some Find 'Sunshine' Amid Rain," *The* [Louisville] *Courier-Journal*, June 29, 2007, p. 6K.

25. Quoted in Jessica Blanchard and Christine Frey, "District Vows to Seek Out Diversity Answers," *Seattle Post-Intelligencer*, June 29, 2007, p. A1.

26. See Emily Heffter, "First Day of School for Chief," *Seattle Times*, July 10, 2007, p. B1.

27. See Emily Heffter, "Law firm wants school district to pay $1.8M," *Seattle Times*, Sept. 6, 2007, p. B5.

28. Chris Kenning and Andrew Wolfson, "Lawyer in schools case seeks fees, bonus," *The* [Louisville] *Courier-Journal*, July 29, 2007, p. 1A.

29. Quoted in Antoinette Konz, "Schools adopt guidelines for assignment plan," *The* [Louisville] *Courier-Journal*, Sept. 11, 2007.

BIBLIOGRAPHY

Books

Frankenberg, Erika, and Gary Orfield (eds.), *Lessons in Integration: Realizing the Promise of Racial Diversity in American Schools*, University of Virginia Press, 2007.
Twelve essays by 19 contributors examine the educational and social effects of desegregation and the disadvantages to students in segregated schools. Orfield is co-director of the Civil Rights Project, UCLA Graduate School of Education and Information Studies (formerly, the Harvard Civil Rights Project); Frankenberg is a study director for the project. Includes notes, 46-page bibliography.

Loveless, Tom, *The Tracking Wars: State Reform Meets School Policy*, Brookings Institution Press, 1999.
The director of the Brown Center on Educational Policy at Brookings depicts tracking as a traditional educational practice and detracking as "a gamble" that may hurt rather than help students in low-achievement schools. Includes detailed notes.

Oakes, Jeannie, *Keeping Track: How Schools Structure Inequality* (2nd ed.), *Yale University Press*, 2005.
The director of urban schooling at UCLA's Graduate School of Education and Information Studies updates the landmark critique of tracking that launched a detracking reform movement after its publication in 1985. Includes detailed notes.

Patterson, James T., Brown v. Board of Education: *A Civil Rights Milestone and Its Troubled Legacy*, Oxford University Press, 2001.

An emeritus professor of history at Brown University gives a compact account of the landmark school desegregation case and a legacy described as "conspicuous achievement" along with "marked failures."

Reese, William J., *America's Public Schools: From the Common School to "No Child Left Behind," Johns Hopkins University Press*, 2005.
A professor of educational-policy studies at the University of Wisconsin-Madison provides an accessible overview of the history of U.S. public education from Horace Mann's advocacy of the "common school" through 20th-century developments.

Thernstrom, Abigail, and Stephan Thernstrom, *No Excuses: Closing the Racial Gap in Learning, Simon & Schuster*, 2003.
The authors decry the persistent achievement gap between white and black students but discount the importance of racial isolation in schools as a cause. Includes extensive statistical information, notes. Both authors are senior fellows with the Manhattan Institute; Abigail Thernstrom is vice chair of the U.S. Civil Rights Commission, Stephan Thernstrom a professor of history at Harvard.

Articles

Simmons, Dan, "A Class Action: Leaders Tried to Rein In Effects of Poverty in Public Schools; Voters Were in No Mood for Busing," *La Crosse* (Wis.) *Tribune*, Jan. 21, 2007, p. 1.
The story and an accompanying sidebar ("Balance by Choice") examine the history and current status of the La Crosse school district's 15-year experiment with socioeconomic integration.

Reports and Studies

Kahlenberg, Richard D., "Rescuing *Brown v. Board of Education*: Profiles of Twelve School Districts Pursuing Socioeconomic School Integration," *Century Foundation*, June 28, 2007, www.tcf.org.

The 42-page report describes the mixed results of socioeconomic integration in 12 school systems, with lengthy treatment of three: La Crosse, Wis.; Cambridge, Mass.; and Wake County (Raleigh), N.C. For a book-length treatment, see Kahlenberg, *All Together Now: Creating Middle-Class Schools through Public School Choice* (Brookings Institution Press, 2001).

Linn, Robert L., and Kevin G. Welner (eds.), "Race-Conscious Policies for Assigning Students to Schools: Social Science Research and the Supreme Court Cases," *National Academy of Education*, June 29, 2007, www.naeducation.org/Meredith_Report.pdf.
The 58-page report details social-science research on the effects of racial diversity in schools and finds "general support" for the conclusion that the overall academic and social effects of increased racial diversity are "likely to be positive."

Orfield, Gary, and Chungmei Lee, "Historic Reversals, Accelerating Resegregation, and the Need for New Integration Strategies," *UCLA Civil Rights Project*, Aug. 29, 2007, www.civilrightsproject.ucla.edu.
The 50-page report finds "accelerating isolation" of African-American and Latino students in public schools and recommends a variety of measures to counter the trend, including an attack on housing segregation, socioeconomic integration of schools and congressional initiatives "to require and/or to support racial progress."

On the Web

The *Courier-Journal* has an extensive compilation of articles, photographs and information on the course of school desegregation in Louisville and Jefferson County (www.courier-journal.com/desegregation). Current coverage can be found on the Web sites of Seattle's two newspapers, the *Seattle Times* (http://seattletimes .nwsource.com/html/education/) and the *Seattle Post-Intelligencer* (http://seattlepi.nwsource.com/).

For More Information

American Educational Research Association, 1430 K St., N.W., Suite 1200, Washington, DC 20005; (202) 238-3200; www.aera.net. National research society encouraging scholarly research in efforts to improve education.

Center for Individual Rights, 1233 20th St., N.W., Suite 300, Washington, DC 20036; (202) 833-8400; www.cir-usa.org. Nonprofit public-interest law firm opposed to racial preferences.

Center for Equal Opportunity, 7700 Leesburg Pike, Suite 231, Falls Church, VA 22043; (703) 442-0066; www.ceousa.org. Think tank devoted to equal opportunity and racial harmony.

Century Foundation, 41 E. 70th St., New York, NY 10021; (212) 535-4441; www.tcf.org. Public-policy institution promoting methods for socioeconomic integration in education.

Mexican American Legal Defense and Educational Fund, 634 S. Spring St., Los Angeles, CA 90014; (213) 629-2512; www.maldef.org. Protects and promotes the civil rights of Latinos living in the United States.

NAACP Legal Defense and Educational Fund, 99 Hudson St., Suite 1600, New York, NY 10013; (212) 965-2200; www.naacpldf.org. Serves as legal counsel on issues of race, with emphasis on education, voter protection, economic justice and criminal justice.

National School Boards Association, 1680 Duke St., Alexandria, VA 22314; (703) 838-6722; www.nsba.org. Seeks to foster excellence and equity in public education by working with school board leadership.

Here is contact information for the school districts involved in the Supreme Court decision, *Parents Involved in Community Schools v. Seattle School District No. 1:*

Jefferson County Public Schools, VanHoose Education Center, 3332 Newburg Rd., P.O. Box 34020, Louisville, KY 40232-4020; (502) 485-3949; www.jefferson.k12.ky.us.

Seattle School District No. 1, 2445 Third Ave. South, Seattle, WA 98134; (206) 252-0000; www.seattleschools.org.

Reparations Movement

Should Payments Be Made for Historical Wrongs?

David Masci

Children were among the survivors in April 1945 when Russian soldiers liberated the Nazi concentration camp at Auschwitz, Poland, where hundreds of thousands of Jews were murdered. Billions of dollars have been paid to Holocaust survivors.

5

From *CQ Researcher*, June 22, 2001.

Rep. John Conyers Jr. is not a man who gives up easily. Six times since 1989, the feisty 19-term Michigan Democrat has introduced a measure in the House of Representatives to create a commission to study paying reparations to African-American descendants of slaves. Each time, the bill has died.

But Conyers is optimistic. He claims that beating the same legislative drum so long has helped bring the reparations issue to the attention of the American people.

"Twelve years ago, most people didn't even know what reparations were, and now it's a front-burner issue," he says. "It's like those first [unsuccessful] bills making Martin Luther King's birthday a holiday: You have to build up a critical mass of support, or you don't get anyplace."

Indeed, several local governments have passed resolutions favoring reparations, and the issue has caught the attention of a growing cadre of prominent black advocates and scholars, who have begun holding conferences and symposia on the subject. "It's time to address this issue we've so long denied — the lingering effects of slavery," said Johnnie Cochran, former counsel for O.J. Simpson and a member of a "dream team" of attorneys preparing to sue the federal government and others for slavery reparations.[1]

In addition, several African nations are trying to put the issue on the agenda of the upcoming United Nations World Conference Against Racism, in Durban, South Africa. They hope the United States and former colonial powers like Britain and France will increase aid to African countries to compensate for centuries of slave trading.

Seeking Justice for Australia's Aborigines

Australian Olympic gold medal winner Cathy Freeman knew all about the "stolen generation" of Aborigines. Her grandmother was one of the thousands of youngsters taken from their parents by white authorities.

Winning the 400-meter dash at last year's Summer Games gave Freeman a chance to speak out on the centuries of mistreatment of Australia's indigenous people.

Aborigines have lived in Australia for at least 40,000 years, most likely migrating from Southeast Asia. Their downfall as a people began in 1788, when British ships brought 1,000 settlers, including more than 500 convicts from overcrowded jails. Clashes began almost immediately, but the Aborigines' primitive weapons were no match for British guns and mounted soldiers.

Because the convicts provided free labor, the white settlers treated the Aborigines as little more than useless pests. Those who were not killed were driven away to fenced reservations in the most inhospitable parts of the "outback" territory. Crimes against Aborigines often went unpunished.

Aborigines, who make up 2 percent of Australia's largely white population of 19 million, were not allowed to vote until 1962; they were not counted in the census until 1967. Moreover, Aborigines' life expectancy is 20 years less than the national average and they occupy the lowest rung of the nation's economic ladder.

But in 1992, they won a significant victory when courts recognized that the Aborigines had "owned" Australia before whites arrived. Today, they own more than 15 percent

Olympic gold medalist Cathy Freeman has used her celebrity to call attention to her fellow Aborigines.

of the continent, mostly in the remote northern territory.

Nevertheless, some Aboriginal leaders are seeking reparations for perhaps the worst injustice perpetrated against their group — the state-sponsored abduction of Aboriginal children from their parents.

From the early 1900s until the 1970s, as many as 100,000 Aboriginal children were taken from their parents to be raised among whites in orphanages or foster families. State and federal laws that permitted the practice were based on the belief that full-blooded Aborigines would eventually die out and that assimilating the children into white society was the best way to save them.

In 1997, the Australian Human Rights and Equal Opportunity Commission reported that many of the children had been physically and sexually abused and suffered long-term psychological damage from the loss of family and cultural ties.

But Australian Sen. John Herron called the 1997 report "one-sided" and said the stories about removing Aboriginal children from their families was greatly exaggerated."[1]

His comments stung Aden Ridgeway, the only Aborigine senator in Parliament, who angrily compared Herron's statements to "denying the Holocaust."[2]

"They were denying they had done anything wrong, denying that a whole generation was stolen," Freeman said. "The fact is, parts of people's lives were taken away."[3]

Herron recognizes the removal of Aboriginal children as a blemish on Australia's history, but he claims many were taken with their parents' consent and for their own welfare.

Until 50 years ago, debates over reparations for victims of persecution were largely theoretical. But in the wake of World War II, reparations increasingly have been seen as a viable means of addressing past injustices — not just to Jews slaughtered in the Holocaust but to Japanese-Americans, Native Americans and even

Australian Aborigines. In fact, the debate over slavery reparations comes on the heels of a string of victories for groups seeking restitution.

In 1988, for instance, Congress passed a law authorizing the U.S. government to apologize for interning Japanese-Americans during the war and award $20,000 to

He believes amends are the responsibility of states and churches and has suggested that reparations claims be filed individually via the courts.

But reparations proponents say it is difficult to prove abuse in the absence of documents and witnesses. They cite the first stolen-generations case, brought last year, which was dismissed for lack of evidence.

Many advocates for the Aborigines favor creation of a national compensation board to adjudicate all "stolen generation" claims.

But Prime Minister John Howard dismisses the idea. He refuses to issue an apology, stating today's Australians should not be held responsible for the mistakes of past generations. He also points to a $63 million government program designed to reunite families of the stolen generation.

However, former Prime Minister Malcolm Fraser says an apology is essential. "We can't undo the past, but we can, in an apology, recognize the fact that many actions in the past did a grave injustice to the Aboriginal population of Australia. We have a commitment to recognize that and other past injustices in walking together into a new future."[4]

Last year, the government spent $1.5 billion on health, education, housing and job-training programs for Aborigines.

But monetary payments and programs are not enough, say some reparations supporters. Geoff Clark, chairman of the Aboriginal and Torres Strait Islander Commission, which oversees indigenous affairs, wants the government not only to apologize but also to sign a treaty with the indigenous population that would provide limited autonomy for Aboriginal communities. His group cites similar treaties in the United States and Canada.

Howard says a treaty would be too divisive. "One part of Australia making a treaty with another part is to accept that we are in effect two nations," he said in a radio interview last year."[5]

Ridgeway supports the treaty. "I think the prime minister's kidding himself if he thinks that a treaty's going to be divisive. The goal is about a formal document that better defines black and white relations and the unfinished business of reconciliation."[6]

At a rally during the 2000 Olympics in Sydney, an Aborigine spokesman calls for the resignation of Prime Minister John Howard, who opposed reparations for mistreated indigenous Australians.

A national election later this year is widely expected to usher in a new prime minister. Howard's rival has supported the idea of a government apology to the Aborigines.

— *Scott Kuzner*

[1] "Separated, But Not a Generation," *Illawarra Mercury*, Aug. 19, 2000, p. 9.

[2] Mitchell Zuckoff, "Golden Opportunity, Australian Aboriginal Activists Hope to Exploit the Olympics to Publicize Their Demands for an Apology, Cash Reparations and Limited Sovereignty," *The Boston Globe*, Sept. 18, 2000, p. 1E.

[3] Michael Gordon, "Beginning Of The Legend," *Sydney Morning Herald*, Sept. 25, 2000, p. 10.

[4] Malcolm Fraser, "Apology Must Be First Step," *Sydney Morning Herald*, April 8, 1999, p. 15.

[5] Tony Wright and Kerry Taylor, "PM Rules Out 'Divisive' Treaty," *The Age*, May 30, 2000, p. 2.

[6] *Ibid.*

each surviving victim. More recently, European countries and companies from Bayer AG to Volkswagen have paid billions of dollars to victims of Nazi Germany's effort to exterminate Europe's Jews and other "undesirables."

Now it is time for slavery reparations, proponents say. Randall Robinson, author of the bestseller *The Debt: What America Owes to Blacks*, argues that acknowledging the nation's debt to African-Americans for slavery and a subsequent century of discrimination will help heal the country's existing racial divide. "We cannot have racial reconciliation until we make the victims of this injustice whole," says Robinson, president of TransAfrica, a Washington, D.C.-based black advocacy group.

Besides raising a moral question, reparations for slavery is also an economic issue, Robinson says. Many of the problems facing black America are directly linked to slavery and the 100 years of forced segregation that followed emancipation in 1865, he says. "It's foolish to argue that the past has nothing to do with the present," Robinson says. "There's a reason why so many African-Americans are poor: It's because a terrible wrong occurred in our history that produced a lasting inequality." Reparations will help right that wrong, advocates say, by helping black Americans reach social and economic parity.

But other black Americans warn that paying reparations for slavery will drive a new wedge between blacks and whites, leading to greater racial polarization. "Doing something like this would create a tremendous amount of resentment among whites," says Walter Williams, chairman of the Economics Department at George Mason University in Fairfax, Va.

Williams says whites and other Americans would understandably be opposed to paying restitution for a crime that ended more than 135 years ago and to a community now making great social and economic strides. "Blacks have come so far; this is nothing but counterproductive," he says.

Opponents also argue that, rather than correcting economic disparity, reparations would take money and attention away from more pressing social and economic issues facing black Americans, such as a substandard education system and high incarceration rates for young African-American men. "This would be such a huge waste of resources, at a time when so much needs to be done in education and other areas," Williams says.

To counter such arguments, slavery reparations advocates have begun modeling their efforts on successful techniques used by Holocaust victims. Recent battles for Holocaust-related reparations have netted survivors and their families more than $10 billion in compensation for slave labor, recovered bank accounts and unclaimed life insurance policies.

But some argue that compensating victims of injustice cheapens their suffering. Indeed, a group of mostly Jewish-American scholars and journalists has criticized some of the efforts to obtain relief for Holocaust survivors. They say the lawyers and Jewish groups involved

have turned the legitimate quest for restitution into a shameless money grab that degrades the memory of the millions who perished.

"Fighting for money makes it much harder to see a tragedy in the right light," says Melissa Nobles, a professor of political science at the Massachusetts Institute of Technology (MIT) in Boston.

"They have hijacked the Holocaust and appointed themselves saviors of the victims — all in the name of money," says Norman Finkelstein, a history professor at Hunter College in New York City and author of *The Holocaust Industry: Reflections on the Exploitation of Jewish Suffering.*

Finkelstein points out that those representing the victims have used hardball tactics to "blackmail" Germany, Switzerland and other countries into paying huge sums to satisfy what are often dubious claims. Besides cheapening the historical legacy of the Holocaust, he argues, such actions could potentially trigger an anti-Semitic backlash in Europe.

Supporters say they are only working aggressively to obtain some small measure of justice for the victims. "We are trying to compensate slave laborers and return the assets of survivors," says Elan Steinberg, executive director of the World Jewish Congress, one of the groups leading the Holocaust reparations efforts. "In doing this, we must uncover the truth, which is often hard for these countries to confront."

He says Holocaust victims should not be denied their assets or rightful compensation just because confronting European countries with their past might lead to an anti-Jewish backlash. "Survivors have a right to pursue legitimate claims," he insists. "This is about justice."

"It is good that we try to make some effort to acknowledge someone's suffering, even if it is inadequate," says Tim Cole, a professor of 20th century European history at the University of Bristol in England. At the very least, reparations are important symbolic gestures to the victims from the victimizers, he adds.

As the debate over reparations continues, here are some of the questions experts are asking:

Should the United States pay reparations to African-American descendants of slaves?

For much of its 250-year history on these shores, slavery was America's most divisive and controversial issue. The

Founding Fathers fought over the status of African slaves when drafting both the Declaration of Independence and the Constitution. And of course, in 1861 slavery helped trigger the nation's most costly conflict, a four-year Civil War that tore the country apart.

Today, few Americans of any race would disagree that slavery was the most shameful and tragic episode in American history. Many would also agree that African-Americans as a whole, including the descendants of slaves, are still suffering from its effects.

Proponents say compensation is justified on a variety of levels, beginning with the fact that African-Americans remain severely handicapped by the legacy of slavery, lagging behind the nation as a whole in virtually every measure. As a result, supporters say, they need and deserve extra help to overcome the economic and social disadvantages they face.

"Our entire economic sector has been and remains truncated because of slavery," says Ronald Walters, a political science professor at the University of Maryland. "We need something to help reverse this terrible harm done to blacks in this country."

"You have an enormous, static and fixed inequality in America due to a 350-year human-rights crime," Robinson says. "We have an obligation to compensate the people still suffering for the wrong that occurred."

Robinson, Walters and others argue that reparations are justified by the fact that the United States grew prosperous largely through the toil of unpaid African-Americans. "Exports of cotton, rice and tobacco swelled the coffers of the U.S. Treasury, yet the people who produced it were never paid," Robinson says.

However, an overwhelming majority of Americans do not believe the nation owes black Americans reparations. A March poll found that 81 percent of registered voters oppose reparations, while only 11 percent support them.[2]

Some Americans feel that the nation has already paid reparations for slavery by passing civil rights and affirmative action laws and by funding myriad social programs designed to help African-Americans and other disadvantaged peoples. "Since the War on Poverty in the 1960s,

the nation has spent $6 trillion on fighting poverty," Williams says.

Others dismiss the whole idea of reparations for slavery out of hand, citing the potentially astronomical cost. Compensating for slavery's injustices could cost as much as $10 trillion, according to some estimates, dwarfing the estimated $10 billion paid to Holocaust victims so far.

Nevertheless, supporters say, reparations would ease African-Americans' feeling that the nation cares little about their plight. "The socio-economic inequality that exists today because of slavery means that the American promise of egalitarianism remains unfulfilled for blacks," Walters says. "It would make the idea of America and American democracy meaningful to blacks."

Paying reparations would benefit the entire nation by creating a more conducive environment for racial reconciliation, supporters say. "We'll never have any harmony or stability between the races until there is commitment to make the victim whole," Robinson says. "Whites need to realize that we'll have no chance of cohering as a nation in the future unless we deal with this issue now."

> "Whites need to realize that we'll have no chance of cohering as a nation in the future unless we deal with this issue now."
>
> — *Randall Robinson, President, TransAfrica*

Conyers agrees that paying reparations would encourage racial healing — for both blacks and whites. "This could create a bridge that unlocks understanding and compassion between people," he says.

But opponents say compensating slavery victims will have exactly the opposite effect — creating new grounds for racial polarization. "I can't think of a better fortification for racism than reparations to blacks," says George Mason University's Williams. "To force whites today, who were not in any way responsible for slavery, to make payments to black people — many of whom may be better off [than the whites] — will create nothing but great resentment."

"It would create a huge backlash against black people, which is something they don't really need," says Glen Loury, director of the Institute of Race and Social Division at Boston University. "It would also be seen as just another example of black people's inability 'to get over it and move on.'"

Indeed, opponents say, reparations might even have the reverse effect: They could significantly weaken the nation's commitment to lifting poor black Americans out of poverty. "This would be a Pyrrhic victory for African-Americans," says Loury, who is black. "It would undermine the claim for further help down the road, because the rest of America will say: 'Shut up: You've been paid.'"

In addition, Loury says, pushing for restitution detracts from the real issues facing the black community. "This whole thing takes the public's attention away from important issues, like failing schools and the fact that so many African-Americans are in jail."

Have efforts to collect reparations for Holocaust victims gone too far?

In the last five years, efforts to compensate and recover stolen property for Holocaust victims and their heirs have increased dramatically. What started in the mid-1990s as an action to recover money in long-dormant Swiss bank accounts has snowballed into a host of lawsuits and settlements against European insurance companies, German and American manufacturers and art galleries around the world.[3]

By and large, these actions have been hailed as a great victory for victims of oppression. Yet a small but growing circle of critics questions the efforts. They charge the lawyers working on behalf of Holocaust victims — as well as the World Jewish Congress, the International Commission on Holocaust Era Insurance Claims (known as the Claims Conference) and other groups — with exploiting a historical tragedy for monetary gain.

"This whole thing has gone way too far," says Gabriel Shoenfeld, senior editor of *Commentary*, a conservative opinion magazine that examines issues from a Jewish perspective. "This is a case of a just cause that has been traduced by overzealous organizations and some rather unscrupulous lawyers."

Hunter College's Finkelstein goes further, branding those who work on behalf of survivors as "the Holocaust industry" and their actions "nothing short of a shakedown racket."

Shoenfeld and Finkelstein are troubled by the fact that Jewish groups and attorneys working on the cases have taken it upon themselves to represent Holocaust survivors. "Groups like the World Jewish Congress don't really represent anyone," Finkelstein says. "They weren't elected by anyone to do this, and most Jews don't even know who they are."

He argues that such groups are using the survivors' high moral status as a cudgel to beat countries and corporations into submission. "They've wrapped themselves in the mantle of the needy Holocaust victims against the greedy, fat Swiss bankers and Nazi industrialists," Finkelstein says. "They are out of control and reckless."

Shoenfeld says the claims often are either overblown, dubious or simply not valid. "It's clear that they're trying to humiliate these countries into giving in," he says.

Shoenfeld cites a recent case against Dutch insurers, who had already settled with the Netherlands' Jewish community for unpaid wartime insurance policies. "These guys then came in and tried to unfairly blacken Holland's reputation by painting their behavior during the war in an unfavorable light, without acknowledging all of the good things Dutch people did for Jews during that time," he says. "It was all an effort to blackmail them, to extract more money from them."

> "I can't think of a better fortification for racism than reparations to blacks."
>
> — *Walter Williams,*
> *Chairman, Economics Department,*
> *George Mason University*

Even the much-publicized victory against the Swiss banks was marred by unscrupulous tactics, Finkelstein contends. After forcing the banks to set up a commission headed by former U.S. Federal Reserve Chairman Paul A. Volcker to investigate claims, they demanded a settlement before the commission finished its work, he says.

The Swiss caved in and paid $1.25 billion, Finkelstein says, because the groups were creating public hysteria and had American politicians threatening an economic boycott. "They honed this strategy against the Swiss and then turned to the French, Germans and others and used it successfully against them."

Such heavy-handed tactics create unnecessary ill will against European Jews, critics say. "By bludgeoning the Europeans into submission, the Holocaust industry is fomenting anti-Semitism," Finkelstein says.

Shoenfeld says the tactics have already spurred an anti-Semitic backlash in Germany and Switzerland. "Don't Jews have enough problems in the world without

For Native Americans, a Different Struggle

Unlike African-Americans, Native Americans are not seeking a huge settlement to right the wrongs of the past. Instead, they're working on the present.

"We don't want reparations," says John Echohawk, executive director of the Native American Rights Fund, an Indian advocacy group in Boulder, Colo. "What we do want is the government to honor its duty to us — and we want our land and our water back." They also want up to $40 billion they say the government owes them.

Tribes have been making land claims against the government for more than a century. Today, dozens of claims are being dealt with (*see p. 105*).

But the biggest fight for restitution has come over allegations of government mishandling of a huge trust fund for Native Americans. Indian advocates say the federal government will end up owing between $10 billion and $40 billion to Native Americans when the matter is cleared up.

Since 1887, the federal government's Bureau of Indian Affairs (BIA) has managed many of the natural resources on Indian lands, such as oil and mineral deposits and grazing and water rights. Proceeds from the sale or use of these resources are, in theory at least, put into a trust fund administered by the government on behalf of members of the tribes who own the assets — some 500,000 Native Americans throughout the country.

In the 1970s, Elouise Cobell, a member of the Blackfoot tribe, began to question the government's management of these accounts. Other Indians had long suspected mismanagement, but no one had challenged the BIA officials who controlled the fund.

Over the next two decades, Cobell, who has an accounting background, concluded that billions of dollars had been lost, and that many Indians were being cheated out of money that was rightfully theirs. Her efforts to get BIA officials to pay attention to the problem came to naught. "They tried to belittle me and intimated that I was a dumb Indian," she says.

In 1996, after years of what Cobell calls stonewalling by federal officials, she and four other Native Americans filed a class action suit in federal court against the Department of the Interior, which controls BIA. "The suit was a last resort,

Penny Manybeads stands beside her hogan at the Navajo Indian reservation in Tuba City, Ariz., in 1993. Native Americans want the government to pay for the mismanagement of their natural resources trust fund.

because no one would listen to us," Echohawk says. "No one did anything."

The plaintiffs charged that many records had been destroyed; that officials had improperly invested much of the money coming into the trust; and that no effort was made to keep individual Indians informed about the individual accounts the government kept for them.[1] These claims were later buttressed by a government official, who acknowledged that trust managers could not locate some 50,000 account holders because of poor recordkeeping.

Even before the suit was filed, the federal government had made some attempts to address the problem. In 1994, Congress passed the Native American Trust Fund Accounting and Management Reform Act, authorizing the appointment of a special trustee to manage and reform the fund. But the first such trustee, former Riggs Bank President Paul Homan, resigned in protest in 1999, complaining that the Interior Department was not adequately committed to reform.

Meanwhile, Cobell's suit against the government succeeded. In December 2000, a federal court ruled against the Interior Department and took control of the trust fund. "The government kept arguing that they were doing the best they could, but that just wasn't true," Echohawk says. "Fortunately, the court didn't believe them."

The government lost a subsequent appeal. Most recently, the new Bush administration decided not to continue to appeal the ruling, ending resistance to a court-administered solution.

The parties now must decide how much the government owes the trust fund. "We hope we can avoid a protracted legal battle over damages and settle out of court," Echohawk says, adding that Bush's decision not to continue appealing the ruling is a good sign the administration is committed to solving the problem.

Still, Echohawk is wary. "I'm cautious because until now, the government has fought us every inch of the way," he says. "Federal stonewalling and neglect are part of the story of the American Indian."

---

[1] Colman McCarthy, "Broken Promises Break Trust," *The Baltimore Sun*, March 7, 1999.

bringing upon themselves the wrath of major European powers?" he asks.

But groups pursuing Holocaust reparations say their opponents are misguided. "How can anyone ask [if] we are going too far in attempting to get restitution for people who were driven from their homes, forced into hiding, persecuted and forced to work?" asks Hillary Kessler-Godin, director of communications for the Claims Conference in New York City.

Supporters also argue that their tactics are not "heavy-handed" or designed to blackmail European countries. "We're not out to humiliate anyone," says the World Jewish Congress's Steinberg. "But sometimes the truth is hard and difficult for everyone to accept."

For instance, it would not serve the truth or the victims to sugarcoat Holland's dismal record of protecting Jews during the Holocaust, Steinberg says. "Holland had the worst record of any Western European country," he argues. "Eighty percent of its Jews were wiped out."

He also points out that his group rushed to settle the Swiss case before the Volcker commission finished its work in order to begin repaying survivors before they died. "Many survivors are very old and dying at such a rapid rate — some 10,000 to 15,000 a year. We had to move on this," he says. The commission will continue its work, so that all 55,000 Holocaust-era accounts can be investigated and paid out, he adds.

Proponents also counter the criticism that their actions foment anti-Semitism. "Anti-Semitism is not caused by Jewish actions, but by people who don't like Jews," Kessler-Godin says. "To temper our actions on behalf of people who have suffered the worst form of anti-Semitism possible in the name of not causing anti-Semitism defies logic."

"Holocaust survivors should not have to abrogate their rights simply for political expediency," Steinberg adds, pointing out that most people, regardless of their religious background, understand and support his group's efforts. "At the end of the day, most non-Jews — except those who represent the banks or insurance companies — see this as an act of justice."

Does putting a price tag on suffering diminish that suffering?

On Dec. 7, 1998, the leader of one of the preeminent Jewish organizations in the United States shocked many American Jews by publicly questioning efforts to obtain reparations for Holocaust survivors. In a *Wall Street Journal* editorial, Abraham Foxman, national director of the Anti-Defamation League, argued that when "claims become the main focus of activity regarding the Holocaust, rather than the unique horror of 6 million Jews, including 1.5 million children, being murdered simply because they were Jewish, then something has gone wrong."[4]

Foxman worried that the drive to obtain restitution would shift modern attitudes about the Holocaust from one of reverence for the victims and their suffering to an accounting of their material losses.

"I fear that all the talk about Holocaust-era assets is skewing the Holocaust, making the century's last word on the Holocaust that the Jews died, not because they were Jews, but because they had bank accounts, gold, art and property," he wrote. "To me that is a desecration of the victims, a perversion of why the Nazis had a Final Solution, and too high a price to pay for a justice we can never achieve."[5]

Foxman's editorial provoked an immediate response from many prominent Jews. Nobel Peace Prize winner Elie Wiesel argued that compensating Holocaust survivors does not sully their memory but is the right thing to do.

"It is wrong to think of this as about money," said Wiesel, a Holocaust survivor himself. "It is about justice, conscience and morality."[6]

But critics point out that reparations, almost by their nature, are tainted, because they mix the sacredness of a people's suffering and pain with the world's greatest source of corruption: money. "Although there might be a way to handle this whole thing with dignity, it inexorably becomes a sordid business," Finkelstein says. "I believe money always corrupts things."

"There is a real danger here that most people will say: Hey wait a minute. This is all really about money," says MIT's Nobles. "Money can profoundly obscure the nature of a tragedy."

Some critics also contend that monetary reparations can do victims more harm than good. "People who have been victimized need to become free internally in order to move beyond the tragedy that has occurred," says Ruth Wisse, a professor of Yiddish and comparative literature at Harvard University. "In this sense, reparations can be harmful because they make victims less dependent on themselves."

Instead of monetary payments, she says, nations should take steps to resolve the political problems that led to the suffering in the first place. "Reparations should be made on political terms, not economic terms," she says. For example, she said a country like Turkey, which many historians say exterminated more than a million Armenians at the beginning of the 20th century, might want to help protect Armenia from outside threats.

But advocates for reparations argue that the money is more a powerful symbol than a primary motive. "We're really talking about justice," says the University of Bristol's Cole. "It's a symbolic act, a gesture."

Although, Cole says, "no amount of money can ever compensate for the suffering of history's victims," restitution can aid them in some small way. "There are things we can do to ease people's suffering or bring them some sense that justice is being done."

"Of course you can't put a price tag on suffering," says the University of Maryland's Walters. "But what you can do is ask: What will bring the victims a measure of dignity? Isn't that the most important thing?"

Proponents also contend that, in the real world where victims of past oppression may still be suffering, monetary compensation can make a huge difference in their lives. For instance, says Kessler-Godin, many Eastern European Holocaust survivors live in poverty and need assistance. "It's OK for Abraham Foxman, living his comfortable American life, to say that it cheapens the memory of victims, but there are people who are living hand to mouth who don't have that luxury."

Finally, supporters say, forgoing reparations allows the victimizers to retain their financial wealth. "When you argue that a victim shouldn't pursue restitution, you are essentially rewarding the oppressors," Steinberg says.

BACKGROUND

Ancient Notion

The payment of reparations for genocide or other injustices is a relatively new phenomenon, which began with Germany's 1951 pledge to aid Israel and to compensate individual victims of the Holocaust. "Before World War II, nations saw what they did to other people during wartime as a natural byproduct of war," MIT's Nobles says. "The vanquished simply had to accept what had happened to them."

But while the use of reparations may be a relatively new remedy, the ideas behind them have a long, if circuitous, intellectual pedigree stretching back for millennia. For instance, the ancient Greeks and Romans explored the notion that the weak and oppressed deserve sympathy and possibly assistance. The 4th century B.C. Athenian philosopher Plato addressed this issue in his most famous dialogue, *The Republic*. A generation later Aristotle, another Athenian philosopher, wrote that the best kind of government was one that helped those who had been deprived of happiness.[7]

Judeo-Christian doctrine also grappled with what individuals and society owe to the downtrodden and oppressed. For instance, in the *New Testament*, Jesus Christ singled out the persecuted as being particularly deserving of compassion and assistance.[8]

The first modern articulation of these principles came in the 18th century during the Enlightenment. Ironically, it was the intellectual father of free market economics — Scottish philosopher Adam Smith — who wrote most forcefully and eloquently about guilt and the resulting sympathy it causes.

In his 1759 treatise, *The Theory of Moral Sentiments*, he wrote: "How selfish soever man may be supposed, there are evidently some principles in his nature, which interest him in the fortunes of others, and render their happiness necessary to him, though he derives nothing from it, except the pleasure of seeing it. Of this kind is pity or compassion, the emotion we feel for the misery of others, when we either see it, or are made to conceive it in a very lively manner."[9]

Smith argued further that this sympathy is a cornerstone of justice. It is necessary for creating and maintaining general social order, he believed.

Native Americans

In the 18th and 19th centuries, compassion for the plight of others — whether out of Christian duty or to promote the greater good — fueled movements to abolish slavery and the slave trade in Europe and the United States. Later, these impulses led the United States, albeit very slowly, to consider compensating

CHRONOLOGY

1945-1980 *After World War II, West Germany moves to pay restitution to Jewish survivors of the Holocaust.*

1948 Congress passes the Japanese-American Evacuations Claims Act to compensate Japanese-Americans who lost property as a result of being interned during World War II.

1951 West German Chancellor Konrad Adenauer proposes paying assistance to Israel and reparations to Jewish survivors of the Nazi Holocaust.

1953 Israel and West Germany agree on payment of reparations and aid. Over the next nearly 50 years, Germans will pay more than $60 billion in Holocaust-related restitution.

1956 Swiss government asks banks and insurers to reveal their Holocaust-related assets. The companies say such "dormant accounts" hold less than 1 million Swiss francs.

1962 A second request for an accounting of Holocaust-related assets leads to the discovery of about 10 million Swiss francs in dormant accounts.

1965 West Germany ends state-to-state payments to Israel. Holocaust survivors continue to receive payments from German government through the present.

1980s-Present *Oppressed groups begin seeking reparations.*

1980 Congress creates the Commission on Wartime Relocations and Internment of Civilians to study possible reparations for Japanese-Americans interned during World War II.

1987 National Coalition of Blacks for Reparations in America (N'COBRA) is founded.

1988 Congress passes the Civil Liberties Act, which apologizes for the wartime internment of Japanese-Americans and authorizes the payment of $20,000 to surviving internees. Eventually, 80,000 Japanese-Americans receive an apology and a check.

1989 Rep. John Conyers Jr., D-Mich., introduces legislation to create a commission to study the African-American reparation issue. He will reintroduce the bill five more times in the coming years.

1990 The first Japanese-American internees begin receiving reparations checks.

1995 European and American media exposés document the role of Swiss banks in financing the Nazi war effort and in failing to make restitution to Holocaust survivors.

October 1996 Class action suit is filed in New York federal court against Swiss banks, seeking funds from "dormant accounts" of Holocaust victims.

1998 Though not an apology, President Clinton says in a speech at a Ugandan village school that it was wrong for European Americans to have received "the fruits of the slave trade."

August 1998 Swiss government agrees to pay $1.25 billion to settle claims against Swiss banks.

December 1998 In a *Wall Street Journal* op-ed piece, Anti-Defamation League national director and Holocaust survivor Abraham Foxman questions the tactics employed by those seeking reparations for Holocaust survivors.

December 1999 The German government and corporations that used slave labor during the war establish a $4.3 billion fund to compensate surviving slave laborers.

2000 TransAfrica founder Randall Robinson publishes *The Debt: What America Owes to Blacks*, a bestselling book arguing for reparations for slavery.

2001 Conservative commentator David Horowitz creates a controversy on many American campuses when he tries to publish an ad in college newspapers entitled "Ten Reasons Why Reparations for Slavery is a Bad Idea — and Racist, Too."

2002 Prominent African-American attorneys promise to sue the federal government and private companies for slavery reparations.

Native Americans for the government's taking of their land and the resulting destruction of much of their population and culture.

The expansion of the American frontier during the 19th century resulted in American Indians being forcibly moved to reservations, where many remain today. Millions of acres, primarily in the Great Plains, were taken from tribes with little or minimal compensation.

But the U.S. government did not consider compensating Native Americans for the loss of this property until 1946, when Congress established a Claims Commission to handle Indian land claims. The body soon became bogged down in the flood of claims, many of which were substantial. When the commission was eliminated in 1978, it had adjudicated only a fraction of the disputes between tribes and the government and had paid Native Americans only token compensation for the lost land.[10]

Meanwhile, the courts became much more sympathetic to Indian claims. In 1980, for instance, the Supreme Court awarded the Sioux $122 million for the theft of lands in South Dakota's Black Hills. It remains the largest award for a Native American land claim in U.S. history. (*See story, p. 101.*)

Today, Native Americans are still pressing land claims, particularly in the Eastern United States. "Many of these claims revolve around treaties made between states and Indian nations early in the country's history," says John Echohawk, executive director of the Native American Rights Fund, an Indian advocacy group in Boulder, Colo. Since the U.S. Constitution leaves the power to negotiate Indian treaties with the federal government, many of these agreements with the states are now being challenged, he adds.

One of the biggest such disputes involves three bands of Oneida Indians, who are trying to recover 300,000 acres of land in central New York state. The case hinges on a treaty negotiated in 1838.

Restitution to "Comfort Women"

On the other side of the globe, victims of a more recent tragedy — Japan's sexual enslavement of thousands of Asian women during World War II — are also seeking restitution. An estimated 200,000 "comfort women" were forced to serve the Japanese military at its far-flung outposts. They claim they were kidnapped or tricked into

THE WHITE HOUSE
WASHINGTON

A monetary sum and words alone cannot restore lost years or erase painful memories; neither can they fully convey our Nation's resolve to rectify injustice and to uphold the rights of individuals. We can never fully right the wrongs of the past. But we can take a clear stand for justice and recognize that serious injustices were done to Japanese Americans during World War II.

In enacting a law calling for restitution and offering a sincere apology, your fellow Americans have, in a very real sense, renewed their traditional commitment to the ideals of freedom, equality, and justice. You and your family have our best wishes for the future.

Sincerely,

G Bush

GEORGE BUSH
PRESIDENT OF THE UNITED STATES

OCTOBER 1990

In October 1990, Japanese-Americans interned during World War II received this letter of apology from President George Bush, in addition to a check for $20,000.

working as sexual slaves for the Japanese soldiers, who beat and raped them.

In 1995, then Japanese Prime Minister Tomiici Murayama officially apologized for the practice, but the government has yet to pay any reparations to the surviving women.

Other groups that have been victimized, like Armenians, also want restitution. And still others — like Latinos, Chinese-Americans and women in the United States — who suffered varying degrees of discrimination over the years, have not organized significant reparations movements, in part because their suffering is perceived

AFP Photo

South Korean "comfort women" who were forced to provide sex for Japanese soldiers in World War II demand compensation during a protest at the Japanese Embassy in Seoul last April.

as being different from the official policies that led to genocide or slavery.

Japanese-Americans

On Feb. 19, 1942, less than three months after the Japanese bombing of Pearl Harbor, President Franklin Delano Roosevelt signed Executive Order 9066, authorizing the removal of Japanese immigrants and their children from the western half of the Pacific coastal states and part of Arizona.

Within days, the government began removing 120,000 Japanese-Americans — two-thirds of them U.S. citizens — from their homes and businesses. Many were forced to sell their property at far below market value in the rush to leave. All were eventually taken to hastily built camps in Western states like California, Idaho and Utah, where most remained until the war was almost over. Some young Japanese-American men were allowed to leave the camps to serve in the armed forces — and many did so with valor — and a handful of mostly young internees were also permitted to relocate to Midwestern or Eastern states.

The camps were Spartan, but in no way resembled Nazi concentration camps or Stalinist Russia's gulags. Still, the internees were denied their freedom and, in many cases, their property.

During this time, internee Fred Korematsu and several other Japanese-Americans challenged the constitutionality of the internment. Korematsu's case ultimately found its way to the Supreme Court, which ruled that during

national emergencies like war Congress and the president had the authority to imprison persons of certain racial groups.

After the war, Congress passed the Japanese-American Evacuations Claims Act of 1948 to compensate those who had lost property because of their internment. Over the next 17 years, the government paid $38 million to former internees.[11]

But efforts to make the government apologize for its wartime actions and pay reparations to internees over and above the property claims remained on a back burner until the 1970s. During that decade, Japanese-American activists — led by the community's main civic organization, the Japanese-American Citizens League (JACL) — began building support for redress.

Initially, only about a third of Japanese-Americans favored reparations. Many felt the painful war years should be forgotten. Others worried that vocal demands, coupled with growing fears among the U.S. public over the rising economic power of Japan, would provoke another backlash against Japanese-Americans.[12]

But by the end of the decade, a majority of Japanese-Americans supported the effort, and the JACL began effectively lobbying Congress for redress. In 1980, Congress created the Commission on Wartime Relocations and Internment of Civilians to study the issue.

During public hearings over the next two years, the commission heard emotional testimony as former internees shared their personal sagas. Publicity generated by the hearings helped awaken the American public to the injustice done to the internees.

One former internee, Kima Konatsu, told about her family's experience while incarcerated near Gila River, Ariz. "During that four years we were separated [from my husband] and allowed to see him only once," Konatsu told the commission. Eventually he became ill and was hospitalized, she said. "He was left alone, naked, by a nurse after having given him a sponge bath. It was a cold winter and he caught pneumonia. After two days and two nights, he passed away. Later on, the head nurse told us that this nurse had lost her two children in the war and that she hated Japanese."[13]

In 1983, the commission concluded that there had been no real national security reason to justify relocating or incarcerating the Japanese-Americans, and that the action had caused the community undue hardship. A second report four months later recommended that the government apologize for the internment and appropriate $1.5 billion to pay each surviving internee $20,000 in reparations.[14]

That same year, a new National Council for Japanese-American Redress (NCJAR) emerged, which opposed what it saw as the JACL's accommodationist approach to reparations. NCJAR filed a class action suit against the government on behalf of the internees, demanding $27 billion in damages. But the suit was dismissed in 1987 on procedural grounds.[15]

Nevertheless, the lawsuit created restitution momentum in Congress, where support had been building since issuance of the commission's 1983 reports. Because many former internees were elderly, proponents argued that something should be done quickly, before most of the intended beneficiaries died.[16]

In 1988, Congress passed the Civil Liberties Act, which authorized $1.25 billion over the next 10 years to pay each internee $20,000. The law also contained an apology to Japanese-Americans who had been incarcerated[17] (*see p. 105*).

On Oct. 9, 1990, the government issued its first formal apologies and checks to Japanese-Americans in a moving ceremony in Washington, D.C. A tearful Sen. Daniel K. Inouye, D-Hawaii — a Japanese-American who lost an arm fighting for the United States during World War II — told the internees and assembled guests that day: "We honor ourselves and honor America. We demonstrated to the world that we are a strong people — strong enough to admit our wrongs."[18]

Since then, some 80,000 former internees have received compensation.[19]

The Holocaust

In many ways, the modern debate over reparations began on Sept. 27, 1951. On that day West German Chancellor Konrad Adenauer appeared before the country's legislature, or Bundestag, and urged his fellow Germans to make some restitution for the "unspeakable crimes" Germany had committed against the Jewish people before and during World War II. His proposal — to provide assistance to the newly founded state of Israel as well as restitution to individual Holocaust survivors — was supported by both his own Christian Democratic party and the opposition Social Democrats.

Japanese-Americans wait for housing after being sent to the Manzanar, Calif., internment camp in March 1942 following the Japanese attack on Pearl Harbor. The U.S. later paid $20,000 to each person confined.

Ironically, West Germany's offer of reparations was much more controversial in Israel, where a sizable minority, led by then opposition politician Menachem Begin, opposed taking "blood money" from Holocaust perpetrators. Begin and others argued that by receiving compensation from the Germans, Israel would literally be selling the moral high ground.[20]

But Israeli Prime Minister David Ben Gurion argued forcefully that Israel had a duty to see that Germany did not profit from its heinous crimes. "He understood that we are obligated to ensure that murderers are not inheritors," says the World Jewish Congress's Steinberg.

Ben Gurion prevailed, in part because Israel desperately needed funds to resettle European Jews who had survived the Holocaust. The German government began paying restitution to Holocaust survivors around the world in 1953 and has since paid out about $60 billion for both individual claims and aid to Israel. The state-to-state payments ended in 1965, but the German government still sends monthly pension checks to about 100,000 Holocaust survivors.

After West Germany's agreement with Israel, little was done to obtain further restitution for Holocaust victims. Many who had survived the camps were more concerned with getting on with their new lives and wanted to forget about the past. In addition, the Soviet Union and its Eastern bloc allies — where most Holocaust victims had

Italian-Americans Were Also Mistreated

Japanese-Americans were not the only ethnic group to suffer from discrimination during World War II. Many Italian-Americans also were victimized in the name of national security.

The United States was at war with Italy from the end of 1941 until it surrendered to the Allies in 1943. During that time, some 600,000 Italian immigrants were classified as "enemy aliens," even though many had sons fighting for the United States against Italy, Germany and Japan.

Tens of thousands were subjected to search and arrest, and 250 were interned in camps. In California, an evening curfew was imposed on more than 50,000 Italian-Americans. Some 10,000 were forced to move away from areas near military installations. Authorities even impounded the boats of Italian-American fishermen.

While generally recognized as a gross violation of civil liberties, the federal government's mistreatment of Italians was much less far-reaching than the internment suffered by 120,000 Japanese. Indeed, more German-Americans were interned — about 11,000 in Texas, North Dakota and elsewhere. Perhaps that's why Italian-American groups have not demanded reparations. Instead, they have asked the government to "acknowledge" what happened.

In 2000, Congress agreed, passing legislation authorizing the Justice Department to conduct an investigation into the episode. The department's work is expected to be finished by the end of the year.

---

come from — made no effort to aid the quest for restitution. Even the United States was content to let the issue lie, partly in order to focus on integrating West Germany and other Western allies into a Cold War alliance.[21]

Still, the issue did not disappear entirely. In Switzerland — a banking and finance mecca and a neutral country during the war — the government was taking small, inadequate steps to discover the extent of Holocaust-related wealth. Many Jews killed by the Germans had opened accounts in Swiss banks and taken out insurance policies from Swiss companies before the war as a hedge against the uncertainty created by the Nazi persecution.

In 1956, the Swiss government surveyed its banks and insurance companies to determine the value of accounts held by those who had died or become refugees as a result of the Holocaust. The companies replied that there were less than a million Swiss francs in those accounts.

In 1962, the government once again requested an accounting of Holocaust-related assets. This time, the companies came up with about 10 million francs, some of which was paid to account holders or their heirs. In the 1960s, '70s and '80s, other efforts by individuals seeking to recover Swiss-held assets were largely unsuccessful because the banks and insurers required claimants to have extensive proof of account ownership, proof that often had been lost or destroyed during the war.

But in the 1990s the situation changed dramatically. First, the collapse of communist regimes throughout Eastern Europe opened up previously closed archives containing Holocaust-related records. In addition, many Holocaust survivors lost their reticence about pursuing claims, in part because films like "Schindler's List" brought greater attention to their plight and made it easier to go public.

In the mid-1990s, journalists and scholars began uncovering evidence that Switzerland had been a financial haven for Nazi officials, who had deposited gold looted from Holocaust victims in Swiss banks. The investigation stimulated new interest in dormant bank accounts and insurance policies.

In 1996 a class action suit on behalf of victims and their heirs was filed in New York against Swiss banks and insurance companies. Swiss efforts to get the suit dismissed failed. Meanwhile, pressure from the U.S. Congress and local officials threatening economic sanctions against the companies forced the banks and insurers to acknowledge the existence of a large number of dormant accounts. By 1999, the Swiss had negotiated a settlement to set aside $1.25 billion to pay out dormant accounts and fund other Holocaust-related philanthropies.

The Swiss case prompted other Holocaust claims. For instance, in 1998 U.S. and European insurance regulators, Jewish groups and others formed a commission — headed by former Secretary of State Lawrence Eagleburger — to investigate claims against European insurance companies outside Switzerland.

The commission was an attempt to bypass lawsuits and to get the insurers — which include some of Europe's largest, like Italy's Generali and Germany's Allianz — to pay elderly claimants before they died. So far, the companies have paid out very little in compensation, because of bureaucratic wrangling at the commission and unwillingness on the part of survivors to accept what have in many cases been only small offers of restitution from the companies.[22]

Meanwhile, former prisoners who had been forced to work without pay for German manufacturers during the war began seeking restitution for their labor. The Nazis had drafted an estimated 12 million people — including 6 million mostly Jewish concentration camp inmates — to provide unpaid labor for some of the biggest names in German industry, including giant automaker Volkswagen. Many were worked to death.[23]

Initially Germany and then-Chancellor Helmut Kohl resisted efforts to pay reparations to slave laborers, citing the 1953 settlement with Israel. But in 1998 the country elected a new leader, Gerhard Schröeder, who authorized negotiations to settle the issue.

Last July, the German government and companies that had used slave labor established a $4.3 billion fund to compensate an estimated 1.5 million survivors. The deal, negotiated with German and American lawyers for the slave laborers and ratified in the Bundestag on May 30, indemnifies German industry from further lawsuits on behalf of slave laborers.

CURRENT SITUATION

Reparations for Slavery

Efforts to compensate African-Americans for slavery began formally on Jan. 16, 1865, months before the Civil War ended. On that day, Union General William Tecumseh Sherman issued Special Field Order 15, directing his soldiers — who were then marching through the South — to divide up confiscated Confederate farms into 40-acre plots and redistribute the land to slaves. Farm animals were also to be redistributed.

But Sherman's promise of "40 acres and a mule" was never realized. Four months after the order was signed,

President Abraham Lincoln was assassinated. His successor, Southerner Andrew Johnson, largely opposed reconstruction and quickly rescinded Sherman's order. More than 40,000 slaves were removed from farms they had recently occupied.

In the years since Special Field Order 15, the idea of compensating African-Americans arose only occasionally in the public arena and attracted little attention. But lately the idea has gained considerable steam, propelled by several high-profile events, such as academic conferences on the subject and the threat of reparations lawsuits by prominent black attorneys.

In addition, Chicago, Detroit and Washington, D.C., have passed resolutions supporting federal reparations legislation. And slavery reparations has become a hot topic on college campuses, as more and more scholars study the idea. "This is the fourth paper I've delivered on reparations this year alone," University of San Diego Law Professor Roy Brooks said at a May conference on the issue. "That suggests there's much to say about the subject and that reparations is a hot issue internationally."[24]

The lawsuits being prepared by several prominent black attorneys and advocates are expected to be filed early next year. They are the brainchild of a legal team that includes TransAfrica's Robinson, O.J. Simpson attorney Cochran, Harvard University Law School Professor Charles Ogletree and Alexander Pires, who recently won a $1 billion settlement from the Department of Agriculture on behalf of black farmers who were denied government loans.

"The history of slavery in America has never been fully addressed in a public forum," Ogletree said. "Litigation will show what slavery meant, how it was profitable and how the issue of white privilege is still with us. Litigation is a place to start, because it focuses attention on the issue."[25]

The team wants the federal government to officially apologize for slavery and for the century of state-supported discrimination — such as the South's segregationist "Jim Crow" laws — that followed emancipation. Moreover, the lawyers are likely to ask for some kind of monetary remedy, although no agreement has been reached either on how much is owed or how reparations would be dispersed.

Estimates vary wildly over how much black Americans are owed for slavery. Larry Neal, an economics professor at the University of Illinois at Urbana-Champaign, has

Rep. John Conyers Jr., D-Mich., wants Congress to create a commission on reparations for descendants of slaves. "Twelve years ago, most people didn't even know what reparations were, and now it's become a front-burner issue," he says.

calculated that the United States owes African-Americans $1.4 trillion in back wages for work completed before emancipation. Georgetown University Business School Professor Richard America, however, estimates the debt is closer to $10 trillion.[26]

Robinson doesn't want direct cash payments to African-Americans, especially people like himself, who are in the middle- or upper-income brackets. He favors establishment of a trust fund to assist underprivileged blacks. "The question we need to be asking is: How do we repair the damage?" Robinson asks. "We need a massive diffusion of capital to provide poor African-American youth with education — from kindergarten through college — and some sort of fund to promote economic development."

Most legal experts do not expect Cochran, Ogletree and the others to succeed, noting that the claim is almost 150 years old and thus the statute of limitations expired long ago.

"Even in a friendly court, there are going to be statute of limitations problems," Tulane University Law School Professor Robert Wesley says.[27] Moreover, experts point out, under the doctrine of sovereign immunity governments are protected from most legal actions.

Still, some legal scholars say the suit is not wholly a pipe dream, noting that civil rights attorneys in the 1950s and '60s also faced long odds in their battle to end race discrimination. "This will be a daunting task, but it is certainly not impossible," says Robert Belton, a Vanderbilt University law professor.

Even if the suit does not ultimately lead to redress or an apology, it may succeed on another level, says David Bositis, senior political analyst at the Joint Center for Political and Economic Studies, a think tank focusing on African-American issues. "Even if they just got some federal district judge to hear the case, it would become a much larger news item and so would stimulate discussion and debate," he says. "They would consider that a victory."

The black legal team is also planning to sue private companies that benefited from slavery, including banks, insurance companies, shipping firms and other businesses that may have profited from the slave trade.

Research by New York City lawyer and activist Deadria Farmer-Paellmann revealed that several insurance companies — including Aetna and New York Life — insured slave owners against the loss of their "property."

"If you can show a company made immoral gains by profiting from slavery, you can file an action for unjust enrichment," she said.[28] Her work coincides with a new California law requiring all insurance companies in the state to research past business records and disclose any connections to slavery.

In addition, a growing chorus of civil rights leaders, including the Rev. Jesse L. Jackson, has called on insurers to pay some form of restitution. "We call on the insurance companies to search their national files and disclose any and all policies issued to insure slave owners during the period of slavery," Jackson said.[29]

Some black leaders have suggested that culpable corporations establish scholarship funds for underprivileged black students.

But, while Aetna has publicly apologized for insuring owners against the loss of slaves, it has refused to provide compensation, arguing that slavery was legal when the policies were issued. New York Life is withholding comment until it finishes reviewing its historical records.

AT ISSUE

Should the U.S. government apologize to African-Americans for slavery?

YES Rep. Tony P. Hall
D-Ohio

Written for The *CQ Researcher*, June 2001

America's history has changed the course of humanity. As an enemy of tyrants, an advocate of liberty and a defender of freedoms, America has proven herself again and again. Our achievements stir other peoples' pride, and our history bestows upon us the courage to conquer new challenges.

But our achievements and our history are blemished by the shameful decades when U.S. laws permitted the enslavement of African-Americans. This long chapter ensured that many of the hands that built our young nation were not those of full participants in an emerging American dream, but of men, women and children forced to obey the tyranny of "masters."

In recent years, we have apologized for racist medical experiments that inflicted pain and eventually death on many young, innocent men in Tuskegee, Ala. We have paid reparations for forcibly interning thousands of Japanese-Americans during World War II. And we helped to broker an apology and reparations for victims of the Holocaust.

Of course, the fact we have acknowledged these wrongs doesn't make up for the pain of the past. But if what we've done in these cases wasn't sufficient to fulfill that impossible goal, it was necessary to restore the goodwill needed to change our future. In giving these and other Americans the dignity of an honest admission that our nation was wrong, these apologies have given us all a measure of healing.

Nearly 14 decades after slavery was abolished, its legacy still reverberates through Americans' daily lives. Neither former slaves nor slave owners are alive today, and few Americans trace their own roots to slavery. But all Americans bear slavery's bitter burdens — the lingering racial tensions, the stubborn poverty and dysfunction that is disproportionately high among African-Americans, the persistence that justice has not yet been done.

"I am sorry" are the first words uttered by anyone sincere about righting a wrong. And yet in the case of our nation's greatest moral failing, we have yet to say these words. We have pursued countless policies toward the goal of racial healing. We have been enriched by the determination of African-Americans to overcome the problems rooted in their ancestors' enslavement. But neither their success, nor the blood spilled in our Civil War, excuses our country's continuing silence.

Some critics say an apology may open old wounds. Some say that paying reparations is essential to atonement. But no one can say those three words don't ring true.

NO Robert W. Tracinski
Fellow, Ayn Rand Institute,
Marina del Rey, Calif.

June 2001

An apology for slavery on behalf of the nation presumes that whites today, who mostly oppose racism and never owned slaves, still bear a collective responsibility — simply by belonging to the same race as the slaveholders of the Old South. Such an apology promotes the very idea at the root of slavery: racial collectivism.

Slave owners were certainly guilty of a grave injustice. But by what standard can other whites be held responsible for their ideas and actions? By what standards can today's Americans be obliged to apologize on the slaveholders' behalf? The only justification for such an approach is the idea that each member of the race can be blamed for the actions of every other member, that we are all just interchangeable cells of the racial collective.

Critics of the proposed apology oppose it, not because it embraces this racist premise but because it does not go far enough. They want to apply the notion of racial collectivism in a more "substantial" form, by increasing welfare and affirmative-action programs designed to compensate for the wrongs of slavery. Such compensation consists of punishing random whites, by taxing them and denying them jobs and promotions in order to reward random blacks.

The ultimate result of this approach is not racial harmony or a color-blind society but racial warfare. It is precisely this kind of mentality that has devastated the Balkans, with each ethnic tribe continually exacting revenge on the other in retaliation for centuries-old grievances.

The idea of a national apology for slavery merely reinforces this same kind of racial enmity in America. By treating all whites as the stand-ins or representatives for slaveholders, it encourages the view of blacks and whites as a collective of victims pitted against an opposing and hostile collective of oppressors, with no possibility for integration or peaceful coexistence.

The only alternative to this kind of racial Balkanization is to embrace the opposite principle: individualism. People should be judged based on their choices, ideas and actions as individuals, not as "representatives" of a racial group. They should be rewarded based on their own merits — and they must not be forced to pay, or to apologize, for crimes committed by others, merely because those others have the same skin color.

Americans both black and white should reject the notion of a collective guilt for slavery. They should uphold the ideal of a color-blind society, based on individualism, as the real answer to racism.

South Carolina Gov. Jim Hodges helps to break ground for an African-American monument last year in Columbia. In spite of efforts by several states to come to terms with the history and contributions of black Americans, many advocates for slavery reparations say that only restitution will close the racial divide.

OUTLOOK

Starting a Dialogue

Those working to obtain reparations for slavery often compare the fight with the long, uphill struggle faced by civil rights activists in the 1950s and '60s. "The relative powerlessness of our community is not a new thing for African-Americans," the University of Maryland's Walters says. "We've been here before and have won, and I think we're going to win this time, too."

"The uneasiness that some express about reparations is the same uneasiness that we had about integration and about a woman's right to choose," Harvard's Ogletree said. "We've gained some important mainstream viability, but these things take time."[30]

For now, reparations proponents say that they hope to get the government to consider the issue, just as it did for Japanese-American internees and Holocaust survivors. "Right now this is about process," Walters says. "With Japanese-Americans, nothing really happened until after the government took some time to study the issue."

But opponents and others are confident the effort will fail. "This is going to die out because it makes no sense," George Mason's Williams says. "Conyers' bill is languishing in Congress and will continue to languish in Congress,

because white politicians cannot sell this to white America."

MIT's Nobles agrees. "The best they can hope for from Congress is some sort of formal apology," she says. A claim based on an injustice that occurred so long ago is simply too nebulous to warrant serious consideration by lawmakers or judges, she says. "This isn't like the case of Japanese-Americans, where you had direct survivors of the act in question. [The former internees'] suffering was identifiable and for a specific period of time — four years — making it much less complicated."

Efforts against private firms — like insurance companies — have a better chance of producing some monetary reward, she predicts. "Eventually, some company will feel the heat, cave in and set up some sort of trust fund or something," she says, adding that Cochran, Ogletree and the other attorneys are unlikely to quit without something to show for their efforts. "To prove that all of this [effort] was worthwhile, they're going to work for a real win."

Others agree the movement will probably achieve at least some of its goals. "The less sophisticated supporters may think that they're going to win reparations, but the more sophisticated ones know that, in the near term, the chance of this happening is very unlikely," says Bositis, of the Joint Center for Political and Economic Studies.

"For these more realistic people, the principal thing they are trying to do is to start a dialogue on the issue, to get people talking about it," he concludes.

NOTES

1. Quoted in Jane Clayson, "Some Civil Rights Leaders Say Descendants of Slaves Should Be Compensated," CBS News: "The Early Show," Jan. 11, 2001.

2. Larry Bivins, "Debate on Reparations for Slavery Gaining Higher Profile," Gannett News Service, April 21, 2001.

3. For background, see Kenneth Jost, "Holocaust Reparations," *The CQ Researcher*, March 26, 1999, pp. 257-280.

4. Quoted in Abraham H. Foxman, "The Dangers of Holocaust Restitution," *The Wall Street Journal*, Dec. 7, 1998.

5. Quoted in *Ibid.*

6. Mortimer Adler, *Aristotle for Everybody* (1978), p. 126.

7. Quoted in Arthur Spiegelman, "Leaders of Fight for Holocaust Reparations Under Attack," *The Houston Chronicle*, Dec. 27, 1998

8. Matthew 5:10.

9. Adam Smith, *The Theory of Moral Sentiments* (1759), pp. 47-48.

10. Elazar Barkan, *The Guilt of Nations: Restitution and Negotiating Historical Injustices* (2000), p. 183.

11. Mitchell T. Maki, *et al.*, *Achieving the Impossible Dream: How Japanese-Americans Obtained Redress* (1999), p. 54.

12. Barkan, *op. cit.*, p. 34.

13. Maki, *op. cit.*, p. 107.

14. *Ibid.*

15. *Ibid.*, pp. 121-128.

16. Christine C. Lawrence, ed., *1988 CQ Almanac* (1988), p. 80.

17. *Ibid.*

18. Maki, *op. cit.*, p. 213.

19. *Ibid.*, p. 214.

20. Barkan, *op. cit.*

21. Jost, *op. cit.*

22. Henry Weinstein, "Spending by Holocaust Claims Panel Criticized," *Los Angeles Times*, May 17, 2001.

23. "Key Dates in Nazi Slave Labor Talks," *The Jerusalem Post*, May 21, 2001.

24. Quoted in Erin Texeira, "Black Reparations Idea Builds at UCLA Meeting," *Los Angeles Times*, May 12, 2001.

25. Quoted in Tamar Lewin, "Calls for Slavery Restitution Getting Louder," *The New York Times*, June 4, 2001.

26. Kevin Merida, "Did Freedom Alone Pay a Nation's Debt?" *The Washington Post*, Nov. 28, 1999.

27. Quoted in Tovia Smith, "Legal Scholars Considering Class Action Lawsuit to Seek Restitution for Descendants of African Slaves," Weekend Edition Saturday, National Public Radio, April 1, 2001.

28. Quoted in Lewin, *op. cit.*

29. Quoted in Tim Novak, "Jackson: Companies Owe Blacks," *The Chicago Sun Times*, July 29, 2000.

30. Quoted in Lewin, *op. cit.*

BIBLIOGRAPHY

Books

Barkan, Elazar, *The Guilt of Nations: Restitution and Negotiating Historical Injustices*, W.W. Norton, 2000.
A professor of history at Claremont Graduate University has written an excellent and thorough history of restitution efforts in the 20th century, from attempts by Holocaust survivors to recover stolen property to the campaign to compensate "comfort women" forced to provide sex to Japanese soldiers. Barkan also examines the intellectual origins of the reparations movement.

Finkelstein, Norman G., *The Holocaust Industry: Reflections on the Exploitation of Jewish Suffering*, Verso, 2000.
Finkelstein, a professor of political theory at Hunter College, charges lawyers and Jewish groups with exploiting the Holocaust for financial and political gain, using unethical and immoral tactics. He contends that much of the money "extorted" from European companies and countries is not going to survivors, and that the entire process is degrading the historical legacy of the Holocaust.

Maki, Mitchell T., Harry H. L. Kitano and S. Megan Berthold, *Achieving the Impossible Dream: How Japanese Americans Obtained Redress*, University of Illinois Press, 1999.
The authors trace the history of efforts to get the U.S. government to pay reparations to Japanese-Americans interned during World War II.

Robinson, Randall, *The Debt: What America Owes to Blacks*, Plume, 2000.
The president of TransAfrica argues for reparations for African-Americans, writing: "If . . . African Americans will not be compensated for the massive wrongs and social injuries inflicted upon them by their government, during and after slavery, then there is no chance that America can solve its racial problems — if solving these

problems means, as I believe it must, closing the yawning economic gap between blacks and whites in this country."

Articles

Bivis, Larry, "Debate on Reparations for Slavery Gaining Higher Profile," Gannett News Service, April 21, 2001.
The article examines African-Americans' growing call for reparations.

Dyckman, Martin, "Our Country has Paid the Bill for Slavery," St. Petersburg Times, June 25, 2000.
Dyckman makes a strong case against reparations to black Americans, arguing that the Union soldiers who died in the Civil War to free the slaves paid the country's debt to African-Americans.

Jost, Kenneth, "Holocaust Reparations," The CQ Researcher, March 26, 1999.
Jost gives an excellent overview of the debate over reparations for the survivors of the Nazi Holocaust. His description of the fight over dormant bank accounts and insurance policies in Switzerland is particularly illuminating.

McTague, Jim, "Broken Trusts: Native Americans Seek Billions They Say Uncle Sam Owes Them," Barron's, April 9, 2001.
McTague examines the Native American lawsuit against the federal government for decades of mishandling of the trust fund derived from the lease and sale of natural resources on Indian lands. The tribe recently won a judgment against the federal government, and the suit may result in native tribes receiving up to $10 billion.

Merida, Kevin, "Did Freedom Alone Pay a Nation's Debt?" The Washington Post, Nov. 28, 1999.
Merida examines the movement to obtain reparations for the African-American descendants of slaves, providing a good historical overview of efforts to compensate newly freed slaves after the Civil War.

Schoenfeld, Gabriel, "Holocaust Reparations — A Growing Scandal," Commentary Magazine, Sept. 2000.
The magazine's senior editor takes Jewish groups to task for their hardball tactics against Germany and other European countries in their Holocaust reparations efforts. He worries they will foment bad feeling in Europe against Jews and Israel.

Trounson, Rebecca, "Campus Agitator," Los Angeles Times, April 10, 2001.
The article chronicles the controversy surrounding recent attempts by conservative commentator David Horowitz to place ads in college newspapers that argue against reparations for African-Americans.

Zipperstein, Steven J., "Profit and Loss," The Washington Post, Sept. 24, 2000.
A professor of Jewish studies at Stanford University accuses author Norman G. Finkelstein of making wild and unsubstantiated charges in The Holocaust Industry (see above). "Imagine an old-style rant, with its finely honed ear for conspiracy, with all the nuance of one's raging, aging, politicized uncle," he writes.

For More Information

Anti-Defamation League, 823 United Nations Plaza, New York, NY 20017; (212) 490-2525; www.adl.org. Fights anti-Semitism and represents Jewish interests worldwide.

Conference on Jewish Material Claims Against Germany, 15 East 26th St., Room 906, New York, NY 10010; (212) 696-4944; www.claimscon.org. Pursues reparations claims on behalf of Jewish victims of the Nazi Holocaust.

Japanese American Citizens League (JACL), 1765 Sutter St., San Francisco, CA 94115; (415) 921-5225. www .jacl.org. The nation's oldest Asian-American civil rights group fights discrimination against Japanese-Americans.

Joint Center for Political and Economic Studies, 1090 Vermont Ave., N.W., Suite 1100, Washington, DC 20005; (202) 789-3500; www.jointcenter.org. Researches and analyzes issues of importance to African-Americans.

National Coalition of Blacks for Reparations in America, P.O. Box 62622, Washington, DC 20029; (202) 635-6272; www.ncobra.com. Lobbies for reparations for African-Americans.

Native American Rights Fund, 1712 N St., N.W., Washington, DC 20036; (202) 785-4166; www.narf.org. Provides Native Americans with legal assistance for land claims.

TransAfrica, 1744 R. St., N.W., Washington DC 20009; (202) 797-2301; www.transafricaforum.org. Lobbies on behalf of Africans and people of African descent around the world.

U.S. Holocaust Memorial Museum, 100 Raoul Wallenberg Place, S.W., Washington, DC 20024; (202) 488-0400; www.ushmm.org. Preserves documentation and encourages research about the Holocaust.

World Jewish Congress, 501 Madison Ave., 17th Floor, New York, NY 10022; (212) 755-5770; www.worldjewish congress.org. An international federation of Jewish communities and organizations that has been at the forefront of negotiations over Holocaust reparations.

American Indians

Are They Making Meaningful Progress at Last?

Peter Katel

Jerolyn Fink lives in grand style in the housing center built by Connecticut's Mohegan Tribe using profits from its successful Mohegan Sun casino. Thanks in part to booming casinos, many tribes are making progress, but American Indians still face daunting health and economic problems, and tribal leaders say federal aid remains inadequate.

From *CQ Researcher*, April 28, 2006.

It's not a fancy gambling palace, like some Indian casinos, but the modest operation run by the Winnebago Tribe of Nebraska may just help the 2,300-member tribe hit the economic jackpot.

Using seed money from the casino, it has launched 12 businesses, including a construction company and an Internet news service. Projected 2006 revenues: $150 million.

"It would be absolutely dumb for us to think that gaming is the future," says tribe member Lance Morgan, the 37-year-old Harvard Law School graduate who runs the holding company for the dozen businesses. "Gaming is just a means to an end — and it's done wonders for our tribal economy."

Indian casinos have revived a myth dating back to the early-20th-century Oklahoma oil boom — that Indians are rolling in dough.[1] While some of the 55 tribes that operate big casinos indeed are raking in big profits, the 331 federally recognized tribes in the lower 48 states, on the whole, endure soul-quenching poverty and despair.

Arizona's 1.8-million-acre San Carlos Apache Reservation is among the poorest. The rural, isolated community of about 13,000 people not only faces devastating unemployment but also a deadly methamphetamine epidemic, tribal Chairwoman Kathleen W. Kitcheyan, told the Senate Indian Affairs Committee in April.

"We suffer from a poverty level of 69 percent, which must be unimaginable to many people in this country, who would equate a situation such as this to one found only in Third World countries," she said. Then, speaking of the drug-related death of one of her own grandsons, she had to choke back sobs.

Conditions on Reservations Improved

Socioeconomic conditions improved more on reservations with gambling than on those without gaming during the 1990s, although non-gaming reservations also improved substantially, especially compared to the U.S. population. Some experts attribute the progress among non-gaming tribes to an increase in self-governance on many reservations.

Socioeconomic Changes on Reservations, 1990-2000*
(shown as a percentage or percentage points)

	Non-Gaming	Gaming	U.S.
Real per-capita income	+21.0%	+36.0%	+11.0%
Median household income	+14.0%	+35.0%	+4.0%
Family poverty	-6.9	-11.8	-0.8
Child poverty	-8.1	-11.6	-1.7
Deep poverty	-1.4	-3.4	-0.4
Public assistance	+0.7	-1.6	+0.3
Unemployment	-1.8	-4.8	-0.5
Labor force participation	-1.6	+1.6	-1.3
Overcrowded homes	-1.3	-0.1	+1.1
Homes lacking complete plumbing	-4.6	-3.3	-0.1
Homes lacking complete kitchen	+1.3	-0.6	+0.2
College graduates	+1.7	+2.6	+4.2
High school or equivalency only	-0.3	+1.8	-1.4
Less than 9th-grade education	-5.5	-6.3	-2.8

* The reservation population of the Navajo Nation, which did not have gambling in the 1990s, was not included because it is so large (175,000 in 2000) that it tends to pull down Indian averages when it is included.

Source: Jonathan B. Taylor and Joseph P. Kalt, "Cabazon, The Indian Gaming Regulatory Act, and the Socioeconomic Consequences of American Indian Governmental Gaming: A Ten-Year Review, American Indians on Reservations: A Databook of Socioeconomic Change Between the 1990 and 2000 Censuses," Harvard Project on American Indian Economic Development, January 2005

- Nearly one in five Indians age 25 or older in tribes without gambling operations had less than a ninth-grade education. But even members of tribes with gambling had a college graduation rate of only 16 percent, about half the national percentage.[5]
- Death rates from alcoholism and tuberculosis among Native Americans are at least 650 percent higher than overall U.S. rates.[6]
- Indian youths commit suicide at nearly triple the rate of young people in general.[7]
- Indians on reservations, especially in the resource-poor Upper Plains and West, are the nation's third-largest group of methamphetamine users.[8]

The immediate prognosis for the nation's 4.4 million Native Americans is bleak, according to the Harvard Project on American Indian Economic Development. "If U.S. and on-reservation Indian per-capita income were to continue to grow at their 1990s' rates," it said, "it would take half a century for the tribes to catch up."[9]

Nonetheless, there has been forward movement in Indian Country, though it is measured in modest steps. Among the marks of recent progress:

- Per-capita income rose 20 percent on reservations, to $7,942, (and 36 percent in tribes with casinos, to $9,771), in contrast to an 11 percent overall U.S. growth rate.[10]
- Unemployment has dropped by up to 5 percent on reservations and in other predominantly Indian areas.[11]
- Child poverty in non-gaming tribes dropped from 55 percent of the child population to 44 percent (but the Indian rate is still more than double the 17 percent average nationwide).[12]

"Our statistics are horrific," says Lionel R. Bordeaux, president of Sinte Gleska University, on the Rosebud Sioux Reservation in South Dakota. "We're at the bottom rung of the ladder in all areas, whether it's education levels, economic achievement or political status."[2]

National statistics aren't much better:

- Indian unemployment on reservations nationwide is 49 percent — 10 times the national rate.[3]
- The on-reservation family poverty rate in 2000 was 37 percent — four times the national figure of 9 percent.[4]

More than two centuries of court decisions, treaties and laws have created a complicated system of coexistence between tribes and the rest of the country. On one level, tribes are sovereign entities that enjoy a government-to-government relationship with Washington. But the sovereignty is qualified. In the words of an 1831 Supreme Court decision that is a bedrock of Indian law, tribes are "domestic dependent nations."[13]

The blend of autonomy and dependence grows out of the Indians' reliance on Washington for sheer survival, says Robert A. Williams Jr., a law professor at the University of Arizona and a member of North Carolina's Lumbee Tribe. "Indians insisted in their treaties that the Great White Father protect us from these racial maniacs in the states — where racial discrimination was most developed — and guarantee us a right to education, a right to water, a territorial base, a homeland," he says. "Tribes sold an awful lot of land in return for a trust relationship to keep the tribes going."

Today, the practical meaning of the relationship with Washington is that American Indians on reservations, and to some extent those elsewhere, depend entirely or partly on federal funding for health, education and other needs. Tribes with casinos and other businesses lessen their reliance on federal dollars.

Unlike other local governments, tribes don't have a tax base whose revenues they share with state governments. Federal spending on Indian programs of all kinds nationwide currently amounts to about $11 billion, James Cason, associate deputy secretary of the Interior, told the Senate Indian Affairs Committee in February.

But the abysmal conditions under which many American Indians live make it all too clear that isn't enough, Indians say. "This is always a discussion at our tribal leaders' meetings," says Cecilia Fire Thunder, president of the Oglala Sioux Tribe in Pine Ridge, S.D. "The biggest job that tribal leaders have is to see that the government lives up to its responsibilities to our people. It's a battle that never ends."

Indeed, a decades-old class-action suit alleges systematic mismanagement of billions of dollars in Indian-owned assets by the Interior Department — a case that has prompted withering criticism of the department by the judge (*see p. 134*).

Government officials insist that, despite orders to cut spending, they've been able to keep providing essential services. Charles Grim, director of the Indian Health

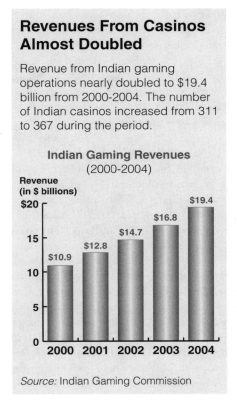

Revenues From Casinos Almost Doubled

Revenue from Indian gaming operations nearly doubled to $19.4 billion from 2000-2004. The number of Indian casinos increased from 311 to 367 during the period.

Indian Gaming Revenues
(2000-2004)

Revenue (in $ billions)

Year	Revenue
2000	$10.9
2001	$12.8
2002	$14.7
2003	$16.8
2004	$19.4

Source: Indian Gaming Commission

Service, told the Indian Affairs Committee, "In a deficit-reduction year, it's a very strong budget and one that does keep pace with inflationary and population-growth increases."

In any event, from the tribes' point of view, they lack the political muscle to force major increases. "The big problem is the Indians are about 1 percent of the national population," says Joseph Kalt, co-director of the Harvard Project. "The voice is so tiny."

Faced with that grim political reality, Indians are trying to make better use of scarce federal dollars through a federally sponsored "self-governance" movement. Leaders of the movement say tribes can deliver higher-quality services more efficiently when they control their own budgets. Traditionally, federal agencies operate programs on reservations, such as law enforcement or medical services.

But since the 1990s, dozens of tribes have stepped up control of their own affairs both by building their own businesses and by signing self-governance "compacts" with the federal government. Compacts provide tribes with large chunks of money, or block grants, rather than individual grants for each service. Then, with minimal federal oversight, the tribes develop their own budgets and run all or most services.

The self-governance trend gathered steam during the same time that Indian-owned casinos began booming. For many tribes, the gambling business provided a revenue stream that didn't flow from Washington.

According to economist Alan Meister, 228 tribes in 30 states operated 367 high-stakes bingo halls or casinos in 2004, earning an estimated $19.6 billion.[14]

The gambling houses operate under the 1988 Indian Gaming Regulatory Act (IGRA), which was made possible by a U.S. Supreme Court ruling upholding tribes' rights to govern their own activities.[15] A handful of tribes are doing so well that $80 million from six tribes in 2000-2003 helped fuel the scandal surrounding one-time Washington super-lobbyist Jack Abramoff, whose clients were among the most successful casino tribes.[16]

If the Abramoff scandal contributed to the notion of widespread Indian wealth, one reason may be the misimpression that tribes don't pay taxes on their gambling earnings. In fact, under the IGRA, federal, state and local governments took in $6.3 billion in gambling-generated tax revenues in 2004, with 67 percent going to the federal government. In addition, tribes paid out some $889 million in 2004 to state and local governments in order to get gambling operations approved.[17]

The spread of casinos has prompted some cities and counties, along with citizens' groups and even some casino-operating tribes, to resist casino-expansion plans.

The opposition to expansion is another reason tribal entrepreneur Morgan doesn't think gaming is a good long-range bet for Indians' future. His vision involves full tribal control of the Indians' main asset — their land. He argues for ending the "trust status" under which tribes can't buy or sell reservation property — a relic of 19th-century protection against rapacious state governments.

Indian Country needs a better business climate, Morgan says, and the availability of land as collateral for investments would be a big step in that direction. "America has a wonderful economic system, probably the best in the world, but the reservation tends to be an economic black hole."

As Indians seek to improve their lives, here are some of the issues being debated:

Is the federal government neglecting Native Americans?

There is wide agreement that the federal government bears overwhelming responsibility for Indians' welfare, but U.S. and tribal officials disagree over the adequacy of the aid Indians receive. Sen. John McCain, R-Ariz., chairman of the Senate Indian Affairs Committee, and Vice Chairman Byron L. Dorgan, D-N.D., have been leading the fight for more aid to Indians. "We have a full-blown crisis . . . particularly dealing with children and elderly, with respect to housing, education and health care," Dorgan told the committee on Feb. 14. He characterized administration proposals as nothing more than "nibbling around the edges on these issues . . . making a few adjustments here or there.' "

Administration officials respond that given the severe federal deficit, they are focusing on protecting vital programs. "As we went through and prioritized our budget, we basically looked at all of the programs that were secondary and tertiary programs, and they were the first ones on the block to give tradeoffs for our core programs in maintaining the integrity of those," Interior's Cason told the committee.

For Indians on isolated reservations, says Bordeaux of the Rosebud Sioux, there's little alternative to federal money. He compares tribes' present circumstances to those after the buffalo had been killed off, and an Army general told the Indians to eat beef, which made them sick. "The general told them, 'Either that, or you eat the grass on which you stand.'"

But David B. Vickers, president of Upstate Citizens for Equality, in Union Springs, N.Y., which opposes Indian land claims and casino applications, argues that accusations of federal neglect are inaccurate and skirt the real problem. The central issue is that the constitutional system is based on individual rights, not tribal rights, he says. "Indians are major recipients of welfare now. They're eligible. They don't need a tribe or leader; all they have to do is apply like anybody else."

Pat Ragsdale, director of the Bureau of Indian Affairs (BIA), acknowledges that Dorgan's and McCain's criticisms echo a 2003 U.S. Commission on Civil Rights report, which also called underfunding of Indian aid a crisis. "The government is failing to live up to its trust responsibility to Native peoples," the commission concluded. "Efforts to bring Native Americans up to the standards of other Americans have failed in part because of a lack of sustained funding. The failure manifests itself in massive and escalating unmet needs."[18]

"Nobody in this government disputes the report, in general," says Ragsdale, a Cherokee. "Some of our tribal communities are in real critical shape, and others are prospering."

The commission found, for example, that in 2003 the Indian Health Service appropriation amounted to $2,533 per capita — below even the $3,803 per capita appropriated for federal prisoners.

Concern over funding for Indian programs in 2007 centers largely on health and education. Although 90 percent of Indian students attend state-operated public schools, their schools get federal aid because tribes don't pay property taxes, which typically fund public schools. The remaining 10 percent of Indian students attend schools operated by the BIA or by tribes themselves under BIA contracts.

"There is not a congressman or senator who would send his own children or grandchildren to our schools," said Ryan Wilson, president of the National Indian Education Association, citing "crumbling buildings and outdated structures with lead in the pipes and mold on the walls."[19]

Cason told the Indian Affairs Committee the administration is proposing a $49 million cut, from $157.4 million to $108.1 million, in school construction and repair in 2007. He also said that only 10 of 37 dilapidated schools funded for replacement by 2006 have been completed, with another 19 scheduled to finish in 2007. Likewise, he said the department is also behind on 45 school improvement projects.

McCain questioned whether BIA schools and public schools with large Indian enrollments would be able to meet the requirements set by the national No Child Left Behind Law.[20] Yes, replied Darla Marburger, deputy assistant secretary of Education for policy. "For the first time, we'll be providing money to . . . take a look at how students are achieving in ways that they can tailor their programs to better meet the needs of students." Overall, the Department of Education would spend about $1 billion on Indian education under the administration's proposed budget for 2007, or $6 million less than in 2006.

Controversial Whiteclay, Neb., sells millions of cans of beer annually to residents of the nearby Pine Ridge Reservation in South Dakota. Alcohol abuse and unemployment continue to plague the American Indian community.

AP Photo/William Lauer

McCain and Dorgan are also among those concerned about administration plans to eliminate the Indian Health Service's $32.7 million urban program, which this year made medical and counseling services available to some 430,000 off-reservation Indians at 41 medical facilities in cities around the nation. (*See sidebar, p. 126.*) The administration argues that the services were available through other programs, but McCain and Dorgan noted that "no evaluation or evidence has been provided to support this contention."[21]

Indian Health Service spokesman Thomas Sweeney, a member of the Citizen Potawatomi Nation of Oklahoma, says only 72,703 Indians used urban health centers in 2004 and that expansion of another federal program would pick up the slack.[22]

In Seattle, elimination of the urban program would cut $4 million from the city's Indian Health Board budget, says Executive Director Ralph Forquera. "Why pick on a $33 million appropriation?" he asks. In his skeptical view, the proposal reflects another "unspoken" termination program. You take a sub-population — urban Indians — and eliminate funding, then [you target] tribes under 1,000 members, and there are a lot of them. Little by little, you pick apart the system."

The IHS's Grim told the Senate committee on Feb. 14 the cuts were designed to protect funding that "can be used most effectively to improve the health status of American Indian and Alaskan Native people."

Have casinos benefited Indians?

Over the past two decades, Indian casinos have become powerful economic engines for many tribal economies. But the enthusiasm for casinos is not unanimous.

"If you're looking at casinos in terms of how they've actually raised the status of Indian people, they've been an abysmal failure," says Ted Jojola, a professor of planning at the University of New Mexico and a member of Isleta Pueblo, near Albuquerque. "But in terms of augmenting the original federal trust-responsibility areas — education, health, tribal government — they've been a spectacular success. Successful gaming tribes have ploughed the money either into diversifying their economies or they've augmented funds that would have come to them anyway."

Tribes with casinos near big population centers are flourishing. The Coushatta Tribe's casino near Lake Charles, La., generates $300 million a year, enough to provide about $40,000 to every member.[23] And the fabled Foxwoods Resort Casino south of Norwich, Conn., operated by the Mashantucket Pequot Tribe, together with Connecticut's other big casino, the Mohegan Tribe's Mohegan Sun, grossed $2.2 billion just from gambling in 2004.[24]

There are only about 830 Coushattas, so their benefits also include free health care, education and favorable terms on home purchases.[25] The once poverty-stricken Mashantuckets have created Connecticut's most extensive welfare-to-work program, open to both tribe members and non-members. In 1997-2000, the program helped 150 welfare recipients find jobs.[26]

Most tribes don't enjoy success on that scale. Among the nation's 367 Indian gambling operations, only 15 grossed $250 million or more in 2004 (another 40 earned $100 million to $250 million); 94 earned less than $3 million and 57 earned $3 million to $10 million.[27]

"We have a small casino that provides close to $3 million to the tribal nation as a whole," says Bordeaux, on the Rosebud Sioux Reservation. The revenue has been channeled into the tribe's Head Start program, an emergency home-repair fund and other projects. W. Ron Allen, chairman of the Jamestown S'Klallam Tribe in Sequim, Wash., says his tribe's small casino has raised

living standards so much that some two-dozen students a year go to college, instead of one or two.

Efforts to open additional casinos are creating conflicts between tribes that operate competing casinos, as well as with some of their non-Indian neighbors. Convicted lobbyist Abramoff, for example, was paid millions of dollars by tribes seeking to block other tribal casinos.[28]

Some non-Indian communities also oppose casino expansion. "We firmly believe a large, generally unregulated casino will fundamentally change the character of our community forever," said Liz Thomas, a member of Tax Payers of Michigan Against Casinos, which opposes a casino planned by the Pokagon Band of Potawotami Indians Tribe in the Lake Michigan town of New Buffalo, where Thomas and her husband operate a small resort.

"People are OK with Donald Trump making millions of dollars individually," says Joseph Podlasek, executive director of the American Indian Center of Chicago, "but if a race of people is trying to become self-sufficient, now that's not respectable."

Nevertheless, some American Indians have mixed feelings about the casino route to economic development. "I don't think anyone would have picked casinos" for that purpose, says the University of Arizona's Williams. "Am I ambivalent about it? Absolutely. But I'm not ambivalent about a new fire station, or Kevlar vests for tribal police fighting meth gangs."

"There's no question that some of the money has been used for worthwhile purposes," concedes Guy Clark, a Corrales, N.M., dentist who chairs the National Coalition Against Legalized Gambling. But, he adds, "If you do a cost-benefit analysis, the cost is much greater than the benefit." Restaurants and other businesses, for example, lose customers who often gamble away their extra money.

Even some Indian leaders whose tribes profit from casinos raise caution flags, especially about per-capita payments. For Nebraska's Winnebagos, payments amount to just a few hundred dollars, says CEO Morgan. What bothers him are dividends "that are just big enough that you don't have to work or get educated — say, $20,000 to $40,000."

But there's no denying the impact casinos can have. At a January public hearing on the Oneida Indian Nation's attempt to put 17,000 acres of upstate

New York land into tax-free "trust" status, hundreds of the 4,500 employees of the tribe's Turning Stone Resort and Casino, near Utica, showed up in support. "When I was a kid, people worked for General Motors, General Electric, Carrier and Oneida Ltd.," said casino Human Resources Director Mark Mancini. "Today, people work for the Oneida Indian Nation and their enterprises."[29]

For tribes that can't build independent economies any other way, casinos are appealing. The 225,000-member Navajo Nation, the biggest U.S. tribe, twice rejected gaming before finally approving it in 2004.[30] "We need that infusion of jobs and revenue, and people realize that," said Duane Yazzie, president of the Navajos' Shiprock, N.M., chapter.[31]

But the Navajos face stiff competition from dozens of casinos already in operation near the vast Navajo reservation, which spreads across parts of Arizona, New Mexico and Utah and is larger than the state of West Virginia.

Would money alone solve American Indians' problems?

No one in Indian Country (or on Capitol Hill) denies the importance of federal funding to American Indians' future, but some Indians say it isn't the only answer.

"We are largely on our own because of limited financial assistance from the federal government," said Joseph A. Garcia, president of the National Congress of American Indians, in his recent "State of Indian Nations" speech.[32]

Fifty-two tribal officials and Indian program directors expressed similar sentiments in March before the House Appropriations Subcommittee on the Interior. Pleading their case before lawmakers who routinely consider billion-dollar weapons systems and other big projects, the tribal leaders sounded like small-town county commissioners as they urged lawmakers to increase or restore small but vital grants for basic health, education and welfare services.

"In our ICWA [Indian Child Welfare Act] program, currently we have a budget of $79,000 a year," said Harold Frazier, chairman of the Cheyenne River Sioux, in South Dakota. "We receive over 1,300 requests for assistance annually from 11 states and eight counties in South Dakota. We cannot give the type of attention to these requests that they deserve. Therefore, we are requesting $558,000."

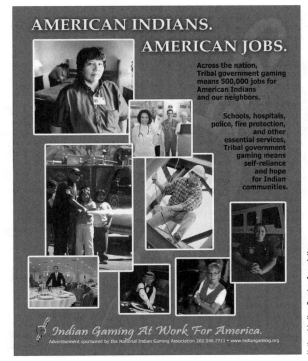

A National Indian Gaming Association advertisement touts the benefits of tribal gaming operations to American Indian communities. Some 228 tribes in 30 states operated 367 high-stakes bingo halls or casinos in 2004.

To university President Bordeaux, federal funding is vital because his desolate reservation has few other options for economic survival. "What's missing is money," he says.

Money is crucial to improving Indians' health, says Dr. Joycelyn Dorscher, director of the Center of American Indian and Minority Health at the University of Minnesota-Duluth. Especially costly are programs to combat diabetes and other chronic diseases, says Dorscher, a Chippewa. While health programs have to be carefully designed to fit Indian cultural patterns, she says, "Everything comes down to time or money in the grand scheme of things."

But with funding from Washington never certain from year to year, says the Harvard Project's Kalt, "The key to economic development has not been federal funding" but rather 'tribes' ability to run their own affairs."

For tribes without self-government compacts, growing demands for services and shrinking funding from

Washington make keeping the dollars flowing the highest priority. "We're always afraid of more cutbacks," says Oglala Sioux President Fire Thunder.

But an Indian education leader with decades of federal budgetary negotiations acknowledges that problems go beyond funding shortfalls. "If you ask students why they dropped out, they say, 'I don't see a future for myself,' " says David Beaulieu, director of Arizona State University's Center for Indian Education. "Educators need to tie the purposes of schooling to the broad-based purposes of society. We're more successful when we tie education to the meaning of life."

The University of Arizona's Williams says a tribe's success and failure may be tied more to the way its government is organized than to how much funding it gets.

Williams says the first priority of tribes still using old-style constitutions should be reorganization, because they feature a weak executive elected by a tribal council. "That's what the BIA was used to," he explains. "It could play off factions and families, and the economic system would be based on patronage and taking care of your own family." Under such a system, he adds, "there's not going to be any long-term strategic planning going on."[33]

Yet other needs exist as well, says the American Indian Center's Podlasek. "It's so difficult for us to find a place to do a traditional ceremony," he says. "We had a traditional healer in town last month, and he wanted to build a sweat lodge. We actually had to go to Indiana. Doing it in the city wasn't even an option."

BACKGROUND

Conquered Homelands

Relations between Indian and non-Indian civilizations in the Americas began with the Spanish Conquistadors' explorations of the 1500s, followed by the French and British. By turns the three powers alternated policies of enslavement, peaceful coexistence and all-out warfare against the Indians.[34]

By 1830, with the Europeans largely gone, white settlers moved westward into Georgia, Mississippi and Alabama. Unwilling to share the rich frontier land, they pushed the Indians out. President Andrew Jackson backed the strategy, and Congress enacted it into the Indian Removal Act of 1830, which called for moving the region's five big tribes into the Oklahoma Territory.

If the law didn't make clear where Indians stood with the government, the treatment of Mississippi's Choctaws provided chilling evidence. Under a separate treaty, Choctaws who refused to head for Oklahoma could remain at home, become citizens and receive land. In practice, none of that was allowed, and Indians who stayed in Mississippi lived marginal existences.

Georgia simplified the claiming of Cherokee lands by effectively ending Cherokee self-rule. The so-called "Georgia Guard" reinforced the point by beating and jailing Indians. Jackson encouraged Georgia's actions, and when Indians protested, he said he couldn't interfere. The lawsuit filed by the Cherokees eventually reached the Supreme Court.

Chief Justice John Marshall's 1831 majority opinion, *Cherokee Nation v. Georgia*, would cast a long shadow over Indians' rights, along with two other decisions, issued in 1823 and 1832. "Almost all Indian policy is the progeny of the conflicting views of Jackson and Marshall," wrote W. Dale Mason, a political scientist at the University of New Mexico.[35]

In concluding that the court couldn't stop Georgia's actions, Marshall defined the relationship between Indians and the U.S. government. While Marshall wrote that Indians didn't constitute a foreign state, he noted that they owned the land they occupied until they made a "voluntary cession." Marshall concluded the various tribes were "domestic dependent nations." In practical terms, "Their relations to the United States resembles that of a ward to his guardian."[36]

Having rejected the Cherokees' argument, the University of Arizona's Williams writes, the court "provided no effective judicial remedy for Indian tribes to protect their basic human rights to property, self-government, and cultural survival under U.S. law."[37]

Along with the *Cherokee* case, the other two opinions that make up the so-called Marshall Trilogy are *Johnson v. M'Intosh* (also known as *Johnson v. McIntosh*), and *Worcester v. State of Georgia*.[38]

In *Johnson*, Marshall wrote that the European empires that "discovered" America became its owners and had "an exclusive right to extinguish the Indian title of occupancy, either by purchase or by conquest. The tribes of Indians inhabiting this country were fierce savages. . . . To leave

CHRONOLOGY

1800s *United States expands westward, pushing Indians off most of their original lands, sometimes creating new reservations for them.*

1830 President Andrew Jackson signs the Indian Removal Act, forcing the Cherokees to move from Georgia to Oklahoma.

1832 Supreme Court issues the last of three decisions defining Indians' legal status as wards of the government.

1871 Congress makes its treaties with tribes easier to alter, enabling non-Indians to take Indian lands when natural resources are discovered.

Dec. 29, 1890 U.S. soldiers massacre at least 150 Plains Indians, mostly women and children, at Wounded Knee, S.D.

1900-1950s *Congress and the executive branch undertake major shifts in Indian policy, first strengthening tribal governments then trying to force cultural assimilation.*

1924 Indians are granted U.S. citizenship.

1934 Indian Reorganization Act authorizes expansion of reservations and strengthening of tribal governments.

1953 Congress endorses full assimilation of Indians into American society, including "relocation" from reservations to cities.

1960s-1980s *In the radical spirit of the era, Native Americans demand respect for their traditions and an end to discrimination; federal government concedes more power to tribal governments, allows gambling on tribal lands.*

1969 American Indian Movement (AIM) seizes Alcatraz Island in San Francisco Bay to dramatize claims of injustice.

July 7, 1970 President Richard M. Nixon vows support for Indian self-government.

Feb. 27, 1973 AIM members occupy the town of Wounded Knee on the Pine Ridge, S.D., Sioux Reservation, for two months; two Indians die and an FBI agent is wounded.

1988 Indian Gaming Regulatory Act allows tribes to operate casinos under agreements with states.

1990s *Indian-owned casinos boom; tribal governments push to expand self-rule and reduce Bureau of Indian Affairs (BIA) supervision.*

1994 President Bill Clinton signs law making experimental self-governance compacts permanent.

March 27, 1996 U.S. Supreme Court rules states can't be forced to negotiate casino compacts, thus encouraging tribes to make revenue-sharing deals with states as the price of approval.

June 10, 1996 Elouise Cobell, a member of the Blackfeet Tribe in Montana, charges Interior Department mismanagement of Indian trust funds cheated Indians out of billions of dollars. The case is still pending.

Nov. 3, 1998 California voters uphold tribes' rights to run casinos; state Supreme Court later invalidates the provision, but it is revived by a 1999 compact between the tribes and the state.

2000s *Indian advocates decry low funding levels, and sovereignty battles continue; lobbying scandal spotlights Indian gambling profits.*

2000 Tribal Self-Governance Demonstration Project becomes permanent.

2003 U.S. Commission on Civil Rights calls underfunding for Indians a crisis, saying federal government spends less for Indian health care than for any other group, including prison inmates.

Feb. 22, 2004 *Washington Post* reports on Washington lobbyist Jack Abramoff's deals with casino tribes.

March 29, 2005 U.S. Supreme Court blocks tax exemptions for Oneida Nation of New York on newly purchased land simply because it once owned the property.

April 5, 2006 Tribal and BIA officials testify in Congress that methamphetamine addiction is ravaging reservations.

Budget Cuts Target Health Clinics

When Lita Pepion, a health consultant and a member of the Blackfeet Nation, learned that her 22-year-old-niece had been struggling with heroin abuse, she urged her to seek treatment at the local Urban Indian Clinic in Billings, Mont.

But the young woman had so much trouble getting an appointment that she gave up. Only recently, says Pepion, did she overcome her addiction on her own.

The clinic is one of 34 federally funded, Indian-controlled clinics that contract with the Indian Health Service (IHS) to serve urban Indians. But President Bush's 2007 budget would kill the $33-million program, eliminating most of the clinics' funding.

Indians in cities will still be able to get health care through several providers, including the federal Health Centers program, says Office of Management and Budget spokesman Richard Walker. The proposed budget would increase funding for the centers by nearly $2 billion, IHS Director Charles W. Grim told the Senate Indian Affairs Committee on Feb. 14, 2006.[1]

But Joycelyn Dorscher, president of the Association of American Indian Physicians, says the IHS clinics do a great job and that, "It's very important that people from diverse backgrounds have physicians like themselves."

Others, however, including Pepion, say the clinics are poorly managed and lack direction. Ralph Forquera, director of the Seattle-based Urban Indian Health Institute, says that while the clinics "have made great strides medically, a lack of resources has resulted in services from unqualified professionals." In addition, he says, "we have not been as successful in dealing with lifestyle changes and mental health problems."

Many Indian health experts oppose the cuts because Indians in both urban areas and on reservations have more health problems than the general population, including 126 percent more chronic liver disease and cirrhosis, 54 percent more diabetes and 178 percent more alcohol-related deaths.[2]

Indian health specialists blame the Indians' higher disease rates on history, lifestyle and genetics — not just on poverty. "You don't see exactly the same things happening to other poor minority groups," says Dorscher, a North Dakota Chippewa, so "there's something different" going on among Indians.

In the view of Donna Keeler, executive director of the South Dakota Urban Indian Health program and an Eastern Shoshone, historical trauma affects the physical wellness of patients in her state's three urban Indian clinics.

Susette Schwartz, CEO of the Hunter Urban Indian Clinic in Wichita, Kan., agrees. She attributes Indians' high rates of mental health and alcohol/substance abuse to their long history of government maltreatment. Many Indian children in the 19th and early 20th centuries, she points out,

---

them in possession of their country was to leave the country a wilderness."[39]

However, Marshall used the 1832 *Worcester* opinion to define the limits of state authority over Indian tribes, holding that the newcomers couldn't simply eject Indians.

"The Cherokee nation . . . is a distinct community occupying its own territory . . . in which the laws of Georgia can have no force," Marshall wrote. Georgia's conviction and sentencing of a missionary for not swearing allegiance to the state "interferes forcibly with the relations established between the United States and the Cherokee nation."[40] That is, the federal government — not states — held the reins of power over tribes.

According to legend, Jackson remarked: "John Marshall has made his decision — now let him enforce it." Between Jackson's disregard of the Supreme Court and white settlers' later manipulation of the legal system to vacate Indian lands, the end result was the dispossession of Indian lands.

Forced Assimilation

The expulsions of the Native Americans continued in the Western territories — especially after the Civil War. "I instructed Captain Barry, if possible to exterminate the whole village," Lt. Col. George Green wrote of his participation in an 1869 campaign against the White Mountain Apaches in Arizona and New Mexico. "There

were taken from their parents and sent to government boarding schools where speaking native languages was prohibited. "Taking away the culture and language years ago," says Schwartz, as well as the government's role in "taking their children and sterilizing their women" in the 1970s, all contributed to Indians' behavioral health issues.

Keeler also believes Indians' low incomes cause their unhealthy lifestyles. Many eat high-fat, high-starch foods because they are cheaper, Pepion says. Growing up on a reservation, she recalls, "We didn't eat a lot of vegetables because we couldn't afford them."

Opponents of the funding cuts for urban Indian health centers also cite a recent letter to President Bush from Daniel R. Hawkins Jr., vice president for federal, state and local government for the National Association of Community Health Centers. He said the urban Indian clinics and community health centers are complementary, not duplicative.

While Pepion does not believe funding should be cut entirely, she concedes that alternative health-care services are often "better equipped than the urban Indian clinics." And if American Indians want to assimilate into the larger society, they can't have everything culturally

Native Americans in downtown Salt Lake City, Utah, demonstrate on April 21, 2006, against the elimination of funding for Urban Indian Health Clinics.

AP Photo/Salt Lake Tribune

separate, she adds. "The only way that I was able to assimilate into an urban society was to make myself do those things that were uncomfortable for me," she says.

But Schwartz believes a great benefit of the urban clinics are their Indian employees, "who are culturally competent and sensitive and incorporate Native American-specific cultural ideas." Because of their history of cultural abuse, it takes a long time for Native Americans to trust non-Indian health providers, says Schwartz. "They're not just going to go to a health center down the road."

Dorscher and Schwartz also say the budget cuts could lead to more urban Indians ending up in costly emergency rooms because of their reluctance to trust the community health centers. "Ultimately, it would become more expensive to cut the prevention and primary care programs than it would be to maintain them," Dorscher says.

— Melissa J. Hipolit

[1] Prepared testimony of Director of Indian Health Service Dr. Charles W. Grim before the Senate Committee on Indian Affairs, Feb. 14, 2006.

[2] Urban Indian Health Institute, "The Health Status of Urban American Indians and Alaska Natives," March 16, 2004, p. v.

seems to be no settled policy, but a general policy to kill them wherever found."[41]

Some military men and civilians didn't go along. But whether by brute force or by persuasion, Indians were pushed off lands that non-Indians wanted. One strategy was to settle the Indians on reservations guarded by military posts. The strategy grew into a general policy for segregating Indians on these remote tracts.

Even after the Indians were herded onto lands that no one else wanted, the government didn't respect reservation boundaries. They were reconfigured as soon as non-Indians saw something valuable, such as mineral wealth.

The strategy of elastic reservation boundaries led to the belief — or rationalization — that reservations served

no useful purposes for Indians themselves. That doctrine led to a policy enshrined in an 1887 law to convert reservations to individual landholdings. Well-meaning advocates of the plan saw it as a way to inculcate notions of private property and Euro-American culture in general.

All tribal land was to be divided into 160-acre allotments, one for each Indian household. The parcels wouldn't become individual property, though, for 25 years.

Indian consent wasn't required. In some cases, government agents tried persuading Indians to join in; in others, the divvying-up proceeded even with many Indians opposed. In Arizona, however, the government backed off from breaking up the lands of the long-settled Hopis,

Disease Toll Higher Among Indians

American Indians served by the Indian Health Service (IHS) — mainly low-income or uninsured — die at substantially higher rates than the general population from liver disease, diabetes, tuberculosis, pneumonia and influenza as well as from homicide, suicide and injuries. However, Indians' death rates from Alzheimer's disease or breast cancer are lower.

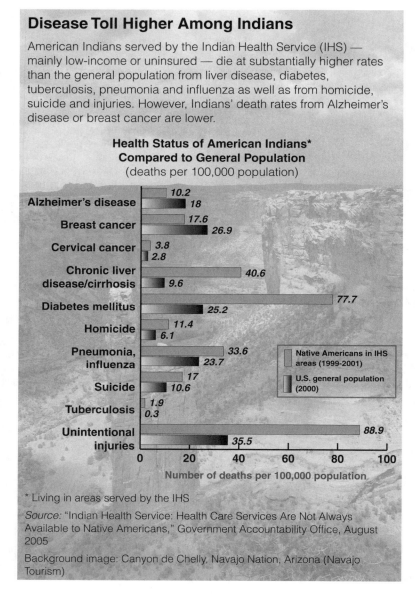

Health Status of American Indians*
Compared to General Population
(deaths per 100,000 population)

	Native Americans in IHS areas (1999-2001)	U.S. general population (2000)
Alzheimer's disease	10.2	18
Breast cancer	17.6	26.9
Cervical cancer	3.8	2.8
Chronic liver disease/cirrhosis	40.6	9.6
Diabetes mellitus	77.7	25.2
Homicide	11.4	6.1
Pneumonia, influenza	33.6	23.7
Suicide	17	10.6
Tuberculosis	1.9	0.3
Unintentional injuries	88.9	35.5

Number of deaths per 100,000 population

* Living in areas served by the IHS

Source: "Indian Health Service: Health Care Services Are Not Always Available to Native Americans," Government Accountability Office, August 2005

Background image: Canyon de Chelly, Navajo Nation, Arizona (Navajo Tourism)

The bleak period ended with President Franklin D. Roosevelt. In his first term he appointed a defender of Indian culture, John Collier, as commissioner of Indian affairs. Collier pushed for the Indian Reorganization Act of 1934, which ended the allotment program, financed purchases of new Indian lands and authorized the organization of tribal governments that enjoyed control over revenues.

Termination

After World War II, a new, anti-Indian mood swept Washington, partly in response to pressure from states where non-Indians eyed Indian land.

Collier resigned in 1945 after years of conflict over what critics called his antagonism to missionaries proselytizing among the Indians and his sympathies toward the tribes. The 1950 appointment of Dillon S. Myer — fresh from supervising the wartime internment of Japanese-Americans — clearly reflected the new attitude. Myer showed little interest in what Indians themselves thought of the new policy of shrinking tribal land holdings. "I realize that it will not be possible always to obtain Indian cooperation. . . . We must proceed, even though [this] may be lacking."[42]

Congress hadn't authorized a sweeping repeal of earlier policy. But the introduction of dozens of bills in the late 1940s to sell Indian land or liquidate some reservation holdings entirely showed which way the winds were blowing. And in 1953, a House Concurrent Resolution declared Congress' policy to be ending Indians' "status as wards of the United States, and to grant them all of the rights and privileges pertaining to American citizenship." A separate law granted state jurisdiction over Indian reservations in five Midwestern and Western states and extended the same authority to other states that wanted to claim it.[43]

who resisted attempts to break up their territory. The vast Navajo Nation in Arizona, Utah and New Mexico was also left intact.

While widely reviled, the "forced assimilation" policy left a benign legacy for the affected Indians: the grant of citizenship. Beyond that, the era's Indians were restricted to unproductive lands, and with little means of support many fell prey to alcoholism and disease.

The following year, Congress "terminated" formal recognition and territorial sovereignty of six tribes. Four years later, after public opposition began building (spurred in part by religious organizations), Congress abandoned termination. In the meantime, however, Indians had lost 1.6 million acres.

At the same time, though, the federal government maintained an associated policy — relocation. The BIA persuaded Indians to move to cities — Chicago, Denver and Los Angeles were the main destinations — and opened job-placement and housing-aid programs. The BIA placed Indians far from their reservations to keep them from returning. By 1970, the BIA estimated that 40 percent of all Indians lived in cities, of which one-third had been relocated by the bureau; the rest moved on their own.[44]

Activism

Starting in the late 1960s, the winds of change blowing through American society were felt as deeply in Indian Country as anywhere. Two books played a crucial role. In 1969, Vine Deloria Jr., member of a renowned family of Indian intellectuals from Oklahoma, published his landmark history, *Custer Died For Your Sins*, which portrayed American history from the Indians' viewpoint. The following year, Dee Brown's *Bury My Heart at Wounded Knee* described the settling of the West also from an Indian point of view. The books astonished many non-Indians. Among young Indians, the volumes reflected and spurred on a growing political activism.

It was in this climate that the newly formed American Indian Movement (AIM) took over Alcatraz Island, the former federal prison site in San Francisco Bay (where rebellious Indians had been held during the Indian Wars), to publicize demands to honor treaties and respect Native Americans' dignity. The takeover lasted from Nov. 20, 1969, to June 11, 1971, when U.S. marshals removed the occupiers.[45]

A second AIM-government confrontation took the form of a one-week takeover of BIA headquarters in Washington in November 1972 by some 500 AIM members protesting what they called broken treaty obligations. Protesters charged that government services to Indians were inadequate in general, with urban Indians neglected virtually completely.

Another protest occurred on Feb. 27, 1973, when 200 AIM members occupied the village of Wounded Knee

Native American children and adults in the Chicago area keep in touch with their cultural roots at the American Indian Center. About two-thirds of the nation's Indians live in urban areas.

American Indian Center/Warren Perlstein

on the Oglala Sioux's Pine Ridge Reservation in South Dakota. U.S. soldiers had massacred at least 150 Indians at Wounded Knee in 1890. AIM was protesting what it called the corrupt tribal government. And a weak, involuntary manslaughter charge against a non-Indian who had allegedly killed an Indian near the reservation had renewed Indian anger at discriminatory treatment by police and judges.

The occupation soon turned into a full-blown siege, with the reservation surrounded by troops and federal law-enforcement officers. During several firefights two AIM members were killed, and an FBI agent was wounded. The occupation ended on May 8, 1973.

Self-Determination

Amid the surging Indian activism, the federal government was trying to make up for the past by encouraging tribal self-determination.[46]

In 1975, Congress passed the Indian Self-Determination and Education Assistance Act, which channeled federal contracts and grants directly to tribes, reducing the BIA role and effectively putting Indian communities in direct charge of schools, health, housing and other programs.

And to assure Indians that the era of sudden reversals in federal policy had ended, the House in 1988 passed a resolution reaffirming the "constitutionally recognized government-to-government relationship with Indian tribes." Separate legislation set up a "self-governance demonstration project" in which eligible tribes would sign "compacts" to run their own governments with block grants from the federal government.[47]

By 1993, 28 tribes had negotiated compacts with the Interior Department. And in 1994, President Bill Clinton signed legislation that made self-governance a permanent option.

For the general public, the meaning of newly strengthened Indian sovereignty could be summed up with one word: casinos. In 1988, Congress enacted legislation regulating tribal gaming operations. That move followed a Supreme Court ruling (*California v. Cabazon*) that authorized tribes to run gambling operations. But tribes could not offer a form of gambling specifically barred by the state.

The law set up three categories of gambling operations: Class I, traditional Indian games, controlled exclusively by tribes; Class II, including bingo, lotto, pull tabs and some card games, which are allowed on tribal lands in states that allow the games elsewhere; and Class III, which takes in casino games such as slot machines, roulette and blackjack, which can be offered only under agreements with state governments that set out the size and types of the proposed casinos.

Limits that the Indian Gaming Regulatory Act put on Indian sovereignty were tightened further by a 1996 Supreme Court decision that the Seminole Tribe couldn't sue Florida to force negotiation of a casino compact. The decision essentially forced tribes nationwide to make revenue-sharing deals with states in return for approval of casinos.[48]

Meanwhile, particularly on reservations from Minnesota to the Pacific Northwest, a plague of methamphetamine addiction and manufacturing is leaving a trail of death and shattered lives. By 2002, Darrell Hillaire, chairman of the Lummi Nation, near Bellingham, Wash., said that members convicted of dealing meth would be expelled from the tribe.[49]

But the Lummis couldn't stop the spread of the scourge on other reservations. National Congress of American Indians President Garcia said early in 2006: "Methamphetamine is a poison taking Indian lives, destroying Indian families, and razing entire communities."[50]

CURRENT SITUATION
Self-Government

Some Indian leaders are advocating more power for tribal governments as the best way to improve the quality of life on reservations.

Under the Tribal Self-Governance Demonstration Project, made permanent in 1994, tribes can replace program-by-program grants by entering into "compacts" with the federal government, under which they receive a single grant for a variety of services. Some 231 tribes and Alaskan Native villages have compacts to administer a total of about $341 million in programs. Of the Indian communities now living under compacts, 72 are in the lower 48 states.[51]

Under a set of separate compacts, the Indian Health Service has turned over clinics, hospitals and health programs to some 300 tribes and Alaskan villages, 70 of them non-Alaskan tribes.

The self-governance model has proved especially appropriate in Alaska, where the majority of the native population of 120,000 is concentrated in 229 villages, many of them remote, and compact in size, hence well-suited to managing their own affairs, experts say.

Another advantage of Alaska villages is the experience they acquired through the 1971 Alaska Native Claims Settlement Act, which granted a total of $962 million to Alaska natives born on or before Dec. 18, 1971, in exchange for giving up their claims to millions of acres of land. Villages formed regional corporations to manage the assets. In addition, all Alaska residents receive an annual dividend ($946 in 2005) from natural-resource royalty income.[52]

"The emergence of tribal authority is unprecedented in Indian Country's history," says Allen, of the Jamestown S'Klallam Tribe, one of the originators of the self-governance model. "Why not take the resources you have available and use them as efficiently as you can — more efficiently than currently being administered?"[53]

But the poorer and more populous tribes of the Great Plains and the Southwest have turned down the self-governance model. "They can't afford to do it," says Michael LaPointe, chief of staff to President Rodney Bordeaux of the Rosebud Sioux Tribe. "When you have a lot of poverty and not a lot of economic activity to generate tribal resources to supplement the unfunded mandates, it becomes impossible."

In contrast with the Jameston S'Klallam's tiny membership of 585 people, there are some 24,000 people on the Rosebud Siouxs' million-acre reservation. The tribe does operate law enforcement, ambulances and other services under contracts with the government. But it can't afford to do any more, LaPointe says.

A combined effect of the gambling boom and the growing adoption of the self-governance model is that much of the tension has gone out of the traditionally strained relationship between the BIA and tribes. "BIA people are getting pushed out as decision-makers," Kalt says. Some strains remain, to be sure. Allen says he senses a growing reluctance by the BIA to let go of tribes. "They use the argument that that the BIA doesn't have the money [for block grants]," he says.

BIA Director Ragsdale acknowledges that tougher financial-accounting requirements sparked by a lawsuit over Interior Department handling of Indian trust funds are slowing the compact-approval process. (*See "Trust Settlement" on p. 134.*) But, he adds, "We're not trying to hinder self-governance."

Limits on Gambling

Several legislative efforts to limit Indian gaming are pending. Separate bills by Sen. McCain and House Resources Committee Chairman Richard Pombo, R-Calif., would restrict tribes' ability to acquire new land for casinos in more favorable locations.

More proposals are in the pipeline. Jemez Pueblo of New Mexico wants to build a casino near the town of Anthony, though the pueblo is 300 miles away.[54]

In eastern Oregon, the Warm Springs Tribe is proposing an off-reservation casino at the Columbia River Gorge. And in Washington state, the Cowlitz and Mohegan tribes are planning an off-reservation casino near Portland.[55] The process has been dubbed "reservation shopping."

Under the Indian Gaming Regulatory Act of 1988, a tribe can acquire off-reservation land for casinos when it is:

- granted as part of a land claim settlement;
- granted to a newly recognized tribe as its reservation;

- restored to a tribe whose tribal recognition is also restored; or
- granted to a recognized tribe that had no reservation when the act took effect.

The most hotly debated exemption allows the secretary of the Interior to grant an off-reservation acquisition that benefits the tribe without harming the community near the proposed casino location. Both Pombo and McCain would repeal the loophole created by this so-called "two-part test." Under Pombo's bill, tribes acquiring land under the other exemptions would have to have solid historic and recent ties to the property. Communities, state governors and state legislatures would have to approve the establishment of new casinos, and tribes would reimburse communities for the effects of casinos on transportation, law enforcement and other public services.

McCain's bill would impose fewer restrictions than Pombo's. But McCain would give the National Indian Gaming Commission final say over all contracts with outside suppliers of goods and services.

The bill would also ensure the commission's control over big-time gambling — a concern that arose from a 2005 decision by the U.S. Court of Appeals for the District of Columbia that limited the agency's jurisdiction over a Colorado tribe. The commission has been worrying that applying that decision nationwide would eliminate federal supervision of casinos.

McCain told a March 8 Senate Indian Affairs Committee hearing that the two-part test "is fostering opposition to all Indian gaming."[56]

If the senator had been aiming to soften tribal opposition to his bill, he didn't make much headway. "We believe that it grows out of anecdotal, anti-Indian press reports on Indian gaming, the overblown issue of off-reservation gaming, and a 'pin-the-blame-on-the-victim' reaction to the Abramoff scandal," Ron His Horse Is Thunder, chairman of the Standing Rock Sioux Tribe of North Dakota and South Dakota, told the committee. He argued that the bill would amount to unconstitutional meddling with Indian sovereignty.

But the idea of restricting "reservation-shopping" appeals to tribes facing competition from other tribes. Cheryle A. Kennedy, chairwoman of the Confederated Tribes of the Grand Ronde Community of Oregon, said

Urban Indians: Invisible and Unheard

Two-thirds of the nation's 4.4 million American Indians live in towns and cities, but they're hard to find.[1] "Indians who move into metropolitan areas are scattered; they're not in a centralized geographical area," says New Mexico Secretary of Labor Conroy Chino. "You don't have that cohesive community where there's a sense of culture and language, as in Chinatown or Koreatown in Los Angeles."

Chino's interest is professional as well as personal. In his former career as a television journalist in Albuquerque, Chino, a member of the Acoma Pueblo, wrote an independent documentary about urban Indians. His subjects range from a city-loving San Franciscan who vacations in Hawaii to city-dwellers who return to their reservations every vacation they get. Their lives diverge sharply from what University of Arizona anthropologist Susan Lobo calls a "presumption that everything Indian is rural and long, long ago."[2]

Indian society began urbanizing in 1951, when the Bureau of Indian Affairs (BIA) started urging reservation dwellers to move to cities where — it was hoped — they would blend into the American "melting pot" and find more economic opportunity and a better standard of living.[3]

But many found the urban environment oppressive and the government assistance less generous than promised. About 100,000 Indians were relocated between 1951 and 1973, when the program wound down; unable to fit in, many fell into alcoholism and despair.[4]

Still, a small, urban Indian middle class has developed over time, partly because the BIA began systematically hiring Indians in its offices. Indians keep such a low profile, however, that the Census Bureau has a hard time finding them. Lobo, who consulted for the bureau in 1990, recalls that the agency's policy at the time was to register any household where no one answered the door as being in the same ethnic group as the neighbors. That strategy worked with urban ethnic groups who tended to cluster together, Lobo says, but not with Native Americans because theirs was a "dispersed population."

By the 2000 census that problem was resolved, but another one cropped up. "American Indians are ingenious at keeping expenses down — by couch-surfing, for instance," Lobo says. "There's a floating population that doesn't get counted because they weren't living in a standard residence."

But other urban Indians live conventional, middle-class lives, sometimes even while technically living on Indian land. "I am highly educated, a professor in the university, and my gainful employment is in the city of Albuquerque," says Ted Jojola, a professor of planning at the University of New Mexico (and a member of the Census Bureau's advisory committee on Indian population). "My community [Isleta Pueblo] is seven minutes south of Albuquerque. The reservation has become an urban amenity to me."

Some might see a home on Indian land near the city as a refuge from discrimination. "There have been years where you couldn't reveal you were native if you wanted to get a job," says Joseph Podlasek, executive director of the American Indian Center of Chicago.

Joycelyn Dorscher, president of the Association of American Indian Physicians, recalls a painful experience several years ago when she rushed her 6-year-old daughter to a hospital emergency room in Minneapolis-St. Paul, suspecting appendicitis. The young intern assigned to the case saw an Indian single mother with a sick child and apparently assumed that the daughter was suffering from neglect. "She told me if I didn't sit down and shut up, my daughter would go into the [child-protective] system," recalls Dorscher, who at the time was a third-year medical student.

Even Chino, whose mainstream credentials include an M.A. from Princeton, feels alienated at times from non-Indian city dwellers. He notes that Albuquerque officials ignored Indians' objections to a statue honoring Juan de Oñate, the 16th-century conqueror who established Spanish rule in what is now New Mexico. "Though native people protested and tried to show why this is not a good idea," Chino says, "the city went ahead and funded it."[5]

In the long run, Chino hopes a growing presence of Indian professionals — "we're not all silversmiths, or weavers" — will create more acceptance of urban Indians and more aid to combat high Indian dropout rates and other problems. "While people like having Indians in New Mexico and like visitors to get a feel for the last bastion of native culture," he says, "they're not doing that much for the urban Indian community, though we're paying taxes, too."

---

[1] Urban Indians were 64 percent of the population in 2000, according to the U.S. Census Bureau. For background, see, "We the People: American Indians and Alaska Natives in the United States," U.S. Census Bureau, 2000, p. 14, www.census.gov/prod/2006pubs/censr-28.pdf.

[2] "Looking Toward Home," *Native American Public Telecommunications*, 2003, www.visionmaker.org.

[3] Donald L. Fixico, *The Urban Indian Experience in America* (2000), pp. 9–11.

[4] *Ibid.*, pp. 22–25.

[5] Oñate is especially disliked at Acoma, Chino's birthplace, where the conqueror had the feet of some two-dozen Acoma men cut off in 1599 after Spanish soldiers were killed there. For background, see Wren Propp, "A Giant of Ambivalence," *Albuquerque Journal*, Jan. 25, 2004, p. A1; Brenda Norrell, "Pueblos Decry War Criminal," *Indian Country Today*, June 25, 2004.

Should tribes open casinos on newly acquired land?

YES — Ernest L. Stevens, Jr.
Chairman, National Indian Gaming Association

From statement before U.S. House Committee on Resources, Nov. 9, 2005

Indian gaming is the Native American success story. Where there were no jobs, now there are 553,000 jobs. Where our people had only an eighth-grade education on average, tribal governments are building schools and funding college scholarships. Where the United States and boarding schools sought to suppress our languages, tribal schools are now teaching their native language. Where our people suffer epidemic diabetes, heart disease and premature death, our tribes are building hospitals, health clinics and wellness centers.

Historically, the United States signed treaties guaranteeing Indian lands as permanent homes, and then a few years later, went to war to take our lands. This left our people to live in poverty, often on desolate lands, while others mined for gold or pumped oil from the lands that were taken from us.

Indian gaming is an exercise of our inherent right to self-government. Today, for over 60 percent of Indian tribes in the lower 48 states, Indian gaming offers new hope and a chance for a better life for our children.

Too many lands were taken from Indian tribes, leaving some tribes landless or with no useful lands. To take account of historical mistreatment, the Indian Gaming Regulatory Act (IGRA), provided several exceptions to the rule that Indian tribes should conduct Indian gaming on lands held on Oct. 17, 1988.

Accordingly, land is restored to an Indian tribe in trust status when the tribe is restored to federal recognition. For federally recognized tribes that did not have reservation land on the date IGRA was enacted, land is put into trust. Or, a tribe may apply to the secretary of the Interior. The secretary consults with state and local officials and nearby Indian tribes to determine whether an acquisition of land in trust for gaming would be in the tribe's "best interest" and "not detrimental to the surrounding community."

Now, legislation would require "newly recognized, restored, or landless tribes" to apply to have land taken in trust through a five-part process. Subjecting tribes to this new and cumbersome process discounts the fact that the United States mistreated these tribes by ignoring and neglecting them, taking all of their lands or allowing their lands to be stolen by others.

We believe that Congress should restore these tribes to a portion of their historical lands and that these lands should be held on the same basis as other Indian lands.

NO — State Rep. Fulton Sheen, R-Plainwell
Michigan House of Representatives

From statement to U.S. House Committee on Resources, April 5, 2006

The rampant proliferation of tribal gaming is running roughshod over states' rights and local control and is jeopardizing everything from my own neighborhood to — as the Jack Abramoff scandal has demonstrated — the very integrity of our federal political system.

In 1988, Congress passed the Indian Gaming Regulatory Act (IGRA) in an effort to control the development of Native American casinos and, in particular, to make sure that the states had a meaningful role in the development of any casinos within their borders. At that time, Native American gambling accounted for less than 1 percent of the nation's gambling industry, grossing approximately $100 million in revenue.

Since that time, the Native American casino business has exploded into an $18.5 billion industry that controls 25 percent of gaming industry revenue. Despite this unbridled growth, IGRA and the land-in-trust process remain basically unchanged.

When Congress originally enacted IGRA, the general rule was that casino gambling would not take place on newly acquired trust land. I believe Congress passed this general rule to prevent precisely what we see happening: a mad and largely unregulated land rush pushed by casino developers eager to cash in on a profitable revenue stream that is not burdened by the same tax rates or regulations that other businesses have to incur. "Reservation shopping" is an activity that must be stopped. And that is just one component of the full legislative overhaul that is needed.

IGRA and its associated land-in-trust process is broken, open to manipulation by special interests and in desperate need of immediate reform. It has unfairly and inappropriately fostered an industry that creates enormous wealth for a few select individuals and Las Vegas interests at the expense of taxpaying families, small businesses, manufacturing jobs and local governments.

Our research shows that while local and state governments receive some revenue-sharing percentages from tribal gaming, the dollars pale in comparison to the overall new costs to government and social-service agencies from increased infrastructure demands, traffic, bankruptcies, crime, divorce and general gambling-related ills.

I do not think this is what Congress had in mind. Somewhere along the way, the good intentions of Congress have been hijacked, and it is time for this body to reassert control over this process. It is imperative that Congress take swift and decisive steps today to get its arms around this issue before more jobs are lost and more families are put at risk.

Harvard Law School graduate Lance Morgan, a member of Nebraska's Winnebago Tribe, used seed money from his tribe's small casino to create several thriving businesses. He urges other tribes to use their casino profits to diversify. "Gaming is just a means to an end," he says.

her tribe's Spirit Mountain Casino could be hurt by the Warm Springs Tribes' proposed project or by the Cowlitz and Mohegan project.[57]

Pombo's bill would require the approval of new casinos by tribes that already have gambling houses up and running within 75 miles of a proposed new one.

The House Resources Committee heard another view from Indian Country at an April 5 hearing. Jacquie Davis-Van Huss, tribal secretary of the North Fork Rancheria of the Mono Indians of California, said Pombo's approval clause would doom her tribe's plans. "This provision is anti-competitive," she testified. "It effectively provides the power to veto another tribe's gaming project simply to protect market share."

Trust Settlement

McCain's committee is also grappling with efforts to settle a decade-old lawsuit that has exposed longstanding federal mismanagement of trust funds. In 1999, U.S. District Judge Royce Lamberth said evidence showed "fiscal and governmental irresponsibility in its purest form."[58]

The alternative to settlement, McCain and Dorgan told the Budget Committee, is for the case to drag on through the courts. Congressional resolution of the conflict could also spare the Interior Department further grief from Lamberth. In a February ruling, he said Interior's refusal to make payments owed to Indians was "an obscenity that harkens back to the darkest days of United States-Indian relations."[59]

Five months later, Lamberth suggested that Congress, not the courts, may be the proper setting for the conflict. "Interior's unremitting neglect and mismanagement of the Indian trust has left it in such a shambles that recovery may prove impossible."[60]

The court case has its roots in the 1887 policy of allotting land to Indians in an effort to break up reservations. Since then, the Interior Department has been responsible for managing payments made to landholders, which later included tribes, for mining and other natural-resource extraction on Indian-owned land.

But for decades, Indians weren't receiving what they were owed. On June 10, 1996, Elouise Cobell, an organizer of the Blackfeet National Bank, the first Indian-owned national bank on a reservation, sued the Interior Department charging that she and all other trust fee recipients had been cheated for decades out of money that Interior was responsible for managing. "Lands and resources — in many cases the only source of income for some of our nation's poorest and most vulnerable citizens — have been grossly mismanaged," Cobell told the Indian Affairs Committee on March 1.

The mismanagement is beyond dispute, said John Bickerman, who was appointed to broker a settlement. Essentially, Bickerman told the Senate Indian Affairs Committee on March 28, "Money was not collected; money was not properly deposited; and money was not properly disbursed."

As of 2005, Interior is responsible for trust payments involving 126,079 tracts of land owned by 223,245 individuals — or, 2.3 million "ownership interests" on some 12 million acres, Cason and Ross Swimmer, a special trustee, told the committee.

Bickerman said a settlement amount of $27.5 billion proposed by the Indian plaintiffs was "without foundation." But the Interior Department proposed a settlement

Ho-Chunk, Inc.

of $500 million based on "arbitrary and false assumptions," he added. Both sides agree that some $13 billion should have been paid to individual Indians over the life of the trust, but they disagree over how much was actually paid.

Supreme Court Ruling

Powerful repercussions are expected from the Supreme Court's latest decision in a centuries-long string of rulings involving competing claims to land by Indians and non-Indians.

In 2005, the high court said the Oneida Indian Nation of New York could not quit paying taxes on 10 parcels of land it owns north of Utica.[61]

After buying the parcels in 1997 and 1998, the tribe refused to pay property taxes, arguing that the land was former tribal property now restored to tribal ownership, and thereby tax-exempt.[62]

The court, in an opinion written by Ruth Bader Ginsburg, concluded that though the tribe used to own the land, the property right was too old to revive. "Rekindling the embers of sovereignty that long ago grew cold" is out of the question, Ginsburg wrote. She invoked the legal doctrine of "laches," in which a party who waits too long to assert his rights loses them.[63]

Lawyers on both sides of Indian law cases expect the case to affect lower-court rulings throughout the country. "The court has opened the cookie jar," Williams of the University of Arizona argues. "Does laches only apply to claims of sovereignty over reacquired land? If a decision favoring Indians is going to inconvenience too many white people, then laches applies — I swear that's what it says." Tribes litigating fishing rights, water rights and other assets are likely to suffer in court as a result, he argues.

In fact, only three months after the high court decision, the 2nd U.S. Circuit Court of Appeals in New York invoked laches in rejecting a claim by the Cayuga Tribe. Vickers of Upstate Citizens for Equality says that if the 2nd Circuit "thinks that laches forbids the Cayugas from making a claim because the Supreme Court said so, you're going to find other courts saying so."

In Washington, Alexandra Page, an attorney with the Indian Law Resource Center, agrees. "There are tribes in the West who have boundary disputes on their reservations; there are water-law cases where you've got people looking back at what happened years ago, so the Supreme Court decision could have significant practical impact. The danger is that those with an interest in limiting Indian rights will do everything they can to expand the decision and use it in other circumstances."

OUTLOOK

Who Is an Indian?

If advocates of Indian self-governance are correct, the number of tribes running their own affairs with minimal federal supervision will keep on growing. "The requests for workshops are coming in steadily," says Cyndi Holmes, self-governance coordinator of the Jamestown S'Klallam Tribe.

Others say that growth, now at a rate of about three tribes a year, may be nearing its upper limit. "When you look at the options for tribes to do self-governance, economics really drives whether they can," says LaPointe of the Rosebud Sioux, whose tribal government doesn't expect to adopt the model in the foreseeable future.

But the longstanding problems of rural and isolated reservations are not the only dimension of Indian life. People stereotypically viewed as tied to the land have become increasingly urban over the past several decades, and the view from Indian Country is that the trend will continue.

That doesn't mean reservations will empty out or lose their cultural importance. "Urban Indian is not a lifelong label," says Susan Lobo, an anthropologist at the University of Arizona. "Indian people, like everyone else, can move around. They're still American Indians."

For Indians, as for all other peoples, moving around leads to intermarriage. Matthew Snipp, a Stanford University sociologist who is half Cherokee and half Oklahoma Choctaw, notes that Indians have long married within and outside Indian society. But the consequences of intermarriage are different for Indians than for, say, Jews or Italians.

The Indian place in American society grows out of the government-to-government relationship between Washington and tribes. And most tribes define their members by what's known as the "blood quantum" — their degree of tribal ancestry.

"I look at it as you're kind of USDA-approved," says Podlasek of the American Indian Center. "Why is no other race measured that way?"

Podlasek is especially sensitive to the issue. His father was Polish-American, and his mother was Ojibway. His own wife is Indian, but from another tribe. "My kids can be on the tribal rolls, but their kids won't be able to enroll, unless they went back to my tribe or to their mother's tribe to marry — depending on what their partners' blood quantum is. In generations, you could say that, by government standards, there are no more native people."

Snipp traces the blood-quantum policy to a 1932 decision by the Indian Affairs Commission, which voted to make one-quarter descent the minimum standard. The commissioners were concerned, Snipp says, reading from the commission's report, that thousands of people "more white than Indian" were receiving "shares in tribal estates and other benefits." Tribes are no longer bound by that decision, but the requirement — originally inserted at BIA insistence — remains in many tribal constitutions.

On the Indian side, concern over collective survival is historically well-founded. Historian Elizabeth Shoemaker of the University of Connecticut at Storrs calculated that the Indian population of what is now the continental United States plummeted from a top estimate of 5.5 million in 1492 to a mere 237,000 in 1900. Indian life expectancy didn't begin to rise significantly until after 1940.[64]

Now, Indians are worrying about the survival of Indian civilization at a time when Indians' physical survival has never been more assured.

Even as these existential worries trouble some Indian leaders, the living conditions that most Indians endure also pose long-term concerns.

Conroy Chino, New Mexico's Labor secretary and a member of Acoma Pueblo, says continuation of the educational disaster in Indian Country is dooming young people to live on the margins. "I'm out there attracting companies to come to New Mexico, and these kids aren't going to qualify for those good jobs."

Nevertheless, below most non-Indians' radar screen, the Indian professional class is growing. "When I got my Ph.D. in 1973, I think I was the 15th in the country," says Beaulieu of Arizona State University's Center for Indian Education. "Now we have all kinds of Ph.D.s, teachers with certification, lawyers." And Beaulieu says he has seen the difference that Indian professionals make in his home state of Minnesota. "You're beginning to see an educated middle class in the reservation community,

and realizing that they're volunteering to perform lots of services."

In Albuquerque, the University of New Mexico's Jojola commutes to campus from Isleta Pueblo. Chairman of an advisory committee on Indians to the U.S. Census Bureau, Jojola shares concerns about use of "blood quantum" as the sole determinant of Indian identity. "A lot of people are saying that language, culture and residence should also be considered," he says.

That standard would implicitly recognize what many Indians call the single biggest reason that American Indians have outlasted the efforts of those who wanted to exterminate or to assimilate them. "In our spirituality we remain strong," says Bordeaux of the Rosebud Sioux. "That's our godsend and our lifeline."

NOTES

1. For background, see "The Administration of Indian Affairs," *Editorial Research Reports 1929* (Vol. II), at *CQ Researcher Plus Archive*, CQ Electronic Library, http://library.cqpress.com.

2. For background see Phil Two Eagle, "Rosebud Sioux Tribe, Demographics," March 25, 2003, www.rosebudsiouxtribe-nsn.gov/demographics.

3. "American Indian Population and Labor Force Report 2003," p. ii, Bureau of Indian Affairs, cited in John McCain, chairman, Senate Indian Affairs Committee, Byron L. Dorgan, vice chairman, letter to Senate Budget Committee, March 2, 2006, http://indian.senate.gov/public/_files/Budget5.pdf.

4. Jonathan B. Taylor and Joseph P. Kalt, "American Indians on Reservations: A Databook of Socioeconomic Change Between the 1990 and 2000 Censuses," Harvard Project on American Indian Economic Development, January 2005, pp. 8-13; www.ksg.harvard.edu/hpaied/pubs/pub_151.htm. These data exclude the Navajo Tribe, whose on-reservation population of about 175,000 is 12 times that of the next-largest tribe, thus distorting comparisons, Taylor and Kalt write.

5. *Ibid.*, p. 41.

6. McCain and Dorgan, *op. cit.*

7. "Injury Mortality Among American Indian and Alaska Native Youth, United States, 1989-1998,"

Morbidity and Mortality Weekly Report, Centers for Disease Control and Prevention, Aug. 1, 2003, www.cdc.gov/mmwr/preview/mmwrhtml/mm5230a2.htm#top.

8. Robert McSwain, deputy director, Indian Health Service, testimony before Senate Indian Affairs Committee, April 5, 2006.

9. *Ibid.*, p. xii.

10. Taylor and Kalt, *op. cit.*

11. *Ibid.*, pp. 28-30.

12. *Ibid.*, pp. 22-24.

13. The decision is *Cherokee Nation v. Georgia*, 30 U.S. 1 (1831), http://supreme.justia.com/us/30/1/case.html.

14. Alan Meister, "Indian Gaming industry Report," Analysis Group, 2006, p. 2. Publicly available data can be obtained at, "Indian Gaming Facts," www.indiangaming.org/library/indian-gaming-facts; "Gaming Revenues, 2000-2004," National Indian Gaming Commission, www.nigc.gov/TribalData/GamingRevenues20042000/tabid/549/Default.aspx.

15. The ruling is *California v. Cabazon Band of Mission Indians*, 480 U.S. 202 (1987), http://supreme.justia.com/us/480/202/case.html.

16. For background, see Susan Schmidt and James V. Grimaldi, "The Rise and Steep Fall of Jack Abramoff," *The Washington Post*, Dec. 29, 2005, p. A1. On March 29, Abramoff was sentenced in Miami to 70 months in prison after pleading to fraud, tax evasion and conspiracy to bribe public officials in charges growing out of a Florida business deal. He is cooperating with the Justice Department in its Washington-based political-corruption investigation. For background see Peter Katel, "Lobbying Boom," *CQ Researcher*, July 22, 2005, pp. 613-636.

17. Meister, *op. cit.*, pp. 27-28. For additional background, see John Cochran, "A Piece of the Action," *CQ Weekly*, May 9, 2005, p. 1208.

18. For background, see, "A Quiet Crisis: Federal Funding and Unmet Needs in Indian Country," U.S. Commission on Civil Rights, July, 2003, pp. 32, 113. www.usccr.gov/pubs/na0703/na0731.pdf.

19. Ryan Wilson, "State of Indian Education Address," Feb. 13, 2006, www.niea.org/history/SOIEAddress06.pdf.

20. For background see, Barbara Mantel, "No Child Left Behind," *CQ Researcher*, May 27, 2005, pp. 469-492.

21. McCain and Dorgan, *op. cit.*, pp. 14-15.

22. According to the Health and Human Services Department's budget proposal, recommended funding of $2 billion for the health centers would allow them to serve 150,000 Indian patients, among a total of 8.8 million patients. For background, see "Budget in Brief, Fiscal Year 2007," Department of Health and Human Services, p. 26, www.hhs.gov/budget/07budget/2007BudgetInBrief.pdf.

23. Peter Whoriskey, "A Tribe Takes a Grim Satisfaction in Abramoff's Fall," *The Washington Post*, Jan. 7, 2006, p. A1.

24. Meister, *op. cit.*, p. 15.

25. Whoriskey, *op. cit.*

26. For background see Fred Carstensen, *et al.*, "The Economic Impact of the Mashantucket Pequot Tribal National Operations on Connecticut," Connecticut Center for Economic Analysis, University of Connecticut, Nov. 28, 2000, pp. 1-3.

27. "Gambling Revenues 2004-2000," National Indian Gaming Commission, www.nigc.gov/TribalData/GamingRevenues20042000/tabid/549/Default.aspx.

28. Schmidt and Grimaldi, *op. cit.*

29. Alaina Potrikus, "2nd Land Hearing Packed," *The Post-Standard* (Syracuse, N.Y.), Jan. 12, 2006, p. B1.

30. For background see "Profile of the Navajo Nation," Navajo Nation Council, www.navajonationcouncil.org/profile.

31. Leslie Linthicum, "Navajos Cautious About Opening Casinos," *Albuquerque Journal*, Dec. 12, 2004, p. B1.

32. For background, see "Fourth Annual State of Indian Nations," Feb. 2, 2006, www.ncai.org/News_Archive.18.0.

33. For background see Theodore H. Haas, *The Indian and the Law* (1949), p. 2; thorpe.ou.edu/cohen/tribalgovtpam2pt1&2.htm#Tribal%20Power%20Today.

34. Except where otherwise noted, material in this section is drawn from Angie Debo, *A History of the Indians of the United States* (1970); see also, Mary H. Cooper, "Native Americans' Future," *CQ Researcher*, July 12, 1996, pp. 603-621.

35. W. Dale Mason, "Indian Gaming: Tribal Sovereignty and American Politics," 2000, p. 13.

36. *Cherokee Nation v. Georgia, op. cit.,* 30 U.S.1, http://supct.law.cornell.edu/supct/html/historics/USSC_CR_0030_0001_ZO.html.

37. Robert A. Williams Jr., *Like a Loaded Weapon: the Rehnquist Court, Indians Rights, and the Legal History of Racism in America* (2005), p. 63.

38. *Johnson v. M'Intosh*, 21 U.S. 543 (1823), www.Justia.us/us21543/case.html; *Worcester v. State of Ga.*, 31 U.S. 515 (1832), www.justia.us/us/31/515/case.html.

39. *Johnson v. M'Intosh, op. cit.*

40. *Worcester v. State of Ga., op. cit.*

41. Quoted in Debo, *op. cit.*, pp. 219-220.

42. Quoted in *ibid.*, p. 303.

43. The specified states were Wisconsin, Minnesota (except Red Lake), Nebraska, California and Oregon (except the land of several tribes at Warm Springs). For background, see Debo, *op. cit.*, pp. 304-311.

44. Cited in Debo, *op. cit.*, p. 344.

45. For background see Troy R. Johnson, *The Occupation of Alcatraz Island: Indian Self-Determination and the Rise of Indian Activism* (1996).

46. For background, see Mary H. Cooper, "Native Americans' Future," *CQ Researcher*, July 12, 1996, pp. 603-621.

47. For background see "History of the Tribal Self-Governance Initiative," Self-Governance Tribal Consortium, www.tribalselfgov.org/Red%20Book/SG_New_Partnership.asp.

48. Cochran, *op. cit.*

49. For background see Paul Shukovsky, "Lummi Leader's Had It With Drugs, Sick of Substance Abuse Ravaging the Tribe," *Seattle Post-Intelligencer*, March 16, 2002, p. A1.

50. "Fourth Annual State of Indian Nations," *op. cit.*

51. Many Alaskan villages have joined collective compacts, so the total number of these agreements is 91.

52. For background see Alexandra J. McClanahan, "Alaska Native Claims Settlement Act (ANCSA)," Cook Inlet Region Inc., http://litsite.alaska.edu/aktraditions/ancsa.html; "The Permanent Fund Dividend," Alaska Permanent Fund Corporation, 2005, www.apfc.org/alaska/dividendprgrm.cfm?s=4.

53. For background see Eric Henson and Jonathan B. Taylor, "Native America at the New Millennium," Harvard Project on American Indian Development, Native Nations Institute, First Nations Development Institute, 2002, pp. 14-16, www.ksg.harvard.edu/hpaied/pubs/pub_004.htm.

54. Michael Coleman, "Jemez Casino Proposal At Risk," *Albuquerque Journal*, March 10, 2006, p. A1; Jeff Jones, "AG Warns Against Off-Reservation Casino," *Albuquerque Journal*, June 18, 2005, p. A1.

55. For background see testimony, "Off-Reservation Indian Gaming," House Resources Committee, Nov. 9, 2005, http://resourcescommittee.house.gov/archives/109/full/110905.htm.

56. Jerry Reynolds, "Gaming regulatory act to lose its 'two-part test,' " *Indian Country Today*, March 8, 2006.

57. Testimony before House Resources Committee, Nov. 9, 2005.

58. Matt Kelley, "Government asks for secrecy on its lawyers' role in concealing document shredding," The Associated Press, Nov. 2, 2000.

59. "Memorandum and Order," Civil Action No. 96-1285 (RCL), Feb. 7, 2005, www.indiantrust.com/index.cfm?FuseAction=PDFTypes.Home&PDFType_id=1&IsRecent=1.

60. "Memorandum Opinion," Civil Action 96-1285 (RCL), July 12, 2005, www.indiantrust.com/index.cfm?FuseAction=PDFTypes.Home&PDFType_id=1&IsRecent=1.

61. Glenn Coin, "Supreme Court: Oneidas Too Late; Sherrill Declares Victory, Wants Taxes," *The Post-Standard* (Syracuse), March 30, 2005, p. A1.

62. *Ibid.*

63. *City of Sherrill, New York, v. Oneida Indian Nation of New York*, Supreme Court of the United States, 544 U.S._(2005), pp. 1-2, 6, 14, 21.

64. Elizabeth Shoemaker, *American Indian Population Recovery in the Twentieth Century* (1999), pp. 1-13.

BIBLIOGRAPHY

Books

Alexie, Sherman, *The Toughest Indian in the World*, Grove Press, 2000.
In a short-story collection, an author and screenwriter draws on his own background as a Spokane/Coeur d'Alene Indian to describe reservation and urban Indian life in loving but unsentimental detail.

Debo, Angie, *A History of the Indians of the United States*, *University of Oklahoma Press*, 1970.
A pioneering historian and champion of Indian rights provides one of the leading narrative histories of the first five centuries of Indian and non-Indian coexistence and conflict.

Deloria, Vine Jr., *Custer Died For Your Sins: An Indian Manifesto*, *University of Oklahoma Press*, 1988.
First published in 1969, this angry book gave many non-Indians a look at how the United States appeared through Indians' eyes and spurred many young Native Americans into political activism.

Mason, W. Dale, *Indian Gaming: Tribal Sovereignty and American Politics*, *University of Oklahoma Press*, 2000.
A University of New Mexico political scientist provides the essential background on the birth and early explosive growth of Indian-owned gambling operations.

Williams, Robert A., *Like a Loaded Weapon: The Rehnquist Court, Indians Rights, and the Legal History of Racism in America*, *University of Minnesota Press*, 2005.
A professor of law and American Indian Studies at the University of Arizona and tribal appeals court judge delivers a detailed and angry analysis of the history of U.S. court decisions affecting Indians.

Articles

Bartlett, Donald L., and James B. Steele, "Playing the Political Slots; How Indian Casino Interests Have Learned the Art of Buying Influence in Washington," *Time*, Dec. 23, 2002, p. 52.
In a prescient article that preceded the Jack Abramoff lobbying scandal, veteran investigative journalists examine the political effects of some tribes' newfound wealth.

Harden, Blaine, "Walking the Land with Pride Again; A Revolution in Indian Country Spawns Wealth and Optimism," *The Washington Post*, Sept. 19, 2004, p. A1.
Improved conditions in many sectors of Indian America have spawned a change in outlook, despite remaining hardships.

Morgan, Lance, "Ending the Curse of Trust Land," *Indian Country Today*, March 18, 2005, www.indiancountry.com/content.cfm?id=1096410559.
A lawyer and pioneering tribal entrepreneur lays out his vision of a revamped legal-political system in which Indians would own their tribal land outright, with federal supervision ended.

Robbins, Ted, "Tribal cultures, nutrition clash on fry bread," "All Things Considered," *National Public Radio*, Oct. 26, 2005, transcript available at www.npr.org/templates/story/story.php?storyId=4975889.
Indian health educators have tried to lower Native Americans' consumption of a beloved but medically disastrous treat.

Thompson, Ginger, "As a Sculpture Takes Shape in New Mexico, Opposition Takes Shape in the U.S.," *The New York Times*, Jan. 17, 2002, p. A12.
Indian outrage has clashed with Latino pride over a statue celebrating the ruthless Spanish conqueror of present-day New Mexico.

Wagner, Dennis, "Tribes Across Country Confront Horrors of Meth," *The Arizona Republic*, March 31, 2006, p. A1.
Methamphetamine use and manufacturing have become the scourge of Indian Country.

Reports and Studies

"Indian Health Service: Health Care Services Are Not Always Available to Native Americans," *Government Accountability Office*, August 2005.
Congress' investigative arm concludes that financial shortfalls combined with dismal reservation conditions, including scarce transportation, are stunting medical care for many American Indians.

"Strengthening the Circle: Interior Indian Affairs Highlights, 2001-2004," *Department of the Interior* **(undated).**
The Bush administration sums up its first term's accomplishments in Indian Country.

Cornell, Stephen, *et al.,* **"Seizing the Future: Why Some Native Nations Do and Others Don't,"** *Native Nations Institute, Udall Center for Studies in Public Policy, University of Arizona, Harvard Project on American Indian Economic Development, John F. Kennedy School of Government, Harvard University,* **2005.**
The authors argue that the key to development lies in a tribe's redefinition of itself from object of government attention to independent power.

For More Information

Committee on Indian Affairs, U.S. Senate, 838 Hart Office Building, Washington, DC 20510; (202) 224-2251; http://indian.senate.gov/public. A valuable source of information on developments affecting Indian Country.

Harvard Project on American Indian Economic Development, John F. Kennedy School of Government, 79 John F. Kennedy St., Cambridge, MA 02138; (617) 495-1480; www.ksg.harvard.edu/hpaied. Explores strategies for Indian advancement.

Indian Health Service, The Reyes Building, 801 Thompson Ave., Suite 400, Rockville, MD 20852; (301) 443-1083; www.ihs.gov. One of the most important federal agencies in Indian Country; provides a wide variety of medical and administrative information.

National Coalition Against Legalized Gambling, 100 Maryland Ave., N.E., Room 311, Washington, DC 20002; (800) 664-2680; www.ncalg.org. Provides anti-gambling material that touches on tribe-owned operations.

National Indian Education Association, 110 Maryland Ave., N.E., Suite 104, Washington, DC 20002; (202) 544-7290; www.niea.org/welcome. Primary organization and lobbying voice for Indian educators.

National Indian Gaming Association, 224 Second St., S.E., Washington, DC 20003; (202) 546-7711; www.indiangaming.org. Trade association and lobbying arm of the tribal casino industry.

Self-Governance Communication and Education Tribal Consortium, 1768 Iowa Business Center, Bellingham, WA 98229; (360) 752-2270; www.tribalselfgov.org. Organizational hub of Indian self-governance movement; provides a wide variety of news and data.

Upstate Citizens for Equality, P.O. Box 24, Union Springs, NY 13160; http://upstate-citizens.org. Opposes tribal land-claim litigation.

The fence blocks illegal border crossings near Ciudad Juarez (right side of fence) and El Paso, Texas. The planned 670-mile fence along the U.S.-Mexican border includes a mix of pedestrian and vehicle barriers. Supporters call the fence a vital first step in securing the U.S. border; opponents say it is a waste of money that threatens wildlife and forces undocumented immigrants to take more dangerous desert routes into the U.S.

From *CQ Researcher*,
September 19, 2008.

7

America's Border Fence

Will It Stem the Flow of Illegal Immigrants?

Reed Karaim

In the arid landscape near Naco, Ariz., America's new border fence already looks timeworn. A rusted brown the color of the distant Huachuca Mountains, spray-painted here and there with directions for maintenance crews, it snakes up and down rugged hills, disappearing into the distance. Besides its length, the most surprising thing about the fence is how unimpressive it appears. Our nation's highly publicized first line of defense against illegal entry, now being built up and down the U.S.-Mexican border, looks in some places like something that might guard a construction site.

But to Border Patrol Agent Mike Scioli the fence marks a new day. "It's a huge improvement," he said recently, while showing a reporter the 14-foot-high fencing near Naco and the accompanying new roads, lights and other improvements. "It makes a huge difference in our ability to do our job. It changes the game."

A few miles away, Bill Odle, a retired Marine whose house sits only a hundred yards or so from a stretch of fence erected last fall, views the fence quite differently. Odle has lived on the border since 1997 and is familiar with the evidence and even the sight of illegal immigrants stealing across. He regularly picks up the trash they leave behind and fixes livestock fences they've damaged. But it's the border fence itself that raises his ire.

"It's ugly. It doesn't work. It costs too much," Odle said, contemplating the steel-mesh barrier from his driveway. "It's the perfect government project."

The 670 miles of barriers the government plans to have in place along the U.S.-Mexican border by the end of the year does more than separate two nations: It sharply divides U.S. opinion about

Border Fence Affects Four States

The U.S.-Mexican border fence is slated to span 670 miles across four states — Texas, New Mexico, Arizona and California — by the end of 2008. More than half of the barricade will be designed to stop pedestrians, and the rest will block vehicular traffic. Nearly half of the fence will be located in Arizona.

Length of Border Fence
(in miles, by state)

Total Mileage: 370   300

California: 78, 12
New Mexico: 13, 101
Texas: 149, 0
Arizona: 130, 187

Anti-pedestrian fencing
Anti-vehicle fencing

Source: Bureau of Customs and Border Protection

how we should approach illegal immigration and border security. That division becomes evident even in what the barricade is called. The government and supporters of the structure call it a "fence"; opponents disparagingly call it a "wall."

A March 2008 Associated Press poll found Americans almost evenly split over the Secure Border Initiative, with 49 percent favoring the fence and 48 percent opposing it. But only 44 percent believe it will make a difference, while 55 percent do not.[1]

That sentiment may partly reflect skepticism about the effectiveness of the effort. The "fence" is really a melange of barriers — built along several different stretches of the border — designed to hamper immigrants crossing illegally on foot and in vehicles. Some of the earliest portions are solid metal, consisting of corrugated steel once used in Vietnam-era aircraft landing mats. More recent sections are often made of wire mesh reinforced by concrete-filled poles or taller concrete-filled poles planted six inches apart. The height ranges from 12 to 18 feet. Vehicle barriers are lower and often resemble the crossed metal defenses erected by the Germans on the beaches of Normandy during World War II.

The longest continuous segment is 22.5 miles, according to Barry Morrissey, a Bureau of Customs and Border Protection (CBP) spokesman. The United States had constructed 338 miles of fencing as of Aug. 13, 2008.[2] Homeland Security Secretary Michael Chertoff has said 670 miles will be in place by the end of 2008 — stretching across about one-third of the 1,950-mile-long U.S.-Mexican border. Roughly 370 miles of the fence will be designed to stop pedestrians and 300 miles of it to stop vehicular traffic.[3] At least 28 miles of the fence will consist of high-tech sensors and cameras that will create a "virtual fence" in parts of the Arizona desert. However, Homeland Security recently sent that project back to the drawing board after the initial effort proved neither high-tech nor particularly effective.[4]

But even as National Guard engineering units and private contractors work to meet Chertoff's ambitious completion timetable, everything about the fencing — from design to location to the very notion itself — has proven controversial. Some prefer a double layer of more formidable fencing along nearly the entire length of the border.[5] Others object to the wall on humanitarian grounds, believing it only forces illegal migrants to try crossing in more dangerous or remote desert areas or along the Pacific and Gulf of Mexico coasts. In both cases, they say, the death toll — which has been climbing for years — is likely to rise further.[6]

"The fence doesn't stop migration along the border, it simply displaces migration," says Nestor Rodriguez, co-director of the Center for Immigration Research at the University of Houston.

The fence has attracted a widely disparate group of opponents. A coalition of civic leaders from 19 Texas border communities has sued to halt construction, claiming the federal government has improperly seized land for the fence. The Defenders of Wildlife and the Sierra Club are trying to halt the fence because of concern over what it will to do wildlife and environmentally sensitive habitat.

"This thing might not be very effective at stopping people, but it's stopping wildlife in its tracks," says Matt Clark, the Southwestern representative of Defenders of Wildlife. (*See sidebar, p. 154, and "Current Situation," p. 156.*)

While critics attack from all directions, supporters concentrate their defense of the fence along two fronts: its important role in halting illegal immigration and bolstering border security at a time of increased threats from terrorists and drug smugglers.

"It sends a message we are finally getting serious about our borders," says Rosemary Jenks, director of governmental affairs for Numbers USA, a group that advocates reducing both illegal and legal immigration.

Few think a fence alone will stem the tide of illegal immigrants across the Southern border, estimated by the Pew Hispanic Center at about 850,000 people annually between 2000 to 2006.[7] But supporters believe properly placed fencing, backed by more surveillance equipment and an expanded Border Patrol (projected to reach 18,319 agents by the end of 2008) can largely halt the flow of illegal human traffic.[8]

The history of the economic, demographic and cultural forces that finally led America to fence off more than a third of its border with Mexico is nearly as long and serpentine as the fence itself. In fact, the fence can be viewed as the physical manifestation of two powerful political currents: heightened U.S. attention to national security after the terrorist attacks of Sept. 11, 2001, and a rapidly integrating global economy that has left many Americans vulnerable to competition from foreign workers, both here and abroad.

The forerunner of the fence building now under way began in a far more limited fashion near San Diego in the 1990s. Congress adopted the idea as a national approach to the border when it passed the Secure Fence Act of 2006, which called for double-layer fencing along specific sections of the border. The law was subsequently modified to give Chertoff wide discretion in where and when to install fencing.

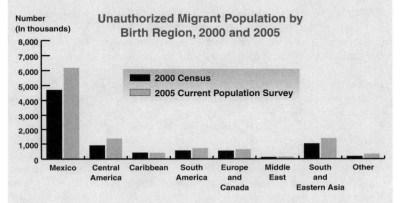

Undocumented Population Rose

The nation's unauthorized migrant population increased by more than 3 million between 2000 and 2005 — a jump of nearly 33 percent, according to the 2005 Current Population Survey. The increases were among immigrants from every region in the world except the Caribbean. Mexico led the way with more than 6.2 million immigrants in 2005, more than all other regions combined.

Unauthorized Migrant Population by Birth Region, 2000 and 2005

Number (In thousands)

■ 2000 Census
▨ 2005 Current Population Survey

Source: Jeffrey S. Passel, "The Size and Characteristics of the Unauthorized Migrant Population in the U.S.," Pew Hispanic Center, March 2006

Work is under way in all four states along the border — California, Arizona, New Mexico and Texas. But two states will get most of the barrier: Texas will get 149 miles of pedestrian fencing by the end of 2008, according to the CBP, while Arizona will end up with 317 miles (130 miles of pedestrian fencing and 187 miles of vehicular barriers), covering 84 percent of the state's 377-mile border with Mexico.

The CBP estimates that pedestrian fencing costs about $4 million to $5 million per mile, depending on the terrain, while vehicle fencing costs $2 million to $3 million. But the Government Accountability Office (GAO) says the final costs will be higher.[9] Although the long-term price tag is difficult to estimate, the U.S. Army Corps of Engineers predicts the 25-year cost could range from $16.4 million to $70 million per mile, depending on the amount of damage done to the fence by illegal border crossers and the elements.[10] Thus the quarter-century cost to taxpayers for 670 miles of fence could reach as high as $46.9 billion, or nearly seven times the size of the annual budget of the Environmental Protection Agency.

Does the Border Fence Deter Would-be Terrorists?

Some believe terrorists are more likely to enter legally.

The Border Patrol annually rounds up a smattering of illegal entrants from nearly every country in the world, including Middle Eastern countries considered hotbeds of terrorist activity. Indeed, the Internet buzzes with reports of Korans and prayer rugs found along the U.S.-Mexican border.

But so far, no one in the U.S. government has tied any terrorist act to anyone who crossed the border illegally. The 9/11 hijackers all entered the United States on temporary visas, arriving through regular ports of entry. Other foreign terrorists or would-be terrorists apprehended in the United States have followed similar routes into the country.

Many immigration and security experts believe the Southwestern border remains an unattractive option for terrorists plotting their path into the United States. "We have lots of data on terrorist travel. They like to travel the way everybody else travels. They like predictability. They like to know what they're going to face," says James Jay Carafano, a senior defense and counterterrorism analyst for the conservative Heritage Foundation. "That's not to say a terrorist can't try to use a smuggler to get across the border, but they're far more likely to use the legal ports of entry."

Carafano believes a border fence makes sense for immigration control in limited areas but that the cost and effort necessary to build nearly 700 miles of fence is diverting resources that could be better used to improve infrastructure and screening procedures at ports of entry. "Fixating myopically on the wall is just bad public policy," he says. "Looking for terrorists by standing watch on the border is stupid. It's looking for a needle in a haystack."

But Michael Cutler, a former Immigration and Naturalization Service special agent and now a fellow at the Center for Immigration Studies, thinks the danger of terrorists sneaking across the U.S.-Mexican border shouldn't be discounted. "If you're doing risk analysis, any place where somebody could reasonably expect to enter the United States is a place where you want to shore up security," he says. "And

when you look at how many people cross that border every week, and the evidence of Islamists they've found there, then I think you've got to consider it a threat."

Cutler is concerned that Hezbollah and other terrorist groups may have a presence in the "tri-border region" in South America — the area where Argentina, Paraguay and Brazil meet, which includes an immigrant population from the Middle East. He believes the region could provide a Latin American base for Islamic terrorists who could use the Southwestern border to enter the United States. However, the credibility of such a threat is debated in security circles.

Rey Koslowski, director of the Research Program on Border Control and Homeland Security at the University at Albany, in New York, says U.S. efforts to tighten security at ports of entry — particularly a new system intended to make it more difficult for those on the government's terrorist "watch list" to board airplanes bound for the United States — could make the Southwestern border more attractive to "established terrorists." If they did end up contemplating that route, then the border fence might help deter them, Koslowski adds, since it would make their capture — and identification — more likely.

Still, he believes al Qaeda and other terrorist organizations would probably choose a different strategy: sending individuals who don't have a criminal record and thus would be less likely to generate a "watch list" hit. "Such individuals would be in a better position to enter through ports of entry, at lower levels of risk," Koslowski says.

But Ira Mehlman, a spokesman for the Federation for American Immigration Reform (FAIR), which favors less immigration — legal or illegal — says the "general sense of chaos" along the U.S.-Mexican border created by the large number of illegal migrants makes it an attractive target for terrorists.

"The fact that it hasn't happened yet doesn't mean it isn't going to happen," he says. "The presumption ought to be that if we leave any areas unguarded, our enemies will take advantage of them."

Moreover, if Chertoff's goal is to be met, construction will have to average more than a mile a day for the rest of this year. Many supporters and opponents are skeptical, but government officials are confident they'll meet the self-imposed deadline.

"We are on track to complete this project by the end of the year," says Jason Ahern, CBP deputy commissioner, "and then we'll assess where we need to consider putting additional miles of fence."

Meanwhile, as the fence rises, here are some of the questions being asked:

Can a border fence stem the flow of illegal immigrants?

The border below San Diego was being overwhelmed by illegal immigrants in the early 1990s when the U.S. government began building pedestrian fencing in the area. The initial fence did not have the impact supporters had hoped, but when it was backed up with a second and third layer of fencing, along with surveillance equipment and an increased Border Patrol presence, the results were dramatic.

At the Border Patrol's Imperial Beach and Chula Vista stations, which had been ground zero of the illegal migrant explosion, apprehensions plummeted from 294,740 people in 1994 to 19,035 in 2004.[11] (*See graph, p. 148.*) Apprehensions are considered one of the best measures of the overall number of migrants trying to cross illegally, and supporters of the fence cite these statistics, along with similar ones in the Border Patrol's Yuma, Ariz., sector.

"A fence is a clearly proven technology that, when deployed properly and used in conjunction with other enforcement strategies, clearly works," says Dan Stein, president of the Federation for American Immigration Reform (FAIR), which supports even stronger measures to stop illegal immigrants. "The Yuma fence is triple fencing, and nobody gets over it. You can build a fence that's essentially impenetrable."

Skeptics point out the increases in personnel and equipment may have had as much to do with the success as the fencing. But Deputy Commissioner Ahern says the fence was always intended to work in conjunction with other resources. "We have what we call the three legs of our stool: tactical infrastructure [the fence], technology and personnel," he says. "It's that combination that's effective."

Agent Scioli believes the fence will deter some migrants and smugglers, but he says it makes his job easier even if illegal migrants make it over the top, because catching border crossers is an equation involving time and distance. Agents are trained in "cutting sign" — following the footprints and other pieces of evidence migrants leave as they pass through the desert. If agents are late to the trail, their chances of success drop dramatically.

"Yes, I've heard what people say. 'Show me a 14-foot fence, and I'll show you someone with a 15-foot ladder,'" Scioli says. "But even if they do get over this fence, it takes time. Now, when I'm on their trail, maybe it only takes minutes to catch them, rather than hours."

The Border Patrol's comprehensive approach sounds impregnable. But to Odle, the ex-Marine who lives along the border, the reality is different. Almost all of the new fencing around Naco, as along most of the border, is a single layer that largely stands alone — a one-legged stool he sees doing little good. The remote-controlled cameras and motion sensors that have been in the desert for some time don't seem particularly effective, he says, and his stretch of the border is still only lightly patrolled. "The Border Patrol, their presence has lessened considerably since they built the wall," he says.

Odle does credit the vehicle barriers with stopping smugglers from driving across the desert the way they once did. But the rest fails to impress him. If anything, he believes illegal migration may have increased slightly in the area since the fence went up. "I've seen women and kids as well as guys climbing over it," he says. "I could put up with the damn thing if it worked, but it doesn't."

Criticism of the fence grows even stronger when its effectiveness is measured on a national scale. "It can slow down or deter migration in some areas that are very popular for border crossing, as it did in San Diego, but that doesn't mean it stops migration along the whole border," notes Rodriguez of the Center for Immigration Research.

National statistics back this assertion. The Border Patrol made 1.2 million apprehensions in 1992 along the entire Southern border and about the same number in 2004, suggesting that increased enforcement in the San Diego sector and other areas made little difference in the overall number of immigrants trying to cross illegally.[12]

The more recent squeeze in Yuma also has been met with increased activity elsewhere. Fence supporters counter that's because much of the new fencing is still

A vehicle barrier lines the south side of Interstate 8 at the Imperial Dunes, just north of the U.S.-Mexican border near Winterhaven, Calif. Some 300 miles of border fencing are designed to stop vehicles.

inadequate. They note that before the Secure Fence Act of 2006 was revised last year, it required double layers of fencing along specified parts of the border. "They took out that language," says NumbersUSA's Jenks, "which would have made a big difference."

Fencing and stepped-up patrolling are effective, say fence supporters, when the government is willing to commit sufficient resources to the task. "We don't argue that the fence alone is the solution," says Jenks. "The fence is one part of the solution. But there are vast amounts of land . . . where fencing is feasible and where it would do a tremendous amount of good. We need more fence along the border."

But stepped-up border enforcement alone is bound to fail, says Wayne Cornelius, director of the Center for Comparative Immigration Studies at the University of California, San Diego, which favors lower U.S. immigration levels. "A continuous barrier is impossible because of the terrain; even the government recognizes that," he says. Besides, he continues, a continuous border would only create added pressure at the maritime borders, which is already happening. "We've had about two dozen boats washing up or interdicted in San Diego County since last August. And those were only the boats that were found."

Moreover, Canada does not require Mexicans to produce a visa when entering Canada.[13] For a continuous Southern-border fence to work, says Rey Koslowski,

director of the Research Program on Border Control and Homeland Security at the University at Albany in New York, "The U.S. would have to build another fence on the much longer 5,525-mile U.S.-Canadian border or persuade the Canadian government to end free travel from Mexico."

But even that wouldn't completely solve the problem, because 45 percent of all illegal immigrants entered the United States legally but did not leave in accordance with the terms of their visas, according to the Pew Hispanic Center.[14]

The most recent study by the Center for Comparative Immigration Studies found that 91 percent of the villagers interviewed in San Miguel Tlacotepec, a city in Southern Mexico, believed it is "very dangerous" to cross the border without documents. And nearly a quarter of the interviewees knew someone who had died trying to get into the United States.

Yet such awareness didn't make a difference.[15] "Being aware of the physical risks, being aware of someone who actually died in the crossing, knowing about the Border Patrol's increased efforts to interdict people — none of these things discouraged them," says Cornelius.

In fact, Cornelius says, the interviews revealed that increased border enforcement has ended up discouraging illegal immigrants from returning home because of the danger now involved.

"The undocumented population has tripled during the period of concentrated border enforcement," he says. "We were at 3.9 million in 1995, and now we're over 12 million. To me, that's the most significant evidence that this approach has failed."

Would blocking all illegal immigrants hurt or benefit the U.S. economy?

Both supporters and critics of the border fence agree that as long as U.S. businesses continue to hire illegal immigrants for higher salaries than they can earn at home, workers will continue to risk their lives to enter the United States.

But a divide quickly reemerges in discussions about the impact those immigrants have on the U.S. economy. Some see illegal immigrants doing work that U.S. citizens spurn, filling a host of hard, low-paying, but essential service and trade jobs that allow the rest of us to live comfortably. That view was encapsulated in the 2004 movie "A Day Without a Mexican," a comedy that shows the California economy grinding to a halt when the state's immigrants mysteriously disappear. (The film attracted almost no attention in the United States but was a hit and won several awards in Mexico.)

Others, however, believe illegal immigrants are driving down U.S. wages, draining state and federal treasuries by collecting government payments to which they're not entitled and contributing to rising health-care and law-enforcement costs. These sentiments are strong enough to have transformed CNN anchor Lou Dobbs — who proudly waves the anti-illegals flag — into a populist hero to millions of Americans. Dobbs ties the illegal immigrant surge to larger economic forces, chiefly globalization, and the "sellout" by U.S. policymakers to powerful business interests, which are all part of what he calls a "war on the middle class." Dobbs particularly claims that the North American Free Trade Agreement (NAFTA), which lowered trade barriers between the United States, Mexico and Canada, has sent U.S. jobs to Mexico and lowered American wages.

Kathleen Staudt, a political science professor at the University of Texas, El Paso, says immigrants make a convenient target during tough economic times. But she believes overheated rhetoric has kept many Americans from seeing the role illegal immigrants play in the economy. "If we were forced to do without this labor, I think the economies of many border towns would begin to die," she says, "and the price of many mainstream goods and services would go up dramatically."

However, Stein, at the Federation for American Immigration Reform, says the laws of supply and demand would bring clear rewards to U.S. workers. "If the people here illegally had to leave, wages would rise, and employers would suddenly have incentives to provide things like health care again," he says. "It would be a great windfall for the rising tide of less-skilled workers in the country, who would have a chance to reestablish their role in the middle class."

But would Americans really take jobs in meatpacking plants, janitorial services, yard care, food service, construction and other trades now dependent on illegal labor? Staudt doubts it. "I think the chamber of commerce in many cities would begin to lobby very hard for relaxed [immigration] rules allowing more people in to fill these jobs," she says.

That has already happened in Arizona, which passed a law last year imposing stiff, new sanctions against employers who hire illegal immigrants. Since then, the hospitality and agriculture industries have reported worker shortages.[16] Some business groups have sued to overturn the law, and some of the original sponsors are even calling for reducing penalties on businesses that violate the law.[17]

Opponents of illegal immigrants say businesses' economic distress is just the result of the economic system adjusting to new realities. "It's not a crime for employers to have to raise wages to get people to do certain jobs," says Stein.

But Gordon Hanson, an economist at the University of California, San Diego, who has studied the impact of immigrant labor on the workforce, says, "The United States has done a pretty good job of educating itself out of low-end work. Only 8 percent of the U.S. labor force lacks a high-school education. You don't graduate from high school to go to work in a poultry plant."

America also has one of the highest incarceration rates in the developed world, Hanson adds, further reducing the low-end labor supply.[18] If illegal immigrant labor is cut off, "you're not going to fill all those jobs with native workers," he says. "In industries where work can be exported, you're going to lose jobs."

Wages will rise in the service industries where jobs can't be exported — such as maids, dishwashers, gardeners, waiters and 7-11 clerks — but so will the costs to consumers, Hanson says. While illegal labor hurts low-skilled U.S. workers, it helps higher-skilled workers by providing them with cheaper goods and services, such as home and child care. "In families with two educated workers," Hanson says, "it allows whoever would be the stay-at-home spouse to stay in the workforce at lower cost."

The question of how much illegal immigration costs taxpayers also is hotly disputed. The Federation for American Immigration Reform estimates that in just three areas — schooling, medical care and incarceration — illegal immigrants cost local governments $36 billion a year.[19] Other estimates are lower, but most economists agree illegal workers are a net cost to local governments, especially in communities with large illegal populations.

The costs are incurred, in part, because illegal workers are less likely to have health insurance than U.S. citizens and because their children are more likely to need special

Arrests Shift After Border Improvements

After the U.S.-Mexican border was strengthened in San Diego in the early 1990s, arrests of illegal immigrants in the region — which includes Imperial Beach and Chula Vista — dropped dramatically. At the same time, however, apprehensions in Tucson skyrocketed to 491,000 in 2004. Because of the shift of illegal immigration to Tucson, the overall number of illegal migrants — 630,000 — apprehended in the San Diego and Tucson border regions remained about the same in 2004 as in 1992.

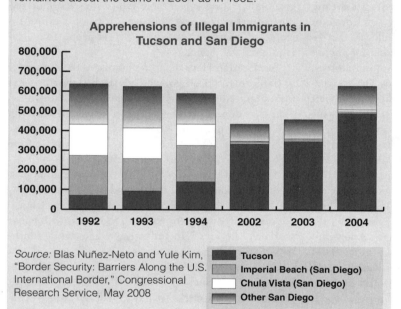

Apprehensions of Illegal Immigrants in Tucson and San Diego

Source: Blas Nuñez-Neto and Yule Kim, "Border Security: Barriers Along the U.S. International Border," Congressional Research Service, May 2008

Legend:
- Tucson
- Imperial Beach (San Diego)
- Chula Vista (San Diego)
- Other San Diego

immigrants pay more into the federal treasury in taxes and Social Security taxes — since they usually have fake Social Security cards — than they receive in benefits. A study by Standard & Poor's, a credit-rating and research firm, noted the U.S. Social Security Administration places $6 billion to $7 billion in a special account for unclaimed benefits annually — an amount analysts believe mostly comes from illegal immigrants who pay Social Security taxes but cannot legally claim Social Security or Medicare benefits.[23]

When all the economic pluses and minuses are taken into account, Hanson says, "You get something that's close to a wash. There are distributional shifts within the economy — some employers and consumers who will be hurt, some workers and state and local governments that will benefit. But our best sense is that the net economic impact isn't huge."

Does the fence harm U.S relations with Mexico and other countries?

About a century ago, Mexican strongman Porfirio Diaz surveyed his nation's already long and troubled relationship with its neighbor to the north and observed, "Poor Mexico, so far from God and so close to the United States."

Much has changed in both countries since Diaz's dictatorial reign. Mexico's politics are far more vibrant, peaceful and democratic. America no longer interferes as bluntly as it once did in its neighbor's affairs, and NAFTA ties the two countries together economically with Canada.

But in more than one sense, Diaz's melancholy observation feels as timeless as ever. "Mexico has never been the actor that drives the relationship," says Tony Payan, an assistant professor of international relations and foreign policy at the University of Texas, El Paso. "It's always been unilateral action by the United States, and then Mexico is left to react."

assistance in school. With average incomes significantly below the national average, most studies indicate illegal workers pay less in state and local taxes than they collect in services.[20]

However, the impact appears limited. The Congressional Budget Office estimates that public spending for illegal immigrants generally accounts for less than 5 percent of state and local spending on law enforcement, education and health care.[21]

The impact on the federal budget is less clear. A Center for Immigration Studies report put the net cost to the federal government for services provided to illegal immigrants — such as Medicare, food stamps, subsidized school lunches, federal aid to public schools and increased costs to the federal court and prison systems — at about $10 billion annually.[22] But other analysts say illegal

Mexico made its unhappiness with the border fence clear from the beginning. In 2005, then-Mexican President Vicente Fox called the idea "shameful" when it began gaining traction in Congress. "It's not possible that in the 21st century we're building walls between two nations that are neighbors, between two nations that are brothers," Fox said at an event for migrants in his home state of Guanajuato.[24]

Mexican officials already were distressed by the rising death toll among illegal migrants, which began after U.S. border enforcement activities were stepped up in the mid-1990s. By sealing off the areas of heaviest illegal crossing, the Border Patrol drove border crossers into more remote and deadly terrain, particularly the Arizona desert.

Illegal immigrant deaths along the border have climbed steadily, according to the U.S. Border Patrol and Mexican consular offices, rising to 472 in 2005, compared to an average of about 200 in the early 1990s.[25] The totals are widely believed to be undercounted, however, because they reflect only bodies recovered by the U.S. and Mexican border patrols. In the rugged expanses of the Southwestern desert, many are likely never found.[26]

Mexico has officially complained about the expansion of fencing. "We certainly recognize that they would prefer not to have a fence between our two countries," says Customs Deputy Commissioner Ahern. "But they acknowledge that we need to secure our country, that it's our responsibility and our sovereign right."

The two countries continue to cooperate along the border, with Mexican officials working with their U.S. counterparts on the International Boundary Waters Commission to ensure that fence construction along the Rio Grande River does not impede water flow or drainage. The two countries also continue to work together to battle violent crime and drug smuggling along the border. "We've had a great relationship with them there," Ahern says.

His comments dovetail with public statements offered by President George W. Bush and Mexican President Felipe Calderon during the North American Leaders Summit in Louisiana last April. Both said the relationship between the two countries remains strong and collaborative, despite Mexican concerns over U.S. immigration policy.[27]

But some observers are skeptical. "I think there's almost total disillusionment right now among Mexico's ruling elites," says Ed Williams, a retired political science professor from the University of Arizona. "They've recognized that this is the reality and that haranguing isn't going to change anything, but there's enormous disappointment."

The disappointment is particularly profound, he adds, because Mexico initially believed Bush's time as governor of Texas and his close relationship with Fox signaled an era of closer ties between the two countries once he was elected.

Some fence proponents acknowledge the bond between the United States and its Southern neighbor has been damaged, but they blame Mexican attitudes. "U.S.-Mexico relations are headed for hard times because they insist on respect, but what we want is a mutuality of respect," says FAIR's Stein, "and for some reason they seem to think it's a one-way street. They want a special policy for Mexican nationals."

Americans often take their neighbors — both to the north and south — for granted, even though the Mexicans and Canadians are more important to the U.S. economy than is generally realized. Canada and Mexico are America's top two trading partners as well as, respectively, the largest and third-largest suppliers of crude oil to the United States.

Williams believes dismay over U.S. border policies extends to Canada, too. "The policy elites in both Canada and Mexico are increasingly exasperated with the United States, and therefore a whole host of relationships are jeopardized by a feeling of ill will that characterizes the current situation," he says.

At the end of the Louisiana summit, Bush and Calderon, along with Canadian Prime Minister Stephen Harper, issued a joint communiqué pledging, among other things, to coordinate long-term infrastructure plans along their borders and to "deepen cooperation on the development and application of technology to make our borders both smarter and more secure."[28]

Although the communiqué painted a picture of three partners marching together into the future, Payan at the University of Texas believes the real picture is different. "What you have is an elephant in the middle with two mice sleeping on either side. Canada and Mexico are always going to have to move in such a way that the elephant doesn't squash them," he says. "But the image is a little more complicated than it first seems because the elephant is afraid of mice. And, right now, the U.S. is viewing its neighbors as potential threats."

BACKGROUND

Building Walls

Nations have been building walls or fences along their borders more or less since nations began.

Consider Hadrian's Wall, built in the second century AD along Roman Britain's frontier. The wall was made of turf and stone instead of steel and concrete, but its commonly accepted purpose sounds familiar: to keep the poorer "barbarians" of ancient Scotland from invading the civilized and more prosperous empire.

The Great Wall of China built over several hundred years was a similar, even more expansive effort. Much like the U.S. border fence, it wasn't one structure but a series of walls totaling about 4,000 miles along strategic stretches of the border, designed to keep out the Mongols and other nomadic tribes from Central Asia.

More recently, the Berlin Wall appears to have been built for the opposite reason: to keep residents inside communist East Berlin. However, as former University of Arizona political science Professor Williams points out, East Germany claimed the wall was designed to protect East Berliners from the "alien influences of capitalism."

American history is replete with its own examples of walls, notes Williams, who edited an upcoming special issue of the university's *Journal of the Southwest* entitled, "Fences."[29] The Jamestown settlers and the Pilgrims built palisades — fences of pointed wooden stakes — around their small communities to keep out the Native Americans and wild animals.

Through the centuries, barriers have been erected along borders "to protect 'us' from 'them,' " Williams says. "The same things are always said about the people on the other side of the fence — they're barbarians or savages or an alien force."

The question is whether they work. After all, the Berlin Wall fell, the Romans eventually abandoned Hadrian's Wall, the Manchu finally conquered China and even the massive fortifications of the French Maginot Line, built between the world wars, were rendered ineffectual when the Germans simply went around them — an approach critics of the U.S. border fence say illegal migrants already are taking.

But such unequivocal dismissal, popular with critics of the U.S. fence, ignores the long periods during which certain fortifications proved effective. In his book about the Roman Empire, historian Derek Williams says after Hadrian's Wall was built, "Decades passed without emergency." The Berlin Wall fulfilled its function for more than 40 years, he adds, and the Great Wall of China for much longer.[30]

"It would be very comfortable for my liberal consciousness to say these things don't work," says Williams. "But that's not the case. They do work."

But even if walls and fences work, says Maribel Alvarez, a folklorist at the University of Arizona's Southwest Center, the U.S. barriers still create a simplistic view of the border. "It's a view locked in an either/or perspective," she says. "The border is treated as an untamed badlands. It assumes that in this badlands someone with higher knowledge needs to impose an order that is lacking."

Some of the rhetoric from Washington concerning the Southwestern border certainly fits Alvarez's description. Rep. Tom Tancredo, R-Colo., a strong opponent of illegal immigration, summed up the view in an article for *Human Events* magazine, titled "Mexico's Lawless Border Poses Huge Test for Washington."[31]

But history may provide an unexpected lesson, says Mary Beard, a classics scholar at Cambridge University in England. The Romans' view of frontiers was more complex than those who cite Hadrian's Wall as a forerunner of the U.S. fence would have it. The Romans did not see borders as clear divisions, Beard wrote in *The Times of London*, but rather as "frontier zones" where the empire gradually disappeared into foreign territory.[32]

Contacted by e-mail, Beard notes that one connection between Hadrian's Wall and "Bush's wall" is that both are partly symbolic in intent. Critics of the U.S. fence have argued it is primarily a political gesture intended to appease anti-immigration sentiment. Similarly, Hadrian's Wall was clearly designed as much to impress the Romans behind it as those on the other side, notes historian Williams.[33]

But Beard's description of the fluid nature of Roman borders, which were largely unfortified, describes the U.S.-Mexican border for much of its history.

Bracero Program

Until the 1990s, most of America's border with Mexico was largely invisible. The Rio Grande provided a natural border in Texas. In the deserts of Arizona, New Mexico and inland California, an occasional stone obelisk or a

CHRONOLOGY

Pre-1950s *The U.S. restricts immigration based on race and national origin.*

1882 Chinese Exclusion Act suspends immigration of Chinese laborers for 10 years — the first law in U.S. history to restrict immigration based on nationality.

1921 A rising tide of isolationism prompts the Emergency Quota Act, which limits annual immigration from any one country to 3 percent of existing U.S. population from that country. It sharply reduces immigration from Eastern and Southern Europe.

1924 Congress enacts the Johnson-Reed Act, further tightening quotas for Europeans and excluding immigrants from Asia altogether. . . . The Labor Appropriation Act establishes the Border Patrol, with 450 officers responsible for guarding both borders with Mexico and Canada.

1942 Facing labor shortages during World War II, the United States initiates the Bracero Program, which imports Mexican workers for farm labor and other jobs.

1950s-1960s *America begins to deal with large-scale illegal immigration.*

1954 Facing growing illegal immigration from Mexico, the government initiates "Operation Wetback." Authorities sweep through Mexican-American barrios, and thousands of immigrants are returned to Mexico.

1964 Congress ends Bracero Program.

1965 Immigration and Nationality Act of 1965 abolishes immigration quotas based on national origin but gives preference to relatives of U.S. citizens, permanent resident aliens, scientists and workers with skills in short supply.

1970s-1990s *America offers amnesty to illegal aliens and begins to consider a border fence.*

1986 President Ronald Reagan signs Immigration Reform and Control Act of 1986 giving amnesty, under certain circumstances, to illegal immigrants who have been in the United States since 1982.

1990 The Border Patrol begins erecting a 14-mile fence to deter illegal entries and drug smuggling near San Diego.

1993 A Sandia Laboratory study says a three-tiered fence along parts of the border would discourage or delay border crossers and channel others into areas the Border Patrol could more easily control.

1994 Operation Gatekeeper increases the number of Border Patrol agents near San Diego.

1996 Congress passes the Illegal Immigration Reform and Immigrant Responsibility Act, which gives the government broad authority to construct barriers along the border and authorizes a secondary layer of fencing in San Diego.

2000-Present *Congress sweeps aside legal restrictions and directs the administration to build fencing.*

2002 Congress allows Immigration and Naturalization Service (INS) funds to be used to buy land for border fencing and to construct the fences.

2003 The INS is abolished, and its functions are transferred to the newly created Department of Homeland Security.

2005 Congress passes the REAL ID Act authorizing the Homeland Security secretary to waive all legal requirements in order to expedite the construction of border barriers.

2006 Border Patrol apprehends 1.2 million illegal migrants along U.S.-Mexican border. . . . Secure Fence Act authorizes construction of a total of 850 miles of fencing along the border.

2007 Consolidated Appropriations Act gives the secretary of Homeland Security greater freedom to decide how much fencing to build along the Southern border and where and when to build it.

2008 Homeland Security Secretary Michael Chertoff reaffirms 670 miles of fencing will be in place by the end of the year.

Border-town Life Becomes More Difficult

Cross-border exchanges may be in jeopardy.

On clear afternoons, Tony Zavaleta sometimes stands on the porch of his home outside Brownsville, Texas, gazes across the Rio Grande and watches one of his cousins working his farm on the other side of the river.

"I've got all kinds of family across the river," says Zavaleta, vice president for external affairs at the University of Texas, Brownsville. "In fact, at 3 o'clock today I'm going to the bridge to pick up a cousin, and we're going to Starbucks to have coffee."

The U.S.-Mexico border looks like a clearly drawn line on a map, but up close the delineation is blurred. The two nations are connected by history, economy and, most significantly, a border population with extensive and often deep roots in both nations.

"We have family business, family dealings, intermarriages, social events on both sides of the border, and that is the case for literally hundreds of thousands of people," says Zavaleta, whose family traces its heritage on both sides of the river back to the 18th century.

These strong relationships have created what many describe as a unique border culture — one they believe is threatened by the new border fence. "We're one community, and we've historically operated as one community," says Chad Foster, mayor of Eagle Pass, Texas, about his city's relationship with Piedras Negras, immediately across the border. "We have individuals who live in Piedras Negras but pay tuition so their kids can go to school in Eagle Pass. We have people who live in Eagle Pass and run plants in Piedras Negras. We've always gone back and forth."

The border between the United States and Mexico remains the busiest in the world, with more than 220 million legal crossings a year. But casual interchange between the two nations, the lifeblood of border culture, has been growing more difficult in recent years, particularly with the beefed-up border security since the Sept. 11 terrorist attacks. Now, many fear a further stifling of the relationship.

"You wouldn't think it would affect everyday, legal crossing," says Zavaleta, "but it has already done that."

Foster says the fence sends a signal: "You're not welcome."

When combined with longer waits at the legal ports of entry due to tighter security and inadequate staffing, they say, the fence creates the sense that crossing the border is best avoided — a feeling that could have serious economic implications for border communities.

Tom Fullerton, an economics professor at the University of Texas, El Paso, has studied the financial relationships between cities located across from each other on the border. In El Paso, he attributes an average of $900 million annually in retail sales to Mexicans crossing the border to shop in the United States.

few strings of barbed wire were often all that signified the transition from one nation to another.

Sparsely populated and little traveled for most of its history, the Sonoran Desert in Arizona and New Mexico seemed to need little more than that. The United States did not even establish the Border Patrol until 1924, when it hired 450 agents. In some border towns, the two countries were no more than a street apart.

People from both countries moved back and forth with little government attention until World War I created a significant shortage of labor in the United States. Congress created a program allowing the temporary admission of nearly 77,000 Mexican "guest workers." The legislation began a pattern of "recruitment in times of labor shortage followed by massive restrictions and deportations," writes Katherine Fennelly, a member of the League of Women Voters' Immigration Study Committee.[34]

When joblessness rose during the Depression in the late 1920s, thousands of Mexican immigrants were deported. But when World War II left the United States with another labor shortage, the country reversed course and created the Bracero Program — Spanish for "laborer" — to bring in Mexicans, mainly to work in agriculture and on the railroads.

The program brought in more than 400,000 workers a year during its 22-year history.[35] But illegal immigration

Business also travels the other way. "I don't know the number of people I've met who routinely go to the dentist in Nogales [Mexico] because it's cheaper," says folklorist Maribel Alvarez, an assistant professor at the University of Arizona's Southwest Center.

Betty Perez, who operates a small ranch a couple of miles from the border near Roma, Texas, says many ranchers go across the border "to buy a good bull or sell a good bull or a horse. There's a lot of horse business down there."

Fullerton says it's difficult to estimate the economic consequences of the border fence, but with trade liberalization, Mexicans now can find almost anything they might buy in the United States at home. "It's possible they'll say, 'We'll just stay here and not worry about going into this country where we're not really welcome,' " he notes.

That would be just fine for many fence supporters, including those living along the border. Ed Williams, a retired University of Arizona political science professor, points out the existence of a border culture does not imply universal mutual appreciation. "While many borderlands people have been sympathetic to their brethren across the line, others have always been suspicious," he says. "There are people in the border communities who say, 'Build that damn wall.' "

Patricia Escobar, left, of Los Angeles, visits through the fence with her daughter Rosa, who lives in Tijuana, Mexico.

But opinion does not necessarily divide strictly along racial lines. "You can find a lot of people with Spanish surnames who will say, 'Keep those Mexicans out,' " says Zavaleta. "And a lot of Anglos feel that's bad for business."

But Alvarez, who edits the center's "Borderlore" blog, notes the breadth of the population whose lives have been lived on both sides of the border. "You have the ranchers. You have the Native Americans. You have the bohemians that come to the desert to write and paint," she says. "You have a very grounded working class that crosses back and forth almost daily."

Border towns even have shared fire departments and other civic institutions. "Laredo and Nuevo Laredo, prior to the 1980s, was essentially like a spot on the Canadian border or between two Scandinavian countries," says Fullerton. "That's how closely intertwined they were. They even shared a minor league baseball team."

But when people living on the border reminisce about earlier, less-security-conscious days, they most often cite the personal exchanges that built a sense of a shared land. "I remember when my grandfather decided he wanted to give me a horse as a gift," says Zavaleta. "He just had a ranch hand ride it across the river. I was 14, and I remember standing on the riverbank and watching that horse come across from my grandfather. You wouldn't do that today."

grew at the same time, particularly in the late-1940s and '50s as Mexicans came north to take advantage of America's postwar economic boom. In reaction, Immigration and Naturalization Commissioner Gen. Joseph Swing initiated "Operation Wetback" in 1954, with federal and local authorities sweeping through Mexican-American barrios looking for illegal immigrants. Thousands were deported.[36]

When the Bracero Program ended in 1965, legal entry became more difficult for Mexican farmworkers. But work in U.S. fields and orchards remained plentiful, so many Mexicans began to travel into the United States seasonally without legal documents.

'Tortilla Curtain' Rises

As illegal immigration grew, certain border cities became the favorites for border crossers. By 1978 the problem had become bad enough in El Paso, Texas, that the government erected 12.5 miles of chain-link fence — the "Tortilla Curtain" — along the border. The Border Patrol has expanded infrastructure along the border since, with lighting and more agents on the ground, but the fence remains in place, says Tom Fullerton, an economist at the University of Texas, El Paso. "You can't go more than 30 feet without finding spots where either holes have been cut or repaired," he says.

Critics Say Fence Disrupts Wildlife

Border fence is 'stopping wildlife in their tracks.'

The San Pedro River in Arizona — one of only two major rivers that flow north from Mexico into the United States — provides habitat to an astonishing variety of birds and small mammals. It also serves as a watering hole for deer, mountain lions, bobcats and possibly even jaguars as they range across the arid Sonoran Desert in Mexico and the United States.

The U.S. government recognized the importance of the San Pedro and the surrounding landscape when it created the San Pedro Riparian National Conservation Area — a 57,000-acre refuge for the animals and plants of the region's fragile desert riparian ecosystem, one of the few remaining in the American Southwest.

But today the area is also home to a section of the new border fence, slicing the desert landscape in half as it stretches east from the riverbank. Much of America's new fencing is being built on environmentally sensitive public lands, which critics fear could have disastrous consequences, especially for wildlife.

"You can call this a fence, but to animals it's an impenetrable barrier," says Matt Clark, Southwest representative for Defenders of Wildlife, an organization dedicated to the preservation of wild animals and native plants. "It's between 14 and 18 feet tall; it goes on for miles; it's not something they can jump over or circumvent. It might not be very effective at stopping people, but it's stopping wildlife in their tracks."

Border barriers are being built or are planned for portions of Arizona's Cabeza Prieta National Wildlife Refuge and the Organ Pipe National Monument. In Texas, new fencing is planned near Big Bend National Park and on the Lower Rio Grande Valley National Wildlife Refuge. In California, the federal government is even filling in a canyon, Smuggler's Gulch, with more than 2 million cubic yards of dirt so it can run a fence across it.

Environmental concerns differ by area, but in general the fence divides the breeding and hunting territories of many species, separating animals from food, water or potential mates, according to wildlife advocates. Sometimes the animals have already had their habitat reduced or disrupted by development, and their populations cannot afford to be split in two.

"With isolation comes a lack of genetic exchange — a lack of genetic diversity, which makes these populations less fit to survive," says Clark.

The impact of new border barriers could be particularly acute in the Lower Rio Grande Valley refuge, according to Scott Nicol, a member of the Texas-based No Border Wall citizens' coalition.

The 90,000-acre refuge consists of 115 separate plots along the Rio Grande River, designed so wildlife can use the river as a corridor to move from one plot to another. But they would be blocked if the government builds new barriers

Some see the Tortilla Curtain as the primitive forerunner of today's fence. Before the U.S. government embraced the idea, however, policy would once again veer in a different direction. During the Reagan administration, "Congress allowed people who had been in the United States illegally for a number of years to apply for citizenship," says Staudt, of the University of Texas, El Paso.[37]

But the Immigration Reform and Control Act of 1986 — what some call the "amnesty bill" — did little to stem the flow of illegal immigrants, so anti-immigration sentiment continued to grow in Border States. The Clinton administration reacted with operations "Hold the Line" in El Paso in 1993 and "Gatekeeper" in San Diego the following year. Border Patrol agents and

technology were concentrated in these areas, and fencing was either built or reinforced.[38]

Both operations dramatically reduced illegal immigration in the targeted locations, although illegal crossings did not fall significantly overall. But Congress seemed to judge the approach a success. A series of bills then expanded the Border Patrol, increased money for security measures and, after 9/11, gave the new Homeland Security secretary the authority to ignore laws that might slow fence construction.

Although President Bush pushed for a comprehensive immigration-reform package that would have included guest-worker and limited-amnesty programs, Congress remained focused on enforcement. The Secure Fence Act

along the river levees as now planned, Nicol says. "You put a wall there that keeps animals from getting to the river," he explains, "and the individual plots are not large enough to support them."

Among the rare or endangered species threatened by the fence, says Clark, are jaguars, Sonoran pronghorn antelopes, ocelots, jaguarundi, flat-tailed horned lizards and the Cactus Ferruginous Pygmy Owl. A bird may seem an unlikely victim of a 14-foot fence, but wildlife advocates say the fence threatens the habitat for many birds. "You have barriers that can catch debris and sediment, create artificial dams, shifting water flows, impacting the vegetation," Clark says. "All of this does damage."

Department of Homeland Security Secretary Michael Chertoff has used authority granted by Congress to waive compliance with environmental laws in several areas as he proceeds with the fence, a move that upset local officials and led to a lawsuit by Defenders of Wildlife and the Sierra Club. (*See "Current Situation," p. 156.*)

Customs and Border Protection officials say they are still working to protect native plants and animals. "Even though the secretary used his waiver authority to keep moving this process forward, we're not disregarding environmental considerations at all," says Jason Ahern, Customs and Border Protection deputy commissioner. "We're

The ability of the jaguar and other animals to range between Mexico's Sonoran Desert and the Southwestern United States may be blocked by the border fence.

looking at what we need to do to mitigate risk to the environment. Our goal is to make sure we leave the environment in better condition than we found it."

The border fence is being built in several different styles. Some of the most recent, described as "bollard" fencing, is made of round, concrete-filled poles spaced six inches apart in a staggered pattern. In Arizona, bollard fencing is being constructed in the washes, which run with water in the rainy season. Border Patrol officials believe bollard fences are more eco-friendly, because water can flow around the poles and because small animals and reptiles can pass between them. But environmentalists doubt this will be enough to prevent erosion and habitat damage.

The fence's advocates point out that illegal immigrants are already damaging fragile desert lands. "When hundreds of thousands of people are hiking through pristine ecosystems, setting fires, dumping trash and abandoning vehicles, building a fence that can drastically reduce that destruction is a good thing," says Rosemary Jenks, governmental affairs director for NumbersUSA, which supports reducing both legal and illegal immigration.

But trails and trash can be cleaned up, Clark says. "The wall has significantly more impact," he adds, "because of its magnitude and because it's permanent."

of 2006 mandated double-layer security fencing along significant parts of the border. That requirement was later modified to give Secretary Chertoff more latitude, but the message was clear: America was building a border fence.

Facing the Fence

In 2006, more than 90 percent of the 1.2 million illegal migrants apprehended by the Border Patrol were caught along the border with Mexico — nearly 88 percent of them Mexicans. But U.S. authorities also picked up nearly 150,000 people from 197 other countries. (*See graphic, p. 143.*)

The largest number, after Mexicans, came from Central America. In 2006, there were 46,329 illegal immigrants

from El Salvador, 33,365 from Honduras and 25,135 from Guatemala. Many were twice illegal, having first entered Mexico without papers and then the United States.

The arduous and dangerous effort to enter the United States is a sign of border-crossers' determination. In *Enrique's Journey, The Story of a Boy's Dangerous Odyssey to Reunite with His Mother*, journalist Sonia Nazario traced the 1,600-mile cross-Mexico migration made by thousands of Central American children following their mothers to the United States. Many were turned back repeatedly but refused to quit. Enrique, the boy she followed, finally succeeded in making it all the way into the United States on his eighth attempt.[39]

Nazario's book also illuminated a little-noticed trend: An increasing number of women have been making the journey alone, followed by an increasing number of their children. Nazario estimates about 48,000 children a year enter the United States illegally. Mexican railroad workers report children as young as 7 trying to cross their country alone traveling to the United States.[40]

With little or no knowledge of what they are facing, these illegal migrants seem unlikely to give up their journey because of the fence. The Center for Comparative Immigration Studies found similar determination. Briseida, a 24-year-old woman from Oaxaca, recounted being caught six times in a single month before making it into the United States.[41]

Research also indicates that most illegal immigrants had jobs in Mexico but thought the United States offered greater opportunity. "Ninety-three percent of undocumented Mexican immigrants left jobs in Mexico," says Robert Pastor, director of the Center for North American Studies at American University in Washington. "They're not coming to the United States for jobs. They're coming because they can earn six to 10 times more."

CURRENT SITUATION

Local Blowback

America's new border fence may represent a national commitment by the Bush administration, but it's also a matter of local politics. For many who live on the border, the fence isn't being built along some abstract line, it's going through their community, or neighborhood or even backyard.

In the Rio Grande Valley in Texas, in particular, local concerns are sparking a battle that pits communities in President Bush's home state against his administration. The Texas Border Coalition, made up of mayors, economists and business leaders from 19 municipalities and 10 counties in the valley, in May sued the Department of Homeland Security, alleging it is ignoring due process and abusing private property rights in its rush to put up the fence.

"We didn't want to file this lawsuit, but we felt we had no choice," says coalition Chairman Chad Foster, the mayor of Eagle Pass, a border town of about 22,000. "We just want the government to follow the law."

The anti-fence blowback has been triggered by tactics adopted by the Department of Homeland Security to speed construction. When some property owners refused to give the Corps of Engineers permission to survey for the fence on their land, the Corps sent landowners letters threatening a lawsuit and raising the possibility of seizing their property through eminent domain.[42]

Landowners responded by challenging the government in court. "I don't think they counted on anybody standing up to them," says Eloisa Tamez, who lives on a three-acre plot along the Rio Grande that has been in her family for nearly 250 years. "We're not big, powerful people here. We respect our government. But we're not just going to lay down and let the bulldozer roll over us."

In January, a federal judge ordered 10 property owners along the border — including Tamez — to permit the surveying, but only after denying the government the right to take the land without a hearing.[43] The government's actions against individual landowners, however, are not the only ones provoking indignation.

In Eagle Pass, for example, the City Council met with Homeland Security in 2006 over the department's plans to leave a city park and golf course south of the proposed barrier. "They were going to cede our municipal golf course and a city park to Mexico," he says. "We had a resolution to oppose it, and they said they would allow us to delete the fence. But they came back a year later and sued us. We can't trust them."

Because the fence is being located on or outside of flood control levees, in several Texas locations the preliminary site is inside the U.S. border. In the small town of Granjeno, for instance, about 35 landowners found they might end up on the wrong side of the border fence.[44] In Brownsville, the proposed fence will run through the University of Texas campus, leaving some facilities south of the barrier. Campus officials say they are working with Homeland Security to resolve the situation.[45]

Homeland Security said it places a high priority on feedback from local residents. Since May 2007, the agency has held 100 meetings with local officials and 600 with individual property holders along the Southwest border.[46]

CBP Deputy Commissioner Ahern says siting the fence has been a painstaking process. "We looked at enforcement data," he says. "We looked at geography. We looked at landscape. We looked at alternatives. This was a thoughtful

AT ISSUE

Is a border fence the answer to the illegal immigration problem?

YES   Rep. Duncan Hunter, R-Calif.

Written for *CQ Researcher*, September 2008

A battle is being waged for control of the U.S.-Mexican border between the U.S. Border Patrol and criminals who utilize this largely unprotected land corridor to carry narcotics and other contraband into the United States. Citizens on both sides of the border, whose safety is seriously threatened by escalating violence, are caught in the middle.

Last year drug-war violence claimed least 2,500 lives in Mexico, and numerous U.S. citizens reportedly have been kidnapped and murdered by Mexican criminals linked to the drug trade. The local sheriff in the Laredo, Texas, border community compared conditions to a "war zone" and said his officers appear "outgunned" by the drug cartels.

Border Patrol agents are also at risk, because they often are the first to encounter these criminals. Since 2001, assaults against agents have nearly tripled, from 335 to 987 in 2007. Four agents and three other border security officials were killed last year, and two agents have been killed so far in 2008.

The land corridor between Tijuana, Mexico, and San Diego, Calif., has been overrun by smugglers and criminals. It wasn't until my legislation mandating construction of the San Diego border fence that the armed gangs and drug cartels lost control of this smuggling route. Since then, conditions on both sides of the border have improved.

Since construction of the border fence began in 1996, San Diego County has become one of the most secure and responsibly enforced border regions. Smuggling of people and narcotics in this area has decreased by more than 90 percent, and violent crime has declined by 53 percent.

Such a high level of effectiveness illustrates that fencing — supported with the right mix of personnel and technology — is an excellent border enforcement tool.

The Department of Homeland Security (DHS) is accelerating fence construction in several areas along the border, rightly utilizing its broad waiver authority to expedite completion in locations subject to unnecessary delays and litigation. DHS expects to meet its goal of 670 miles of new fence by the end of this year, but overall a lot of work remains in creating an enforceable border.

Moving forward, it would be wise to extend this infrastructure to other smuggling routes and heavily transited areas of the U.S.-Mexican border. Not only is it the quickest and easiest way to control the border, but it's also proven to be the most effective.

NO   Rep. Silvestre Reyes, D-Texas
Former El Paso Sector Chief,
U.S. Border Patrol

Written for *CQ Researcher*, September 2008

I am acutely aware of the challenges of securing our borders, having served for more than 26 years with the U.S. Border Patrol. I have not only patrolled the U.S.-Mexican border but also supervised thousands of hard-working, dedicated Border Patrol agents and initiated a successful deterrence strategy called Operation Hold the Line. I also supported fencing certain strategic areas to augment enforcement. I strongly feel, however, that erecting nearly 700 miles of fencing on our Southern border is wasteful, irresponsible and unnecessary, and I voted against the Secure Fence Act.

Hundreds of miles of fencing will do little to curb the flow of undocumented immigrants and could even increase demand for human smuggling. It will only provide a false sense of security for supporters of a hard line on immigration reform. With construction expected to exceed $1.2 billion and lifetime maintenance of up to $50 billion, the exorbitant cost of this border fence would be better invested in additional Border Patrol agents, equipment and technology.

As the only member of Congress with a background in border control, I have worked to educate my colleagues that existing policies and the border fence will do little to honor our legacy as a nation of immigrants and will threaten our nation's security. I have worked with the Department of Homeland Security (DHS), hosted many leaders at annual border conferences and have emphasized that border communities must be consulted in fencing decisions.

Unfortunately, DHS Secretary Michael Chertoff recently made the troubling announcement that he intends to waive more than 30 federal environmental laws to expedite construction of the fence. This approach continues DHS's continued disregard for border communities and undermines decades-old policies that have preserved many of our region's most valuable environmental assets, cultural sites and endangered wildlife.

After Secretary Chertoff's decision, I joined 13 of my colleagues in submitting an *amicus* brief to the U.S. Supreme Court, asking the justices to hear an appeal challenging the secretary's waiver authority.

Our nation needs comprehensive immigration reform with three main components: strengthened border security; an earned path to legalization along with tough, strictly enforced sanctions against employers who hire undocumented immigrants; and a guest worker program. Hundreds of miles of border fencing is not the answer.

and detailed analysis by both local and national Border Patrol leadership."

But some Texans believe politics plays a role. The Texas Border Coalition lawsuit asserts that Homeland Security is violating the Fifth Amendment's Equal Protection provision by "giving certain politically well-connected property owners a pass on having the border fence built on their property," according to the coalition's Web site.

Specifically, the coalition refers to media reports the fence is being built through city and county-owned land while bypassing land owned by Dallas billionaire Ray Hunt, a close friend of President Bush who recently donated $35 million to help build the George W. Bush Memorial Library at Southern Methodist University.

The coalition's allegations brought a sharp response from Ahern. "I reject the idea out of hand," he says. "Our analysis of where to locate the fence was based on the operational and tactical requirements in a given area, not on who owned the land or whether they were influential individuals."

Legal Challenges

Even as construction continues, however, Chertoff faces another challenge that has the active support of several members of Congress. Last spring Chertoff used the broad authority granted him by Congress to waive more than 30 environmental-, historical- and cultural-protection laws and regulations to enable fence construction to proceed.

"Criminal activity at the border does not stop for endless debate or protracted litigation," Chertoff said in the statement announcing the decision.[47]

The Sierra Club and Defenders of Wildlife already had sued Homeland Security over an earlier, more limited waiver allowing fence construction to continue in the San Pedro Riparian National Conservation Area in Arizona, home to many rare and endangered species of plants and animals. The environmental groups feared that the fence would block migratory patterns and access to water and habitat for several endangered animals and that construction could harm certain rare plants. (*See sidebar, p. 154.*)

A federal judge ruled against their claim, which challenged the constitutionality of the secretary's waiver authority. The fence is now up in the conservation area. After Chertoff expanded his use of waivers to cover construction of the entire fence, the environmental groups

asked the Supreme Court to hear their case; in July the court refused to take the case.

Before the court's decision, however, the lawsuit had been joined by 14 Democratic House members, including Mississippi Rep. Bennie Thompson, chairman of the Homeland Security Committee, and several lawmakers from border districts. Their friend-of-the-court briefs argued that Congress overstepped its constitutional bounds when it allowed the secretary to ignore laws.

On the other side, Rep. Peter King, R-N.Y., ranking minority member of the House Homeland Security Committee, backed Chertoff's use of waivers. "He's acting entirely within the law, and any attempts to impede the fence's progress through frivolous litigation will only serve to lessen the security of our country," King said.[48]

Noah Kahn, an expert on federal lands at Defenders of Wildlife, says Chertoff's decision to bypass laws intended to provide a thorough review of environmental and cultural impacts makes it impossible to determine whether there were other options, such as better use of surveillance technology in environmentally sensitive areas. "One of the basic problems is the complete lack of transparency in the way the Department of Homeland Security has carried out this entire process," says Kahn. "They've completely ignored not just communities and other public partners but even other federal agencies in their deliberations."

Cindy Alvarez, who oversaw an environmental assessment of the fence in the San Pedro conservation area, defends the agencies building the fence. "Once the waiver came into play, it took it out of our hands," says Alvarez, assistant field manager of the U.S. Bureau of Land Management's Tucson office. "But that said, the Border Patrol and the Corps of Engineers are continuing to try to be good land stewards while meeting the nature of their missions. They are continuing to work with us."

Homeland Security's critics are skeptical. "The only reason you waive the laws is because you're planning on breaking them," says Scott Nicol, a member of the No Border Wall Coalition, a citizens' group in Texas.

The Tohono O'odham Indian Nation, which straddles the border, has also been concerned about Chertoff's use of waivers. The tribe has so far agreed to allow vehicle barriers, but not pedestrian fencing, on tribal lands but is weighing its options concerning the waivers, says Pete Delgado, a tribal spokesman. With more fencing planned for environmentally and culturally sensitive areas in both Texas and California, further legal challenges to Chertoff's authority and the fence's route seem almost inevitable.

Straddling the Fence

Nothing illustrates the complicated political fault lines that run through the border fence debate better than the way the presidential nominees have straddled the issue.

By voting for the Secure Fence Act of 2006, both GOP candidate Sen. John McCain, R-Ariz., and Democratic contender Sen. Barack Obama, D-Ill., voted to authorize the dramatic expansion of border fencing now under way. A year later, presumably busy campaigning, they missed the key votes on the Consolidated Appropriations Act, which gave the Homeland Security secretary more latitude on when and where to locate the fencing.

Since then, McCain and Obama have sent conflicting messages about what they think now that the fence is actually being built. Obama's campaign Web site calls for preserving "the integrity of our borders" and says the candidate supports "additional personnel, infrastructure and technology on the border and at our ports of entry."

But when a question about the border fence came up during a primary campaign debate with Sen. Hillary Rodham Clinton, D-N.Y., in Texas, Obama struck a skeptical note about the fence now being built. After Clinton criticized the Bush administration's approach and called for more personnel and better technology instead of a physical barrier, Obama agreed. "There may be areas where it makes sense to have some fencing," Obama said. "But for the most part, having [the] border patrolled, surveillance, deploying effective technology, that's going to be the better approach."[49]

McCain's campaign Web site calls for "securing the border through physical and virtual barriers." But the word "fence" can't be found on McCain's Border Security Web page. In interviews, however, McCain has said he supports building a border fence in areas where it's necessary, while he believes technology can more effectively do the job in others.

Anti-immigrant groups have criticized McCain for supporting President Bush's failed comprehensive immigration reform package, which included a path for many illegal immigrants in the United States to gain citizenship. The sensitive nature of the issue in Republican circles was clear at a town meeting in Texas, when McCain was asked how he would balance individual property rights with border security.

"This meeting is adjourned," McCain joked, before saying he would look into the issue.[50] Earlier, he said he hoped federal and local officials could work together to resolve their differences over the fence.

Neither candidate's campaign press office responded to requests for further information clarifying their candidate's position.

OUTLOOK

Demographic Solution

What goes up can always come down — even if it is 670 miles long and built by the U.S. government of double-layered steel. And many critics of the border fence say that's just what will happen.

"The United States eventually will have to tear down the wall they built because the forces of globalization drawing us together are much stronger than the forces trying to tear us apart," says Payan, at the University of Texas, El Paso.

Others, particularly those concerned with the fence's impact on the environment, place their faith in technology. "Ultimately, we're going to be a lot less dependent on physical infrastructure," says Bob Barnes, a senior policy adviser at the Nature Conservancy. "Particularly in open country, virtual fencing — sensors, cameras and other surveillance technology — is a lot more mobile and can react to changing patterns of immigration more easily."

Customs and Border Protection Deputy Commissioner Ahern says the agency will continue using sensors, remote-controlled cameras, unmanned surveillance planes and other high-tech hardware. But he believes there will always be a need for fencing.

"No matter how good our technology is, in some of these areas of the border [illegal crossings are] going to be too easy," he says. "So, especially in urban environments, we're always going to need that tactical infrastructure, some kind of physical barrier."

But illegal immigration is about more than the border. It also reflects economic and political conditions in two countries, and that's where some experts believe the most significant changes will be seen, Payan suggests. Rodriguez, at the University of Houston's Center for Immigration

Research, notes that the rapidly growing U.S. Latino population is likely to make anti-immigrant political posturing less acceptable in the future.[51]

At the same, he says, a little noticed demographic trend within Mexico could also shift the equation. The Mexican birthrate has been falling for decades and, Rodriguez says, is expected to decline to the replacement rate by 2050.[52] Then, the country will no longer have the surplus labor it now exports to the United States. "If you think there are too many Mexicans," he says, "the problem eventually is that there's not going to be enough Mexicans to do the dirty work."

Other analysts believe further economic integration between the two nations will regularize the labor flow. "I can't help but think that in the future there will be a time when the North American continent will resemble the European Union," says Staudt, at the University of Texas.

Meanwhile, what happens to the border fence? Back in Eagle Pass, Texas, Mayor Foster had the most cynical view. Given the estimates of up to $47 billion to maintain it over the next 25 years, he believes it will simply be abandoned. "I think it gets turned into barbecue grills on both sides of the border," Foster says.

NOTES

1. The Associated Press poll, conducted by Ipsos Public Affairs, of 1,103 adults on March 3-5, 2008. The poll had a margin of error of +/- 3.1 percent.

2. From the Department of Homeland Security Web site, border fence update page, www.dhs.gov/xprevprot/programs/border-fence-southwest.shtm.

3. Testimony of Department of Homeland Security Secretary Michael Chertoff before the House Subcommittee on Homeland Security Appropriations, April 10, 2008. The text is available at www.dhs.gov/xnews/testimony/testimony_1207933887848.shtm.

4. See Arthur H. Rotstein, "US scraps $20 million prototype of virtual fence," The Associated Press, April 23, 2008, www.cbsnews.com/stories/2008/04/23/tech/main4037342.shtml?source=related_story. Also see Brady McCombs, "'Virtual fence' work is halted," *Arizona Daily Star*, Aug. 19, 2008, www.azstarnet.com/metro/253456.

5. See the Border Fence Project Web site, www.borderfenceproject.com/index.shtml, one of several citizens' groups that propose fencing the entire border.

6. See the Humane Borders Web site, www.humaneborders.org/, one of several organizations that object to the fence.

7. Estimates of the annual number of illegal border crossers and the total illegal population vary widely. But an analysis of Census Bureau data by the Pew Hispanic Center in March 2006 seems to provide the best, impartial estimate of annual illegal migration. The report, "The Size and Characteristics of the Unauthorized Migrant Population in the United States," also estimated the total illegal immigrant population in the United States at 11.5 million to 12 million.

8. "Homeland Security — DHS Has Taken Actions to Strengthen Border Security Programs and Operations, but Challenges Remain," testimony before the Subcommittee on Homeland Security, House Committee on Appropriations, Government Accountability Office, pp. 16, March 6, 2008.

9. "Secure Border Initiative, The Importance of Applying Lessons Learned to Future Projects," Government Accountability Office, testimony before House Homeland Security Subcommittees on Management, Investigations and Oversight and Border, Maritime and Global Counterterrorism, Feb. 27, 2008, p. 2.

10. Blas Nuñez-Neto and Yule Kim, "Border Security: Barriers along the U.S. International Border, Congressional Research Service, May 13, 2008, p. 33.

11. *Ibid.*, pp. 14-15.

12. *Ibid.*, p. 2.

13. Ray Koslowski, "Immigration Reforms and Border Security Technologies," Social Science Research Council, July 31, 2006. For background, see Mary H. Cooper, "Rethinking NAFTA," *CQ Researcher*, June 7, 1996, pp. 481-504, and David Masci, "U.S.-Mexico Relations," *CQ Researcher*, Nov. 9, 2001, pp. 921-944.

14. "Modes of Entry for the Unauthorized Migrant Population," Pew Hispanic Center, Fact Sheet, May 22, 2006, http://pewhispanic.org/files/factsheets/19.pdf.

15. Wayne Cornelius, *et al.*, "Controlling Unauthorized Immigration from Mexico: The Failure of Prevention through Deterrence and the Need for Comprehensive Reform," Center for Comprehensive Immigration Studies, June 10, 2008, pp. 2-3.

16. Becky Pallack and Mariana Alvarado Avalos, "Employer-sanctions law starting to have the intended effect," *Arizona Daily Star*, Dec. 23, 2007.

17. Howard Fischer, "Some who voted for sanctions seek rollback," *Arizona Daily Star*, Jan. 18, 2008, p. A1.

18. For background, see Peter Katel, "Prison Reform," *CQ Researcher*, April 6, 2007, pp. 289-312, and Charles S. Clark, "Prison Overcrowding," *CQ Researcher*, Feb. 4, 1994, pp. 97-120.

19. "The Cost to Local Taxpayers for Illegal or 'Guest' Workers," Federation for American Immigration Reform, 2006, www.fairus.org.

20. Melissa Merrell, "The Impact of Unauthorized Immigrants on the Budgets of State and Local Governments," Congressional Budget Office, December 2007, p. 3.

21. *Ibid.*, p. 3.

22. Steven Camarota, "The High Cost of Cheap Labor, Illegal Immigration and the Federal Budget," Center for Immigration Studies, August 2004, p. 1.

23. Robert McNatt and Frank Benassi, Standard & Poor's Ratings Direct, as cited in *Business Week*, "Econ 101 on Illegal Immigrants," April 2006, www .businessweek.com/investor/content/apr2006/ pi20060407_072803.htm.

24. "US border fence plan 'shameful' " BBC News (online), Dec. 19, 2995, http://news.bbc.co.uk/ 2/hi/americas/4541606.stm.

25. Nuñez-Neto and Kim, *op. cit.*, p. 40.

26. Wayne Cornelius, "Death at the Border: The Efficacy and 'Unintended' Consequences of U.S. Immigration Control Policy 1993-2000," Center for Comparative Immigration Studies, *Working Paper 27*, December 2001.

27. "President Bush Meets with President Calderon of Mexico," White House press release, April 21, 2008, www.whitehouse.gov/news/releases/2008/04/ 20080421-6.html.

28. "Joint Statement by President Bush, President Calderon, Prime Minister Harper," White House press release, April 22, 2008, www.whitehouse.gov/ news/releases/2008/04/20080422-4.html.

29. *Journal of the Southwest*, Vol. 50, No. 3, University of Arizona, autumn 2008.

30. Derek Williams, *The Reach of Rome, A History of the Roman Imperial Frontier, 1st-5th Centuries AD* (1996), p. 111.

31. Tom Tancredo, "Mexico's Lawless Border Poses Huge Test for Washington," *Human Events*, Feb. 6, 2006.

32. Mary Beard, "Don't Blame Hadrian for Bush's Wall," *Times Literary Supplement*, April 30, 2007, http:// timesonline.typepad.com/dons_life/2007/04/dont_ blame_hadr.html.

33. Williams, *op. cit.*, p. 108.

34. Katherine Fennelly, "U.S. Immigration, A Historical Perspective," *The National Voter*, February 2007, p. 5.

35. Andorra Bruno, "Immigration: Policy Considerations Related to Guest Worker Programs," Congressional Research Service, June 27, 2007, p. 1.

36. PBS Interactive Border Timeline, www.pbs.org/ kpbs/theborder/history/timeline/20.html.

37. For background, see Hank Donnelly, "Immigration," *Editorial Research Reports*, June 13, 1986, available at *CQ Researcher Plus Archive*. Also see Kenneth Jost, "Cracking Down on Immigration," *CQ Researcher*, Feb. 3, 1995, pp. 97-120; and Alan Greenblatt, "Immigration Debate," *CQ Researcher*, Feb. 1, 2008, pp. 97-120.

38. "Border Patrol History," U.S. Customs and Border Protection, www.cbp.gov/xp/cgov/border_security/ border_patrol/border_patrol_ohs/history.xml.

39. Sonia Nazario, *Enrique's Journey, The Story of a Boy's Dangerous Odyssey to Reunite With his Mother* (2006).

40. *Ibid.*, pp. 5-6.

41. Cornelius, *et al.*, *op. cit.*, June 10, 2008, p. 2.

42. Ralph Blumenthal, "In Texas, Weighing Life with a Border Fence," *The New York Times*, Jan. 13, 2008. For background, see Kenneth Jost, "Property Rights," *CQ Researcher*, March 4, 2005, pp. 197-220.

43. "Opponents of Border Fence Lose Round in Court," The Associated Press, *The New York Times*, Jan. 29, 2008.

44. Alicia Caldwell, The Associated Press, "Border Fence Could Cut through Backyards," *USA Today*, Nov. 11, 2007.

45. See "Updated Border Fence Information," University of Texas, Brownsville, www.utb.edu.

46. "DHS Exercises Waiver Authority to Expedite Advancement in Border Security," Department of Homeland Security press release, April 1, 2008.

47. *Ibid.*

48. "Key House Democrats Join Suit Against Use of Waivers for Border Fence," *Congressional Quarterly Today*, April 16, 2008.

49. A transcript of the Feb. 21, 2008, debate in Austin, Texas, is available on the CNN Web site, www.cnn .com/2008/POLITICS/02/21/debate.transcript/ index.html.

50. Michelle Roberts, "McCain sidesteps border fence, property rights question," *The Dallas Morning News*, Feb. 27, 2008.

51. For background, see David Masci, "Latinos' Future," *CQ Researcher*, Oct. 17, 2003, pp. 869-892.

52. For past and projected Mexican birthrates by decade, see *Statistical Yearbook for Latin America and the Caribbean, 2007*, United Nations Economic Commission for Latin America and the Caribbean.

BIBLIOGRAPHY

Books

Martinez, Ruben, *Crossing Over, A Mexican Family on the Migrant Trail*, Picador, 2001.
A writing teacher and award-winning journalist follows immigrants as they cross illegally into the United States.

Nazario, Sonia, *Enrique's Journey: the Story of a Boy's Dangerous Odyssey to Reunite with his Mother*, Random House, 2006.
A *Los Angeles Times* reporter won a Pulitzer prize for the articles that formed the basis for this book about a Honduran boy's illegal journey to the United States.

Williams, Derek, *The Reach of Rome, A History of the Roman Imperial Frontier 1st-5th Centuries AD*, St. Martin's Press, 1996.
An English writer spent 15 years researching and writing his study of Roman frontiers. Chapter 5 provides an exhaustive look at Hadrian's Wall.

Articles

Archibold, Randal C., and Julia Preston, "Despite Growing Opposition, Homeland Security Stands by its Fence," *The New York Times*, May 21, 2008, p. A18, www.nytimes.com/2008/05/21/washington/21fence .html.
An update on the progress of the border fence looks at the unhappiness in the Texas Rio Grande Valley over the way Homeland Security is routing the fence.

Fennelly, Katherine, "U.S. Immigration, a Historical Perspective," *The National Voter*, February 2007, p. 4, www.lwv.org/AM/Template.cfm?Section=Immig ration1&TEMPLATE=/CM/ContentDisplay.cfm& CONTENTID=8708.
This history of U.S. immigration laws and their consequences was published in a League of Women Voters periodical.

Garreau, Joel, "The Walls Tumbled by Time," *The Washington Post*, Oct. 27, 2006, p. C1, www .washingtonpost.com/wp-dyn/content/article/2006/ 10/26/AR2006102601826.html.
The reporter describes historic fences and walls and their fate, published the day after President George W. Bush signed the Secure Fence Act of 2006 into law.

McNatt, Robert, and Frank Benassi, "Econ 101 on Illegal Immigrants," a special report from S&P rating services, *Business Week*, April 7, 2006, www.business-week.com/investor/content/apr2006/pi20060407_ 072803.htm.
Standard & Poor's analyzes how illegal immigrants affect government revenues and expenditures.

Pallack, Becky, and Mariana Alvarado Avalos, "Employer-sanctions law starting to have the intended effect," *Arizona Daily Star*, Dec. 23, 2007, www.eller. arizona.edu/docs/press/2007/12/ArizonaDailyStar_ Employer-sanctions_law_ starting_to_have_intended_ effect_Dec23_2007.pdf.

An Arizona law that includes stiff sanctions for employers hiring illegal immigrants leaves some employers short of workers.

Wood, Daniel B., "Where U.S.-Mexico Border Fence is Tall, Border Crossings Fall," *The Christian Science Monitor*, **April 1, 2008, p. 1, www.csmonitor.com/ 2008/0401/p01s05-usgn.html.**
Beefing up border fencing in San Diego and Yuma has reduced illegal crossings.

Reports and Studies

Cornelius, Wayne, *et al.*, **"Controlling Unauthorized Immigration From Mexico: The Failure of 'Prevention through Deterrence' and the Need for Comprehensive Reform,"** *Center for Comparative Immigration Studies*, **June 10, 2008, www.immigrationpolicy.org/ images/File/misc/CCISbriefing061008.pdf.**
The study examines motivations and concerns of immigrants as they cross the border, drawn from 3,000 interviews with villagers in Mexico.

Koslowski, Rey, "Immigration Reforms and Border Security Technologies," *Social Science Research Council*, **July 31, 2006, http://borderbattles.ssrc.org/ Koslowski/.**
An associate professor of political science and public policy at the Rockefeller College of Public Affairs in New York reviews the effectiveness of new technology along the U.S.-Mexican border.

Nuñez-Neto, Blas, and Yule Kim, "Border Security: Barriers Along the U.S. International Border," *Congressional Research Service*, **May 13, 2008, www .fas.org/sgp/crs/homesec/RL33659.pdf.**
Congressional researchers examine the history of barriers built by the United States along the Southwestern border, including legislative action, construction, costs and effectiveness.

Stana, Richard, *et al.*, **"Homeland Security: DHS Has Taken Actions to Strengthen Border Security Programs and Operations, but Challenges Remain,"** *U.S. Government Accountability Office*, **March 6, 2008, www.gao.gov/new.items/d08542t.pdf.**
The report assesses security along the U.S. border, including at ports of entry and between legal entry points.

For More Information

Border Region Modeling Project, http://academics.utep.edu/Default.aspx?tabid=2883. A research program in the Economics Department at the University of Texas, El Paso, that analyzes the economies of four urban areas that have communities that straddle both sides of the border.

The Center for Comparative Immigration Studies, www.ccis-ucsd.org. An academic institute at the University of California, San Diego, devoted to the comparative analysis of the causes and effects of immigration and refugee flows throughout the world.

Center for Immigration Studies, 1522 K St., N.W., Suite 820, Washington, DC 20005-1202; (202) 466-8185; www.cis.org. A think tank that publishes research on immigration issues; strives for "fewer immigrants but a warmer welcome for those admitted."

Defenders of Wildlife, 1130 17th St., N.W., Washington, DC 20036; (202) 682-9400; www.defenders.org. National nonprofit organization dedicated to the protection of all native animals and plants in their natural communities.

Federation for American Immigration Reform, 25 Massachusetts Ave., N.W., Suite 330, Washington, DC 20001; (202) 328-7004; www.fairus.org. Nonprofit citizens group that supports improved border security to stop illegal immigration and reduce legal immigration to about 300,000 people a year.

Humane Borders, 740 E. Speedway Blvd., Tucson, AZ 85719; (520) 628-7753; www.humaneborders.org. A faith-based citizens group that operates more than 80 emergency water stations along the border as part of an effort to offer humanitarian assistance to those in distress in the desert.

National Immigration Law Center, 3435 Wilshire Blvd., Suite 2850, Los Angeles, CA 90010; (213) 639-3900; www.nilc.org. Protects and promotes the rights of low-income immigrants and their families; analyzes immigration policies.

NumbersUSA, 1601 N. Kent St., Suite 1100, Arlington, VA 22209; (703) 816-8820; www.numbersusa.com. A nonprofit, activist organization that supports reducing immigration, both legal and illegal.

Pew Hispanic Center, 1615 L St., N.W., Suite 700, Washington, DC 20036-5610; (202) 419-3600; http://pewhispanic.org. A nonpartisan research organization supported by the Pew Charitable Trusts, dedicated to improving understanding of the U.S. Hispanic population; a leading repository of statistics and studies on illegal immigration.

The Southwest Center, http://web.arizona.edu/~swctr/. A research center at the University of Arizona that sponsors projects designed to enhance understanding of U.S.-Mexican trans-border culture and history.

Texas Border Coalition, www.texasbordercoalition.org. A coalition of mayors and other civic leaders from communities along the U.S.-Mexican border; advocates for individuals and communities unhappy with the Department of Homeland Security's plans for the border fence.

A Chinese supervisor (right) oversees Africans working on a Chinese-funded road project in Addis Ababa, Ethiopia, in April 2007. Sino-African trade has increased more than sixfold in recent years, bringing Chinese investment and cheap consumer goods to the continent but generating fears China could become Africa's newest colonizer.

AFP/Getty Images/Simon Maina

From *CQ Global Researcher*, January 2008.

China in Africa

Is China Gaining Control of Africa's Resources?

Karen Foerstel

8

B illboards displaying elephants, lions and giraffes roaming African savannas hung from every street corner. Wood-carvings of antelopes and other safari animals lined the streets of the main shopping district. And everywhere posters proclaimed, "Africa, the Land of Myth and Miracles."[1]

The three-day Forum on China-Africa Cooperation in Beijing in November 2006 ranked among China's biggest extravaganzas in years, with 43 of Africa's 53 heads of state attending the meeting to discuss how the two regions could expand economic, political and social ties.[2]

No expense — or detail — was spared. African drummers and Chinese acrobats greeted delegates as they entered the Great Hall of the People for the opening ceremonies. A 30-foot image of the Egyptian Sphinx looked down on passersby in downtown Beijing. Even the grass around the airport and conference venues was touched up with green paint.[3]

But China was offering its visitors more than just a good time. President Hu Jintao pledged to double China's assistance to Africa by 2009, an economic package that also included:

- Preferential loans and credits to Africa totaling $5 billion;
- A promise to increase two-way trade to more than $100 billion by 2010;
- A $5 billion development fund to encourage Chinese companies to invest in Africa;
- Cancellation of debts owed to China from the least-developed African countries;

China Is Making Oil Deals Throughout Africa

China is negotiating oil deals with 13 of the 19 African countries with proven oil reserves. Africa's total reserves are estimated at 103 billion barrels, or about the same as Kuwait.

African Countries with Oil Reserves

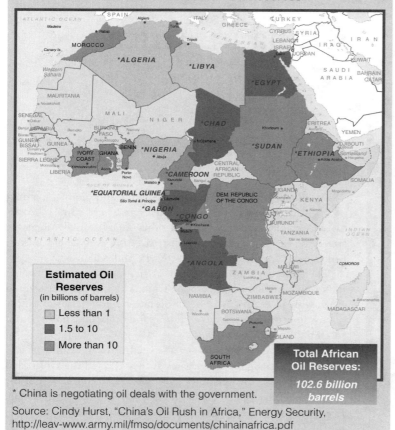

Estimated Oil Reserves
(in billions of barrels)

- Less than 1
- 1.5 to 10
- More than 10

Total African Oil Reserves:
102.6 billion barrels

* China is negotiating oil deals with the government.

Source: Cindy Hurst, "China's Oil Rush in Africa," Energy Security, http://leav-www.army.mil/fmso/documents/chinainafrica.pdf

- Doubling exports to China from Africa's least developed countries, which receive zero-tariff treatment, and
- Construction of 30 hospitals, 30 malaria treatment centers and 100 schools in rural Africa.[4]

Apart from the promised government aid, Chinese companies and African governments and firms signed $1.9 billion in business agreements.[5]

"China is opening itself up to Africa, coming with assistance," said Zimbabwe's President Robert Mugabe.

"We have nothing to lose but our imperialist chains."[6]

Many African leaders feel the same. After a history of often brutal and rapacious colonization and failed economic policies imposed upon them by the West, African nations are increasingly turning East. China presents itself as a partner that has never colonized Africa nor enslaved any African. And it emphasizes the fact that it is a developing country, so it understands the many issues Africa's developing nations face.

Since the Beijing forum, China-Africa trade has increased almost 30 percent, and Chinese diplomats have held nearly nonstop meetings with African leaders.[7] In early 2007, Foreign Minister Li Zhaoxing took a seven-nation tour across Africa to discuss public health, education, agribusiness and other areas of economic cooperation.[8] A month later, President Hu opened a Chinese-built hospital in Cameroon, a Chinese-funded malaria treatment center in Liberia and a Chinese-language after-school program in Namibia.[9] In September, representatives from 48 African countries met with their Chinese counterparts at U.N. headquarters in New York — the first such meeting of its kind between Africans and the Chinese.[10]

"African nations never had this level of attention before," says Chris Alden, head of the China in Africa program at the South African Institute of International Affairs and author of a new book, *China in Africa*. "African leaders have often been treated by the West as tin-pot dictators. Now they are being treated by China with a level of respect that all leaders crave."

And the attention is paying off — for both sides. Chinese firms have won contracts worth more than $30 billion for infrastructure projects in Africa, and nearly 800 Chinese companies now operate in Africa.[11]

In 2005, Africa's economy grew a record 5.2 percent, which many credit at least in part to China's growing engagement.[12]

"If these trends continue, China will be the dominant economic trader across the continent," says Alden.

But many wonder whether China — while certainly helping Africa develop — is also becoming the continent's newest colonizer, extracting its vast natural resources, supporting corrupt governments for financial gain and making the African economy dependent on Chinese aid. Chinese exports — often surplus products that can be sold well below cost — are flooding African markets and putting many local manufacturers and companies out of business. Likewise, thousands of Chinese workers are streaming into Africa to build roads, hospitals and other infrastructure, displacing the African labor force. By some estimates, from 750,000 to 1 million Chinese now live and work in Africa.[13]

"The relationship between China and Africa does resemble the standard European relationship — you pay as little as you can for the resources you need," says Patrick Smith, editor and publisher of *Africa Confidential*, a London-based publication focusing on African issues and events. "There is a real risk of them becoming like Western colonizers."

While African leaders are embracing Chinese products and aid, average Africans increasingly are opposing the growing presence of China in their back yard. During the 2006 presidential election in Zambia, opposition candidate Michael Sata made China — and its growing control over the country's copper mines — a major platform of his campaign.

"Zambia is becoming a province — no, a district — of China," Sata said during his campaign.[14]

He threatened to cut diplomatic ties with China and instead support the Chinese breakaway state of Taiwan and its claim to regain its seat in the United Nations. Ultimately, Sata lost the election, garnering 28 percent of the vote. But his opposition Patriotic Front party won key seats in Zambia's mining regions.[15]

Anti-Chinese sentiment in Zambia grew in 2005 after 46 workers died in an explosion at a Chinese-owned copper mine. The blast was blamed on poor safety conditions.[16]

In addition to copper, timber, minerals and oil are all in high demand by China's rapidly growing economy.

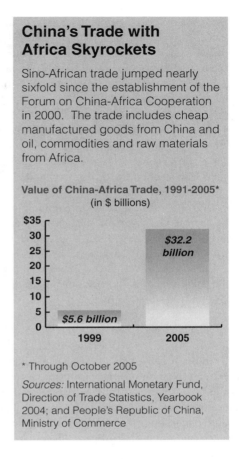

China's Trade with Africa Skyrockets

Sino-African trade jumped nearly sixfold since the establishment of the Forum on China-Africa Cooperation in 2000. The trade includes cheap manufactured goods from China and oil, commodities and raw materials from Africa.

Value of China-Africa Trade, 1991-2005*
(in $ billions)

$5.6 billion (1999)
$32.2 billion (2005)

* Through October 2005

Sources: International Monetary Fund, Direction of Trade Statistics, Yearbook 2004; and People's Republic of China, Ministry of Commerce

And as the Middle East becomes increasingly unstable, China and the West both are looking to Africa for oil supplies. Now the world's second-largest oil consumer behind the United States, China has negotiated oil deals in more than a dozen African nations and buys nearly a third of its oil from Africa — an amount likely to grow quickly.[17]

"The single, biggest future worry [for the West] is access to petroleum resources," says Stephen Chan, a professor of international relations at the University of London's School of Oriental and African Studies. "China is buying [oil-producing] acreage and putting a lot of sweeteners in the deals. . . . The real danger is about 20 years up the line. You will have intense competition."

China's growing thirst for oil has led it to deal with resource-rich nations that have been ostracized by the West for human-rights abuses. Sudan, for instance, where more than 200,000 people have died in fighting in the Darfur region since 2003, is one of China's biggest oil suppliers.[18] China repeatedly has blocked efforts by the West to impose sanctions against Sudan and until recently was reluctant even to pressure the Sudanese government to curb the fighting.

The West has condemned China's failure to demand that African nations comply with democratic, environmental or human-rights standards before receiving financial aid. Without such demands, the West says, loans and investments will benefit despotic regimes but do little for average Africans.

"There can be no sustainable development without good governance. Development is much more than just financial aid," says Amadeu Altafaj, a spokesman for the European Commission. "There must be links between security and development, social issues and development, the environment and development. China is not doing that" in its dealings in Africa.

But even as the West criticizes China's policy of non-interference, it is taking notice of China's rapid success in Africa and beginning to play catch-up. In an obvious effort to counterbalance Beijing's spectacular Forum on China-Africa Cooperation, the European Union (EU) this past December hosted the EU-Africa Summit, which brought leaders from 53 African nations to Lisbon, Portugal, to discuss how to strengthen and expand political and strategic ties with Europe.[19] Although the EU says the summit was not a reaction to China's influence in Africa, the EU's own summary paper about the summit opens by describing China's growing trade and economic power in Africa:

"China . . . has rapidly emerged as Africa's third most important trade partner [behind the United States and the European Union] with total trade amounting to about €43 billion [about $32 billion] in 2006. . . . If the EU wants to remain a privileged partner and make the most of its relations with Africa, it must be willing to reinforce, and in some areas reinvent, the current relationship — institutionally, politically and culturally. . . . [I]t is now time to move on from a strategy for Africa towards **a political partnership *with* Africa."[20]** As China's influence continues to grow across the African continent, here are some of the questions analysts are beginning to ask:

Is China benefiting Africa's economy?

While the $70-billion U.S. trade with Africa overshadows China's $55.5 billion total, business between China and Africa is growing at a much faster pace.[21] Sino-African trade more than quintupled between 1999 and 2004 — rising from roughly $5.6 billion to $29.5 billion — while U.S.-African trade doubled to $58.9 billion during that same period.[22]

Beijing, meanwhile, has overtaken the World Bank in lending to Africa. In 2005, for instance, China committed $8 billion in loans to Nigeria, Angola and Mozambique while the World Bank distributed just $2.3 billion throughout the continent.[23]

China's increasing investments in Africa's oil fields, roads and telephone networks appear to have helped the currency of many African nations to rise in value. According to the Standard Bank Group, the Kenyan shilling, Nigerian naira, Zambian kwacha, Angolan kwanza and Ghanaian cedi have all gained strength this year.[24]

At the same time, China's growing exports to Africa have inundated the continent with low-cost consumer goods. Televisions, washing machines and cell phones are now available to many Africans who previously couldn't afford such items. But critics say the influx of cheap goods is forcing many African retailers and manufacturers out of business.

"A large proportion of our population is very poor, so they have to buy the cheapest products available. So, yes, there is a positive impact," says Brian Brink, executive director of the South African Textile Federation. "But if that continues, there won't be anyone with jobs and money in their pockets. [Chinese goods are] destroying a lot more jobs" than they are creating.

As a result, tensions between African and Chinese merchants are on the rise. Fist fights and even riots have been reported in street markets across the continent, according to Brink and Chan. And migrant Chinese workers create additional tensions among average Africans by forming isolated communities across the continent.

"The Chinese tend to live in enclaves and don't contribute to the local economies where they're living," says Elizabeth Economy, director of Asian studies at the influential Council on Foreign Relations, a New York-based think tank. "If you export labor, people expect [them] to buy things [on the local market]. But the Chinese are very self-sufficient. It doesn't breed a sense that it's benefiting the local people."

And although Sino-African trade is growing rapidly, most African nations have a mounting trade deficit with China.[25] Many also worry that China's massive loans to African nations will plunge the continent deeper into debt. In 2006, the EU's European Investment Bank and the International Monetary Fund (IMF) warned that China's emergence as a major creditor was creating a wave of new debt for African countries, and the U.S. Treasury Department labeled China a "rogue creditor" practicing "opportunistic lending."[26]

"Africa sells raw materials to China, and China sells manufactured products to Africa. This is a dangerous equation that reproduces Africa's old relationship with colonial powers," said Moeletsi Mbeki, deputy chairman of the South African Institute of International Affairs. "The equation is not sustainable for a number of reasons. First, Africa needs to preserve its natural resources to use in the future for its own industrialisation. Secondly, China's export strategy is contributing to the de-industrialisation of some middle-income countries."[27]

Chinese officials tried to allay those concerns in May 2007, when Shanghai hosted the annual meeting of the African Development Bank. "We are truly sincere in helping Africa speed up economic and social development for the benefit of the African people and its nations," said Chinese Premier Wen Jiabao.[28] China then pledged an additional $20 billion for African infrastructure development over the next three years.[29]

China had already invested billions in Africa's infrastructure. In Angola — desperate to rebuild after a 27-year civil war — China International Fund Ltd., a Hong Kong construction company, funded a $300 million project to repair the heavily damaged Benguela Railroad. In Sierra Leone, also recovering after years of conflict, China has paid for the construction and repair of government buildings, bridges, hydroelectrical facilities, Sierra Leone University and the national football stadium.[30]

Oil-Rich Countries Get China's Transport Help

Energy-hungry China is giving low-interest loans to oil-rich sub-Saharan countries to help overhaul aging roads and rail lines. Major projects funded in 2006 included:

- $1 billion to repair Nigerian rail lines and supply new equipment;

- Rebuilding nearly half of Angola's 754 roads;

- $500 million to overhaul Angola's railways and

- An offer of $1.5 billion to upgrade other parts of Angola's transportation network.

Source: Raphael Kaplinsky, et al., "The Impact of China on Sub Saharan Africa," Institute of Development Studies, April 2006

Western nations either have been reluctant to invest in these war-torn countries or demand preconditions many African nations are unwilling or unable to meet. "The Chinese are doing more than the G-8 to make poverty history," said Sahr Johnny, Sierra Leone's ambassador to Beijing, referring to the world's eight largest economies. "If a G-8 country had wanted to rebuild the stadium, we would still be holding meetings. The Chinese just come and do it. They don't hold meetings about environmental impact assessment, human rights, bad governance and good governance."[31]

Nicole Lee, director of TransAfrica, a Washington D.C., organization that promotes human-rights policies that benefit Africans and those of African descent, says China gives African leaders more power to decide what is best for their countries. "They can make their own choices and don't have to take loans from the U.S. with all these conditions and attachments," Lee says. "There may be some bad impacts from China, but African countries are being treated as partners, not subjects."

Indeed, she notes, Western preconditions on aid do not guarantee benefits to Africans. Often, those conditions — such as requiring aid recipients to slash public-sector work or privatize businesses — are designed only to "ensure that multinational corporations are getting rich off the privatization of Africa," says Lee. "But they are not always good for the lower or middle classes."

The Council on Foreign Relations' Economy says Africans have "a lot of mixed feelings" about China.

AFP/Getty Images/Peter Parks

Chinese soldiers and engineers train in China before shipping out to Darfur in western Sudan. China recently agreed to send engineers, medics and transportation specialists to join U.N. peacekeepers in the war-torn region, partly to rebut Western criticism that China enables genocidal atrocities in Darfur by trading arms to the Sudanese government for oil. China has more than 1,200 peacekeepers building infrastructure and monitoring troubled villages in Africa.

"Certain people benefit, some don't. But the more China engages, the more the picture is mixed."

Do China's policies threaten human rights in Africa?

China's drive for oil and natural resources has prompted it to forge close relationships with many governments that have been condemned by the West for corruption and human-rights abuses.

In 2003, China gave Angola a $2 billion loan in exchange for 10,000 barrels of oil a day, with no strings attached.[32] That allowed Angola to avoid good-governance conditions demanded by the IMF before it would provide aid. Shortly after the loan was granted, Transparency International ranked Angola as one of the world's most corrupt nations.[33]

In Sudan — where the government is accused of condoning years of wholesale rape, murder and pillaging by Arab *mujahadeen* in the Darfur region — China has invested billions in the oil sector, imports 60 percent of Sudan's oil and is Sudan's largest source of weapons.[34]

In May 2007, the United States imposed economic sanctions against Sudan, barring 30 companies controlled by the Sudanese government from using the U.S.

banking system. The sanctions also specifically prohibited three individuals — including Sudan's minister for humanitarian affairs — from doing business with U.S. companies or individuals.[35]

Until recently, China had been reluctant to leverage its billions in investments to demand that the Sudanese government halt the murder and destruction in Darfur. Instead, China had followed a policy of "non-interference" in countries where it does business, refusing to become involved in internal conflicts and often ignoring human-rights abuses, corruption or other social problems.

China respects the sovereignty of African nations to "independently resolve African problems," according to the declaration adopted by China and 48 African nations during the 2006 Beijing forum.[36]

"Business is business. We try to separate politics from business," Chinese Deputy Foreign Minister Zhou Wenzhong said in 2004, when asked about his government's cooperation with Sudan. "Secondly, I think the internal situation in the Sudan is an internal affair, and we are not in a position to impose upon them."[37]

That attitude rankles human-rights groups. Amnesty International says the principle of non-interference in the internal affairs of another country "must not become an excuse to remain silent when such states violate the human rights of their people. . . . Economic profits for China should not be built on the killings and displacement of Africans."[38]

Besides buying Africa's natural resources without demanding reforms, China provided one-tenth of the arms bought in Africa between 1996 and 2003.[39] In 2004, China sold arms to Zimbabwe, ignoring a U.S. and EU arms embargo imposed because of human-rights abuses. In Zimbabwe, where acute food and commodities shortages threaten social collapse and unemployment has reached 80 percent, China sold $200 million worth of military aircraft and vehicles.[40] Chinese businesses also reportedly designed Mugabe's 25-room mansion and provided radio-jamming equipment to block anti-government broadcasts.[41]

In the past year, however, China has begun to distance itself from Mugabe and other governments condemned by the West. Li Guijin, China's special envoy for Africa, announced last September that Beijing had halted development aid to Zimbabwe and would only provide humanitarian assistance. "China in the past provided substantial development assistance, but owing to the dramatic currency revaluations and rapid deterioration of economic conditions, the economic outcomes of these projects have not been so good."[42]

Meanwhile, after years of blocking U.N. efforts to impose sanctions on Sudan, China now is joining Western forces in peacekeeping missions. In 2007, China sent hundreds of engineers, medics and transport specialists to join U.N. forces sent in to keep peace in Sudan until 2011. It is China's longest peacekeeping mission to date. Across Africa, China now has more than 1,200 peacekeepers building infrastructure and monitoring troubled villages.[43]

"China's policy of non-interference is coming apart at the seams," says Smith of *Africa Confidential*, because it is finding that doing business with corrupt, unstable governments is often less than profitable. Continued fighting in Sudan threatens oil production, and China is losing money on its investments in Zimbabwe, he says.

And, as China strives to become a global superpower, it apparently is beginning to pay more attention to Western criticism. "China wants to be seen as a serious, international player," Smith says.

China contends that — as a developing nation that has overcome imperialism — it has a sincere interest in helping Africans also succeed and thrive. In fact, China considers "economic rights" and "rights of subsistence" as the most important human rights for citizens in developing nations, more important than the personal, individual rights promoted by the West.[44]

China sent its first medical team to Algeria in 1963 and has since dispatched more than 15,000 medical professionals to 47 African countries. In addition, China has sent more than 500 teachers to Africa and trained more than 1,000 Africans in various professional skills. Each year, China provides more than 1,500 scholarships for African students.[45]

Chinese officials and others cite the hypocrisy they see in Western nations that criticize China for supporting tyrants in Africa while they themselves do business with despots elsewhere. "The United States is in Saudi Arabia," says Economy of the Council on Foreign Relations. "Chevron is in Burma. I'm certainly not an apologist for China, but before we call the kettle black we have to be very, very careful."

Are China and the West headed for a showdown over Africa's natural resources?

Western countries buy much more of Africa's oil than China does. China bought only 9 percent of Africa's petroleum exports in 2006, while the United States took 33 percent and Europe 36 percent.[46]

But both China and the West are growing increasingly dependent on African oil as oil-rich Middle Eastern nations become less stable. China already imports more oil from Angola than it does from Saudi Arabia, and the United States has nearly doubled its oil imports from Africa since 2002.[47] In 2006, Africa provided more than 15 percent of U.S. oil imports. Experts say recent explorations in the Gulf of Guinea region show potential reserves that could supply 25-35 percent of U.S. imports within the next decade.[48]

As China's economy expands, its future oil needs are expected to have consequences for the West on several levels. "Chinese demand is driving up commodity prices," says Alden at the South African Institute of International Affairs. "It's making the cost of energy more expensive for the West."

Ian Taylor, a professor of international relations at Scotland's University of St. Andrews, said there might be another concern for the West. "Chinese oil diplomacy in Africa has two main goals: in the short-term, secure oil supplies to help feed growing domestic demand back in China; and in the long-term position China as a global player in the international oil market," Taylor wrote. "The recent upsurge in Chinese oil diplomacy may be linked to Chinese strategists at the national level who may well first and foremost be paying attention to the long-term goal of being in charge of oil resources at their source in a strategy to manipulate future prices."[49]

Some say China's strategy to bypass international market pricing by controlling products at the source does not stop at oil but includes nearly every natural resource Africa has to offer. "Thus the price that China pays for specific commodities will be negotiated at source with recipient governments rather than the price determined by the 'market,'" charges a report conducted by the Centre for Chinese Studies at Stellenbosch University in South Africa. "This is the underlying factor of China's strategic engagement of African commodity- and energy-endowed economies."[50]

Voracious China Threatens the Environment

African forests are most at risk.

While China is focusing largely on Africa's oil, it is also reaching deeply into Africa's forests. China imports half of all the tropical trees being logged around the world, making it the world's largest importer of tropical timber. In the past 10 years, China's wood imports have jumped more than 400 percent — much of it harvested under conditions outlawed by local and regional laws from forests around the globe.[1]

Nearly half — 46 percent — of Gabon's forest exports go to China, making it Gabon's largest timber trading partner.[2] Although Gabonese law requires timber to be processed before exportation — increasing its export value — China, with its abundance of cheap home-grown labor, wants only unprocessed logs. As a result, China encourages "flagrant disregard for the law," according to the Web site of GlobalTimber .org.uk, which compiles data and studies on the international trade of wood products. According to the group, 80 percent of Gabon's timber exports to China are illegal.

China's timber imports from other African nations are just as shady, according to the group. Eighty percent of wood exports from Cameroon to China are illegal, as are 90 percent of the wood exports from Equatorial Guinea and Congo, the group says.[3]

Ironically, China's growing demand for wood stems from recent policies it has enacted to protect its own forests. After deadly floods along the Yangtze River in 1998, the Chinese government instituted environmental protections aimed at preventing future disasters, including new restrictions on timber harvesting and reforestation projects to combat erosion.[4] While those strategies may be helping to protect China's forests, they are prompting China to look elsewhere for timber.

China's demand for oil also has caused environmental degradation in Africa's forests. Gabon recently forced China's Sinopec oil company to stop exploring for oil in a national forest after the company was found to be polluting, dynamiting and carving roads through the forest.[5]

African governments often are reluctant to prosecute China for its environmental activities because they "want the investments," says Elizabeth Economy, director of Asia studies at the New York-based Council on Foreign Relations.

But with pressure mounting from environmentalists, Beijing last August issued new guidelines to encourage Chinese logging companies working overseas to carry out their operations in a sustainable manner.[6] In November,

Others, however, say China is not deliberately trying to push Western companies out of Africa's oil market but has simply made the most of the opportunities available to it to meet its energy needs.

"There is a race for these resources," says Helmut Reisen, coordinator of the Finance for Development Unit at the Organization for Economic Cooperation and Development in Paris. But he says China has monopolized African oil markets "only where the West deliberately leaves an empty space. Zimbabwe, Sudan, Angola — that's exactly where the Chinese have jumped in."

The vast economic resources of China's state-controlled oil companies have enabled China to attach billions in development aid to oil contracts and out-bid international companies for rights to Africa's petroleum reserves. For example, in 2004, as India was preparing to close a $620 million deal to buy shares in an oil field in

Angola, China at the last minute offered an additional $2 billion in aid for various projects in Angola. Not surprisingly, China got the contract.[51]

"The Chinese don't just go after the extractive resources," says Alden. "They produce a whole package. They build roads, hospitals and other things."

BP and ExxonMobil refused to comment for this report on China's growing hold on African oil. But during a September 2007 speech before the German Council for Foreign Policy, BP's regional president for Asia, Gary Dirks, said the West should not be concerned.

"Some rather simplistically see China as the root cause of rising oil prices. Others doubt the adequacy of the world's energy resources to meet the growing Chinese demand," Dirks said. "My own more narrow perspective is that the world has enough energy resources to meet growing energy demand for the foreseeable future,

China and Brazil announced they would give Africa free satellite imaging of the continent to help it respond to threats from deforestation, desertification and drought.[7]

And in June, B&Q — one of China's largest home-improvement retail chains — announced it would guarantee that timber products in all its 60 stores come from legal sources. Moreover, the company pledged that within three years all its product lines will come from certified, ecologically responsible forestry operations. The move won high praise from the environmental group Greenpeace.[8]

But there is still concern that China will continue to put its need for resources above its concern for habitat protection, and that African leaders — desperate for Chinese investments — will ignore environmental regulations.

In October, environmental activists in Gabon expressed outrage over a deal they say could destroy one of the most beautiful natural waterfalls in central Africa. The watchdog organization Environment Gabon said the deal between Gabon and a Chinese iron mining consortium would exempt from taxes for 25 years the Belinga iron ore mining project — run by a predominantly Chinese company — and free it from responsibility for any "environmental consequences."[9]

The project is set to be powered by a hydroelectric dam built at the spectacular Kongou Falls. No environmental-impact studies have been conducted — as required by Gabonese law — but construction has already begun, authorized by Gabon's Ministry of Mines.[10]

The Chinese firm reportedly is ready to conduct environmental assessments if authorities request it. But Gabonese officials say the socio-economic benefits of the project outweigh environmental concerns.

"Belinga just reveals the tensions born of overlapping interests between the necessary development of the country and protecting the environment, as well as Chinese penetration into Africa," said a government official.[11]

[1] Tamara Stark and Sze Pang Cheung, "Sharing the Blame: Global Consumption and China's Role in Ancient Forest Destruction," Greenpeace, March 28, 2006, p. 1.

[2] Michelle Chan-Fishel, "Environmental Impact: More of the Same?," *African Perspectives of China in Africa*, p. 146.

[3] GlobalTimber.org.uk.

[4] Alex Kirby, "Plan to tame Yangtze floods," BBC News Online, Oct. 12, 2001.

[5] Ian Taylor, "China's environmental footprint in Africa," chinadialogue, Feb. 2, 2007.

[6] "China issues rules on overseas logging by its companies," Associated Press Worldstream, Aug. 29, 2007.

[7] "China, Brazil give Africa free satellite land images," Agence France-Presse, Nov. 28, 2007.

[8] "Greenpeace applauds B&Q's initiative to clean up timber trade in China," Greenpeace press release, June 12, 2007.

[9] Francesco Fontemaggi, "Chinese iron mine project in Gabon pits greens against developers," Agence France-Presse, Oct. 16, 2007.

[10] *Ibid.*

[11] *Ibid.*

including from China, provided adequate investment is made in a timely manner."[52]

EU spokesman Altafaj agrees. "Most African countries are smart enough to diversify portfolios. We don't fear a monopoly."

But others say there is evidence the West is more than just concerned about China's oil investments in Africa. The United States, they charge, is in fact beginning to use its military to maintain control over Africa's oil. In October 2007, the United States announced creation of AFRICOM, a new military headquarters devoted solely to Africa. It will be located near the Gulf of Guinea — home to one of the largest untapped oil reserves in the world.[53]

By some estimates, by 2010 the gulf will contribute at least one out of every five new barrels of oil used on the global market.[54] The oil fields are scattered off the coast of southwest Africa in territorial waters claimed by Nigeria, Angola, Gabon, Equatorial Guinea and others.

AFRICOM's Web site denies that the new military force has anything to do with oil or China. Its homepage includes the question: "Is this an effort by the United States to gain access to natural resources (for example, petroleum)? Is this in response to Chinese activities in Africa?" AFRICOM's reply: "No. Africa is growing in military, strategic and economic importance in global affairs. We are seeking more effective ways to bolster security on the continent, to prevent and respond to humanitarian crises, to improve cooperative efforts with African nations to stem transnational terrorism, and to sustain enduring efforts that contribute to African unity."[55]

But many are skeptical. "I think it has everything to do with China and oil," says TransAfrica's Lee. "China has between 10 to 20 oil platforms off the coast. That is

AP Photo/Rebecca Blackwell

Senegalese shop assistants in Dakar wait for clients under the watchful eye of the Chinese owner's sister — a visible sign of China's deep penetration into Africa's economies. Up to 800 Chinese companies operate in Africa — buying oil and raw materials, building infrastructure and helping China become a player in the continent's telecommunications and textile industries.

an absolute threat to our own energy interests in the Gulf of Guinea. The United States does not want to give up its hold there."

U.S. Rep. Marcy Kaptur, a Democrat from Ohio, agrees. "The hot, new area, of course, for exploration is Africa, and I imagine that may be a reason President Bush this week announced a new U.S-Africa Command," Kaptur told House colleagues last February. "China is interested in Africa's natural resources, including oil. And now the Bush administration is trying to play catch-up."[56]

BACKGROUND

Breaking Colonial Ties

China's first encounter with Africa dates back to the early 15th century, when Admiral Zheng He led some 300 ships on seven journeys across the globe. Although his celebrated expeditions between 1405 and 1423 took him as far as the eastern coast of Africa, China had little to do with Africa for the next 500 years. Western nations, on the other hand, spent those centuries enslaving Africans and later colonizing the continent and extracting its raw materials to supply the needs of an industrializing Europe.

For more than 300 years, Europeans ran a lucrative and brutal trans-Atlantic slave trade, bringing an estimated 10 million Africans to the Americas — mainly Brazil.[57] After Britain abolished slavery in 1807, the Europeans began exploring Africa's interior, and by the late 1800s Europe's "Scramble for Africa" was in full swing. The colonial powers — primarily Britain, France, Belgium, Portugal and Germany — competed for vast tracts of Africa. And while they did build roads, railroads and other infrastructure — primarily to facilitate their exploitation of Africa's vast resources — millions of Africans died in the process.

As European nations expanded their control over Africa, they began to fear competition from one another for the continent's resources. In 1884, the European powers gathered at the so-called Berlin Conference to divvy up control of the continent. By 1902, all but 10 percent of Africa was under European control.[58]

But by mid-century the colonial powers had been weakened by the First and Second World Wars and could no longer afford to maintain vast colonies abroad.[59] Before World War II, Africa had only three independent countries: Liberia — which was founded by freed American slaves and declared itself independent in 1847; Ethiopia, which was never colonized by a European power; and Egypt, which had achieved independence in 1922.[60]

As Europe's colonies around the world gained independence after World War II, Mahatma Gandhi's struggle for Indian independence — achieved in 1947 — inspired similar efforts across Africa in the 1950s.[61]

During that time, China began reaching out to Africa. In 1955, emerging independent African and Asian countries gathered in Indonesia for the Bandung Conference — the first meeting of Third World nations — to promote Afro-Asian economic and cultural cooperation and spur political autonomy from the West. Attendees also launched the Non-Aligned Movement, pledging to support neither the United States nor the Soviet Union in their Cold War struggles.[62] Chinese Prime Minister Zhou Enlai played a particularly strong role in the conference and launched China's first foray into international politics. The first Sino-African diplomatic ties were established with Egypt in 1956, and within 10 years China had solidified relations with more than a dozen African countries.[63]

In the early 1960s, as African countries were gaining their independence, Zhou made a 10-country tour across the continent offering China's support. His trip was seen in part as a way to ensure Africa's opposition to Taiwan and to counter growing influence from the United States and Soviet Union, which supported "proxy" wars in Africa as offshoots of the global Cold War. China began sending doctors to Africa and provided aid to more than 800 projects across the continent, ranging from sports stadiums and the Tanzam railway — between Tanzania and Zambia — to providing scholarships to African students to study in Beijing.[64]

"People forget how much goodwill China gained in Africa during this liberation era," says Chan of London's School of Oriental and African Studies. "Africans were struck by the message Zhou Enlai put to them. It sustained the relationship between Africa and China. There was a genuine solidarity and empathy involved. Africans never forgot that."

Along with its ideological goal of spreading the "people's revolution" against Western imperialism, Communist China's outreach to Africa was also an attempt to counter Soviet influence. For instance, in Rhodesia (now Zimbabwe) — which did not gain its independence from Britain until 1980 — China backed the liberation movement of Robert Mugabe's Zanu party, while the Soviet Union backed that of Joshua Nkomo's Zapu party. In response, Mugabe's party turned profoundly anti-Soviet.

When Mugabe was elected prime minister in March 1980, Zimbabwe's close relationship with China was cemented. The two countries announced diplomatic ties on April 18, the day Zimbabwe won its independence from Britain. Shortly after that, Foreign Minister Simon Muzenda visited Beijing to thank the government for its support, and Mugabe himself went to Beijing the following year.[65]

Colonialism's Legacy

By the early 1980s, China had established diplomatic ties with nearly 40 African nations. However, during the political turmoil that followed the death of Chairman Mao Zedong in September 1976, China turned inward,

West Is Still Africa's Biggest Trade Partner

Sub-Saharan Africa's trade with China — the value of both exports and imports — has grown dramatically since 2000, but its trade with industrialized countries is still far bigger. Africa's trade with China reached nearly $50 billion in 2006, or about one-seventh of its trade with the West.

Sub-Saharan Africa's Trade with China and the Industrialized Countries, 1980-2006

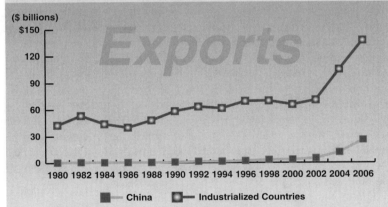

Source: Raphael Kaplinsky, et al., "The Impact of China on Sub Saharan Africa," Institute of Development Studies, www.uk.cn/uploadfiles/2006428172021581.doc

A Chadian soldier mans a Chinese-made armored vehicle in April 2006 that reportedly was seized from rebel forces. Chad has accused neighboring Sudan — which gets most of its arms from China — of forming a new rebel army to attack Chad. China provided one-tenth of all arms bought in Africa between 1996 and 2003.

and its influence and involvement in Africa waned.[66] But China's ideological goal of revolution and independence in Africa had been largely achieved. And having forged strong relationships with African leaders, China was not as fearful of Taiwan's influence in the region.

Despite their independence, African nations still faced many problems. Many lacked the technical and administrative skills needed to create healthy economies, and support structures — such as higher education, communications and armed forces — were poorly developed.[67]

During the post-independence era, the United States thought Africa did not have sufficient natural resources to warrant large U.S. investments, which could have helped to stabilize and strengthen the new African nations. "It is highly unlikely that most African countries will obtain external assistance or investment on anything approaching the scale required for sustained economic development," said a 1965 CIA assessment. "No African raw materials or other resources are essential to U.S. security."[68]

After the colonial rulers left, ethnic violence erupted across Africa in nations where colonizers had drawn artificial boundaries without regard to traditional tribal territories.

Many of the new African countries also embraced socialism, prompting the United States — fearful that the continent might tilt toward the Soviet Union — to provide economic and military support to anti-communist despots or rebel groups. The beneficiaries of U.S. funding during this period included notoriously corrupt strongmen such as Mobuto Sese Seko of Zaire (now the Democratic Republic of Congo), Jonas Savimbi of Angola and Hiseene Habre of Chad.[69]

In the 1980s, African nations borrowed heavily from the West. By 1986 Africa's foreign debt had reached $162 billion, and interest payments alone were eating up two-thirds of all the money the continent received in foreign aid. By 1989, the World Bank and International Monetary Fund (IMF) were forcing 30 heavily indebted sub-Saharan African nations to submit to "structural adjustment" programs designed to institute more market-oriented policies.[70]

The countries were forced to lower the value of their currencies to make their exports more attractive, shrink bloated budgets and bureaucracies and privatize state-run enterprises. But the spending limits kept many economies in deep recession and hurt Africa's poor. And although the requirements were initially said to be temporary, they soon become permanent World Bank and IMF policy.[71]

As the 1980s came to a close, African nations grew disillusioned with Western financial aid and the economic and political strings it carried. Many African leaders felt China could offer an alternative model in which "bread comes before the freedom to vote," in the words of Ndubisi Obiorah, director of the Center for Law and Social Action in Lagos, Nigeria.[72]

China's Return

As the 1990s dawned, Africa's economy continued to falter, Taiwan reached out to African leaders for support in regaining its seat in the United Nations and China re-emerged across the continent.

Earlier, African nations grateful for China's support during their struggles for independence had voted in 1971 to strip Taiwan of its U.N. seat and re-assign it to China. But in the 1990s, several African leaders began playing politics with their allegiances, switching back and forth between China and Taiwan. As a result, both Asian governments sent economic aid to Africa in hopes of winning African support at the U.N.[73] In 1996, Senegal moved

C H R O N O L O G Y

1400s-1900s *Chinese explorers make first contact with Africa. Europeans expand across Africa, enslaving, colonizing and exploiting natural resources.*

1405-1423 Chinese Admiral Zheng He reaches the east coast of Africa.

1515 Portugal ships the first slaves from Africa to colonies in the Americas.

1884-1885 German Chancellor Otto von Bismarck convenes major Western powers to negotiate colonial control of Africa.

1914 Europeans finalize plan to divide Africa among themselves into 50 countries. Great Britain colonizes much of eastern and southern Africa, while France takes much of West Africa, and Portugal takes Mozambique and Angola.

1950s-1960s *African nations begin fighting for — and gaining — independence. China establishes diplomatic relations with more than a dozen African nations by 1969.*

1955 Africa-Asia summit in Bandung, Indonesia, promotes economic and cultural cooperation and opposes "colonialism in all of its manifestations."

1956 China establishes diplomatic relations with Egypt, the first official Sino-African ties.

1959 China establishes diplomatic relations with Sudan; then with eight more African countries, including Uganda, Congo, Kenya and Somalia.

1963-1964 Chinese Prime Minister Zhou Enlai makes a 10-country tour across Africa offering China's support for the continent's growing independence.

1980s-1990s *After turning inward following Mao Zedong's death in 1976, China reemerges and rapidly expands its outreach to Africa.*

1980 After years of support from China during its struggle for independence, Zimbabwe and China establish

diplomatic relations on the same day Zimbabwe gains its independence.

1983 China establishes diplomatic ties with Angola.

1996 Chinese President Jiang Zemin tours six African nations, promising financial aid "without political strings."

1998 China begins a 957-mile-long pipeline in Sudan, the largest foreign oil project in China's history.

2000s *China invests billions in Africa, securing its hold across the continent.*

2000 Forum on China-Africa Cooperation (FOCAC) is founded, sparking increased trade between the two regions.

2003 FOCAC holds its second ministerial meeting in Ethiopia, during which China cancels $1.27 billion in African debt and vows to increase overall Sino-African trade to $28 billion by 2006. . . . China gives Angola $2 billion in exchange for 10,000 barrels of oil a day, allowing Angola to avoid IMF good-governance requirements.

2004 Trade between China and Africa reaches $29.5 billion. . . . China becomes second-largest consumer of oil, behind United States. . . . China sells Zimbabwe $200 million in arms, despite U.S., EU embargoes.

2005 Nigeria signs $800-million deal to supply 30,000 barrels of crude oil per day to China.

2006 Forty-eight African nations attend FOCAC's Third Ministerial Meeting in Beijing, where Chinese President Hu Jintao announces $5 billion in preferential loans and credits to Africa and pledges to increase Sino-Chinese trade to $100 billion by 2010.

2007 China hosts African Development Bank's annual meeting in Shanghai, promising $20 billion for infrastructure development in Africa over the next three years. . . . European Union holds an EU-Africa Summit in Lisbon, Portugal, amid controversy over the attendance of Zimbabwean President Robert Mugabe, condemned by the West as a dictator and suppressor of human rights.

China Floods Africa with Cheap Textiles

Hundreds of thousands of Africans have lost their jobs.

Since China began exporting large quantities of cheap clothing and fabric to Africa about seven years ago, more than 80 percent of Nigeria's textile factories have been forced to shut down, and an estimated 250,000 workers have been laid off.[1]

"It's very serious," says Brian Brink, executive director of the South African Textile Federation. The Chinese can supply materials at prices that are "very much below" local prices, and sometimes even "below the cost of raw materials. That's usually bloody impossible."

Africa's textile and clothing industry — perhaps more than any other sector — has been hit hardest by China's economic expansion across the continent. And South Africa and Nigeria have suffered the most.

In South Africa, textile business membership in Brink's federation has declined by nearly half — dropping from 75 to just 40 in the past seven years. If the trend continues, Brink says, the 150,000 textile and apparel workers across Southern Africa face a troubled future.

"Those who are less resilient will pack up and close their doors," he says. "There will be others that survive in areas that China is not yet operating in, such as in the technical areas, products supplied to technical specifications. China is not there — yet."

About 90 percent South Africa's clothing imports come from China, according to the federation, most of it surplus items from orders destined for the U.S. market. That's what allows China to sell them in Africa for below cost — despite South African regulations that prohibit such "dumping" trade practices.

Brink said relations between Chinese businessmen in South Africa and local textile workers have grown so tense that fist fights regularly break out in local markets. In the face of growing resentment that Africans feel toward Chinese businesses, Beijing officials have voluntarily agreed to cut back on textile exports to South Africa and to provide technical training and assistance to African textile manufacturers.

"The Chinese government does not encourage Chinese enterprises to take other countries' markets by purely increasing the quantity of their exports," President Hu Jintao said during an eight-nation tour of Africa in early 2007.[2]

Meanwhile, Chinese Commerce Minister Bo Xilai met last fall with his counterparts from Benin, Cote d'Ivoire,

Mali, Senegal and Togo to discuss how China can help the cotton industry in West Africa. In addition to sharing technology and sending experts to help increase production, China pledged to build clothing and textile factories and import more cotton from West Africa to boost textile jobs in Africa.[3]

Cheap Clothing Means Lost Jobs

Since China began exporting low-cost clothing to Africa, many textile workers in Southern Africa have lost their jobs. More than half the textile workers in Swaziland, for instance, lost their jobs between 2004 and 2005.

Decline in Textile Jobs in Southern Africa, 2004-2005

	2004	2005	% decline
Kenya	34,614	31,745	9.3
Lesotho	50,217	35,678	28.9
S. Africa	98,000	86,000	12.2
Swaziland	32,000	14,000	56.2

Source: Raphael Kaplinsky and Mike Morris, "Dangling by a Thread: How Sharp Are the Chinese Scissors?" Institute of Development Studies, University of Sussex, Brighton, England, 2006

Brink says those moves will help Africa's textile industry but won't solve all the problems. He admits that many African retailers are contributing to the flood of cheap Chinese goods by undervaluing or not declaring imports in order to avoid paying duties.

"It's not just China being efficient. It's not just the little beavers working hard," Brink says. "There is illegal activity, and that takes two to tango. We have to get our own house in order."

---

[1] Chris Alden, *China in Africa*, p. 81.

[2] "China, Africa build new partnership on old ties," Xinhua General News Service, Oct. 2, 2007.

[3] "Chinese minister meets officials on boosting cotton industry in west Africa," Xinhua News Agency, Oct. 2, 2007.

its embassy from Beijing to Taipei, Taiwan's capital — for the third time — after receiving a large development aid package. Gambia got $48 million from Taiwan the previous year when it moved its embassy from China to Taipei.[74]

Shortly after the Senegal move, Chinese President Jiang Zemin made a six-nation tour of Africa, promising financial assistance "without political strings" and pledging that "hand in hand the two sides will march towards the 21st century."[75] During the trip he offered Zaire $10 million for a cobalt and copper mining project, plus a "gift" of $3.6 million.[76] Also in 1996, China announced a $24 million investment in a gold mine in Sudan, despite U.N. Security Council sanctions against the country for "terrorist" activities.[77]

Besides countering Taiwan's influence, China was interested in Africa's consumer markets for its burgeoning exports and commercial enterprises. China's economy has grown an average of 9 percent each year over the last two decades.[78]

In 2000, the Forum on China-Africa Cooperation (FOCAC) was founded to promote stronger trade and investment relations between both the public and private sectors in China and Africa. It was wildly successful: Sino-African trade more than quintupled between 1999 and 2004 — from $5.6 billion to $29.5 billion — and continued to grow to $32.2 billion by the end of October 2005.[79] At the second FOCAC meeting in 2003, China promised to help train 10,000 African professionals,[80] cancel $1.27 billion in debt to 31 African nations and increase overall Sino-African trade to $28 billion by 2006 — a target that was far exceeded.[81] During the third FOCAC meeting in Beijing in 2006, China dramatically pledged to increase Sino-African trade to $100 billion by 2010 and to pour billions more into financial aid, infrastructure development and social services.

China also has expanded its cultural ties to Africa, offering more than 18,000 government-sponsored scholarships to Africans through 2005, signing 65 cultural agreements with African countries, implementing 151 cultural exchanges and organizing visits by performing-arts troupes from each African region.[82]

"China is the largest developing country, and Africa is home to the largest number of developing countries," President Hu told the 2006 FOCAC summit. "Building

Kidnapped Chinese oil workers land in Addis Ababa, Ethiopia, last April after being released. Anti-government rebels held the six men for nearly a week after attacking a Chinese oil refinery in Ethiopia. Attacks on Chinese businesses have been on the rise in Africa.

strong ties between China and Africa will not only promote development of each side but also help cement unity and cooperation among developing countries and contribute to establishing a just and equitable, new international political and economic order."

He added: "We in China will not forget Africa's full support for restoring the lawful rights of the People's Republic of China in the United Nations. Nor will we forget the sincere and ardent wish of African countries and people for China to realise complete and peaceful reunification and achieve the goal of building a modern nation."[83]

Resource Envy

Many analysts believe China's biggest motivation for expanding its influence in Africa is its growing need for natural resources. Until the 1990s, China could meet its own energy needs by tapping its massive oil reserves in Daqing in northern China.[84] It also relied heavily on coal. But because of coal's low efficiency and negative environmental impacts, China has increasingly switched to gas and oil.

Once Asia's largest oil exporter, China became a net importer of oil in 1993. Between 1995 and 2005 oil consumption in China doubled to 6.8 million barrels per day.[85] In 2003, China became the world's second-largest

Oil Comprises More of Sino-African Trade

Oil represented 85 percent of Africa's exports to China in 2005, more than twice the amount 10 years ago.

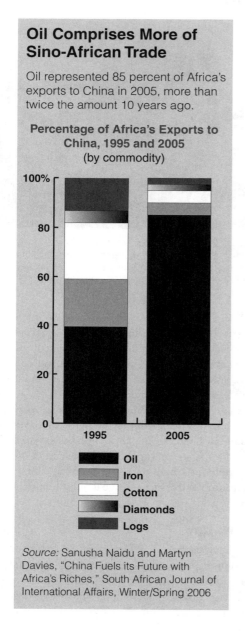

Percentage of Africa's Exports to China, 1995 and 2005 (by commodity)

Legend:
- Oil
- Iron
- Cotton
- Diamonds
- Logs

Source: Sanusha Naidu and Martyn Davies, "China Fuels its Future with Africa's Riches," South African Journal of International Affairs, Winter/Spring 2006

workers to Sudan to build a 957-mile pipeline, the largest contracted foreign oil project in China's history.[86] The project — Sudan's first step into oil exploration — was seen as a possible panacea to the war-torn country's problems.[87] Since then, China has become the leading developer of Sudan's oil reserves, importing 60 percent of the country's output.[88]

Using a combination of political prowess and technological contributions, China also has made oil deals with Angola, Equatorial Guinea, Gabon, Nigeria and others.[89] To gain a foothold in Nigeria, for instance — where Western companies had dominated the oil reserves for decades — China has promised to build and launch a communication satellite. In 2005, China and Nigeria signed an $800 million deal to supply 30,000 barrels of crude oil per day to China. More recently, China and Nigeria agreed China would provide a $4 billion infrastructure investment package in exchange for first-refusal rights on four oil blocks. Many believe China could easily replace some Western firms when their drilling licenses come up for renewal.[90]

Besides oil, China has an unquenchable thirst for minerals needed to produce everyday items, such as door knobs, faucets and cell phones for its 1.3 billion population.[91] "Anywhere there are extractive resources, if China hasn't moved in yet, they will," says Alden, of the South African Institute of International Affairs.

In 2004, China bought 14 percent of Africa's timber exports and 85 percent of its cobalt.[92] South Africa is China's fourth-largest supplier of iron ore. Gabon, South Africa and Ghana are among China's top five manganese suppliers and together account for more than a third of its total manganese imports. Minerals accounted for 97 percent of Sierra Leone's exports to China in 2005 and 87 percent of Zambia's. Minerals accounted for 92 percent of Tanzania's exports to China in 2004.[93]

"China's primary goal is to import from Africa those key raw materials that will sustain its booming economy," says David Shinn, former U.S. ambassador to Ethiopia and Burkina Faso and currently an adjunct professor at The George Washington University. "The Communist Party is more or less predicating its future on maintaining booming economic growth, and if it should stumble, then I think the party is in danger of losing power."[94]

oil consumer, behind the United States, and its oil demand is expected to continue growing steadily.

China has spent the last 10 years negotiating deals with African nations to secure oil supplies. In 1998, China sent 7,000 Chinese engineers and construction

CURRENT SITUATION

Communism to Capitalism

Today, China's outreach to Africa is no longer driven by ideological goals but by the economic and energy resources it needs to become a global superpower. "The West is worried about the impact of Chinese capitalism, not communism," says Alden.

China is Africa's third-largest trading partner, behind the European Union and the United States.[95] And it's doing everything it can to gain on the competition.

In the first quarter of 2007 senior Chinese officials — including President Hu and then-Foreign Minister Li — visited 15 African countries.[96] Besides hosting the African Development Bank's annual meeting in May and promising $20 billion for infrastructure development, Beijing pledged $8 million to the World Health Organization to beef up African countries' capacity to respond to public health emergencies.[97] In September China agreed to lend the Republic of Congo $5 billion in exchange for access to the country's extensive timber, cobalt and copper. Congo said the loan will help build roads, hospitals, housing and universities.[98]

Meanwhile, China is strengthening its political ties with Africa. In September, the first annual political consultation meeting between Chinese and African foreign ministers was held at U.N. headquarters in New York. Foreign ministers and representatives from 48 African countries attended the event chaired by Chinese Foreign Minister Yang Jiechi and Egyptian Foreign Minister Ahmed Aboul Gheit.[99]

"China has a long history of relationships with African countries," says Economy, of the Council on Foreign Relations. "The development aspect — providing doctors and engineers — has remained fairly constant. But now there's an extraordinary jump in the level of Chinese business deals. They're not pushing communism anymore."

Africa Reacts

African governments are welcoming China's financial aid and business investments. The African Union accepted China's offer to build — free of charge — a new conference center for the organization next to its headquarters in Addis Ababa, Ethiopia.[100]

Youngsters — some only 8 years old — work at a copper mine in the Democratic Republic of Congo. The mineral-rich country's huge copper deposits are helping to fuel China's economic boom. To help move the minerals, China is investing $5 billion in Congo to build nearly 2,000 miles of roads and rail lines plus 31 hospitals, 145 health clinics, two new universities and 5,000 housing units.

For many Africans, China has become the new symbol of prosperity, replacing the United States as the land of opportunity. "The United States is a nice place to visit," said Ahmet Mohamet Ali, a trader in Chad who returned from his first trip to China in October. "China is a place to do business."[101]

Direct flights to more than 20 African cities leave weekly from Beijing, Shanghai, Guangzhou and Hong Kong. Regular flights from the United States, on the other hand, serve only eight African cities.[102]

In fall 2007, Chinese officials held a university exposition in the Kenyan capital of Nairobi to recruit even more African students for study in China. African students made up about 2.3 percent of the 162,000 foreign students in China last year. The Chinese government, which already allocates one-fifth of its international scholarships to Africans, plans to double the number of scholarships for Africa to 4,000 by 2009.

According to the official Xinhua news agency, more than 8,000 African students studied Mandarin last year.[103]

Violence against China and its businesses in Africa, however, is increasing. President Hu was forced to cancel a February 2007 trip to Zambia because of threats of massive protests against China's growing hold over the

Tons of fish were seized from two Chinese ships caught in Ivory Coast waters in December 2007. Fishing groups claim Chinese fleets are exploiting Africa's resources by illegally "bottom trawling" — which some equate with clear-cutting the ocean bottom of all flora and fauna.

country's copper mines and poor labor policies toward mine workers.[104] In the past year, numerous Chinese businesses in Africa have been attacked. Rebels attacked a Chinese-run oil refinery in Ethiopia, killing 74 and kidnapping six Chinese employees. In Nigeria — where militants are seeking greater local share of oil revenues — 16 Chinese oil workers were kidnapped in three separate incidents. And gunmen in Kenya killed a Chinese engineer working on a highway project and injured another. Chinese officials, however, have pledged not to let the attacks hinder their business investments in Africa.[105]

Competition Heats Up

Western nations continue to criticize China's business practices in Africa while stepping up their own efforts to reach out to the continent.

"The increasing presence of China in Africa has worked as kind of a wake-up call among some European nations," says the European Commission's Altafaj. "We had a feeling that many Europeans didn't put Africa as high as it should be on its list."

In December, the European Union hosted an EU-Africa Summit in Lisbon, Portugal, in order to develop joint strategies on such issues as trade, human rights, climate change and security. The meeting had originally been scheduled for 2003 but was cancelled because of controversy over whether Zimbabwe's President Mugabe should

be allowed to attend. Western countries condemn Mugabe as a dictator who uses violence against his opponents and has expropriated land from white farmers and plunged the country into economic collapse. The same controversy threatened to derail the December summit when Prime Minister Gordan Brown vowed that neither he nor any senior British cabinet member would attend if Mugabe participated.[106]

African leaders angrily threatened to boycott the summit if Mugabe was excluded and accused the West of resorting to its colonial ways. "This is again another way of manipulating Africa," Gertrude Mongella, the Tanzanian president of the Pan-African Parliament, said in response to Brown's boycott. "Zimbabwe is a nation which got independence. In the developed countries there are so many countries doing things which not all of us subscribe to. We have seen the Iraq War — not everyone accepts what is being done in Iraq."[107]

Despite Brown's opposition, other European leaders were quick to insist that Mugabe be allowed to attend. "There has been enough moralization from Europe," says Altafaj. "We should not underestimate the negative impact of former colonizers lecturing Africans. This summit will be a good opportunity to have conversations about good governance. We do not intend to give lectures." Earlier, German Chancellor Angela Merkel said it was up to African leaders to decide who should represent them at the summit — a sign of the growing pressure European countries feel to strengthen ties with Africa in the wake of China's influence.[108]

And U.S. Treasury Secretary Henry Paulson made a six-day tour to Ghana, South Africa and Tanzania in November to "shine a light" on a part of the world that investors have overlooked. At the end of the tour, President Bush pledged $250 million to start three government funds that will invest in African debt, stocks and companies.[109]

Robert Mosbacher, Jr., president of the Overseas Private Investment Corp., which will administer the government funds, said U.S. companies had to do "a bit of catch-up" in Africa after having focused in recent years on Eastern Europe, Russia and parts of Latin America. "There's no doubt the U.S. can do more to take advantage of growth opportunities in Africa," he said.[110]

As the West is taking notice of China's activities in Africa, China is beginning to listen to Western criticism

AT ISSUE

Is China becoming Africa's newest colonizer?

YES
Adama Gaye
Visiting Fellow, Johns Hopkins
University, School of Advanced and
International Studies, and author,
China-Africa: The Dragon and the Ostrich

Written for *CQ Global Researcher*, December 2007

Every time the colonial question is raised in relation to China's ties with Africa, the Chinese refute it. But the question cannot be easily whisked away.

Now casting itself as the world's largest developing country, China associates its destiny with that of Africa, insisting that both were once humiliated by foreign imperialists and colonial rulers.

But despite its claim that it wants to contribute to Africa's development, a closer look shows another face of China. No longer promoting "international proletarianism," China now strives to gain access to Africa's natural resources and isolate Taiwan. In the process, a colonial power with an Asian face may have entered the continent. And like previous colonizers, China, too, is in Africa to achieve a colonial strategy.

China's goal in Africa is geared toward fulfilling narrow national interests, and the goodwill surrounding it can be perceived as the softer side of a hard-core project. For all its debt cancellation and financial support of Africa, China gets even more in return. While grabbing Africa's natural resources, China dumps its cheap exports in Africa. So far, China's business investments have not reversed the unequal terms of trade that attracted criticism for Western colonizers of the past. The ports, refineries and railways being built by the Chinese serve China's eagerness to "exfiltrate" Africa's resources. And its equity investments in energy and mining industries are all part of its long-term interests.

Meanwhile, cynicism is China's watchword. Under the guise of non-interference and respect for sovereignty, China closes its eyes to lapses in good leadership, corruption, arms sales and violations of human rights and democratic norms.

Giving legitimacy to "rogue states" and providing loans under dubious conditions, China has indirectly rehabilitated political authoritarianism in Africa. Many African leaders now brag about China's achievements in poverty alleviation and economic recovery. Hailing this "model" from the East, they say that it "works" and does not "dictate." Contrasting it to the "failed" Western solutions, these leaders are too happy to have found in China their new tutor. They are no longer orphans of the demise of the Cold War nor do they need to go, bowl in hands, begging the now-discredited World Bank and International Monetary Fund.

Yet the ruthless, capitalistic behavior of China's businessmen in Africa is bound to produce a backlash. Soft-power alone will not prevent it.

NO
Ronald D. Palmer
Former U.S. Ambassador
to Togo and Mauritius

Written for *CQ Global Researcher*, December 2007

Colonialism consists of intricate politico-economic-juridical and socio-cultural structures. Traditional colonizing powers maintained authority and control by ruthless use, as necessary, of police power. By this definition, China is clearly not seeking to colonize Africa.

But China is seeking to increase its influence in Africa. For more than 50 years, China has had a strategy of developing soft power in Africa. They have been quietly making a place for themselves across the continent. The Chinese have established hundreds of businesses across the continent and have poured billions into roads, bridges and other infrastructure. Chinese officials meet regularly with African leaders.

We are seeing the product of years of careful planning. The Chinese worked closely with many African nations during their struggles for independence in the 1950s and '60s. Understanding Africa's resentment toward Western colonialists and the possibilities of exploiting that resentment, China moved into an influence vacuum when colonialism ended.

In desperate need of oil and working hard to become a global superpower, China is doing whatever it needs to do to achieve those goals. In the process, China has made mistakes, rousing the anger of some Africans and prompting many to accuse it of colonialism. Through grants and loans, the Chinese government has helped many small Chinese businesses open up shop in Africa, competing with Africans and forcing many workers to lose their jobs. And Chinese businesses in Africa are known for their poor labor rights and low wages.

But China doesn't have any intention of colonizing Africa. The Chinese are firmly planted in their own environment. Their concerns are with their homeland.

And Africans will not allow themselves to be re-colonized. Already, we have seen Africans protesting Chinese policies that hurt their livelihoods. Africans will simply not put up with another colonial power. By 2020, Africa will still be Africa. It will not be China. Africans don't plan to be dominated again. Africans will retain their concept of who they are and who they want to be.

Does China want to have influence? Yes. Does China need to use its military to colonize Africa? No. They've demonstrated that their investments in Africa's infrastructure can win and influence people. The Chinese are doing things the West did in the past to profit from Africa's resources. But the Chinese are doing it better and without the need to colonize.

To protest the genocide in Darfur, actress Mia Farrow holds an Olympic-style torch at a rally last Dec. 10 outside the Chinese Embassy in Washington. Activists are pressuring Beijing — which hosts the Olympics this summer — to use its influence in oil-rich Sudan to stop the killing.

of its dealings with African nations. After years of blocking U.N. sanctions against Sudan, China last year agreed to send more than 300 peacekeepers as part of the U.N. mission to end years of bloodshed in Darfur.[111]

In fact, President Bush's special envoy to Sudan, Andrew Natsios, last fall credited China for its work to help end the fighting in Darfur. It was Chinese influence, Natsios said, that finally convinced the Sudanese government to accept a July Security Council resolution to authorize a 26,000-member U.N. military and civilian peacekeeping operation in Darfur. "The Chinese are like a locomotive

that is speeding up," he said. "They are even doing things we didn't ask them to do."[112]

Many observers say China is working hard to improve its global image with the approach of the 2008 Olympics in Beijing. "It's about reputational risks, especially with the build-up to the Olympics," says Alden, of the South African Institute of International Affairs. "They don't want to be seen as an evil face."

OUTLOOK

Belle of the Ball

China is expected to honor the promises it made at the Beijing summit to rapidly expand its business, cultural and infrastructure investments across Africa. In part, that commitment is dictated by China's need for resources. By 2020, analysts say, China will have 120 million private cars on the road and be forced to import at least 60 percent of its oil.[113]

But Western countries also are expected to invest more financial and diplomatic energy in Africa. "The West is already beginning to get off their duffs. This could mean greater trade and aid from the West," Alden says. "I sense the West is going to increasingly feel China as a source of pressure and provide more assistance and government investment to Africa in the coming years."

Increased attention from both the East and the West will undoubtedly inject much-needed infrastructure and economic support into developing Africa, which could benefit both sides. For decades the West has ignored the continent's potential as a business and political partner, generally seeing African governments as too corrupt or too weak to provide healthy investment environments. Or they saw Africa as a disaster zone — plagued by famine and disease — worthy of humanitarian assistance rather than financial investment. But China has proven that Africa can be a powerful ally.

"It's not too late [for the West], but it's getting late," says the European Commission's Altafaj. "We better upgrade our relationship now — for the benefit of both sides."

But along with China and the West, India, Russia, Brazil and others also are expected to look increasingly toward Africa as their energy needs grow and business opportunities expand. Russian trade with Africa has tripled since 2000, up to $3 billion a year. Russia also has invested $3.5 billion in oil exploration across the continent in recent years, and new energy deals in Algeria have been accompanied by $4 billion in arms sales.[114]

Meanwhile, Africa is relishing its newfound international popularity — opening its doors to a multitude of investors. "Angola and others have discovered it's in their best interest to stay diversified," says Reisen at the Organization for Economic Cooperation and Development. "You don't want to replace one monopolizer with another."

But some fear the new flood of investments — especially from countries such as China that put no restrictions on the funding — will actually feed the continent's already serious corruption problem.

"The Chinese are much more prone to do business in a way that today Europeans and Americans do not accept — paying bribes and all kinds of bonuses under the table," said Gal Luft, codirector of the Institute for the Analysis of Global Security, a Washington educational organization focusing on energy security. "These are things that have been rampant throughout Africa. . . . It will be much easier for those countries to work with Chinese companies rather than American and European companies that are becoming more and more restricted by this 'publish what you pay' initiative and others calling for better transparency."[115]

International pressure is also forcing China to play a bigger role in confronting human-rights abuses in Africa. China has already softened its policy of "non-interference" and sent peacekeepers to Darfur. "The pressure on China is immense, especially with the Olympics coming up" in China, says the Council on Foreign Relations' Economy. "China is getting the message that it's not enough just to be a global superpower."

It is unclear, however, whether China's recent actions to protect human rights in Africa is simply a short-term public relations campaign or a long-term change in policy. "If you're a glass half-full person, then you'll say there won't be that much difference between Western policy and Chinese policy in the future," says Alden. "If you're a glass half-empty person, you'd say it's just window dressing."

But Africans say the onus is not just on China. Africans themselves must act to ensure they do not fall prey to yet another colonial power.

"China's stance on Africa is likely to harden in the long term, with more manipulation and exploitation and less

benefit for the continent," said Moreblessings Chidaushe, a lobby and advocacy program officer with the African Forum and Network on Debt and Development, based in Harare, Zimbabwe. "One way out would be the development of a comprehensive African policy on China."

Chidaushe called on the African Union to "increase African countries' security" and make it easier for them to deal with China — which she called a "superpower wannabe" — rather than making individual approaches "that are easily susceptible to manipulation."[116]

Some say China's growing involvement in Africa is giving leaders across the continent the power they need to improve social conditions and human rights. "Human rights cannot be imposed upon a nation. It's indigenous," says TransAfrica's Lee. "China is opening more options for these governments and for their people. Africans now have more room, more flexibility to determine how they can improve their countries."

But even those who question China's motives, business practices and human-rights policies say the renewed interest could benefit the continent economically, politically and socially. "Africans will rise up significantly in the coming years," says Chan at the University of London's School of Oriental and African Studies. "They will rise up with the assistance of everyone — not just China."

NOTES

1. Jonathan Watts, "The savannah comes to Beijing as China hosts its new empire," *The Guardian* (London), Nov. 4, 2006, p. 24; "China-Africa Forum Opens in Beijing Today," *Ghanaian Chronicle*, Nov. 3, 2006.

2. Bates Gill, Chin-hao Huang and J. Stephenson Morrison, "Assessing China's Growing Influence in Africa," *China Security*, Summer 2007, World Security Institute, p. 3, http://yaleglobal.yale.edu/ about/pdfs/china-africa.pdf.

3. "China-Africa Forum Opens in Beijing Today," *op. cit*.

4. "China announces package of aid measures for Africa at historic summit," Xinhua News Agency, Nov. 4, 2006.

5. "Chinese, African entrepreneurs sign billion-dollar worth agreements," Xinhua News Agency, Nov. 5, 2006.

6. Watts, *op. cit.*; also see http://news.xinhuanet.com/english/2006-12/08/content_5452301.htm.

7. Sarah DiLorenzo, "China thanks Africans for help stopping Taiwan vote, heralds 30 percent trade increase," The Associated Press, Sept. 27, 2007.

8. Bates Gill, Chin-hao Huang and J. Stephenson Morrison, "China's Expanding Role in Africa and Implications for the United States," Center for Strategic and International Studies, January, 2007.

9. Danna Harman, "China Takes Up Civic Work in Africa," *The Christian Science Monitor*, June 27, 2007, p. 1.

10. "Full text of joint communiqué of Sino-African ministerial political consultations," Xinhua Economic News Service, Sept. 27, 2007.

11. "Promoting Growth in Africa: Working with China," British Department for International Development Fact Sheet, October 2006; also see Sanusha Naidu and Martyn Davies, "China Fuels its Future with Africa's Riches," *South African Journal of International Affairs*, Winter/Spring 2006, pp. 69-83.

12. Esther Pan, "Backgrounder: China, Africa and Oil," Council on Foreign Relations, Jan. 26, 2007.

13. Statistics come from Chris Alden and Helmut Reisen.

14. Chris Alden, *China in Africa* (2007), p. 75.

15. *Ibid.*

16. "Blast Kills 46 at a Copper Mine in Zambia," Reuters, April 21, 2005.

17. Cindy Hurst, "China's Oil Rush in Africa," Institute for the Analysis of Global Security, July 2006, p. 3.

18. Barbara Slavin, "Olympics seen as leverage for Darfur; China moving to solve crisis," *USA Today*, Sept. 21, 2007, p. 6A.

19. "An Awkward Meeting: Europe and Africa," the Economist.com, Dec. 9, 2007. www.economist.com/world/africa/displaystory.cfm?story_id=10273503.

20. "Communication from the Commission to the European Parliament and the Council: From Cairo to Lisbon — The EU-Africa Strategic Partnership," Commission of the European Communities, June 26, 2007, p. 3.

21. Heidi Vogt, "Chinese Mark on Africa Means Commerce," The Associated Press, Sept. 2, 2007.

22. Peter Brookes and Ji Hye Shin, "China's Influence in Africa: Implications for the United States," Heritage Foundation, Feb. 22, 2006, p. 6.

23. Harman, *op. cit.*

24. Jake Lee, "China inflows give African currencies a boost," *International Tribune Herald*, June 5, 2007, p. 18.

25. "China's Interest and Activity in Africa's Construction and Infrastructure Sectors," Centre for Chinese Studies, Stellenbosch University, South Africa, Nov. 2006, p. 7.

26. Brookes and Shin, *op. cit.*, p. 6.

27. Quoted in Firoze Manji and Stephen Marks, *African Perspectives on China in Africa* (2007), p. 5, available at www.fahamu.org/downloads/cia_download.pdf.

28. "China defends its role in Africa," *East African Business Week*, May 28, 2007.

29. Gill, Huang and Morrison, "Assessing China's Growing Influence in Africa," *op. cit.*, p. 5.

30. Stellenbosch University, *op. cit.*, pp. 21, 33.

31. Richard Beeston, "West could learn from straightforward approach," *The Times* (London), Nov. 2, 2006, p. 42.

32. Don Lee, "China Barrels Ahead in Oil Market," *Los Angeles Times*, Nov. 14, 2004, p. C1.

33. Peter Ford, "China woos African trade," *The Christian Science Monitor*, Nov. 3, 2006, p. 1.

34. Hurst, *op. cit.*, p. 7; and Slavin, *op. cit.*

35. Deb Riechmann, "Bush announces new sanctions against Sudan for its role in Darfur," The Associated Press, May 29, 2007.

36. "Beijing Summit adopts declaration, highlighting China-Africa strategic partnership," Forum on China-Africa Cooperation press release, Nov. 6, 2006.

37. Howard W. French, "China in Africa: All Trade, With No Political Baggage," *The New York Times*, Aug. 8, 2004, p. 4.

38. "Appeal by Amnesty International to the Chinese government on the occasion of the China-Africa Summit for Development and Cooperation," AI Index: AFR 54/072/2006, Nov. 1, 2006.

39. Pan, *op. cit.*

40. Jane Macartney, "Beijing turns its back on embattled Robert Mugabe," *The Times* (London), Sept. 19, 2007, p. 34; also see Brookes and Shin, *op. cit.*, p. 4.

41. Abraham McLaughlin, "A rising China counters US clout in Africa," *The Christian Science Monitor*, March 30, 2005, p. 1.

42. Macartney, *op. cit.*, p. 4.

43. Harman, *op. cit.*

44. Margaret C. Lee, Henning Melber, Sanusha Naidu and Ian Taylor, "China in Africa," *Current African Issues*, No. 33, Nordiska Afrikainstitutet, Uppsala, Sweden, p. 11.

45. For statistics on China's assistance to Africa, see the Forum on China-Africa Cooperation, http://english.focacsummit.org/.

46. David Shinn, "Africa, China, the United States, and Oil," Center for Strategic and International Studies Africa Policy Forum, May 8, 2007.

47. Guy Raz, "New U.S. Command in Africa Faces Skeptics, National Public Radio, Oct. 18, 2007; and Shinn, *op. cit.*

48. Christopher Thompson, "The Scramble for Africa's Oil," *The New Statesman*, June 14, 2007. www.newstatesman.com/200706180024.

49. Lee, Melber, Naidu and Taylor, *op. cit.*

50. Naidu and Davies, *op. cit.*

51. Hurst, *op. cit.*, p. 10.

52. See www.bp.com/genericarticle.do?categoryId=98&contentId=7036566.

53. Raz, *op. cit.*

54. Manji and Marks, *op. cit.*, p. 18.

55. See www.africom.mil/africomFAQs.asp.

56. "Big Oil and Energy Independence," *Congressional Record*, Feb. 8, 2007, p. H1404, www.govtrack.us/congress/record.xpd?id=110-h20070208-53.

57. See "The Trans-Atlantic Slave Trade," from About.com: African History, http://africanhistory.about.com/library/weekly/aa080601a.htm.

58. For background on European colonization of Africa and the Berlin Conference, see U.K.'s Channel 4 feature, "Empire's Children: The Scramble for Africa," at www.channel4.empireschildren.co.uk.

59. For background, see David Masci, "Aiding Africa," *CQ Researcher*, Aug. 29, 2003, pp. 697-720.

60. For background on Africa's fight for independence, see the BBC, "The Story of Africa: Independence," at www.bbc.co.uk/worldservice/africa/features/storyofafrica.

61. *Ibid.*

62. Slobodan Lekic, "Historic Asia-Africa conference was marked by superpower hostility, tragedy," The Associated Press, April 24, 2005.

63. For background on diplomatic relations between China and Africa, visit http://english.focacsummit.org.

64. Manji and Marks, *op. cit.*, p. 35.

65. Joshua Eisenman, "Zimbabwe: China's African ally," China Brief 5 (15), the Jamestown Foundation, July 5, 2007.

66. Stellenbosch University, *op. cit.*, p. 13.

67. Masci, *op. cit.*, p. 710.

68. For background, see Peter Katel, "Ending Poverty," *CQ Researcher*, Sept. 9, 2005, pp. 733-760.

69. *Ibid.*

70. Masci, *op. cit.*, p. 749; also see Kathy Koch, "Economic Turnabout in Africa," *Editorial Research Reports*, Nov. 7, 1986, available in CQ Researcher Plus Archive, www.cqpress.com.

71. Katel, *op. cit.*, p. 749.

72. Manji and Marks, *op. cit.*, p. 44.

73. "Africa and Asia. Hallo, China — or is it Taiwan?" *The Economist*, Sept. 14, 1996, p. 44.

74. Jonathan Manthorpe, "Asia courts Africa in Chinese rivalry," *The Vancouver Sun* (British Columbia), June 5, 1996, p. A1.

75. "Visiting Chinese president pledges support with no strings attached," BBC, May 27, 1996.

76. *The Economist, op. cit.*

77. David Hecht, "Taiwan Loses 1 Big African Nation But Still Has 8 Little Ones," *Africa News*, Dec. 5, 1996.

78. Pan, *op. cit.*

79. Brookes and Shin, *op. cit.*, pp. 5-6.

80. For background, visit FOCAC's Web site at http://english.focacsummit.org/.

81. Alden, *op. cit.*, p. 31.

82. For background on China's aid to Africa, see http://english.focacsummit.org/.

83. "Full text: Address by Hu Jintao at the Opening Ceremony of the Beijing Summit of The Forum on China-Africa Cooperation," http://english.focacsummit.org/2006-11-04/content_4978.htm.

84. Hurst, *op. cit.*, p. 3.

85. Lee, Melber, Naidu and Taylor, *op. cit.*, p. 14.

86. "Set to Build Pipeline for Sudan," Xinhua News Agency, July 31, 1998.

87. Michela Wrong, "Sudan looks to oil for new life-blood," *Financial Times*, June 11, 1998, p. 4.

88. Hurst, *op. cit.*, p. 7.

89. *Ibid.*, p. 6.

90. *Ibid.*, p. 11.

91. Manji and Marks, *op. cit.*, p. 143.

92. Naidu and Davies, *op. cit.*

93. Stellenbosch University, *op. cit.*, p. 74.

94. Sebastian Junger, "Enter China the Giant," *Vanity Fair*, July 2007, p. 126.

95. Lee, Melber, Naidu and Taylor, *op. cit.*, p. 41.

96. Gill, Huang and Morrison, *op. cit.*, p. 3.

97. *Ibid.*, p. 6.

98. China opens coffers for minerals," BBC, Sept. 18, 2007, http://news.bbc.co.uk/2/hi/africa/7000925.stm.

99. "Chinese, African foreign ministers launch consultation mechanism at UN," BBC Worldwide Monitoring, Sept. 27, 2007.

100. David White, "The China Factor: A spectacular resurgence," *Financial Times*, Nov. 20, 2006, www.ft.com/cms/s/0/e6afc19a-6e5d-11db-b5c4-0000779e2340,dwp_uuid=1f2588a0-765d-11-db-8284-0000779e2340.html.

101. Stephanie McCrummen, "Struggling Chadians Dream Of a Better Life — in China," *The Washington Post*, Oct. 6, 2007, p. A17, www.washingtonpost.com/wp-dyn/content/article/2007/10/05/AR2007100502484.html.

102. Heidi Vogt, "Chinese Mark on Africa Means Commerce," The Associated Press, Sept. 2, 2007, www.mcclatchydc.com/staff/shashank_bengali/story/20987.html.

103. Shashank Bengali, "To soften its image, China courts African students," McClatchy News Service, Nov. 4, 2007.

104. Danna Harman, "In Sudan, China Focuses on Oil Wells, Not Local Needs," *The Christian Science Monitor*, June 25, 2007, p. 11, www.csmonitor.com/2007/0625/p11s01-woaf.htm.

105. Anita Powell, "Ethiopia Blames Eritrea for Attack," The Associated Press, April 25, 2007.

106. "Zimbabwe poses dilemma for EU-Africa summit host," Agence France-Presse, Nov. 25, 2007.

107. Philip Webster and David Charter, "Brown offers summit a lifeline: I'll go — but only if Mugabe stays away," *The Times* (London), Sept. 21, 2007, p. 21, www.timesonline.co.uk/tol/news/world/africa/article2496374.ece.

108. Tracy McVeigh, "Mugabe can attend summit," *The Guardian* (London), Oct. 12, 2007, p. 6.

109. "U.S. funds to purchase Africa debt and stocks," *The International Herald Tribune*, Nov. 20, 2007.

110. Alec Russell, "US business worried over China's expansion in Africa," *Financial Times*, Nov. 20, 2007, p. 5, www.ft.com/cms/s/0/93944ea8-96f3-11dc-b2da-0000779fd2ac,dwp_uuid=5cdb1d20-feea-11db-aff2-000b5df10621.html.

111. Mohamed Hasni, "Darfur rebels tell China peace-keepers to go home," Agence France-Presse, Nov. 25, 2007.

112. William C. Mann, "China Credited with Progress on Darfur," The Associated Press, Sept. 19, 2007.

113. Hurst, *op. cit.*, p. 3.

114. Owen Matthews, "Racing for New Riches," *Newsweek*, Nov. 19, 2007, www.newsweek.com/id/68910.

115. Hurst, *op. cit.*, p. 15.

116. Manji and Marks, *op. cit.*, pp. 110-111.

BIBLIOGRAPHY

Books

Alden, Chris, *China in Africa, Zed Books*, 2007.
The head of the China in Africa program at the South African Institute of International Affairs offers a comprehensive overview of China's new engagement in Africa, examining China's motives, Africa's reaction and the ultimate outcome of the new relationship.

Lee, Margaret C., Henning Melber, Sanusha Naidu and Ian Taylor, *China in Africa: Current African Issues No. 3, Nordic Africa Institute*, 2007.
The authors, all researchers with extensive experience in African and Asian studies, examine China's scramble for Africa's resources, its economic investments in the continent and case studies on Uganda and South Africa.

Manji, Firoze, and Stephen Marks (eds.), *African Perspectives on China in Africa, Fahamu*, 2007.
Essays by some of Africa's leading academics and activists look at a variety of issues arising from China's growing influence across the continent — from environmental impacts to colonialism to economic growth.

Articles

Gill, Bates, Chin-hao Huang and J. Stephenson Morrison, "Assessing China's Growing Influence in Africa," *China Security*, Vol. 3, No. 3, summer 2007, World Security Institute, pp. 3-21, www.wsichina.org/cs7_all.pdf.
The authors explore China's rapidly growing engagement in Africa over the past decade and highlight milestones that have led to their strong relationship.

Harman, Danna, "China Takes up Civic Work in Africa," *The Christian Science Monitor*, June 27, 2007, p. 1, www.csmonitor.com/2007/0627/p01s05-woaf.html.
Is China helping or hurting Africa? Both sides of the debate are presented.

Junger, Sebastian, "Enter China, the Giant," *Vanity Fair*, July 2007, p. 126.
A best-selling author examines China's activities in Sudan and Darfur.

Naidu, Sanusha, and Martyn Davies, "China Fuels its Future with Africa's Riches," *South African Journal of International Affairs*, Vol. 13 (2), winter/spring 2006, www.ccs.org.za/downloads/Naidu%20and%20Davies%20-%20SAIIA%20-%20Vol%2013.2.pdf.
Scholars at the Center for Chinese Studies in South Africa examine China's growing reliance on African resources and the opportunities and threats China's search for energy is creating for Africans.

Shinn, David H., "Africa, China, the United States and Oil," *Center for Strategic and International Studies Online Africa Policy Forum*, May 8, 2007, http://forums.csis.org/africa/index.php?s=Shinn&searchbutton=Go%21.
A former U.S. ambassador to Ethiopia and Burkina Faso discusses the role oil plays in the relationships among China, Africa and the United States.

Vogt, Heidi, "Chinese Mark on Africa Means Commerce," *The Associated Press*, Sept. 2, 2007, www.usatoday.com/news/world/2007-09-02-2865007898_x.htm.
A reporter provides an overview of the pros and cons of the proliferation of Chinese businesses and citizens working in Africa.

Reports and Studies

Brooks, Peter, and Ji Hye Shin, "China's Influence in Africa: Implications for the United States," *The Heritage Foundation Backgrounder, No. 1916*, Feb. 22, 2006, www.heritage.org/Research/AsiaandthePacific/bg1916.cfm.
Scholars at a conservative Washington think tank outline China's rapidly expanding political, social and economic influence across Africa and warn of threats to U.S. goals in the region.

Hurst, Cindy, "China's Oil Rush in Africa," *The Institute for the Analysis of Global Security*, July 2006, http://leav-www.army.mil/fmso/documents/chinainafrica.pdf.
A U.S. Navy officer and political-military research analyst offers an excellent overview of China's growing reliance on African oil.

Kaplinsky, Raphael, Dorothy McCormick and Mike Morris, "The Impact of China on Sub Saharan Africa," *U.K. Department for International Development*, April 2006, www.uneca.org/eca_programmes/acgd/Overview_Report.pdf.

The report examines why China and Africa are strengthening their ties and details China's impact on Africa's trade, textile and energy sectors.

Pan, Esther, "China, Africa and Oil," *Backgrounder for the Council on Foreign Relations*, Jan. 26, 2007, www.cfr.org/publication/9557/china_africa_and_oil.html?breadcrumb=%2Fpublication%2Fpublication_list%3Ftype%3Dbackgrounder%26page%3D5.
A researcher at the Council on Foreign Relations addresses some of the most frequently asked questions about China in Africa.

For More Information

African Union, P.O. Box 3243, Addis Ababa, Ethiopia; +251 11 551 77 00; www.africa-union.org. A diplomatic organization that fosters economic and social cooperation among 53 African nations and other governments.

Center for Strategic and International Studies, 1800 K St., N.W., Washington, DC 20006; (202) 887-0200; www.csis.org. A nonprofit public policy research institution that provides analysis on defense, security and international issues.

Council on Foreign Relations, 1779 Massachusetts Ave., N.W., Washington, DC 20036; (202) 518.3400; www.cfr.org. A nonpartisan think tank that offers extensive resources, data and experts on foreign policy issues.

Department for International Development, 1 Palace St., London SW1E 5HE, UK; +44 020 7023 0000; www.dfid.gov.uk. The United Kingdom agency working on international development issues.

Directorate General for External Trade, European Union, 200 rue de la Loi-Wetstraat, B-1049 Brussels, Belgium, 00 800 67891011; http://ec.europa.eu/trade/. Oversees the European Commission's global trade policy.

Forum on China-Africa Cooperation, No. 2, Chaoyangmen Nandajie, Chaoyang District, Beijing, 10070; +86-10-65961114; www.focac.org/eng. A Ministry of Foreign Affairs organization that works to strengthen economic, social and political ties between China and Africa.

Institute for the Analysis of Global Security, P.O. Box 2837, Washington, DC 20013; (866) 713-7527; www.iags.org. A nonprofit educational organization focusing on energy security.

South African Institute of International Affairs, P.O. Box 31596, Braamfontein, 2017, South Africa; +27 (011) 339-2021; www.saiia.org.za. Its China in Africa Project studies the emerging relationship between China and Africa.

Textile Federation of South Africa, P.O. Box 53, Bruma, 2026, South Africa; +27 (011) 454-2342; www.texfed.co.za. The trade association for South Africa's textile businesses; offers information about the economic stability of the industry, particularly China's impact.

Ilan Halimi, a French Jew, was kidnapped and killed by a gang in Paris. He was found naked, handcuffed and covered with burn marks and died on the way to a hospital. The case spurred national outrage and huge marches protesting the rise of anti-Semitism in France.

Anti-Semitism in Europe

Are Israel's Policies Spurring a New Wave of Hate Crimes?

Sarah Glazer

O n Feb. 22, Mathieu Roumi, a 19-year-old French Jew, was tortured for nine hours in a basement in a Paris suburb by a group of young men, including several Muslims, who wrote "dirty Jew" on his face and forced him to eat cigarette butts and suck on a condom-covered stick.[1]

The incident bore eerie parallels to the 2006 murder of Ilan Halimi, a 23-year-old Jewish cell phone salesman who was kidnapped and killed by a gang in Paris after three weeks of torture. Halimi was found naked, covered in bruises, knife slashes and burns; he died on the way to the hospital.[2]

Both Halimi and Roumi were abducted in their own neighborhoods in Paris' low-income Bagneux quarter. Halimi had been abducted by a gang calling itself the Barbarians, which had tried unsuccessfully to extort a ransom of 3 million Euros ($4.5 million) from Halimi's family. Unlike Halimi, however, Roumi knew his attackers and was ultimately released.

When police raided the apartments of gang leader Youssouf Fofana and other gang members charged with Halimi's killing, they discovered anti-Semitic, neo-Nazi and radical Muslim, or Islamist, literature. Fofana continued to send anti-Semitic letters to the judge overseeing the case.

Gang members later admitted they selected Halimi assuming he was "one of these rich Jews" — although Halimi's family actually was of only modest means, defying the stereotype.[3]

The Halimi case spurred a storm of controversy about the state of anti-Semitism in France and was seen by the Jewish community as the culmination of a wave of anti-Jewish attacks on individuals and synagogues that has surged since 2000 — just after the start of

From *CQ Global Researcher*, June 2008.

Individuals Targeted in Many Incidents

Forty percent of the 632 major attacks and violent incidents against Jews worldwide in 2007 targeted specific individuals, while 22 percent targeted cemeteries and memorials. More than half of the incidents were nonviolent — involving vandalism, graffiti or slogans.

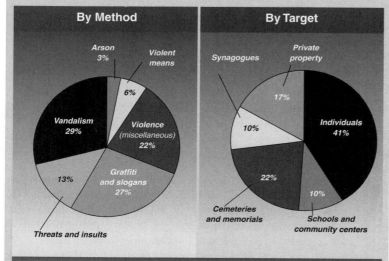

Anti-Semitic Attacks and Incidents Worldwide, 2007

By Method

Arson 3%
Violent means 6%
Vandalism 29%
Violence (miscellaneous) 22%
13%
Graffiti and slogans 27%
Threats and insults

By Target

Synagogues
Private property 17%
10%
Individuals 41%
22%
10%
Cemeteries and memorials
Schools and community centers

Total No. of Incidents Worldwide in 2007: 632

Source: Stephen Roth Institute, 2007

the second Palestinian intifada, or uprising, against Israel's occupation — according to the Stephen Roth Institute for the Study of Contemporary Anti-Semitism and Racism in Tel Aviv.[4] It also raised questions about a new source of anti-Semitism in Europe — radical, anti-Zionist Muslims.

In fact, the institute's latest report on global anti-Semitism found mixed trends in 2007: Anti-Jewish incidents of all kinds slowed and even declined a bit from the previous year in a handful of countries, and it was the quietest year the French Jewish community has known since the rise in attacks began in 2000.[5] But violent attacks on individuals continued to rise, causing some Jewish groups and experts to worry that Europe appears to be adjusting to a new, high level of violent hate incidents and blatant anti-Jewish rhetoric.

Although anti-Semitic incidents overall declined last year in Britain,[6] Belgium and Germany,[7] major attacks and

violent incidents against Jews in Western Europe — including attacks on individuals and vandalizing of Jewish property — reached a new high — 352 incidents, or more than quadruple the number in 1999, according to the institute.[8] For instance, while France experienced a 33 percent drop in anti-Semitic acts of all kinds, major violent attacks on French individuals and property quadrupled from 2 to 8; violent, anti-Semitic offenses in Germany jumped more than 50 percent.[9]

A British parliamentary inquiry raised concern in 2006 about a "widespread change in mood and tone when Jews are discussed" in the media, at universities and in other public settings.

"We are concerned that anti-Jewish themes and remarks are gaining acceptability in some quarters in public and private discourse in Britain, and there is a danger that this trend will become more and more mainstream," the report warned.[10]

Many young people in the Jewish community tolerated living with verbal and physical assaults — so much so, the report found, that many incidents weren't even reported, particularly in orthodox Jewish neighborhoods. "The routineness of anti-Semitism was most shocking — how it became accepted as a normal part of life," says John Mann, chair of the Parliamentary Committee Against Anti-Semitism.

A month before the report's release on Aug. 9, 2006, Jasmine Kranat — a 13-year-old Jewish girl riding home from school on a bus — was asked by teenagers demanding money whether she was Jewish. The teenagers punched her in the face until she lost consciousness, and no one on the bus offered her assistance.[11]

Middle East or Muslim-related news events — such as the 9/11 terrorist attacks in the United States or the 2006 Lebanon war between Israel and Hezbollah — appear to trigger anti-Jewish violence in Europe, notes Mark Gardner, a spokesman for the Community Security Trust, a London-based group that tracks anti-Semitic incidents in Britain.

"Our fear is that since 2000 there have been so many trigger events that the net effect is a considerable increase in underlying anti-Semitic incidents," contributing to a high, ongoing base level, says Gardner. "In 2007 there were no trigger events, yet it was still the second-worst year on record" since his organization began recording them in 1984. Even with the slight drop in anti-Jewish incidents in Britain last year, the 547 incidents that did occur — which included assaults, hate mail, anti-Semitic graffiti and verbal abuse — amounted to twice as many as in 1999. And, disturbingly, 114 of the 2007 incidents were violent assaults — the highest number since 1984.[12]

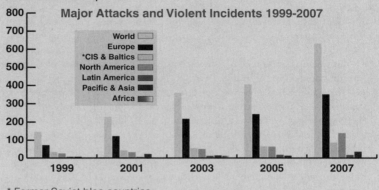

Most Anti-Semitic Attacks Occur in Europe

Major anti-Semitic attacks and violent incidents worldwide jumped more than fourfold between 1999 and 2007. North America saw more than a fivefold increase — from 25 in 1999 to 140 in 2007 — but more than half of the 632 major attacks worldwide last year occurred in Europe.

Major Attacks and Violent Incidents 1999-2007

Legend: World, Europe, *CIS & Baltics, North America, Latin America, Pacific & Asia, Africa

* Former Soviet bloc countries

Source: Stephen Roth Institute, 2007

Last year many religious Jews, identifiable by their dress, were attacked and injured by Arabs or North Africans, according to the Roth Institute. For example, on Sept. 7, Rabbi Zalman Gurevitch was stabbed in the stomach in Frankfurt am Main, Germany, by someone he described as an Arab speaker who shouted "[Pig] Jew, I will kill you."[13]

A great deal of this violence apparently is stimulated by opposition to the existence of Israel, or anti-Zionism, which is shared both by Muslims and by much of Europe's intellectual elite, according to the Roth Institute's latest report on anti-Semitism worldwide. "The fact that anti-Zionism has become politically correct in some sectors encourages not only anti-Semitic activists of the left and right but also young, second- or third-generation Muslims who have been exposed (via satellite TV and the Internet) to hate preachers from the Arab world," the report says.[14]

Franco Frattini, the European Union (EU) commissioner responsible for combating racism and anti-Semitism in Europe, has attributed half of all documented anti-Semitic incidents in Europe to "radical Islamic elements."[15]

The U.S. State Department calls anti-Zionist political cartoons and news commentary that appear after Israeli-Palestinian flareups the "new anti-Semitism," a term adopted by critics of the European left and even included in a working definition of anti-Semitism agreed to by EU states in January 2005.[16] These critics have savaged the liberal European media and leftist activists for what they consider their one-sided sympathizing with the Palestinians.

"Zionism is now a dirty word in Britain, and opposition to Israel has become a fig leaf for a resurgence of the oldest hatred," Melanie Phillips, a commentator for the British *Daily Mail*, recently charged.[17]

Some find this new type of anti-Semitism particularly disturbing because they fear it arouses European racial canards that existed before and during World War II. Political cartoons in newspapers and on the Internet have revived caricatures reminiscent of medieval beliefs in the Jew as child-killer and employed Nazi-like imagery to portray Jewish Israelis as cruel and bloodthirsty in countries as varied as Norway, Greece and England.[18]

So many familiar anti-Jewish stereotypes appeared in the mainstream media during the Lebanon war in 2006 that British scholar David Hirsch described the period as "the summer in which anti-Semitism entered the mainstream."[19]

Hate rhetoric coming out of the Middle East is often beamed into Europe via Syrian and Egyptian satellite TV

Who Are Israel's Harshest Critics?

Liberal British Jews oppose Palestinian occupation.

At a March meeting in London of activists opposed to Israel's occupation of Palestinian territories, attendees could buy fair-trade, organic Palestinian olive oil soap, with revenues going to widows in Ramallah.

But this was not a meeting directed at London's large Muslim population. It featured a panel of Israeli protesters who have come to view their nation's treatment of the Palestinians as incompatible with a democratic, racially equitable society. And it was organized primarily by liberal-left British Jewish groups critical of Israel, such as Jews for Justice for Palestinians.

About 200 mostly middle-aged Jews crowded into the room, the kind of rumpled, intellectual audience one might expect at a talk at New York's famous 92nd Street Y. Palestinian psychiatrist Eyad El-Sarraj, director of the Gaza Community Mental Health Program, described on a live phone line how Israel's blockade had left Gazans so short of bottled water and water filters that they were forced to drink salty, polluted tap water.

"Imagine living in a prison that you're not allowed to leave, and the prison is bombed," he told the hushed room. As for the violence, he said, "I cry for the children killed in Gaza," but also "I cry when my people celebrated in the streets" over the killing of children in Jerusalem.

Parallels to apartheid South Africa were frequently drawn by the speakers as photos flashed across a screen of impoverished Palestinians confronting armed soldiers at checkpoints and standing dwarfed by Israel's security wall dividing it from Palestinian villages. The overwhelmingly sympathetic crowd applauded calls for a boycott of Israeli academics and of companies that benefit from the occupation of Palestinian territories.

Michael Kustow, a British writer and organizer of the event, anticipated criticism from the British Jewish community. "Those of us who criticize Israel do not think we're disloyal or self-hating," he maintained. "We're trying to return Israel to . . . its own values."

Harsh criticism of Israel is common on campuses in Great Britain, which often comes as a shock to visiting American Jewish students. "I've been very surprised at the amount of anti-Israel programming at the institutional level," says Naomi Berlin, a student at Tufts University in Medford, Mass., spending her junior year at Oxford. "When you say Israel, you get words like 'occupation,' 'apartheid,' 'racist.'"

Berlin cited two highly controversial debates organized this academic year by the eminent Oxford Union Debating Society. One, a November forum on free speech featuring Holocaust denier David Irving, was picketed by Jewish students. Another, a debate on whether Israel should exist, invited two prominent critics of Israel to argue in favor of Israel's existence. One of them actually switched sides during the debate and argued against Israel's right to exist.

stations and the Internet, but it has been getting less attention from the liberal press than it once did, says Charles Small, director of the Yale Initiative for the Interdisciplinary Study of Antisemitism. As an example, Small cites the lack of coverage for a recent speech by Iranian President Mahmoud Ahmadinejad calling Israel "filthy bacteria," in language reminiscent of Nazi demands for eradication of Jews.[20]

"On the one hand, you have a genocidal movement" coming out of the Muslim world, says Small, "and on the other you have acquiescence in Europe. . . . I think increasingly because of anti-Semitism among the elite in Europe, particularly in the U.K. and France, you have this dual-loyalty issue coming in. As Israel becomes more and more tarnished as an apartheid, Nazi-like state, you also have the accusation that Jews are loyal to this entity."

In England, the majority of perpetrators identified in connection with anti-Semitic incidents are not disaffected Muslims but white youths, according to criminologist Paul Iganski of Britain's Lancaster University. Although he agrees the Middle East conflicts serve as trigger events, incidents often start with a mundane irritation such as road rage or a dispute over a parking spot — which "becomes aggravated by deep-seated anti-Semitic feeling," he says. "There is a reservoir of anti-Semitic bigotry there simmering below the surface."

Adam Parker, a first-year student from Manchester who co-founded the Israeli Cultural Society at Oxford this year, helped organize a protest against the Irving event. "I think it was a disgrace," he says.

Yair Zivan, campaigns director for the Union of Jewish Students, claims anti-Zionism on campus "often spills over into anti-Semitism." According to Zivan, three anti-Semitic incidents were reported at Manchester University when Jewish students protested a resolution to "twin" their student union with Palestinian An-Najah University, where some students have become suicide bombers, Zivan says.

The harshest critics of Israel at places like Oxford are Jewish professors, notably Israeli Professor of International Relations Avi Shlaim, who charges that Israel's aim in its current blockade of Gaza is "to starve the people of Gaza into submission."[1]

Seth Anziska, an American Oxford graduate student in Middle Eastern studies, says, "Europeans — and the British in particular — have a much more pessimistic outlook" about the peace process between Israel and the Palestinians than Americans. But he adds, "In some ways, it's more realistic."

Yet some prominent British Jews aren't buying it. Shalom Lappin, a professor of computational linguistics at King's College, London, who has written on the history of British Jews, dismisses groups like Jews for Justice for Palestinians. He sees them as part of a long tradition of what he calls "a survival strategy" among British Jews to gain acceptance from the British establishment by not provoking anger.

"I don't doubt their sincerity," he says, "but they're celebrated with open access to *The Guardian* and the *London*

Demonstrators outside England's famed Oxford Union Debating Society protest the presence of British writer David Irving, a notorious Holocaust denier, at a debate on freedom of speech.

Review of Books and paraded across campuses as 'the good Jews,' not the 'tribal and bad Jews.' "

"I'm proud to be Jewish," responds the organization's chair, Dan Judelson, who said he became active after his daughter was born. "That sense of Jewish injustice and treating people equitably was something I wanted to pass on to my daughter."

---

[1] Avi Shlaim, "Free Speech? Not for Critics of Israel," *The Jewish Chronicle*, Feb. 29, 2008.

For example, anti-Semitic taunts now ring out at soccer stadiums throughout Europe, where so-called soccer hooligans have traditionally sympathized with the extreme right, according to two recent reports. In the Netherlands, supporters of the traditionally Jewish soccer team Ajax Amsterdam are regularly taunted by fans of opposing teams with Hitler salutes and chants of "Hamas, Hamas, Jews to the gas!"[21]

In a recent report, British MP Mann found that anti-Semitic cheers and paraphernalia are proliferating at Europe's soccer stadiums in part because of the increasing tendency of fans to travel across borders and share anti-Jewish attitudes on the Internet. "We're not prepared to

tolerate that; we're meeting with football authorities to take action to stamp this out," Mann says.

However, some experts downplay such concerns, noting that Jews no longer face discriminatory laws in Europe, while Muslims and other minorities are far more likely to face prejudice in employment and housing.

And liberal critics of Israel are leery of what they see as a tendency to equate criticism of Israel's policies with anti-Semitism. "This redefining devalues the word [anti-Semitism] itself. You desensitize people — they become confused," objects Antony Lerman, executive director of the Institute for Jewish Policy Research, a London-based think tank.[22] (*See "At Issue," p. 213.*)

Vandals spray-painted a star of David hanging from a gallows on this gravestone at the only remaining Jewish cemetery in Bialystok, Poland. Defacing Jewish gravestones is a frequent outlet for expressions of anti-Semitism.

"I'm critical of what is done [by Israel] in the occupied territories, but I've never seen myself as an anti-Semite," says Lerman. "I feel as if I'm being bracketed in with anti-Semites."

Here are some of the questions about anti-Semitism and other forms of prejudice being debated across Europe:

Is anti-Semitism on the rise in Europe?

Some Jewish groups and experts point to the surge in reported anti-Semitic incidents since 2000, particularly violent attacks on individuals and anti-Jewish imagery in the press, as a sign that anti-Semitism is growing.[23]

In addition, the European Union's Agency for Fundamental Rights (FRA) and other Europe-wide groups have documented increases in anti-Semitism.[24]

In June 2007, the Parliamentary Assembly of the Council of Europe issued a resolution noting "the persistence and escalation of anti-Semitic phenomena. . . . [F]ar from having been eliminated, anti-Semitism is today on the rise in Europe. It appears in a variety of forms and is becoming commonplace."[25]

The data are somewhat problematic, however, because Jewish communities that are best organized and living in open, democratic societies tend to report the highest number of incidents. Assiduous reporting by Jewish groups in

Britain, for instance, makes that country look worse than nations that are less transparent, such as those in Eastern Europe with a long tradition of anti-Semitism in both the church and government. For example, in Belarus, government enterprises produce and distribute anti-Semitic material, but the nation does not rank high on comparative international charts. In addition, figures compiled by law-enforcement agencies or community groups often do not measure anti-Semitic attitudes, such as those captured in political cartoons.[26] (*See graph, p. 192.*)

A recent State Department report makes a distinction between traditional anti-Semitism — which draws on older ideas of Jews as racially inferior, bloodthirsty or Christ killers — and the "new anti-Semitism," which relies primarily on anti-Zionist language but sometimes also incorporates older stereotypes such as Jews as world conspirators.

Eastern European countries tend to specialize in older forms of anti-Semitism. According to a June 2007 report by Human Rights First, extreme, nationalist political groups in Eastern Europe recently have adopted 19th-century anti-Semitic language. The group singled out Poland, Ukraine and Hungary as countries where certain Orthodox and Roman Catholic institutions have encouraged anti-Semitism.[27] (*See "Background" and sidebar, p. 200, for more detail on Poland.*)

In Poland, recent attention has focused on anti-Semitic remarks broadcast on Catholic Radio Maryja, part of the Polish media empire run by the Rev. Tadeusz Rydzyk of the Catholic missionary order Redemptorists. Rydzyk was quoted most recently calling Jews greedy and responsible for lobbies that control the Polish president.[28]

The Rydzyk empire's audience is estimated to be approaching 3 million mostly elderly Poles. Polls show Polish seniors are more likely than young people to hold anti-Semitic views, such as the belief that Jews killed Christ, observes Michal Bilewicz, a social psychologist at Warsaw University's Centre for Research on Prejudice. "We have demography on our side," he says.

Polls also suggest that many traditional stereotypes are commonly held in both Western and Eastern Europe. Anti-Defamation League polls show substantial percentages in many countries believe traditional conspiracy theories about Jews, such as that they have too much power in the business world or in international financial markets.[29]

The most heated debate in Europe, however, has focused on the new anti-Semitism, which often emanates from radical Muslims, relies on anti-Zionism and is concentrated in Western European countries like Great Britain and France, according to advocates of the term.

These experts say they are most concerned about the type of anti-Semitism promoted by radical Muslims known as Islamists, who often appeal to left-leaning European intellectuals for support of the Palestinian liberation movement.

In a 2005 interview, French philosopher and political scientist Pierre-André Taguieff, who helped coin the term "the new anti-Semitism," said all Jews have come to be seen as "more or less hidden Zionists; Zionism equals colonialism, imperialism and racism; therefore the Jews are colonialists, imperialists and racists, openly or not." Zionism, says Taguieff, "became the incarnation of absolute evil."[30]

Like Taguieff, critics in England and Germany have charged that anti-Semitic comments by Muslim groups are often ignored by the liberal media and by leftist academics who support the Palestinians' liberation movement.

For example, in a recent book, *Jihad and Jew-Hatred*, political scientist Matthias Küntzel reports trial testimony showing that 9/11 leader Mohammed Atta and fellow plotters were convinced that "the Jews" sought world domination. The plotters saw New York City as the center of world Jewry, making it their obvious target.[31]

Yet that testimony was widely ignored in the German and international media, according to Küntzel. "If we had the same quotes by the Oklahoma [City] bomber — by far-right white perpetrators — I think it would have made headlines. But if the very same anti-Semitism is displayed by Muslims, people think perhaps this is Israel's fault, and we just have to tackle the Middle East problem and it will vanish again," says Küntzel, a research associate at the Vidal Sassoon International Center for the Study of Antisemitism at Hebrew University in Jerusalem.

It's no accident, he says, that al Qaeda leader Osama bin Laden quotes left-leaning American intellectual Noam Chomsky, a strong critic of Israel's Palestinian politics. "This is the most dangerous aspect of this Islamism ideology," Küntzel says. In an effort to appeal to the European

Demonstrators in Paris protest racism and anti-Semitism in February 2006. The sign says "Anti-Semitic barbarism. Our child murdered." The photograph is of Ilan Halimi, the Jewish Frenchman murdered in Paris.

left, he maintains, Islamist leaders "put themselves in the same role as communism [once played] — as the only potent force against global capitalism. They want to build a broad alliance in order to fight against America and Israel."

Leftist criticism of Israelis as powerful oppressors with Nazi-like characteristics can spur anti-Semitic violence, suggests British journalist Phillips. For example, in a widely reported incident in 2005, when a Jewish reporter approached London's former far-left Mayor Ken Livingstone with a question, the mayor snapped, "What did you do before? Were you a German war criminal?" When the reporter said he was Jewish, Livingstone compared him to a "concentration camp guard."

Later, several perpetrators of anti-Semitic attacks mentioned those comments, according to the Community Security Trust, which tracks anti-Semitic incidents in Britain and provides security advice to Jewish schools and other institutions.[32]

"The Jewish organizations — particularly Jewish-defense organizations — are highlighting how these themes on campuses, Web sites and classrooms have physical manifestations: That can be a swastika on a wall or a physical attack like the one in Paris," says Ben Cohen, the American Jewish Committee's associate director for tackling anti-Semitism and extremism and the editor of a new Web site, www.z-word.com, focusing on anti-Zionism.

However, some observers think the significance of anti-Semitic acts counted by Jewish groups is often overplayed. "Every time someone smears anti-Semitic graffiti on a synagogue wall in France we are warned that 'the unique evil' is with us once more, that it is 1938 all over again," New York University historian Tony Judt recently wrote. "We are losing the capacity to distinguish between the normal sins and follies of mankind — stupidity, prejudice, opportunism, demagogy and fanaticism — and genuine evil. . . . After all, if we see evil everywhere, how can we be expected to recognize the real thing?"[33]

In a similar vein, a prominent French historian, Patrick D. Weil, of the National Center for Scientific Research (CNRS) at the University of Paris, downplays the significance of the recent kidnapping in Paris and paints a positive picture of the general climate in France. "It is in France that you have the most open society with respect to Jews," he says, citing surveys that find French Muslims and French people generally rate at the top of European countries when asked if they have a favorable view of Jews. "But it doesn't mean at the local individual level or at the margin you won't have activist anti-Semitism from some very small segments of the population," he adds.

Bagneux, the poor suburb where Roumi lived and was kidnapped, is integrated, with Jews living alongside Arabs, and Roumi apparently knew his attackers. News reports indicate he was "not a saint," Weil points out, but was involved in some petty criminality like his attackers. "The fact that people [of different ethnic origin] live all together is perhaps good for the integration of society, but it can also produce these extreme attitudes and acts," says Weil. Such assaults may stem as much from the rising tendency of people in France to identify with their own ethnic group, he suggests, which affects other minorities as well.

Experts critical of Israel downplay the levels of anti-Semitism in Europe. "I don't think the evidence is there to suggest that the growth is as bad as many people do claim," says Lerman, at the Institute for Jewish Policy Research. "Quite a few research institutions in Europe and the U.S. have spoken of anti-Semitism as being so extreme it's like being back at *Kristallnacht* on the eve of the Holocaust — which I find unnecessary. I personally would say in the last year or so it's reached a plateau."

Is anti-Zionism a cover-up for anti-Semitism?

Increasingly, groups such as the American Jewish Committee charge that inflammatory anti-Zionist language is being used in Europe as a pretext for anti-Semitism. Anti-Defamation League Director Abraham Foxman has charged that in Britain, hostility towards Jews often "is camouflaged as criticism of Israel."[34]

"The canard," in Foxman's words, that Israel resembles apartheid-era South Africa — reflected in February's "Israel Apartheid Week" organized on British campuses by Muslim students — is "fueling dislike, distrust, hatred of Jews," Foxman has written.[35]

Critics in Britain and France have charged that members of the liberal intelligentsia, in their eagerness to make common cause with the Palestinians, have turned a blind eye to the anti-Semitism that is part of Islamist rhetoric.

"Essentially, you see the movement into the mainstream of ideas that until 10 years ago were confined to the far left and the far right," says Shalom Lappin, a professor at King's College in London and one of the founders of a group of academics, the Euston Manifesto, which has protested against British anti-Semitism. "They place Israel and Jews at the center of the Jewish conspiracy, part of the lobby used to subvert foreign policy. . . . It's sweeping campuses; it lends toxicity to public debate."

French philosopher and political scientist Taguieff contends that anti-Jewish stereotypes and accusatory themes originally drawn from Palestinian nationalism "have become more and more widespread since the 1970s in the French public arena . . . as well as in the West more generally." This new anti-Semitism, he said, often relies on anti-Zionist themes, using metaphors like "cancer" to describe Israel and creating what he called the most recent form of "eliminationist" anti-Semitism.[36]

Weil of CNRS is skeptical of the concept. "I think what we call a new anti-Semitism resembles the old one — the same kind of theory of the plot of the *Protocols of the Learned Elders of Zion*," says Weil, referring to the infamous anti-Semitic literary hoax alleging a Jewish plot to achieve world domination. "Some people call it new because it comes from Arabs."

British journalist Phillips has charged that "Language straight out of the lexicon of medieval and Nazi Jew-hatred has become commonplace in acceptable British discourse, particularly in the media." For her, "the most

striking evidence that hatred of Israel is the latest muta-
tion of anti-Semitism is that it resurrects the libel of the
world Jewish conspiracy, a defining anti-Semitic motif
that went underground after the Holocaust."[37]

For example, she cites the left-leaning *New Statesman*
magazine's investigation into the "Zionist" lobby in
Britain, which it headlined the "Kosher Conspiracy" and
illustrated on its Jan. 14, 2002, cover with a gold Star of
David piercing the Union Jack.[38] *The Guardian*, Britain's
leading liberal daily, published a cartoon on July 19,
2006, depicting a huge fist, armed with brass knuckles
shaped like Stars of David, hammering a bloody child.[39]
A cartoon in *The Independent* in 2003 showing former
Israeli leader Ariel Sharon biting the head off a Palestinian
baby won first prize in the British Political Cartoon
Society's annual competition for that year.[40]

Some critics say such drawings of Jews killing children are reminiscent of the imagery of the "blood libel,"
the medieval European belief that Jews murdered Gentile
children to obtain their blood for religious rituals —
sparking massacres of Jews throughout history.

But not all Jews see these media images as intention-
ally ill-motivated. "What that proves is there's a great
deal of criticism of Israel, some of which spills over into
odious anti-Semitism," says Dan Judelson, chair of Jews
for Justice for Palestinians, a British group. "It's not a
type of deep-seated, visceral hatred of the Jews; it's just
intellectual laziness."

Judelson's is one of several groups of generally left-
leaning Jews who have been active in criticizing Israel's
actions towards the Palestinians. He says Israel's defenders equate criticism of Israel with anti-Semitism as a way
of "de-legitimizing" sincere criticism. And he takes issue
with a commonly used definition of anti-Semitism from
the European Union's monitoring arm, which encompasses "denying the Jewish people their right to self-
determination, e.g. by claiming that the existence of a
State of Israel is a racist endeavor."[41] Not all Jews define
self-determination as having a Jewish state, he points
out. (*See sidebar, p. 194–195.*)

Groups like Judelson's have been criticized for marching for Palestinian liberation with Muslim activists who
carried placards linking a swastika to a Star of David
with an equal sign. Judelson says whenever he's confronted Muslim marchers about this kind of imagery,
they have responded by changing their symbols.

But other observers, including a former Islamist, say
liberal Jewish groups are naïve about the ultimate motives
of such Muslim activists. Rashad Ali, a former director in
the command structure of the radical Islamist group
Hizb-ut-Tahrir Britain, says the group would capitalize
on sentiments against Israel for its own political ends.

During the conflict between Israel and Lebanon, he
says, "We'd always know we can get a Jewish rabbi to talk
about the atrocities in Israel; then we'd take over and say
what we need is the Caliphate" — which Ali describes as
a dictatorship in which laws would be based on Islamic
religious interpretation. (When asked which groups such
a rabbi would come from, Ali mentioned Neturei Karta,
an orthodox Jewish group that opposes the establishment of the state of Israel before the coming of the
Messiah.)

At least one radical Islamist group has been careful to
replace the word "Jew" with "Zionist" in its leaflets and
Web sites in order to appeal to more mainstream critics
of Israel, says Ali, now head of research and policy at the
Quilliam Foundation, a new London-based group aimed
at fighting extremist forms of Islam. He has printed out
an online leaflet that he said Hizb had recently removed
from its Web site following wide distribution. Entitled
"The Muslim Ummah will never submit to the Jews,"
the leaflet is replete with anti-Semitic stereotypes such as
"The Jews are cowards, they are a people of money and
not a people of fighting."

Formerly, anti-Semitic language was used heavily
"because it has a lot of currency in Islamist crowds,"
Ali says. But after then-Prime Minister Tony Blair
declared he wanted to ban Hizb, the group underwent
a public re-imaging. "They didn't change any of their
ideas, but they realized the need to re-brand themselves for public media consumption. They started to
tailor their language to say the 'Zionist state,' not 'the
Jewish state.' "

But is anti-Zionism always anti-Semitism? NYU historian Judt, a British Jew and an outspoken critic of
Israel, recently argued that by "shouting anti-Semitism
every time someone attacks Israel or defends the
Palestinians, we are breeding cynics" and risk losing
the attention of those who need to recognize genuine
genocidal evil.

"When people chide me and others for criticizing
Israel too forcefully, lest we rouse the ghosts of prejudice,

Confronting the Past in Poland

Accounts of pogroms rouse anti-Semitic ghosts.

Anti-Semitism in Poland today is almost entirely about history. Unlike France and England, where Israel's treatment of the Palestinians is often the source of anti-Jewish feeling, the most recent debates in Poland have centered on Poles' responsibility for the deadly fate of their Jewish neighbors during and after the Holocaust.

In Poland today, "The problem of the Jews is the problem of the past," says Anna Bikont, a Polish journalist with the leading daily newspaper *Gazeta Wyborcza*, who has written about Polish reactions to the revelations that Poles in the town of Jedwabne killed Jewish neighbors during the war.

The most prominent Jewish issue in the Polish media since the fall of communism in 1989 has been the infamous massacre. On July 10, 1941, about 400 people were forced into a barn on the town's outskirts and burned alive by their Polish neighbors. During the communist era, the incident was blamed on the Nazis; even the monument at the site made no mention of Poles' part in the massacre.

But in 2001, the publication of the book *Neighbors*, by Jan T. Gross, a Polish Jewish historian now at Princeton University, revealed documentary evidence that residents of the town were primarily to blame for the deaths of up to 1,600 of their Jewish neighbors.[1] When news reports made clear that Poles had carried out the deadly pogrom, with only a little encouragement from the Nazis, the "bombshell" shocked the Polish public, according to Hanna Kwiatkowska, who has analyzed anti-Semitism in the right-wing Polish press for her doctoral thesis at University College, London.

The ensuing discussion encouraged the press, which denied that Poles ever participated in the crime, to launch a full-blown anti-Semitic campaign. Seven years later Jedwabne continues to serve as an anti-Semitic tool and litmus test of "real Poles," according to Kwiatkowska.[2]

The newspaper *Nasz Dziennik*, which is part of a conservative Catholic media empire in Poland, charged that Jews were using "lies" about the massacre to blackmail Poland into paying them "billions of dollars" in restitution. The theme of "Jewish profiteers" has persisted several years later in the paper's coverage.[3] While such views were confined mainly to the right-wing press, skepticism about Poles' guilt in the event was surprisingly widespread in Poland. In 2002, 35 percent of respondents said the Germans had murdered the Jews in Jedwabne, while 38 percent believed the townspeople had been forced by the Germans to launch the pogrom.[4]

"We have an old and strong tradition of anti-Semitism," which Poles use to define their national identity, says Bikont. "To be very Polish you have to be different from the Jew." She cites typical stereotypes: "The Jews are so intelligent, they like to manipulate other people; the Polish people are honest and supported one another. The Jews didn't fight in the diaspora; the Poles were always very brave."

But Bikont says views about responsibility for the past seem to be changing among young people. In a recent poll, *Gazeta Wyborcza* asked if Poles should examine their conscience in connection with actions against Jews in the past. Only 14 percent of respondents old enough to have been alive in World War II answered yes, but 37 percent of 18- to 24-year-olds answered in the affirmative, Bikont reports. (The audience for the most anti-Semitic newspapers and radio programs is composed largely of elderly pensioners, who have been forced into reduced circumstances since the fall of communism.)

Shortly after the revelations about Jedwabne, residents in their forties, most with family links to the original murderers, clung angrily to the town's innocence and blamed the new account on Jewish journalists or Jews seeking money or political power, Bikont reported.

When Bikont questioned residents about Jews who had lived on their street, a typical response was, "Now, don't you try to threaten us. We have all the papers proving our ownership of this house."[5] (Gross suggests that Poles' attacks on Jews during and after the war were partly motivated by Poles' coveting and subsequent confiscation of Jewish property.)

The family of a resident who revealed more details to the press about the residents' part in the massacre was forced to move away after they were ostracized, called "Jewish lapdogs" and received death threats, according to Bikont. Some elderly residents who concurred in Gross' account were told by the local priest they would not be buried in the Catholic cemetery, she adds.[6]

Gross' latest historic revelation describes how a few Jewish survivors of the Holocaust, destitute and emaciated, returned to their Polish hometowns after the war, only to be attacked and sometimes murdered by residents, who often had occupied former Jewish homes.[7] In the most horrifying instance, an estimated 42 people, including a mother with her baby and a pregnant woman, were shot or stoned to death by residents of Kielce in 1946. Until the release of Gross' account in January, many people in Poland believed the Kielce massacre had been provoked by the communists.

At a recent meeting in Kielce to discuss Gross's book, Bikont said only a few people spoke in virulently anti-Semitic tones. "Many people talked about feelings of guilt about things in Kielce" — a contrast from her interviews in Jedwabne several years ago, where she met mainly denial.

"I think Jedwabne opened up something in Poland," she says. "It's really changed."

Poland's chief rabbi, Michael Schudrich, has a different take on Kielce. "People forget that in the postwar period the Nazis had so succeeded in destroying morality in society that one of the normal options to resolve a conflict was killing the other person."

In a recent U.S. State Department report, Poland is criticized for desecrations last year at one of the country's largest Jewish cemeteries. Vandals in Czestochowa spray-painted about 100 gravestones with swastikas, "SS" and "Jews out."[8]

The report doesn't say, Schudrich notes, that "the mayor of the town was out there with me and teens scrubbing off the swastikas" shortly afterwards. "Yeah, bad things happen," but the question is, "How does the rest of society react?" Harking back to the Holocaust, he observes, "Genocide happens when the good are silent."

Neglect, rather than vandalism, is the main threat to Jewish cemeteries in communities where no Jews remain, says Bikont. Some have been used to dump garbage, while others have been dug up for building sites. In a few towns, Polish Jews are trying to restore crumbling cemeteries. Bikont also points out that it's no longer dangerous to be a Jew in Poland.

At the same time, however, Kwiatkowska finds it "a worrying sign" that Poland's second-most-popular daily newspaper, *Rzeczpospolita*, gave a platform to right-wing voices in response to Gross's recent revelations about Kielce. It could be a nod towards the current, conservative government, which partially owns the paper.[9]

But Schudrich has a more optimistic outlook. In May 2006, he was attacked in the most serious anti-Semitic incident in Poland in years. Schudrich, who wears a kepah (Jewish skullcap), was walking on the street after Sabbath prayers when a man, later identified with right-wing causes,

Then-Polish President Aleksander Kwasniewski lays a wreath at a new monument to mark the place where Poles massacred Jews from the town of Jedwabne, Poland, in 1941. Kwasniewski addressed relatives of the victims and apologized in the name of Poland.

yelled "Poland for Poles," a well-known anti-Semitic slogan from before the war, historically followed by "Jews to Palestine!"

When Schudrich confronted the man and asked why he had yelled that, the rabbi was punched and pepper-sprayed. After the incident, Schudrich received a call from the prime minister and an invitation to the presidential palace, where government officials condemned the incident before the Polish media. His attacker served two months in jail.

"It did happen," but "much more important was the response — universal condemnation," Schudrich said in an interview last year.[10]

Asked about the incident recently, he added, "And no such attack has happened again. If anti-Semitism is rampant, it should be happening every other day."

[1] Jan T. Gross, *Neighbors: The Destruction of the Jewish Community in Jedwabne, Poland* (2002). In 2002, the Institute of National Memory (IPN) in Poland disputed Gross's figure of 1,600 deaths (the pre-war Jewish population in Jedwabne) after an investigation, suggesting it was only in the hundreds, but concluded the real figure would never be known. See "'Fear': An Exchange," *The New York Times*, Aug. 20, 2006. For an estimate that half of adult men, plus some women and children, witnessed or participated in the massacre and an estimate that some 400 were killed in the barn, see, Peter S. Green, "Polish Town Still Tries to Forget its Dark Past," *The New York Times*, Feb. 8, 2003.

[2] Hanna Kwiatkowska, "Conflict of Images. Conflict of Memories. Jewish Themes in the Polish Right-Wing Nationalistic Press in the Light of Articles from Nasz Dziennik 1998-2007," unpublished doctoral thesis.

[3] *Ibid.*

[4] *Ibid.*

[5] Anna Bikont, "Seen from Jedwabne," www1.yadvashem.org/download/about_holocaust/studies/bikont.pdf.

[6] *Ibid.*

[7] Jan T. Gross, *Fear: Anti-Semitism in Poland after Auschwitz* (2007).

[8] "Contemporary Global Anti-Semitism: A Report Provided to the United States Congress," U.S. State Department, March 2008, p. 17, www.state.gov/g/drl/rls/102406.htm.

[9] Hanna Kwiatkowska, "Book Reviews: Jan T. Gross, *Fear,*" East European Jewish Affairs, April 1, 2007, pp. 119-121, www.informaworld.com.

[10] "Insight: Interview with Michael Schudrich, chief rabbi of Poland," *San Francisco Chronicle* podcast, May 4, 2007, www.sfgate.com/cgi-bin/blogs/sfgate/detail?blogid=5&entry_id=16203.

Young Poles Turn to Judaism

"People treat it like something exotic."

If you walked into the only active synagogue in Warsaw during morning prayers, many of those praying would probably have been brought up as Catholics. Most would have discovered only as adults that they had Jewish family roots.

In a country where over 90 percent of its more than 3 million Jews perished under the Nazis, where Jewish concentration camp survivors who returned to their villages were murdered by their Polish neighbors and where communist oppression reigned for decades, it was for many years dangerous to reveal one's Jewish heritage.[1]

But since 1989, as the collapse of communism in Poland made it safe for families to reveal their Jewish ties to their children and as interest in their lost culture has grown, a growing number of young Poles have been drawn to Judaism, even some with no known Jewish heritage.

"It's a fun thing . . . oriental. People treat it like something exotic with a secret language no one understands," says Krzystof Izdebski, 27, a lawyer and secretary of Zoom, a Warsaw cultural group aimed at bringing young Jewish Poles together. "Also, there are people who have empathy for the Jews; they are taught about the *Shoah* [Holocaust] in school and want to pay tribute. The majority of Zoom's 126 members, ages 16-35, only discovered their Jewish heritage in their teens, or even later, according to Izdebski.

Of an estimated 5,000-10,000 Jews who participate in Jewish religious life in Poland today, more than 60 percent did not discover they were Jewish until adulthood, estimates Michael Bilewicz, a social psychologist at Warsaw University who studies Polish Jewish identity. (Some estimates place the number of Jews in Poland much higher, around 20,000, as a result of the growing number discovering they have Jewish roots.[2])

The discovery of Jewish roots is often problematic, especially if it breaches a deeply held family secret. Anna Bikont, a 54-year-old Warsaw journalist, was 35 when she discovered that her mother was Jewish but had survived the war on "the Aryan side" in Poland, married to a Christian.

When Bikont decided to raise her children as Jews and send them to a Jewish school, her mother at first refused to have any contact with her. "She was anxious and furious," Bikont recalls. "All her life she did all she could [to make sure] that my sister and I wouldn't be Jews." Today, Bikont's 19-year-old daughter Ola identifies strongly with Judaism, is a member of Zoom and has applied for Israeli citizenship.

The variety of reasons for this enduring secrecy reflects the historical difficulty of being Jewish in Poland. During the war, many Jewish children were given to Christian families by parents who would not survive the Holocaust. Some Jewish families passed as Christians with false identity papers and after the war were still afraid to reveal their true identity. Those Jewish families who stayed after the war or returned as communists from the Soviet Union were more likely to be secular or atheistic in a Catholic country known for its hostility toward Jews. And some children of Jewish communists rebelled against their parents' generation by participating in the Catholic opposition that gave rise to the Solidarity anticommunist movement. (Adam Michnik, editor of Warsaw's *Gazeta Wyborcza*, a leading Polish newspaper, is the most famous Solidarity leader with Jewish roots.)

In an attempt to curry favor with the Soviet Union, the communist government in Poland responded to the 1967 Six-Day Israeli war with an anti-Semitic campaign in 1967-68, accusing Jews of loyalty to the Zionist state, blaming Jews for student protests against the regime, firing Jewish workers and confiscating property. Of Poland's 30,000 remaining Jews, about 20,000 emigrated in 1968-69.[3]

What's driving young Poles to reconnect with Jewish culture or religion — especially if their link is as tenuous as a grandparent they never knew? "The need to belong to a defined and exotic ethnic group is very common," Bilewicz found in an ongoing study of young Polish Jews.[4] Poland's homogeneous population is 90 percent ethnically Polish, white and Christian, he points out, so "being Jewish gives a sense of being distinctive."

I tell them that they have the problem exactly the wrong way around. It is just such a taboo that may itself stimulate anti-Semitism," Judt recently asserted.[42]

But British MP Mann argues that anti-Zionism in the press and public discussion stirs up deeper hatred than criticism of other countries because it is fundamentally racist, not just making a political point.

"Why are young Jewish kids abused in the streets when there's conflict in Lebanon?" he asks. "Young Chinese kids are not abused when there's conflict in Tibet. People feel free

The desire to get in touch with a family tradition broken during the Holocaust is also important, he says. Ironically, it's often religious Catholics who feel most comfortable making the switch to religious Judaism, he notes, because they already believe in God. Indeed, Zoom has some members who consider themselves Jews but also attend Catholic church, according to Izdebski.

Chief Rabbi of Poland Michael Schudrich says he knows of a handful of Poles with no Jewish family heritage who have converted to Judaism. "They simply believe Judaism helps them find God and brings morality into their lives."

The movement may also reflect a growing curiosity among Poles generally about a people that virtually disappeared. Many Poles have never laid eyes on a Jew, notes Bikont. "In Poland, many young people are now interested in Jewish history," she says. "It's very new, and it's very strong. We have five or six new plays about Jews written by young people this year." A Jewish cultural festival attracts thousands to Krakow every year.

The recent Jewish revival dates back to the early 1990s, when young Poles who had just discovered their Jewish family connections found the elderly regulars at Polish synagogues less than welcoming toward people who knew nothing about the faith, according to Bilewicz.

Schudrich, then a dynamic young American rabbi, started to offer "a new way of being Jewish," Bilewicz says — organizing Shabbat dinners, translating prayers into Polish and introducing guitar music to services.

Today, Rabbi Schudrich estimates that thousands of Jews have discovered they have Jewish roots since the fall of

Members of Czulent, a group for young Polish Jews in Krakow, pose in front of graffiti referring to "Jude Gang" (literally "Jewish Gang"), the name taken by fans of Krakow's soccer team. The team's fan club protected Jews during the Nazi era and represents a positive link with Jews in Poland. "We decided to take the photo here to show we are not afraid to tell people we are Jewish," says Czulent's Anna Makowka.

Courtesy Czulent

communism. "The question is, what are they going to do about it? That's what we do: Try to create programming and an environment that will empower them to look into their Jewish heritage."

In this vein, cultural associations like Zoom in Warsaw and Czulent* in Krakow — organized by young Poles who returned from Israel wanting to know more about their newfound Judaism — organize Jewish holiday parties, seminars on Judaism and multicultural dialogues. These gatherings offer a way for young Poles to connect to Judaism as a culture — not necessarily by conversion. They also offer companionship for new entrants to a tiny minority group that has lost most of its communal memory.

Young people who suddenly discover their Jewish background often have to overcome a feeling of alienation from Poles around them, Czulent's Web site acknowledges. "Sometimes it's better to have a beer together than to go to lectures," says Izdebski. "Or go for Shabbat dinner to someone's home, so you don't feel so alone in Polish society."

---

* Czulent is the name of a traditional Sabbath dish of slow-cooking meat and beans, http://czulent.org.

---

[1] See Tony Judt, *Postwar* (2007), p. 804. According to Judt, 97.5 percent of Poland's Jews were exterminated.

[2] See Stephen Roth Institute for the Study of Antisemitism and Racism, "Poland 2006," p. 1, and "Poland" 1997, p. 1, at www.tau.ac.il/Anti-Semitism/asw2006/poland.htm. The 2006 report estimates 5,000-10,000 Jews in Poland.

[3] Judt, *op. cit.*, pp. 434-435.

[4] Cohen Center for Modern Jewish Studies, Brandeis University, "Taglit-Birthright Israel International," http://cmjs.org/Project.cfm?idProject=18.

to criticize China or Israel, but the consequences are very different. That is because of the language used. . . . There is a difference: It's stoked by anti-Semitic discourse, and the language used in attacking Israel is a big part of that," he says. "It creates this legitimacy for racist abuse."

Recently, Small at Yale's Initiative for the Interdisciplinary Study of Antisemitism and a colleague decided to test whether there is a statistical correlation between Israel-bashing and anti-Semitic attitudes in a survey of 500 people in 10 European countries.[43] The results,

Middle Ages *Ritual-murder rumors incite pogroms; Jew are persecuted during Spanish Inquisition.*

1144 Blood-libel charge emerges in England.

1218 English Church requires Jews to wear special badges to identify them as non-Christians.

1247 Pope declares ritual-murder allegations fraudulent.

1290 Jews expelled from England.

1492-1498 Jews expelled from Spain, then Portugal and France.

18th Century *Some European Jews are emancipated during Enlightenment.*

1791 France gives Jews equal rights.

19th Century *Ottoman Empire declares religious tolerance; Russian pogroms scatter Jews to Western Europe; "Dreyfus affair" spurs Zionism.*

1839 Ottoman sultan decrees equality for Jews, Christians.

1879 German journalist Wilhelm Marr coins term "anti-Semitic."

1880 First wave of Russian Jews arrives in England.

1894-99 Capt. Alfred Dreyfus, a French Jew, is falsely accused of treason. Affair radicalizes Austrian Jewish journalist Theodor Herzl, who later leads Zionist movement.

Early 20th Century *Britain restricts Jewish immigration, declares support for Jewish homeland.*

1903 "Protocols of the Learned Elders of Zion" — an anti-Semitic literary hoax — appears in Russia.

1906 Britain's Aliens Act of 1905 limits Jewish refugees.

1917 Balfour Declaration states British support for Jewish homeland in Palestine.

1930s *Nazis begin persecuting Jews, followed by systematic eradication.*

1933 Nazis begin restricting Jews' rights; Dachau concentration camp opens.

Nov. 9-10, 1938 A night of mob attacks on German Jews, known as *Kristallnacht* ("Night of Broken Glass") destroys Jewish businesses and synagogues. Some 30,000 Jews are sent to concentration camps, launching the Nazi plan to eradicate Europe's Jews.

1940s *Six million Jews die in Nazi concentration camps; Vichy French hand over Jews to Nazis; Allied propaganda and press barely mention Jews.*

July 1940 Vichy regime initiates anti-Jewish laws.

July 10, 1941 Poles kill Jewish neighbors in Jedwabne.

1942 Mass gassings begin at Auschwitz-Birkenau camp; Polish Jews are deported to concentration camps; Vichy government deports 13,000 French Jews to Auschwitz.

Postwar 1940s *Anti-Semitism continues.*

1945 Soviet troops liberate Auschwitz-Birkenau; Nuremberg war trials begin.

1946 Jews returning to Poland are murdered by former neighbors.

1960s-1980s *Holocaust enters public consciousness; fall of communism opens door for Eastern European Jews to reveal family roots.*

1962 Israel kidnaps former Nazi official Adolf Eichmann in Argentina, prosecutes and later hangs him for his role in killing Jews.

1968-1969 Polish communist regime invokes anti-Semitism to suppress student protests.

January 1979 "Holocaust" TV series raises awareness of war-time atrocities among millions of West Germans.

1985 Documentary "Shoah" raises awareness in France.

1989 Communist regimes fall in Eastern Europe.

1990s-2000s *Anti-Jewish crimes surge in Europe as Arab-Israeli tensions escalate; anti-Israel resolutions are debated in international, national arenas.*

1991 U.N. General Assembly overturns 1975 resolution declaring Zionism "racism."

1995 President Jacques Chirac acknowledges French responsibility in sending Jews to concentration camps.

2000 Second Palestinian uprising spurs anti-Semitic crimes; European Union begins tracking anti-Jewish incidents.

2004 Organization for Security and Co-operation in Europe declares that events in the Middle East do not justify anti-Semitism.

Feb. 13, 2006 Kidnapped French Jew Ilan Halimi dies after being found tortured in Paris suburb; national outrage ensues.

Sept. 7, 2006 British report finds anti-Semitism increasing.

Feb. 14, 2008 Report shows anti-Semitic incidents in Britain dropped slightly in 2007.

Feb. 22, 2008 French Jew Mathieu Roumi is kidnapped and tortured in Paris.

May 2008 British professors' union revives debate over boycotting Israel.

---

published in the *Journal of Conflict Resolution*, showed an "off-the-charts" correlation with beliefs that Israel purposely kills children or that Israel is an apartheid state, he says. "In many countries, people who hold such beliefs are 13 times more likely to be anti-Semitic than the average population," reports Small.

Is anti-Semitism as severe as racial discrimination against other minorities in Europe?

"Would you feel safe, accepted [and] welcome today as a 'Paki' in parts of England? A black in Switzerland? Or would you not feel safer more integrated, more accepted as a Jew?" historian Judt recently asked.[44]

Although attacks like the recent kidnappings of two young French Jews are disturbing, young Arabs and Africans frequently face harassment in France — often several times a day — including interference from police, according to Weil of CNRS. Most people concede that European Jews — largely assimilated, educated and middle class — do not face the kinds of job, housing or personal discrimination faced by darker-skinned immigrants.

Those most concerned about the state of anti-Semitism today concede it does not approach the social discrimination faced by other minorities. But some experts contend that anti-Semitism has always been different in nature from other kinds of racial discrimination. Since the 19th

century, anti-Semitism has not just been about looking down on Jews as an inferior race, notes Ruth Wisse, a professor of Yiddish and comparative literature at Harvard University and author of the 2007 book *Jews and Power*. It's also been the polar opposite: attributing great power to Jews as a global conspiracy controlling government, banks and the media. As such, Jews often served as a convenient scapegoat for a society's social ills, she says.

Following this logic, the Nazis called for killing all Jews as a way of cleansing society of all evil, something Iran's Ahmadinejad has repeatedly called for, notes historian Küntzel. By contrast, no head of state today calls for the killing of all blacks as a way to solve society's ills, he notes. "Therefore anti-Semitism is the most dangerous" of these phenomena and the threats of Ahmadinejad are to be taken seriously, he says.

Yet, while assaults on individual Jews have clearly risen in recent years in Britain, the Institute for Jewish Policy Research's Lerman says the attacks against other groups, especially Muslims, are far worse. They are rarely captured in statistics, however, because other ethnic communities are less organized in collecting the data, according to Lerman.

In London, a Jewish person is three times as likely to be the subject of racial attack as a non-Jewish white person, but Arabs, blacks and Asians are 9 to 12 times more

Some Poles Hid Jews From the Nazis

More than 70 people are alive today thanks to Jerzy Kozminski.

*E*ditor's note: During a recent trip to Poland, CQ Global Researcher *contributing writer Sarah Glazer interviewed 83-year-old Jerzy Kozminski, whose family in Warsaw had helped hide several members of her own family during the Nazi occupation.*

In the winter of 1942, a gas company meter reader — a member of the underground Council for Aid to Jews — approached a Christian Polish family living in a small house in German-occupied Warsaw and asked if they would be willing to hide three Jews.

The family agreed, even though it was widely known that Poles who hid Jews would be executed by the Nazis — along with their entire families. The Kozminskis had just enough room to house the two men, watchmakers, and one of their wives, recalls 83-year-old Jerzy Kozminski — then a 17-year-old living with his father, stepmother and 2-year-old stepbrother. But the family could not afford to feed three more people.

So when the two watchmakers ran short of watch parts — essential for buying their food on the black market — they asked young Jerzy to seek help from an acquaintance in the Jewish ghetto, Samuel Glazer — a cousin of mine — who had owned a shirt factory in Lodz before the war.

Donning a yellow Jewish armband, which the Nazis required all Jews to wear, Jerzy crept into the Jewish ghetto for the first of numerous trips as a courier. Once, a guard sprayed him with submachine fire as he began scaling the ghetto wall; another time, as he emerged on the "Aryan" side of the wall, he was grabbed by an undercover officer, whom he paid off with a small bribe.

Samuel asked if Jerzy's family would hide his large extended family of seven. Jerzy's father agreed, and the Kozminskis rented a larger house on the outskirts of Warsaw and dug a basement bunker where the family could hide.

The Glazers paid smugglers to get them out of the ghetto on April 19, 1943, the day the Warsaw ghetto uprising began, just as residents were being ordered to gather for the fateful transfer to the Treblinka death camp. Only one family member didn't make it out: Samuel's sister-in-law, Anda Herling, the mother of a 10-year-old daughter, was caught by guards while escaping, and the family never saw her again.

Later, Jerzy led another four members of the Glazer family to a safe hiding place in Warsaw, where he continued

to look after them. The Kozminskis also took in other groups of Jews for varying periods of time.

Eleven members of the Glazer family survived the war hidden in the Kozminski house and their Warsaw hiding place until liberation by the Russians. All told, Kozminski is credited with saving more than 20 Jews.[1] He has been honored by the Yad Vashem Institute in Jerusalem as one of the Righteous Among the Nations — non-Jews who risked life or liberty to rescue Jews during the Holocaust.

Today, the retired engineer with a keen, blue-eyed gaze and a smile playing around his lips remembers many of his close calls with a sense of humor. After three residents of the Warsaw apartment where Samuel's elderly father was hiding were arrested on the street, the Glazers feared he was in danger of being discovered by police. It was vital to move the old man to a new hiding place. But his long beard would instantly identify him as an Orthodox Jew. Kozminski remembers with a chuckle that the old man's son Sewek shaved off the beard over his father's vigorous protests. Then, disguised as a peasant with a handlebar mustache in an old-fashioned cap and boots, the old man followed Kozminski to his home through the streets of Warsaw without being discovered.

It was difficult to hide the fact that so many people were living in the house, especially since large amounts of food had to be purchased. On at least one occasion, Kozminski remembers his little brother blurting out cheerfully at the local store, "There is no one living in our basement."

"The neighbors knew someone was there, but they didn't know who," Kozminski believes. If those hidden had been Polish underground partisans, he points out, the neighbors knew that denouncing the family would put them at risk of being killed by the Polish resistance.

Kozminski says he does not like the word "hero" and tends to brush off the idea that he did anything out of the ordinary. Indeed, in his view, "This rescue was a patriotic act" at a time when Poles were suffering under Nazi occupation. "Many people in Poland did things against the Germans."

In his modesty, Kozminski is typical of other Poles who saved Jews, of whom more than 6,000 have received the Righteous award.[2] In their insistence that they did nothing unusual, "I sense a stubborn belief in human decency being not the exception but the rule," suggests Konstanty Gebert, founder of the Polish-Jewish monthly *Midrasz*. "[A]nd were the Righteous to be considered exceptional, this belief would fail."[3]

Simple humanity may be another explanation. Kozminski's father had many Jewish friends while a student in Switzerland, the son recalls, and had once been in love with a Jewish girl — or so his wife used to tease him.

Moreover, Kozminski's stepmother, "was a woman who couldn't say 'No' " if someone came to her door seeking help, recalls Gita Baigelman, 86, of New York City, one of Samuel's surviving sisters, who met the Kozminski family after the war.[4]

When asked about the Poles who murdered their Jewish neighbors in notorious pogroms during and after the war, Kozminski displayed his only flare of anger during a recent interview, declaring, "The pope said that a Christian, if an anti-Semite, is not a Christian."

After joining the Polish resistance, Kozminski was caught by the Nazis in October 1943 while on a gun-buying run. When he failed to return home, the Glazers feared their hiding place would be revealed, Baigelman recalls. What they didn't know was that Jerzy had been questioned by the Gestapo but had kept their secret.

After his interrogation, Kozminski was sent to Auschwitz and then to the Mauthausen concentration camp. Upon the camp's liberation by the Americans in May 1945, he emerged emaciated, unable to eat, his health broken by starvation. By happy coincidence, he located Samuel, who was once again running a clothing factory in Lodz. The Glazers sent him to a doctor, who gradually restored his health.

One theme that is often overlooked in rescue accounts is the extent to which Jewish families aided those who hid them. As Kozminski remembers it, the Glazers "promised to help me recover; they delivered on their word."[5]

In 1964, Samuel and his family, who had moved to Israel, invited Jerzy's stepmother Theresa to stay with them. Then a widow, she took them up on their invitation, married a Jewish man, converted to Judaism and lived out the rest of her life in the Jewish homeland. She was made an honorary citizen of Tel Aviv and buried in a cemetery for distinguished citizens.

In 1996, when the Anti-Defamation League honored Kozminski for the rescue, it estimated that more than 70 people around the world — the descendants of those he saved — were alive because of his efforts.[6]

Halinka Herling, the 10-year-old whose mother did not survive the escape from the ghetto, is now a grandmother living in Israel.

CQ Press/Sarah Glazer

Jerzy Kozminski, now 83, helped hide several members of the author's family in Warsaw during the Nazi occupation.

Kozminski proudly displays a photograph of Halinka surrounded by her smiling grandchildren, which he received after he was reunited with her two years ago. This, he declares, is his reward. "God gave me the present of the grandchildren of Halinka on my 81st birthday," he says, adding he could not imagine a better gift.

— *Sarah Glazer*

[1] Jerzy Kozminski, "The Memories of a Righteous Man" (unpublished memoir, undated). Those rescued include 11 members of the extended Glazer family, the three-member Seifman family and eight Jews housed for three weeks.

[2] A total of 6,066 people from Poland were honored with the award, more than any other nation. However, Poland also had the largest number of Jews of any country in Europe before the Holocaust, www1.yadvashem.org/righteous_new/statistics.html.

[3] "Recalling Forgotten History: For Poles Who Rescued Jews During the Holocaust," album prepared to accompany a ceremony honoring the Righteous at the Polish National Opera in cooperation with the Museum of History of Polish Jews, Oct. 10, 2007, published by the Chancellery of the President of the Republic of Poland.

[4] Gita Baigelman was living in the Lodz ghetto, from where she was transferred to Ravensbrück concentration camp and a labor camp in Germany. She met the Kozminskis after the war.

[5] Kozminski, *op. cit.*

[6] Anti-Defamation League, press release, "ADL Honors Christian Rescuers of Jews During the Holocaust Who Had the Courage to Care," Nov. 22, 1996, www.adl.org/PresRele/ChJew_31/2857_31.asp.

likely to be attacked, according to police authorities cited by Lerman. A recent speech by the Archbishop of Canterbury proposing adoption of sharia law for Muslims in England for personal matters like marriage was followed by a storm of hostile protest, including some 500 incidents against Muslims in Britain ranging from verbal abuse to attacks on mosques, according to Lerman.

Lerman sees these attacks, like anti-Semitic crimes, as part of "the rise of racism generally. More has to be done to combat racism."

But some scholars of anti-Semitism think there's something unique that distinguishes it from other forms of racism. Hitler, of course, spoke of the inferior racial nature of Jews and their need to be eliminated in his quest for Aryan racial purity. "People love to talk about that form of anti-Semitism — that was the only form that was defeated," says Wisse.

It's more important, she suggests, to defend against the tendency to use Jews as a scapegoat for everything that's wrong with capitalism and modernity.

"It's an anti-modernist ideology that says, 'You think emancipation, democracy, is such a terrific force, but it's only a vehicle for the Jews to take us over.' " In Wisse's view, "The horror is that this organization of politics against the Jews is much more important to the Arabs than it ever was to Europe" because anti-Semitism has become the "glue" that ties disparate Muslim countries together.

Meanwhile, discrimination against Muslims — dubbed "Islamophobia" — has been garnering growing government and press attention. A 2006 report by the EU's European Monitoring Centre on Racism and Xenophobia said that while discrimination and incidents against European Muslims remain underdocumented and underreported, Muslims in the European Union "frequently suffer different forms of discrimination which reduce their employment opportunities and affect their educational achievement."[45]

Indeed, several columnists have recently described Muslims as "the new Jews" of Britain in connection with events seen as discriminatory against Muslims. After several Muslims were arrested in connection with an alleged terrorist plot, Mohammad Naseem, chairman of the Birmingham Central Mosque, told the press that Britain was becoming a "police state" and compared the police raids to the persecution of Jews in Germany.[46]

But when the EU's racism-monitoring arm investigated incidents of Islamophobia following 9/11, it found very few incidents of physical assaults on Muslims in most countries. (Only in the U.K. was a significant rise in attacks on Muslims reported.)[47] Historian David Cesarani of Royal Holloway, University of London, says this is a significant contrast from the spikes in attacks on Jews following events like the invasion of Afghanistan and Israeli incursions into the West Bank and Gaza Strip.

In addition, while Muslim immigrants may experience poverty and social discrimination, as Jewish immigrants once did, Muslims today are often connected to powerful foreign governments, while diaspora Jews historically had no homeland. When Muslims in Denmark were offended in September 2005 by cartoons depicting the Prophet Mohammed, for example, they could appeal to governments of Muslim countries, triggering an international wave of protests.

In addition, Cesarani notes, Jews historically never constituted a rival military or economic force to Europe, whereas Europeans rightfully feared Muslim power during the Ottoman Empire. Today, European reactions to Muslims are to some degree accurate perceptions of the real menace of Islamic terrorism, according to Cesarani.

"Islamophobia is incommensurable with anti-Semitism because Jews as Jews never espoused the attitudes ascribed to them by anti-Semites" or threatened a state in the name of Judaism, he argues. "Islamophobia may be an inappropriate . . . reaction to a grossly inflated 'threat,' but the danger of terrorism by Islamists is real, and there are several conflicts in the world in which Islamic militants are at war in the name of Islam."[48]

BACKGROUND

'Blood Libel' Slander

The accusation that Jews killed Christians, usually children, to obtain their blood for religious rituals originated in England in 1144, when Jews were accused of a ritual murder during the Passover period. This fabricated slander would become one of the most common incitements to anti-Jewish riots and killings throughout Europe during the Middle Ages, despite a papal bull in 1247 that declared such accusations false.[49]

The blood libel accusation lasted well into the 20th century, providing the ostensible cause for a pogrom as late as 1946 against Jewish survivors returning to their homes in Kielce, Poland. The accusation: The Jews planned to use the blood from the murder of a small boy to bake matzo for Passover.

In England and other European countries these seemingly spontaneous riots occurred as Jews were being denied equal rights with Christians. Restrictions imposed on Jews owning land and their exclusion from craft guilds made them dependent upon money lending and other forms of commerce, providing a historical basis for the stereotype of the Jew as greedy money-lender, notably the character of Shylock in Shakespeare's "Merchant of Venice."[50]

In 1218 England became the first European country to implement a church decree that Jews wear a badge to distinguish them from Christians, a directive the Nazis revived when they required all Jews to wear a yellow Jewish star.[51]

In 1290, King Edward expelled all Jews from England, ending their official presence in Britain for the next 400 years — the first large-scale deportation of Jews from a country in Europe. In 1656, British political leader Oliver Cromwell achieved limited recognition for Jews in England, many of whom were descended from Spanish and Portuguese Jews, known as "Conversos," who had fled the Inquisition and been converted to Christianity to prevent discovery.

In a recent paper delivered at Yale, Lappin of Kings College argues that Britain mistakenly perceives itself as a society tolerant of Jews. While the year 1492 is infamous in history for Spain's expulsion of the Jews, notes Lappin, Britain's own expulsion is generally not mentioned in British school curriculum.

History, he says, reveals a "deeply rooted view of Jews as fundamentally alien to British life." For decades, if not centuries, Jews' social acceptability has been "conditional upon suppression of one's Jewish associations and cultural properties," Lappin argues.[52]

With each new influx of Jews, the British government imposed further legal restrictions, such as banning land ownership or citizenship — notably in 1753 and again in 1768 after pogroms in Poland and the Ukraine brought waves of impoverished East European Jews to London.

In the 19th century, while British reformers crusaded for abolition of the slave trade, giving women the vote and establishing workers' rights, no political movement

AFP/Getty Images/Ralf Succo

Exactly 68 years after a Nazi mob destroyed Munich's main synagogue, members of the city's Jewish community and Israeli Rabbi Mei Lau, left, deliver Torahs to a new Munich synagogue in 2006. Germany's growing Jewish community opened the synagogue amid a resurgent debate about rising anti-Semitism in Germany.

supported Jewish emancipation, according to Lappin. Rather, Anglo-Jewish leaders pursued a strategy of "quiet diplomatic engagement."[53]

For example, between 1847 and 1852, banker Lionel Rothschild was prevented three times from taking the House of Commons seat to which he was elected. Rothschild was only allowed to enter the House 11 years after his first election and only after the Commons made an exception — suspending the required Christian oath for members of Parliament. Then, from 1880 to 1905 a large wave of Jewish immigrants escaping pogroms in Russia stimulated a strong anti-immigrant sentiment. The Aliens Act of 1905 was the first of several 20th-century measures aimed at limiting entry into the country.

Restricting Jewish Refugees

Britain's attitude towards Jewish refugees during the Nazi regime was more hostile than sympathetic, Lappin argues, in contrast to the country's reputation as a welcoming refuge. After the Nazis took power in Germany in 1933, British officials, like other Western governments, were flooded with requests from German Jews seeking to escape the regime. However, throughout the pre-war period, Britain maintained its system of rigorous controls on immigration, keeping Jewish immigration to a minimum except for those who could fill jobs in which labor was needed — notably female servants.

Nazis Exported Anti-Semitism to the Middle East

Hitler repackaged anti-Semitism as anti-Zionism.

On Nov. 2, 1917, Britain's foreign minister, Lord Balfour, announced Britain's support for the establishment in Palestine of a national home for the Jewish people.

The Balfour Declaration is often cited as the start of the Jewish-Arab conflict — and some would say it was the original source of anti-Israel sentiment in Europe.[1] But as political scientist Matthias Küntzel points out in his recent book, *Jihad and Jew-Hatred*, it wasn't clear that it would turn out that way. Some Arab leaders initially supported Zionist settlements, hoping Jewish immigration would bring economic development.

Before 1937, when the German government first decided it needed to turn the Arabs against the Jews, Jews held prominent positions in business and government in Egypt.[2] Indeed, in 1839 the sultan of the Ottoman Empire had decreed equality for Jews and Christians, and in 1856 such equality was established in law, motivated partly by the Ottoman elite's desire to draw closer to European civilization and to modernize.[3]

But some Arab leaders violently opposed Jewish immigration and the prospect of a Jewish homeland. In the decade leading up to 1936, the mufti of Jerusalem, Amin al-Husseini, the highest religious authority in Palestine, incited Palestinian Arabs to violence against Jews with the aim of ending Jewish immigration and destroying the prospect of a Jewish majority ruling the area. This movement culminated in the 1936-39 Arab revolt, which included anti-Semitic demonstrations, riots, bombings and raids on Jewish villages.[4]

As perhaps the leading inciter of hatred against Jews in the Arab world, the mufti became the region's most committed supporter of Nazism and "a local henchman of the Nazis," according to Küntzel, a research associate at the Vidal Sassoon International Center for the Study of Antisemitism at Hebrew University, Jerusalem.[5]

By 1938, amid mounting tension in Europe, the continuing flight of Jews from Germany to Palestine was provoking renewed Arab violence, including attacks against British fortifications, attacks on Jews and Jewish reprisals. The mufti fled Palestine in 1938 to avoid arrest by the British for his part in the Arab revolt. He spent most of the war in Berlin, recruiting Bosnian Muslims for the SS, the semi-military Nazi organization that oversaw Hitler's extermination of the Jews. From 1939 to 1945, the mufti's Arabic radio broadcasts, which mixed anti-Semitic propaganda with quotes from the *Koran*, made his station the most popular in the Arab world.[6]

The mufti also agreed with the Nazi policy of exterminating the Jews. In 1943, as a propaganda stunt, SS leader Heinrich Himmler wanted to permit 5,000 Jewish children to emigrate to Palestine, in exchange for 20,000 German prisoners. The mufti fought against the plan, and the children were sent to the gas chambers.[7]

The Nazis funded the burgeoning growth of Muslim fundamentalism, helping the radical Muslim Brotherhood distribute Arabic translations of *Mein Kampf*, Hitler's autobiographical political treatise, and the forged *Protocols of the Learned Elders of Zion* and helped fan anti-Zionist flames in the Arab world.[8]

In Germany, a mutual-admiration society appeared to have developed between the mufti and Hitler, who described the mufti inaccurately as having blond hair and blue eyes, to emphasize that he was not a member of an inferior race. Hitler had also expressed his antagonism to Zionism in *Mein Kampf.*

Küntzel argues that the idea of Jews as an all-powerful, dominating world force was essentially a Western idea exported to the Middle East by the Nazis in an effort to turn Muslims against Jews and Zionism. After all, the *Koran* portrays Jews primarily as a defeated force, and for centuries

In 1938, the "Kindertransports" brought about 10,000 Jewish children from Germany and Austria to Britain. These efforts often are cited as proof of British efforts to help the Jews. However, because of British immigration rules — not German restrictions — the children were forced to come without their parents, according to Lappin. As a result, many of these children became orphans at the end of the war.

Jews were treated as second-class citizens in most Arab countries.

But in a recent review of Küntzel's book, Jeffrey Goldberg, a journalist who writes about the region for *The Atlantic*, disagrees, arguing that plenty of anti-Jewish ideas were organic to Muslim thought. And he doesn't buy Küntzel's view that this history explains much Arab hostility towards Israel today. "Jews today have actual power in the Middle East, and Israel is not innocent of excess and cruelty," he writes.[9]

In Europe, Hitler's propaganda machine didn't begin waging a public war on Zionism until 1944, according to Michael Berkowitz, a professor of modern Jewish history at University College, London. In his 2007 book *The Crime of My Very Existence*, Berkowitz argues that Nazi leaders refashioned anti-Semitism as anti-Zionism as part of a broader tactic of painting Jews as criminals. Zionism was painted as the guise for a criminal conspiracy to create a Jewish world government. The Nazis often concocted specific charges against Jews based on technical aspects of tax laws and currency-exchange regulations in addition to charges of petty criminality.[10]

The criminality charges, Berkowitz argues, were chosen because Nazis feared their project of wiping out the Jews for racial reasons would not be universally compelling among German citizens who might be friendly with Mr. Stern the baker or Mrs. Morgen the neighbor. By contrast, the "law and order" motive for assailing an ethnic group was much more persuasive and survives today in stereotypical attitudes toward other ethnic groups, like blacks in the United States or West Indians in Britain, Berkowitz observes.

By 1944, as Nazis feared they were losing the war and would face international outrage at the genocide of the Jews, Zionism "was reconfigured as the apex of Jewish evil and organized criminality to rationalize the decimation of 6 million" Jews, he writes.[11]

Toward the end of the war, when the Nazis had nearly annihilated European Jews, they were searching for new enemies. As a Nazi propagandist put it at the time, once the Jews were all gone, momentum and sympathy for anti-Semitism would be lost: "When asked, young 20-year-old officers say that they have never yet knowingly seen a Jew.

Adolf Hitler meets with Grand Mufti Amin el-Husseini.

Therefore they find no interest . . . in the Jewish problem as it has been presented to them up to now."[12]

Most significantly for today, the Nazis' anti-Zionism represented "a new form of anti-Jewish discourse," Berkowitz writes, one that "contributed to the evil brew of post-1948 Arab anti-Semitism."[13]

---

[1] See www.yale.edu/lawweb/avalon/mideast/balfour.htm.

[2] The stimulus for Nazi support of Arabs was the British Peel Commission's 1937 partition plan, providing for a Jewish state, which the Germans feared would increase power for world Jewry. See Matthias Küntzel, *Jihad and Jew-Hatred* (2007), p. 29.

[3] *Ibid.*, p. 33.

[4] Martin Gilbert, *Churchill and Jews* (2007), p. 102.

[5] Küntzel, *op. cit.*, p. 101.

[6] *Ibid.*, pp. 34-35.

[7] *Ibid.*, p. 36.

[8] See www.hitler.org/writings/Mein_Kampf/.

[9] Jeffrey Goldberg, "Seeds of Hate," *New York Times Book Review*, Jan. 6, 2008, www.nytimes.com/2008/01/06/books/review/Goldberg-t. html?_r=1&oref=slogin.

[10] Michael Berkowitz, *The Crime of My Very Existence: Nazism and the Myth of Jewish Criminality* (2007), p. xviii.

[11] Berkowitz, *op. cit.*, pp. 112-113, xix.

[12] *Ibid.*, p. 133.

[13] *Ibid.*, p. 113.

By then, approximately 60,000 Jewish refugees remained in Britain, while another 10,000-20,000 had entered and then re-emigrated or were deported. Lappin notes that while the U.S. government's attitude towards aiding Jews shifted in early 1944 due in part to public pressure from American Jewish groups, the British Jewish community consistently refrained from publicly challenging the government on its handling of refugees.

AP Photo

In a dramatic gesture that helped to raise Europe's consciousness about the Holocaust, West Germany's Chancellor Willy Brandt kneels before the Jewish Heroes' monument in Warsaw, Poland, on Dec. 6, 1970.

In addition, the postwar Labor government refused to accept survivors beyond token numbers. Fewer than 5,000 survivors were admitted from 1945-50 under a family-reunification program, even as Britain was admitting 365,000 non-Jewish immigrants to solve its severe labor shortage. Foreign Secretary Ernest Bevin insisted Jews would not be easily assimilated into British life and that admitting large numbers would aggravate anti-Jewish sentiment stemming from Britain's conflict with Zionists in Palestine.[54]

Ironically, many of the most vocal anti-Zionists among today's British leftists insist that a solution to the Jewish refugee problem during the Holocaust should have been found in European countries rather than in Palestine — "obtuse to the fact that their own political precursors" helped to block Jewish immigration to Britain, Lappin observes.[55]

Forged 'Protocols'

The forgery known as the "Protocols of the Learned Elders of Zion" is the most famous document to libel the Jews. The tract purportedly comprises the minutes from 24 sessions of a conference supposedly held by representatives from the 12 tribes of Israel and led by a Grand Rabbi, whose apparent purpose is to lay out a plan for Jewish world conquest.

It first appeared in Russia in 1903 and again in 1905, inspired partly by the first Zionist congress, held in 1897 under the leadership of Theodor Herzl, an Austro-Hungarian Jewish journalist considered the father of Zionism. The protocols initially were used to blame the Jews for the 1905 Russian Revolution, but the tract soon proved adaptable to other situations where Jews were the target of blame.

"The Nazis saw its value immediately," writes Stephen Eric Bronner, a professor of political science at Rutgers University. The document provides a glimpse into what makes anti-Semitism unique by presenting the Jew as a kind of "chameleon," in Bronner's words. "The Jew is not simply a capitalist or a communist revolutionary, but the Jew is now any enemy required by the anti-Semite."[56]

Herzl, Paris correspondent for the liberal Viennese daily newspaper *Neue Frei Presse*, covered the notorious 1894 trial of Capt. Alfred Dreyfus, a French Jew falsely accused of spying for the Germans. During the trial Herzl witnessed anti-Jewish demonstrations in which cries of "Death to the Jews" were common. The Dreyfus Affair, as it is known, became a watershed event for Jews in France, who felt increasingly vulnerable to anti-Semitism — even though Dreyfus was pardoned in 1899 and his innocence officially recognized in 1906.

A secular Jew, Herzl decided that if anti-Semitism was so entrenched in the capitals of the European Enlightenment, Jews had no hope of assimilating in Europe. In 1896, he published *Der Judenstaat* (The Jewish State), in which he argued that Jews needed to create their own state. In 1897 he organized the First Zionist Congress in Basel, Switzerland, which voted to establish a "publicly and legally secured home" for the Jews in Palestine.[57]

Herzl had a utopian vision of the future homeland, imagining in his 1902 novel *Altneuland* (Old-New Land) an Israel much like his home city of Vienna, an intellectual café society of opera-going, German-speaking Jews. He also imagined that Arabs in Palestine would welcome the gifts of science and improved hygiene brought by the Jews.[58] But Arab opposition to the influx of Jews only hardened over time, leading to the development of the Palestine national liberation movement. (*See sidebar, p. 210.*)

Numerous theories have been put forward in trying to explain the success of anti-Semitism during the Nazi period, some reaching back to much earlier historical

Is anti-Zionism a cover-up for anti-Semitism?

YES

Ben Cohen
*Associate Director, Department on
Anti-Semitism and Extremism, American
Jewish Committee; editor, www. z-word.com*

Written for *CQ Global Researcher*, June 2008

Anti-Zionism has gained greater visibility over the last decade, but it is not an unknown phenomenon historically. In communist Europe, remnants of Jewish communities that perished during the Nazi Holocaust were frequently persecuted in the name of anti-Zionism.

These days, anti-Zionist views are heavily concentrated among the educated elite. If you regard anti-Zionism as one more expression of hatred towards Jews, this is somewhat puzzling, because anti-Semitism — particularly after the Holocaust — is widely perceived to be more beer hall than bistro.

Anti-Semites regard Jews as a malign social force that controls the banks, media and governments. But most of Zionism's mainstream critics say they are only concerned with the Jewish state, not demented fantasies about what Jews are up to.

So can we construct an unbreachable partition between anti-Semitism and anti-Zionism? The answer is "No," and here is why:

- You can't disavow anti-Semitism as a vulgar form of bigotry and then invoke the age-old themes of anti-Semitic conspiracy theory. After assuring us their arguments were not anti-Semitic, U.S. academics John Mearsheimer and Stephen Walt upended decades of political science research by advancing a monocausal theory of U.S. foreign policy in the Middle East: The powerful "Israel Lobby" cajoles the United States into doing things it otherwise wouldn't do.
- Anti-Zionism is founded upon a caricature of Israel as the apartheid-like child of a colonial enterprise. But Zionism's goal is to guarantee, after centuries of horrendous persecution, the freedom and security of Jews, not the subjugation of non-Jews.
- Before Israel's creation in 1948, there was a vibrant debate about the desirability of a Jewish state. But to be an anti-Zionist now is to question the legitimacy of only Israel, out of nearly 200 states worldwide. In a world of disintegrating polities from Iraq to the Democratic Republic of Congo, why should only Israel's existence be subject to debate?

No serious supporter of Israel claims that mere criticism is anti-Semitism. There is, however, a vital distinction between a rational critique of Israeli policies and demonization, which too often is stimulated by or evokes anti-Semitism.

NO

Antony Lerman
*Director, Institute for
Jewish Policy Research*

Written for *CQ Global Researcher*, June 2008

Anti-Zionism and hostility to Israel can be anti-Semitic if they are expressed using the symbols of the anti-Semitic figure of the Jew or of Jewry as a whole. For example, if Zionism is characterized as a worldwide Jewish conspiracy, or a plan straight out of the forged, anti-Semitic "Protocols of the Learned Elders of Zion," that is anti-Semitism.

But to believe that anti-Zionism and anti-Semitism are one and the same ignores the history of Zionism.

For decades Zionism was supported only by a minority of Jews. The rest were either indifferent or manifestly opposed to the whole idea of the establishment of a Jewish state. Anti-Zionism was therefore a perfectly respectable position to hold, and one that continues to be held today by hundreds of thousands of strictly orthodox Jews and many secular Jews with left-liberal perspectives.

Equating anti-Zionism and anti-Semitism — what has become known as the "new anti-Semitism" — fundamentally subverts the shared understanding of what anti-Semitism is, built up painstakingly through research and study by scholars over many years: It drains the word anti-Semitism of any useful meaning. The advocates of the concept of a new anti-Semitism argue that it is anti-Semitic to either criticize Israeli policies or deny Israel's right to exist, even if one does not hold beliefs historians have traditionally regarded as an anti-Semitic view: hatred of Jews per se, belief in a worldwide Jewish conspiracy, belief that Jews created communism and control capitalism, belief that Jews are racially inferior and so on.

Those who argue that anti-Zionism and anti-Semitism are one claim they don't say criticism of Israeli policies is illegitimate. However, in practice this view virtually proscribes any such thing.

As the Oxford academic Brian Klug has written, anti-Zionism and hostility to Israel — if based on a political cause or moral code that is not anti-Jewish per se — is not anti-Semitic. And arguing that it is harms the all-important struggle to combat anti-Semitism. If people feel unfairly stigmatized as anti-Semitic simply for speaking out about the plight of the Palestinians and the Israeli government's role in causing their suffering, they could become cynical and alienated whenever the problem of anti-Semitism is raised.

roots. Austrian-born American historian Raul Hilberg contends the Germans greeted Nazi anti-Semitism without suspicion as to its ultimate goal because it drew on old forms of anti-Semitism that had been part of Christian writings since the 16th century, when Martin Luther railed against what he saw as recalcitrant Jews because of their resistance to Christianity.[59]

The term "anti-Semitism" was coined in 1879 by German journalist and Jew-hater Wilhelm Marr, who wished to emphasize the "scientific," ethnic character of his opposition to Jews. Like the Nazis that followed him, Marr saw the Jews as a threatening race, incapable of assimilating, that had seized control of the German economy and society. "Semite" was his preferred term for Jews because it sounded scientific, neutral and modern.[60]

The Nazis, drawing on these ideas, believed exterminating Jews would cleanse humanity and save the world from a lethal threat to European morality and culture. Jews were allegedly a satanic race involved in a conspiracy for world domination that would lead to extinction of so-called "Aryan" civilization.

Holocaust Denial

By the end of 1942, Allied governments were aware of concentration camps holding thousands of Jewish prisoners across Europe and that six camps were devoted exclusively to killing. But in 1943, Jews were barely mentioned in Allied propaganda.[61]

Nor were Jews discussed much in the press. In Britain, where the photo of British troops liberating the Nazi camp Bergen-Belsen became a familiar image, the skeleton-like survivors shown on cinema newsreels were not generally identified as Jews.[62]

Not until Israel captured and tried Nazi official Adolf Eichmann in the early 1960s did the horrifying nature of European Jewry's fate enter public consciousness. For example, there is no mention of genocide in the charter under which the major Nazi war criminals were tried at Nuremberg. The term Holocaust did not come into use to describe the extermination of the Jews until several years after the war.

"Today we find this difficult to understand, but the fact is that the Shoah — the attempted genocide of the Jews of Europe — was for many years by no means the fundamental question of postwar intellectual life in Europe. . . . Indeed most people — intellectuals and others — ignored it as much as they could," writes historian Judt.[63]

However, it was no mystery that 6 million Jews had been put to death during World War II — a fact widely accepted within a few months of the war, Judt notes in *Postwar: A History of Europe Since 1945.*[64]

In France, less than 3 percent of the 76,000 Jews deported in 1940-44 survived. In the Netherlands, which had 140,000 Jews before the war, fewer than 5,000 returned. In Germany, just over 21,000 of the country's 600,000 Jews remained after the war.[65]

But even the remnants of returning Jews were "not much welcomed," Judt notes. "After years of anti-Semitic propaganda, local populations everywhere were not only disposed to blame 'Jews' in the abstract for their own suffering but were distinctly sorry to see the return of men and women whose jobs, possessions and apartments they had purloined."[66]

In Paris in 1945, hundreds of people protested when a returning Jewish deportee tried to reclaim his occupied apartment, screaming "France for the French!"[67]

Postwar Poland's Anti-Semitism

Poland was perhaps the most dangerous country for returning Jews. Although it had the largest concentration of Jews before the war — more than 3 million — 97.5 percent of them had been exterminated under the Nazis.[68]

In his recent book, *Fear*, Princeton historian Jan T. Gross estimates that after the war, 500-1,600 Jews returning to their hometowns in Poland — sick, traumatized and destitute, often from concentration camps — were killed by Poles upon their arrival.[69] (*See sidebar, p. 200.*)

Why did Poles attack their returning neighbors after the war? During the Nazi persecution and following the Jews' deportation to concentration camps, many Poles benefited materially, moving into Jewish homes and seizing their possessions. (Sometimes the property was pitiful: Gross describes a 1945 letter from a surviving Polish Jew asking a Polish court to make his neighbor return the two eiderdown quilts and pillows he had left in his safekeeping.[70])

As Jews returned, Poles often feared this property would be reclaimed. The Poles' "widespread collusion" in Nazi plunder and murder of the Jews — and suppressed guilt about it — generated virulent anti-Semitism after the war, in Gross' view.[71] "Jews were perceived as a threat to the material status quo, security and peaceful conscience of their Christian fellow-citizens," he writes.[72]

More people witnessed the death of Jews in Poland than in any other country, since it was the site of Auschwitz and other major concentration camps. But in some cases, Poles also participated in the killings.

During the Soviet occupation of Poland, many Poles believed the Jews had betrayed Poland, collaborating with the Russians while the Poles were fighting and being deported to Siberia. In recent years, some Poles cited this version of history, which Gross discredits, as the reason behind the massacres.[73]

In addition, Polish national identity depended to some extent on stories Poles told about their own suffering during the war, and "comparative victimhood" continued to poison relationships with the few remaining Jews after the war.[74]

In fact, the communist period became yet another period in which the memory of the Jews' suffering was suppressed in official accounts, and many Jews were afraid to reveal their origins. In the 1960s, a student uprising against the communist regime was denounced as being perpetrated by Zionist agents. The 1968 campaign also drew on the myth of "Judeo-communism," in which Jews were believed to have cooperated with the Stalinists. By the end of 1968, two-thirds of Poland's Jews had been driven away.[75]

Facing the Holocaust

The trials of Eichmann and of Auschwitz guards in the early 1960s triggered renewed interest in the Holocaust in countries like Germany and the Netherlands, where silence had reigned. The postwar baby boomers were curious about recent history and skeptical of the story told by the "silent generation" of their parents, Judt notes.

During the 1960s and '70s, several events helped to put the Jews' suffering in the German spotlight, according to Judt: The Six-Day Arab-Israeli War of 1967, Chancellor Willy Brandt dropping to his knees at the Warsaw Ghetto memorial and the telecast in Germany in 1979 of an American miniseries, "Holocaust."[76]

Twenty million German viewers saw the series — well over half the population. From then on, writes Judt,

AFP/Getty Images/Gali Tibbon

English Football Association Chief Executive Brian Barwick (left) and Noel White (2nd-left), chairman of the association's International Committee, and representatives of fans lay wreaths on March 23, 2007, at the "Hall of Remembrance" at the Yad Vashem Holocaust Memorial in Jerusalem commemorating the 6 million Jews killed by the Nazis during World War II. The association says it is committed to reducing anti-Semitism at soccer matches.

"Germans would be among the best-informed Europeans on the subject of the Shoah and at the forefront of all efforts to maintain public awareness of their country's singular crime." Compared to 1968, when a little over 400 school groups visited Dachau, by the 1970s more than 5,000 a year were visiting the former concentration camp, located 10 miles outside of Munich.[77]

As Judt notes, some major European countries — the Netherlands, Belgium, Norway, Italy — could claim that their orders to deport and execute Jews came from the Germans. The exception was France. Marshal Philippe Petain's Vichy regime, elected in July 1940 by the French parliament, initiated its own anti-Jewish laws in 1940 and 1941. French authorities rounded up the country's Jewish population; most Jewish deportees from France never saw a foreign uniform until they were handed over to Germans for the final shipment to Auschwitz.

Not until 1995 did President Jacques Chirac break a 50-year silence and acknowledge for the first time that the French were responsible for rounding up nearly 13,000 Jews — more than 4,000 of them children — for deportation to Auschwitz in July 1942.[78]

Chirac's acknowledgement followed publication in the late 1960s and mid-'70s of several books by foreign historians demonstrating that the Vichy crimes were French, not German initiatives.

President Charles de Gaulle's 1967 press conference after Israel's victory in the Six-Day War, when he referred to Jews as "a people sure of themselves and domineering" provoked outrage among French Jews and contributed to a new level of awareness of French Jews.[79] Marcel Ophuls's film "The Sorrow and the Pity," about the trials of high-ranking French officials, and a 1985 documentary film, "Shoah," by the French director Claude Lanzmann, also had a dramatic impact.

Anti-Semitism Re-emerges

Immediately after World War II, Austria and West Germany, led by anti-Nazi parties, barred Nazis from political participation and banned overt support of Nazi ideology. On May 8, 1948, the Austrian government banned Nazi activities. West Germany prohibited public expression of Nazi beliefs, banned Nazis from the political process and outlawed swastikas.

In the 1960s, however, extremist, neo-Nazi groups re-emerged in both countries. After German reunification in the 1990s, the groups gained followers among disaffected teenagers from the former East Germany. Such groups tended to merge with skinheads, a far-right youth subculture that developed in Britain during the "rude boy" music scene of the 1960s.[80] Skinheads re-surfaced in the late 1970s with white-power, racist, anti-Semitic overtones. The term "skinhead" described the close-cropped hairdo adopted by its adherents, sometimes accompanied by leather boots and tattoos. Skinheads were known for creating violent confrontations with non-whites, Muslims, Jews and gays — a movement that soon spread to the rest of Europe and North America.

The German National Democratic Party (NPD) is Germany's oldest and most influential right-wing party. In 2006, after receiving 7.3 percent of the vote in the regional parliamentary elections for Mecklenburg-Western Pomerania, the party launched an online news show on its Web site featuring videos, for example, of a memorial march in honor of Hitler's deputy Rudolf Hess.[81] The party holds weekly demonstrations and meetings of extreme-right sympathizers, including neo-Nazis and skinheads, according to the Stephen Roth Institute. To get around the legal bans on Nazi activity, the groups recruit East German youth using music — including music videos and far-right music portals on the Web — sponsoring trips to concerts and offering free beer. At a 2006 NPD event, an Iranian flag was hoisted to demonstrate the party's solidarity with the Iranian government's denial of the Holocaust — a way to express that view without violating German law against Holocaust denial.[82]

Between 2001 and 2005 anti-Semitic incidents increased in eight European countries — Austria, Belgium, Denmark, France, Germany, Netherlands, Sweden and Britain. At the same time, anti-Jewish crimes increased significantly in France between 2001 and 2006, but only slightly in Germany and Sweden.[83]

Although many perceive that today's anti-Semitic hate crimes are perpetrated by disaffected Muslims instead of right-wing skinheads, the European Union's monitoring agency says the shift is "difficult to substantiate," noting that several countries prohibit investigating ethnic or religious backgrounds of criminal suspects.[84]

According to the EU Agency for Fundamental Rights, the most troubling development in European attitudes has been the increase since 2005 in the number of respondents questioning the loyalty of Jewish citizens, as recorded in surveys by the Anti-Defamation League. Last year, the percentage of those believing Jews are "more loyal to Israel than to this country" rose in the United Kingdom, Austria, Belgium, Hungary, the Netherlands and Switzerland.[85]

Today there is no single hand directing anti-Semitic propaganda worldwide, as there was under the Nazis or under the Soviet Union in the 1970s or '80s. Anti-Semitism today generally does not have the power of the state behind it, except for governments in the Muslim world like Iran with its official discrimination against Jews.

International Action

Since the beginning of its upsurge in 2000, anti-Semitism in Europe has been monitored and surveyed continually, and analyzed at international conferences and by Europe-wide organizations. Since 2003, the 56-nation Organization for Security and Co-operation in Europe (OSCE) has held six major conferences on anti-Semitism. A conference in April 2004 produced the "Berlin Declaration," which stated that "international developments . . . including those in Israel or elsewhere in the Middle East, never justify anti-Semitism."[86]

In 2003 the OSCE recommended that member states actively collect data on hate crimes, including anti-Semitic incidents, and it has established a special envoy to combat anti-Semitism.

On March 1, 2007, the EU established the Agency for Fundamental Rights, to collect reliable and comparable data on racism and anti-Semitism. In 2000, its forerunner agency, the European Monitoring Centre on Racism and Xenophobia, established a system to help states collect and analyze data. However, only four out of 27 member states — Germany, France, the Netherlands and Great Britain — have mechanisms for accurate data collection on anti-Semitic incidents, the agency reported last year.[87]

In April 2007, the Council of the European Union agreed that member states should harmonize their minimal criminal provisions against racist agitation, including Holocaust denial. The final document, if adopted, would give countries two years to incorporate these provisions into their national laws.[88]

On June 27, 2007, the Parliamentary Assembly of the Council of Europe issued a resolution noting that it "remains deeply concerned about the persistence and escalation of anti-Semitic phenomena."[89]

In response to the Iranian government's sponsorship of an international conference aimed at denying the Holocaust, the U.N. General Assembly in January 2007 declared Holocaust denial "tantamount to approval of genocide in all its forms."[90]

In 1991, the General Assembly had overturned a 1975 resolution declaring Zionism "a form of racism." However, according to a recent State Department report, the assembly has established bureaucracies "with the sole mandate of singling out Israel as a violator of the human rights of others." In its first 16 months, which ended on Sept. 30, 2007, the U.N. Human Rights Commission adopted 15 anti-Israel decisions but has taken little action against notorious human-rights violators like Myanmar, complains the State Department. The report also charges that Muslim countries have used the U.N. system to "demonize Israelis implicitly, and Jews generally," an approach, the department warns, which may be "fueling anti-Semitism."[91]

In response to rising anti-Semitism worldwide, the U.S. Congress passed the Global Anti-Semitism Review Act of 2004, which requires the State Department to document and combat anti-Semitic acts internationally.

The act also established a special envoy to combat anti-Semitism.

CURRENT SITUATION

Britain Reacts

Countries today vary widely in their legal approaches to combating anti-Semitism. Six European countries, including France and Germany, impose criminal penalties on certain forms of anti-Semitic expression, such as denial of the Holocaust. British MP Mann, chair of the committee on anti-Semitism in Parliament, says he wants to shut down Web sites spewing anti-Semitic ideas, several of which originate in the United States. So far, the U.S. government has resisted these efforts because they would conflict with constitutional protection for freedom of speech.

A British parliamentary inquiry produced a report in September 2006 finding that "violence, desecration of property and intimidation directed towards Jews is on the rise."

The report found that only a minority of police forces in Britain can record anti-Semitic incidents. According to Mann, a new national data-gathering and reporting system will shortly be in place to correct this.[92]

The panel also complained that only a few anti-Semitic incidents are being prosecuted as racial harassment, which carries increased penalties, and called on the Crown Prosecution Service to address the problem. The Service released an investigation in May that found the low number of prosecutions resulted from the inability to identify suspects and the unwillingness of victims to pursue prosecution. To reverse the trend, the Service is encouraging the Jewish community and police to pursue these crimes.[93]

Noting that anti-Semitic incidents in Britain declined by 8 percent in 2007 from the previous year, Mann says, "We're bringing the problem down to more reasonable levels, where it can be dealt with more routinely."

A campaign for an academic boycott of Israel, the focus of much campus-based anti-Zionism in Britain, died last year after a legal opinion found that the movement would violate discrimination laws. The proposed boycott by the University and College Union — which would have barred Israeli academics from coming to British universities and prevented British academics from participating in Israeli conferences — provoked international outrage and charges of anti-Semitism.

However, it appears the debate is being re-ignited. In May, delegates to the union's annual congress passed a motion asking members "to consider the moral and political implications of educational links" with Israel in light of Israel's policies towards the Palestinians.[94] Union leaders said the motion's goal was "to provide solidarity with Palestinians," not to boycott Israel.[95] But Stop the Boycott Coalition, formed of academics and Jewish and non-Jewish groups, fought the motion, saying it constituted a thinly veiled illegal boycott.

Whatever the motion's impact, observers say boycott proposals are likely to come back in the form of "divestment" resolutions on campuses vowing not to purchase Israeli products. In February, the student union of the London School of Economics was one of the first to pass such a resolution, which called for students to lobby the school to divest from Israel and from companies that "provide military support for the occupation."[96]

In February, a report on the continued presence of anti-Semitic soccer chants came out just as Avram Grant, the Israeli manager of the Chelsea soccer team, received a package said to contain a lethal white powder and a threatening note describing him as "a backstabbing Jewish bastard" who would die "a very slow and painful death."[97]

French Anti-Semitism?

While overall anti-Semitic incidents in France decreased 32 percent for the first eight months of 2007 compared to the same period the previous year, several troubling developments have led to government action.

The 2006 kidnapping and death of the 23-year-old Halimi led to a government report to then-Prime Minister Dominique de Villepin stressing the gravity of anti-Semitic propaganda. The Education Department also ratified inclusion of Holocaust studies, anti-Semitism and Jewish-Arab relations in the 2007 school curriculum.[98]

In February President Nicolas Sarkozy proposed making every 10-year-old French student honor one of the 11,000 Jewish children from France killed in the Holocaust, by learning about the selected child's background and fate. The proposal provoked a storm of protests from experts, including some prominent Jews, who said it would be too traumatic for young children. France's education

minister later softened the proposal so that entire classes would adopt one child.

But Sarkozy defended the plan, saying "We must tell a child the truth."[99]

Sarkozy had been toying with this idea since serving as interior minister under President Chirac, when he was astonished by the high number of anti-Semitic incidents.[100]

Many are particularly disturbed by the growing popularity of French comedian Dieudonné M'bala M'bala, who claims the African slave trade was a Jewish enterprise and that France is ruled by Zionists and neo-Zionists.

After Halimi's death, French groups monitoring anti-Semitism said the words of the comedian, who made an abortive bid for the presidency, had influenced the killers. Dieudonné (as he is known), is of Afro-Caribbean descent and is a folk hero among black and Arab immigrants. A great many attacks against Jews occur in their neighborhoods.[101]

Jean-Marie Le Pen, leader of the right-wing National Front Party, wooed Muslim immigrants by receiving Dieudonné at his party convention in 2006. (In February, Le Pen, widely known for his anti-Semitism, received a suspended prison sentence for saying that the Nazi occupation of France was "not particularly inhumane.")[102] Last March, a Paris court fined Dieudonné 5,000 euros for saying Jews had been slave traders and were now bankers and terrorists.[103]

However, in the presidential balloting in May, Le Pen won only 10 percent of the vote — his worst showing since 1974 — and failed to qualify for a second round. In June, his party failed to win a single seat in the legislative elections.[104]

In February, 21 people were charged in Halimi's kidnapping and murder, including Muslim immigrants from North Africa and immigrants from Congo and the Ivory Coast. The gang's self-proclaimed leader, Fofana, who was eventually found and arrested in the Ivory Coast, told police he organized Halimi's kidnapping but has denied killing him. No trial date has been set.[105]

Meanwhile, six people are being held in connection with Roumi's February kidnapping and torture, also in the Bagneux quarter.[106] In both cases, money appears to have been a substantial part of the motive.

In Bagneux, following Halimi's murder, a social worker said the belief that "all Jews are rich is an anti-Semitic prejudice that didn't exist in the neighborhood 20 years ago."[107]

OUTLOOK

Growing Discomfort

By many measures, life for Jews in Europe has never been better. They no longer fear any political party agitating for discrimination against them or for their deportation, as in past centuries.

But Jews also maintain a historical consciousness that a comfortable middle-class life can suddenly become a mirage, as it did in Germany, France and Poland in the late 1930s. To one another, Jews often speak of having, at least metaphorically, a bag packed under the bed, "just in case." Indeed, Jews increasingly are emigrating from France to Israel — 2,400 in 2004; 3,000 in 2005 — indicating a growing sense of discomfort as attacks on Jews and religious property have risen.[108]

As the Middle East conflict continues, anti-Jewish and anti-Zionist attitudes are likely to gain even more force. A conference last month in Jerusalem marking the 60th anniversary of Israel's creation treated global threats like terrorism and Iran as especially harmful to Israel and Jews.

"Cataclysms always seem to affect Jews first," said Stuart E. Eizenstat, a senior official in the Clinton and Carter administrations and author of an essay that formed the basis for the conference. "Go back to the Black Plague. It was not a Jewish issue, but it had particular impact on Jews because they were blamed for it."[109]

Some fear that European leftists will continue to court the growing population of young Muslims — who are often hostile to Jews — as the new working class, contributing to the new anti-Semitism. By contrast, the French Jewish population is small and aging, and many French Jews adhere to the traditional stance of "being Jewish at home and a citizen outside," making them a less strident political faction.

Nevertheless, the French left appears to be "turning away from the unholy alliance with Islamic fundamentalism," especially as the anti-Semitic content of Islamic ideology is exposed, noted a 2005 analysis from the Stephen Roth Institute.[110] Indeed, French historian Weil suggests this alliance is no longer a problem, though it's understandable how it happened.

"There was a cognitive impossibility for some people, especially some Jews who fought against racism and colonialism in the past, to suddenly acknowledge that anti-Semitism could come from the people they were defending

for so many years," who themselves suffered from racism, he observes. "It took time for some people on the left. It was, 'Oh my God, how can this happen?'"

In Eastern Europe, notably Poland, while the older generation continues to do battle with its Jewish ghosts, the younger generation is showing greater curiosity and openness toward Jewish culture, and some are even returning to Jewish roots. (*See sidebar, p. 202.*) Many hope that will change the overall climate for the better.

Meanwhile, in Central and Eastern Europe left-wing anti-Semites are joining right-wing nationalists to protest globalization, which they blame on Jewish financiers.[111]

Officials in Europe and in international bodies have become more conscious of anti-Semitism, arguing that where it is tolerated other forms of racism will follow. "We're making it less acceptable by challenging it and doing things about it," says British MP Mann. But he adds, "We're not complacent."

NOTES

1. Brett Kline, "Echoes of Halimi in French Suburb," *JTA*, March 6, 2008, www.jta.org.

2. "The Terrible Tale of Ilan Halimi," *The Economist*, March 4, 2006.

3. Stephen Roth Institute for the Study of Contemporary Antisemitism and Racism, "Antisemitism Worldwide 2006," p. 6, www.tau .ac.il/Anti-Semitism/asw2006/gen-analysis.pdf.

4. Stephen Roth Institute, "France 2006," p. 12, www.tau.ac.il/Anti-Semitism/asw2006/france.htm.

5. Daniel Ben Simon, "Anti-Semitism in France/ Calm Interrupted," *Haaretz*, March 6, 2008, www .haaretz.com/hasen/spages/961302.html.

6. Community Security Trust, press release, "Antisemitic hate incidents remain at unacceptably high level," Feb. 14, 2008, www.thecst.org.uk.

7. Stephen Roth Institute, "Antisemitism Worldwide 2007," 2008, p. 1.

8. *Ibid.*, Appendices: "Major Attacks and Violent Incidents 1999-2007." Major attacks are defined as attacks and attempted attacks by violent means such as shooting, arson, or firebombing. Major violent incidents include harassment of individuals,

vandalizing Jewish property and street violence not involving a weapon.

9. *Ibid.*, pp. 1, 7.

10. All-Party Parliamentary Group Against Antisemitism, "Report of the All-Party Parliamentary Inquiry into Antisemitism," September 2006, www.thepcaa.org/report.pdf.

11. Office of the Special Envoy to Monitor and Combat Anti-Semitism, U.S. Department of State, "Contemporary Global Anti-Semitism: A Report Provided to the United States Congress," March 2008, p. 77. See "Action Heroes," *Telegraph Magazine*, June 2, 2007, www.telegraph.co.uk.

12. Community Security Trust, "Antisemitic Incidents Report 2007," 2008, www.thecst.org.uk.

13. Stephen Roth Institute, "Antisemitism Worldwide, 2007," *op. cit.*, p. 6.

14. *Ibid.*, p. 6.

15. *Ibid.*, p. 6. Frattini is EU Commissioner for Justice, Freedom and Security.

16. Stephen Roth Institute, *op. cit.*, p. 12.

17. Melanie Phillips, "Britain's Anti-Semitic Turn," *City Journal*, autumn 2007, www.city-journal.org/html/17_4_anti-semitism.html.

18. U.S. Department of State, *op. cit.*, pp. 28-35. See p. 35 for cartoons in *Guardian* and Norwegian press.

19. Stephen Roth Institute, "Antisemitism Worldwide 2006," *op. cit.*, p. 5.

20. *Jerusalem Post* staff and Michael Lando, "Amadinejad: Israel Filthy Bacteria," *Jerusalem Post*, Feb. 20, 20008, www.jpost.com/servlet/Satellite?pagename=JPost%2FJPArticle%2FShowFull&cid=1203343707673.

21. Yves Pallade, *et al.*, "Antisemitism and Racism in European Soccer," American Jewish Committee Berlin Office, May 2007, p. 10.

22. www.jpr.org.uk.

23. U.S. Department of State, *op. cit.*, p. 3.

24. European Agency for Fundamental Rights, "Anti-Semitism: Summary Overview of the Situation in the European Union 2001-2007," January 2008, *FRA Working Paper*, http://fra.europa.eu.

25. U.S. Department of State, *op. cit.*, p. 3.

26. *Ibid.*, p. 3.

27. *Ibid.*, p. 31.

28. Vanessa Gera, "Israel Urges Poland, Catholic Church to Condemn Polish Priest for Anti-Semitic Comments," The Associated Press, July 30, 2007.

29. U.S. Department of State, *op. cit.*, pp. 22, 28.

30. "Pierre-André Taguieff on the New Anti-Zionism," interview in *Observatoire du Communautarisme*, Sept. 7, 2005, www.zionism-israel.com/ezine/New_Antizionism.htm. Taguieff's 2002 book published in France *La nouvelle judeophobie* (The New Judephobia) was published in English translation in 2004 under the title *Rising from the Muck: The New Anti-Semitism in France.*

31. Matthias Küntzel, *Jihad and Jew Hatred: Islamism, Nazism and the Roots of 9/11* (2007), p. 129.

32. Phillips, *op. cit.*

33. Tony Judt, "On the 'Problem of Evil' in Postwar Europe," *New York Review of Books*, Feb. 14, 2008, pp. 33-36, www.nybooks.com/articles/21031.

34. Abraham H. Foxman, "Britain's Jewish Problem," *New York Sun*, May 18, 2005, at www.adl.org/ADL_Opinions/Anti_Semitism_Global/20050518-NY+Sun.htm.

35. *Ibid.*

36. Pierre-André Taguieff, *Rising from the Muck: The New Anti-Semitism in Europe* (2004), pp. 12-17.

37. Phillips, *op. cit.*

38. See Dennis Sewell, "A Kosher Conspiracy," newstatesman.com, Jan. 14, 2002, www.newstatesman.com/200201140009.

39. U.S. Department of State, *op. cit.*, p. 35.

40. "Report of the All-Party Parliamentary Inquiry into Antisemitism," *op. cit.*, p. 35.

41. "EUMC Working Definition of Anti-Semitism," *ibid.*, p. 6.

42. Judt, *op. cit.*, pp. 33-36.

43. Edward H. Kaplan and Charles A. Small, "Anti-Israel Sentiment Predicts Anti-Semitism in Europe," *Journal of Conflict Resolution*, August 2006, www.h-net.org/~antis/papers/jcr_antisemitism.pdf.

44. Judt, *op. cit.*

45. "EUMC Presents Reports on Discrimination and Islamophobia in the EU," European Monitoring Centre on Racism and Xenophobia, Dec. 18, 2006, www.fra.europa.eu/fra/index.php?fuseaction= content.dsp_cat_content&catid=43d8bc25bc89d &contentid=4582ddc822d41. The report found only one member state, the United Kingdom, publishes criminal justice data that specifically identify Muslims as victims of hate crimes.

46. "Cameron to Meet Mosque Leaders," *Birmingham Daily Mail*, Feb. 5, 2007, www.birminghammail .net/news/tm_headline=cameron-to-meet-city-mosque-leaders&method =full&objectid=185770 92&siteid=50002-name_ page.html.

47. David Cesarani, "Are Muslims the New Jews? Comparing Islamophobia and Anti-Semitism in Britain and Europe," draft discussion paper delivered to the Yale Initiative for the Interdisciplinary Study of Antisemitism, March 27, 2008, www .yale.edu/yiisa/Cesarani_Paper.pdf.

48. *Ibid.*, p. 12.

49. Jan T. Gross, *Fear* (2007), p. 149.

50. Shalom Lappin, "This Green and Pleasant Land: Britain and the Jews," delivered to the Yale Initiative for the Interdisciplinary Study of Anti-Semitism, Nov. 29, 2007, p. 7, at www.yale.edu/ yiisa/lappin_yiisa072.pdf.

51. *Ibid.*, p. 6.

52. *Ibid.*, p. 12.

53. *Ibid.*

54. Lappin, *op. cit.*, p. 18. In the period immediately following the war, the British government kept legal restrictions on the 60,000 refugees still in the country — as aliens without full rights to seek employment until 1948. This group included people who had served in the British army or worked for the war effort in other ways.

55. *Ibid.*, p. 19.

56. Stephen Eric Bronner, "Libeling the Jews: Truth Claims, Trials and the Protocols of Zion," in Debra Kaufman, *et al.*, eds., *From the Protocols of the Learned Elders of Zion to Holocaust Denial Trials* (2007), pp. 15-17.

57. David Remnick, "Blood and Sand," *The New Yorker*, May 5, 2008, p. 72.

58. Jeffrey Goldberg, "Unforgiven: Israel Confronts its Existential Fears," *The Atlantic*, May 2008, pp. 34-51, p. 42. Also See Martin Gilbert, *Churchill and the Jews* (2007).

59. Michael Berkowitz, *The Crime of My Very Existence: Nazism and the Myth of Jewish Criminality* (2007), p. xvii.

60. Robert S. Wistrich, "European Anti-Semitism Reinvents Itself," American Jewish Committee, May 2005, www.ajc.org. Originally, the term Semite referred to peoples from ancient southwestern Asia who spoke Hebrew, Aramaic, Arabic or Amharic.

61. Henry Feingold, "The Surprising Historic Roots of Holocaust Denial," in Debra Kaufman, *et al.*, *op. cit.*, pp. 66-79.

62. Tony Judt, *Postwar: A History of Europe since 1945* (2007), p. 807. Also see B. W. Patch, "Anti-Semitism in Germany," in *Editorial Research Reports*, Aug. 2, 1935, available in *CQ Researcher Plus Archive*, www .library.cqpress.com.

63. Judt, *New York Review of Books, op. cit.*, p. 33.

64. Judt, *Postwar, op. cit.*, p. 804.

65. *Ibid.*

66. *Ibid.*

67. *Ibid.*, p. 805.

68. *Ibid.*, p. 804.

69. Gross, *op. cit.*, p. 35.

70 *Ibid.*, p. 42.

71. *Ibid.*, p. xiv.

72. *Ibid.*, p. 247.

73. See Gross, *op. cit.*, and Peter S. Green, "Polish Town Still Tries to Forget its Dark Past," *The New York Times*, Feb. 8, 2003.

74. Judt, *op. cit.*, p. 823.

75. *Ibid.*

76. *Ibid.*, p. 811.

77. *Ibid.*

78. Tom Reiss, "Letter from Paris: Laugh Riots," *The New Yorker*, Nov. 19, 2007, pp. 44-50, www.newyorker .com/reporting/2007/11/19/071119fa_fact_reiss.

79. Judt, *Postwar, op. cit.*, p. 817.

80. For background, see R. L. Worsnop, "Neo-Nazism in West Germany," *Editorial Research Reports*, April

12, 1967, available at *CQ Researcher Plus Archives*, www.library.cqpress.com. See "Neo-Nazi Skinheads," Anti-Defamation League, www.adl.org/hate-patrol/njs/neonazi.asp.

81. Stephen Roth Institute, "Germany 2006," at www.tauc.il/Anti-Semitism, p. 2.

82. *Ibid.*, pp. 4, 6, 7.

83. European Agency for Fundamental Rights, *op. cit.*, p. 18. The report specifies that only these three countries collect sufficient criminal data to analyze a trend, www.libertysecurity.org/IMG/pdf_Antisemitism_Overview_Jan_2008_en.pdf.

84. *Ibid.*, p. 21.

85. *bid.*, p. 17.

86. U.S. Department of State, *op. cit.*, p. 3.

87. Stephen Roth Institute, *op. cit.*, 2007, p. 18.

88. *Ibid.*, p. 16.

89. U.S. Department of State, *op. cit.*, p. 68.

90. *Ibid.*, p. 69.

91. *Ibid.*, pp. 47, 48-50.

92. All-Parliamentary Group against Anti-Semitism, *op. cit.*

93. The Crown Prosecution Service, press release, "CPS Publishes Response to All-Party Parliamentary Inquiry into Antisemitism," May 6, 2008, www.cps.gov.uk/news/pressreleases/134_08.html.

94. Francis Beckett, "Israel, administration or pay?" *The Guardian*, May 27, 2008, http://education.guardian.co.uk.

95. University and College Union, press release, "UCU Delegates vote for International Solidarity," May 28, 2008, www.ucu.org.uk.

96. Simon Rocker, "LSE Student Union in New Drive to Encourage Divestment from Israel," *The Jewish Chronicle*, Feb. 22, 2008, p. 5, http://education.guardian.co.uk/higher/worldwide/story/0,2268513,00.html.

97. Dana Gloger and Simon Griver, "Racist Death Threats Don't Scare Us, Say Avram's Family," *The Jewish Chronicle*, Feb. 22, 2008, p. 2, www.thejc.com/home.aspx?ParentId=m11&SecId=11&AId=58231&ATypeId=1.

98. European Agency for Fundamental Rights, *op. cit.*

99. The Associated Press, "French Government Softens Sarkozy Plan to Honor Holocaust Victims," *Haaretz*, Feb. 18, 2008, www.Haaretz.com.

100. Daniel Ben-Simon, "Analysis: Sarkozy's Holocaust Education Plan Baffles Jews," *Haaretz*, Feb. 19, 2008, www.Haaretz.com.

101. Reiss, *op. cit.*

102. Reuters, "France's Le Pen Gets Suspended Jail Term for Comments on Nazi Occupation," *Haaretz*, Feb. 20, 2008, www.haaretz.com/hasen/spages/952527.html.

103. Stephen Roth Institute, "France 2006," *op. cit.*

104. *Ibid.*

105. Daniel Ben-Simon, "21 Charged with Kidnap, Murder of Jewish Man," *Haaretz*, Feb. 20, 2008, www.haaretz.com/hasen/spages/955962.html.

106. Ingrid Rousseau, "6 Held in Anti-Semitic Attack in France," *USA Today*, March 5, 2008, www.usatoday.com/news/world/2008-03-05-2346559257_x.htm.

107. Reiss, *op. cit.*

108. Stephen Roth Institute, "France 2006," *op. cit.*

109. Ethan Bronner, "At 60, Israel Redefines Roles for Itself and for Jews Elsewhere," *The New York Times*, May 8, 2008, p. A23.

110. Jean-Yves Camus, "The French Left and Political Islam: Secularism Versus the Temptation of an Alliance," Stephen Roth Institute, 2005, p. 13, www.tau.ac.il/Anti-Semitism/asw2005/camus.html.

111. Stephen Roth Institute, 2007, *op. cit.*, p. 35.

BIBLIOGRAPHY

Books

Berkowitz, Michael, *The Crime of My Very Existence: Nazism and the Myth of Jewish Criminality, University of California Press,* **2007.**
A professor of modern Jewish history at University College, London, traces how the Nazis used accusations of criminality and a Zionist conspiracy to justify murdering the Jews.

Gross, Jan T., *Fear: Anti-Semitism in Poland after Auschwitz, Random House Trade Paperbacks,* **2007.**
A Princeton University historian analyzes why Poles killed their Jewish neighbors returning to Poland after the war.

Judt, Tony, *Postwar: A History of Europe Since 1945, Pimlico,* **2007.**

This history of postwar Europe by a New York University historian contains an excellent epilogue cataloguing the hostility to Jews who remained in Europe after the war.

Kaufman, Debra, *et al.***, *From the Protocols of the Learned Elders of Zion to Holocaust Denial Trials: Challenging the Media, Law and the Academy,* Valentine Mitchell, 2007.**
This collection of essays on Holocaust denial and anti-Semitism grew out of a conference at Northeastern University in 2001.

Küntzel, Matthias, *Jihad and Jew-Hatred: Islamism, Nazism and the Roots of 9/11,* **Telos Press Publishing, 2007.**
Anti-Semitism in today's jihadist movement and its Nazi roots are discussed in this account by a German political scientist.

Taguieff, Pierre André, *Rising from the Muck: The New Anti-Semitism in Europe,* **Ivan R. Dee, 2004.**
A French philosopher and historian of ideas at France's Center for Scientific Research (CNRS) charges that anti-Zionist rhetoric in France has become the "New Anti-Semitism."

Articles

Judt, Tony, "The 'Problem of Evil' in Postwar Europe," *New York Review of Books,* **Feb. 14, 2008, pp. 33-35.**
Historian Judt asks whether the threat of anti-Semitism today is exaggerated, especially when linked to criticism of Israel.

Kline, Brett, "Echoes of Halimi in a French Suburb," *JTA* **(Jewish Telegraphic Agency), March 6, 2008, www.jta.org.**
Jews in Paris respond to the torture of a young Jewish man in the Paris suburbs in February.

Phillips, Melanie, "Britain's Anti-Semitic Turn," *City Journal,* **autumn 2007, www.city-journal.org.**
A British journalist claims that anti-Semitism is growing and that anti-Israel actions like the proposed academic boycott of Israel are inherently anti-Semitic.

Reiss, Tom, "Letter from Paris: Laugh Riots," *The New Yorker,* **Nov. 19, 2007, pp. 44-50.**
Some experts fear that the popularity of French comedian Dieudonné M'Bala M'Bala, whose routines have become increasingly anti-Jewish, may be tapping a reservoir of anti-Semitic feeling in France.

Reports and Studies

***All-Party Parliamentary Group against Antisemitism,* "Report of the All-Party Parliamentary Inquiry into Antisemitism," September 2006, www.thepcaa.org/report.html.**
A parliamentary investigation calls on the British government to tackle a disturbing rise in anti-Semitism.

***European Union Agency for Fundamental Rights,* "Anti-Semitism: Summary Overview of the Situation in the European Union 2001-2007," updated version January 2008, http://fra.europa.eu/fra/material/pub/AS/Antisemitism_Overview_Jan_2008_en.pdf.**
The arm of the European Union responsible for monitoring racism and anti-Semitism compiled data on anti-Semitic incidents from government and community organizations within EU countries. The most recent data for most countries were from 2006.

Mann, John, and Johnny Cohen, "Antisemitism in European Football: A Scar on the Beautiful Game," *The Parliamentary Committee Against Antisemitism,* **2008, www.johnmannmp.com/publications.**
A report lists examples of anti-Jewish behavior at soccer stadiums as well as "good practices" aimed at curbing the behavior.

Pallade, Yves, *et al.***, "Antisemitism and Racism in European Soccer,"** *American Jewish Committee Berlin Office,* **May 2007.**
The problem of anti-Semitic incidents and chanting continues in soccer stadiums, according to this report, which also describes some initiatives to counteract them.

***Stephen Roth Institute for the Study of Contemporary Antisemitism and Racism,* "Antisemitism Worldwide."**
The institute's annual report contains statistics and analysis on anti-Jewish incidents around the world.

***U.S. Department of State,* "Contemporary Global Anti-Semitism: A Report Provided to the United States Congress," March 2008, www.state.gov/documents/organization/102301.pdf.**
The State Department's mandated report on anti-Semitism worldwide shows anti-Jewish incidents are increasing.

For More Information

American Jewish Committee, 165 E. 56th St., New York, NY 10022; (212) 751-4000; www.ajc.org. Monitors anti-Semitism in Europe through offices in Berlin, Brussels, Geneva and Paris.

Anti-Defamation League, 605 Third Ave., New York, NY 10158; (212) 692-3900; www.adl.org. Monitors anti-Semitism around the world.

Community Security Trust; 020-8457-9999; www.thecst.org.uk. A U.K.-based group that provides physical security for British Jews and monitors anti-Semitism in Britain.

Engage; www.EngageOnline.org.uk. A British group that challenges anti-Semitism in unions and universities and opposes an academic boycott of Israeli academics.

European Jewish Congress, 78 Avenue des Champs-Elysées, 75008 Paris, France; 33-1-43-59-94-63; www.eurojewcong.org/ejc. A Paris-based group that coordinates 40 elected Jewish leaders in Europe to represent their concerns, including anti-Semitism.

Institute for Jewish Policy Research, 79 Wimpole St., London W1G 9RY, United Kingdom; +44-20-7935-8266; www.jpr.org.uk. A think tank promoting multiculturalism and the role of Jews in Europe.

Jews for Justice for Palestinians, P.O. Box 46081, London W9 2ZF, United Kingdom; www.jfjfp.org. Opposes the Israeli occupation.

Middle East Media Research Institute, P.O. Box 27837, Washington, DC 20038; (202) 955-9070; www.memri.org. A Washington-based group with offices in London and Rome that translates messages coming from the Middle East in Arabic, Persian and Turkish.

Office of Special Envoy to Monitor and Combat Anti-Semitism, U.S. Department of State, 2201 C St., N.W., Washington, DC 20520; (202) 647-4000; www.state.gov/g/drl/seas. Advocates for U.S. policy on global anti-Semitism.

Parliamentary Committee Against Antisemitism, P.O. Box 4015, London W1A 6NH, United Kingdom; 020-7935-8078; www.thepcaa.org. A committee of the British Parliament that monitors anti-Semitism in Britain and issues annual reports on the subject.

Quilliam Foundation; 020-7193-1204; www.quilliamfoundation.org. London-based think tank created by former activists of radical Islamic organizations that aims to counter extremism among Muslims in the West.

Stephen Roth Institute, Tel Aviv University, P.O. Box 39040, Ramat Aviv, Tel Aviv 69978, Israel; 972-3-6408779; www.tau.ac.il/Anti-Semitism. Publishes annual reports on anti-Semitism worldwide.

Yale Institute for the Interdisciplinary Study of Anti-semitism, Yale University, 77 Prospect St., New Haven, CT 06520; (203) 432-5239; www.yale.edu/yiisa. A center for research on anti-Semitism that presents papers on European anti-Semitism by prominent experts.

The Z-word, 165 E. 56th St., New York, NY 10022; (212) 751-4000; www.z-word.com. Independent online journal created by the American Jewish Committee focusing on the link between anti-Zionism and anti-Semitism.

10

Anti-Americanism

Is Anger at the U.S. Growing?

Samuel Loewenberg

President George W. Bush lands on the aircraft carrier *USS Abraham Lincoln* in May 2003 and declares the formal end to combat in Iraq. Many critics abroad blame Bush and the Iraq War — now entering its fifth year — for the decline in U.S. prestige.

From *CQ Global Researcher*, March 2007.

Soon after the Sept. 11, 2001, terrorist attacks, the cover of *Newsweek* pictured a turbaned child holding a toy machine gun. The headline read: "The Politics of Rage: Why Do They Hate Us?"[1]

Since then, versions of that question — simultaneously plaintive and rhetorical — have been repeated throughout the U.S. media. The most common answer often reflected the views of Harvard scholar Samuel P. Huntington, who described an inevitable schism between Christianity and Islam in his seminal 1993 essay, "Clash of Civilizations."[2]

But America's critics are far more diverse, and their criticisms more differentiated, than can be explained away by a simple East vs. West conflict. Today not only radical Eastern Islamists but also more and more Latin Americans and former close allies in Europe are finding America and its policies reprehensible.

Some of the most outspoken voices come from Europe, where dismissive attitudes about the mixing bowl of people in the New World have long been a staple of intellectual preening. Since the 17th century, America has been depicted as a haven for uncouth debauchers, religious zealots and puffed-up nationalists. Only after World War II, when America emerged into a position of military and economic might, did it became an object of both desire and envy.

As the United States flexed its muscles over the subsequent decades, others began to perceive it as a threat to their own national sovereignty and identity. America was too big, too influential, too sure of its virtues. Protesters around the world began to attack all three facets of American influence — economic, political and cultural. By the end of the Cold War, the United States was the only

225

remaining superpower, and even more vulnerable to accusations of arrogance and bullying.

In 1999 this sole superpower was symbolically attacked on a much smaller — and non-lethal — scale than it was on Sept. 11, 2001, when French protesters dismantled a McDonald's restaurant in the town of Millau, turning farmer and union leader José Bové into an international hero.[3]

"Look," Bové said later, "cooking is culture. All over the world. Every nation, every region, has its own food cultures. Food and farming define people. We cannot let it all go, to be replaced with hamburgers. People will not let it happen."[4]

That act of cultural theater preceded many others, and by 2003, as the United States led the invasion into Iraq, America was regularly being pilloried as an international villain, damned for its military excursions and held up as a convenient target for all sorts of global discontent.[5]

The indictment against America, writes Andrei S. Markovits, a Romania-born professor of comparative European politics at the University of Michigan, "accuses America of being retrograde on three levels":

- Moral: America is viewed as the purveyor of the death penalty and of religious fundamentalism, while Europe abolished the death penalty in favor of rehabilitation and adheres to an enlightened secularism;
- Social: America is viewed as the bastion of unbridled "predatory capitalism," as former German Chancellor Helmut Schmidt put it, while Europe is the home of the considerate welfare state; and
- Cultural: America is viewed as common, prudish and prurient, Europe as refined, savvy and wise.[6]

Those bleak assessments of the United States have played out in innumerable protests in recent years. When tens of thousands of leftist protesters from around the world gathered in Porto Alegre, Brazil, during the World Economic Forum in February 2002, they waved signs declaring "No blood for oil," and "Bush is #1 Terrorist." Raucous anti-globalization protests have followed the meetings of the World Trade Organization and the G8 from Doha to Davos to Seattle.

When 70,000 protesters gathered in Berlin's Alexanderplatz in March 2003, a banner proclaimed: "We Aren't Allowed to Compare Bush to Hitler. Too Bad!"[7]

When 2,000 Pakistanis in Islamabad rallied against Danish cartoons that had caricatured the Prophet Muhammad in 2006, they also shouted "Death to America!" and torched an effigy of President George W. Bush, as if Bush himself had commissioned the works.[8]

This was a long way from the moment after the 9/11 attacks, when the globe was in brief solidarity with the United States, as epitomized by the famous banner headline in the French newspaper *Le Monde*, "We are all Americans."[9]

Something had changed.

In just a few years, what once seemed to be a clash of two halves of the globe had metastasized into a clash between America and the rest of the world. These sentiments were not coming from isolated pockets of religious fundamentalists but from America's longstanding allies throughout the world. In Europe, anti-U.S. sentiment had reached record levels.

The Iraq invasion "did not create anti-Americanism but it increased it and gave it form," according to Professor Gérard Grunberg, deputy director of Sciences Po, a political institute in Paris.[10]

Many clearly think that negative attitudes toward the United States are now at an all-time high. "Anti-Americanism is deeper and broader now than at any time in modern history. It is most acute in the Muslim world, but it spans the globe," according to a recent survey by the Pew Research Center for People & the Press.[11] In another Pew poll, Europeans gave higher approval ratings to China than to the United States.[12]

Yet much of the anti-American hostility disguises the fact that many of the most vociferous European critics really don't know much about the USA. As British scholar Tony Judt, director of the Remarque Institute at New York University, points out, Europeans complain about their own governments' policies by saying they have been influenced by America.[13]

But on both sides of the Atlantic, says Judt, even in the supposed age of "globalization," there is a massive ignorance about the reality of politics, and of everyday life. "We don't actually understand each other any better than we did in the 1930s."

How did America go, in the eyes of many, from being the symbol of democracy, freedom and opportunity — an ideal to strive for — to an example to be avoided? Judt calls anti-Americanism the "master narrative" of the current age, in which declared opposition to the United States became a uniting factor for disparate critics of economic, cultural and foreign policies around the globe. In America they had found "a common target."

But these days, the overwhelming source of anti-American sentiment, not only in Europe but also throughout the world, is U.S. foreign policy, especially the Bush administration's pursuit of the war in Iraq.

Resentment of the policies and personalities in the Bush administration cannot be overstated. Even President Richard M. Nixon's transgressions were mostly identified as domestic problems (the Watergate scandal), while the Vietnam War was seen as part of larger Cold War politics and did not evoke the same strong anti-American sentiment as Iraq does today.

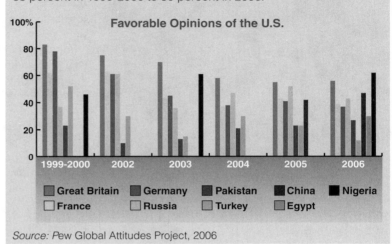

America's Global Image Slips

Since the beginning of the Bush administration in 2001, favorable opinions of the United States have declined in many countries. In Great Britain — an ally in the war in Iraq — approval levels fell from 83 percent in 1999-2000 to 56 percent in 2006.

Favorable Opinions of the U.S.

Legend: Great Britain, Germany, Pakistan, China, Nigeria, France, Russia, Turkey, Egypt

Source: Pew Global Attitudes Project, 2006

Although there certainly was European criticism about the American war in Vietnam, Americans did not hear about it on a daily basis, as they do with criticisms of the war in Iraq. Instant television reporting and the Internet bring the war as well as its critics into homes every hour. Now, says Judt, "Whatever catastrophes the Americans are involved in overseas are immediately visible, with no time lag."

Another foreign conflict strongly identified with the United States and a recurrent theme at anti-war protests around the globe is the Israeli-Palestinian stalemate. European and Middle Eastern criticism of U.S. support of Israel ranges from humanitarian concerns about Palestinian rights to demagoguery invoking a Jewish-American-capitalist conspiracy.

"This didn't come from nothing," says Markovits. In his new book, *Uncouth Nation: Why Europe Dislikes America*, he traces the origins of anti-American sentiment to the 19th century, when European elites feared the pugnacious, young country.

For Americans, it is easy to dismiss criticism of U.S. policies as simply an irrational ideology, Markovits writes. But the term "anti-Americanism" is misleading,

he says, because it lumps together rational criticisms, whether one agrees with them or not, with a disembodied, ideological opposition to an idea of America, in which the country stands as a symbol for a variety of foreign, cultural and political discontents.

As Markovits notes, "Anti-Americanism is a particularly murky concept because it invariably merges antipathy toward what America does with what America is — or rather is projected to be in the eyes of its beholders." In contrast to classical stereotypes, which usually depict powerless minorities, the United States does, in fact, have great political, economic and cultural power. This makes it especially difficult to disentangle the perception from the reality. Critics of America assume that the expansion of this power, rather than a more benign exercise of it, is always the top priority of the American government. This is particularly true when it comes to the view, shared by much of the globe, that the United States is too tightly connected to Israel.

As Beirut's *Daily Star* said after the United States deposed Saddam Hussein: "Having waged an 'illegitimate' war on Iraq that has stoked anti-American feelings around the world, challenged and ignored international

French activist and farmer José Bové has a following in Solomiac, France, after attempting to rip up a crop of genetically modified maize. Bové gained fame for destroying a French McDonald's restaurant in 1999.

law and the United Nations . . . the Bush administration is not about to 'offer Iraq on a golden platter to an opposition group or to the U.N. Security Council.'

"It will deny others a say in shaping post-war Iraq, and it won't withdraw its forces on request . . . . Israel, of course, will be an exception, and is the only U.S. partner whose participation in shaping post-war Iraq is 'guaranteed.' That is because Israel was the main reason for which the war was waged."[14]

Trying to sort out real criticisms of the United States from the political symbolism that makes up much anti-Americanism is a daunting task. But for America's many critics around the globe, the daily carnage in Iraq has confirmed that America, having found no weapons of mass destruction in Iraq, is now on a reckless crusade.

In the week after the Sept. 11, attacks, Bush declared, "this crusade, this war on terrorism, is going to take a while."[15] While the term "crusade" went largely unnoticed in the United States, it alarmed many around the world with its evocation of the ancient wars between Christianity and Islam.

As Americans seek to understand global criticism of the United States, here are some of the key issues being debated:

Is the United States the primary force behind globalization policies that harm other countries?

Before there was anti-Americanism there was anti-globalization. For many critics, they are mostly the same.[16]

Globalization is the umbrella term for the rapidly increasing social, technological, cultural and political integration of nation-states, corporations and organizations around the world.

Its supporters believe that globalization is a positive engine of commerce that brings increased standards of living, universal values, multiculturalism and technology to developing countries. Globalization's critics claim it is a slave to corporate interests, harms the environment and tramples human rights and the economic and ethical claims of the poor and working classes.

It's no surprise, then, that America has become the country most vilified by the anti-globalization movement. After all, U.S. brands like McDonald's, Marlboro and Nike are among the most recognized in the world.

Globalization does have its defenders, and at least one links the movement to an old socialist tradition in Europe. "Globalization simply means freedom of movement for goods and people," wrote the late French journalist and philosopher Jean-Francois Revel, "and it is hard to be violently hostile to that.

"But behind the opposition to globalization lies an older and more fundamental struggle against economic liberalization and its chief representative, the United States. Anti-globalism protests often feature an Uncle Sam in a stars-and-stripes costume as their supreme scapegoat."

Lashing out at America through targeting its products had roots in the Cold War. For example, some Eastern Bloc countries prohibited Coca-Cola but not Pepsi, because Coke was so strongly identified with the United States. But the movement reached its peak at the turn of the 21st century with global protests against the World Trade Organization, against the incursion of McDonald's and Starbucks and against acceptance of genetically modified foods from the United States.[17]

Championing the pure-food cause was Great Britain's Prince Charles. In 1999, after representatives of 20 African countries had published a statement denying that gene technologies would help farmers to produce the food they needed, Charles came to their defense: "Are we going to allow the industrialization of life itself, redesigning the natural world for the sake of convenience? Or should we be adopting a gentler, more considered approach, seeking always to work with the grain of nature?"[18]

Reluctance to accept American products and economic power has brought together critics from the left and the right. For both, "America represents the ideal of unfettered capitalism itself," says Fernando Vallespin, director of the Sociological Research Centre of Spain, a nonpartisan think tank in Madrid. "For those on the left, the concern is for labor exploitation. For those on the right, it is the loss of national sovereignty."

Resentment of the American economic model is particularly strong in Europe, which is currently confronting painful and unpopular adjustments to its own long-held social-welfare state model. Politicians, unions and disenfranchised workers in France, Italy and Spain say they do not want to adopt the "Anglo-Saxon" model, a reference not to Germany or England but to the United States. Spaniards are vociferous critics of the American way of life, says Vallespin, "but on the other hand we are probably one of the most American in terms of our patterns of consumption."

Cost-cutting proposals that seem to erode Europe's time-honored cradle-to-grave welfare privileges — such as fees for seeing a doctor or reducing the meal allowances of factory workers — have been denounced as "American." But in truth, most policies are still far from American-style capitalism.

In Germany, American business interests are seen as a double threat. After a recent buying spree of distressed companies by hedge funds, most of them American, German Vice Chancellor Franz Muentefering said the funds "fall like a plague of locusts over our companies, devour everything, then fly on to the next one."

Muentefering's statement was widely scrutinized, with some critics suggesting that the image of locusts preying on German companies evoked sentiments that were not only anti-American but also anti-Semitic.

There is no doubt the United States has been leading the current charge to deregulate markets, but it is still wrong to blame it for the world's economic inequalities, says Charles Kupchan, a professor of international affairs at Georgetown University and the former director for European affairs at the National Security Council during the Clinton administration.

He points out that large corporations in nearly every European country have been globalizing. In fact, the precursor

AFP/Getty Images

Yankee mice Mickey and Minnie reign at Disneyland Paris during Disney's 100th anniversary. Despite protests against American cultural imports by French intellectuals, more people visit the Paris theme park than any other Disney attraction in the world.

to modern globalization was not the commercial efforts of the United States but European imperialism of the past 500 years. A large part of that was the economic domination and exploitation of Latin America and Africa.

The remnants of Europe's imperialist past continue to earn big profits for European countries, with Spain holding powerful telecom and banking concessions in Latin America, and the French profiting off mining and agricultural interests in their former colonies in Africa. Yet, curiously, the focus of the anti-globalization debate continues to revolve around the United States.

"There is an unjustifiable equation between globalization and Americanization," says Kupchan.

Spanish Blame Bombing on War in Iraq

Spain's support of U.S. seen as critical factor

On the morning of March 11, 2004, a coordinated bomb attack on four rush-hour trains in Madrid killed 191 people and injured more than 1,700.

Spain had lived through decades of terrorism from the Basque separatist group ETA, but these bombers were not seeking independence; they were attempting to intimidate the Spanish government. In February 2007, Spanish authorities put 29 men on trial for the bombings, claiming they belonged to a local cell of Islamic militants aligned with al Qaeda.

In sharp contrast to the American reaction after the Sept. 11, 2001, terrorist attacks, Spanish citizens did not view the assault as part of a war between Islam and the West. Instead, many turned their anger toward the United States and their own government, which had supported the U.S.-led invasion of Iraq.

"We didn't want to go to war, but we did because of [former Prime Minister José Maria] Aznar," said Miguel Barrios, a 45-year-old maintenance worker who was in one of the bombed trains. "They didn't pay attention to the anti-war movement."[1]

It became clear that in an effort to stay aligned with the interests of the United States, the world's sole superpower, the Spanish government had run against the will of its own people. In the wake of the railroad attacks that Spanish government was voted out. The new prime minister, José Luis Rodriguez Zapatero, withdrew Spain's 1,300 troops from Iraq within weeks, risking a rupture of the close alliance Spain had enjoyed with the U.S.

"Mr. Bush and Mr. Blair will reflect on our decision," said Zapatero. "You cannot justify a war with lies. It cannot be."

People felt the war in Iraq had never been Spain's business, said Miguel Bastenier, a columnist for *El Pais*, Spain's largest newspaper. "Aznar was doing what Bush wanted without any particular reason for Spain to be there.

"There was undoubtedly the feeling that Spain was being punished for its association with the aggressive policies of the United States," and that "their country had been targeted by Muslim terrorists because it was now seen as being allied with the Jewish state."

In 2002, when war in Iraq was still only imminent, millions of Spaniards had taken to the streets to protest the coming invasion; polls showed more than 80 percent opposed to supporting the United States.

"Bush wants to go into Iraq to get the oil," said Virgilio Salcedo, a 29-year-old computer programmer who came to the rally in Madrid with his parents. "Everybody knows

At the same time, the U.S. government, under both the current Bush administration and the Clinton presidency, pushed often and hard on behalf of U.S. business interests.

The most famous attempt, which failed spectacularly, was the U.S. attempt to open Britain to bioengineered foods. The lobbying attempt, led by former Clinton U.S. Trade Representative Mickey Kantor, ran up against deeply held British attitudes of reverence for pristine nature.

"These senior executives thought they could just walk in and buy [British officials] a glass of champagne and charm them," said Evie Soames, a British lobbyist who represented the U.S. company Monsanto, which was attempting to sell its genetically modified seeds in England for several years.[19]

More recent American lobbying efforts have borne fruit. In 2001 the European Union tried to impose a strict safety-testing regime on chemical manufacturers; the Bush administration mounted a massive lobbying campaign that mobilized American embassies across Europe and Asia. The final, much scaled-back, version of the testing regime will save U.S. chemical companies billions of dollars.

Perhaps the biggest global concern about U.S. economic interests has been the perception that the U.S.-led invasion of Iraq was driven by America's thirst for petroleum. Notably, the most ubiquitous slogan, "No blood for oil," popped up at protests in the United States and abroad during the first Persian Gulf War in 1991 as well as the current war.

In a scathing commentary about President Bush's belief that he is on a direct mission from God, Henry

that he doesn't want to help the people there."

"We think our president has sold out the country to the Americans," said Susanna Polo, a 30-year-old economist.

"Aznar is Bush's dog," added Raquel Hurtado, a 19-year-old economics student.[2]

Even for those most deeply affected by 9/11, like 53-year-old Rosalinda Arias, whose sister died in the World Trade Center attacks, U.S. motives were suspect. "It is all business. They want petroleum; they want to bring U.S. imperialism," said Arias, owner of a restaurant in Madrid.

For the many older people attending the rally, memories of the Franco dictatorship were still fresh, including America's support of the fascist regime in the 1930s. Now they had little faith in Bush administration claims that America was going to liberate Iraq.

"There are lots of dictatorships that have been backed by the USA," said Carlos Martin, a 67-year-old

A tear rolls down a girl's cheek during a rally in Madrid following terrorist bombings in March 2004 that killed nearly 200 people. Her message: "Peace, not terrorism."

translator of Italian literature. "I can't imagine how the Iraqi people are feeling now. They were bombed in 1991, then they had 12 years of horrible sanctions, and now they are being bombed again. I can't imagine they will look at the Americans as liberators."

Some of the protesters' worst fears were realized as the U.S. Coalition Forces invaded and subdued Baghdad in 2003, then settled into the current quagmire.

But Spain did not seek revenge against the killing of 191 of its citizens. A 40-year-old teacher named Valeria Suarez Marsa gave a softer voice to the public mood. "It is more important then ever to call for peace," she said. "The bombs reminded us of that urgency."

Getty Images/Ian Waldie

---

[1] The author covered the Madrid protests in 2002.

[2] Quoted in Samuel Loewenberg, "A Vote for Honesty," _The Nation_, March 18, 2004.

A. Giroux, a professor of communications at Canada's McMaster University, wrote: "Surrounded by born-again missionaries . . . Bush has relentlessly developed policies based less on social needs than on a highly personal and narrowly moral sense of divine purpose."[20]

In the months before the invasion of Iraq in March 2003, _The Economist_ summed up the anti-Bush sentiment: "Only one thing unsettles George Bush's critics more than the possibility that his foreign policy is secretly driven by greed. That is the possibility that it is secretly driven by God . . . . War for oil would merely be bad. War for God would be catastrophic."[21]

Is the United States threatening other cultures?

Any American who has traveled abroad for any length of time will be familiar with the following exchange: "Oh,

you're American. I hate Americans." Or, the rhetorical litmus-test question: "What do you think of your president?" This, however, is soon followed by "I love New York" or "Have you ever been to Disneyland?"

For decades, America's most influential export has not been cars or televisions, but culture. This can be mass media like Hollywood movies and hip-hop music, fast-food restaurants that are often seen as crass and objectionable, or soft drinks such as Coca-Cola.

While these cultural products have long been embraced on a worldwide scale, they have also raised concerns that their appeal would diminish traditions and habits that other cultures hold dear. This love-hate relationship with American popular culture and consumerism was reflected in a 2005 Pew study that found "72 percent of French, 70 percent of Germans and 56

U.S. Lags in Foreign Aid

When foreign aid donations are measured as a percentage of gross national income, the U.S. ranks behind 20 other major donors.

Country	Foreign Aid as a Percentage of Gross National Income
Norway	0.87%
Luxembourg	0.85%
Denmark	0.84%
Sweden	0.77%
Netherlands	0.74%
Portugal	0.63%
France	0.42%
Belgium	0.41%
Ireland	0.39%
Switzerland	0.37%
United Kingdom	0.36%
Finland	0.35%
Germany	0.28%
Spain	0.26%
Canada	0.26%
Australia	0.25%
Austria	0.24%
Greece	0.23%
New Zealand	0.23%
Japan	0.19%
United States	0.16%
Italy	0.15%

Source: Larry Nowels, "Foreign Aid: Understanding Data Used to Compare Donors," Congressional Research Service, May 23, 2005

percent of Britons regard the spread of American culture negatively. In all of these countries, paradoxically, large majorities of respondents — especially young people — say they like American movies and other cultural exports."[22]

The University of Michigan's Markovits says resentment of U.S. culture has deep roots among European elites. "Many of the components of European anti-Americanism have been alive and well in Europe's intellectual discourse since the late 18th century," he writes. "The tropes about Americans' alleged venality, mediocrity, uncouthness, lack of culture and above all inauthenticity have been integral and ubiquitous to European elite opinion for well over 200 years. All of these 'Americanizations' bemoan an alleged loss of purity and authenticity for Europeans at the hands of a threatening and unwelcome intruder who — to make matters worse — exhibits a flaring cultural inferiority."[23]

"The fear is that what's happening in America will happen in Europe, and that left to their own devices

people will go to vulgar theme parks and shop at Wal-Mart," says Nick Cohen, a liberal British columnist. At its roots, this strain of anti-Americanism is a conservative ideology, he says. European elites were concerned that Americans had forsaken the church and the social hierarchy, according to Cohen, the author of a book reassessing European social liberals, *What's Left? How Liberals Lost Their Way.*

Nowhere is the ambivalence toward American culture more apparent than in France. When a Walt Disney theme park opened near Paris in 1994, French critics called it "a cultural Chernobyl." Yet today it rivals the Eiffel Tower as the country's most popular tourist destination. Without doubt, the biggest symbol of American cultural effrontery for the French is McDonald's. Yet the French are the biggest consumers of Big Macs in Europe.[24]

When France was making a national celebrity of farmer-activist Bové in 1999, the quality of McDonald's cheeseburgers was not the big issue; the enemy was the corporation. But food in France has deep and sentimental roots.

At a protest gathering on Bové's behalf, *The New York Times* interviewed a 16-year-old French lad who had come mostly for the carnival atmosphere. "But my father was a farmer," he said, "and I am here representing my family, too. We believe in what Mr. Bové believes in. We don't want the multinationals to tell us what to eat."[25]

In the 19th and early 20th centuries, when millions of Europeans sought their fortunes in the United States, American culture promised relief from the restrictions of European social hierarchies. "America was a hope, especially for the lower classes, in those times," says Detlev Claussen, a professor of social theory, cultural studies and sociology at Germany's Leibniz Hannover University. In the wake of World War I, Germans embraced American jazz, literature and art.

Nazi propaganda enthusiastically portrayed Americans as evil capitalists during World War II, but attitudes mellowed after the war when, despite the continued presence of the American military, the U.S. Marshall Plan helped rebuild Europe. Even in the 1960s and '70s, Germans were enthralled by American history and pop culture and established hundreds of re-enactment clubs that staged "Wild-West" shootouts and sympathetic portrayals of Indians.

The positive view of America began to change only in the Vietnam War era of the late 1960s, says Claussen. Even then, Germans made a distinction between disdain for American policies and adoration of cultural icons like Bob Dylan and the Rev. Martin Luther King Jr.

Now even those distinctions are eroding. The new anti-Americanism, Claussen says, stems from a sense of disappointment in the American utopia, tinged with envy of its political and economic power. Many Germans, he says, have simply given up on the idea of a virtuous America as a land of promise.

"When you can make no distinction between politics and culture, when you say, 'I don't like America, full stop,' that's real anti-Americanism," he says.

Is the "American Century" over?

On Feb. 7, 1941, in an editorial in *Life* magazine entitled "The American Century," media magnate Henry Luce advocated that the United States enter World War II and begin a global crusade on behalf of the values of freedom, opportunity, self-reliance and democracy.[26]

The concept of the "American Century," a potent ideal even before Luce's epochal essay, encompasses the modern history of American dominance, from the Spanish-American War to World War II, the Cold War and America's emergence as the world's only superpower in the 1990s.

These days, many are questioning whether the United States has squandered its position atop the global hierarchy. Rivals have emerged, even as the Soviet Union, once a contender, has dissolved. The European Union has been revitalized by the membership of new former Soviet-bloc countries. China and India, with their massive populations, are rapidly becoming developed countries. Perhaps the American "empire," like the Roman Empire and others before it, is already locked into inevitable decline.

Time recently devoted a cover story to China which concluded that, "in this century the relative power of the U.S. is going to decline, and that of China is going to rise. That cake was baked long ago."[27]

For the time being, however, the United States is the world's richest country and leading economy, with a gross domestic product (GDP) of $13 trillion. Its armed forces are stationed in 40 countries, its corporations and its charities operate throughout the globe and its technology arguably remains the most innovative. America is still a magnet for millions around the world, but its image has been badly tarnished by the Iraq War.

"There is a perception in the rest of the world that the U.S. is no longer capable of being the global leader that it once was," says Julia E. Sweig, director of Latin America studies at the Council on Foreign Relations and author of the 2006 book *Friendly Fire: Losing Friends and Making Enemies in the Anti-American Century.*

For many, that would be no great loss. No one likes the king of the hill for long. America (at least as a concept) is genuinely unpopular. A Pew survey found that "favorability ratings for the United States continue to trail those of other major countries. In Europe, as well as in predominantly Muslim countries, the U.S. is generally less popular than Germany, France, Japan and even China. In Western Europe, attitudes toward America remain considerably more negative than they were in 2002, prior to the Iraq War."[28]

"The tendency now is to view the U.S. as a threat to international stability," says Georgetown University's Kupchan.

Muslims in Southeast Asia, for example, no longer look up to the United States, says Farish A. Noor, a history professor at the Centre for Modern Oriental Studies in Berlin. "That's gone. It's completely erased now. An entirely new image of America has been constructed by the Islamists."

Of course, the damage to America's status did not begin with the invasion of Iraq. Still alive is the memory of the war in Vietnam, as well as America's Cold War support of totalitarian regimes, such as Augusto Pinochet's in Chile and Saddam Hussein's in Iraq (when Iraq was fighting Iran). In Latin America, many blamed the United States for encouraging the "dirty war" of the 1970s and '80s in Argentina and for supporting right-wing paramilitary squads in Nicaragua against the Marxist Sandinista junta.

At the same time, the United States cut back many "soft power" programs in cultural, economic and humanitarian

CHRONOLOGY

1700s–1800s *Europeans express disdain over U.S. independence.*

1768 Dutch philosopher Cornelius de Pauw describes America as "a Moronic Spirit" and the people "either degenerate or monstrous."

1776 English radical Thomas Day decries American hypocrisy: "If there be an object truly ridiculous in nature, it is an American patriot, signing resolutions of independency with the one hand, and with the other brandishing a whip over his affrighted slaves."

1842 British writer Charles Dickens lambastes oppressive Northern cities, Southern ignorance and Mississippi River pollution in *American Notes*.

1901–1980 *U.S. industrial power helps win world wars; Cold War begins.*

1919 Allies defeat Germany in World War I after U.S. enters war in 1917.

June 6, 1944 American forces lead invasion of Europe on D-Day; millions extend thanks to GIs.

August 1945 U.S. drops atomic bombs on Hiroshima and Nagasaki, forcing Japan to surrender. . . . Post-war U.S.-funded Marshall Plan provides development assistance to war-ravaged Europe.

1961 U.S. involvement in Vietnam begins, sparking anti-U.S. sentiment.

1967 Israel wins Six-Day War against Egypt, Jordan and Syria, begins occupation of West Bank and Gaza Strip. U.S. support for Israel feeds anti-Americanism.

1979 Shah overthrown in Iran. U.S. declared "The Great Satan."

1980s–1990s *Soviet Union collapses. U.S. involvement in Central America misfires. Resentment of world's sole superpower grows.*

1981 U.S.-trained Salvadoran soldiers massacre 800 women and children and elderly people in the country's bloody civil war; U.S. blamed.

Nov. 9, 1989 Berlin Wall falls. Citizens of newly reunited German capital dance to American TV star David Hasselhoff's "Looking for Freedom."

1989 U.S. arrests former American ally Gen. Manuel Noriega of Panama for drug trafficking.

1999 Negotiations conclude for Kyoto global warming pact; U.S. signs but Congress refuses to ratify.

1999 Farmer José Bové destroys a McDonald's in southern France as a consumer protest. Protests are held against globalization, multinational corporations and U.S. products.

2000s *President George W. Bush begins a unilateralist foreign policy, alienating allies.*

Sept. 11, 2001 Terrorists hijack four airplanes and crash three into the World Trade Center and the Pentagon. . . . In October a worldwide, U.S.-led coalition invades Afghanistan.

2002 In France, Thierry Meyssan's bestseller *L'Effroyable Imposture* (*The Terrible Fraud*) alleges the U.S. was behind the Sept. 11 attacks. . . . Venezuelan strongman Hugo Chavez, temporarily toppled in an aborted coup, accuses Bush administration of backing the revolt. . . . American companies abroad are vandalized.

2003 Millions march in Europe to protest U.S-led invasion of Iraq. . . .

2004 U.N. Secretary-General Kofi Annan calls Iraq invasion "illegal." . . . Abu Ghraib prison abuses shock the world. . . . Terrorists bomb Madrid trains.

2005 U.S. sends disaster aid to Indonesia and Pakistan, gaining goodwill. . . . Terrorists bomb London buses.

2006 British television airs a mock documentary about the imagined assassination of President Bush.

Feb. 10, 2007 Russian President Vladimir Putin denounces U.S. expansionism and military spending.

March 8, 2007 President Bush begins five-nation Latin American tour, sparking protests across the region.

aid in Latin America. Many of these were replaced with aggressive law-and-order programs that were part of the American government's war on drugs, and, after Sept. 11, the "war on terror."

And even before al Qaeda's 9/11 attacks, foreigners were critical of the U.S. rejection of global treaties, including the Kyoto Protocol for climate change, the creation of the International Criminal Court and rules for curbing biological weapons. Some of these treaties were actually rejected during the Clinton administration. The impression was strong that the United States would go it alone, because it thought it could.

It was at that point that many nations began to view the United States as "a delinquent international citizen."[29]

Some analysts wonder if the end of the American Century will begin in the Americas. Stepping into the hemispheric leadership vacuum, leftist President Hugo Chavez of Venezuela mocks President Bush as "the little gentleman" from the North and works at consolidating the region under his own oil-rich leadership.

American involvement in Latin America, long treated as a vast raw-material commodities mart by U.S. businesses, had already alienated many South and Central American countries, and, more recently, many Latin Americans have blamed U.S.-backed free-market economic policies for destabilizing their economies.

In 2005 Chavez even attempted to turn old-style American "soft power" on its head, offering and delivering 17 million gallons of heating oil to low-income families in New York and New England.

President Bush's March 2007 diplomatic swing through Latin American was intended to soothe feelings, but his administration's neglect, says Sweig, "has ripped off the Band-Aid that had covered up latent wounds for a long time."

As Bush was addressing an audience in Uruguay on March 10, Chavez led a counter rally in Argentina in which he called Bush a "political corpse." Alluding to the fact that he had previously called Bush "the devil" at the United Nations, Chavez bragged that, "He does not even smell of sulfur anymore; what [smells] is the scent of political death, and within a very short time it will become cosmic dust and disappear."[30]

In Muslim nations, the fiery rhetoric of the Bush administration's war on terror sparked a new depth of hostility. Among predominantly Islamic countries in Southeast Asia, which had previously looked on the U.S. as liberators, the Bush administration "squandered five decades of goodwill," says Noor. "So much of this has been personalized in Bush. He is like an icon of everything that is bad about the U.S."

Because of the war in Iraq and the festering Palestinian question, hatred for America on the Arab "street," as well as among Islamists, is raw and without nuance. But it is instructive to hear voices from a recent *New York Times* report about a new al Qaeda training camp for jihadists at a Palestinian refugee camp north of Beirut.

" 'The United States is oppressing a lot of people,' the group's deputy commander, Abu Sharif, said in a room strewn with Kalashnikovs. 'They are killing a lot of innocents, but one day they are getting paid back.'

" 'I was happy,' Hamad Mustaf Ayasin, 70, recalled in hearing last fall that his 35-year-old son, Ahmed, had died in Iraq fighting American troops near the Syrian border. 'The U.S. is against Muslims all over the world.'

"On the streets of the camp, one young man after another said dying in Iraq was no longer their only dream."

It was suicide.

" 'If I had the chance to do any kind of operation against anyone who is against Islam, inside or outside of the U.S., I would do the operation,' " said 18-year-old Mohamed.[31]

In England, *The Guardian* noted the continuing concern about the United States' use of its power during the months leading up to the invasion of Iraq. "Of course, enemies of the U.S. have shaken their fist at its 'imperialism' for decades," the paper editorialized. "They are doing it again now, as Washington wages a global 'war against terror' and braces itself for a campaign aimed at 'regime change' in a foreign, sovereign state.

"What is more surprising, and much newer, is that the notion of an American empire has suddenly become a live debate inside the U.S. And not just among Europhile liberals either, but across the range — from left to right."[32]

BACKGROUND

The Ungrateful Son

The story begins in Europe. The roots of antagonism toward the New World grew among the nations that first

At a Berlin Café, Musing About America

"We were hoping America would not elect Bush"

*P*renzlauer Berg was once on the gritty side of town, in East Berlin, when Berlin was a divided city. The Berlin Wall was torn down nearly 20 years ago, and few signs of it remain.

Prenzlauer Berg is now fashionable, but there's still a certain working-class feel to it. On a rainy afternoon last February three friends met for coffee at the Wasser und Brot (Water and Bread), a barely decorated neighborhood café frequented mostly by local workmen, artists, students and retirees.

Baerbel Boesking is a 45-year-old actress, originally from Lower Saxony; Robert Lingnau, 33, is a composer and writer. Petra Lanthaler, 30, is a psychologist. She came to Berlin four years ago from northern Italy.

They sipped tea and coffee and smoked, musing about the United States, George Bush and the future of relations with those increasingly alienating Americans:

Is America different from other countries?

ROBERT: America is very powerful so it has more impact on us than any other country. All of the oil stuff, all of the pollution, the politics.

BAERBEL: Since the student protests here in the 60s, many people still think of the United States as an imperialist, capitalist power. People think Americans are just

superficial, and Bush has only made that worse. But I know that not all Americans are superficial, like [filmmaker] Michael Moore, for instance.

PETRA: I don't think the American people are superficial. As far as I know, there are also many people in the United States who are rebelling against Bush.

Did your impression of America change after Sept. 11?

ROBERT: I think that the American government in some way participated or co-arranged for 9/11, or at least they knew certain things in advance and didn't act to prevent it. They wanted to install the Patriot Act, so that the government could take more control over people's lives. With the terrorist threat, people let the Patriot Act go through. Meanwhile, Bush is cutting billions from Medicare but putting more and more money into the war in Iraq.

BAERBEL: I often hear things like this from my friends. Many of them have the opinion that this whole thing, 9/11, was self-done by the U.S. itself. These are really educated people, it's horrible. This is an unbelievable point of view, like people who believe that the landing on the moon was just a Hollywood production.

ROBERT: I have two degrees actually. I think the Americans landed on the moon, but I don't think the

colonized it. America was the repository of the old world's disenfranchised and discontented, after all.

It was 18th-century British author Samuel Johnson who famously declared, "I am willing to love all mankind except an American." And another Briton, the 19th-century playwright George Bernard Shaw, quipped that "an asylum for the sane would be empty in America." Austria's Sigmund Freud, the father of psychoanalysis, was not enamored of the United States either. "A mistake," he called it, "a gigantic mistake."[33]

While some Americans might take pride in being loathed by European intellectuals, most have been mystified by, if not indifferent to the barbs. European anti-American feeling, argues the University of Michigan's Markovits, stems from the Europeans' sense that they have lost their own power and influence, and the subsequent search for a

contemporary identity in a differently aligned global pecking order.

"Unlike elsewhere in the world," he said, "at least until very recently, America represented a particularly loaded concept and complex entity to Europeans precisely because it was, of course, a European creation."

The son, in other words, had rejected the father; America had "consciously defected from its European origins," Markovits says.

European conservatives and elites were miffed at America's rejection of the strictures of European class and religious hierarchies, the very things that people rebelled against when they emigrated to America.

One of the first Anti-American sentiments was the "degeneracy hypothesis," the belief that humidity and other atmospheric conditions in America created weak and

government did their best to prevent what happened. I don't think they wrote the script for what happened, but in a way they participated in order to get the Patriot Act through and for what came after.

PETRA: I don't want to believe that a government would do that. It's true that after 9/11 the U.S. took advantage of these fears of terrorism.

Anti-war demonstrators sometimes have signs comparing Bush to Hitler.

BAERBEL: Bush is not equal to Hitler. You can't compare somebody to Hitler.

ROBERT: You can compare Stalin to Hitler, but not Bush.

BAERBEL: You can compare Mao, this new guy in Korea and Saddam Hussein, but it is crazy to say that Bush is like Hitler.

BAERBEL: I was watching a television debate between Bush and [Sen. John] Kerry [D-Mass.], and Bush said that his role model was Jesus. He's got a long way to go. I don't think Jesus would have started a war with Iraq. I'm a Christian, too.

What do you think about American culture?

PETRA: The first words that come into my mind are big size. The shops are much bigger, the portions are much bigger, everything is bigger. People are bigger. But I know that's a really superficial answer because I've never actually been to America. I am impressed by their

scientific research. They think much more globally than Europeans do.

ROBERT: They don't seem to think globally about pollution and global warming. For me, there are two things that constitute my everyday life: that's jazz music and Apple Macintosh. That's what I think of when I think about U.S. culture. Both native American art forms.

BAERBEL: I had an American boyfriend once. From Kansas.

Do you think relations between America and Europe will improve with a new president in 2008?

BAERBEL: Yes, if it's a Democrat. It's really good you have term limits in the United States. We had Helmut Kohl for 16 years.

ROBERT: But if Jeb Bush gets elected, this is like 16 years of Kohl.

PETRA: All of my friends, most everybody I knew, we were really hoping that America would not elect Bush for the second term. It was really disappointing.

ROBERT: My hope for the next president is that he didn't study at Yale and that he hasn't been a member of Skull and Bones [the exclusive secret society].

It was still raining and cold when the friends left the smoky warmth of the Wasser und Brot. It wasn't their anti-Americanism that stood out but how much they knew about America and American life. And it begged the question: Would Americans know half as much about Germany, even the name of the chancellor?

---

morally inferior animals and human beings. The court philosopher to Frederick II of Prussia, Cornelius de Pauw, argued in 1768 about Americans that, "the weakest European could crush them with ease."[34]

As American industry rose in the late 19th century, the speed of American life became a major threat to European traditions of craftsmanship. "The breathless haste with which they work — the distinctive vice of the new world — is already beginning ferociously to infect old Europe and is spreading a spiritual emptiness over the continent," observed the German philosopher Friedrich Nietzsche.[35]

The notion that the mixing of races was bringing down the level of capability in Americans was another major thrust of anti-Americanism. Blacks and "low quality" immigrants, it was said in European salons, would lead to ultimate dissolution.

Arthur de Gobineau, a French social thinker, declared that America was creating the "greatest mediocrity in all fields: mediocrity of physical strength, mediocrity of beauty, mediocrity of intellectual capacities — we could almost say nothingness."[36]

After World War I, allies of the United States, France and Great Britain, found themselves massively in debt to the brash and newly powerful Americans, which generated resentment. These sentiments spread during the Great Depression. Sometimes the bias took on anti-Semitic overtones, including the widely held theory that the American government was ruled by a Jewish conspiracy.[37]

After World War II, the U.S. Marshall Plan helped rebuild Europe. Yet as American power grew while Europe licked its wounds, the United States became a scapegoat for an increasing sense of weakness among those nostalgic

Pakistani protesters burn the American flag and a mock Israeli flag to protest the Israeli attack on southern Lebanon in August 2006. Anti-American sentiment often ties the U.S. and Israel together as partners in the exploitation and humiliation of other countries.

for their former empires. It was then that the global spread of American cultural, economic, and political power — rock 'n' roll, McDonald's and U.S. military bases — established the United States as a symbol of global authority, and one to be resisted.

Religious Differences

The staying power of American religiosity created another divide between Europe and the United States. Historian Huntington's "clash of civilizations" theory postulated that the big divide was between Christianity and Islam. But one of the deepest rifts between Europe and the United States centered on the relationship between religion and government.

Europeans had begun abandoning churchgoing in the 1950s and no longer felt that religion should play a role in political affairs.[38] But a large majority of Americans not only continued to go to church but also maintained the belief that religious tenets should provide moral direction to their elected leaders.

Many Europeans have been aghast at what they viewed as American religious fervor, particularly when it has seemed to influence government policy. "An American president who conducts Bible study at the White House and begins Cabinet sessions with a prayer may seem a curious anachronism to his European allies, but he is in tune with his constituents," write Judt and French scholar Denis Lacorne.[39]

Even in Spain, which has one of the most conservative religious establishments in Europe, American evangelicals'

penchant for focusing on sexual issues does not resonate. In 2005, for example, a large majority of the Spanish population voted to legalize gay marriage, a key moral issue to some conservative American Christians.

Policies and traditions that regularly mix church and state in the United States — prayer in schools, God in the Pledge of Allegiance and the open displays of faith by President Bush — "were really shocking to the average Spaniard," says Charles Powell Solares, a deputy director at the Elcano Royal Institute, a think tank in Madrid. He says that 90 percent of Spaniards are in favor of a radical separation between church and state.

On the other hand, polls in Indonesia, Pakistan, Lebanon and Turkey reveal that the majority of people in Muslim countries believe the United States is secular and ungodly.[40]

Foreign Affairs Bully?

Muslims and Americans have not always been adversaries. The United States, after all, supported Islamists in Afghanistan in their fight against the Soviet Union in the 1980s, as well as Bosnian Muslims against Christian Orthodox Serbia in the 1990s.

Moreover, the United States maintains strong relationships with Saudi Arabia, Jordan and Egypt, and Muslim immigrants continue to flow into America — from Pakistan, Bangladesh, Afghanistan, India and even Iraq.

In Indonesia and Malaysia, home to some of the world's largest Muslim populations, anti-Americanism is a recent phenomenon. For most of the postwar 20th century, the United States was seen as an anti-colonial power because of its role in liberating those countries from Japan.

"It's not a coincidence that the Malaysian flag looks like the American flag," says Noor of Berlin's Centre for Modern Oriental Studies.

The advance of high-speed communications has been a key factor in the attitude shift in Southeast Asia. "New media, especially satellite television and the Internet, reinforce negative images of the U.S. through a flood of compelling, highly graphic images," said Steven Simon, a Middle East scholar at the Council on Foreign Relations. "Some of these images present the Muslims as victims; others as victors. All tend to frame events as segments of an ongoing drama between good and evil."[41]

This "us vs. them" dynamic had its genesis in Europe. "Many of these originated outside the Muslim world entirely," Simon told the House International Relations Committee. They were "introduced to the region by Nazi and Soviet propaganda in mid-20th century."

Most notoriously, the British-appointed mufti of Jerusalem, Haj Amin al-Husayni, made a pact with the German government in the 1930s and spread ill will throughout the region against the Western allies, including the United States. Great Britain, of course, was already an object of scorn and resentment for its heavy-handed colonial administration of Muslim territory.

Simon also noted that after Britain pulled out of the Middle East in the 1940s and America began to vie for influence during the Cold War, the United States inherited the animosity that Muslim countries had against Britain, their former conquerors. "The substitution of American power in the region for British authority was bound to tar the U.S. with the imperialist brush," Simon said.

American Exceptionalism

Americans' self-image has been rooted in the certitude that their country is different — a beacon of personal, political and economic freedom in the world. This idea really came of age during World War II, when American industrial power, along with Soviet manpower, liberated Europe. Then the Yanks were cheered and admired, but some scholars believe that the roots of anti-American feelings by many Europeans stem from this U.S. "salvation."

A residue of that feeling remains in France, which truly had been liberated. Germany, however, had been the enemy, and even during the height of the Cold War in the 1960s and '70s, many West Germans deeply resented the presence of American military bases.

Even though the American army's airlift of supplies had saved West Berlin, few thought of the United States as having saved them from the Nazis or the Soviets, says Claussen, at Leibniz Hannover University, and West German politicians were loath to suggest that "America has liberated us."

Spain until recently was America's closest ally in continental Europe, but enmity toward the United States has existed since the 1950s, says Powell Solares, at Madrid's Elcano Royal Institute. Spain never viewed America as a liberator because the country was largely uninvolved with World War II. Instead, they tend to condemn the U.S. for supporting fascist Gen. Francisco Franco as part of its Cold War policy.

A female U.S. Army soldiers frisks a Kurdish woman at a checkpoint in Ramadi, Iraq, in October 2004. Several people had been killed in clashes between rebels and U.S. troops. The War in Iraq underlies much of the spiraling anti-American sentiment around the world today.

AFP/Getty Images/Patrick Baz

"And that means that Spaniards have never associated the U.S. with freedom and democracy," says Powell Solares, citing polls from the 1960s and '70s in which Spaniards viewed the United States as a bigger threat to world peace than the Soviet Union.

After the collapse of the Soviet Union in 1991 the former republics of the Soviet Union and its satellite nations emerged with more solidarity with the United States than most of the countries of Western Europe. Except for Great Britain, Eastern European nations have contributed more troops per capita to the Coalition Forces in the invasions of Afghanistan and Iraq. Several have allegedly allowed controversial secret CIA prisons on their soil.

When U.S. Secretary of Defense Donald Rumsfeld distinguished between the "Old Europe" and "New Europe" in 2003, he was paying homage to the willingness of the newly liberated nations to aid the United States, in contrast to the recalcitrance of Germany and France — Old Europe.[42] French officials labeled the secretary's bluntness as "arrogance."

Anti-Americanism got only a short reprieve in the aftermath of the 9/11 attacks.

"Initially, there was a spontaneous outpouring of sympathy and support for the United States," Pew researchers found. "Even in some parts of the Middle East, hostility toward the U.S. appeared to soften a bit. But this reaction proved short-lived. Just a few months after the attacks, a Global Attitudes Project survey of opinion leaders around

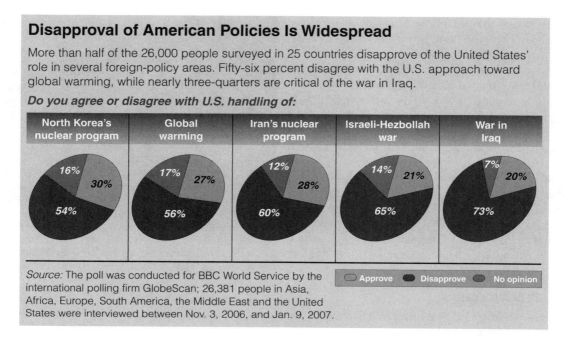

Disapproval of American Policies Is Widespread

More than half of the 26,000 people surveyed in 25 countries disapprove of the United States' role in several foreign-policy areas. Fifty-six percent disagree with the U.S. approach toward global warming, while nearly three-quarters are critical of the war in Iraq.

Do you agree or disagree with U.S. handling of:

| North Korea's nuclear program | Global warming | Iran's nuclear program | Israeli-Hezbollah war | War in Iraq |

Source: The poll was conducted for BBC World Service by the international polling firm GlobeScan; 26,381 people in Asia, Africa, Europe, South America, the Middle East and the United States were interviewed between Nov. 3, 2006, and Jan. 9, 2007.

the world found that, outside Western Europe, there was a widespread sense that U.S. policies were a major cause of the attacks."

In Venezuela, President Chavez cynically suggested, "The hypothesis that is gaining strength . . . is that it was the same U.S. imperial power that planned and carried out this terrible terrorist attack or act against its own people and against citizens of all over the world. Why? To justify the aggressions that immediately were unleashed on Afghanistan, on Iraq."[43]

CURRENT SITUATION

Missteps and Failures

Because of their self-proclaimed virtues and their emphasis on human rights, Americans are often held to higher expectations on the world stage than are other nations. When they fail to perform to those standards, they are doubly condemned. Many who see U.S. foreign policy floundering are as disappointed as they are angry.

Some of the criticisms of the United States — such as the allegations that the government was behind the 9/11 attacks — are so irrational that there is no way to answer them. But there are inescapable realities that will not go away.

America's credibility on human rights has been severely damaged by prisoner abuse at Abu Ghraib, the U.S.-run Baghdad prison for terrorism suspects, and alleged mistreatment at the Guantanamo Bay detention camp in Cuba, as well as by CIA renditions and secret detention camps in Eastern Europe.[44] Its reputation for competence has been trampled by revelations that Iraq's alleged weapons of mass destruction had been trumped up by an overeager White House yearning for battle. Most jarring of all is the bloodshed in Iraq that has claimed at least 34,000 Iraqis and more than 3,000 American troops.[45]

After the revelations at Abu Ghraib, Patrick Sabatier of the French newspaper *Liberation* wrote, "One can lose a war in places other than battlegrounds. The torture that took place in the Abu Ghraib prison is a major defeat for the U.S. The photographs fan the fires of anti-American hate in the Arab world. Elsewhere they trigger reactions of disgust, and take away from the coalition's small dose of moral legitimacy, gained by toppling Saddam's regime."[46]

Even Americans themselves no longer defend the U.S position in Iraq, Pew researchers found. "As to whether the removal of Saddam Hussein from power made the world a safer place," the survey said, "views are also lopsidedly negative. In no country surveyed, including the

AT ISSUE

Will anti-Americanism wane after President Bush leaves office?

YES Dr. Farish A. Noor
Professor of History, Centre for Modern Oriental Studies, Berlin

Written for *CQ Global Researcher*, March 2007

It is undeniable that the image of the United States of America has declined significantly in Southeast Asia during President George Bush's term. Over the past two years I have witnessed more than two-dozen anti-American demonstrations in Malaysia and Indonesia, where the issues ranged from Malaysia's protracted negotiations with the USA on the Free Trade Agreement to America's actions in Afghanistan and Iraq. At almost all of these demonstrations effigies of George Bush and Condoleeza Rice were paraded and sometimes set alight.

Historically America was seen as a liberator and savior in the Southeast Asian region, especially in its role against the Japanese imperial army during the Second World War and its efforts to prevent the Western European colonial powers (Britain, France and the Netherlands) from recolonizing their former colonies Malaya, Indonesia, Vietnam, Burma and the Philippines.

Admiration for America, the American way of life and American values was at its peak during the postcolonial developmental era of the 1960s to 1980s, when Southeast Asian countries sent tens of thousands of students to the U.S. for further education. The American economic model became the framework for the postcolonial economies of the region; and America was doubly thanked for helping to keep the region safe from communism.

Yet, America today is seen as the enemy of Islam, and for Muslim-majority countries like Malaysia, Indonesia and Brunei this poses new problems for bilateral relations. One major factor that has worsened the situation was the use of bellicose rhetoric by the Bush administration in its unilateral "war on terror," which was couched in terms of a "crusade." Subsequent actions and misjudgments (such as the invasion of Iraq without sufficient consultation with Muslim countries) and the deteriorating security condition in Iraq and Afghanistan have merely compounded the problem even more.

Much of the damage, however, is due to the unilateralist character of a Bush administration that was seen as cavalier, gung-ho and insensitive to Muslim concerns. Thanks in part to the overreach and over-projection of the image of Bush in this campaign, however, much of the controversy surrounding the war on terror, the invasion of Afghanistan and Iraq, etc. has been associated with President Bush himself on a personal level.

There is every reason to believe that some of the anti-Americanism we see in Southeast Asia today will wane with a change of administration. But this also depends on whether the next U.S. government can bring the campaigns in Afghanistan and Iraq to a close with minimum loss of life.

NO Manjeet Kripalani
Edward R. Murrow Press Fellow, Council on Foreign Relations; India Bureau Chief, BusinessWeek

Written for *CQ Global Researcher*, March 2007

The favorability rating of the U.S. in the eyes of the world has fallen precipitously since the Iraq invasion, and continues to decline as the war wears on.

Will America ever recover its lost reputation? Perhaps, but it will take years. The perception of the U.S. is that of a power in descent, a nation spent in the ignominious and outmoded task of building Empire. The ideals and positive force that the U.S. represented have been discredited since 2003, given the fundamentalist fervor with which they have been pursued.

That's not the best option in an increasingly complex world. Getting a global consensus on crises like Darfur, trade imbalances, terrorism and Middle East peace in a world without the powerful moral authority of the U.S. will be more difficult. But it has created space for other leadership to step up to the task.

This ascendant world comprises powers like Russia, but more widely the countries of Asia — notably China, India and even Japan. As the beneficiary of past American ideals, Japan has developed goodwill over decades through aid, anti-war sensitivities and the potential to be the stable "America" in Asia.

China and India are both poor, developing countries — but much of today's world looks more like them than it does the U.S.-dominated developed world. Their experiences are being closely watched by their peers, with whom there are centuries-old cultural and historic ties.

In this new world order, the U.S.' tarnished image really doesn't matter. America is still a powerful country, and these same ascendant nations are meshed with it economically and politically. China is in a tight economic embrace with America. Japan is still militarily protected by the U.S. and is its strongest, staunchest ally in Asia.

India, after years of hostile relations with the U.S., has turned pragmatic. Since 2001, America's popularity in India has been on the rise. That's because Indians, affected by terrorism for decades, view Washington as fighting their war for them. And despite domestic pressure, President Bush has continued to support the outsourcing of back-office jobs to India. The signing of the nuclear deal last December is surely good for U.S. business and Indian consumers. But its symbolism is far greater: Its confidence in India's non-proliferation record has ensured that democratic India will wholeheartedly embrace the U.S. economically, technologically and politically.

This ensures that in the future, no matter how much moral authority the U.S. loses, its wagon is hitched firmly to the stars of these ascendant nations — and vice versa.

Political theater plays out in Paris as orange-jump-suited Amnesty International protesters call on the United States to close the Guantanamo Bay, Cuba, prison camp.

United States, does a majority think the Iraq leader's overthrow has increased global security."[47]

Another strike against the American war in Iraq is its duration — longer now than World War II. And the carnage can be seen daily on television. "If the war had had a quick or favorable ending, people would have forgotten about it. But it is in the news every day," says Vallespin, at the Sociological Research Centre of Spain.

Support for Israel

For many Americans and Europeans, Israel cannot be forsaken. It is a place of immense historical and spiritual importance, and was established to right grievous historic wrongs. This is felt not only by America's 3 million Jews but also by an overwhelming number of the country's Christians.

Muslim nations, however, and many other non-Muslim countries, see Israel as a regional bully propped up by the United States. Pew surveys found that many people "suspect the United States of deliberately targeting Muslim nations and using the war on terror to protect Israel," as well as to gain control of Middle East oil.[48]

Clear evidence of a biased relationship was seen in the fact that the United States announced a $10 billion military-aid package to Israel on the same day that the U.S. military began its assault on Iraq in 2003.

"To announce this package on the same day that Iraq is bombed is as stupid as it is arrogant," said Nabeel Ghanyoum, a military analyst in Syria. "This is effectively telling the Arab world, 'Look we are bombing Iraq as we please, and we are giving Israel as much financial aid [as] it wants.' "[49]

In his study of the links between anti-Israeli sentiment and anti-Americanism, the University of Michigan's Markovits found that the crucial link was made after the Israeli victory in the 1967 war, while America was embroiled in Vietnam.

"Israel became little more than an extension of American power to many, especially on Europe's political left," he wrote. "Israel was disliked, especially by the left, not so much because it was Jewish but because it was American. And as such it was powerful."[50]

A Good Neighbor?

There have been positive moments in the past few years. The Council on Foreign Relations' Simon says that there was an upsurge in America's standing in 2004, when it provided substantial aid in the wake of the devastating Southeast Asian tsunami. The perception that this aid was "unconditional," he said, had a "sharply positive effect" on perceptions of the United States.

Noor at the Centre for Modern Oriental Studies in Berlin disagrees. He says he visited storm-damaged areas of Indonesia and Pakistan after the disaster and perceived even this seemingly altruistic venture was a public-relations disaster for the United States.

"They showed up on aircraft carriers and other warships," he says, "and the soldiers sent to help the victims were still wearing their combat fatigues from the Iraq War." It would have been far wiser to send civilian aid workers rather than the military, he says, who were regarded by many storm victims as emissaries of the imperial United States. "America is now seen [there] as something alien."

The Remarque Institute's Judt says that the U.S. government's disdain for international institutions has had a lasting negative effect, particularly among America's longtime allies. The Bush administration created an "in-your-face America," he says, that conveyed the message: "Not only do the things we do annoy you, but we don't care. We are going to do what we do, and you can take it or leave it."

For example, during his short stint as U.S. envoy to the United Nations, Ambassador John Bolton was criticized — and also praised — for his straight-from-the-shoulder diplomacy, including his disparagement of the United Nations itself. "The Secretariat building in New York has 38 stories," he famously once said. "If it lost 10 stories, it wouldn't make a bit of difference." [51] Bolton was blamed by some U.N. officials for quietly sabotaging the organization's reform initiative by stirring differences between poor and rich countries.

"He sometimes makes it very difficult to build bridges because he is a very honest and blunt person," said South Africa's ambassador, Dumisani Shadrack Kumalo, chairman of a coalition of developing nations. He said it sometimes appeared that "Ambassador Bolton wants to prove nothing works at the United Nations."[52] Bolton resigned in December 2006.

In addition, both Noor and Latin America expert Sweig at the Council on Foreign Relations say the U.S. reputation for generosity has been hurt by drastic cuts in foreign-assistance programs under the U.S. Agency for International Development (AID), as well as cuts in funds for libraries, scholarships and other cultural activities. Private giving by Americans remains the highest per capita in the world, and American foreign-development aid is the highest in the developed world in pure dollar terms, but the level of aid sinks very low when measured as a percentage of GDP.[53]

Such aid programs in many cases were replaced by "War on Terrorism" initiatives, including a $300 million propaganda campaign from the Pentagon. The psychological-warfare operation included plans for placing pro-American messages in foreign media outlets without disclosing the U.S. government as the source.[54]

Alarmist rhetoric is a poor substitute for help, says Noor, because the United States no longer has people on the ground in Muslim countries who know the cultures and the languages. When they were in effect and fully funded, he says, U.S. aid programs were so successful that Islamist movements in those countries have mimicked them. "They borrowed the tactics of the Peace Corps."

Missed Opportunities

By linking Israel and the United States into a single, fearsome conspiracy, anti-American activists have created strange bedfellows: fundamentalist Muslims, socialists and Western pacifists. Left-leaning groups used to find common cause in socialist ideals. Now, "anti-Americanism is the glue that holds them together, and hatred of Israel is one aspect," said Emmanuele Ottolenghi, a research fellow at the Centre for Hebrew and Jewish studies at Oxford University in England.[55]

While America's close relationship with Israel was often questioned outside the United States, the U.S. role in opposing the Soviet Union during the Cold War more

Venezuelan President Hugo Chavez fulminates about the United States at Miraflores Palace, Caracas, in 2006. Chavez, who is attempting to form an alternative coalition of South American countries opposed to the United States, insults and belittles the American president at every opportunity.

than outweighed it, says Georgetown University's Kupchan. Now, he says, the old bonds don't count for so much.

"The World War II generation is dying off; the reflexive support of the transatlantic partnership of that generation is disappearing. You have a new generation of Europeans for whom the United States is not the savior from the Nazis and the Soviets that it was for their parents," says Kupchan.

Meanwhile, even with a new U.S. presidential election nearing, fears remain strong in Europe about the actions of the Bush administration in its remaining months. Of particular concern is the possibility of a dangerous new U.S. offensive against Iran, which says it will continue developing nuclear energy.

"We think that the growing tensions between the two countries are made more dangerous by George Bush's detachment from the electorate: There's a real risk that he may strike at Iran before he leaves power," John Micklethwait, editor of *The Economist,* recently wrote.[56]

OUTLOOK

Lasting Damage?

When prosecutors in Munich decided in January to charge CIA counterterrorism operatives with kidnapping a German citizen, Khalid el-Masri, the newspaper *Sueddeutsche Zeitung* declared: "The great ally is not allowed to simply send its thugs out into Europe's streets." Indeed,

Craig Whitlock reported, the decision "won widespread applause from German politicians and the public."[57]

In the wake of such incidents, many at home and abroad are asking how — and even if — the United States can repair its image and its relations with its allies. Some analysts believe that the coming new presidential administration, whether Republican or Democratic, can do it through diligent cooperation and outreach. Others say the damage is so severe that it would take decades.

"When Bush goes, assuming that there isn't a war with Iran, it will be possible for the next president to exercise damage control," says Remarque Institute Director Judt.

Sweig of the Council on Foreign Relations sees a longer road ahead. "It will be the work of a generation to turn this around," she says.

Gerard Baker, U.S. editor for the *Times of London*, posits a more complex future. "Somewhere, deep down," he writes, "tucked away underneath their loathing for George Bush, in a secret place where the lights of smart dinner-party conversation and clever debating-society repartee never shine, the growing hordes of America-bashers must dread the moment he leaves office.

"When President Bush goes into the Texas sunset, and especially if he is replaced by an enlightened, world-embracing Democrat, their one excuse, their sole explanation for all human suffering in the world will disappear too. And they may just find that the world is not as simple as they thought it was."[58]

Critics agree that as long as the United States remains the world's greatest economic and military force, it will often be blamed for its negative impact on other countries, and seldom thanked for positive contributions. The inferiority complex that the University of Michigan's Markovits says drives Europe's brand of anti-Americanism will probably continue to fester until the EU can learn to assert itself in global affairs when humanitarian as well as military demands are compelling.

The Israeli-Palestinian conflict also will remain a problem and a source of agitation against U.S. policy, as long as Israel insists on occupying Palestinian land, America supports its right to do so and Palestinian politicians are unable to bring their angry streets to a compromise solution for statehood. The problem is multi-faceted.

But, as Powell Solares at Madrid's Elcano Royal Institute points out, much of the global public sees only one thing: "The perception that the main problem with the Arab-Israeli conflict is that the U.S. will always back Israel."

Iraq looms over all questions about the future. "The U.S. presence in Iraq will seriously impede American efforts to influence hearts and minds," Simon, the Middle East expert at the Council on Foreign Relations, told a House subcommittee last September. "Our occupation will reinforce regional images of the United States as both excessively violent and ineffectual."[59]

But what will follow the "American Century" in the near future if the United States has lost the trust of the world?

"It may be that the United States has not shown itself worthy or capable of ensuring the unity of a civilization whose laws have governed the world, at least for the last few centuries," writes Jean Daniel in *Le Nouvel Observateur* in Paris.

"But since a united Europe capable of taking over this mission hasn't yet emerged," Daniel continues, "all we can do is hope that the American people will wake up and rapidly call a halt to these crude interventionist utopias carelessly dredged out of the Theodore Roosevelt tradition. Utopias that, in the words of an American diplomat, have made George W. Bush and his brain trust 'lose their intelligence as they turned into ideologues.' "[60]

NOTES

1. See Fareed Zakaria, "The Politics of Rage: Why Do They Hate Us?" *Newsweek*, Sept. 24, 2001.

2. Samuel P. Huntington, "The Clash of Civilizations?" *Foreign Affairs*, summer 1993; www.foreignaffairs .org/19930601faessay5188/samuel-p-huntington/ the-clash-of-civilizations.html.

3. James Keaten, "French Farmer José Bové Leads New McDonald's Protest," The Associated Press, Aug. 13, 2001; www.mcspotlight.org/media/press/mcds/ theassociatedpr130801.html.

4. Quoted in David Morse, "Striking the Golden Arches: French Farmers Protest McDonald's Globalization," *The Ecologist*, Dec. 31, 2002, p. 2; www.socsci.uci.edu/~cohenp/food/frenchfarmers .pdf.

5. For background, see Mary H. Cooper, "Hating America," *CQ Researcher*, Nov. 23, 2001, pp. 969-992.

6. Andrei S. Markovits, "European Anti-Americanism (and Anti-Semitism): Ever Present Though Always Denied," Working Paper Series #108. Markovits is Karl W. Deutsch Collegiate Professor of Comparative Politics and German Studies at the University of Michigan.

7. Paul Hockenos, "Dispatch From Germany," *The Nation*, April 14, 2003; www.thenation.com/doc/20030414/hockenos.

8. "Pakistani Cartoon Protesters Chant Anti-American Slogans," FoxNews.com, Feb. 21, 2006; www.foxnews.com/story/0,2933,185503,00.html.

9. Jean-Marie Colombani, "We Are All Americans," *Le Monde*, Sept. 12, 2001.

10. Quoted in Denis Lacorne and Tony Judt, *eds.*, *With Us or Against Us: Studies in Global Anti-Americanism* (2005).

11. "Global Opinion: The Spread of Anti-Americanism," *Trends 2005*, p. 106; Pew Research Center for People and the Press, Jan. 24, 2005; http://people-press.org/commentary/display.php3?Analysis ID=104.

12. "U.S. Image Up Slightly, But Still Negative American Character Gets Mixed Reviews," Pew Research Center for People and the Press, June 23, 2005; http://pewglobal.org/reports/display.php?Report ID=247.

13. Lacorne and Judt, *op. cit.*

14. "War in Iraq: Winning the Peace," *The* [Beirut] *Daily Star*, April 6, 2006, from Worldpress.com; www.worldpress.org/Mideast/1041.cfm.

15. Peter Ford, "Europe Cringes at Bush 'Crusade' Against Terrorists," *The Christian Science Monitor*, Sept. 19, 2001.

16. For background, see "Brian Hansen, "Globalization Backlash," *CQ Researcher*, Sept. 28, 2001, pp. 961-784.

17. For background, see Sarah Glazer, "Slow Food Movement," *CQ Researcher*, Jan. 26, 2007, pp. 73-96, and David Hosansky, "Food Safety," *CQ Researcher*, Nov. 1, 2002, pp. 897-920.

18. Quoted in *The Daily Mail*, June 1, 1999, BBC Online Network; http://news.bbc.co.uk/2/hi/uk_news/358291.stm.

19. Quoted in Sam Loewenberg, "Lobbying Euro-Style," *The National Journal*, Sept. 8, 2001.

20. Henry A. Giroux, "George Bush's Religious Crusade Against Democracy: Fundamentalism as Cultural Politics," *Dissident Voice*, Aug. 4, 2004; www.dissidentvoice.org/Aug04/Giroux0804.htm.

21. "God and American diplomacy," *The Economist*, Feb. 8, 2003.

22. Pew Research Center, *op. cit.*, Jan. 24, 2005.

23. Markovits, *op. cit.*

24. "Burger and fries à la française," *The Economist*, April 15, 2004.

25. Suzanne Daley, "French Turn Vandal Into Hero Against US." *The New York Times*, July 1, 2000.

26. Henry Luce, "The American Century," *Life*, Feb. 7, 1941.

27. Michael Elliott, "China Takes on the World," *Time*, Jan. 11, 2007.

28. "America's Image Slips, But Allies Share U.S. Concerns Over Iran, Hamas; No Global Warming Alarm in the U.S., China," Pew Research Center for People and the Press, June 13, 2006; http://pewglobal.org.

29. Lacorne and Judt, *op. cit.*

30. "Hugo Chavez: Latin America Rises Against the Empire," March 10, 2007, from audio transcript on TeleSUR; http://latinhacker.gnn.tv/blogs/22178/Hugo_Chavez_Latin_America_Rises_Against_the_Empire.

31. Souad Mekhennet and Michael Moss, "New Face of Jihad Vows Attacks," *The New York Times*, March 16, 2007.

32. "Rome AD . . . Rome DC?" *The Guardian*, Sept. 18, 2002; www.guardian.co.uk/usa/story/0,12271,794163,00.html.

33. Quoted in Judy Colp Rubin, "Is Bush Really Responsible for Anti-Americanism Around the World," Sept. 27, 2004, George Mason University's History Network; http://hnn.us/articles/7288.html.

34. Cornelius de Pauw, "Recherches philosophiques sur les Américains ou Mémoires interessants pour servir à l'histoire de l'espèce humaine," London, 1768.

35. Friedrich Nietzsche, *The Gay Science*, sec. 329 (1882).

36. Arthur Gobineau, (Count Joseph Arthur de Gobineau) and Adrian Collins [1853-55] 1983. *The Inequality of Human Races*, Second edition, reprint.

37. Barry Rubin and Judith Colp Rubin, *Hating America: A History* (2004).

38. Lacorne and Judt, *op. cit.*, p. 26.

39. *Ibid.*

40. Pew Research Center, *op. cit.*, June 23, 2005.

41. Testimony before House International Relations Committee, Sept. 14, 2006.

42. Quoted in "Outrage at 'Old Europe' Remarks," BBC Online, Jan. 23, 2003.

43. "Theory That U.S. Orchestrated Sept. 11 Attacks 'Not Absurd,' " The Associated Press, Sept. 12, 2001, www.breitbart.com/.

44. For background, see Peter Katel and Kenneth Jost, "Treatment of Detainees," *CQ Researcher*, Aug. 25, 2006, pp. 673-696.

45. For background, see Peter Katel, "New Strategy in Iraq," *CQ Researcher*, Feb. 23, 2007, pp. 169-192.

46. Patrick Sabatier, Liberation, Paris, Quoted in WorldPress.com, "Iraq Prisoner Abuse Draws International Media Outrage," May 12, 2004; www.worldpress.org/Mideast/1861.cfm.

47. Pew Research Center, *op. cit.*, June 23, 2005.

48. Pew Research Center, *op. cit.*, Jan. 24, 2005.

49. Firas Al-Atraqchi, "Disillusion, Anger on the Arab Street," *Dissident Voice Online*, March 21, 2007; www.dissidentvoice.org/Articles3/Atraqchi_Arab Street.htm.

50. Markovits, *op. cit.*

51. Quoted in Anne Applebaum, "Defending Bolton," *The Washington Post*, March 9, 2005, p. A21.

52. Quoted in Peter Baker and Glenn Kessler, "U.N. Ambassador Bolton Won't Stay," *The Washington Post*, Dec. 6, 2006, p. A1.

53. "Review of the Development Cooperation Policies and Programmes of United States," Organization for Economic Cooperation and Development, 2006.

54. Matt Kelley, "Pentagon Rolls Out Stealth PR," *USA Today*, Dec. 14, 2005.

55. Glenn Frankel, "In Britain, War Concern Grows Into Resentment of U.S. Power; Anxiety Over Attack on Iraq Moves to Political Mainstream," *The Washington Post*, Jan. 26, 2003, p. A14.

56. John Micklethwait, "Letter to Readers," *The Economist*, Feb. 8, 2007.

57. Craig Whitlock, "In Another CIA Abduction, Germany Has an Uneasy Role," *The Washington Post*, Feb. 5, 2007, p. A11.

58. Gerard Baker, "When Bush Leaves Office," *Times of London*, TimesOnline, March 2, 2007.

59. Testimony before International Relations Subcommittee on the Middle East, Sept. 14, 2006.

60. Jean Daniel, "Our American 'Enemies,' " *La Nouvel Observateur*, Sept. 23, 2003, quoted on WorldPress.org.

BIBLIOGRAPHY

Books

Cohen, Nick, *What's Left? How Liberals Lost Their Way, Fourth Estate*, 2007.
A well-known liberal British columnist for *The Observer* and *The New Statesman* gives a scathing critique of anti-Americanism among the British Left, the anti-globalization movement and intellectuals who have become apologists for militant Islam.

Garton Ash, Timothy, *Free World: America, Europe and the Surprising Future of the West, Random House*, 2004.
In an engaging critique of anti-American sentiment, a former journalist who runs the European Studies Centre at Oxford University argues that in the post-Cold War world, America is the "other" against which Europeans try to define their own identity.

Joffe, Josef, *Uberpower: The Imperial Temptation of America, W. W. Norton*, 2006.
The editor and publisher of *Die Zeit,* a German weekly, and a fellow in international relations at the Hoover Institution, provides a European intellectual's insight into the envy at the heart of anti-Americanism and its parallels with classical anti-Semitism.

Katzenstein, Peter, and Robert Keohane, eds., *Anti-Americanisms in World Politics*, Cornell University Press, 2006.
Two international-relations scholars bring together the insights of historians, social scientists and political scientists.

Kohut, Andrew, and Bruce Stokes, *America Against the World: How We Are Different and Why We Are Disliked*, Times Books, 2006.
Kohut, director of the Pew Research Center for the People and the Press, and Stokes, international economics columnist for *National Journal,* provide a comprehensive survey of public opinions about America from around the world.

Kupchan, Charles, *The End of the American Era: U.S. Foreign Policy and the Geopolitics of the Twenty-first Century*, Vintage, 2003.
A former National Security Council staffer and a senior fellow at the Council on Relations argues that with the rise of China and the European Union America can no longer afford to have a unilateralist foreign policy.

Lacorne, Denis, and Tony Judt, eds., *With Us or Against Us: Studies in Global Anti-Americanism*, Palgrave Macmillan, 2005.
Essays by 11 scholars analyze anti-American sentiment in Western and Eastern Europe, the Middle East and Asia.

Markovits, Andrei S., *Uncouth Nation: Why Europe Dislikes America*, Princeton University Press, 2007.
A professor of comparative politics and German studies at the University of Michigan, Ann Arbor, writes provocatively about the anti-Americanism in everyday European life.

Revel, Jean-Francois, *Anti-Americanism*, Encounter Books, 2003.
Revel, a leading French intellectual, castigates his countrymen for pointing their fingers at America when they should be dealing with their own current and historical problems.

Sweig, Julia, *Friendly Fire: Losing Friends and Making Enemies in the Anti-American Century*, Public Affairs, 2006.
The director of Latin American studies at the Council on Foreign Relations argues that American policies in Latin America, including sponsoring dictators and condoning human-rights violations, set the stage for the current animosity toward the U.S.

Articles

Judt, Tony, "Anti-Americans Abroad," *The New York Review of Books*, May 2003.
The director of the Remarque Institute at New York University examines the rage for new books in France attacking America.

Reports and Studies

"America's Image Slips, But Allies Share U.S. Concerns Over Iran, Hamas," *Pew Research Center*, 2006; http://pewglobal.org/reports/display.php?ReportID=252.
The latest poll by the Pew Global Attitudes Project finds that while anti-Americanism had dipped in 2005, it began rising again.

"Foreign Aid: An Introductory Overview of U.S. Programs and Policy," *Congressional Research Service, Library of Congress*, 2004; http://fpc.state.gov/documents/organization/31987.pdf.
This study of American foreign aid includes data on humanitarian, military and bilateral-development aid.

"Worldviews 2002," *German Marshall Fund of the United States and The Chicago Council on Foreign Relations*, 2002; www.worldviews.org.
A comprehensive survey of contrasting European and American public opinion following the Sept. 11 terrorist attacks finds that Europeans believed U.S. foreign policy contributed to the attacks.

For More Information

Centre for Modern Oriental Studies, Kirchweg 33, 14129 Berlin, Germany; +49-(0)-30-80307-0; www.zmo.de. German think tank conducting comparative and interdisciplinary studies of the Middle East, Africa, South and Southeast Asia.

Council on Foreign Relations, 58 E. 68th St., New York, NY 10065; (212) 434-9400; www.cfr.org. Promotes a better understanding of the foreign-policy choices facing the United States and other governments.

Elcano Royal Institute, Príncipe de Vergara, 51, 28006 Madrid, Spain; +34-91-781-6770; www.realinstitutoelcano .org. Non-partisan Spanish institution generating policy ideas in the interest of international peace.

Pew Global Attitudes Project, 1615 L St., N.W., Suite 700, Washington, DC 20036; (202) 419-4400; www .pewglobal.org. Assesses worldwide opinions on the current state of foreign affairs and other important issues.

USC Center on Public Diplomacy, USC Annenberg School, University of Southern California, 3502 Watt Way, Suite 103, Los Angeles, CA 90089-0281; (213) 821-2078; http://uscpublicdiplomacy.com. Studies the impact of government-sponsored programs as well as private activities on foreign policy and national security.

11

Crisis in Darfur

Is There Any Hope for Peace?

Karen Foerstel

Villages continue to be attacked and burned in Darfur by the notorious Arab janjaweed militia — aided by aerial bombing by the Sudanese government — despite a two-year-old peace agreement between the government and rebel groups. The prosecutor for the International Criminal Court recently said the government's "scorched earth" tactics amount to genocide, but others say there is insufficient evidence that civilians have been targeted because of their ethnicity.

Courtesy of Brian Steidle

From *CQ Global Researcher*, September 2008.

It was mid-afternoon when helicopters suddenly appeared and opened fire on the terrified residents of Sirba, in Western Darfur. Then hundreds of armed men riding horses and camels stormed the village, followed by 30 military vehicles mounted with weapons.

"The cars . . . were shooting at everyone, whether a woman, man or child," said Nada, one of the survivors. "They were shooting at us even when we were running away."[1]

Almost simultaneously, another attack was taking place a few miles away in the town of Abu Suruj. Witnesses say Sudanese soldiers and members of the notorious *janjaweed* militia shot people, set homes on fire and stole livestock. Many died in flames inside their huts. Three-quarters of the village was burned to the ground, as government planes bombed the town and surrounding hills where residents had fled for cover.

But that wasn't all. In a third nearby village, Silea, women and girls were raped and two-thirds of the town was destroyed by fire. Among the victims was Mariam, 35, who was shot as she tried to stop looters.

"They told me to leave and not to take anything, and then one of the men on a Toyota shot me, and I fell down," she said. Her father found her and took her by horse-drawn cart to a regional clinic. "I was pregnant with twins, and I lost them while we made the trip," she said. "I lost so much blood."[2]

In all, nearly 100 people were killed and 40,000 civilians driven from their homes in a single day, according to Human Rights Watch (HRW), a global advocacy group. The Sudanese military said the strikes were in retaliation against the Justice and Equality

Conflict Continues Despite Cease-Fire Accords

Darfur is an ethnically diverse area about the size of France in western Sudan — Africa's largest country. It has been wracked by decades of tension — and more recently open warfare — over land and grazing rights between the nomadic Arabs from the arid north and predominantly non-Arab Fur, Masalit and Zaghawa farmers in the more fertile south. A third of the region's 7 million people have been displaced by the conflict, which continues despite numerous cease-fire agreements. The United Nations has set up several camps inside Darfur and in neighboring Chad for those fleeing the violence.

Sources: USAID satellite imagery, Aug. 13, 2007; United Nations Office for the Coordination of Humanitarian Affairs, June 2, 2008

While HRW criticized the rebels for operating around populated areas, it strongly condemned the Sudanese government for targeting civilians and using a "scorched earth" policy to clear the region and make it easier to go after JEM positions.[3]

Indeed, civilians have been targeted and terrorized throughout the long and bloody fighting in Darfur between non-Arab rebel groups who want to overthrow the Sudanese government and government troops backed by Arabic *janjaweed* militias.* During the peak fighting between 2003 and 2005, from 200,000 to 400,000 people — mostly civilians — died from armed attacks as well as famine and disease. More than 2.4 million Sudanese — about a third of the population — have been forced to flee their homes since 2003; tens of thousands now live in refugee camps across the region.[4]

But the same-day attacks in the three villages did not occur during the period of peak fighting. They occurred on Feb. 8 of this year, nearly two years after rebels and the government signed the Darfur Peace Agreement (DPA) in May 2006.

The continuing conflict has sparked the world's largest humanitarian mission, with more than 17,000 aid workers now stationed in Darfur.[5] And the situation is deteriorating. Observers predict next year will be one of the worst ever.

Growing banditry and lawlessness have made much of Darfur — a region

Movement (JEM), an anti-government rebel group that had recently launched a military offensive in the region, attacking a police station, killing three civilians and detaining local officials.

* The word *janjaweed*, which means devil on a horse, is used to describe horsemen from the nomadic Arab tribes in Darfur that have been armed and supported by the Sudanese government.

in western Sudan as large as France — inaccessible to aid workers.[6] Rising food prices, drought and a poor cereal harvest also are combining to form what Mike McDonagh, chief of the U.N. Office for Coordination of Humanitarian Affairs, described as a "perfect storm."[7]

Already, conditions are dire:

- In the first five months of this year, 180,000 Darfuris were driven from their homes.[8]
- More than 4.2 million people in Darfur now rely on humanitarian aid for food, water and medical care.[9]
- Attacks against aid workers have doubled since last year.[10] (*See chart, p. 259.*)
- The U.N. World Food Program was forced to cut its food rations in Darfur by 40 percent this year because of repeated attacks by armed gangs.[11]
- About 650,000 children — half of the region's children — do not receive any education.[12]

While attacks on civilians have decreased since the peace deal was signed, international watchdog groups say the drop has little to do with increased security. "A third of the population has been displaced, so targets are fewer," says Selena Brewer, a researcher with Human Rights Watch. "But there are far more perpetrators."

The fighting between non-Arab rebels and the Arab-led government's forces — backed by the *janjaweed* — has morphed into all-out lawlessness. The two main rebel groups — the JEM and the Sudanese Liberation Army/Movement (SLA/M) — have splintered into more than a dozen factions that fight among themselves as much as against the government. Moreover, some disaffected *janjaweed* fighters have joined the rebels, and

Lack of Resources Hampers Peacekeepers

More than a year after the U.N. authorized the largest peacekeeping force in the world in Darfur, the joint U.N.-African Union (UNAMID) force has received only 37 percent of the nearly 32,000 military, police and civilian personnel that were authorized and 72 percent of the funds. Much of the force's equipment has been delayed by Sudanese customs, hijacked by bandits or simply not provided by international donors. For instance, by the end of May not a single military helicopter had been donated to the force.

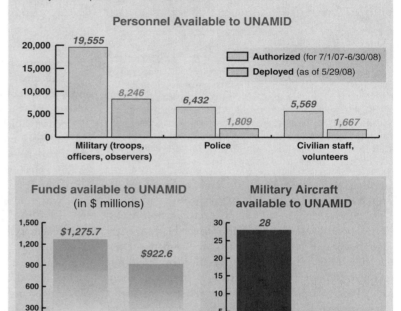

Source: U.N. Security Council, June 2008

skirmishes between ethnic tribes are increasing. Bandits attack civilians, aid workers and international peacekeepers almost at will.[13]

"We no longer know who is attacking," says Denise Bell, a Darfur specialist with Amnesty International USA.

To make matters even more complicated, Darfur has become the staging ground for a proxy war between Sudan and its western neighbor Chad. The two governments support opposing groups in the region with the goal of launching coup attempts against one

During a 2007 visit to Sudan, Chinese President Hu Jintao reviews Sudanese troops with President Omar Hassan al-Bashir. In the run-up to the Beijing Olympics this summer, China came under intense international pressure to use its economic clout as Sudan's biggest oil buyer and weapons supplier to convince Bashir to stop the slaughter in Darfur. Hu convinced Bashir to allow joint U.N.-African Union peacekeeping forces to enter Darfur, but critics say China could do much more.

another. As arms pour into the area, civilians are the primary victims.

Many describe the conflict as Arabs vs. non-Arabs. "The *janjaweed* . . . would tell us that the black Africans were a lesser race and that they shouldn't be there . . . and that they would drive them out or kill them," said former U.S. Marine Capt. Brian Steidle, whose book about his six months as an unarmed military observer in Darfur was made into an award-winning documentary.[14]

But most observers say the situation is more complicated than that. Nearly all Darfuris speak Arabic, and nearly all are Muslims. Generations of intermarriage have resulted in little physical difference between the groups, and not all Arab tribes have joined the *janjaweed* while some Arab groups have even been targeted themselves — although most of the victims are from the non-Arab Fur, Masalit and Zaghawa ethnic groups.

But poverty, drought and the ongoing conflict have led to increased tensions between Arab groups, who are mainly nomadic, and non-Arabs, who are mainly farmers, as they compete for dwindling land and water resources.[15] The Sudanese government is widely accused of doing all it can to inflame these historical tensions and grow support among its Arab political base in Darfur by arming and recruiting the *janjaweed* to clear the region of non-Arabs.

But most agree race has little to do with government motives. "It's all about divide to rule. It's just the government using one lot of poor people against another lot of poor people," says Gillian Lusk, associate editor of the London-based newsletter *Africa Confidential.* "It's not about ethnic supremacy. If the so-called Arabs don't help the government, it will kill them, too. It's just renting them."

Although Sudan says its attacks in Darfur comprise a "counterinsurgency" campaign, the prosecutor for the International Criminal Court (ICC) refuted that claim in July when he sought an indictment against Sudanese President Omar Hassan Al-Bashir for genocide and crimes against humanity.[16]

"The most efficient method to commit genocide today in front of our eyes is gang rapes, rapes against girls and rapes against 70-year old women," Chief ICC Prosecutor Luis Moreno-Ocampo said as he described the brutality of the war in Darfur. "Babies born as a result have been called *janjaweed* babies, and this has led to an explosion of infanticide." In addition, he said, "Al-Bashir is executing this genocide without gas chambers, without bullets and without machetes. The desert will do it for them. . . . Hunger is the weapon of this genocide as well as rape."[17]

Many hope the prosecutor's action will pressure Sudan to halt its attacks in Darfur. But others fear an indictment would prompt Bashir to prevent peacekeepers and Western aid organizations from working in Darfur.

"[An indictment] would have very serious consequences for peacekeeping operations, including the political process," U.N. Secretary-General Ban Ki-moon said. "I'm very worried. But nobody can evade justice."[18]

While the ICC is considering charging Bashir with genocide, many aid groups, governments and the United Nations have avoided using the "G-word" to describe the situation in Darfur. Some say the reluctance stems from the fact that international law requires countries to take action to "prevent and punish" genocide. But others, including Amnesty International, say that despite the obvious atrocities, there is insufficient evidence civilians were targeted because of their ethnicity.[19]

The international community also disagrees on how to solve the crisis. While the United States and the United Nations have sanctioned the Bashir government, the move has largely been opposed by China, Russia,

AP Photo/*The Citizens' Voice*/Kristen Mullen

Arab nations and the African Union (AU) — a political and economic coalition of African countries.

"China is uniquely positioned to fix this," says Alex Meixner, director of government relations for the Save Darfur Coalition. "They have a fair amount of leverage over Bashir." China buys two-thirds of Sudan's petroleum — much of which comes from the south — and is its largest supplier of weapons. But as a member of the U.N.'s Security Council, China repeatedly has used its veto threat to block action against Sudan.[20]

Over the past year, however, as the Beijing Olympics brought international attention to China's human-rights policies — its government has played a more active role in trying to solve the crisis. It appointed a special envoy to help negotiate a peace settlement and helped convince Sudan to allow a joint U.N.-African Union peacekeeping force — known as UNAMID — to enter Darfur. In July China sent 172 engineers to join the peacekeeping force, bringing China's participation in the mission to more than 300 personnel.[21]

Nearly a year into their mission, however, the force is severely undermanned, underequipped and under constant attack. Although authorized to have 26,000 military and police peacekeepers — the largest deployment in the world — fewer than half that number have been deployed and not a single military helicopter has been donated to the force. (*See graph, p. 251.*)[22]

Darfur is "a test case for international response — or the inability of the international community to respond — to this type of situation," says Imani Countess, senior director for public affairs at TransAfrica Forum, which campaigns for human rights in Africa. "It's a damning indictment against the government of Sudan, because it refuses to end the violence. But it's also a pretty damning indictment of the international community."

And while the international community stands by, the situation in Darfur threatens to destabilize the entire region. Millions of refugees from the area are creating economic and political chaos in Sudan and neighboring countries, and the region's porous borders have turned Darfur into the headquarters for rebels from Chad and the Central African Republic.

The growing crisis also threatens to undo the precarious 2005 Comprehensive Peace Agreement (CPA) that ended the bloody 20-year civil war between North and South Sudan — Africa's longest civil war.

"A lot of attention has been diverted to Darfur," causing backsliding and insufficient funding for implementing the peace agreement, says Bell of Amnesty International. "Darfur threatens to overshadow the CPA. If the CPA falls, the country falls. The international community needs to be much more aware of that."

In June, Jan Eliasson — the U.N.'s special envoy to Darfur — resigned, blaming himself, the U.N. and the international community for not doing enough to bring peace to the region. He said attention has been too narrowly focused on Darfur alone and that a more comprehensive strategy — addressing the many tensions and conflicts across the region — must now be pursued.

"This simply cannot go on," Eliasson said. "A new generation in Sudan may be doomed to a life in conflict, despair and poverty. The international community should have learned enough lessons from other conflicts where the populations were left to stagnate and radicalize in camps."[23]

As the situation deteriorates in Darfur, these are some of the questions being asked:

Has genocide occurred in Darfur?

In July 2004, the U.S. Congress declared the violence in Darfur "genocide" and urged President George W. Bush to do the same. But for months afterward, Secretary of State Colin L. Powell studiously avoided using the word, on the advice of government lawyers.

Under the International Convention on the Prevention and Punishment of Genocide, any signatory country — including the United States — which determines that genocide is occurring must act to "prevent and punish" the genocide. However, while some believe the 1948 treaty requires military intervention to stop the killing, others believe economic sanctions alone are permitted.[24]

The Bush administration used the word to describe what is happening in Darfur only after religious groups launched a lobbying and media campaign condemning the Sudanese government for "genocide." In May 2004, the U.S. Holocaust Memorial Museum issued a "genocide alert" for Darfur, and two months later the American Jewish World Service and the Holocaust Museum founded the Save Darfur Coalition — an alliance of

AFP/Getty Images/Khaled Desouki

AFP/Getty Images/Ashraf Shazly

Defying the Court

Surrounded by security guards, Sudanese President Omar Hassan al-Bashir (center, top), greets supporters in North Darfur just days after the chief prosecutor at the International Criminal Court accused him of masterminding genocide in the region. Bashir dismissed the accusations as lies and vowed not to cooperate with the court. Soon after the accusation, the Sudanese government convicted and sentenced to death more than three dozen rebels — including these prisoners (bottom) — in connection with a daring attack last May on Khartoum, the capital, in which more than 200 people were killed.

secular and religious groups calling for international intervention to halt the violence.[25] That August, 35 evangelical Christian leaders said genocide was occurring in Darfur and asked the administration to consider sending troops.[26]

A month later, Powell finally capitulated, telling the Senate Foreign Relations Committee, "We concluded — I concluded — that genocide has been committed in Darfur and that the government of Sudan and the *janjaweed* bear responsibility — and genocide may still be occurring."[27] Powell then called on the U.N. to take action for the "prevention and suppression of acts of genocide."[28] A week later, the United States pushed a resolution through the General Assembly threatening Sudan with economic sanctions if it did not protect civilians in Darfur.[29]

But most other governments and international humanitarian groups — including Amnesty International — say genocidal intent has not been proven.

"There is a legal definition of genocide, and Darfur does not meet that legal standard," former President Jimmy Carter said last year. "The atrocities were horrible, but I don't think it qualifies to be called genocide. If you read the law textbooks . . . you'll see very clearly that it's not genocide, and to call it genocide falsely just to exaggerate a horrible situation — I don't think it helps."[30]

Not surprisingly, Sudan denies targeting ethnic groups in Darfur, instead blaming the massive deaths on tribal conflict, water disputes and collateral military damage. "We do not deny that atrocities have taken place," says Khalid al-Mubarak, a media counselor at the Sudanese Embassy in London. "We do deny that they have been planned or systematic. They happened in an area out of reach of the central government. The government could not have planned or controlled it."

A U.N. commission investigating the conflict also said genocidal intent has not been proven, but it did say Sudanese forces working with *janjaweed* militias had "conducted indiscriminate attacks, including killing of civilians, torture, enforced disappearances, destruction of villages, rape and other forms of sexual violence, pillaging and forced displacement."[31]

"I don't think it matters [whether you call it genocide or not]," says *Africa Confidential's* Lusk. "In terms of legitimizing intervention, it might be important. But no one wants to get involved anyway."

In a joint statement in May, the three leading American presidential candidates at the time — Sens. Barack Obama, D-Ill., Hillary Rodham Clinton, D-N.Y., and John McCain, R-Ariz., — called the situation in Darfur "genocide" and promised, if elected, to intervene.[32]

Some other U.S. politicians — including Democratic vice presidential nominee and Foreign Relations

Committee Chairman Sen. Joseph R. Biden, of Delaware — have called for military intervention to halt the mass killings.[33] Susan Rice, a foreign policy adviser to Obama, has called for legislation authorizing the use of force.[34]

But experts say the international backlash against the Iraq War — including the abuse of Muslim prisoners at Abu Ghraib prison by U.S. soldiers — makes intervention in another Muslim country unlikely anytime soon, whether the word genocide is used or not. "Sudan can say all this 'genocide' stuff is a conspiracy to steal [their] oil," says Peter Moszynski, a writer and aid worker with 25 years of experience in Sudan. "With the Iraq backlash, Bashir became bulletproof."

Sudan is Africa's fifth-largest oil producer, with proven reserves of 5 billion barrels. Experts say in the next few years Sudan's daily production could reach 700,000 barrels — enough for nearly 30 million gallons of gasoline a day — about 10 percent of U.S. daily needs.[35]

The United States is also in the awkward position of balancing its national-security interests against calls to end the genocide. Since the Sept. 11, 2001, terrorist attacks in the United States, Sudanese officials have worked closely with the CIA and other intelligence agencies to provide information on suspected terrorists. Although Sudan is on the U.S. list of "state sponsors of terrorism," a 2007 State Department report called Sudan "a strong partner in the War on Terror."[36]

"I am not happy at all about the U.S. working with Sudan," says El-Tahir El-Faki, speaker of the JEM legislative assembly. "Definitely it is genocide in Darfur. They are targeting ethnic people with the aim of eliminating people. . . . It will be contrary to American interest supporting a government that is killing people."

Regardless of what the violence is called, most agree the label is meaningless if nothing is done to stop the killing. "It's like walking down the street and you see someone being beaten up. You don't stop and think whether it's bodily harm or not. You stop and help and let the lawyers figure out the legal side later," says James Smith, head of the Aegis Trust, a British group that works to halt genocide. "Stopping genocide is more of a political and moral question than a legal one."

"The legal framework exists to prevent or mitigate genocide if the political will is sufficient," he continues. "However, politicians and diplomats create legal ambiguity to mask their disinterest in protecting lives in certain far-away countries."

Would arresting Sudanese President Bashir do more harm than good?

In July, when he asked the International Criminal Court to charge Bashir with genocide and other war crimes, the ICC prosecutor cast aside all the debate over how to label the violence in Darfur. Bashir's motives were "largely political," ICC prosecutor Luis Moreno-Ocampo said. "His pretext was a 'counterinsurgency.' His intent was genocide. . . . He is the mastermind behind the alleged crimes. He has absolute control."[37]

The court is expected to decide this fall whether to accept the charges and issue an arrest warrant. Many heralded the prosecutor's unprecedented request — the first genocide indictment sought for a sitting head of state — as a critical first step to peace in Darfur.

"Darfur has had very little justice of any kind. They've been let down by the African Union, by the U.N. peacekeeping force, by other countries," says *Africa Confidential's* Lusk. "It's about time a small sign of justice appeared on the horizon. Impunity has reigned for 19 years. This action says this is not a respectable government."

But others fear an indictment could spark reprisal attacks against foreign peacekeepers and aid workers by the Sudanese government and could block a peace settlement. Sudan's U.N. ambassador, Abdalmahmood Abdalhaleem Mohamad, said the charges would "destroy" efforts towards a peace agreement in Darfur. "Ocampo is playing with fire," he said. "If the United Nations is serious about its engagement with Sudan, it should tell this man to suspend what he is doing with this so-called indictment. There will be grave repercussions."[38]

Sudanese officials said that while they would not retaliate with violence, they could not guarantee the safety of any individual. "The U.N. asks us to keep its people safe, but how can we guarantee their safety when they want to seize our head of state?" asked Deputy Parliament Speaker Mohammed al-Hassan al-Ameen.[39]

The Sudanese government, which refused to hand over two other officials indicted for war crimes last year by the ICC, said it would not cooperate with the ICC's latest efforts either.

The United Nations evacuated staff from the region shortly after Ocampo made his announcement.[40]

Climate Change Blamed for Darfur Conflict

Nomads and farmers battle for scarce water and arable land.

For generations, Arab nomads in Darfur enjoyed a symbiotic relationship with their farming non-Arab neighbors. As the seasons changed, the nomads would bring their livestock from the arid north to the greener lands to the south during the dry season and then lead them back north during the rainy season. The non-Arabs, who came from several different ethnic groups, would allow the nomads to graze camels, sheep and goats on their farmlands, and in exchange the livestock would provide fertilizer for the farmers' crops.[1]

That relationship, however, began to change about 75 years ago. And today, what had once been a convenient alliance between nomads and farmers has exploded into a bloody war between Darfur's Arabs and ethnic African tribes.

While many blame the bloodshed on political or ethnic divisions, others say climate change lies at the root of the devastation. "It is no accident that the violence in Darfur erupted during the drought," U.N. Secretary-General Ban Ki-moon said. "Until then, Arab nomadic herders had lived amicably with settled farmers."[2]

Most people use "a convenient military and political shorthand" to describe Darfur as an ethnic conflict between Arab militias fighting black rebels and farmers, Ban explained. And, while the conflict involves a complex set of social and political causes, it "began as an ecological crisis, arising at least in part from climate change," he said.

According to the U.N., average precipitation in Sudan has declined 40 percent since the early 1980s.[3] Signs of desertification began emerging as far back as the 1930s. A lake in El-Fashir in northern Darfur reached its lowest water level in 1938, after which wells had to be drilled to tap into underground water supplies. Villages in northern Darfur increasingly were evacuated because of disappearing water supplies.[4]

In the 1980s a severe drought and famine made the northern areas nearly impossible to cultivate, forcing nomadic tribes to migrate even further south and increasingly encroach upon their farming neighbors' more fertile lands.[5] To prevent damage from the nomad's passing herds, the farmers began to fence off their shrinking fertile plots. Violent land disputes grew more and more common.

"Interestingly, most of the Arab tribes who have their own land rights did not join the government's fight," said David Mozersky, the International Crisis Group's project director for the Horn of Africa.[6]

Representatives from the five permanent members of the U.N. Security Council — Britain, China, France, Russia and the United States — met with U.N. officials to discuss the safety of the peacekeeping force in Darfur, which evacuated non-essential staff and cut back on operations that could endanger civilian staff.[41]

Meanwhile, the African Union (AU), the Arab League and others asked the U.N. to delay the ICC legal action, which some say could be used as a bargaining chip to force Bashir to end the killing. "We are asking that the ICC indictment be deferred to give peace a chance," Nigerian Foreign Affairs Minister Ojo Maduekwe said after an emergency meeting on the issue by the African Union's Peace and Security Council in July. China and Russia also support deferring ICC action.[42]

Others fear the request for delay could produce its own backlash — among the rebels. Leaders of JEM and one of the SLA's factions said they will no longer recognize AU efforts to mediate peace because of its request for a deferral. "The African Union is a biased organization and is protecting dictators and neglecting the African people," said Khalil Ibrahim, president of JEM.[43]

Former U.S. Special Envoy for Sudan Andrew Natsios agrees an indictment could derail peace negotiations and make it impossible to hold free and fair elections, scheduled next year. "The regime will now avoid any compromise or anything that would weaken their already weakened position, because if they are forced from office they'll face trials before the ICC," Natsios wrote. "This indictment may well shut off the last remaining hope for a peaceful settlement for the country."[44]

The United States — which, like Sudan, has never ratified the treaty creating the ICC — nevertheless said Sudan must comply with the ICC. But the U.S. envoy to

A new report by the European Commission predicts that increasing drought and land overuse in North Africa and the Sahel — the semi-arid swath of land stretching from the Atlantic Ocean to the Horn of Africa — could destroy 75 percent of the region's arable land. As land and water resources disappear, the report said, such violent conflicts will increase around the world.[7]

"Already today, climate change is having a major impact on the conflict in and around Darfur," the report said.[8]

Economist Jeffrey Sachs, director of the Earth Institute at Columbia University, said Darfur is an example of the conflicts that increasingly will erupt because of climate change.

"What some regard as the arc of Islamic instability, across the Sahel, the Horn of Africa, Yemen, Iraq, Pakistan and Afghanistan, is more accurately an arc of hunger, population pressures, water stress, growing food insecurity and a pervasive lack of jobs," Sachs wrote earlier this year, using Darfur as an example of a conflict sparked by climate change.[9]

But others say climate change is just an excuse used by the Sudanese government to relieve itself of responsibility. Politics is the real cause of the bloodshed in Darfur, many say, with President Omar Hassan al-Bashir's government bearing full blame for the ongoing violence.

"Jeffrey Sachs and Ban Ki-moon said it's essentially environmental. How dare they?" says Gillian Lusk, associate editor of the London-based newsletter *Africa Confidential*. "The essential issue is the Sudan government went in there and killed people." And any attempts "to turn it into a primary ethnic or environment issue are dangerous."

Still, many international leaders say Darfur is a warning sign of growing environmental degradation. "Climate change is already having a considerable impact on security," French President Nicolas Sarkozy told an international governmental conference in April. "If we keep going down this path, climate change will encourage the immigration of people with nothing towards areas where the population does have something, and the Darfur crisis will be only one crisis among dozens."[10]

[1] Stephan Faris, "The Real Roots of Darfur," *The Atlantic*, April 2007, www.theatlantic.com/doc/200704/darfur-climate.

[2] Ban Ki-moon, "A Climate Culprit in Darfur," *The Washington Post*, June 16, 2007, p. A15.

[3] *Ibid.*

[4] M. W. Daly, *Darfur's Sorrow* (2007), pp. 141-142.

[5] Gerard Prunier, *Darfur: The Ambiguous Genocide* (2005), pp. 49-50.

[6] Faris, *op. cit.*

[7] "Climate Change and International Security," The High Representative and the European Commission, March 14, 2008, p. 6, http://ec.europa.eu/external_relations/cfsp/doc/climate_change_international_security_2008_en.pdf.

[8] *Ibid.*

[9] Jeffrey Sachs, "Land, Water and Conflict," *Newsweek*, July 14, 2008.

[10] "Climate change driving Darfur crisis: Sarkozy," Agence France-Presse, April 18, 2008, http://afp.google.com/article/ALeqM5h7l_NjlMjZF-QWDOwxIbibX5AeuA.

the United Nations has been vague on whether the United States would support a deferral. "We haven't seen anything at this point that could have the support of the United States," said U.S. Ambassador to the United Nations Zalmay Khalilzad. "We certainly do not support impunity for crimes."

But he added, "As you know also, we're not a member of the ICC. So there are various factors in play here. And as I said, I don't see any action on this in the council that would provide impunity anytime in the foreseeable future."[45]

Others point out that efforts to solve the crises diplomatically were faltering long before the ICC prosecutor's recommendations. "The process hasn't gotten anywhere," says veteran aid worker Moszynski. "If we're going to say 'never again,' we've got to do it. Someone must be held accountable.

In any case, he added, the pending ICC charges — and potential indictments — have turned Bashir into an international "pariah," making it nearly impossible for him to play any leadership role on the international stage.

Is China blocking peace in Darfur?

In the year leading up to the Beijing Olympics, U.S. government leaders, human-rights activists and Hollywood's elite used the international sporting event as a platform to criticize China's policy toward Darfur.

China is Sudan's biggest trading partner, weapons supplier and oil-industry investor. It has built a 957-mile-long pipeline in Sudan — one the largest foreign oil projects in China's history. It also has constructed three arms factories in Sudan and provided small arms, anti-personnel mines, howitzers, tanks, helicopters and

After years of fighting the Sudanese government, rebels in Darfur — like these from the Sudanese Liberation Army/ Movement (SLA/M) — have splintered into more than a dozen factions that fight among themselves as much as against the government. Meanwhile, bandits are attacking civilians, aid workers and international peacekeepers almost at will, contributing to rampant lawlessness in the region.

ammunition. China also has done more than any other country to protect Khartoum from U.N. sanctions.[46]

China "potentially has the most influence with Sudan," says Amnesty International's Bell. "People who are the main [economic] players are able to dictate the rate of progress that is made."

American actress Mia Farrow last year branded the Beijing Olympics the "Genocide Olympics," and Hollywood producer Steven Spielberg stepped down as one of the event's artistic advisers, citing the ongoing violence in Darfur.[47] Last May, a bipartisan group of 108 members of Congress warned the Chinese government that if China did not pressure Sudan to do more to help Darfur, protests and boycotts could destroy the Olympics.

"[We] urge you to protect your country's image from being irredeemably tarnished, through association with a genocidal regime, for the purpose of economic gains," the group wrote. "[U]nless China does its part to ensure that the government of Sudan accepts the best and most reasonable path to peace, history will judge your government as having bank-rolled a genocide."[48]

The day after the letter was sent, China appointed a special envoy for Darfur and since then has made several moves to mitigate the crisis.[49] In addition to sending 315 engineers to join the UNAMID peacekeeping force to build roads, bridges and wells, China last May donated more than $5 million in humanitarian aid and in February handed over a $2.8 million package of financial and development aid.[50] According to China's official news agency, China has given a total of $11 million in humanitarian aid to Darfur, and Chinese companies have spent about $50 million on development projects in the region, including 53 miles of water pipelines.[51]

"We have done as much as we can," said China's assistant foreign minister Zhai Jun. "China remains committed to resolving the Darfur issue and has made unremitting efforts."[52]

But many say China could do much more, and that its millions of dollars in arms sales to Sudan feed the continuing violence. "They've taken some action, but not nearly enough," says Meixner of the Save Darfur Coalition. "They sent engineers to UNAMID, but they're kind of milking that. I look at that as China's having kept these engineers in their back pocket until right before the Olympics."

More meaningful, he says, would be an immediate halt or reduction in China's arms sales to Sudan. According to Amnesty International, China sold Sudan $24 million worth of arms and ammunition in 2005, plus $59 million worth of parts and aircraft equipment.[53]

In March 2005, the U.N. banned the sale of weapons to any combatants for use in Darfur.[54] But earlier this year the BBC reported that China had been providing trucks being used by the Sudanese military in Darfur. China admitted that 212 trucks were exported to Sudan in 2005 but said all were for civilian use and were only later equipped with guns in a defensive move by the government to stave off rebel attacks.[55]

"The Western media and in particular the activities of some nongovernmental organizations have caused China's role to be distorted," said China's Special Envoy to Darfur, Liu Guijin.[56]

China, which repeatedly has opposed or abstained from U.N. votes to sanction or condemn Sudan's actions in Darfur, says diplomacy and humanitarian support are the best path to peace. It has expressed "great concern" over the ICC prosecutor's request for an arrest warrant against Bashir and is considering supporting an effort to delay further action by the court.[57]

Some say such "subtle diplomacy" has persuaded Sudan to reduce military attacks in Darfur and improved conditions for civilians. Former U.S. Envoy Natsios told a

Senate hearing last year that Beijing complemented rather than undercut Washington's sanctions-based policy and said China had convinced Sudan to accept UNAMID peacekeepers. "There has been a lot of China-bashing in the West, and I'm not sure, to be very frank with you, that . . . it's very helpful," he told the committee.[58]

Others say that while China is a powerful player in Sudanese affairs, Beijing alone cannot be blamed for the continuing violence. "The finger is pointed first at the Sudan government, and then China . . . and then many other countries," says *Africa Confidential's* Lusk.

John Prendergast, co-chair of the anti-genocide ENOUGH Project, agreed. "Unless China and the U.S. are both exerting much more pressure on Sudan, the crisis will continue to spiral out of control," he said. "China has unique economic leverage, while the U.S. retains leverage based on its ability to confer or withdraw legitimacy."[59]

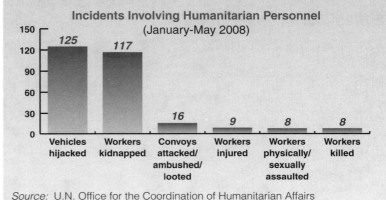

Aid Workers Face Danger

Eight humanitarian workers in Darfur were killed and 117 kidnapped within the first five months of 2008. Rising lawlessness has made parts of Darfur inaccessible to the 17,000 aid workers stationed in Darfur to help the more than 4 million people affected by the ongoing fighting between government and rebel forces, militia attacks and inter-tribal fighting.

Incidents Involving Humanitarian Personnel (January-May 2008)

Vehicles hijacked	125
Workers kidnapped	117
Convoys attacked/ambushed/looted	16
Workers injured	9
Workers physically/sexually assaulted	8
Workers killed	8

Source: U.N. Office for the Coordination of Humanitarian Affairs

BACKGROUND

Ostrich Feathers, Ivory and Slaves

The name Darfur comes from the Arabic word "dar," meaning home, and the name of the principal ethnic group of the region, the non-Arab Fur. For centuries, however, Darfur has been home to a wide range of people — both Arab and non-Arab. Darfur is at the crossroads of Africa and the Middle East, and Islamic traders as well as pilgrims traveling to Mecca have long traversed the province — leaving their cultural and religious imprint.[60] Today, around 90 percent of all Darfuris are Muslim.[61] After generations of intermarriage between Arabs and non-Arabs, it is nearly impossible to discern the ethnic ancestry of the people of Darfur, other than through cultural traditions: "Arabs" tend to be nomadic and "non-Arabs" tend to be farmers. Blurring the lines even further, it is not uncommon for people to call themselves Arab one day and non-Arab another.[62]

Around 1650, a Fur sultanate was established, and the region became a prosperous trading center for such goods as ostrich feathers, ivory and black slaves.[63] Over the next two centuries, the sultanate spread across 80 percent of the area known today as Darfur, encompassing 40 to 90 different ethnic groups or tribes.[64] The sultanate was considered one of the region's most powerful kingdoms, wholly separate in culture and heritage from the rest of modern-day Sudan.

In 1899, Egypt and Britain — which had occupied Egypt since 1882 — assumed joint authority over Sudan with the British taking the South and Egyptians taking the North. Even before Sudan came under joint control, Egyptian rulers had for decades occupied northern Sudan, amassing great wealth, largely from kidnapping black Africans from the South and selling them into slavery. Southern resentment against the North for the brutal slave trade remains today.[65]

Sudan's division between Britain and Egypt set the stage for the clashing cultures and religions that would later lead to the Sudanese civil war that raged for more than 20 years. The Egyptian North — with a higher concentration of Arabic population — was predominantly Islamic, while those in the South were animists or

CHRONOLOGY

1899-1956 *Colonization sows seeds of poverty and division.*

1899 Britain takes control of mostly Christian southern Sudan; Egypt takes the predominantly Muslim north.

1916 Sudan annexes Darfur.

1956 Britain and Egypt turn control of Sudan over to northern Arab elites.

1957-Early '70s *Multiple coups switch control of Sudan between military and civilian governments; Darfur remains neglected as civil war rages in the east.*

1964 Civilians overthrow Sudan's military government.

1965 Chadian fighters establish bases in Darfur after civil war breaks out in neighboring Chad.

1969 Gen. Jaafar al-Nimeiri takes control of Sudan in military coup.

1972 Sudan's civil war ends when peace agreement is signed in Addis Ababa.

Late '70s-'80s *Darfur serves as staging ground for Chadian rebels; Libya arms Darfuri rebels; rising Islamic extremism sparks renewed civil war in eastern Sudan; famine and drought devastate Darfur.*

1976 Libyan-backed Darfuri rebels attack Khartoum, are defeated. Government tracks down and kills alleged sympathizers in Darfur.

1983 Nimeiri imposes sharia law and nullifies peace agreement, triggering new civil war in eastern Sudan.

1984 Drought devastates Darfur; Arabs and non-Arabs fight over land, water.

1985 Civilian uprising overthrows Nimeiri.

1989-1999 *Civil war intensifies; U.S.-Sudanese tensions increase.*

1989 Gen. Omar Hassan al-Bashir seizes power, embraces militant Islam and hosts al Qaeda's Osama bin Laden.

1993 U.S. lists Sudan as a state sponsor of terrorism.

1996 Sudan expels bin Laden under U.S. pressure.

1997 China agrees to build oil refinery in Khartoum, becomes Sudan's leading weapons supplier.

1998 U.S. bombs Khartoum pharmaceutical factory, claiming it produces chemical weapons, which is never proven.

2000-2005 *War breaks out in Darfur. U.S. says genocide is occurring in Darfur. Civil war in eastern Sudan ends.*

2001 President George W. Bush appoints former Sen. John C. Danforth, R-Mo., as special envoy to Sudan to try to settle the civil war.

2003 Darfur rebels attack North Darfur's capital, marking start of war in Darfur. A cease-fire is reached in the civil war between northern and southern Sudan.

2004 U.S. House of Representatives labels the fighting in Darfur as "genocide." . . . U.N. imposes arms embargo on Darfur and endorses deployment of African Union (AU) peacekeepers.

2005 Sudan's 20-year civil war in the east ends with signing of peace accord.

2006-Present *Darfuri peace deal dissolves; rebel groups splinter; peacekeepers fail to control chaos.*

2006 Darfur Peace Agreement is signed by government and one rebel group.

2007 U.N. creates joint U.N.-AU peacekeeping force.

2008 During run-up to Beijing Olympics, human-rights activists accuse China of abetting genocide in Darfur. . . . International Criminal Court considers indicting Bashir for genocide and war crimes.

Christians. British missionaries were dispatched to spread the Christian faith in the South.

In 1916, Darfur was annexed by Sudan, merging two states with vastly different cultures and political structures.[66] "There was the problem of differential integration: Darfur is not the Sudan," says Gerard Prunier, author of the book *Darfur: The Ambiguous Genocide.* "Darfur was the easternmost sultanate in Africa, not part of the Nile Valley" as is the rest of Sudan.

And the colonial authorities did nothing to help integrate Darfur into their new state, largely ignoring the former sultanate and giving various tribes semi-autonomous rule over their individual lands. But tribal leaders were often illiterate and corrupt and did little to help Darfur. By 1935, only four government primary schools existed in all of Darfur.[67] Health care and economic development also were non-existent under the colonial rulers, who actually boasted of keeping Darfur poor and powerless.

"We have been able to limit education to the sons of chiefs and native administration personnel," wrote Philip Ingleson, governor of Darfur from 1935 to 1944, "and we can confidently look forward to keeping the ruling classes at the top of the educational tree for many years to come."[68]

Independence and Instability

After World War II, Britain began withdrawing from Sudan and reconnecting the North and South. The British handed power over to northern Arab elites in Khartoum, which became the center of government.[69] Once again, Darfur was ignored.

"Darfur had no say whatsoever over the structure or features of an independent Sudan," Prunier says.

In fact, much of the conflict in Darfur has its roots in the post-independence history of eastern Sudan, which involved a long-running civil war between the Arab- and Muslim-dominated North and the oil-rich, Christian and animist South. Darfur also became a political pawn in strategic maneuverings by Sudan, Chad and Libya, with each country arming rebel groups in the region to further their parochial interests.

Within months of Sudan's independence in January 1956, the consolidation of power in the Arab North sparked rebellion in the South. Over the next 10 years, a series of political coups alternated the government in Khartoum between military and civilian power, as civil war continued between the North and the South. Yet successive administrations continued to ignore growing poverty and dissent in Darfur. In 1972 the military government of Gen. Jaafar Nimeiri signed a peace agreement in Addis Ababa, Ethiopia, providing substantial power- and wealth-sharing between the North and South but offering nothing to the Darfuris.

However, the North-South tensions remained, and growing conflict in neighboring Chad created even more instability in Sudan. Arab rebels from Chad who opposed their country's Christian government used Darfur as a home base for their own civil war. Libyan leader Muammar Qaddafi — hoping to create a powerful Arab belt stretching into central Africa — supported the Chadian rebels and proposed a unified Arab state between Libya and Sudan, but Nimeiri rejected the offer. Angered by Nimeiri's rejection and Sudan's agreement to end the civil war with the Christians in South Sudan, Qaddafi labeled Nimeiri a traitor to the Arab cause and began arming militant Arab organizations in Darfur who opposed the governments of both Chad and Sudan.

In 1976, Libyan-backed rebels attacked Nimeiri's government in Khartoum but were defeated in three days. The Sudanese military then hunted down and killed Darfuri civilians accused of sympathizing with the insurgents.[70]

Suddenly, after years of neglect, Darfur was getting the attention of Sudan's political leaders — but not the kind it had wanted. The ongoing violence also catapulted Darfur's various local tribes into the broader polarized conflict between "Arabs" and "non-Arabs," depending on which regime they supported.[71]

Making matters worse, a drought and famine in the early 1980s plunged Darfur deeper into poverty and desperation. For the next two decades, the nomadic "Arabs" and the farming "non-Arabs" increasingly fought over disappearing land and water resources. (*See sidebar, p. 256.*) The Arab-led government in Khartoum frequently intervened, providing arms to its nomadic Arab political supporters in Darfur, who in turn killed their farming neighbors.[72]

Another Civil War

After the failed coup by Libyan-backed Arab rebels in 1976, Nimeiri tried to appease radical Islamic groups who

Arabs Criticized for Silence on Atrocities

Islamic countries also lag in donations, troop support.

The thin, white-haired man living in a U.N. refugee camp in Chad was soft-spoken but fervent as he thanked Americans "and the free world" for the food, medicine and other donations sent to the victims of the conflict in Darfur.

But, he asked a visiting filmmaker intently, tears trickling down his face, "Where are the Arab people? I am Muslim. We receive nothing from Islamic people."[1]

While nations around the world have criticized the Arab-dominated Sudanese government for not halting the rapes and murders of Muslims in the beleaguered region, other Arab governments have been largely silent about the atrocities being committed against Muslims by other Muslims.

"The Islamic world's response to the daily killings and suffering of millions of Muslims in Darfur has been largely silent — from both civil society as well as the institutions and majority of Islamic governments," said the newly formed Arab Coalition for Darfur, representing human-rights groups from 12 Muslim countries. "The Islamic world must decide to end its wall of silence, before it is too late."[2] The coalition made its statement in June before the Organization of the Islamic Conference, an intergovernmental organization of 57 Muslim nations.

Moreover, among the world's Arab governments — many of them awash in petrodollars — only the United Arab Emirates (UAE) earmarked any money ($100,000) specifically for aid to Darfur this year.* The rest of the international community donated more than $100 million,

according to ReliefWeb, run by the U.N. Office for the Coordination of Humanitarian Affairs, including $28 million from the European Commission and $12 million from the United States.[3]

Moreover, only 587 of the 12,000 U.N. peacekeepers in Darfur have come from nations belonging to the 22-member Arab League. Of those, 508 were from Egypt, and the rest came from Jordan, Mauritania, Yemen and Libya.[4]

Amjad Atallah, senior director for international policy and advocacy with the Save Darfur Coalition, charges that the Arab League is more worried about protecting Arab leaders than about representing ordinary Arabs. "They seem to have a more compelling need to come to the defense of Arab states than for the people suffering under the regimes," says Atallah.

For its part, the Arab League did help convince Sudan to allow peacekeepers from the joint U.N.-AU peacekeeping mission into Darfur. And in 2004, an Arab League Commission of Inquiry into Darfur publicly condemned military attacks against civilians as "massive violations of human rights." But after Sudan complained, the statement was removed from the Arab League Web site.[5]

And in July, when the International Criminal Court prosecutor sought to indict Sudanese President Omar Hassan al-Bashir for genocide and war crimes, the Arab League expressed "solidarity with the Republic of Sudan in confronting schemes that undermine its sovereignty, unity and stability." The group said the charges would undermine ongoing negotiations to stop the violence in Darfur, and that Sudan's legal system was the appropriate place to investigate abuses in Darfur.[6] The league turned down several requests to be interviewed for this article.

---

* The UAE and Saudi Arabia, however, did contribute a total of $44 million to Sudan as a whole — about 3 percent of the $1.3 billion contributed to Sudan by the international community.

felt he was disloyal to the dream of a united Arab front. He named leading Islamist opposition leaders to important government posts, including extremist Hassan al-Turabi as attorney general.[73]

The discovery of oil in Southern Sudan in the late 1970s added to the pressure from the increasingly Islamic government to back away from the Addis Ababa peace agreement, because the Arab authorities in the North did not want to share the profits with the Christian South,

as the peace deal stipulated. In 1983, Nimeiri ordered the 11-year-old agreement null and void, began imposing strict Islamic law, or sharia, across the country and transformed Sudan into an Islamic state.[74] Southern opposition groups formed the Sudan People's Liberation Army (SPLA) and civil war broke out again.

In 1985 civilians overthrew Nimeiri, and hopes began to emerge for a new peace settlement. But in yet another coup in 1989, Bashir seized power with the help of the

While Arab governments have been muted in their criticism of the situation in Darfur, the citizens of Arab countries are more outspoken. According to a poll last year, a vast majority of the public in Morocco, Egypt, Saudi Arabia, the UAE, Turkey and Malaysia think their countries should do more to help Darfur. And more than three-quarters of the Muslim respondents said Arabs and Muslims should be as concerned about the situation in Darfur as they are about the Arab-Israeli conflict.

"The poll shatters the myth that Arabs and Muslims don't care about Darfur," said James Zogby, president of the Arab American Institute, which commissioned the poll. "While they fault news coverage for not being extensive enough, Arabs and Muslims feel compelled by the images and stories they see coming out of Darfur. The poll clearly illustrates a great degree of concern among Muslims, even rivaling that of another longstanding issue to Arabs and Muslims, the Arab-Israel conflict."[7]

Last year, the institute launched an Arabic-language television advertising campaign calling for increased action to help the people of Darfur. The commercial, which featured first-hand accounts in Arabic from victims of the violence in Darfur, concluded by saying, "Palestine, Lebanon, Iraq — Darfur. We must pray for them all."[8]

Getty Images/Marco DiLauro

Darfuri refugees pray at an improvised mosque in a refugee camp in Chad. Arab governments have been largely silent about the Muslim-on-Muslim violence in Darfur and have contributed little aid to the victims.

[1] Quoted from "The Devil Came on Horseback" documentary film, Break Thru Films, 2007.

[2] "Arab Panel Scolds Islamic World for Darfur Silence," Agence France-Press, June 20, 2008, http://news.yahoo.com/s/afp/20080620/wl_mideast_afp/sudandarfurunrestrightsislamoic_080620190222. The coalition represents human-rights groups from Egypt, Jordan, Bahrain, Algeria, Iraq, Yemen, Syria, Libya, Mauritania, Kuwait, Saudi Arabia and the Palestinian territories.

[3] "Sudan 2008: List of all commitments/contributions and pledges as of 18 August 2008," U.N. Office for the Coordination of Humanitarian Affairs, http://ocha.unog.ch/fts/reports/daily/ocha_R10_E15391_asof__08081816.pdf.

[4] "UN Mission's Contributions by Country," United Nations, June 2008, www.un.org/Depts/dpko/dpko/contributors/2008/jun08_5.pdf.

[5] Nadim Hasbani, "About The Arab Stance Vis-à-vis Darfur," *Al-Hayat*, March 21, 2007, International Crisis Group, www.crisisgroup.org/home/index.cfm?id=4722.

[6] "Arab League Backs Sudan on Genocide Charges," The Associated Press, July 19, 2008, http://www.usatoday.com/news/world/2008-07-19-Sudan_N.htm.

[7] "Majorities in six countries surveyed believe Muslims should be equally concerned about Darfur as the Arab-Israeli conflict," Arab American Institute, press release, April 30, 2007, www.aaiusa.org/press-room/2949/aaizogby-poll-muslims-across-globe-concerned-about-crisis-in-darfur.

[8] "AAI Launches Darfur Ads Aimed at Arabic-Speaking International Community," Arab American Institute, press release, Jan. 8, 2007, www.aaiusa.org/press-room/2702/aai-launches-darfur-ads-aimed-at-arabic-speaking-international-community.

National Islamic Front (NIF) and its leader, former Attorney General Turabi.[75]

Then-Gen. Bashir and the NIF embraced militant Islam and welcomed foreign jihadists, including Osama bin Laden. In 1993, the United States added Sudan to its list of state sponsors of terrorism, and President Bill Clinton imposed economic sanctions against Sudan in 1996 and 1997. In 1998, after U.S. embassies were bombed in Kenya and Tanzania, the United States bombed a Khartoum pharmaceutical factory claiming it was producing chemical weapons. The allegation was never proven.[76]

Meanwhile, Bashir and the NIF launched a bloody counterinsurgency against the South, which became one of the deadliest wars in modern history. An estimated 2 million people died before the fighting ended in 2003. At least one out of every five Southern Sudanese died in the fighting or from disease and famine caused by the

Human-rights advocates in London call on the international community to stop the violence in Darfur. The conflict erupted in 2003, when ethnic Africans in western Sudan took up arms against the central government in Khartoum, accusing it of marginalizing them and monopolizing resources.

war. Four million people — nearly 80 percent of the Southern Sudanese population — were forced to flee their homes.[77]

Throughout the war, China sold arms to Sudan, and in 1997 China — whose domestic oil-production capacity had peaked — agreed to build an oil refinery near Khartoum and a massive pipeline from southern Sudan to Port Sudan on the Red Sea in the north.[78] Bashir declared that the "era of oil production" had begun in Sudan and that the country would soon become economically self-sufficient despite the U.S. sanctions.[79]

Darfur Erupts

Darfur, meanwhile, was suffering from economic neglect, and numerous non-Arab tribes faced repression from government-supported militias. In 2000, the non-Arabs began to fight back, especially after the so-called *Black Book* circulated across the region describing how a small group of ethnic northern tribes had dominated Sudan since independence, at the expense of the rest of the country — especially Darfur.

"When we were writing the book, we were not thinking of rebellion. We wanted to achieve our aims by democratic and peaceful means," said Idris Mahmoud Logma, one of authors and a member of the rebel Justice and Equality Movement. "Later, we realized the regime would only listen to guns."[80]

But international attention remained focused on peace prospects between the North and South, overshadowing

the book's impact. The first peace talks began in Nairobi, Kenya, in January 2000. At about the same time, Bashir pushed his former ally, the radical Islamist Turabi, out of power — a move away from religious extremism in the view of the international community.[81]

In 2001, President Bush dispatched former Sen. John C. Danforth, R-Mo., as a special envoy to Sudan to help bring the North and South toward a peace agreement.[82] Just days after the appointment, terrorists attacked the World Trade Center and the Pentagon, prompting Sudan to cooperate with the United States to avoid retaliatory strikes. The two countries soon began sharing intelligence on terrorists, including information about al Qaeda, bin Laden's terrorist organization.[83]

For the next 18 months, as peace negotiators debated splitting wealth and power between the North and South, they never considered sharing any of the pie with Darfur. Moreover, an international community focused on ending the civil war ignored the increasing repression in Darfur and the rebel groups preparing to fight.

In April 2003, just months before a North-South ceasefire was signed in Naivasha, Kenya, Darfuri rebels attacked the airport in El-Fashir, the capital of North Darfur, killing 30 government soldiers and blowing up aircraft. Rebels killed more than 1,000 Sudanese soldiers in the following months.[84]

"The Darfuris saw they had no shot at being part of the process," says Prendergast of the ENOUGH Project. "Leaving these guys out helped reinforce their desire to go to war. Darfur was completely ignored during the first term of the Bush administration, allowing Khartoum to conclude it could do whatever it wanted to in Darfur."

Indeed, Khartoum counterattacked, enlisting the brute force of the desperately poor Arab *janjaweed* militias the government had armed years earlier to settle internal land disputes. Over the next two years, up to 400,000 people died in the conflict by some estimates, and nearly 2.4 million people were displaced.[85] Civilian populations primarily from the Fur, Zaghawa, and Masalit ethnic groups — the same ethnicities as most of the rebel SLA/M and JEM groups — were the main targets.

Through most of the early fighting, global attention remained focused on negotiations to stop the North-South civil war, which officially ended in January 2005 when the government and the SPLA signed the Comprehensive Peace Agreement.

But by then Darfur had already spun out of control. The U.N. human rights coordinator for Sudan the previous April had described the situation in Darfur as "the world's greatest humanitarian crisis," adding "the only difference between Rwanda and Darfur is the numbers involved."[86] Human rights and religious groups had launched a media and lobbying campaign demanding that the international community act. In July 2004, the U.S. House of Representatives called the violence in Darfur "genocide."

A few days later, the U.N. passed its first resolution on Darfur, imposing an arms embargo on militias in the region and threatening sanctions against the government if it did not end the *janjaweed* violence. It also endorsed the deployment of African Union peacekeeping troops.[87] The resolution, the first of a dozen the U.N. would pass regarding Darfur over the next four years, was approved by the Security Council with 13 votes and two abstentions — from China and Pakistan.[88]

"What they've done is produce a lot of pieces of paper," says Brewer, of Human Rights Watch. "But they haven't been reinforced. Khartoum has played a very clever game. They stop aggression just long enough for the international community to look away, and then they start all over again."

Over the past four years rebel groups and Sudanese officials have agreed to a variety of ceasefires and settlements, which one or all sides eventually broke. The most recent — the Darfur Peace Agreement — was reached in May 2006, but only the government and one faction of the SLA/M signed the deal; JEM and another SLA/M faction refused to participate.[89] The SLA/M soon splintered into more than a dozen smaller groups, and fighting grew even worse.[90]

The African Union peacekeepers — under constant attack from rebels and bandits — proved ineffective. So in 2006, the U.N. voted to send international troops to bolster the AU mission. Bashir initially blocked the proposal as a "violation of Sudan's sovereignty and a submission by Sudan to outside custodianship."[91]

But after extended negotiations with China, the AU and the U.N., Bashir finally agreed. In July 2007, the Security Council unanimously voted to send up to 26,000 military and police peacekeepers as part of the joint U.N.-AU force. U.N. Secretary-General Ban heralded the unanimous vote as "historic and unprecedented" and said the mission would "make a clear and positive difference."[92]

But just three months before the peacekeepers began arriving in January 2008, hundreds of rebels in 30 armed trucks attacked a peacekeeping base in the Darfur town of Haskanita, killing at least 10 soldiers, kidnapping dozens more and seizing supplies that included heavy weapons.

"It's indicative of the complete insecurity," said Alun McDonald, a spokesman for the Oxfam aid organization in Sudan. "These groups are attacking anybody and everybody with total impunity."[93]

CURRENT SITUATION

Indicting Bashir

The summer's Olympic Games in Beijing thrust Darfur back into international headlines. Movie stars, activists and athletes have criticized China's continued cozy relationship with the Bashir government and called on the world to stop the violence. Olympic torch-carrying ceremonies in cities around the world were interrupted by protesters complaining about China's support for Sudan and its recent crackdown on dissenters in Tibet.[94]

But even bigger news in the weeks leading up to the Games was the ICC prosecutor's effort to charge Bashir with genocide and war crimes. While the ICC is not expected to decide until later this year whether to indict and arrest Bashir, the decision could be delayed even further if the Security Council agrees with the AU and others that the indictment should be deferred. The council can defer for 12 months — and indefinitely renew the deferral — any ICC investigation or prosecution.[95]

The ICC's move was not its first against Sudanese officials. On March 31, 2005, the United Nations passed a resolution asking the ICC prosecutor to investigate allegations of crimes against humanity and war crimes in Darfur. After a 20-month investigation, the prosecutor presented his evidence to the court in February 2007 and the court agreed two months later to issue arrest warrants for Sudan's former Interior Minister Ahmad Harun and *janjaweed* leader Ali Kushayb.[96] Bashir has refused to hand over either man, and Harun has since been named head the Ministry of Humanitarian Affairs and oversees the government's activities to aid the victims of the atrocities.[97]

More Than 4.2 Million Affected by Crisis

Continued violence forced nearly 180,000 Darfuris to abandon their homes in the first five months of this year, bringing the number affected by the ongoing conflict to 4.2 million. While from 200,000 to 400,000 have been killed, nearly 2.4 million have been displaced. Many now live in U.N. camps inside Sudan — set up for so-called internally displaced persons (IDPs) — or have fled to refugee camps in neighboring Chad.

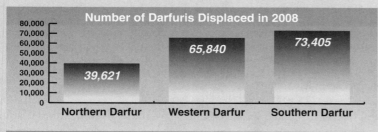

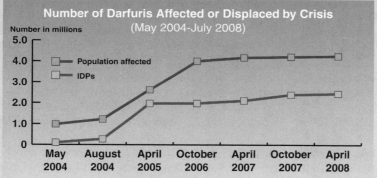

Sources: Sudan — Darfur: Humanitarian Profile, June 2, 2008, U.N. Office for the Coordination of Humanitarian Affairs; United Nations Sudan Information Gateway

This July, just days after the court's announcement about Bashir, the Sudanese president traveled to Darfur and met with 600 refugees from various tribes, including those he is accused of inflicting war crimes against. He promised to send them farming equipment and to free more than 80 rebels imprisoned last May after an attack on Khartoum's twin city Omdurman. Bashir called the prisoners "boys" and said they would be freed and pardoned — although he did not say when.[98]

Sudan also appointed its own prosecutor to investigate war crimes in Darfur and said it was sending legal teams to the region to monitor the situation. Sudan, which is not a signatory of the treaty that created the ICC, said its legal system was adequate to look into alleged abuses in Darfur and that it would pass legislation making genocide a punishable crime in Sudan.[99]

International Betrayal

Despite Secretary-General Ban's confidence in the new UNAMID peacekeeping force, deadly assaults against the mission have occurred almost non-stop. The first UNAMID peacekeeper — a civilian police inspector from Uganda — was killed in May, just four months after the new force began arriving.

On July 9, seven peacekeepers were killed and dozens more injured when their convoy was ambushed by hundreds of horsemen and 40 trucks mounted with machine guns and antiaircraft weapons. The two-hour firefight marked the first time UNAMID had to use force to protect itself, and some observers described it as being near the point of "meltdown."[100]

"The effort being achieved so far is not enough," said, Fadallah Ahmed Abdallah, a Sudanese city official in Darfur working with the peacekeepers. "Sometimes we feel UNAMID itself needs some protection, because UNAMID is not at full strength."[101]

More than a year after the UNAMID force was authorized, only a third of the 26,000 troops are on the ground, and not a single military transport or tactical helicopter among the 28 requested has been deployed to patrol the area — which is the size of France.

On July 31, the day UNAMID's mandate was to expire, the Security Council extended it for a year.[102] Meanwhile, 36 human rights groups — along with Nobel Peace Prize laureate Desmond Tutu and former President Carter — issued a report revealing that countries were not donating helicopters that are desperately needed by UNAMID to restore order.[103] The report said a handful of NATO countries and others that typically contribute aircraft to peacekeeping missions — specifically India, Ukraine, Czech Republic, Italy, Romania and Spain — could easily provide up to 70 helicopters for the mission. (*See graphic, p. 253.*)

"Many of these helicopters are gathering dust in hangars or flying in air shows when they could be saving lives in Darfur," said the report, entitled "Grounded: the International Community's Betrayal of UNAMID."[104]

"It's really shameful," says Brewer of Human Rights Watch. "But it's not just helicopters. They need water, trucks, everything. I don't know whether it's because countries don't have faith in UNAMID, or they don't want to put their troops as risk or if it's fear of being involved in something that will fail."

Brewer also blames the Sudanese government for delaying delivery of peacekeepers' equipment and refusing to accept troops from Western countries. Aside from peacekeepers, aid workers also are being targeted by rebel factions and bandits searching for food and supplies. Eight aid workers were killed in the first five months of 2008, and four times as many aid vehicles were hijacked during the first quarter of this year compared to the same period last year.[105] Armed gangs also attacked 35 humanitarian compounds during the first quarter — more than double the number during the same period last year.[106]

"We are now in the worst situation ever" — even worse than when the government-rebel conflict was at its peak, says Hafiz Mohamed, Sudan program coordinator with Justice Africa, a London-based research and human rights organization. "At least in 2004 we only had two rebel movements. Now we have more than 12 SLA factions and more than four JEM factions. Security-wise, Darfur is worse than in 2004."

In May, SLA Unity rebels arrested a dozen Sudanese government employees in Darfur gathering census information for next year's national elections. The rebels, who believe the census will be inaccurate — depriving Darfur of political representation — vowed to try the census takers in military courts as "enemies," which carries the death penalty.[107]

Rebel attacks also are increasing outside Darfur. Last year JEM — which wants to overthrow the Sudanese government — attacked government positions and kidnapped two foreign workers at a Chinese-run oil field in neighboring Kordofan province. "This is a message to China and Chinese oil companies to stop helping the

Life in the Camps

About a third of the Darfuri population has been forced to flee their homes since 2003, with many now living in refugee camps in Darfur or neighboring Chad. Conditions in the camps, like these near Nyala, are harsh. Children (bottom) attend class at a makeshift outdoor school, but about 650,000 don't attend school at all.

government with their war in Darfur," said JEM commander Abdel Aziz el-Nur Ashr.[108] JEM has said oil revenues are being used to continue the fighting in Darfur.

JEM rebels made their most audacious push against the government in May, when they reached suburban Khartoum before being repelled by Sudanese forces. Sudan immediately cut off diplomatic ties with Chad, which it accused of sponsoring the attack. Chadian officials denied any involvement but accused Sudan of launching a similar attack against their capital three months earlier.[109]

"The entire region is affected by what is happening in Darfur," says Mohamed of Justice Africa. "It's a proxy war.

An African Union (AU) peacekeeper offers bread to two women near the West Darfur town of Murnei. The women said they were raped, beaten and robbed by janjaweed militiamen when they left their refugee camp to gather firewood — a common occurrence in Darfur. After being criticized as ineffective, the AU force has been beefed up this year with 10,000 U.N. military and police peacekeepers. Another 16,000 have been authorized.

Unless we resolve the relationship between Chad and Sudan, we will not have an agreement for peace in Darfur."

Meanwhile, relations between North and South Sudan are worsening. Both sides remain deadlocked over some of the most contentious issues of the 2005 peace treaty, including how to draw the North-South border and how to split oil profits. The South has a large portion of the country's oil reserves while the North has most of the infrastructure. The South has repeatedly accused the North of not sharing oil revenue fairly, while the North has charged the South with mishandling their portion of the funds.[110]

Under the Comprehensive Peace Agreement (CPA), a referendum is scheduled for 2011 on whether the South will secede from the North. Some wonder if tensions between the two sides will hold until then.

"There are real prospects of another North-South war," says Sudan expert Moszynski. "South Sudan is spending 40 percent of their budget on military. They're preparing for the next war with the North. There are a lot of problems in Sudan. In between all of that, they're not going to sort out Darfur."

Mission Impossible?

While the U.N. has been slow to send in troops and materiel, individual governments and private organizations have provided billions of dollars' worth of food, water, housing, medicine and other humanitarian aid to Darfur and the nearby refugee camps in Chad.

In 2004, when the war between rebels and government forces was at its peak, only 230 relief workers were stationed in the region.[111] Today, there are more than 17,000 national and international aid workers from some 80 NGOs, 14 U.N. agencies and the Red Cross/Red Crescent Movement.[112]

"The humanitarian response has been incredible," providing "a staggering amount of money, a staggering number of people," says Brewer. However, she says she sometimes wonders if people are substituting aid for serious "political engagement to find a solution."

And most agree that only political engagement — coming from a unified global community — can solve the ongoing conflict.

"We need more coordinated diplomacy. We can't have different messages coming from France, China, the U.N., the U.S. and African nations," says Meixner of the Save Darfur Coalition. "Bashir can thwart one or two, but if there's a united front, including China and African nations, it's not so easy."

Specifically, he says, multilateral sanctions should be adopted. "Sudan is the test case for multilateralism," he says.

But others say "regime change" is the only viable solution. "I don't think we'll find a political solution for the Darfur crisis if the current government stays in power," says Mohamed of Justice Africa. "Since 1997 we've had six agreements, the CPA, the DPA. This regime will never honor any agreement. . . . If [the international community] managed to overthrow the regime, there is the possibility of a permanent solution."

But Alex de Waal, a program director at the Social Science Research Council in New York and author of *Darfur: A Short History of a Long War*, says global and Arab anger sparked by the Iraq War leaves "zero chance" that the international community will launch any military action against another Muslim country.

However, Obama foreign affairs adviser Rice — a former Clinton-era State Department official — said the U.N. should not let the experience in Iraq deter military action. "Some will reject any future U.S. military action, especially against an Islamic regime, even if purely to halt genocide against Muslim civilians," Rice told a Senate committee in April 2007. "Sudan has also threatened that

AT ISSUE

Would military intervention solve the crisis in Darfur?

YES
Hafiz Mohamed
Sudan Program Coordinator,
Justice Africa

Written for *CQ Global Researcher*, August 2008

The current crisis in Darfur has claimed more than 200,000 lives and displaced millions — due primarily to the Sudanese government's counterinsurgency policy, which uses the *janjaweed* as proxy fighters and bombs villages with government aircraft.

Despite more than 16 U.N. Security Council resolutions and authorization of a joint U.N.-African Union peacekeeping mission in Darfur (UNAMID), the mass killing and displacement of civilians continues. The parties to the conflict have signed many cease-fire agreements since 2004, but all of them have been violated, and even the mechanisms for monitoring the cease-fires have failed. Early last month, peacekeepers were attacked in Darfur, primarily because they were outmanned and outgunned. No country has provided them even with helicopters.

Hardliners within Sudan's National Congress Party still believe in a military solution to the crisis and use any means to defeat the Darfuri armed movements. All their rhetoric about being committed to a peaceful solution is just for public opinion and not a genuine endeavor to achieve a peaceful settlement to the conflict. They will only accept peace if they are pressured to do so or feel the war is unwinable.

The regime is in its weakest position since taking power in 1989 and will only cave when it feels threatened. For example, after the International Criminal Court prosecutor initiated proceedings recently to indict the Sudanese president, the government began mobilizing the public to support the president and seek a peaceful resolution.

There is strong evidence that military intervention is needed to stop the killing of civilians and force the Sudanese government to seriously seek a peaceful solution for the crisis. This could start by imposing a no-fly zone on Darfur, which would prevent the government from using its air force to bomb villages and give air support to the *janjaweed*'s attacks; the normal sequences for the attacks on the villages is to start an attack from the air by using the government bombers or helicopter machine guns, followed by attacks by militia riding horses or camels.

A no-fly zone will stop this, and many lives will be saved. The no-fly zone can start by using the European forces based in neighbouring Chad. The UNAMID forces then can be used to monitor movement on the ground and intervene when necessary to stop the ground attacks on villages.

NO
Imani Countess
Senior Director for Public
Affairs, TransAfrica Forum

Written for *CQ Global Researcher*, August 2008

For the sake of the 2 million displaced peoples and 200,000 killed, the international community should mount a military force that would protect and restore the dignity and livelihoods to those raped, tortured and maimed by the Sudanese government. But whatever peace comes to Sudan will be the result of those who brought the issue to the world stage: Darfurians supported by millions around the globe who are standing in the breach created by the failures and inaction of the nations of the world.

Truth be told, not one major military or economic power is willing to expend the political capital required to solve the crisis in Darfur.

For the United States, Darfur has become "collateral damage" in the global war on terror. The administration states that genocide is occurring, yet it continues to share intelligence with key Sudanese officials implicated in the tragedy in Darfur — sacrificing thousands of Darfuri lives in exchange for intelligence and extraditions of suspected terrorists.

Other Western nations provide plenty of rhetoric and limited sanctions. But they have failed miserably where it counts: providing adequate support for the joint African Union-U.N. peacekeeping force in Darfur. According to AfricaFocus, UNAMID is "understaffed, underequipped, underfunded and vulnerable to attacks." The U.N. authorized up to 19,555 military personnel for the mission, plus 6,432 police and more than 5,000 civilians. But so far fewer than 8,000 troops and 2,000 police have been deployed, along with just over 1,000 civilians. Critical equipment is lacking, and more than half of the $1.3 billion budget was unpaid as of the end of April.

For the international community as a whole — particularly China and India — continued access to Sudan's oil is the major interest.

If military intervention is not the answer, then what will work? Continued pressure from below. In the United States, the Bush administration was compelled to name the crisis "genocide" because of pressure from faith-based, human-rights and social-justice groups. Across the country, divestment activity — modeled after the anti-apartheid campaigns of the 1970s and '80s — has forced U.S. monies out of Sudan. The transnational human-rights movement will continue to pressure governments, businesses and multilateral institutions to move beyond rhetoric to effective human-centered engagement.

al Qaeda will attack non-African forces in Darfur — a possibility, since Sudan long hosted bin Laden and his businesses. Yet, to allow another state to deter the U.S. by threatening terrorism would set a terrible precedent. It would also be cowardly and, in the face of genocide, immoral."[113]

Meanwhile, the U.N. has unsuccessfully tried to resurrect peace talks between the Bashir government and rebel groups. Talks in Libya were called off last October after rebel factions refused to participate.[114]

"The last six months have seen some very negative developments," former U.N. Special Envoy Eliasson said upon his resignation in June. If the international community's energy is not mobilized to halt the fighting, he continued, "we risk a major humanitarian disaster again. The margins of survival are so slim for the people of Darfur."[115] The U.N. could start showing its commitment, he said, by stationing his replacement full time in Sudan. Eliasson had been headquartered in Stockholm.

The new U.N. special envoy, Burkino Faso's foreign minister Djibril Bassole, is hopeful. "This will be a difficult mission," he said after his first visit to Sudan in July. "But it's not mission impossible."[116]

OUTLOOK

Bleak Future

As unstable and violent as the past four years have been for Darfur, the next three could be even more tumultuous — for the entire country.

Under Comprehensive Peace Agreement provisions, elections must be held next year — the first in 23 years. In preparation Sudan conducted its first census since 1993 earlier this year, but many doubt that either the census results — or the vote count — will be accurate.[117]

Displaced Darfuris in refugee camps don't trust the government to take an accurate headcount. Indeed, the huge numbers of displaced persons seem to make both an accurate census and democratic elections nearly impossible.

"It's hard to see how elections can take place in a fair and free way in Darfur," says Lusk of *Africa Confidential*. "Half the people are dead, and the other half are in camps."

"The [displaced] people are concerned that if they register to vote while living in the camps, . . . they will lose their land," says Brewer. "There is great lack of clarity in land law."

Some wonder if the Bashir government will back out of the elections altogether, but Sudanese officials insist the polling will be held. "Rebels said the census should not take place, but it did take place," says Mubarak of the Sudanese Embassy in London. "The elections will go ahead."

But elections will at best do little to help the people of Darfur and at worst prompt further violence from those who oppose the results, say some observers. "The elections will have no impact on Darfur — if they happen," says former U.S. Rep. Howard Wolpe, D-Mich., who directs Africa programs at the Woodrow Wilson Center. "At the end of the day, elections have no impact . . . if you haven't built a sense of cohesion or a way of moving forward."

After the elections, the Sudanese people must brace themselves for another potential upheaval — caused by a planned 2011 referendum on Sudanese unity. While the South appears ready to vote for secession, many say Khartoum will never let that happen.

Others say secession could spell dark times for Darfur. "If the South secedes, [Bashir's National Congress Party] will have greater power in the North, and that is worse for Darfur," says Brewer. "If they vote for power sharing, it could be good for Darfur."

Meanwhile, all eyes are waiting to see whether the ICC will give in to pressure to defer action on Bashir's indictment and how Bashir and the rebel groups will respond to either an indictment or a delay.

The November U.S. presidential election could also bring about some changes. Both McCain and Obama have said they will pursue peace and security for Darfur with "unstinting resolve." And Obama's running mate, Foreign Relations Committee Chairman Biden, was unequivocal last year when he advocated U.S. military intervention. "I would use American force now," Biden said during hearings before his panel in April 2007. "It's time to put force on the table and use it." Biden, who had also pushed for NATO intervention to halt anti-Muslim genocide in Bosnia in the 1990s, said 2,500 U.S. troops could "radically change" the situation on the ground in Darfur. "Let's stop the bleeding. I think it's a moral imperative."[118]

Given the uncertainties of the Sudanese elections, the growing North-South acrimony, the continued fighting between Chad and Sudan and the upcoming ICC decision, most experts say it is nearly impossible to predict what will happen in Darfur in the future.

"Even five years is too far to predict what will happen," says author Prunier. "You have to take it in steps. First look at what happens in 2009, then what happens leading up to the referendum, then what happens after that."

Most agree, however, that whatever future lies ahead for Darfur, it will likely be bleak.

"Sudanese politics is like the British weather: unpredictable from day to day but with a drearily consistent medium-term outlook," de Waal of the Social Science Research Council wrote recently. "There are few happy endings in Sudan. It's a country of constant turbulence, in which I have come to expect only slow and modest improvement. Sometimes I dream of being wrong."[119]

NOTES

1. "They Shot at Us as We Fled: Government Attacks on Civilians in West Darfur," Human Rights Watch, May 2008, p. 18, www.hrw.org/reports/2008/darfur0508/.

2. *Ibid.*, p. 19.

3. *Ibid.*, p. 2.

4. "Darfur Crisis: Death Estimates Demonstrate Severity of Crisis, but Their Accuracy and Credibility Could Be Enhanced," Government Accountability Office, November 2006, pp. 1-2, 7. The U.S. State Department puts the death toll for the period 2003-2005 at between 98,000 and 181,000.

5. "Sudan — Darfur: Humanitarian Profile," United Nations Office for the Coordination of Humanitarian Affairs, June 2, 2008, www.unsudanig.org/library/mapcatalogue/darfur/data/dhnp/Map%201226%20Darfur%20Humanitarian%20Profile%20June%203%202008.pdf.

6. *Ibid.*

7. Sarah El Deeb, "UN warns of bad year in Darfur," The Associated Press, June 22, 2008, www.newsvine.com/_news/2008/06/16/1581306-un-warns-of-bad-year-in-darfur.

8. "Darfur faces potential food crisis unless action taken now, warn UN agencies," UN News Centre, United Nations, June 23, 2008, www.un.org/apps/news/story.asp?NewsID=27114&Cr=darfur&Cr1=.

9. "Darfur 2007: Chaos by Design," Human Rights Watch, September 2007, p. 20.

10. El Deeb, *op. cit.*

11. "Darfur faces potential food crisis," *op. cit.*

12. "Almost Half of All Darfur Children Not in School, Says NGO," BBC Monitoring International Reports, Feb. 29, 2008.

13. Stephanie McCrummen, "A Wide-Open Battle For Power in Darfur," *The Washington Post*, June 20, 2008, p. A1, www.washingtonpost.com/wp-dyn/content/article/2008/06/19/AR2008061903552_pf.html.

14. Quoted from "The Devil Came on Horseback" documentary, Break Thru Films, 2007.

15. Julie Flint and Alex de Waal, *Darfur: A Short History of a Long War* (2005), p. 10.

16. Colum Lynch and Nora Boustany, "Sudan Leader To Be Charged With Genocide," *The Washington Post*, July 11, 2008, p. A1, www.washingtonpost.com/wp-dyn/content/article/2008/07/10/AR2008071003109.html. Also see Kenneth Jost, "International Law," *CQ Researcher*, Dec. 17, 2004, pp. 1049-1072.

17. Quoted in Hussein Solomon, "ICC pressure shows some result; An arrest warrant for Sudan's President Al-Bashir has resulted in a flurry of activity for change in Darfur," *The Star* (South Africa), Aug. 21, 2008, p. 14.

18. "Court Seeks Arrest of Sudan's Beshir for 'genocide,'" Agence France-Presse, July 14, 2008.

19. For background, see Sarah Glazer, "Stopping Genocide," *CQ Researcher*, Aug. 27, 2004, pp. 685-708.

20. For background, see Karen Foerstel, "China in Africa," *CQ Global Researcher*, January 2008, pp. 1-26.

21. Alexa Olesen, "China Appoints Special Envoy for Darfur," The Associated Press, May 11, 2007; "China paper decries Sudan's Bashir arrest move,"

Reuters, July 17, 2008; "China boosts peacekeepers in Darfur," Agence France-Presse, July 17, 2008, http://afp.google.com/article/ALeqM5jxVo9_9z2jJm2wxZW65dyP8CflEw.

22. Neil MacFarquhar, "Why Darfur Still Bleeds," *The New York Times*, July 13, 2008, www.nytimes.com/2008/07/13/weekinreview/13macfarquhar.html.

23. "Darfur's Political Process in 'Troubled State of Affairs,' " U.N. Security Council press release, June 24, 2008, www.un.org/News/Press/docs/2008/sc9370.doc.htm.

24. Glazer, *op. cit.*, p. 687.

25. Neela Banerjee, "Muslims' Plight in Sudan Resonates with Jews in U.S.," *The New York Times*, April 30, 2006, www.nytimes.com/2006/04/30/us/30rally.html.

26. Alan Cooperman, "Evangelicals Urge Bush to Do More for Sudan," *The Washington Post*, Aug. 3, 2004, p. A13, www.washingtonpost.com/wp-dyn/articles/A35223-2004Aug2.html.

27. Glenn Kessler and Colum Lynch, "U.S. Calls Killings in Sudan Genocide," *The Washington Post*, Sept. 10, 2004, p. A1, www.washingtonpost.com/wp-dyn/articles/A8364-2004Sep9.html.

28. "The Crisis in Darfur: Secretary Colin L. Powell, Written Remarks Before the Senate Foreign Relations Committee," Secretary of State press release, Sept. 9, 2004.

29. "Security Council Declares Intention to Consider Sanctions to Obtain Sudan's Full Compliance With Security, Disarmament Obligations in Darfur," U.N. Security Council press release, Sept. 18, 2004, www.un.org/News/Press/docs/2004/sc8191.doc.htm.

30. Opheera McDoom, "Statesmen Say Darfur Violent and Divided," Reuters, Oct. 4, 2007, http://africa.reuters.com/wire/news/usnMCD351991.html.

31. "UN Report: Darfur Not Genocide," CNN.com, Feb. 1, 2005, http://edition.cnn.com/2005/WORLD/africa/01/31/sudan.report/. See also Marc Lacey, "In Darfur, Appalling Atrocity, but Is That Genocide?" *The New York Times*, July 23, 2004, p. 3, http://query.nytimes.com/gst/fullpage.html?res=9B04E0DC163DF930A15754C0A9629C8B63.

32. Hillary Rodham Clinton, John McCain and Barack Obama, "Presidential Candidates' Statement on Darfur," May 28, 2008, www.cfr.org/publication/16359/presidential_candidates_statement_on_darfur.html?breadcrumb=%2Fregion%2F197%2Fsudan.

33. George Gedda, "Biden Calls for Military Force in Darfur," The Associated Press, April 11, 2007.

34. Susan E. Rice, "The Escalating Crisis in Darfur," testimony before the U.S. House Committee on Foreign Affairs, Feb. 8, 2007, www.brookings.edu/testimony/2007/0208africa_rice.aspx.

35. Opheera McDoom, "Analysis — Darfur Scares European Investors Off Sudan's Oil," Reuters, Aug. 3, 2007. One barrel of oil produces 42 gallons of gasoline. Also see Energy Information Administration database, at http://tonto.eia.doe.gov/dnav/pet/pet_cons_psup_dc_nus_mbblpd_a.htm.

36. "US Sanctions on Sudan," U.S. Department of State fact sheet, April 23, 2008, www.state.gov/p/af/rls/fs/2008/103970.htm. Also see "Country Reports on Terrorism," U.S. Department of State, April 30, 2007, Chapter 3, www.state.gov/s/ct/rls/crt/2006/82736.htm.

37. "Situation in Darfur, The Sudan: Summary of the Case," International Criminal Court, July 14, 2008, www.icc-cpi.int/library/organs/otp/ICC-OTP-Summary-20081704-ENG.pdf.

38. Colum Lynch and Nora Boustany, "Sudan Leader To Be Charged With Genocide," *The Washington Post*, July 10, 2008.

39. *Ibid.*

40. Stephanie McCrummen and Nora Boustany, "Sudan Vows to Fight Charges of Genocide Against Its Leader," *The Washington Post*, July 14, 2008, www.washingtonpost.com/wp-dyn/content/article/2008/07/14/AR2008071400112_pf.html.

41. Mohamed Osman, "Sudan Rejects Genocide Charges Against President," The Associated Press, July 14, 2008.

42. Anita Powell, "AU to Seek Delay in al-Bashir Indictment," The Associated Press, July 21, 2008.

43. Opheera McDoom, "Darfur Rebels Condemn AU on ICC Warrant," Reuters, July 22, www.alertnet.org/thenews/newsdesk/L22832812.htm.

44. Andrew Natsios, "A Disaster in the Making," The Social Science Research Council, Making Sense of Darfur blog, July 12, 2008, www.ssrc.org/blogs/darfur/2008/07/12/a-disaster-in-the-making/.

45. "Media Stakeout with Ambassador Zalmay Khalilzad," Federal News Service, July 22, 2008.

46. Foerstel, *op. cit.*, pp. 7, 13. Also see "Sudan," *Political Handbook of the World*, CQ Press (2008).

47. Danna Harman, "Activists Press China With 'Genocide Olympics' Label," *The Christian Science Monitor*, June 26, 2007, www.csmonitor.com/2007/0626/p13s01-woaf.html.

48. "Letter to Chinese President Hu Jintao," Rep. Steven Rothman Web site, May 7, 2007, http://foreignaffairs.house.gov/press_display.asp?id=345.

49. Alexa Olesen, "China Appoints Special Envoy for Darfur," The Associated Press, May 11, 2007.

50. See Jason Qian and Anne Wu, "Playing the Blame Game in Africa," *The Boston Globe*, July 23, 2007, www.iht.com/articles/2007/07/23/opinion/edqian.php; "China boosts peacekeepers in Darfur," *op. cit.*

51. "China envoy: more humanitarian aid to Darfur," Xinhua, Feb. 26, 2008, www.chinadaily.com.cn/china/2008-02/26/content_6483392.htm.

52. Robert J. Saiget, "China says can do no more over Darfur," Agence France-Presse, June 26, 2008, http://afp.google.com/article/ALeqM5gD2S4zFfzj6CZfnluWi5Kq4eFrgw.

53. Danna Harman, "How China's Support of Sudan Shields A Regime Called 'Genocidal,'" *The Christian Science Monitor*, June 26, 2007, www.csmonitor.com/2007/0626/p01s08-woaf. html.

54. Security Council Resolution 1591, United Nations, March 29, 2005, www.un.org/Docs/sc/unsc_resolutions05.htm.

55. "China says BBC's accusation on arms sales to Sudan 'ungrounded,'" Xinhua, July 18, 2008, http://news.xinhuanet.com/english/2008-07/18/content_8570601.htm.

56. Saiget, *op. cit.*

57. Audra Ang, "China urges court to rethink Sudan arrest warrant," The Associated Press, July 15, 2008.

58. Harman, *op. cit.*

59. Lydia Polgreen, "China, in New Role, Presses Sudan on Darfur," *International Herald Tribune*, Feb. 23, 2008, www.iht.com/articles/2008/02/23/africa/23darfur.php.

60. M. W. Daly, *Darfur's Sorrows* (2007), p. 1.

61. "Crisis Shaped by Darfur's Tumultuous Past," PBS Newshour, April 7, 2006, www.pbs.org/newshour/indepth_coverage/africa/darfur/political-past.html.

62. Gerard Prunier, *Darfur: The Ambiguous Genocide* (2007), pp. 4-5.

63. Daly, *op. cit.*, p. 19.

64. Prunier, *op. cit.*, p. 10. Also see Flint and de Waal, *op. cit.*, p. 8.

65. Prunier, *op. cit*, p. 16.

66. *Ibid.*, pp. 18-19.

67. *Ibid.*, p. 30.

68. *Ibid.*

69. Don Cheadle and John Prendergast, *Not On Our Watch* (2007), p. 53.

70. Prunier, *op. cit.*, pp. 45-46.

71. *Ibid.*

72. Cheadle and Prendergast, *op. cit.*, p. 73.

73. *Ibid.*, p. 55.

74. *Ibid.*, p. 56.

75. *Ibid.*, p. 57.

76. Polgreen, *op. cit.*

77. "Sudan: Nearly 2 million dead as a result of the world's longest running civil war," The U.S. Committee for Refugees, April 2001.

78. "Sudan, Oil and Human Rights," Human Rights Watch, September 2003, www.hrw.org/reports/2003/sudan1103/index.htm; "Sudan's President Projects the Export of Oil," *Africa News*, July 13, 1998.

79. "President's Revolution Day Address," BBC Worldwide Monitoring, July 5, 1998.

80. "Crisis Shaped by Darfur's Tumultuous Past," *op. cit.*

81. Prunier, *op. cit.*, p. 88.

82. "President Appoints Danforth as Special Envoy to the Sudan," White House press release, Sept. 6,

2001, www.whitehouse.gov/news/releases/2001/09/20010906-3.html.

83. Polgreen, *op. cit.*

84. Prunier, *op. cit.*, pp. 95-96.

85. "Darfur Crisis," *op. cit.*, p. 1. Also see Sheryl Gay Stolberg, "Bush Tightens Penalties Against Sudan," *The New York Times*, May 29, 2007, www.nytimes.com/2007/05/29/world/africa/29cnd-darfur.html.

86. Gerard Prunier, "The Politics of Death in Darfur," *Current History*, May 2006, p. 196.

87. Security Council Resolution 1556, United Nations, July 30, 2004, www.un.org/Docs/sc/unsc_resolutions04.html.

88. "Security Council Demands Sudan Disarm Militias in Darfur," U.N. press release, July 30, 2004, www.un.org/News/Press/docs/2004/sc8160.doc.htm.

89. "Background Notes: Sudan," U.S. State Department press release, April 24, 2008, www.state.gov/r/pa/ei/bgn/5424.htm.

90. Scott Baldauf, "Darfur Talks Stall After Rebels Boycott," *The Christian Science Monitor*, Oct. 29, 2007, www.csmonitor.com/2007/1029/p06s01-woaf.html.

91. Lydia Polgreen, "Rebel Ambush in Darfur Kills 5 African Union Peacekeepers in Deadliest Attack on the Force," *The New York Times*, April 3, 2007.

92. "Secretary-General Urges All Parties to Remain Engaged, As Security Council Authorizes Deployment of United Nations-African Union Mission in Sudan," U.N. Security Council press release, July 31, 2007, www.un.org/News/Press/docs/2007/sgsm11110.doc.htm.

93. Jeffrey Gettleman, "Darfur Rebels Kill 10 in Peace Force," *The New York Times*, Oct. 1, 2005, www.nytimes.com/2007/10/01/world/africa/01darfur.html.

94. For background, see Brian Beary, "Separatism Movements," *CQ Global Researcher*, April 2008.

95. "Arab League Backs Recourse to UN on Sudan War Crimes," Agence France-Presse, July 21, 2008.

96. "The Situation in Darfur, the Sudan," International Criminal Court fact sheet, www.icc-cpi.int/library/organs/otp/ICC-OTP_Fact-Sheet-Darfur-20070227_en.pdf.

97. "Arrest Now!" Amnesty International fact sheet, July 17, 2007, http://archive.amnesty.org/library/Index/ENGAFR540272007?open&of=ENG-332.

98. Sarah El Deeb, "Sudan's President Pays Visit to Darfur," The Associated Press, July 24, 2008.

99. Abdelmoniem Abu Edries Ali, "Sudan Appoints Darfur Prosecutor," Agence France-Presse, Aug. 6, 2008.

100. Stephanie McCrummen, "7 Troops Killed in Sudan Ambush," *The Washington Post*, July 10, 2008, www.washingtonpost.com/wp-dyn/content/article/2008/07/09/AR2008070900843.html.

101. Jennie Matthew, "Darfur hopes dim six months into UN peacekeeping," Agence France-Presse, June 25, 2008.

102. "Security Council extends mandate of UN-AU force in Darfur," Agence France-Presse, July 31, 2008.

103. "Aid groups urge helicopters for Darfur," Agence France-Presse, July 31, 2008, http://afp.google.com/article/ALeqM5i2aYTRiEePGRmbRqVQbByF28X_RQ.

104. "Grounded: the International Community's Betrayal of UNAMID — A Joint NGO Report," p. 4, http://darfur.3cdn.net/b5b2056f1398299ffe_x9m6bt7cu.pdf.

105. "Sudan — Darfur: Humanitarian Profile," *op. cit.*

106. "Darfur Humanitarian Profile No. 31," Office of U.N. Deputy Special Representative of the U.N. Secretary-General for Sudan, April 1, 2008, p. 4, www.unsudanig.org/docs/DHP%2031_1%20April%202008_narrative.pdf.

107. Opheera McDoom, "Darfur rebels say they arrest 13 census staff," Reuters, May 4, 2008, www.reuters.com/article/homepageCrisis/idUSL04471626._CH_.2400.

108. "Darfur rebels say they kidnap foreign oil workers," Reuters, Oct. 24, 2007, www.alertnet.org/thenews/newsdesk/MCD470571.htm.

109. Shashank Bengali, "Darfur conflict stokes Chad-Sudan tensions," McClatchy-Tribune News

Service, June 14, 2008, www.mcclatchydc
.com/160/story/40518.html.

110. Jeffrey Gettleman, "Cracks in the Peace in Oil-Rich Sudan As Old Tensions Fester," *The New York Times*, Sept. 22, 2007, www.nytimes.com/2007/09/22/world/africa/22sudan.html?fta=y.

111. "Sudan — Darfur: Humanitarian Profile," *op. cit.*

112. "Darfur Humanitarian Profile No. 31," *op. cit.*, p. 6.

113. Susan E. Rice, Testimony before Senate Foreign Relations Committee, April 11, 2007.

114. "Darfur envoys end visit without date for peace talks," Agence France-Presse, April 19, 2008.

115. Steve Bloomfield, "Negotiators quit Darfur, saying neither side is ready for peace," *The Independent* (London), June 27, 2008, www.independent.co.uk/news/world/africa/negotiators-quit-darfur-saying-neither-side-is-ready-for-peace-855431.html.

116. "Darfur mediator arrives for a 'difficult mission,' " *The International Herald Tribune*, July 21, 2008.

117. Opheera McDoom, "Counting begins in disputed Sudan census," Reuters, April 22, 2008, www.reuters.com/article/homepageCrisis/idUSMCD246493._CH_.2400.

118. Presidential Candidates' Statement on Darfur, *op. cit.* Gedda, *op. cit.*

119. Alex de Waal, "In which a writer's work — forged in the heat of chaos — could actually save lives," *The Washington Post*, June 22, 2008, p. BW 11, www.washingtonpost.com/wp-dyn/content/article/2008/06/19/AR2008061903304_pf.html.

BIBLIOGRAPHY

Books

Cheadle, Don, and John Prendergast, *Not On Our Watch, Hyperion*, 2007.
Cheadle, who starred in the African genocide movie "Hotel Rwanda," and human-rights activist Prendergast explore the Darfur crisis, with tips on how to impact international policy. Forward by Holocaust survivor and Nobel Peace Prize-winner Elie Wiesel, and introduction by Sens. Barack Obama, D-Ill., and Sam Brownback, R-Kan.

Daly, M. W., *Darfur's Sorrow, Cambridge University Press*, 2007.
An historian and long-time observer of Sudan traces the complex environmental, cultural and geopolitical factors that have contributed to today's ongoing conflict. Includes a timeline of events in Darfur since 1650.

Flint, Julie, and Alex de Waal, *Darfur: A Short History Of a Long War, Zed Books*, 2005.
Two longtime observers of Sudan and Darfur explore the genesis of today's bloodshed and describe the various actors in the conflict, including the region's many ethnic tribes, the *janjaweed* militia, Libyan leader Muammar Qaddafi and the current Sudanese government.

Prunier, Gerard, *Darfur: The Ambiguous Genocide, Cornell University Press*, 2007.
A French historian who has authored several books on African genocide provides a comprehensive account of the complex environmental, social and political roots of the ongoing fighting in Darfur.

Articles

"Timeline: Conflict in Darfur," *The Washington Post*, June 19, 2008, www.washingtonpost.com/wp-dyn/content/article/2008/06/19/AR2008061902905.html.
This brief narrative outlines the fighting in Darfur and various efforts to find peace over the past five years.

Faris, Stephan, "The Real Roots of Darfur," *The Atlantic Monthly*, April 2007, p. 67.
Climate change and shrinking water supplies have motivated much of the fighting between Darfur's nomadic Arabs and ethnic African farmers.

Macfarquhar, Neil, "Why Darfur Still Bleeds," *The New York Times*, July 13, 2008, p. 5.
A veteran foreign correspondent discusses the many factors fueling the fighting in Darfur and how international leaders now recommend a comprehensive solution.

McCrummen, Stephanie, "A Wide-Open Battle for Power in Darfur," *The Washington Post*, June 20, 2008, p. A1.
The rebellion in Darfur has devolved into chaos and lawlessness that threatens civilians, aid workers and peacekeepers.

Natsios, Andrew, "Sudan's Slide Toward Civil War," *Foreign Affairs*, May/June 2008, Vol. 87, Issue 3, pp. 77-93.
The former U.S. special envoy to Sudan says that while attention is focused on Darfur another bloody civil war could soon erupt between Sudan's north and south.

Prunier, Gerard, "The Politics of Death in Darfur," *Current History*, May 2006, pp. 195-202.
The French historian discusses why the international community has been unable to solve the crisis in Darfur.

Reports and Studies

"Darfur 2007: Chaos by Design," *Human Rights Watch*, September 2007, http://hrw.org/reports/2007/sudan0907/.
Through photographs, maps, first-hand accounts and statistics, the human-rights group summarizes the events that led to the conflict and describes Darfuris' daily struggles.

"Darfur Crisis," *Government Accountability Office*, November 2006, www.gao.gov/new.items/d0724.pdf.
The report analyzes the widely varying estimates on the number of deaths caused by the Darfur conflict and reviews the different methodologies used to track the casualties.

"Displaced in Darfur: A Generation of Anger," *Amnesty International*, January 2008, www.amnesty.org/en/library/info/AFR54/001/2008.
Using interviews and first-hand accounts, the human-rights group vividly describes the death and destruction in Darfur and recommends ways to end the fighting.

"Sudan — Darfur: Humanitarian Profile," *United Nations Office for the Coordination of Humanitarian Affairs*, June 2, 2008, www.unsudanig.org/. . ./darfur/data/dhnp/Map%201226%20Darfur%20Humanitarian%20Profile%20 June%203%202008.pdf.
This frequently updated U.N. Web site provides maps and charts illustrating areas hit worst by the crisis, the number of attacks on humanitarian workers and the number of people affected by the fighting.

"They Shot at Us As We Fled," *Human Rights Watch*, May 2008, www.hrw.org/reports/2008/darfur0508/.
Using first-hand accounts from victims, the report describes how attacks against Darfuri villages in February 2008 violated international humanitarian law.

For More Information

Aegis Trust, The Holocaust Centre, Laxton, Newark, Nottinghamshire NG22 9ZG, UK; +44 (0)1623 836627; www.aegistrust.org. Campaigns against genocide around the world and provides humanitarian aid to genocide victims.

African Union, P.O. Box 3243, Addis Ababa, Ethiopia; +251 11 551 77 00; www.africa-union.org. Fosters economic and social cooperation among 53 African nations and other governments.

Amnesty International, 1 Easton St., London, WC1X 0DW, United Kingdom, +44-20-74135500; www.amnesty.org. Promotes human rights worldwide, with offices in 80 countries.

Council on Foreign Relations, 1779 Massachusetts Ave., N.W., Washington, DC 20036; (202) 518-3400; www.cfr.org. A nonpartisan think tank that offers extensive resources, data and experts on foreign policy issues.

Human Rights Watch, 350 Fifth Ave., 34th Floor, New York, NY 10118-3299; (212) 290-4700; www.hrw.org. Investigates human-rights violations worldwide.

Justice Africa, 1C Leroy House, 436 Essex Road, London N1 3QP, United Kingdom; +44 (0) 207 354 8400; www.justiceafrica.org. A research and advocacy organization that campaigns for human rights and social justice in Africa.

Save Darfur Coalition, Suite 335, 2120 L St., N.W., Washington, DC 20037; (800) 917-2034; www.savedarfur.org. An alliance of more than 180 faith-based, advocacy and humanitarian organizations working to stop the violence in Darfur.

Social Science Research Council, 810 Seventh Ave., New York, NY 10019; (212) 377-2700; www.ssrc.org. Studies complex social, cultural, economic and political issues.

TransAfrica Forum, 1629 K St., N.W., Suite 1100, Washington, DC 20006; (202) 223-1960; www.transafricaforum.org. Campaigns for human rights and sustainable development in Africa and other countries with residents of African descent.

The Obama Presidency

Can Barack Obama Deliver the Change He Promises?

Kenneth Jost and the *CQ Researcher* Staff

The largest crowd in Washington history cheers President Barack Obama after his swearing in on Jan. 20, 2009. An estimated 1.8 million high-spirited, flag-waving people gathered at the Capitol and National Mall, but thousands more were turned away by police due to overcrowding.

From *CQ Researcher*, January 30, 2009.

T hey came to Washington in numbers unprecedented and with enthusiasm unbounded to bear witness and be a part of history: the inauguration of Barack Hussein Obama on Jan. 20, 2009, as the 44th president of the United States and the first African-American ever to serve as the nation's chief executive.

After taking the oath of office from Chief Justice John G. Roberts Jr., Obama looked out at the estimated 1.8 million people massed at the Capitol and National Mall and delivered an inaugural address nearly as bracing as the subfreezing temperatures.

With hardly the hint of a smile, Obama, 47, outlined the challenges confronting him as the fifth-youngest president in U.S. history. The nation is at war, he noted, the economy "badly weakened" and the public beset with "a sapping of confidence."

"Today I say to you that the challenges we face are real," Obama continued in his 18-minute speech. "They are serious and they are many. They will not be met easily or in a short span of time. But know this, America — they will be met."[1] (*See economy sidebar, p. 286; foreign policy sidebar, p. 292.*)

The crowd received Obama's sobering message with flag-waving exuberance and a unity of spirit unseen in Washington for decades. Despite Democrat Obama's less-than-landslide 7 percentage-point victory over John McCain on Nov. 4, hardly any sign of political dissent or partisan opposition surfaced on Inauguration Day or during the weekend of celebration that preceded it. (*See maps, p. 278; poll, p. 280.*)

"It's life-changing for everyone," said Rhonda Gittens, a University of Florida journalism student, "because of who he is,

277

Obama Victory Changed Electoral Map

Barack Obama won nine traditionally Republican states in the November 2008 election that George W. Bush had won easily in 2004, and his electoral and popular vote totals were significantly higher than Bush's. In 2004, Bush won with 50.7 percent of the vote to John Kerry's 48.3 percent. By comparison Obama garnered 52.9 percent to Sen. John McCain's 45.7. In the nation's new political map, the Democrats dominate the landscape, with the Republicans clustered in the South, the Plains and the Mountain states.

Presidential Election, 2004

Democrat: John Kerry
Republican: George W. Bush

Total electoral vote:	
Republican	286
Democrat	251

Total popular vote:	
Republican	62,040,610
Democrat	59,028,444

* One "unfaithful" elector voted for John Edwards.

Presidential Election, 2008

Democrat: Barack Obama
Republican: John McCain

Total electoral vote:	
Democrat	365
Republican	173

Total popular vote:	
Democrat	69,456,897
Republican	59,934,814

* Due to the Nebraska's proportional allocation system, McCain received four electoral votes and Obama one.

Source: Federal Election Commission

because of how he represents everyone." Gittens traveled to Washington with some 50 other members of the school's black student union.

The inaugural crowd included tens of thousands clustered on side streets after the U.S. Park Police determined the mall had reached capacity. The crowd was bigger than for any previous inauguration — at least three times larger than when the outgoing president, George W. Bush, had first taken the oath of office eight years earlier. The total number also exceeded independent estimates cited for any of Washington's protest marches or state occasions in the past.*

The spectators came from all over the country and from many foreign lands. "He's bringing change here," said Clayton Preira, a young Brazilian accompanying three fellow students on a two-month visit to the United States. "He's bringing change all over the world." The spectators were of all ages, but overall the crowd seemed disproportionately young. "He really speaks to young people," said Christian McLaren, a white University of Florida student.

Most obviously and most significantly, the crowd was racially and ethnically diverse — just like the new first family. Obama himself is the son of a

---

* Crowd estimates for President Obama's inauguration ranged from 1.2 million to 1.8 million. Commonly cited estimates for other Washington events include: March on Washington for Jobs and Freedom, 1963, 250,000; President John F. Kennedy's funeral, 1963, 800,000; inauguration of President Lyndon B. Johnson, 1965, 1.2 million; Peace Moratorium, 1969, 250,000; Million Man March, 1995, 400,000-800,000; March for Life, 1998, 225,000; March for Women's Lives, 2004, 500,000-800,000.

black Kenyan father and a white Kansan mother. His wife Michelle, he often remarks, carries in her the blood of slaves and of slave owners. Among those behind the first lady on the dais were Obama's half-sister, Maya Soetoro-Ng, whose father was Indonesian, and her husband, Konrad Ng, a Chinese-American. Some of Obama's relatives from Kenya came as well, wearing colorful African garb.

The vast numbers of black Americans often gave the event the air of an old-time church revival. In quieter moments, many struggled to find the words to convey the significance, both historic and personal. "It hasn't sunk in yet," Marcus Collier, a photographer from New York City, remarked several hours later.

David Moses, a health-care supervisor in New York City, carried with him a picture of his late father, who had encouraged him and his brother to join the anti-segregation sit-ins of the early 1960s in their native South Carolina. "It's the culmination of a long struggle," Moses said, "that still has a long way to go."

Shannon Simmons, who had not yet been born when Congress passed major civil rights legislation in the 1960s, brought her 12-year-old daughter from their home in New Orleans. "It's historic," said Simmons, who made monthly contributions to the Obama campaign. "It's about race, but it's more than that. I believe he can bring about change." (*See sidebar, p. 282.*)

For black Americans, old and young alike, the inauguration embodied the lesson that Obama himself had often articulated — that no door need be viewed as closed to any American, regardless of race. For Obama himself, the inauguration climaxed a quest that took him from the Illinois legislature to the White House in only 12 years.

To win the presidency, Obama had to defy political oddsmakers by defeating then-Sen. Hillary Rodham Clinton, the former first lady, for the Democratic nomination and then beating McCain, the veteran Arizona senator and Vietnam War hero. Obama campaigned hard against the Bush administration's record, blaming Bush, among other things, for mismanaging the U.S. economy as well as the wars in Iraq and Afghanistan.

After a nod to Bush's record of service and help during the transition, Obama hinted at some of those criticisms in his address. "The nation cannot prosper long when it favors only the prosperous," he declared, referencing tax cuts enacted in Bush's first year in office that Obama had called for repealing.

On national defense, "we reject the false choice between our safety and our ideals," Obama continued. The Bush administration had come under fierce attack from civil liberties and human rights advocates for aggressive detention and interrogation policies adopted after the Sept. 11, 2001, terrorist attacks on the United States. (*See "At Issue," p. 302.*)

Despite the attacks, Obama also sounded conservative notes throughout the speech, blaming economic woes in part on a "collective failure to make hard choices" and calling for "a new era of responsibility." Republicans in the audience were pleased. "He wasn't pointing fingers just toward Bush," said Rhonda Hamlin, a social worker from Alexandria, Va. "He was pointing fingers toward all of us."

With the inauguration behind him, Obama went quickly to work. Within hours, the administration moved to institute a 120-day moratorium on legal proceedings against the approximately 245 detainees still being held at the Guantánamo Bay Naval Base in Cuba. Obama had repeatedly pledged during the campaign to close the prison; two days later he signed a second decree, ordering that the camp be closed within one year.

Then on his first full day as president, Obama on Jan. 21 issued stringent ethics rules for administration officials and conferred separately with his top economic and military advisers to begin mapping plans to try to lift the U.S. economy out of its yearlong recession and bring successful conclusions to the conflicts in Iraq and Afghanistan.

By then, the Inauguration Day truce in partisan conflict was beginning to break down. House Republicans pointed to a Congressional Budget Office study questioning the likely impact of the Democrats' $825-billion economic stimulus package, weighted toward spending instead of tax cuts. "The money that they're going to throw out the door, at the end of the day, is not going to work," said Rep. Devin Nunes, R-Calif., a member of the tax-writing House Ways and Means Committee. (*See "At Issue," p. 303.*)

The partisan division raised questions whether Democratic leaders could stick to the promised schedule of getting a stimulus plan to Obama's desk for his signature by the time of the Presidents' Day congressional recess in mid-February. More broadly, the Republicans' stance presaged continuing difficulties for Obama as he turned to other ambitious agenda items, including his repeated pledge to overhaul the nation's health-care system. (*See sidebar, p. 296.*)

Public Gives Obama Highest Rating

Barack Obama began his presidency with 79 percent of Americans having a favorable impression of him — higher than the five preceding presidents. George W. Bush entered office with a 62 percent favorability rating; he left with a 33 percent approval rating, lowest of post-World War II presidents except Harry S. Truman and Richard M. Nixon.

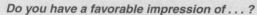

Do you have a favorable impression of . . . ?

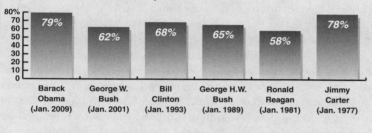

Source: The Washington Post, Jan. 18, 2009

Obama included health care in his inaugural litany of challenges, along with education, climate change and technology. For now, those initiatives lie in the future. In the immediate days after his euphoric inauguration, here are some of the major questions being debated:

Is President Obama on the right track in fixing the U.S. economy?

As president-elect, Obama spent his first full week in Washington in early January first warning of trillion-dollar federal budget deficits for years to come and then making urgent appeals for public support for a close to trillion-dollar stimulus to get the economy moving.

Members of Congress from both parties and advocates and economic experts of all persuasions agree on the need for a good-sized federal recovery program for the seriously ailing U.S. economy. And most agree on a prescription that combines spending increases and tax cuts. But there is sharp disagreement as to the particulars between tax-cutting conservatives and pump-priming liberals, with deficit hawks worried that both of the prescribed remedies could get out of hand.

With the plan's price tag then being estimated somewhere around $800 billion, Obama made his first sustained appeal for public support in a somber, half-hour address on Jan. 8 at George Mason University in Fairfax,

Va., outside Washington. Any delay, he warned, could risk double-digit unemployment. He outlined plans to "rebuild America" ranging from alternative energy facilities and new school classrooms to computerized medical records, but he insisted the plan would not entail "a slew of new government programs." He reiterated his campaign promise of a "$1,000 tax cut for 95 percent of working-class families" but made no mention of business tax cuts being included as sweeteners for Republican lawmakers.

Within days, Obama's plan was taking flack from left and right in the blogosphere. Writing on the liberal HuffingtonPost.com, Robert Kuttner, co-editor of *American Prospect* magazine, denounced the spending plan as too small and the business tax cuts as "huge concessions" in a misguided effort at "post-partisanship." From the right, columnist Neal Boortz accused Obama on the conservative TownHall.com of using the economic crisis as "cover for increased government spending that he's been promising since the day he announced his candidacy."

Allen Schick, a professor of economics at the University of Maryland in College Park and formerly an economics specialist with the Congressional Research Service, sees weaknesses with both components of the Obama plan. "We really have no model to deal with the question of what's the right number" for the stimulus, he says. "And we're not even sure that the stimulus will do the job, especially if a lot of the spending is wasteful."

As for the tax cuts, Schick calls them "harebrained, more intended to look good and buy support than to actually get the economy moving." In particular, he criticized a proposed $3,000 jobs credit for employers. "We know from the past that employers don't hire people for just a few shekels," he says. Eventually, the jobs credit was dropped, but the package still includes business tax breaks such as a $16 billion provision to allow businesses to use 2008 and 2009 losses to offset profits for the previous five years instead of two.

Conservatives favor tax cuts, but not the middle-class tax cut that Obama is proposing. "A well-designed tax cut is the only effective short-term stimulus," says J. D. Foster, a senior fellow at the Heritage Foundation. But Foster, who worked in the Office of Management and Budget in the Bush administration, calls either for extending or making permanent Bush's across-the-board rate cuts, which primarily benefited upper-income taxpayers.

From the opposite side, Chad Stone, chief economist with the liberal Center on Budget Policy and Priorities, endorses Obama's approach. "Tax cuts should be focused on people of low and moderate means, who are much more likely to spend the extra money they get," he says.

Academic economists, however, caution that tax cuts may not deliver a lot of bang for the buck in terms of short-term stimulus. Studies indicate that taxpayers pocketed at least one-third of the $500 tax rebate the government disbursed to counteract the 2001 recession.

Advocates and observers on both sides warn that the spending side of the package may also be less effective than hoped if political forces play too large a role in shaping it. "If it goes to pork, if it goes to green jobs that may sound good in the short term but may not have a market response or a market for them, then it's a waste," Paul Gigot, editorial page editor of *The Wall Street Journal*, said on NBC's "Meet the Press" on Jan. 11.

"If the stuff that gets added is not very effective as stimulus or the things that are good get pulled out, that would not be good," says Stone.

For its part, the budget-restraint advocacy group Concord Coalition sees political forces as driving up the total cost of the package — in spending and tax cuts alike — with no regard for the long-term impact. "Nothing is ever taken off the table," says Diane Lim Rogers, the coalition's chief economist.

Rogers complains of "political pressure to come up with tax cuts even though economists are having trouble figuring out whether they're going to do any good." At the same time, she says spending has to be designed "as thoughtfully as possible, not in a way that the federal government ends up literally just throwing money out the door."

A range of experts also call for renewed efforts to solve the mortgage and foreclosure crisis, saying that homeowners are not going to start spending again without confidence-restoring steps. Indeed, Federal Reserve Chairman Ben Bernanke pointedly told a conference in December that steps to reduce foreclosures "should be high on the agenda" in any economic recovery plan.[2]

Despite questions and concerns about the details, however, support for strong action is all but universal. "We have no choice," said Mark Zandi, chief economist of Moody's Economy.com and a former adviser to the McCain campaign, also on "Meet the Press." "If we don't do something like this — a stimulus package, a foreclosure mitigation plan — the economy is going to slide away."

Is President Obama on the right track in Iraq and Afghanistan?

At the start of his presidential campaign in February 2007, candidate Obama was unflinchingly calling for withdrawing all U.S. combat forces from Iraq within 16 months after taking office. But his tone began changing as he neared the Democratic nomination in summer 2008. And in his first extended broadcast interview after the election, President-elect Obama said on NBC's "Meet the Press" on Dec. 7 only that he would summon military advisers on his first day in office and direct them to prepare a plan for "a responsible drawdown."

Obama also did nothing to knock down host Tom Brokaw's forecast of a "residual force" of 35,000 to 50,000 U.S. troops in Iraq through the end of his term. "I'm not going to speculate on the numbers," Obama said, but he went on to promise "a large enough force in the region" to protect U.S. personnel and to "ferret out any terrorist activity." In addition, Obama voiced disappointment with developments in Afghanistan and said that "additional troops" and "more effective diplomacy" would be needed to achieve U.S. goals there.

Many foreign policy observers are viewing Obama's late campaign and post-election stances as a salutary shift from ideology to pragmatism. "It seems very clear that he will not fulfill his initial pledge to withdraw all U.S. forces from Iraq in 16 months — which is only wise," says Thomas Donnelly, a resident fellow on defense and national security issues at the American Enterprise Institute (AEI).

"I personally have been very impressed with [Obama's] thinking and his way of assembling a national security team," says Kenneth Pollack, director of the Brookings Institution's Saban Center for Middle East Policy. "This is not a man who plays by the traditional American political rules."

First Black President Made Race a Non-Issue

Obama's personal attributes swept voters' doubts aside.

Barack Obama took the oath of office the day after this year's Martin Luther King holiday, and he accepted the Democratic presidential nomination last August on the 45th anniversary of King's celebrated "I Have a Dream" speech.

For millions of Americans, Obama's election as the nation's first African-American president seemed to fulfill the promise of King's "dream" of a nation in which citizens "will not be judged by the color of their skin, but by the content of their character."

"Obviously, for an African-American to win the presidency, given the history of this country . . . is a remarkable thing," Obama said after the election. "If you think about grandparents who are alive today who grew up under Jim Crow, that's a big leap."[1]

While Obama clearly benefited from the sacrifices of the civil rights generation — to which he has paid homage — his politics are different from the veterans of that movement. Older black politicians such as the Rev. Jesse Jackson seemed to base their candidacies mainly on issues of particular concern to African-Americans. But black politicians of Obama's generation, such as Massachusetts Gov. Deval Patrick and Newark Mayor Cory Booker (both Democrats), have run on issues of broader concern — in Obama's case, first on the war in Iraq and later on the economic meltdown.

"The successful ones start from the outside by appealing to white voters first, and work back toward their base of black voters," said broadcast journalist Gwen Ifill, author of the new book *The Breakthrough: Politics and Race in the Age of Obama.*[2]

Black voters initially were reluctant to support Obama — polls throughout 2007 showed Sen. Hillary Rodham Clinton with a big lead among African-Americans — but he picked up their support as it became clear he was the first black candidate with a realistic hope of winning the White House. Clinton's support among blacks dropped markedly in the wake of remarks by former President Bill Clinton that many found demeaning.

But many white Democratic voters remained reluctant to support Obama, particularly in Appalachia. Exit polling during the Pennsylvania primary, for example, showed that 16 percent of whites had considered race in making their pick, with half of those saying they would not support Obama in the fall.[3]

Obama also was bedeviled by videotaped remarks of his pastor, the Rev. Jeremiah Wright, which were incendiary and deemed unpatriotic. But Obama responded with a widely hailed speech on race in March 2008 in which he acknowledged both the grievances of working-class whites and the continuing legacy of economic disadvantages among blacks. Obama said his own life story "has seared into my genetic makeup the idea that this nation is more than the sum of its parts — that out of many, we are truly one."[4]

As the general election campaign got under way, it was clear that race would continue to be a factor. One June poll showed that 30 percent of Americans admit prejudice.[5] And, despite Obama's lead, there was debate throughout the campaign about the so-called Bradley effect — the suggestion that people will lie to pollsters about their true intentions when it comes to black candidates.*

But neither Obama nor Arizona Sen. John McCain, his Republican rival, made explicit pleas based on race, with McCain refusing to air ads featuring Wright. As the campaign wore on, no one forgot that Obama is black — but most doubters put that fact aside in favor of more pressing concerns.

"For a long time, I couldn't ignore the fact that he was black. I'm not proud of that," Joe Sinitski, a 48-year-old Pennsylvania voter, told *The New York Times.* "I was raised to think that there aren't good black people out there."[6] But Sinitski ended up voting for Obama, along with many other whites won over by Obama's personal attributes or convinced that issues such as the economy trumped race.

Exit polls showed that Obama prevailed among those who considered race a significant factor, 53 to 46 percent.[7] "In difficult economic times, people find the price of prejudice is just a little too high," said outgoing North Carolina Gov. Mike Easley, a Democrat.[8]

---

* The Bradley effect refers to Tom Bradley, an African-American who lost the 1982 race for governor in California despite being ahead in voter polls going into the election.

"The Bradley effect really was not a significant factor, despite much concern, fear and hyperventilation about it leading up to the election," says Scott Keeter, a pollster with the Pew Research Center. "Race was a consideration to people, but what it wasn't, invariably, was a negative consideration for white voters. It was a positive consideration for many white voters who saw Obama as a candidate who could help the country toward racial reconciliation."

Michelle Obama holds the Bible used to swear in President Abraham Lincoln as Barack Obama takes the oath of office from Supreme Court Chief Justice John G. Roberts Jr.

AFP/Getty Images/Tim Sloan

Obama carried more white voters than former Vice President Al Gore or Sen. John Kerry of Massachusetts, the two previous Democratic nominees. Still, he could not have prevailed without black and Hispanic voters, particularly in the three Southern states he carried. In Virginia — a state that had voted Republican since 1964 — Obama lost by 21 points among white voters, according to exit polls.

His victory clearly did not bring racial enmity to its end. In December, Chip Saltsman, a candidate for the Republican Party chairmanship, sent potential supporters a CD containing the song "Barack the Magic Negro," a parody popularized by right-wing talk show host Rush Limbaugh during the campaign. And, when Senate Democrats initially balked in January at seating Roland Burris as Obama's replacement, Rep. Bobby Rush, D-Ill, played the race card, warning them not to "hang or lynch the appointee," comparing the move to Southern governors who sought to block desegregation.[9]

But still polls suggest that most Americans believe Obama's presidency will be a boon for race relations. A *USA Today*/Gallup Poll taken the day after the November election showed that two-thirds predicted black-white relations "will eventually be worked out" — by far the highest total in the poll's history.[10]

In the future, white males may no longer be the default inhabitants of America's most powerful position. The present generation and those in the future are likely to grow up thinking it's a normal state of affairs for the country to be led by a black president. "For a lot of African-Americans, it already has made them feel better and more positive about the country and American society," says David Bositis, an expert on black voting at the Joint Center for Political and Economic Studies.

"When you ask my kids what they want to be when they grow up, they always say they want to work at McDonald's or Wal-Mart," said Joslyn Reddick, principal at a predominantly black school in Selma, Ala., a city from which King led an historic march for voting rights in 1965.

"Now they will see that an African-American has achieved the highest station in the United States," Reddick said. "They can see for themselves that dreams can come true."[11]

— Alan Greenblatt,
staff writer, *Governing* magazine

[1] Bryan Monroe, "The Audacity of Victory," *Ebony*, January 2009, p. 16.

[2] Sam Fulwood III, "The New Face of America," *Politico.com*, Jan. 13, 2009.

[3] Alan Greenblatt, "Changing U.S. Electorate," *CQ Researcher*, May 30, 2008, p. 459.

[4] The Obama speech, "A More Perfect Union," is at www.youtube.com/watch?v=pWe7wTVbLUU. The text of the March 18, 2008, speech, "A More Perfect Union," is found in *Change We Can Believe In: Barack Obama's Plan to Renew America's Promise* (2008), pp. 215-232.

[5] Jon Cohen and Jennifer Agiesta, "3 in 10 Americans Admit to Race Bias," *The Washington Post*, June 22, 2008, p. A1.

[6] Michael Sokolove," The Transformation," *The New York Times*, Nov. 9, 2008, p. WK1.

[7] John B. Judis, "Did Race Really Matter?" *Los Angeles Times*, Nov. 9, 2008, p. 34.

[8] Rachel L. Swarns, "Vaulting the Racial Divide, Obama Persuaded Americans to Follow," *The New York Times*, Nov. 5, 2008, p. 7.

[9] Clarence Page, "Hiding Behind Black Voters," *Chicago Tribune*, Jan. 4, 2009, p. 24.

[10] Susan Page, "Hopes Are High for Race Relations," *USA Today*, Nov. 7, 2008, p. 1A.

[11] Dahleen Glanton and Howard Witte, "Many Marvel at a Black President," *Chicago Tribune*, Nov. 5, 2008, p. 6.

Cabinet Includes Stars, Superstars and Surprises

President Obama made his Cabinet selections in record time, and his appointees run the gamut of race, ethnic origin, gender, age and even party affiliation. Those in top posts include Sen. Hillary Rodham Clinton at State and Robert Gates continuing at Defense. Besides Gates, one other Republican was chosen: Transportation's Ray LaHood. New Mexico Gov. Bill Richardson's withdrawal left the Commerce post unfilled along with the director of Drug Control Policy. Cabinet-level appointees include four women, two Asian-Americans, two Hispanics and two African-Americans.

Name, Age Department	Date of Nomination	Date of Confirmation	Previous Positions
Hillary Rodham Clinton, 61, State	Dec. 1	Jan. 21	New York U.S. senator (2001-09); first lady (1993-2001); Arkansas first lady (1979-81, 1983-92)
Timothy Geithner, 47, Treasury	Nov. 24	Jan. 26	President, Federal Reserve Bank of New York (2003-09); under secretary, Treasury (1998-2001)
Robert Gates, 65, Defense*	Dec. 1	Dec. 6, 2006 *	Defense secretary (2006-present); director, CIA (1991-93); deputy national security adviser (1989-91)
Eric Holder, 57, Attorney General	Dec. 1		Deputy attorney general (1997-2001); U.S. attorney (1993-97); judge, D.C. Superior Court (1988-93)
Ken Salazar, 53, Interior	Dec. 17	Jan. 20	Colorado U.S. senator (2005-09); Colorado attorney general (1999-2005)
Tom Vilsack, 58, Agriculture	Dec. 17	Jan. 20	Iowa governor (1999-2007); Iowa state senator (1992-99)
Hilda Solis, 51, Labor	Dec. 19		California U.S. representative (2001-09); California state senator (1995-2001)
Tom Daschle, 61, Health & Human Services	Dec. 11		South Dakota U.S. senator (1987-2005); Senate majority leader (2001, 2001-03); South Dakota U.S. representative (1979-87)
Shaun Donovan, 42, Housing and Urban Development	Dec. 13	Jan. 22	Commissioner, New York City Dept. of Housing Preservation and Development (2004-08); deputy assistant secretary, HUD (2000-01)

Obama invited speculation about a shift toward the center by selecting Clinton and Robert Gates as the two Cabinet members on his national security team along with a retired Marine general, James Jones, as national security adviser. (*See chart, at left.*) Clinton had voted for the Iraq War in late 2002, though she echoed Obama during the campaign in calling for troop withdrawals. As Bush's secretary of Defense, Gates had overseen the "surge" in U.S. forces during 2007.

"This is a group of people who are very sober, very intelligent, fully aware of the importance of Iraq to America's security interests and of the fragility of the situation there," says Pollack.

Some anti-war activists were voicing concern about Obama's seeming shift within days of his election. "Obama has very successfully branded himself as anti-war, but the fact remains that he's willing to keep a residual force in Iraq indefinitely, [and] he wants to escalate in Afghanistan," said Matthis Chiroux of Iraq Veterans Against the War. "My hope is that he starts bringing home the troops from Iraq immediately, but I think those of us in the anti-war movement could find ourselves disappointed."[3]

Since then, however, criticism of Obama's emerging policies has been virtually nonexistent from the anti-war and Democratic Party left. "He seems to be accelerating the withdrawal, which is terrific," says Robert Borosage, co-director of the Campaign for America's Future. Borosage is "concerned" about the residual force in Iraq because of the risk that U.S. troops will become involved in "internecine battles." But he adds, "That's what he's promised, and I think he'll fulfill his promise."

Donnelly and Pollack, however, both view a continuing U.S. role in Iraq as vital. "There's good progress, but a long way to go," says Donnelly. "A huge American role is going to be needed through the four years of the Obama administration." Pollack agrees. "Iraq is far from solved. Whether we like it or not, Iraq is a vital interest for the United States of America."

In his campaign and since, Obama has treated Afghanistan as more important to U.S. interests and harshly criticized the Bush administration for — in his view — ignoring the conflict there. Afghanistan "had had a huge rhetorical place in the Obama campaign," says Donnelly. "The idea being that Afghanistan was the good war, the more important war, and that Iraq was a dead end strategically."

P. J. Crowley, a senior fellow at the liberal think tank Center for American Progress, calls Obama's focus on Afghanistan "correct" but emphasizes the need for a multipronged effort to stabilize and reform the country's U.S.-backed government. "Returning our weight of effort [to Afghanistan] is a right approach," says Crowley, who was spokesman for the National Security Council under President Bill Clinton.

"More troops may help in a narrow sense," Crowley continues, "but I don't think anyone suggests that more troops are the long-term solution in Afghanistan. The insertion of U.S. forces is logical in the short- to mid-term, but it has to be part of a broader strategy."

But Pollack questions the value of any additional U.S. troops at all. "The problems of Afghanistan are not principally military; they are principally political and diplomatic," he says. "Unless this new national security team can create a military mission that is of value to what is ultimately a diplomatic problem, it's going to be tough to justify to the country the commitment of those additional troops."

Name, Age, Department	Date of Nomination	Date of Confirmation	Previous Positions
Ray LaHood, 63, Transportation	Dec. 19	Jan. 22	Illinois U.S. representative (1995-2009); state representative (1982-83)
Steven Chu, 60, Energy	Dec. 15	Jan. 20	Director, Lawrence Berkeley National Laboratory, Dept. of Energy (2004-09); professor, UC-Berkeley (2004-present); Nobel Prize winner, physics (1997)
Arne Duncan, 44, Education	Dec. 16	Jan. 20	C.E.O, Chicago Public Schools (2001-09)
Eric Shinseki, 66, Veterans Affairs	Dec. 7	Jan. 20	Chief of staff, Army (1999-2003)
Janet Napolitano, 51, Homeland Security	Dec. 1	Jan. 20	Arizona governor (2003-09); attorney general (1999-2002)
Rahm Emmanuel, 49, Chief of Staff	Nov. 6	NA	Illinois U.S. representative (2003-09); senior adviser to the president (1993-98)
Lisa Jackson, 46, Environmental Protection Agency	Dec. 15	Jan. 22	Chief of staff, governor of New Jersey (2008-09); commissioner, New Jersey Dept. of Environmental Protection (2006-2008)
Peter Orszag, 40, Office of Management and Budget	Nov. 25	Jan. 20	Director, Congressional Budget Office (2007-08); adviser, National Economic Council (1997-98)
Susan Rice, 44, Ambassador to the United Nations	Dec. 1	Jan. 22	Assistant secretary, State (1997-2001); National Security Council (1993-97)
Ron Kirk, 54, Trade Representative	Dec. 19		Mayor of Dallas (1995-2002)

Department heads are listed in order of succession under Presidential Succession Act; nondepartment heads were given Cabinet-level status.

* Gates was confirmed when first nominated by President George W. Bush and did not have to be re-confirmed.

Compiled by Vyomika Jairam; all photos by Getty Images

Bleak Economy Getting Bleaker

Economists widely agree a stimulus plan is needed.

When Barack Obama took office on Jan. 20, he inherited the most battered U.S. economy since World War II — and one of the shakiest to confront a new president in American history.

And the view from the Oval Office is likely to get bleaker before the gloom begins to lift.

"There are very serious questions on the financial side and apprehension among many parties that there may be more bad news to come," says Kent Hughes, director of the Program on Science, Technology, America and the Global Economy at the Woodrow Wilson Center for Scholars.

Already, Obama has stepped into the worst unemployment picture in 16 years, with the jobless rate at 7.2 percent and 11.1 million people out of work. The economy lost 1.9 million jobs during the last four months of 2008 — 524,000 in December alone.[1]

Economists worry that rising unemployment in manufacturing, construction, retailing and other sectors foreshadows an even more dismal future, at the very least in the short term. Dean Baker, co-director for the Center for Economic and Policy Research, a liberal think tank in Washington, says he expects another million or so jobs to disappear through February, then the pace of job loss to slow if Congress acts to stimulate the economy.

Obama must figure out not only how to get people back to work but also how to restore their confidence in the economy. A punishing credit crisis and cascade of grim news from Wall Street has led consumers to stop spending on everything from restaurant meals to houses and autos.[2]

Home sales have plunged in recent months, foreclosures are hitting record levels and a study by PMI Mortgage Insurance Co. estimates that half of the nation's 50-largest Metropolitan Statistical Areas have an "elevated or high probability" of experiencing lower home prices by the end of the third quarter of 2010 compared to the same quarter of 2008.[3]

Retail sales, a key indicator of consumer confidence, fell in December 2008 for the sixth month in a row, according to the Commerce Department.[4] The International Council of Shopping Centers said chain-store sales in December posted their biggest year-to-year decline since researchers began tracking figures in 1970.[5]

Rebecca Blank, a senior fellow at the Brookings Institution and former member of President Bill Clinton's Council of Economic Advisers, says the unemployment numbers "suggest the economy is still on the way down," and the decline in holiday sales is "surely going to lead to some bankruptcies and belt tightening in the retail sector."

Indeed, such trouble is already occurring. The shopping centers group estimated that 148,000 retail stores closed last year and that more than 73,000 will be shuttered in the first half of 2009.[6] Among the latest examples: Bankrupt electronics chain Circuit City said in January that it was closing its remaining 567 stores, putting some 30,000 employees out of work.

To revive the economy, the new administration — most visibly Obama himself — is urging Congress to quickly approve a stimulus package that could approach $900 billion. Much of the money would likely go toward tax cuts and public infrastructure projects, though how, exactly, the government would allocate it remains a matter of intense political debate.

One thing seems certain, though: The cost of a stimulus package, added to the hundreds of billions of dollars already spent to shore up the nation's flagging financial system, will add to the bulging federal deficit.

"The thing you know for sure is that a stimulus is going to add to the debt, which is [now] quite frightening, and it's going to make it worse," says June O'Neill, an economics professor at the City University of New York's Baruch College

Borosage also worries about an increased U.S. military presence in Afghanistan. "A permanent occupation of Afghanistan is a recipe for defeat," he says.

All of the experts stress that U.S. policy in Afghanistan now plays a secondary part in the fight with the al Qaeda terrorist group, which carried out the 9/11 attacks in the United States. "There is no al Qaeda in Afghanistan," says Donnelly. "Al Qaeda has now reconstituted itself in the tribal areas of northwest Pakistan."

Donnelly questions Afghanistan's importance to U.S. interests altogether but ultimately supports continued U.S. involvement. "The only thing worse than being engaged in Afghanistan," he says, "is turning our backs on it."

and a former director of the Congressional Budget Office (CBO) during the Clinton administration.

In January the CBO projected a $1.2 trillion deficit for the fiscal year. A stimulus plan would add even more pressure on Obama to get federal spending under control. "My own economic and budget team projects that, unless we take decisive action, even after our economy pulls out of its slide, trillion-dollar deficits will be a reality for years to come," Obama said.[7]

The battered economy that confronts President Obama includes record foreclosure rates and plummeting home values. Above, a foreclosed home in Nevada, the state with the nation's highest foreclosure rate.

of the financial markets, more closely resembles the Great Depression than any other recession since then.

Most postwar recessions "were the result of the Fed raising rates," says Baker. "That meant we knew how to reverse it. This one, there's not an easy answer to. We're not going to see [another] Great Depression — not double-digit unemployment for a decade." But in terms of the severity of the problem, Baker adds, the Great Depression is the "closest match" to what confronts the new administration.

— Thomas J. Billitteri

Still, a wide spectrum of economists — including conservatives who typically look askance at government spending — agree that a stimulus plan is necessary.

Martin Feldstein, a Harvard University economist and former chair of the Council of Economic Advisers in the Reagan administration, told a House committee in January that stopping the economic slide and restoring "sustainable growth" requires fixing the housing crisis and adopting a "fiscal stimulus of reduced taxes and increased government spending."[8]

Feldstein pointed out that past recessions started after the Federal Reserve raised short-term interest rates to fight inflation. Once inflation was under control, the Fed cut rates, which spurred a recovery. But the current recession is different, Feldstein said: It wasn't caused by the Fed tightening up on fiscal policy, and thus rate cuts haven't succeeded in reviving the economy.

"Because of the dysfunctional credit markets and the collapse of housing demand, monetary policy has had no traction in its attempt to lift the economy," he said.

That poses an especially daunting challenge for Obama.

Baker of the Center for Economic and Policy Research says that the current crisis, occurring amid a broad collapse

[1] Bureau of Labor Statistics, "Employment Situation Summary," Jan. 9, 2009, www.bls.gov/news.release/empsit.nr0.htm.

[2] For coverage of the economic crisis, see the following *CQ Researcher* reports: Thomas J. Billitteri, "Financial Bailout," Oct. 24, 2008, pp. 865-888; Kenneth Jost, "Financial Crisis," May 9, 2008, pp. 409-432; Marcia Clemmitt, "Regulating Credit Cards," Oct. 10, 2008, pp. 817-840; and Marcia Clemmitt, "The National Debt," Nov. 14, 2008, pp. 937-960.

[3] News release, "PMI Winter 2009 Risk Index Indicates Broader Risk Spreading Across Nation's Housing Markets," PMI Mortgage Insurance Co., Jan. 14, 2009.

[4] Bob Willis, "U.S. Economy: Retail Sales Decline for a Sixth Month," Bloomberg, Jan. 14, 2009, www.bloomberg.com.

[5] V. Dion Haynes and Howard Schneider, "A Brutal December for Retailers," *The Washington Post*, Jan. 9, 2009, p. 2D.

[6] *Ibid.*

[7] Quoted in David Stout and Edmund L. Andrews, "$1.2 Trillion Deficit Forecast as Obama Weighs Options," *The New York Times*, Jan. 8, 2009, www.nytimes.com/2009/01/08/business/economy/08deficit .html?scp=2&sq=deficit&st=cse.

[8] Martin Feldstein, "The Economic Stimulus and Sustained Economic Growth," statement to the House Democratic Steering and Policy Committee, Jan. 7, 2009, www.nber.org/feldstein/Economic StimulusandEconomicGrowthStatement.pdf.

Is President Obama on the right track in winning support for his programs in Congress?

As president of Harvard University, Lawrence Summers clashed so often and so sharply with faculty and others that he was forced out after only five years in office. But when Summers went to Capitol Hill as President-elect Obama's

designee to be top White House economic adviser, the normally self-assured economist told lawmakers that he and other administration officials plan to be all ears.

"All of us have been instructed that when it comes to Congress, to listen and not just talk," Summers told House Democrats in a Jan. 9 meeting to discuss Obama's economic recovery plan.[4]

State Department staffers greet new Secretary of State Hillary Rodham Clinton on her first day of work, Jan. 22, 2009.

Within days after the new Congress was sworn in on Jan. 6, however, lawmakers on both sides of the political aisle were, in fact, taking pot shots at Obama's plan. Republicans were calling for hearings after the plan was unveiled — a move seen as jeopardizing Obama's goal of signing a stimulus bill into law before Congress' mid-February recess. Meanwhile, some Democratic lawmakers were questioning the business tax cuts being considered for the package, calling them examples of what they considered the discredited philosophy of "trickle-down economics."

Despite the criticisms, Obama was upbeat about his relations with Congress in an interview broadcast on ABC's "This Weekend" on Jan. 11. "One of the things that we're trying to set a tone of is that, you know, Congress is a co-equal branch of government," Obama told host George Stephanopoulos. "We're not trying to jam anything down people's throats."

Veteran Congress-watchers in Washington are giving Obama high marks in his dealings with Capitol Hill so far, while also praising Congress for asserting its own constitutional prerogatives.

"Obama is off to a very good start with Congress, and, just as importantly, Congress is off to a good start with him," says Thomas Mann, a senior fellow at the Brookings Institution. "No more [status as a] potted plant for the first branch or an inflated sense of presidential authority by the second, but instead a serious engagement between the players at the opposite ends of Pennsylvania Avenue."

Obama is "in good shape," says Stephen Hess, a senior fellow emeritus at Brookings who began his Washington career as a White House staffer under President Dwight D. Eisenhower in the 1950s. Hess credits Obama in particular with seeking to consult with Republican as well as Democratic lawmakers.

"He was very shrewd after talking with Democrats to talk with Republicans," says Hess, who also teaches at George Washington University. "He has given the opposition the sense that he's open, he's listening. He's reached out to them when he doesn't need them — which of course is the right time to reach out to them."

Norman Ornstein, a resident scholar at the American Enterprise Institute, similarly credits Obama with having gone "further in consulting members of the opposition party than any president I can remember." Writing in the Capitol Hill newspaper *Roll Call*, Ornstein also said Obama is well aware of lawmakers' "issues and sensitivities." For example, Ornstein noted the president-elect's personal apology to Senate Intelligence Committee Chair Dianne Feinstein, D-Calif., for failing to give her advance word in early January of the planned nomination of Leon Panetta to head the Central Intelligence Agency.[5]

The lapse of protocol on the Panetta nomination — which Feinstein later promised to support — may well have been the only avoidable misstep by the Obama team in its dealings with Congress. Criticisms of the economic recovery program as it took shape could hardly have been avoided. And Republican senators naturally looked for ways to find fault with some of Obama's Cabinet nominees — such as their criticism of Attorney General-designate Eric Holder for his role in President Clinton's pardon of fugitive financier Marc Rich and Treasury Secretary-designate Timothy Geithner for his late payment of tens of thousands of dollars in federal income taxes.

A prominent, retired GOP congressman, however, says Obama is doing well so far and predicts the economic crisis may give him a longer than usual pass with lawmakers from both parties. "He has the advantage of a honeymoon, and perhaps the second advantage of the economic conditions of the country, which I think will help the Congress to gather around his program," says Bill Frenzel, a guest scholar at the Brookings Institution and a Minnesota congressman for two decades before his retirement in 1991.

Big-Name Policy 'Czars' Head for West Wing

Appointments may signal decline in Cabinet's influence.

President Barack Obama has tapped several high-profile Washington insiders to fill new and existing senior White House positions, indicating the new administration is shifting policy making from the Cabinet to the influential White House West Wing.

The new so-called policy "czars" include former Sen. Tom Daschle, D-S.D., at the Office of Health Reform (he is also Health and Human Services secretary); former assistant Treasury secretary Nancy Killefer, leading efforts to cut government waste as the nation's first chief performance officer; former Environmental Protection Agency Administrator Carol Browner as the new coordinator of energy and climate policy; and former New York City Council member Adolfo Carrion Jr., who is expected to head the Office of Urban Affairs.

"We're going to have so many czars," said Thomas J. Donohue, president of the U.S. Chamber of Commerce. "It's going to be a lot of fun, seeing the czars and the regulators and the czars and the Cabinet secretaries debate."[1]

In another major West Wing appointment, former Treasury secretary and Harvard President Lawrence Summers becomes director of the existing National Economic Council. In the weeks leading up to the inauguration, analysts noted that Summers, and not then-Treasury secretary-designate Timothy Geithner, was leading then-President-elect Obama's efforts to draft a new financial stimulus package.

But Paul Light, an expert on governance at New York University, questions the role the new "czars" will play. "It's a symbolic gesture of the priority assigned to an issue, and I emphasize the word symbolic," he said. "There've been so many czars over the last 50 years, and they've all been failures. Nobody takes them seriously anymore."[2]

— Vyomika Jairam

---

[1] Michael D. Shear and Ceci Connolly, "Obama Assembles Powerful West Wing; Influential Advisers May Compete With Cabinet," *The Washington Post*, Jan. 14, 2009, p. A1.

[2] Laura Meckler " 'Czars' Ascend at White House," *The Wall Street Journal*, Dec. 15, 2005, p. A6.

"We're talking about both Republicans and Democrats," Frenzel continues. "Democrats are going to want to be independent, and Republicans are going to want to take whacks at him when they can. But I think there is a mood of wanting to help the president when they can for a while."

Ornstein and Hess caution, however, that new presidents cannot expect the honeymoon to last very long. Ornstein writes that Obama's hoped-for supermajority support in Congress "may be doable on stimulus" and "perhaps even on health care." But he says an era of "post-partisan politics" will require "some serious steps" by party leaders and rank-and-file members.

For his part, Hess says Obama may eventually begin to disappoint some within his own party — but not yet. "Democrats will for a while cut him a great deal of slack," Hess explains. "Reason No. 1, he's not George W. Bush. Reason No. 2, they're going to get some of what they want. And reason No. 3, some of those folks have become wiser about the way politics is played in this town."

BACKGROUND

'A Mutt, Like Me'

Barack Obama's inauguration as president represents a 21st-century version of the American dream: the election of a native-born citizen, both black and white, with roots in Kansas and Kenya. Abandoned by his father and later living apart from his mother, Obama was nurtured in his formative years by doting white grandparents and educated in elite schools before turning to community organizing in inner-city Chicago and then to a political career that moved from the Illinois statehouse to the White House in barely 12 years.[6]

Barack Hussein Obama was born in Honolulu on Aug. 4, 1961, to parents he later described in his memoir *Dreams from My Father* as a "white as vanilla" American mother and a "black as pitch" Kenyan father. Barack Obama Sr. and Stanley Ann Dunham married, more or less secretly, after having met as students at the University of Hawaii. Stanley Ann's "moderately liberal" parents

CHRONOLOGY: 1961-2006

1960s-1970s *Obama born to biracial, binational couple; begins education in Indonesia after mother's remarriage, then returns to Hawaii.*

1961 Barack Hussein Obama born on Aug. 4, 1961, in Honolulu; parents Stanley Ann Dunham and Barack Obama Sr. meet as students at University of Hawaii; father leaves family behind two years later for graduate studies at Harvard, return to native Kenya.

1967-1971 Obama's mother remarries, family moves to Indonesia; Obama attends a secular public elementary school with a predominantly Muslim student body until mother decides he should return to Hawaii for schooling.

1971-1979 "Barry" Obama lives with grandparents Stanley and Madelyn Dunham; graduates with honors from Punahou School, one of three black students at the elite private school; enrolls in Occidental College in Los Angeles but transfers later to Columbia University in New York City.

1980s-1990s *Works as community organizer in Chicago, gets law degree, enters politics.*

1983 Obama graduates with degree in political science from Columbia University; floods civil rights organizations with job applications.

1985-1988 Works on housing, employment issues as community organizer in Far South Side neighborhood in Chicago.

Summer 1988 Visits Kenya for first time.

1988-1991 Enrolls in Harvard Law School in fall 1988; graduates in 1991 after serving as president of *Harvard Law Review* — the first African-American to hold that position.

1992-1995 Returns to Chicago; marries Michelle Robinson in 1992; runs voter registration project; works as lawyer, lecturer at University of Chicago Law School.

1995 *Dreams from My Father* is published; mother dies just after publication (Nov. 7, 1995).

1996 Elected to Illinois legislature as senator representing Chicago's Hyde Park area; serves for eight years.

2000-2006 *Enters national political stage as U.S. senator, Democratic keynoter.*

2000 Loses badly in Democratic primary for U.S. House seat held by Rep. Bobby Rush.

2002 Opposes then-imminent war in Iraq.

2004 Gains Democratic nomination for U.S. Senate from Illinois. . . . Wins wide praise for keynote address to Democratic National Convention. . . . Elected U.S. senator from Illinois: third African-American to serve in Senate since Reconstruction.

2005-2006 Earns reputation as hard worker in Senate; compiles liberal voting record; manages Democrats' initiative on ethics reform. . . . *Audacity of Hope* is published (October 2006). . . . Deflects intense speculation about possible presidential bid.

accepted the union. In Kenya — where Barack Sr. already had a wife and child — the family did not. The marriage lasted only two years; Barack left his wife and child behind to go to graduate school at Harvard. Stanley Ann filed for divorce, citing standard legal grounds.

His mother's second marriage, to an Indonesian student, Lolo Soetoro, took young Barry, as he was then called, to his Muslim stepfather's native country at the age of 6. Lolo worked as a geologist in post-colonial Indonesia; his mother taught English. They had a child, Obama's half-sister, Maya. (Maya Soetoro-Ng now teaches high school

history in Honolulu.) Barry attended a predominantly Muslim school that would be falsely depicted as an Isla-mist madrassa during the 2008 campaign. His mother, meanwhile, taught her son about the civil rights struggles in America and eventually sent him back to Hawaii for schooling. The marriage ended later, a victim of cultural and personality differences.

Barry returned to live with grandparents Stanley and Madelyn Dunham — "Gramps" and "Toot" (her nickname came from the Hawaiian word for grandmother). They provided him the stable, supportive home life that he had

CHRONOLOGY: 2007-PRESENT

2007 *Obama enters presidential race as underdog to New York Sen. Hillary Rodham Clinton; nearly matches Clinton in "money primary" in advance of Iowa caucuses.*

Feb. 10, 2007 Obama announces candidacy for Democratic nomination for president at rally in Springfield, Ill., three weeks after Clinton, former first lady, joined race; Democratic field eventually includes eight candidates.

March-December 2007 Democratic candidates engage in 17 debates, with no knockout punches; Obama closes gap with Clinton in polls, fundraising.

2008 *Obama gains Democratic nomination after drawn-out contest with Clinton; beats Republican Sen. John McCain as economic issues take center stage.*

January-February Obama scores upset in Iowa caucuses (Jan. 3); Clinton wins New Hampshire primary (Jan. 9); field narrows to two candidates by end of January.

March-April Clinton wins big-state primaries, including Ohio (March 4) and Pennsylvania (April 22); Obama edges ahead in delegates.

May-June Obama gains irreversible lead after Indiana, North Carolina primaries (May 6); clinches nomination after final primaries (June 2).

July Obama goes to Iraq, reaffirms 16-month pullout timetable; speaks at big rally in Berlin, Germany.

August Obama picks Delaware Sen. Joseph R. Biden as running mate; accepts nomination with speech promising Iraq withdrawal, domestic initiatives; McCain chooses Alaska Gov. Sarah Palin as running mate.

September-October Obama holds his own in three debates with McCain (Sept. 26, Oct. 7, Oct. 15); McCain challenge to go to Washington to push financial bailout plan ends with advantage to Obama.

Nov. 4 Obama victory is signaled with victories in "red states" in East, Midwest; networks declare him winner as polls close in West (11 p.m., Eastern time).

November-December Obama completes Cabinet selections; works on economic recovery plan; vacations in Hawaii.

2009 *Obama inaugurated before largest crowd in Washington history.*

Jan. 5-19 Obama, in Washington, starts public campaign for economic recovery plan. . . . Congress reconvenes with Democrats holding 256-178 majority in House with one vacancy, 57-41 majority in Senate with two seats vacant. . . . More high-level nominations; Commerce post in limbo after Bill Richardson withdraws because of ethics investigation in New Mexico.

Jan. 20 Obama is inaugurated as 44th president; uses inaugural address to detail "serious" challenges at home, abroad; promises that challenges "will be met." . . . President moves quickly over next week to reverse some Bush administration policies; lobbies Congress on economic stimulus package, but Republicans continue to push for less spending, more tax cuts.

somewhat lacked so far. He gained admission to the prestigious Punahou School as one of only three black students. His father visited once — Barack's only time spent with him after the divorce — and spoke to one of his son's classes about life in Africa. Obama's mother came back to Hawaii for studies in anthropology, but when she returned to Indonesia for field work Barack chose to stay in Hawaii.

At Punahou, Obama excelled as a student and played with the state championship basketball team his senior year. He graduated in 1979 and enrolled at Occidental College in Los Angeles. Two years later, he transferred to Columbia University in New York. By now, Obama was well aware of racial issues in the United States — and his ambiguous place in the story. "I learned to slip back and forth between my black and white worlds," he wrote in *Dreams from My Father.* More recently, as president-elect, Obama referred self-deprecatingly to his background. In describing the kind of puppy he would have preferred to get for his two young daughters, but for Malia's allergies, Obama said, "A mutt, like me."

Myriad Global Problems Confront Obama

Two wars, the Middle East and terrorism top the list.

President Barack Obama faces immense foreign-policy challenges — two wars and a turbulent global scene that includes continuing conflict in the Middle East — all against the backdrop of a global economic crisis.

Tens of thousands of U.S. troops are at war in Iraq and Afghanistan. Israel, America's closest Mideast ally, has just suspended a devastating military offensive in the Gaza Strip that could restart at any time. And Islamist terrorism remains a constant threat, with al Qaeda leader Osama bin Laden still at large.[1]

Obama divided his early days in office between wartime matters, the latest Mideast crisis and the economic meltdown. By all indications, he will be walking a tightrope between domestic and international affairs for the foreseeable future.

"A president in these circumstances is going to want to do everything possible to ensure that the transformative and ambitious and very difficult projects of domestic policy that have been designated as the priority for this new administration are not inhibited or disrupted by early failures, in counterterrorism or foreign policy," Steve Coll, president and CEO of the New America Foundation, a nonpartisan think tank, told a pre-inauguration conference on security issues.

Obama's inaugural address restated his commitment to withdraw U.S. forces from Iraq, which is more peaceful after more than five years of war but still violent and torn by political intrigue.[2]

In Afghanistan, however, escalating warfare is tied to another source of U.S. worries: Pakistan. Concern escalated in late November following coordinated terrorist attacks on hotels and other sites in Mumbai — India's financial and cultural capital — which were traced to a jihadist group in Pakistan with deep ties to that country's intelligence agency.[3] Some 175 people were killed and 200 wounded.

The group, Lashkar-e-Taiba, also has at least some operational link to al Qaeda and bin Laden, who is believed to be hiding in Pakistan's northern tribal region, bordering Afghanistan. Another al Qaeda ally, the Taliban guerrillas who are fighting the Afghan government and U.S.

and NATO troops in Afghanistan, use Pakistan as a headquarters.[4]

"Moreover," a government commission on weapons of mass destruction and terrorism said in December, "given Pakistan's tense relationship with India, its buildup of nuclear weapons is exacerbating the prospect of a dangerous nuclear arms race in South Asia that could lead to a nuclear conflict."[5]

The other daunting foreign-policy issue facing the new Obama administration — conflict between Israel and the Palestinians — offers slender prospects for peace. "Two states living side by side in peace and security — right now that stands about as much chance as Bozo the Clown becoming president of the United States," says Aaron David Miller, a former Mideast peace adviser to six secretaries of State.

The biggest obstacle, Miller says, is the "broken and dysfunctional" state of the Palestinian national movement. Fatah, the secular party that runs the West Bank, has a negotiating relationship with Israel. Hamas, the elected Islamist party and militia that initially seized power in an anti-Fatah coup in Gaza in 2007, deems Israel illegitimate. Hamas sponsored or tolerated rocket fire into Israel from Gaza but halted rocketing at the beginning of a cease-fire that began in June 2008. But Israel accused Hamas of building up its arsenal and retaliated by limiting the flow of goods into the region. In December, Hamas announced it wouldn't renew the already shaky truce, blaming the Israeli embargo and military moves. From then on, Hamas stepped up rocketing.

Israel's recent 22-day anti-Hamas offensive in Gaza cost some 1,300 Palestinian lives. The Palestinians estimated the civilian death toll at 40 percent to 70 percent of the fatalities; Israel put the toll at about 25 percent of the total. Israeli fatalities totaled 13, including three civilians.[6]

The scale of Israel's Gaza offensive is renewing calls for the U.S. government to change its relationship to Israel. "The days of America's exclusive ties to Israel may be coming to an end," Miller wrote in *Newsweek* in January. Obama, however, reaffirmed his support for Israel in his Jan. 26 interview with the Arabic-language network Al Arabiya.[7]

Those interests also would require devising a response to what the United States believes is a nuclear arms development project by Iran, which supports Hamas politically and financially — a sign, for some, of how all Middle Eastern issues are interconnected.

"One of the great mistakes we have made has been to believe we can compartmentalize these different policies, that we can somehow separate what is happening between Israel and the Palestinians from what's happening in Iraq and what's happening in Iran and what's happening in Egypt and Saudi Arabia and everywhere else in the Middle East," said Kenneth M. Pollack, a senior fellow at the Brookings Institution and former CIA analyst of the region. "Linkage is a reality."[8]

Another set of connections ties past U.S. support for NATO membership by Ukraine and Georgia to chilled U.S. relations with Russia, which views the potential presence of Western military allies — and U.S. missiles — on its borders as hostile.

Despite the Cold War echoes of that dispute, some foreign-affairs experts argue that Obama actually confronts a less perilous international panorama than some of his recent predecessors. "We don't have the Cold War and World War II," says Michael Mandelbaum, director of the foreign policy program at Johns Hopkins University's School of Advanced International Studies. "Those were existential threats. What the incoming president faces are annoying and troublesome, but not existential threats."

That picture could change if jihadist radicals took over nuclear-armed Pakistan. For now, Mandelbaum argues the biggest international and domestic dangers are one and the same — the economic meltdown.

But success for the huge spending package that Obama wants will require participation by China, America's major creditor. "China has been lending us money by buying our bonds," Mandelbaum says. "That huge stimulus package is not going to work unless we get some cooperation from the Chinese."

Palestinians in Gaza search the rubble of their homes for usable items after an Israeli air strike on Jan. 5, 2009.

In short, the American way of life very much depends on China, Mandelbaum says: "For what Americans care about, for what matters in the world, the issue of where and how we borrow money for the stimulus and where and how we rebalance the economy dwarfs Gaza in importance, and is more important than Iraq and Afghanistan."

— Peter Katel

[1] For coverage of the Iraq and Afghanistan wars, the Middle East and Islamic fundamentalism, see the following *CQ Researcher* reports: Peter Katel, "Cost of the Iraq War," April 25, 2008, pp. 361-384; Peter Katel, "New Strategy in Iraq," Feb. 23, 2007, pp. 169-192; and Peter Katel, "Middle East Tension," Oct. 27, 2006, pp. 889-912. Also see the following *CQ Global Researcher* reports: Roland Flamini, "Afghanistan on the Brink," June 2007, pp. 125-150; Robert Kiener, "Crisis in Pakistan," December 2008, pp. 321-348; and Sarah Glazer, "Radical Islam in Europe," November 2007, pp. 265-294.

[2] Alissa J. Rubin, "Iraq Unsettled by Political Power Plays," *The New York Times*, Dec. 25, 2008, www.nytimes.com/2008/12/26/world/middleeast/26baghdad.html; and Alissa J. Rubin, "Bombs Kill 5 in Baghdad, but Officials Avoid Harm," *The New York Times*, Jan. 20, 2009, www.nytimes.com/2009/01/21/world/middleeast/21iraq.html.

[3] Jane Perlez and Somini Sengupta, "Mumbai Attack is Test for Pakistan on Curbing Militants," *The New York Times*, Dec. 3, 2008, www.nytimes.com/2008/12/04/world/asia/04pstan.html?scp=5&sq=MumbaiLashkar ISI&st=cse.

[4] For a summary and analysis, see K. Alan Kronstadt and Kenneth Katzman, "Islamist Militancy in the Pakistan-Afghanistan Border Region and U.S. Policy," Congressional Research Service, Nov. 21, 2008, http://fpc.state.gov/documents/organization/113202.pdf.

[5] See "World at Risk," Commission on the Prevention of Weapons of Mass Destruction Proliferation and Terrorism, December 2008, p. xxiii.

[6] See Steven Erlanger, "Weighing Crimes and Ethics in the Fog of Urban Warfare," *The New York Times*, Jan. 16, 2009, www.nytimes.com/2009/01/17/world/middleeast/17israel.html?scp=1&sq=Gaza civiliandeathpercent&st=cse; Amy Teibel, "Last Israeli troops leave Gaza, completing pullout," The Associated Press, Jan. 21, 2009, http://news.yahoo.com/s/ap/ml_israel_palestinians.

[7] Aaron David Miller, "If Obama Is Serious, He should get tough with Israel," *Newsweek*, Jan. 3, 2009, www.newsweek.com/id/177716.

[8] Quoted in Adam Graham-Silverman, "Conflict in Gaza Strip Presents Immediate Challenge for New President," *CQ Today*, Jan. 20, 2009.

Barack Obama's riveting, highly personal keynote address at the 2004 Democratic National Convention made him an overnight star and presidential contender.

Graduating from Columbia in 1983 with a degree in political science, Obama decided to take on the so-called Reagan revolution by becoming a community organizer — aiming, as he wrote, to bring about "change . . . from a mobilized grass roots." Obama flooded civil rights organizations to no avail until he was hired in 1985 by Gerald Kellman, a white organizer looking for an African-American to help with community development and mobilization in a Far South Side section of Chicago. Obama's three years in Chicago brought him face to face with the gritty realities of urban life and the disillusionment of the disadvantaged. He later described the time as "the best education I ever had."[7]

Obama enrolled in Harvard Law School in 1988.[8] He wrote nothing about the decision in his memoir and has said little about it elsewhere. Before going, he visited Kenya, where his father had died in an automobile accident six years earlier. Obama described enjoying the meeting with his extended family while acutely conscious of the cultural gap. At Harvard, he excelled as a student, played pick-up basketball and had only a limited social life after meeting his future wife, Michelle Robinson, a lawyer he had met while working for a Chicago law firm as a summer associate. His election in 1990 as president of the *Harvard Law Review* — as a compromise between conservative and liberal factions — marked the first time an African-American had held the prestigious position.

His barrier-breaking gained enough attention to get Obama an invitation from a literary agent, Jane Dystel, to write a book.[9] Obama planned to write about race relations, but in the three years of writing it turned into more of a personal memoir. Obama has said he was unmindful of political consequences in the writing and that he rejected a suggestion from one of his editors to delete references to drug use while in college. The book garnered respectable reviews — and the audio version won a Grammy — but no more than middling sales. Obama's mother read page proofs and lived just long enough to see it published. She died of ovarian cancer in November 1995.[10]

Red, Blue and Purple

Obama needed only 10 years to rise from the back benches of the Illinois legislature to a front seat on the national political stage. His political ambition misled him only once: in a failed run for the U.S. House. But he succeeded in other endeavors on the strength of hard work, personal intelligence, political acumen and earnest efforts to bridge the differences of race, class and partisan affiliation.

Obama entered politics in 1995 as the chosen successor of a one-term state senator, Alice Palmer. But he turned on his mentor when she sought re-election after all, following a losing bid in a special election for a U.S. House seat. Obama successfully challenged signatures on Palmer's nominating petitions and had her disqualified (and the other candidates too) to win the Democratic nomination unopposed and eventual election.

As a Democrat in a Republican-controlled legislature and a liberal with no connection to his party's organization, Obama worked to develop personal ties — some formed in a weekly poker game. Among his accomplishments: ethics legislation, a state earned-income tax credit and a measure, backed by law enforcement, to require videotaped interrogations in all capital cases.[11]

After four years in office, Obama decided in 2000 to mount a primary challenge to the popular and much better known Democratic congressman, Bobby Rush. The race was foolhardy from the outset. But — as Obama recounts in his second book, *The Audacity of Hope* — he suffered a grave embarrassment when he failed to return from a family vacation in Hawaii in time to vote on a major gun control bill in a specially called legislative session. Rush won handily.[12] In the 2008 presidential campaign, Obama's absence on the gun control vote was cited along with many other instances when he voted "present" as evidence of risk-averse gamesmanship on his part — a depiction vigorously disputed by the campaign.

His ambition unquenched, Obama began deciding by fall 2002 to run for the U.S. Senate seat then held by Republican Peter Fitzgerald, a vulnerable incumbent who eventually decided not to seek re-election. In October, at the invitation of a peace activist group, he delivered to an anti-war rally in Chicago his now famous speech opposing the then-imminent U.S. war in Iraq. Obama formally entered the Senate race in 2003 as the underdog to multimillionaire Blair Hull and state Comptroller Dan Hynes. But Hull's candidacy collapsed after allegations of abuse against his ex-wife. Hynes ran a lackluster campaign, while Obama waged a determined, disciplined drive that netted him nearly 53 percent of the vote in a seven-way race.[13]

Obama's debut on the national stage came in July 2004 after the presumptive Democratic presidential nominee, Massachusetts Sen. John Kerry, picked him to deliver the keynote address at the party's convention. Obama drafted the speech himself, according to biographer David Mendell. The night before, he told a friend, "My speech is pretty good." It was better than that. Obama wove his personal story together with verbal images of working-class America to lead up to the passage — rebroadcast thousands of times since — envisioning a unified nation instead of the "pundits'" image of monochromatic "Red States" and "Blue States." The speech "electrified the convention hall," *The Washington Post* reported the next day, and made Obama a rising star to be watched.[14]

By the time of the speech, political fortune had already shone on Obama back in Illinois. Divorce files of his Republican opponent in the Senate race, Jack Ryan, made public in June, showed that Ryan had pressured his wife to go with him to sex clubs and have sex in front of others. Ryan, a multimillionaire businessman, resisted pressure to withdraw for more than a month. Once Ryan bowed out — three days after Obama's speech — GOP leaders had to scramble for an opponent. They eventually lured Alan Keyes, a conservative African-American from Maryland, to be the sacrificial lamb in the race. Obama won with a record-setting 70 percent of the vote to take his seat in January 2005 as only the third African-American to serve in the U.S. Senate since Reconstruction.

Obama entered the Senate with the presidency on his mind but also the recognition that he must succeed first in a club with low tolerance for celebrity without substance. A profile in Congressional Quarterly's *Politics in America* published with his presidential campaign under way in 2007 credited Obama with "a reputation as a hard worker, a good listener and a quick study."[15]

With Democrats in the majority, Obama was designated in 2007 to spearhead the party's work on ethics reform — a role that prompted an icy exchange with his future opponent, Sen. McCain, who had expected to work with Democrats on a bipartisan approach. The eventual package included a ban on senators' discounted trips on corporate jets, but not — as Obama had pushed for — outside enforcement of ethics rules.

Obama had more success working with other Republicans, including Oklahoma's Tom Coburn (Internet access to government databases) and Indiana's Richard Lugar (international destruction of conventional weapons). Overall, however, his voting record was solidly liberal and reliably party-line. In the 2008 race, the McCain campaign repeatedly tried to debunk Obama's image of post-partisanship by challenging him to cite a significant example of departing from Democratic Party positions.

'Yes, We Can'

Obama won the Democratic nomination for president in a come-from-behind victory over frontrunner Hillary Clinton on the strength of fundraising prowess, message control and a pre-convention strategy focused on amassing delegates in caucus as well as primary states. He took an even bigger financial advantage into the general election but pulled away from McCain only after the nation's dire economic news in October drove the undecideds decisively toward the candidate promising "change we can believe in."[16]

Despite intense speculation and Obama's evident interest, he decided to run only after heart-to-heart talks with Michelle while vacationing in Hawaii in December 2006. Michelle's reluctance stemmed from the effects on the family and fear for Obama's personal safety. In the end, she agreed — with one stipulation: Obama had to give up smoking. That promise remains a work in progress. In his post-election appearance on NBC's "Meet the Press" on Dec. 7, Obama promised only that, "you will not see any violations" of the White House's no-smoking rule while he is president.

Daschle Appointment Shows Commitment to Health-Care Reforms

But a vote on a specific plan may be delayed until next year.

"The flaws in our health system are pervasive and corrosive. They threaten our health and economic security," said former Sen. Tom Daschle, D-S.D., President Obama's nominee for secretary of Health and Human Services (HHS), at his initial confirmation hearing before the Senate Health, Education, Labor, and Pensions (HELP) Committee on Jan. 8.[1]

Throughout his campaign, Obama promised to make good-quality health care accessible to all Americans. Many observers see his choice of Daschle — who recently coauthored a book laying out a plan for universal insurance coverage — to lead both HHS and a new White House Office of Health Policy as a sign of the new president's commitment to health-care reform, which he has called the key to economic security.[2] "I talk to hardworking Americans every day who worry about paying their medical bills and getting and keeping health insurance for their families," Obama said.[3]

In the final presidential debate on Oct. 15, 2008, Obama laid out the essence of his health overhaul. "If you've got health insurance through your employer, you can keep your health insurance," he said. "If you don't have health insurance, then what we're going to do is to provide you the option of buying into the same kind of federal pool [of private insurance plans] that [Republican presidential nominee] Sen. McCain and I enjoy as federal employees, which will give you high-quality care, choice of doctors at lower costs, because so many people are part of this insured group," Obama said.[4]

In addition, Obama's plan would:

- require insurance companies to accept all applicants, including those with already diagnosed illnesses — or

"preexisting conditions" — that insurers often decline to cover;
- create a federally regulated national "health insurance exchange" where people could buy coverage from a range of approved private insurers and possibly from a public insurance program as well;
- provide subsidies to help lower-income people buy coverage;
- require all children to have health insurance; and
- require employers except small businesses to either provide "meaningful" coverage to workers or pay a percentage of payroll toward the costs of a public plan.[5]

Points of potential controversy include whether all Americans should be required to buy health coverage.

During the presidential primary campaign, Obama sparred with fellow Democratic candidate Sen. Hillary Rodham Clinton, D-N.Y., who called for a mandate on individuals to buy insurance. Obama disagreed, saying, "my belief is that if we make it affordable, if we provide subsidies to those who can't afford it, they will buy it," and that only children's coverage should be required.[6]

But many analysts, including Daschle, point out that unless coverage is required many people will buy it only after they become sick, making it impossible for health insurance to perform its main task — spreading the costs of care among as many people as possible, not just among those who happen to be sick at a given time.

"The only way we can achieve universal coverage is to require everybody to either purchase private insurance or enroll in a public program," Daschle wrote.[7]

Obama entered the race with a speech to an outdoor rally on a cold Feb. 10, 2007, in Springfield, Ill. After acknowledging the "audacity" of his campaign, Obama laid out a platform of reshaping the economy, tackling the health-care crisis and ending the war in Iraq. He started well behind Clinton in the polls and in organization. In the early debates — with eight candidates in all — Obama himself rated his performance as "uneven," according to *Newsweek*'s post-election account.[17] By December, however, Obama had pulled ahead of Clinton

If Obama ends up authorizing a new government-run insurance plan to compete with private insurers for enrollees, as most Democrats favor, the plan could face tough opposition from Republicans.

"Forcing private plans to compete with federal programs, with their price controls and ability to shift costs to taxpayers, will inevitably doom true competition and could ultimately lead to a single-payer, government-run health-care program," said Sen. Michael Enzi, R-Wyo., the top Republican on the HELP Committee. "Any new insurance coverage must be delivered through private health-insurance plans."[8]

Congressional Democrats stand ready to work with the Obama administration to move health-care reform quickly. Two very influential senators, HELP Committee Chairman Sen. Edward Kennedy, D-Mass., and Finance Committee Chairman Sen. Max Baucus, D-Mont., were already crafting health-reform legislation last year and are expected to begin a strong push for legislation soon. But the press of other business and the time-consuming process of gathering support for a specific plan will put off a vote until the end of this year or the beginning of 2010, predicted Rep. Pete Stark, D-Calif., chairman of the House Ways and Means Health Subcommittee. "I don't think we'll do it in the first 100 days," said Stark.[9]

Ironically, the struggling economy, which leaves many more Americans worried about their jobs and therefore their health coverage, may have opened the door for reform by giving business owners, doctors and others a greater stake in getting more people covered, said Henry Aaron, a senior fellow in economic studies at the centrist Brookings Institution. "Before the economic collapse . . . the odds of national reform were nil," but the nation's economic stress makes it somewhat more likely, especially since Congress has been spending large amounts of money on other industries, Aaron said.[10]

Nevertheless, Aaron and some other analysts say the climate for health-care reform may not be much different from that in 1993 when the tide quickly turned against the Clinton administration's attempt at providing universal health care.

The times are "similar," and despite the desire of many for reform, the details will be painful and will spark push-back, Stuart Butler, vice president of the conservative Heritage Foundation, told PBS' "NewsHour." "When you say, 'We've got to make the system efficient by reducing unnecessary costs' . . . that means people's jobs and . . . doctors are going to rebel against that."[11]

— Marcia Clemmitt

[1] Quoted in "Daschle: Health Care Flaws Threaten Economic Security," CNNPolitics.com, Jan. 8, 2009, www.cnn.com/2009/POLITICS/01/08/daschle.confirmation.

[2] For background see the following *CQ Researcher* reports by Marcia Clemmitt: "Universal Coverage," March 30, 2007, pp. 265-288, and "Rising Health Costs," April 7, 2006, pp. 289-312.

[3] Barack Obama, "Modern Health Care for All Americans," *The New England Journal of Medicine*, Oct. 9, 2008, p. 1537.

[4] Quoted in "In Weak Economy, Obama May Face Obstacles to Health Care Reform," PBS "NewsHour," Nov. 20, 2008, www.pbs.org.

[5] "2008 Presidential Candidate Health Care Proposals: Side-by-Side Summary," health08.org, Kaiser Family Foundation, www.health08.org.

[6] Quoted in Jacob Goldstein, "Clinton and Obama Spar Over Insurance Mandates," *The Wall Street Journal* Health Blog, Feb. 1, 2008, http://blogs.wsj.com.

[7] Quoted in Teddy Davis, "Obama and Daschle at Odds on Individual Mandates," ABC News blogs, Dec. 11, 2008, http://blogs.abcnews.com.

[8] "Enzi Asks Obama Health Cabinet Nominee Daschle Not to Doom Health-Care Competition," press statement, office of Sen. Mike Enzi, Jan. 8, 2009, http://enzi.senate.gov.

[9] Quoted in Jeffrey Young, "Rep. Stark: No Health Reform Vote in Early '09," *The Hill*, Dec. 17, 2008, http://thehill.com.

[10] Quoted in Ben Weyl, "Experts Predict a Health Overhaul Despite Troubled Economy," *CQ Healthbeat*, Dec. 9, 2008.

[11] "In Weak Economy, Obama May Face Obstacles to Health Care Reform," *op. cit.*

in some New Hampshire polling and was in a virtual dead-heat in the all-important "money primary."

The Iowa caucuses on Jan. 3, 2007, gave Obama an unexpected win with about 38 percent of the vote and left only two other viable candidates standing: former North Carolina Sen. John Edwards, who came in second; and Clinton, who finished a disappointing third. Five days later, however, Clinton regained her stride with a 3-percentage-point victory over Obama in the first-in-the-nation New Hampshire primary. Edwards' third-place

Vice President Biden Brings Foreign-Policy Savvy

"I want to be the last guy in the room on every important decision."

The inauguration of Joseph R. Biden Jr. as the 47th vice president of the United States caps a journey almost as improbable as Barack Obama's. During seven terms as a U.S. senator from Delaware, Biden has never lived in Washington, instead commuting daily by train from Wilmington. In 1972, at age 29, he became the sixth-youngest senator ever elected, leading many to believe the White House was in his future.

But after two failed presidential campaigns — in 1988 and in the last election — Biden seemed fated to remain a Senate lifer.

Along the way he rose to become chairman of the Judiciary Committee and gained national prominence while leading the confirmation hearings of Supreme Court nominees Robert Bork and Clarence Thomas. He had also served twice as chairman of the Foreign Relations Committee.

Obama's limited time in the Senate and lack of international experience led to increased speculation that he would select Biden as his running mate to bridge the gap. "[Joe Biden is] a leader who sees clearly the challenges facing America in a changing world, with our security and standing set back by eight years of failed foreign policy," Obama said in introducing Biden as his selection on Aug. 23, 2008.

But the new president has yet to clarify the specific role Biden will play in the new administration. The appointment of Hillary Rodham Clinton as secretary of State all but ensures that Biden, despite his impressive résumé, will not be the point man on foreign policy as initially expected.

Nor does anyone expect him to emulate former Vice President Dick Cheney's muscular role. Upon taking office in 2001, Cheney demanded — and President George W. Bush approved — a mandate to give him access to "every table and every meeting," expressing his voice in "whatever area the vice president feels he wants to be active in," recalls former White House Chief of Staff Joshua B. Bolten.[1]

Cheney's push to expand presidential war-making authority is arguably his most lasting legacy, but he also served as a gatekeeper for Supreme Court nominees, editor of tax proposals and arbiter of budget appeals.

While most vice presidents arrive eager to expand the influence of their position, Biden faces the unusual conundrum of figuring out how to scale it back. "The only value of power is the effect, the efficacy of its use," he told *The New York Times*. "And all the power Cheney had did not result in effective outcomes." But without any direct constitutional authority in the executive branch, Biden does not want to return to the days when vice presidents were neither

finish kept him in the race, but he dropped out on Jan. 30 after finishing third in primaries in Florida and his birth state of South Carolina.

The one-on-one between Obama and Clinton continued through May. Clinton bested Obama in a series of supposedly "critical" late-season primaries — notably, Ohio and Pennsylvania — even as Obama pulled ahead in delegates thanks to caucus state victories and also-ran proportional-representation winnings from the primaries. He turned the most serious threat to his campaign — his relationship with the sometimes fiery black minister, Jeremiah Wright — into a plus of sorts with a stirring speech on racial justice delivered in Philadelphia on March

18. With Clinton's "electability" arguments unavailing, Obama mathematically clinched the nomination on June 3 as the two split final primaries in Montana and South Dakota. Clinton withdrew four days later, promising to work hard for Obama's election.

With nearly three months before the convention, Obama went to Iraq and Europe to burnish his national security and foreign policy credentials. His 16-month timetable for withdrawal now essentially matched the Iraqi government's own position — weakening a Republican line of attack. An address to a huge and adoring crowd in Berlin underscored Obama's promise to raise U.S. standing in the world. The McCain campaign countered

seen nor heard. "I don't think the measure is whether or not I accrete the vestiges of power; it matters whether or not the president listens to me."[2]

And although he says he doesn't seek to wield as much influence as Cheney, many don't expect the loquacious Biden to follow Al Gore either, who in 1992 was assigned a defined portfolio by President Bill Clinton to work on environmental and technology matters. "I think his fundamental role is as a trusted counselor," said Obama senior adviser David Axelrod. "I think that when Obama selected him, he selected him to be a counselor and an adviser on a broad range of issues."[3]

And that's exactly how Biden — who at first balked at accepting the position — wants it. "I don't want to have a portfolio," Biden says. "I don't want to be the guy who handles U.S.-Russian relations or the guy who reinvents government."

"I want to be the last guy in the room on every important decision."

"It's irrelevant what the outside world perceives. What is relevant is whether or not I'm value-added," Biden contends. And very few debate his credentials for the position.

"I'm the most experienced vice president since anybody. Anybody ever serve 36 years as a United States senator?" he asks.[4]

But in all likelihood Biden's first move to Washington will surely be his last.

At age 66, he says he has no plans to pursue the presidency, or return to the Senate for that matter, in 2016 — the last full year of a possible second term for Obama. That suggests he'll truly serve Obama's ambitions rather than his own.

"This is in all probability, and hopefully, a worthy capstone in my career," he said.

— Darrell Dela Rosa

Newly sworn in Vice President Joseph R. Biden, his wife, Jill, and son Beau greet crowds during the Inaugural Parade.

[1] Barton Gellman and Jo Becker, " 'A Different Understanding With the President,' " *The Washington Post*, June 24, 2007, blog.washingtonpost .com/cheney/chapters/chapter_1.

[2] Peter Baker, "Biden Outlines Plans to Do More With Less Power," *The New York Times*, Jan. 14, 2009, www.nytimes.com/2009/01/15/us/ politics/15biden.html?_r=1.

[3] Helene Cooper, "For Biden, No Portfolio but the Role of a Counselor," *The New York Times*, Nov. 25, 2008, www.nytimes.com/2008/11/26/ us/politics/26biden.html.

[4] Baker, *op. cit.*

with an ad mocking Obama's celebrity status. On the eve of the convention, Obama picked Biden as his running mate. The selection won praise as sound, if safe. The four-day convention in Denver (Aug. 25-28) went off without a hitch. Obama's acceptance speech drew generally high marks, but some criticism for its length and predictable domestic-policy prescriptions.

McCain countered the next day by picking Alaska Gov. Sarah Palin as his running mate. The surprise selection energized the GOP base but raised questions among observers and voters about his judgment. For the rest of the campaign, the McCain camp tried but failed to find an Obama weak spot. Obama had already survived personal attacks about ties to Rev. Wright, indicted Chicago developer Tony Rezko and one-time radical William Ayers. He had also fended off attacks for breaking his pledge to limit campaign spending by taking public funds. Improved ground conditions in Iraq shifted the contest from national security — McCain's strength — to the economy: Democratic turf. Obama held his own in three debates and used his financial advantage — he raised a record $742 million in all — to engage McCain not only in battleground states but also in supposedly safe GOP states.

By Election Day, the outcome was hardly in doubt. Any remaining uncertainty vanished when Virginia, Republican since 1968, went to Obama early in the evening. By 9:30, one blog had declared Obama the winner. The networks waited until the polls closed on the West Coast — 11 p.m. in the East — to declare Obama to be the 44th president of the United States. In Chicago's Grant Park, tens of thousands of supporters chanted "Yes, we can," as Obama strode on stage.

"If there is anyone out there," Obama began, "who still doubts that America is a place where all things are possible; who still wonders if the dream of our founders is alive in our time; who still questions the power of our democracy, tonight is your answer."[18]

A Team of Centrists?

President-elect Obama began the 76 days between election and inauguration by hitting nearly pitch-perfect notes in his dealings with official Washington — including President Bush and members of Congress — and with the public at large. Beginning with his first post-election session with reporters, Obama sounded both somber but hopeful in confronting what he continually referred to as the worst economic crisis in generations. He completed his selection of Cabinet appointees in record time before taking an end-of-December vacation with his family in Hawaii. Some discordant notes were sounded as Inauguration Day neared in January. But on the eve of the inauguration, polls showed Obama entering the Oval Office with unprecedented levels of personal popularity and hopeful support. (*See graph, p. 280.*)

Acknowledging the severity of the economic crisis, Obama started the announcement of Cabinet-level appointments on Nov. 24 by introducing an economic team that included New York Federal Reserve Bank President Timothy Geithner to be secretary of the Treasury. Geithner had been deeply involved in the Fed's moves in the financial bailout. Obama also named Summers, who had served as deputy undersecretary of the Treasury in the Clinton administration, as special White House assistant for economic policy.

A week later, Obama introduced a national security team that included Hillary Clinton as secretary of State and Gates as holdover Pentagon chief. Clinton accepted the post only after weighing the offer against continuing in the Senate with possibly enhanced visibility and influence. In addition, the appointment required former President Clinton to disclose donors to his post-presidential foundation to try to reduce potential conflicts of interest with his wife's new role.

Along with Gates, Obama also introduced Gen. Jones, a retired Marine commandant and former North Atlantic Treaty Organization supreme commander, as his national security adviser. He also said that he would nominate Holder, a former deputy attorney general, for attorney general; Gov. Janet Napolitano of Arizona for secretary of Homeland Security; and Susan E. Rice, a former assistant secretary of State, for ambassador to the United Nations with Cabinet rank. Holder was in line to be the first African-American to head the Justice Department.

Other Cabinet nominations followed in rapid succession: New Mexico Gov. Bill Richardson, like Clinton one of the contenders for the Democratic nomination, for Commerce; Gen. Eric Shinseki, a critic of Iraq War policies, for Veterans Affairs; and former Senate Democratic Leader Tom Daschle of South Dakota, for Health and Human Services and a new White House office as health reform czar.

Obama picked Shaun Donovan, commissioner of New York City's housing department, for Housing and Urban Development; outgoing Illinois Rep. Ray LaHood, a Republican, for Transportation; and Chicago public schools Commissioner Arne Duncan, a reformer with good relations with Chicago teacher unions, for Education. Steven Chu, a Nobel Prize-winning scientist and an advocate of measures to reduce global warming, was picked for Energy. Sen. Kenneth Salazar, a Colorado Democrat with a moderate record on environmental and land use issues, was tapped for Interior. Former Iowa Gov. Tom Vilsack, who had supported Clinton for the nomination, was chosen for Agriculture. And Rep. Hilda Solis, a California Democrat and daughter of a union family, was designated for Labor.

As Obama prepared to leave for Hawaii, some supporters were griping about the moderate cast of his selections. "We just hoped the political diversity would have been stronger," Tim Carpenter, executive director of Progressive Democrats of America, told Politico.com. But official Washington appeared to be giving him top marks. *The Washington Post* described the future Cabinet as dominated by "practical-minded centrists who have straddled big policy debates rather than staking out the strongest pro-reform positions."[19]

Obama arrived in Washington on Jan. 4 to enroll daughters Malia, 10, and Natasha ("Sasha"), 7, in the private Sidwell Friends School and begin two hectic work weeks before a long weekend of pre-inaugural events. By then, problems had begun to arise, including a corruption scandal over the selection of Obama's successor in the Senate; the withdrawal of one of his Cabinet nominees; and questions about several of his nominees for top posts.

The Senate seat controversy stemmed from a federal investigation of Illinois Gov. Rod Blagojevich that included tape-recorded comments by the Democratic chief executive that were widely depicted as attempting to sell the appointment for political contributions or other favors. In charging Blagojevich with corruption, U.S. Attorney Patrick Fitzgerald specifically cleared Obama of any involvement. But Obama had been forced to answer questions on the issue from Hawaii and had lined up with Senate Democratic Leader Harry Reid in promising not to seat any Blagojevich appointee. When Blagojevich went ahead and appointed former state Comptroller Roland Burris, an African-American, Reid initially resisted but eventually bowed to the fait accompli and welcomed Burris to the Senate.

Richardson had withdrawn from the Commerce post on Jan. 3 after citing a federal probe into a possible "pay for play" scandal in New Mexico.

Two other Cabinet nominees faced critical questions as Senate confirmation hearings got under way. Treasury Secretary-designate Geithner was disclosed to have failed to pay Social Security and Medicare taxes for several years and to have paid back taxes and interest only after being audited. Attorney General-designate Holder faced questions about his role in recommending that President Clinton pardon fugitive financier Marc Rich and in submitting a pardon application for members of the radical Puerto Rican independence movement FALN. Both seemed headed toward confirmation, however.

CURRENT SITUATION

Moving Quickly

Beginning with his first hours in office, President Obama is moving quickly to put his stamp on government policies by fulfilling campaign promises on such issues as government ethics, secrecy and counterterrorism. Along with the flurry of domestic actions, Obama opened initiatives on the diplomatic front by promising an active U.S. role to promote peace in the Middle East and naming high-level special envoys for the Israeli-Palestinian dispute and the strategically important region of South Asia, including Afghanistan and Pakistan.

In the biggest news of his first days in office, Obama on Jan. 22 signed executive orders to close the Guantánamo prison camp within one year and to prohibit the use of "enhanced" interrogation techniques such as waterboarding by CIA agents or any other U.S. personnel. Human rights groups hailed the actions. "Today is the beginning of the end of that sorry chapter in our nation's history," said Elisa Massimino, executive director and CEO of Human Rights First.

Some Republican lawmakers, however, questioned the moves. "How does it make sense," House GOP Whip Eric Cantor asked, "to close down the Guantánamo facility before there is a clear plan to deal with the terrorists inside its walls?"

An earlier directive, signed late in the day on Jan. 20, ordered Defense Secretary Gates to halt for 120 days any of the military commission proceedings against the remaining 245 detainees at Guantánamo. Separately, Obama directed a review of the case against Ali Saleh Kahlah al-Marri, a U.S. resident and the only person designated as an enemy combatant being held in the U.S.

The ethics and information directives signed on Jan. 21 followed Obama's campaign pledges to limit the "revolving door" between government jobs and lobbyist work and to make government more transparent and accountable.

The new ethics rules bar any executive branch appointees from seeking lobbying jobs during Obama's administration. They also ban gifts from lobbyists to anyone in the administration. Good-government groups praised the new policies as the strictest ethics rules ever adopted. Fred Wertheimer, president of the open-government group Democracy 21, called them "a major step in setting a new tone and attitude for Washington."

On information policy, Obama superseded a Bush administration directive promising legal support for agencies seeking to resist disclosure of government records under the Freedom of Information Act. Instead, Obama called on all agencies to release information whenever possible. "For a long time now, there's been too much secrecy in this city," Obama said at a swearing-in ceremony for senior White House staff.

Obama also signed an executive order aimed at greater openness for presidential records following the

Should Congress and the president create a commission to investigate the Bush administration's counterterrorism policies?

YES Frederick A. O. Schwarz Jr.
Chief Counsel, Brennan Center for Justice, New York University School of Law; co-author, Unchecked and Unbalanced: Presidential Power in a Time of Terror (New Press, 2008)

Written for *CQ Researcher*, January 2009

In his inaugural address, President Obama rejected "as false the choice between our safety and our ideals." Throughout our history, seeking safety in times of crisis has often made it tempting to ignore the wise restraints that make us free and to rush into actions that do not serve the nation's long-term interests. (The Alien and Sedition Acts at the dawn of the republic and the herding of Japanese citizens into concentration camps early in World War II are among many historic examples.) After 9/11 we again overreacted to crisis, this time by descending into practices including torture, extraordinary rendition, warrantless wiretapping and indefinite detention. Each breached American values and thus made America less safe.

Our new president is taking steps to reject these actions. And some say this is all that is needed because we need to look forward. Others clamor for criminal prosecutions because to hold our heads high wrongdoers should be held to account.

But, to me, neither of these positions is right. Prosecution is not likely to be productive, and could well be unfair. At the same time, failure to learn more about how we went wrong poses two dangers: First, if we blind our eyes to the truth, we increase the risk of repetition when the next crisis comes.

Second, clearly and fairly assessing and reporting what went wrong — and right — in our reactions to 9/11 will honor America's commitment to openness and the rule of law. Committing ourselves to a full exploration is consistent with the ethos the new president articulated on his first day in office: "The way to make government responsible is to hold it accountable. And the way to make government accountable is to make it transparent."

For these two reasons, I have recommended that the president and Congress appoint an independent, nonpartisan commission to investigate national counterterrorism policies. This is the best way to achieve accountability and an understanding of how to design an effective counterterrorism policy that comports with fundamental values.

Shortly after his reelection in 1864, President Abraham Lincoln nicely articulated the necessity of learning from the past without seeking punishment: "Let us study the incidents of [recent history], as philosophy to learn wisdom from, and none of them as wrongs to be revenged."

NO David B. Rivkin Jr. and Lee A. Casey
Washington attorneys who served in the Justice Department under Presidents Reagan and George H. W. Bush

Written for *CQ Researcher*, January 2009

A special commission would be both unnecessary and harmful. First, multiple congressional inquiries have already aired and analyzed all of the Bush administration's key legal and policy decisions. Indeed, whether through disclosures, leaks, media and/or congressional investigations, both the process and substance of the administration's war-related decisions have been publicized to an unprecedented extent. If any further inquiry into these policies is necessary, the normal congressional and executive branch investigatory tools are always available, including additional hearings.

Second, a special commission would be fundamentally unfair, beginning — as it would — with the proposition that the Bush policies represent systematic wrongdoing. The Bush policies were based upon well-established case law and reasonable legal extrapolation from the available authorities. Simply because the Supreme Court ultimately decided to change the legal landscape does not mean the Bush administration ignored the law; it did not. Moreover, although there have been many problems and certainly some abuses over the past seven years — Abu Ghraib being a case in point — these have been remarkably rare when compared with past armed conflicts and/or counterterrorism campaigns like the one Britain conducted in Northern Ireland.

A commission would also inevitably involve attacks on career officials in the intelligence community and the departments of Justice and Defense, not merely Bush political appointees. When combined with past investigations, the commission's work would inevitably burden, distract and demoralize the nation's intelligence capabilities. The end result would be the extension of a bureaucratic culture that already favors excessive caution and inaction among our key intelligence and law enforcement officials — the very developments, acknowledged by the 9/11 Commission, as contributing mightily to the analytical, legal and policy failures of 9/11.

Finally, a commission would warp our constitutional fabric and harm civil liberties. While many commissions have operated throughout American history, they have not focused on potential prosecutions. Such a private or quasi-governmental commission would not be constrained by the legal and constitutional limits on Congress and the executive branch, thus raising a host of important constitutional questions.

That the commission's supporters — so determined to vindicate the rights of enemy combatant detainees — seem untroubled by these issues is both ironic and terribly sad.

AT ISSUE

Will Obama's economic stimulus revive the U.S. economy?

YES
Dean Baker
Co-director, Center for Economic and Policy Research

NO
J. D. Foster
Norman B. Ture Senior Fellow in the Economics of Fiscal Policy, The Heritage Foundation

Written for *CQ Researcher*, January 2009

Written for *CQ Researcher*, January 2009

President Obama's stimulus proposal is a very good start toward rescuing the economy. In assessing the plan, it is vitally important to recognize the seriousness of the downturn. The economy lost an average of more than 500,000 jobs a month in the last three months of 2008. In fact, the actual job loss could have been over 600,000 a month due to the way in which the Labor Department counts jobs in new firms that are not in its survey.

The recent announcements of job loss suggest that the rate of job loss may have accelerated even further. It is possible that we are now losing jobs at the rate of 700,000 a month. This is important, because people must understand the urgency of acting as quickly as possible.

With this in mind, the package being debated does a good job of getting money into the economy quickly. According to the projections of the Congressional Budget Office (CBO), 62 percent of the spending in the package will reach the economy before the end of 2010, with most of the rest coming in 2011. This money will be giving the economy a boost when we need it most.

At this point, there is considerable research on the impact of tax cuts, and the evidence suggests that they do not have nearly as much impact on the economy, primarily because a large portion of any tax cut is saved. According to Martin Feldstein, President Reagan's chief economist, just 10 percent of the tax cuts sent out last spring were spent. The rest was saved. Increased savings can be beneficial to household balance sheets, but savings will not boost the economy right now.

There will also be long-term benefits from President Obama's package. For example, the CBO projected we would save more than $90 billion on medical expenses over the next decade by computerizing medical records, which will be financed through the stimulus. In addition, weatherizing homes and offices and modernizing the electrical grid will substantially reduce our future energy use.

The Obama administration projects that this package will generate close to 4 million jobs, and several independent analysts have arrived at similar numbers. This will not bring the economy back to full employment, but it is still a huge improvement over doing nothing.

The cost of this bill sounds large, but it is important to remember that the need is large. If we were to just do nothing, the economy would continue to spiral downward, with the unemployment rate reaching double-digit levels in the near future.

President Barack Obama promises to create 3.5 million new jobs by the end of 2010, and that vow provides a clear measure by which to judge whether his policies work.

U.S. employment stood at about 113 million people in December 2008, so the Obama jobs pledge will be met if 116.5 million people are working by the end of 2010. Reaching this goal will require effective stimulus policies — and the only fiscal policy that can come close to reaching the goal is to cut marginal tax rates.

Obama's target for jobs creation was chosen carefully. Employment peaked at about 115.8 million jobs in November 2007. Obama's jobs pledge at that time was to create 2.5 million jobs, for a total of 116.5 million private sector jobs.

The November 2008 jobs report showed a half-million jobs lost, so his job-creating target rose by a half-million, affirming the 116.5 million target. Then last month's jobs report showed another half-million jobs lost, and the president raised the target again to its current 3.5 million total.

To stimulate the economy, Obama and congressional Democrats have focused on massive new spending programs. However, the federal budget deficit is likely to exceed $2.5 trillion over the next two years even before any stimulus is added. If deficit spending were truly stimulative, the economy would be at risk of overheating by now, not sliding deeper into recession.

Additional deficit spending won't be any more effective than the first $2 trillion, because government spending doesn't create additional demand in the economy. Deficit spending must be financed by borrowing, so while government spending increases demand, government borrowing reduces demand. Worse, since the government's likely to borrow between $3 trillion and $4 trillion over the next two years, the enormous waves of government debt will likely drive interest rates up. That would only prolong the recession and weaken the recovery.

An effective fiscal stimulus would defer the massive 2011 tax hike (higher tax rates on dividends and capital gains are scheduled to kick in), and also cut individual and corporate tax rates further to reduce the impediments to starting new businesses, hiring, working and investing.

To meet his goal, President Obama should junk his ideology and the wasteful spending that goes with it and focus on cutting marginal tax rates. That's the only way to hit his jobs creation target.

congressionally established five-year waiting period after any president leaves office. The order supersedes a Bush administration directive in 2001 by giving the incumbent president, not a former president, decision-making authority on whether to invoke executive privilege to prevent release of the former president's records.

On foreign policy, Obama on his first full day in office turned to the fragile cease-fire in Gaza by placing calls to four Mideast leaders: Egyptian President Hosni Mubarak, Israeli Prime Minister Ehud Olmert, Jordanian King Abdullah and Palestinian Authority President Mahmoud Abbas. Obama offered U.S. assistance to try to solidify the ceasefire that had been adopted over the Jan. 17-18 weekend by Israel and Hamas, the ruling party in Gaza.

Israel had begun an offensive against Hamas on Dec. 27 in an effort to halt cross-border rocket attacks into Israel by Hamas supporters. During the transition, Obama had limited himself to a brief statement regretting the loss of life on both sides. White House press secretary Robert Gibbs said Obama used the calls from the Oval Office to pledge U.S. support for consolidating the cease-fire by preventing the smuggling of arms into Hamas from neighboring Egypt. He also promised U.S. support for "a major reconstruction effort for Palestinians in Gaza," Gibbs said.

The next day, Obama took a 10-block ride to the State Department for Hillary Clinton's welcome ceremony as secretary following her 94-2 Senate confirmation on Jan. 21. As part of the event, Clinton announced the appointment of special envoys George Mitchell for the Middle East and Richard Holbrooke for Afghanistan and Pakistan.

In his remarks, Obama renewed support for a two-state solution: Israel and a Palestinian state "living side by side in peace and security." He also promised to refocus U.S. attention on what he called the "perilous" situation in Afghanistan, where he said violence had increased dramatically and a "deadly insurgency" had taken root.

Returning to domestic issues, Obama on Jan. 23 signed — as expected — an order to lift the so-called Mexico City policy prohibiting U.S. aid to any nongovernmental organizations abroad that provide abortion counseling or services. The memorandum instructed Secretary of State Clinton to lift what Obama called the "unwarranted" restrictions. The policy was first put in place by President Ronald Reagan in 1984, rescinded by President Clinton in 1993 and then reinstituted by President Bush in 2001.

After the weekend, Obama reversed another of Bush's policies on Jan. 26 by directing Environmental Protection Agency Administrator Lisa Jackson to reconsider the request by the state of California to adopt automobile emission standards stricter than those set under federal law. In a reversal of past practice, the Bush administration EPA had denied California's waiver request in December 2007. On the same day, Obama instructed Transportation Secretary Ray LaHood to tighten fuel efficiency standards for cars and light trucks beginning with 2011 model cars.

Working With Congress

President Obama is pressing Congress for quick action on an economic stimulus plan even as bipartisan support for a proposal remains elusive. Meanwhile, the new administration is struggling to find ways to make the financial bailout approved before Obama took office more effective in aiding distressed homeowners and unfreezing credit markets.

House Democrats moved ahead with an $825-billion stimulus package after the tax and spending elements won approval in separate, party-line votes by the House Ways and Means Committee on Jan. 22 and the House Appropriations Committee the day before. The full House was scheduled to vote on the package on Jan. 28 after deadline for this issue, but approval was assured given the Democrats' 256-178 majority in the chamber.

Obama used his first weekly address as president on Jan. 24 — now not only broadcast on radio but also posted online as video on YouTube and the White House Web site — to depict his American Recovery and Reinvestment Plan as critical to get the country out of an "unprecedented" economic crisis. The plan, he said, would "jump-start job creation as well as long-term economic growth." Without it, he warned, unemployment could reach double digits, economic output could fall $1 trillion short of capacity and many young Americans could be forced to forgo college or job training.

Without mentioning the tax and spending plan's minimum total cost, Obama detailed a long list of infrastructure improvements to be accomplished in energy, health care, education and transportation. He mentioned a $2,500 college tax credit but did not note other items in the $225 billion in tax breaks included in the plan — either his long-advocated $1,000 tax break for working families or the various business tax cuts added as sweeteners for Republicans.

Republicans, however, remained unconvinced. Replying to Obama's address, House Minority Leader John Boehner called the plan "chock-full of government programs and projects, most of which won't provide immediate relief to our ailing economy." On "Meet the Press" the next day, the Ohio lawmaker again called for more by way of tax cuts, criticized the job-creating potential of Obama's plan and warned of opposition from most House Republicans.

Appearing on another of the Sunday talk shows, McCain told "Fox News Sunday" host Chris Wallace, "I am opposed to most of the provisions in the bill. As it stands now, I would not support it."

On a second front, the principal members of Obama's economic team are assuring Congress of major changes to come in the second stage of the $700-billion financial rescue plan approved last fall. During confirmation hearings, Treasury Secretary-designate Geithner promised the Senate Finance Committee on Jan. 21 to expect "much more substantial action" to address the problem of troubled banks that has chilled both consumer and corporate credit markets since fall 2008.

Geithner's comments on the financial bailout were overshadowed by sharp questions from Republican senators about the nominee's tax problems while working for the International Monetary Fund. For several years, Geithner failed to pay Social Security and Medicare taxes, which the IMF — as an international institution — does not withhold from employees' pay as domestic employers do. Geithner repeatedly apologized for the mistake and pointed to his payment of back taxes plus interest totaling more than $40,000. In the end, the committee voted 18-5 to recommend confirmation; the full Senate followed suit on Jan. 26 in a 60-34 vote.*

On the bailout, Geithner said he would increase the transparency and accountability of the program once he assumed the virtually unfettered responsibility for dispensing the remaining $350 billion. He acknowledged criticisms that so far the program has benefited large financial institutions but done little for small businesses. He also promised to restrict dividends by companies that receive government help.

---

* Attorney General-designate Holder, Obama's other controversial Cabinet nominee, was expected to be confirmed by the full Senate on Jan. 29 or 30, after deadline for this issue, following the Senate Judiciary Committee's 17-2 vote on Jan. 28 to recommend confirmation.

With many banks still holding billions in troubled assets on their balance sheets, speculation is increasing in Washington and in financial circles about dramatic action by the government. Possible moves include the creation of a government-run "bad bank" to buy distressed assets from financial institutions or even outright nationalization of one or more banks.

"People continue to be surprised by the poor condition of the banks," says Dean Baker, co-director of the Center for Economic and Policy Research, a liberal think tank in Washington. "Whatever plans they may have made a month ago might be seen as inadequate given the severity of the problem of the banking system."

With the stimulus package on the front burner, however, Obama went to Capitol Hill on Jan. 27 for separate meetings to lobby House and Senate Republicans to support the measure. The closed-door session with the full House GOP conference lasted an hour — slightly longer than scheduled, causing the president to be late for the start of the meeting on the other side of the Capitol with Republican senators.

In between meetings, Obama challenged GOP lawmakers to try to minimize partisan differences. "I don't expect 100 percent agreement from my Republican colleagues, but I do hope we can put politics aside," he said.

For their part, House Republican leaders expressed appreciation for the president's visit and his expressed willingness to compromise. But some renewed their opposition to the proposal in its current form. Rep. Tom Price of Georgia, chairman of the conservative House Republican Study Committee, said the proposal "remains rooted in a liberal, big-government ideology."

Obama's meeting with GOP senators came on the same day that the Senate Finance and Appropriations committees were marking up their versions of the stimulus package. The Senate was expected to vote on the proposal over the weekend, giving the two chambers two weeks to iron out their differences if the bill was to reach Obama's desk before the Presidents' Day recess.

OUTLOOK

Peril and Promise

One week after taking office, President Obama is getting high marks from experts on the presidency for carefully stage-managing his first policy initiatives while discreetly moving to set realistic expectations for the months ahead.

"He's started out quite impressively," says Fred Greenstein, professor of politics emeritus at Princeton University in New Jersey and the dean of American scholars on the U.S. presidency. "So far, it's been a striking rollout week."

Other experts agree. "The Obama administration has met expectations for the first week," says Meena Bose, chair of the Peter S. Kalikow Center for the Study of the American Presidency at Hofstra University in Hempstead, N.Y. "There's been virtually no drama, which is an indication of how he intends to run his administration."

"The indications are all positive," says Bruce Buchanan, a professor of political science at the University of Texas in Austin and author of several books on the presidency. Like the others, Buchanan says Obama is holding on to popular support while striving either to win over or to neutralize Republicans on Capitol Hill.

The wider world outside Washington, however, is giving Obama no honeymoon in office. The U.S. economy is continuing to lag, while violence and unrest continue to simmer in three global hot spots: Gaza, Iraq and Afghanistan.

On the economy, Obama has initiated a daily briefing from senior adviser Summers in addition to the daily briefing on foreign policy and national security issues. "Frankly," Obama told congressional leaders on Jan. 23, "the news has not been good." The day before, the Commerce Department had reported that new-home construction fell to its slowest pace since reporting on monthly rates began in 1959. On the same day, new claims for unemployment benefits matched the highest level seen in a quarter-century.[20]

Meanwhile, leading U.S. policy makers were giving downbeat assessments of events in Afghanistan and Iraq. In testimony to the Senate Armed Services Committee, Defense chief Gates warned on Jan. 27 to expect "a long and difficult fight" in Afghanistan. A few days earlier, the outgoing U.S. ambassador to Iraq, Ryan Crocker, warned that what he called "a precipitous withdrawal" could jeopardize the country's stability and revive al Qaeda in Iraq. And special envoy Mitchell left Washington for the Mideast on Jan. 26, just as the fragile cease-fire between Hamas and Israel was jeopardized by the death of an Israeli soldier from a roadside bomb and an Israeli air strike in retaliation.

Obama continues to work at the problems with the same kind of message control that served him well in the election. After reaping a full day's worth of mostly favorable news coverage on the Guantánamo issue, the administration began directing laser-like attention to the economy from Jan. 22 on. For example, the repeal of the Bush administration's ban on funding international groups that perform abortions was announced late on Friday, Jan. 23 — a dead zone for news coverage.

On foreign policy, Obama emphasized the Mitchell and Holbrooke appointments by personally going to the State Department for the announcements. And he underscored the inaugural's outreach to Muslims by granting his first formal television interview as president to the Arabic satellite television network Al Arabiya. Obama called for a new partnership with the Muslim world "based on mutual respect and mutual interest." One of his main tasks, he told the Dubai-based network in an interview aired on Jan. 27, is to communicate that "the Americans are not your enemy."[21]

Obama and his senior aides are also signaling to supporters that some of their agenda items will have to wait. In a pre-inauguration interview with *The Washington Post*, for example, he reiterated his support for a labor-backed bill to make it easier to unionize workers but downgraded it to a post-stimulus agenda item. Similarly, press secretary-designate Gibbs repeated Obama's support for repealing the military's "don't ask, don't tell" policy on homosexuals on the transition's Web site on Jan. 13, but the next day expanded on the answer: "Not everything will get done in the beginning," Gibbs said.[22]

Greenstein and Bose view Obama's inaugural address — which many observers faulted for rhetorical flatness — as a conscious, initial step to lower expectations about the pace of the promised "change we can believe in." Greenstein calls it a "get-down-to-work" address. Obama himself again evoked the inaugural's theme of determination in the face of adversity when he spoke to congressional leaders immediately following the address.

"What's happening today is not about me," Obama said at the joint congressional luncheon on Inauguration Day. "It is about the American people. They understand that we have arrived at a moment of great challenge for our nation, a time of peril, but also extraordinary promise."

"President Obama has done everything he can to tamp down this sense that he somehow walks on water," says Bose. "He has done everything he can to show that he is a man of substance.

"We have to recognize that these challenges aren't going to be met overnight and that we have to have confidence that we're going to meet them," she continues. "Now the question is, 'Can he govern? Can he show results?' "

NOTES

1. The text and video of the inaugural address are available on the redesigned White House Web site: www .whitehouse.gov. Some crowd reaction from Christopher O'Brien of CQ Press' College Division.

2. Quoted in Clea Benson, "An Economy in Foreclosure," *CQ Weekly*, Jan. 12, 2009.

3. Quoted in Aamer Madhani, "Will Obama Stick to Timetable?" *Chicago Tribune*, Nov. 6, 2008, p. 11.

4. Quoted in Shailagh Murray and Paul Kane, "Democratic Congress Shows It Will Not Bow to Obama," *The Washington Post*, Jan. 11, 2009, p. A5.

5. Norman Ornstein, "First Steps Toward 'Post-Partisanship' Show Promise," *Roll Call*, Jan. 14, 2009.

6. For a compact, continuously updated biography, see Barack Obama, www.biography.com. Background also drawn from Barack Obama, *Dreams from My Father: A Story of Race and Inheritance* (2004 ed.; originally published 1995). See also David Mendell, *Obama: From Promise to Power* (2007).

7. Quoted in Serge Kovaleski, "Obama's Organizing Years: Guiding Others and Finding Himself," *The New York Times*, July 7, 2008, p. A1.

8. Background drawn from Jody Kantor, "In Law School, Obama Found Political Voice," *The New York Times*, Jan. 28, 2007, sec. 1, p. 1.

9. Background drawn from Janny Scott, "The Story of Obama, Written by Obama," *The New York Times*, May 18, 2008, p. A1.

10. For a story on his mother's influence on Obama, see Amanda Ripley, "A Mother's Story," *Time*, April 21, 2008, p. 36.

11. See David Jackson and Ray Long, "Showing his bare knuckles: In first campaign, Obama revealed hard-edged, uncompromising side in eliminating party rivals," *Chicago Tribune*, April 4, 2007, p. 1; Rick Pearson and Ray Long, "Careful steps, looking ahead: After arriving in Springfield, Barack Obama proved cautious, but it was clear to many he had ambitions beyond the state Senate," *ibid.*, May 3, 2007, p. 1.

12. See Barack Obama, *The Audacity of Hope: Thoughts on Reclaiming the American Dream* (2006), pp. 105-107.

13. See David Mendell, "Obama routs Democratic foes; Ryan tops crowded GOP field," *Chicago Tribune*, March 17, 2004, p. 1.

14. For the full text of the 2,165-word speech, see http://obamaspeeches.com/002-Keynote-Address-at-the-2004-Democratic-National-Convention-Obama-Speech.htm. For Mendell's account, see *Obama, op. cit.*, pp. 272-285. Obama's conversation with Martin Nesbitt may have been reported first in David Bernstein, "The Speech," *Chicago Magazine*, July 2007; the anecdote is briefly repeated in Evan Thomas, *"A Long Time Coming": The Inspiring, Combative 2008 Campaign and the Historic Election of Barack Obama* (2009), p. 6. For the Post's account, see David S. Broder, "Democrats Focus on Healing Divisions," July 28, 2004, p. A1.

15. *CQ's Politics in America 2008* (110th Congress), www.cnn.com/video/#/video/world/2007/01/22/vause.obama.school.cnn.

16. Some background from Thomas, *op. cit.*

17. *Ibid.*, p. 9.

18. Many versions of the speech are posted on YouTube, including a posting of CNN's coverage.

19. Carpenter was quoted in Carrie Budoff Brown and Nia-Milaka Henderson, "Cabinet: Middle-of-the-roaders' dream?" *Politico*, Dec. 19, 2008; Alec MacGillis, "For Obama Cabinet, a Team of Moderates," *The Washington Post*, Dec. 20, 2008, p. A1.

20. See Kelly Evans, "Home Construction at Record Slow Pace," *The Wall Street Journal*, Jan. 23, 2009, p. A3.

21. See Paul Schemm, "Obama tells Arabic network US 'is not your enemy,' " The Associated Press, Jan. 27, 2009.

22. Obama quoted in Dan Eggen and Michael D. Shear, "The Effort to Roll Back Bush Policies Continues," *The Washington Post*, Jan. 27, 2009, p. A4; Gibbs quoted in, "Obama aide: Ending 'don't ask, don't tell' must wait," CNN.com, Jan. 15, 2009.

BIBLIOGRAPHY

Books by Barack Obama

Dreams from My Father: A Story of Race and Inheritance (Three Rivers Press, 2004; originally published by Times Books, 1995) is a literate, insightful memoir written in the three years after Obama's graduation from Harvard Law School. The three parts chronicle his "origins" from his birth through college, his three years as a community organizer in Chicago and his two-month pre-law school visit to his father's homeland, Kenya.

The Audacity of Hope: Thoughts on Reclaiming the American Dream (Crown, 2006) is a political manifesto written as Obama considered but had not definitively decided on a presidential campaign. The book opens with a critique of the "bitter partisanship" of current politics and an examination of "common values" that could underline "a new political consensus." Later chapters specifically focus on issues of faith and of race. Includes index.

Change We Can Believe In: Barack Obama's Plan to Renew America's Promise (Three Rivers Press, 2008), which includes a foreword by Obama, outlines steps for "reviving our economy," "investing in our prosperity," "rebuilding America's leadership" and "perfecting our union." Also includes texts of seven speeches from his declaration of candidacy on Feb. 7, 2007, to his July 24, 2008, address in Berlin.

Books About Barack Obama

The only objective, full-length biography is ***Obama: From Promise to Power*** (Amistad/Harper Collins, 2007) by David Mendell, the ***Chicago Tribune*** political reporter who began covering Obama in his first race for the U.S. Senate. An updated version was published in 2008 under the title ***Obama: The Promise of Change.***

Two critical biographies appeared during the 2008 campaign: David Freddoso, ***The Case Against Barack Obama: The Unlikely Rise and Unexamined Agenda of the Media's Favorite Candidate*** (Regnery, 2008); and Jerome Corsi, ***The Obama Nation: Leftist Politics and the Cult of Personality*** (Threshold, 2008). Freddoso, a writer with National Review Online, wrote what one reviewer called a "fact-based critique" depicting Obama as "a fake reformer and a real liberal." Corsi, a conservative author and columnist best known for his

book ***Unfit for Command*** attacking Democratic presidential nominee John Kerry in 2004, came under fierce criticism from the Obama campaign and independent observers for undocumented allegations about Obama's background.

Two post-election books chronicle the 2008 campaign. Evan Thomas, ***"A Long Time Coming": The Inspiring, Combative 2008 Campaign and the Historic Election of Barack Obama*** (Public Affairs, 2009) is the seventh in ***Newsweek***'s quadrennial titles documenting presidential campaigns on the basis of reporting by a team of correspondents, with some reporting specifically not for publication until after the election. Chuck Todd and Sheldon Gawiser, ***How Barack Obama Won: A State-by-State Guide to the Historic 2008 Presidential Election*** (Vintage, 2009) gives an analytical overview of the campaign and election with detailed voting analyses of every state. A third title, ***Obama: The Historic Journey***, is due for publication Feb. 16 by ***The New York Times*** and Callaway; the author is Jill Abramson, the ***Times'*** managing editor, in collaboration with the newspaper's reporters and editors.

Other books include John K. Wilson, ***Barack Obama: The Improbable Quest*** (Paradigm, 2008), an admiring analysis of Obama's political views and philosophy by a lawyer who recalls having been a student in Obama's class on racism and the law at the University of Chicago Law School; Paul Street, ***Barack Obama and the Future of American Politics*** (Paradigm, 2009), a critical depiction of Obama as a "power-conciliating centrist"; and Jabiri Asim, ***What Obama Means: For Our Culture, Our Politics, Our Future*** (Morrow, 2009) a depiction of Obama as creating a new style of racial politics — less confrontational than in the past but equally committed to social justice and more productive of results.

Articles
Purdum, Todd, "Raising Obama," *Vanity Fair*, March 2008.

The magazine's national editor, formerly a *New York Times* reporter, provided an insightful portrait of Obama midway through the 2008 primary season.

Von Drehle, David, "Person of the Year: Barack Obama: Why History Can't Wait," *Time*, Dec. 29, 2008.
Time's selection of Obama as person of the year includes an in-depth interview of the president-elect by Managing Editor Richard Stengel, Editor-at-large von Drehle and Time Inc. Editor-in-chief John Huey. The full text is at time.com/obamainterview.

On the Web

The Obama administration unveiled a redesigned White House Web site (www.whitehouse.gov) at 12:01 p.m. on Jan. 20, 2009 — even before President-elect Obama took the oath of office. The "Briefing Room" includes presidential announcements as well as a "Blog" sometimes being updated several times a day. "The Agenda" incorporates Obama's campaign positions, subject by subject. The site includes video of the president's speeches, including the inaugural address as well as the weekly presidential address — previously broadcast only on radio.

For More Information

American Enterprise Institute for Public Policy Research, 1150 17th St., N.W., Washington, DC 20036; (202) 862-5800; www.aei.org. Conservative think tank researching issues on government, economics, politics and social welfare.

Campaign for America's Future, 1825 K St., N.W., Suite 400, Washington, DC 20006; (202) 955-5665; www.ourfuture.org. Advocates progressive policies.

Center for American Progress, 1333 H St., N.W., 10th Floor, Washington, DC 20005; (202) 682-1611; www.americanprogress.org. Left-leaning think tank promoting a government that ensures opportunity for all Americans.

Center for Economic and Policy Research, 1611 Connecticut Ave., N.W., Suite 400, Washington, DC 20009; (202) 293-5380; www.cepr.net. Promotes open debate on key economic and social issues.

Center on Budget and Policy Priorities, 820 First St., N.E., Suite 510, Washington, DC 20002; (202) 408-1080; www.cbpp.org. Policy organization working on issues that affect low- and moderate-income families and individuals.

Concord Coalition, 1011 Arlington Blvd., Suite 300, Arlington, VA 22209; (703) 894-6222; www.concordcoalition.org. Nonpartisan, grassroots organization promoting responsible fiscal policy and spending.

Heritage Foundation, 214 Massachusetts Ave., N.E., Washington, DC 20002; (202) 546-4400; www.heritage.org. Conservative think tank promoting policies based on free enterprise, limited government and individual freedom.

13

Middle-Class Squeeze

Is More Government Aid Needed?

Thomas J. Billitteri

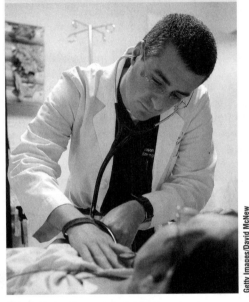

Affordable health care for all Americans is a key element of the budget recently announced by President Barack Obama, along with other policies aimed squarely at helping the middle class. Nearly half of home foreclosures in 2006 were caused, at least partly, by financial issues stemming from a medical problem, according to the advocacy group Families USA. Above, emergency room physician Jason Greenspan cares for a patient in Panorama City, Calif.

From *CQ Researcher*,
March 6, 2009.

Cindy Dreeszen, 41, and her husband may have seemed like unlikely visitors to the Interfaith food pantry last month in affluent Morris County, N.J., 25 miles from New York City. Both have steady jobs and a combined income of about $55,000 a year. But with "the cost of everything going up and up" and a second baby due, the couple was looking for free groceries.

"I didn't think we'd even be allowed to come here," Ms. Dreeszen told *The New York Times*. "This is totally something that I never expected to happen, to have to resort to this."[1]

Countless middle-class Americans are thinking similar thoughts these days as they ponder their suddenly fragile futures.

Millions of families who once enjoyed the American dream of upward mobility and financial security are sliding rapidly down the economic ladder — some into poverty. Many are losing their homes along with their jobs, and telling their children to rethink college.[2] And while today's economic crisis has made life for middle-class households worse, the problems aren't new. Pressure on the middle-class has been building for years and is likely to persist long after the current recession — now 14 months old — is over.

The middle class "is in crisis and decline," says sociologist Kevin Leicht, director of the Institute for Inequality Studies at the University of Iowa.

"Between wages that have been stagnant [in inflation-adjusted terms] since the middle of the 1970s and government policies that are weighted exclusively in the direction of the wealthy, the only thing that has been holding up most of the American middle class is access to cheap and easy credit."

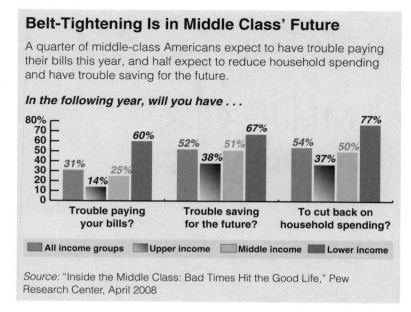

Belt-Tightening Is in Middle Class' Future

A quarter of middle-class Americans expect to have trouble paying their bills this year, and half expect to reduce household spending and have trouble saving for the future.

In the following year, will you have . . .

Source: "Inside the Middle Class: Bad Times Hit the Good Life," Pew Research Center, April 2008

What's at stake goes far beyond economics and family finances, though, experts say. "A large middle class, especially one that is politically active, tends to be a kind of anchor that keeps your country from swinging back and forth," says sociologist Teresa Sullivan, provost and executive vice president for academic affairs at the University of Michigan and co-author of *The Fragile Middle Class: Americans in Debt.* What's more, she says, "there are typical values that middle-class families acquire and pass on to their children," and those values "tend to be very good for democracy."

Right now, though, the middle class is under threat.

In a study of middle-class households, Demos, a liberal think tank in New York, estimated that 4 million families lost their financial security between 2000 and 2006, raising the total to 23 million. Driving the increase, Demos said, were declines in financial assets, then-rising housing costs and a growing lack of health insurance.[6]

"In America the middle class has been a lifestyle, a certain way of life," says Jennifer Wheary, a co-author of the study. "It's been about being able to have a very moderate existence where you could do things like save for your retirement, put your kids through school, get sick and not worry about getting basic care. And those kinds of things are really imperiled right now."

In another study, the Pew Research Center found this year that "fewer Americans now than at any time in the past half-century believe they're moving forward in life."[7]

Among the findings:

• Nearly two-thirds of Americans said their standard of living was higher than that of their parents at the same age, but more than half said they'd either made no progress in life over the past five years or had fallen backward.

• Median household income rose 41 percent since 1970, but upper-income households outperformed those in the middle tier in both income gains and wealth accumulation. The median net worth of upper-income

No official definition of the "middle class" exists. (*See sidebar, p. 322.*) But most Americans — except perhaps the very richest and poorest — consider themselves in that broad category, a fact not lost on Washington policy makers.

Indeed, President Barack Obama announced a 10-year budget on Feb. 28 that takes direct aim at the challenges facing America's middle class and the growing concentration of wealth at the top of the income scale.[3] Key elements of the plan include shifting more costs to the wealthiest Americans and overhauling health care to make it more affordable.[4]

In further recognition of the importance of the middle-class, Obama has named Vice President Joseph R. Biden to chair a new White House Task Force on Middle Class Working Families. It will examine everything from access to college and child- and elder-care issues to business development and the role of labor unions in the economy.[5]

"Talking about the middle class is the closest that American politicians and maybe Americans are willing to go to emphasize the fact that we have growing inequality in this country," says Jacob Hacker, a political scientist at the University of California, Berkeley, and a leading social-policy expert. "A very small proportion of the population is getting fabulously rich, and the rest of Americans are getting modestly richer or not much richer at all."

families rose 123 percent from 1983 to 2004, compared with 29 percent for middle-income families.

- Almost eight in 10 respondents said it was more difficult now for those in the middle class to maintain their standard of living compared with five years ago. In 1986, 65 percent felt that way.

Lane Kenworthy, a sociology and political science professor at the University of Arizona who studies income inequality and poverty, says "the key thing that's happened" to the middle class over the past three decades "is slow income growth compared to general economic growth." Moreover, Kenworthy says a bigger and bigger portion of economic growth has accrued to the wealthiest 1 percent, whether the measure is basic wages or total compensation, which includes the value of employee-sponsored and government benefits.

Even the economic boom leading up to today's recession has proved illusory, new Federal Reserve data show. While median household net worth — assets minus debt — rose nearly 18 percent in the three years ending in late 2007, the increase vanished amid last year's drastic declines in home and stock prices, according to the Fed's triennial "Survey of Consumer Finances." "Adjusting for those declines, Fed officials estimated that the median family was 3.2 percent poorer as of October 2008 than it was at the end of 2004," *The New York Times* noted.[8]

A hallmark of middle-class insecurity reflects what Hacker calls "the great risk shift" — the notion that government and business have transferred the burden of providing affordable health care, income security and retirement saving onto the shoulders of working Americans, leaving them financially stretched and vulnerable to economic catastrophe.

"Over the last generation, we have witnessed a massive transfer of economic risk from broad structures of insurance, including those sponsored by the corporate

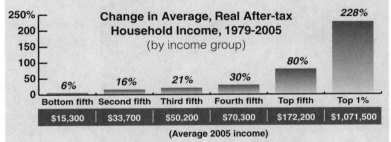

Income Gap Getting Wider

The gap between the wealthiest Americans and everybody else grew to its widest point since at least 1979.* The top 1 percent of households received 70 times as much in average after-tax income as the bottom one-fifth and 21 times as much as the middle one-fifth — in both cases the widest gaps on record. From 1979-2005, the top 1 percent saw its income rise 228 percent compared to a rise of only 21 percent for the middle one-fifth of Americans.

Change in Average, Real After-tax Household Income, 1979-2005
(by income group)

	Bottom fifth	Second fifth	Third fifth	Fourth fifth	Top fifth	Top 1%
Change	6%	16%	21%	30%	80%	228%
Average 2005 income	$15,300	$33,700	$50,200	$70,300	$172,200	$1,071,500

* Data go back only to 1979.

Source: Arloc Sherman, "Income Inequality Hits Record Levels, New CBO Data Show," Center on Budget and Policy Priorities, December 2007

sector as well as by government, onto the fragile balance sheets of American families," Hacker wrote. "This transformation . . . is the defining feature of the contemporary American economy — as important as the shift from agriculture to industry a century ago."[9]

The challenge of solving the problems facing the American middle class will confront policy makers for years to come. Some experts say the key is growth in good jobs — those with good pay, good benefits and good, secure futures. Others argue that solving the nation's health-care crisis is the paramount issue.

One thing is certain, experts say: Leaving the fate of the American middle class to chance is not an option.

"We're believers in hard work, and we're increasingly in a situation where the difference between whether or not a middle-class family prospers comes down to luck, says Amelia Warren Tyagi, co-author of *The Two-Income Trap: Why Middle-Class Mothers and Fathers Are Going Broke.* "And that's an idea that makes us really uncomfortable."

Here are some of the questions that policy makers and average Americans are asking about the middle class:

Getty Images/William Thomas Cain

Vice President Joseph Biden, chair of the new White House Task Force on Middle Class Working Families, listens to a presentation on creating "green" jobs at the University of Pennsylvania on Feb. 27, 2009. President Obama directed the panel to examine issues such as access to college, business development and the role of labor unions in the economy.

Is a stable middle class a thing of the past?

First lady Michelle Obama remembers what some call the good old days of middle-class security.

"I am always amazed," she told a gathering, "at how different things are now for working women and families than when I was growing up. . . . When I was growing up, my father — as you know, a blue-collar worker — was able to go to work and earn enough money to support a family of four, while my mom stayed home with me and my brother. But today, living with one income, like we did, just doesn't cut it. People can't do it — particularly if it's a shift-worker's salary like my father's."[10]

Brookings Institution researchers noted in 2007 that two-thirds of American adults had higher family incomes than their parents did in the late 1960s and early '70s, but a third were worse off. Moreover, they pointed out,

the intergenerational gains largely stemmed from dual paychecks in families.[11]

"Men's earnings have grown little, if at all," while those of women "have risen along with their greater involvement in the work world," they said. "So, yes, today's families are better off than their own parents were. . . . But they are also working more and struggling with the greater time pressures of juggling work and family responsibilities."[12]

At the same time, many economists say the earnings of middle-class working families have not kept pace with gains by the wealthy. They point to Congressional Budget Office data showing that from 1979 through 2005, the average after-tax income of the top 1 percent rose 228 percent, compared with 21 percent for the middle fifth of the population. For the poorest fifth, the increase during the 25-year period was just 6 percent.[13]

Emmanuel Saez, an economist at the University of California, Berkeley, concluded last year that those in the top 1 percent of income distribution captured roughly half of the overall economic growth from 1993 to 2006, and almost three-fourths of income growth in the 2002-2006 period.[14]

"It's the very top of the economic ladder that's pulled away from the rest," Berkeley political scientist Hacker says. "Depending on which source you look at, it's the top 1 percent, or the top one-half of 1 percent, or the top one-tenth of 1 percent that's really received the lion's share of the gain in our economy overall. . . . It would be one thing if we saw middle-class Americans hold onto or even expand their wealth and economic security. But they're more in debt and less secure than they were 20 years ago."

The reasons the middle class is running in place or falling behind can be elusive, though. Kenworthy of the University of Arizona cites a litany of factors — technological changes in the workplace, globalization of trade and the outsourcing of jobs overseas, declining influence of labor unions, slow growth in the proportion of workers with at least a high-school diploma and a stagnant minimum wage — that have helped dampen the economic progress of the middle class. But, he says, social scientists and economists don't have a "good handle on which matter most."[15]

John Schmitt, senior economist at the Center for Economic and Policy Research, a liberal think tank, disputes the notion that technology and globalization are immutable forces that have, in themselves, hurt the middle class. "We've had technological growth at a rapid pace in the United States from the early 1800s," he says, and after World War II the country saw "massive technological innovation," including the introduction of computers.

Those "were huge, potentially disruptive innovations, but we had a social structure that had a lot of protections and guarantees for workers," including "a decent minimum wage, significant union representation" and a strong regulatory framework.

"The real story is that we've made a lot of decisions about economic policy that have had the effect of shifting the playing field toward employers and away from workers at a whole lot of levels," Schmitt says.

As that shift occurred, job security has suffered, many economists say.

In a recent study, Schmitt found that the share of "good jobs" — those paying at least $17 per hour and offering health insurance and a pension — declined 2.3 percentage points in the 2000-2006 business cycle, far more than in comparable periods in the 1980s and '90s. A "sharp deterioration" in employer-provided health plans was a "driving force" in the decline of good jobs, which was most pronounced among male workers, he found.[16]

Meanwhile, career employment — employment with a single employer from middle age to retirement — is no longer the norm, according to researchers at Boston College. Only half of full-time workers ages 58 to 62 are still with the same employer for whom they worked at age 50, they found.[17]

And manufacturing — long a bedrock of middle-class lifestyles — has shrunk from about a third of non-farm employment to only 10 percent since 1950.[18]

Still, interpretations of income and other economic data can vary widely among economists, depending on their political viewpoint. While not diminishing the severe pressures many in the middle class are feeling right now, some conservative economists have a more optimistic view of the jobs issue and long-term middle-class gains in general.

In a study last year, James Sherk, Bradley Fellow in Labor Policy at the Heritage Foundation, challenged the notions "that the era of good jobs is slipping away" and that workers' benefits are disappearing.[19]

"Throughout the economy, jobs paying high wages in fields requiring more education are more available today than they were a generation ago, while low-wage, low-skill jobs are decreasing," he wrote. And, he added, "employer-provided health insurance and pensions are as available now as they were in the mid-1990s. Worker pension plans have improved significantly, with most employers shifting to defined-contribution pensions that provide workers with more money for retirement and do not penalize them for switching jobs."

In an interview, Sherk said that while many middle-class families are struggling today, over the long term they have not, on average, fallen behind overall growth in the economy. Average earnings have risen in step with productivity, he said.

But others are not sanguine about the status of the middle class, long-term or otherwise.

"For quite some time, we've had a sizable minority of the middle class under enormous strain and on the verge of crisis, and since the recent meltdown the proportion of middle-class families in crisis increased exponentially," says Tyagi, who co-authored *The Two-Income Trap* with her mother, Harvard law Professor Elizabeth Warren, chair of a congressional panel overseeing last fall's $700 billion financial bailout. "Many families teetering on the uncomfortable edge have been pushed over."

Is overconsumption at the root of the middle class' problems?

In a recent article about the collapse of the Florida real estate market, *New Yorker* writer George Packer quotes a woman in Cape Coral who, with her husband, had built a home on modest incomes, borrowed against its value, spent some of the money on vacations and cruises, and then faced foreclosure after her husband was laid off.

"I'm not saying what we did was perfect," the woman said. "We spent our money and didn't save it. But we had it, and we didn't see that this was going to happen."[20]

Such vignettes are commonplace these days as the economy plummets and home foreclosures soar. So, too, is the view that many middle-class consumers brought trouble to their own doorsteps by overconsuming and failing to save.

Thomas H. Naylor, a professor emeritus of economics at Duke University and co-author of *Affluenza: The All-Consuming Epidemic*, says the vulnerability of the

Being Middle Class Takes More Income

The minimum income needed for a three-person household to be considered in the middle class was about 40 percent higher in 2006 than in 1969.

Economic Definition of Middle-class Household of Three
(in constant January 2008 dollars)

Year	Income
1969	$31,755 to $63,509
1979	$37,356 to $74,712
1989	$41,386 to $82,771
1999	$45,920 to $91,841
2006	$44,620 to $89,241

Source: "Inside the Middle Class: Bad Times Hit the Good Life," Pew Research Center, April 2008

household debt grew much faster than personal income. Why should we have expected net worth to go up?"

But, Krugman went on to say, until recently Americans thought they were getting wealthier, basing their belief on statements saying their homes and stock portfolios were appreciating faster than the growth of their debts.[21]

In fact, many economists say the picture of consumer behavior and household savings is far more complex than simple theories of overconsumption suggest.

President Obama weighed in at a press conference in early February, saying, "I don't think it's accurate to say that consumer spending got us into this mess." But he added that "our savings rate has declined, and this economy has been driven by consumer spending for a very long time. And that's not going to be sustainable."

Schmitt, of the Center for Economic and Policy Research, contends that what has hurt the middle class the most are steep cost increases of necessities, not spending on luxuries. "There's a lot of argument about overconsumption, but my argument is that consumption of basic necessities is not subject to big price savings," he says. "Housing, education, health care — those are much more expensive than they used to be. That's where people are feeling the pinch."

Housing prices doubled between the mid-1990s and 2007.[22] Average tuition, fees and room-and-board charges at private four-year institutions have more than doubled since 1978-79, to $34,132.[23] And growth in national health expenditures has outpaced gross national product (GNP) growth every year at least since the late 1990s.[24]

One study found that among adults earning $40,000 to $60,000, the proportion of adults spending 10 percent or more of their income on health care doubled between 2001 and 2007, from 18 percent to 36 percent.[25]

"Health care is the epicenter of economic security in the United States today," says Hacker, the University of California political scientist. "It's not the only thing impinging on families finances, but it's one of the areas where the need is greatest."

Economist Robert H. Frank, author of *Falling Behind: How Rising Inequality Harms the Middle Class*, argues that as the wealthiest Americans have acquired bigger and more expensive houses and luxury possessions, their

middle class has been "enhanced by [its] behavior." He blames both consumer excess and the influence of advertising and media.

"On the one hand, consumers have done it to themselves. They've made choices to spend the money," Naylor says. "On the other hand, they've had lots of encouragement and stimulation from corporate America. The big guns are aimed at them, and it's very difficult to resist the temptation."

Pointing to the Federal Reserve's recent "Survey of Consumer Finances," Nobel laureate and *New York Times* economic columnist Paul Krugman wrote that the fact that "the net worth of the average American household, adjusted for inflation, is lower now than it was in 2001" should, at one level, "come as no surprise.

"For most of the last decade America was a nation of borrowers and spenders, not savers. The personal savings rate dropped from 9 percent in the 1980s to 5 percent in the 1990s, to just 0.6 percent from 2005 to 2007, and

behavior has raised the bar for middle-class consumers, leading them to spend more and more of their incomes on bigger houses and upscale goods.

While some of the spending may be frivolous, he says, many consumers have felt compelled to keep up with rising economic and cultural standards — and often for practical reasons: Bigger, more expensive homes typically are in neighborhoods with the best schools, and upscale clothing has become the norm for those who want to dress for success.

"There are people you could say have brought this on themselves," Frank says of the troubles middle-class families are now facing. "If you've charged a bunch of credit cards to the max [for things] that aren't really essential, is that your fault? You bet. But most of it I don't think is. You need a decent suit to go for a job interview. You can buy the cheap suit, but you won't get the call-back. You can break the rules at any turn, but there's a price for that."

In their book on two-income middle-class families, Tyagi and Warren attacked the "rock-solid" myth that "middle-class families are rushing headlong into financial ruin because they are squandering too much money on Red Lobster, Gucci and trips to the Bahamas."[26]

In fact, they wrote, after studying consumer bankruptcy data and other sources, "Today, after an average two-income family makes its house payments, car payments, insurance payments and child-care payments, they have less money left over, even though they have a second, full-time earner in the workplace," than an average single-earner family did in the early 1970s.[27]

One-paycheck households headed by women are among the most vulnerable. In an analysis of 2004 Federal Reserve Board data, the Consumer Federation of America found that the 31 million women who head households had median household income of $22,592, compared with $43,130 for all households. And women on their own had a median net worth of less than $33,000 compared with about $93,000 for all households.[28]

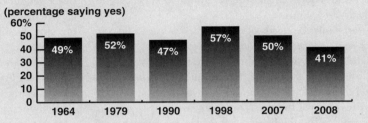

Fewer Americans Say They Are Better Off

The percentage of Americans who said they were better off in 2008 than they were five years earlier dropped to 41 percent in 2008, the lowest confidence level since 1964.

Are you better off now than you were five years ago?

(percentage saying yes)

Year	Percentage
1964	49%
1979	52%
1990	47%
1998	57%
2007	50%
2008	41%

Source: "Inside the Middle Class: Bad Times Hit the Good Life," Pew Research Center, April 2008

Are aggressive new government programs needed to bolster the middle class?

Last year, former Republican Rep. Ernest Istook of Oklahoma criticized then-presidential candidates Hillary Clinton and Obama for arguing that "America is a place where the middle class is repressed" by rising income inequality, stagnating wages, soaring medical and college costs and other woes.

"For both candidates," wrote Istook, a Heritage Foundation fellow, "the answer to all these problems is a rush of new government programs." He pointed to Heritage Foundation studies arguing that wage-growth data have been understated and that the poor are doing better than they were 14 years earlier.

"Convincing Americans that they need government to do all these things," he wrote, "hinges on convincing them that they are victims in need of rescue. . . . It's not enough for America's left to show sympathy for victims of real tragedies like 9/11 or Katrina. Now they must elevate every challenge into a crisis, provoking a sense of desperation that more and bigger government is the answer."[29]

Yet that is not how many policy advocates view the question of government help for the middle class. The pressures weighing on working families — heightened by the current economic crisis — are so great, they argue, that bold government action is needed to keep working Americans from further economic harm.

"We talk about the big financial institutions as too big to fail," says University of California political scientist Hacker. "But most Americans have until recently been apparently viewed as too small to save."

Without policy changes, including ones that make education and health care more affordable and help people build assets, "instability is going to stay," argues Wheary of Demos.

Yet, while the needs of the middle class are a favorite rhetorical device for politicians, they often disagree about the best way to advance those interests. This year's $787 billion stimulus package, which emerged from a cauldron of partisan bickering, is a case in point.

President Obama, speaking to employees of Caterpillar Inc. in February, said the stimulus plan is "about giving people a way to make a living, support their families and live out their dreams. Americans aren't looking for a handout. They just want to work."[30] But Rep. John A. Boehner of Ohio, a key Republican opponent of the president's recovery plan, said it "will do little to create jobs, and will do more harm than good to middle-class families and our economy."[31]

An overhaul of health-care policy is a key priority for many policy experts. Families USA, an advocacy group supporting affordable health care, pointed to research showing that nearly half of home foreclosures in 2006 were caused, at least partly, by financial issues growing out of a medical problem.[32]

Also key, many liberal policy analysts say, is solving what they see as a growing pension crisis, made more perilous for middle-class workers by the Wall Street crash. (*See sidebar, p. 324.*) Rep. George Miller, D-Calif., chairman of the House Education and Labor Committee, says private retirement-savings vehicles like 401(k) plans "have become little more than a high-stakes crap shoot. If you didn't take your retirement savings out of the market before the crash, you are likely to take years to recoup your losses, if at all."[33]

And crucial to the future of the middle class, many experts say, are sound policies for job creation and retention.

"The major policy change we need is to decide that good steady jobs with good wages are a family value," says Leicht of the University of Iowa. "It's good jobs at good wages that last — that's the Rosetta Stone."

Leicht says "our entire system of consumption is built around the idea that you accumulate a lot of debts when you're young, then you get a steady job and your income steadily rises and you gradually pay off your debt as you age." But nowadays, he says, the average job lasts only four to five years. "If you're constantly starting over, you never get out of the hole."

Leicht wants to see a 25 percent break on corporate taxes for businesses that create "high-quality jobs" — ones lasting at least five years and paying at least 30 percent above the median income of a family of four, which in 2007 was $75,675, according to the U.S. Census Bureau.

Kenworthy, the University of Arizona sociologist, advocates temporary "wage insurance" that would "prop up your earnings for a little while if you lost your job and took a new one that paid considerably less."

Not counting the current economic crisis, Kenworthy says, "there really isn't a problem in the United States with long-term unemployment. Most people are able to get a job within six months." Even so, he adds, such jobs often come "at a lower salary."

BACKGROUND

Evolving Concept

During the 2008 presidential campaign, the Rev. Rick Warren, pastor of giant Saddleback Church in Lake Forest, Calif., asked Democrat Obama and Republican John McCain to define "rich."

Obama said that "if you are making $150,000 a year or less as a family, then you're middle class, or you may be poor. But $150 [thousand] down you're basically middle class." He added, though, that "obviously, it depends on [the] region and where you're living." McCain answered the question another way, saying — perhaps with tongue in cheek — that as a definition of rich, "if you're just talking about income, how about $5 million?"[34]

Besides helping to open a window on the candidates' views and personalities, the exchange underscored how highly subjective social and economic class can be.

That's nothing new. For centuries, the concept of a "middle class" has been evolving.

"The middle class first came into existence in early modern Europe as a new social class for which the economic basis was financial rather than feudal — the system in which the nobility owned land and others (serfs, peons) worked it," according to Andrew Hoberek, an associate professor of English at the University of Missouri, Columbia, and author of *The Twilight of the Middle Class: Post World War II American Fiction and White-Collar Work.*[35]

In the United States, the term "middle class" didn't start showing up until the 1830s or 1840s, says Jennifer L. Goloboy, an independent scholar.[36] But years earlier, she says, a segment of the population began to embrace values that would come to define the American middle class, including diligence, frugality, self-restraint and optimism.

"The early republic was such an aspirational time, and it was disproportionately young," Goloboy says. "These young people came to the cities hoping for the best, and they clung to ideas of how they would make it. That's sort of the root of middle-class values. They believed that if they held to these values they were middle class, even if they were not necessarily successful yet."

As the American economy matured in the 20th century, industrialization both nurtured and threatened the nation's budding middle class. Pioneering automaker Henry Ford helped nurture it by paying high wages and encouraging mass consumption of his cars. But the gap between rich and poor remained wide, and industrialization made life precarious for the working class when jobs disappeared.

"The paramount evil in the workingman's life is irregularity of employment," Supreme Court Justice Louis D. Brandeis wrote in 1911.[37] Historian David Kennedy noted that Brandeis' view "was echoed in Robert and Helen Merrell Lynd's classic study *Middletown* a decade later, when they cited 'irregularity of employment' as the major factor that defined the difference between the life trajectories of the working class and the middle class."[38]

During the Great Depression of the 1930s, unemployment soared to 25 percent, and many Americans fell from middle-class stability into destitution. But from the ashes of the Depression came President Franklin D. Roosevelt's New Deal program, which *New York Times* columnist Krugman says created the modern middle class.[39]

"Income inequality declined drastically from the late 1930s to the mid-1940s, with the rich losing ground while working Americans saw unprecedented gains," he wrote.[40]

Consumerism at Its Finest

Some economists say the higher cost of necessities like health care, rather than spending on luxury items like big-screen TVs or new cars, has hit consumers hardest. Moreover, Americans' personal savings rate from 2005 to 2007 was just 0.6 percent — down from 9 percent in the 1980s — with household debt growing faster than personal income.

The New Deal "made America a middle-class society," Krugman wrote this year in *Rolling Stone* magazine. "Under FDR, America went through what labor historians call the Great Compression, a dramatic rise in wages for ordinary workers that greatly reduced income inequality. Before the Great Compression, America was a society of rich and poor; afterward it was a society in which most people, rightly, considered themselves middle class."[41]

After World War II, the U.S. economy blossomed, aided by the GI Bill, which helped millions of former service members buy homes and get college educations. In 1946, construction began on Levittown, one of a series of massive housing developments that became national models of middle-class suburbia.

The postwar boom helped spawn the contemporary notion of the American Dream — a home, a car or two (or three), a good job, paid vacation and a comfortable suburban lifestyle. By 1960, median family income was 30 percent higher in purchasing power than a decade earlier, and more than 60 percent of homes were owner-occupied, compared with 44 percent just before World War II.[42]

Downward Slide

But many economists say the good times began to wane in the 1970s, and for a variety of reasons that can be difficult to untangle. The shift away from manufacturing toward a service economy helped erode middle-class security, as did the increasingly competitive nature of globalization, many economists say. Some also cite the declining power of unions. In 1979, 27 percent of employed wage-and-salary workers in the United States were covered by a collective bargaining agreement, but that figure has steadily declined over the years. It stood at less than 14 percent in 2008.[43]

In remarks tied to formation of his middle-class task force, Obama said, "I do not view the labor movement as part of the problem; to me it's part of the solution. We need to level the playing field for workers and the unions that represent their interest, because we know that you cannot have a strong middle class without a strong labor movement."[44]

Hacker, the University of California political scientist, says that "employers at one time were encouraged by unions, the federal tax code and their own competitive instincts to provide very strong guaranteed benefits to many of their workers in the form of defined-benefit pension plans [and] good health insurance coverage."

But, he says, "over the last generation the work force has changed, and the competitive environment in which employers have operated changed in ways that have made it much less attractive for many employers to provide such

benefits. There used to be a kind of implicit long-term contract in many workplaces, enforced in part by unions, that is no longer there. So it's much more of a free-agent economic culture, which means that it's good for some workers but imposes a lot more risk on all of them."

Many conservatives disagree, though, on the role of unions in helping the middle class. "Numerous studies have shown that unions are not the answer to increasing prosperity for American workers or the economy," the U.S. Chamber of Commerce stated in a paper on the issue. It added: "Organized labor's claims that unionization is a ticket to the middle class cannot be squared with data showing that increased unionization decreases competitiveness and leads to slower job growth."[45]

Besides the issue of union influence, critics often cite Reagan-era economic policies, which included cuts in tax rates for those in upper-income brackets, as contributing to inequality and hurting the middle class.

The criticism is not universal. George Viksnins, a professor emeritus of economics at Georgetown University, argues that so-called Reaganomics was a plus for the middle class. "Perhaps the most significant positive aspect of the Reaganomics program of lower taxes and regulatory reforms is the tremendous increase in employment," he wrote.[46] In an interview, he said that "lowering marginal tax rates held out a lot of hope for young members of the middle class that they might get to keep some of the income" they earned "and didn't need to work quite as hard in sheltering it."

But others see the Reagan years differently. "Yes, there was a boom in the mid-1980s, as the economy recovered from a severe recession," Krugman, the Nobel economist and *Times* columnist, wrote. "But while the rich got much richer, there was little sustained economic improvement for most Americans. By the late 1980s, middle-class incomes were barely higher than they had been a decade before — and the poverty rate had actually risen."[47]

The University of Iowa's Leicht is highly critical of another legacy of the 1980s: deregulation of the banking industry, which he says set the stage for a massive increase in easy credit. The explosion in consumer lending that began in the 1980s helped millions of working Americans buy homes and cars, Leicht acknowledges, but he says the credit binge has come back to haunt the middle class now as home-foreclosure rates and personal bankruptcies soar.

CHRONOLOGY

1800-1929 *Industrial age shifts employment from farm to factory, setting stage for rise of middle class.*

October 1929 Stock market crash marks end of a speculative bubble on Wall Street.

1930-1970 *Great Depression sends unemployment soaring, President Roosevelt crafts New Deal social and economic legislation and postwar boom spurs growth of middle class.*

1933 Unemployment rate reaches 25 percent; Congress passes flood of New Deal legislation.

1935 President Franklin D. Roosevelt signs Social Security Act into law.

1939 Food Stamp program starts.

1944 Roosevelt signs Servicemen's Readjustment Act, or GI Bill, into law; by 1952, the law backed nearly 2.4 million home loans for World War II veterans, and by 1956 nearly 8 million vets had participated in education or training programs.

1946 Construction starts on New York's Levittown, one of three low-cost post-World War II residential communities that would come to define middle-class suburbia.

1960 Median family income is 30 percent higher in purchasing power than a decade earlier, and more than 60 percent of homes are owner-occupied, compared with 44 percent just before World War II.

1970-1995 *Oil shocks, inflation, foreign competition, and other changes mark tougher era for middle-class Americans.*

1979 U.S. manufacturing employment peaks at 21.4 million workers.

1981 President Ronald Reagan fires 11,000 striking members of the Professional Air Traffic Controllers Organization, helping to weaken the power of organized labor; Reagan persuades Congress to pass largest tax cuts in U.S. history.

1981-82 Severe recession rocks U.S. economy, sending the unemployment rate to 10.8 percent, the highest since the Great Depression.

Oct. 19, 1987 Dow Jones Industrial Average loses 23 percent of its value.

1996-Present *Home ownership peaks, and consumer spending soars, but good times end as home values plummet, financial institutions collapse and nation sinks into recession.*

1996 Congress ends 60-year welfare entitlement program, imposing work requirements and putting time limits on cash benefits.

1997 Federal minimum wage raised to $5.15 an hour.

2000 Federal poverty rate falls to 11.3 percent, lowest since 1974.

2001-2006 Housing prices in many cities double, and home-equity loans help lead to soaring consumer spending.

2004 Home-ownership rate peaks at 69 percent.

2008 Federal minimum wage rises to $6.55 an hour; it is set to increase to $7.25 effective July 24, 2009. . . . U.S. seizes Fannie Mae and Freddie Mac, Lehman Brothers files for bankruptcy and Washington Mutual collapses in biggest bank failure in history. . . . President George W. Bush signs $700 billion financial rescue bill but recession deepens.

2009 President Barack Obama announces budget seeking to aid middle class and forms Middle Class Task Force headed by Vice President Joseph Biden; first meeting focuses on "green jobs." . . . Federal unemployment rate rises to 7.6 percent in January (12.6 percent for African-Americans and 9.7 for Hispanics). . . . Labor Department says employers took 2,227 "mass layoff actions" in January, resulting in nearly 238,000 job cuts; from December 2007 through January 2009, mass layoff events totaled more than 25,700. . . . Claims for unemployment benefits exceed 5 million for first time in history. . . . Home foreclosures are reported on 274,399 U.S. properties in January, up 18 percent from January 2008.

What Does 'Middle Class' Really Mean?

Does the definition include income? Number of cars in the garage?

At his first White House press conference, President Barack Obama promised tax relief for "working and middle-class families." But what, exactly, does it mean to be in the "middle class"?

No official definition exists. Politicians, journalists and pundits freely use the term, often without attaching a precise meaning to it. And in opinion polls, most Americans — uncomfortable defining themselves as "rich" or "poor" — place themselves in the category of the middle class, even if their incomes reflect the outer limits of wealth or poverty.

In a report last year, the Pew Research Center noted that the term "middle class" is both "universally familiar" and "devilishly difficult to pin down."

"It is both a social and economic construct, and because these domains don't always align, its borders are fuzzy," Pew said. "Is a $30,000-a-year resident in brain surgery lower class? Is a $100,000-a-year plumber upper middle class?"

In a national survey of more than 2,400 American adults, Pew asked people to define themselves. It found that 53 percent said they were middle class. But, Pew said, "behind the reassuring simplicity of this number lies a nest of anomalies."

For example, it said, 41 percent of adults with annual household incomes of $100,000 or more said they were middle class, as did 46 percent of those with household incomes below $40,000. And of those in between, roughly a third said they were not middle class.

"If being middle income isn't the sole determinant of being middle class, what else is?" Pew added. "Wealth? Debt? Homeownership? Consumption? Marital status? Age? Race and ethnicity? Education? Occupation? Values?"[1]

Christian Weller, an associate professor of public policy at the University of Massachusetts, Boston, and a fellow at the liberal Center for American Progress, says that often, people count the number of cars in a garage or the square footage of a house to judge another person's economic standing. But, he says, "that's not really how people perceive and define middle class. . . . One part of middle class is an aspirational definition: 'I'll be able to send my kids to college, I'll be able to create a better future for my children, and do I have a secure lifestyle right now?'

"That goes beyond just simply having a good job," he says. "That means, do you have health insurance coverage, do you have enough savings, do you own your own home, do you

have retirement savings?" And, Weller adds, "By all those measures middle-class security has been eroding substantially."

Many economists look at the concept of a middle class through the lens of household-income data gathered by the federal government. Median household income was $50,233 in 2007, the latest year for which data are available.[2] That was the midpoint in the distribution, with half of households having more income and half less.[3]

The government also separates household income into five "quintiles," from lowest to highest. Some might consider "middle class" to mean only the third quintile — the one in the very middle — with incomes between $39,101 and $62,000. But many economists consider that view to be too cramped. Some count the third and fourth quintiles, with an upper limit of $100,000 in household income in 2007. Among the broadest definitions of middle class is one encompassing the three income quintiles in the middle, from $20,292 to $100,000.

Of course, using household income to measure the middle class has its own problems. For example, a family might seem solidly middle class based on its income, but parents may be toiling at two jobs each to raise their income level into the middle tier of the distribution tables. They might make good incomes but lack health insurance, putting them and their children at risk of a catastrophic financial collapse. Or they may live in a high-cost region of the country, where a supposed middle-class income of around $50,000 or $60,000 a year simply can't cover the bills.

One thing is certain, say those who have studied the American middle class: Its survival is crucial to the nation's future.

"It is the heart of the country, it's the heart of our democracy, it's the heart of our economy, it's the heart of our population," says Amelia Warren Tyagi, co-author of *The Two-Income Trap: Why Middle-Class Mothers and Fathers Are Going Broke.* "So while it may not be easy to define with precision, it's extremely important."

---

[1] Paul Taylor, et al., "Inside the Middle Class: Bad Times Hit the Good Life," Pew Research Center, April 9, 2008, p. 3, http://pewsocialtrends.org/assets/pdf/MC-Middle-class-report.pdf.

[2] U.S. Department of Commerce, Bureau of the Census, "Historical Income Tables — Households," www.census.gov/hhes/www/income/histinc/h05.html.

[3] In 2007, the United States had about 116,783,000 households.

"Starting in about the mid-1980s, we decided as a nation, through a number of mechanisms, that being loaned money was a perfect substitute for being paid it as long as you could buy things that represented middle-class status like houses and cars," Leicht says.

Impact of Globalization

Like the impact of so-called supply-side Reaganomics, the effects of globalization and trade policy are often hotly debated. While some argue they have, on balance, helped the U.S. economy, others say they have undermined middle-class security. (*See "At Issue," p. 327.*)

In his 2006 book *War on the Middle Class*, CNN anchor Lou Dobbs wrote "[i]n their free-trade fervor, Republicans and Democrats alike, most economists, certainly corporate leaders, and business columnists assure us that the loss of millions of jobs to other countries is the inevitable result of a modern global economy. The result, they promise us, will be a higher standard of living for everyone in America — and especially for the rest of the planet."

But Dobbs went on to say that millions of U.S. manufacturing jobs already had vanished and that many more jobs — including millions of white-collar service positions — were expected to do so in coming years, with the information-technology industry leading the way. "The free-trade-at-any-price enthusiasts once promised us that all those millions of people who lost their positions in manufacturing would find even better ones in the tech industry. But today no one is saying which industry will be the source of replacement for those jobs lost to outsourcing."[48]

C. Fred Bergsten, director of the Peterson Institute for International Economics, appearing on the PBS show "The NewsHour with Jim Lehrer," said studies by his organization have shown that the U.S. economy is $1 trillion a year richer as a result of globalization during the past 50 years.

Nonetheless, Bergsten said "there are losers . . . , costs . . . [and] downsides" to globalization and that the United States "has done a very poor job" in dealing with

Middle Class Enjoys Some of 'Life's Goodies'

More than two-thirds of middle-class Americans enjoy at least three of "life's goodies," such as high-speed Internet and more than one vehicle, according to the Pew Research Center. But half as many middle class as wealthy Americans have vacation homes, household help and children in private school.

Percentage of Americans who have. . .

Item	All incomes	Upper income	Middle income	Lower income
Cable or satellite service	70%	80%	71%	62%
Two or more cars	70	83	72	57
High-speed Internet	66	80	67	50
High-definition or flat screen TV	42	59	42	28
Young child in private school	15	31	14	6
Paid household help	16	36	13	7
A vacation home	10	19	9	4

Source: "Inside the Middle Class: Bad Times Hit the Good Life," Pew Research Center, April 2008

those problems. "You lose your health care when you lose your job. Unemployment insurance is miserably inadequate. Trade-adjustment assistance works, but it doesn't even cover [service] workers who get outsourced, and it's inadequate."

But Thea Lee, policy director and chief international economist at the AFL-CIO, who also appeared on the PBS program, was more critical of globalization than Bergsten. "We've had the wrong kind of globalization," she said. "It's been a corporate-dominated globalization, which has not really served working people here or our trading partners very well. . . . We've seen this long-term, decades-long stagnation of wages and growth of wage inequality in the United States even as we've been in a period of tremendous economic growth, productivity growth, technological improvements and increase in globalization."[49]

However one may interpret the economic history of recent decades, few observers would disagree that the middle class is now caught in the greatest economic downdraft in generations.

"We've really had an erosion of economic security and economic opportunity," and it occurred "very rapidly" after 2001, says Christian Weller, an associate professor of public policy at the University of Massachusetts,

Economic Meltdown Batters Retirement Plans

Reform proposals call for limiting risk to workers.

The economy may look bleak for millions of middle-class Americans, but for those in or near retirement, it's downright scary.

Experts say the steep downturns in stock and real estate values, along with soaring layoffs among older workers, have left millions worrying that they won't have enough income to see them through their golden years. And the crash has underscored what critics see as the weaknesses of 401(k) accounts — tax-advantaged plans that require employees to assume the primary responsibility for building and managing their retirement nest eggs.

"The collapse of the housing bubble, coupled with the plunge in the stock market, has exposed the gross inadequacy of our system of retirement income," Dean Baker, co-director of the Center for Economic and Policy Research, a liberal think tank in Washington, told a House committee in February.[1]

At the same hearing, Alicia H. Munnell, director of the Center for Retirement Research at Boston College, said the center's National Retirement Risk Index, which projects the share of households that will not be able to maintain their living standard in retirement, jumped from 31 percent in 1983 to 44 percent in 2006 and rises to 61 percent when health-care expenses are factored in.

Munnell said that in the two years following the stock market's peak on Oct. 9, 2007, the market value of assets in 401(k) retirement plans and Individual Retirement Accounts fell roughly 30 percent. For people ages 55 to 64, she said, median holdings in 401(k) plans went from a modest $60,000 or so in 2007 to $42,000 at the end of 2008.[2]

Critics have long warned of serious faults in the nation's private system of retirement savings. The number of so-called defined-benefit plans, which provide for guaranteed pensions, has been shrinking, while defined-contribution plans like 401(k)s have risen from supplemental savings vehicles in the early 1980s to what they are now: the main or sole retirement plan for most American workers covered by an employer-sponsored retirement plan.[3]

Jacob S. Hacker, a political scientist at the University of California in Berkeley, said the historical "three-legged stool" of retirement security — Social Security, private pensions and personal savings — is now precarious.

"The central issue for retirement security is . . . the risk," he told a congressional hearing last fall. "Retirement wealth has not only failed to rise for millions of families; it has also grown more risky, as the nation has shifted more of the responsibility for retirement planning from employers and government onto workers and their families.[4]

Several proposals have surfaced for revamping the retirement system, some bolder than others.

Teresa Ghilarducci, a professor at the New School for Social Research in New York, wants Congress to establish "Guaranteed Retirement Accounts," in which all workers not enrolled in an equivalent or better defined-benefit pension plan would participate. A contribution equal to 5 percent of each worker's earnings would go into an account each year, with the cost shared equally between worker and employer. A $600 federal tax credit would offset employees' contributions.

Money in the accounts would be managed by the federal government and earn a guaranteed 3 percent rate of return, adjusted for inflation. When a worker retired, the account would convert to an annuity that provides income until death, though a small portion could be taken in a lump sum at retirement. Those who died before retirement could leave only half their accounts to heirs; those who died after retiring could leave half the final balance minus benefits received.[5]

Boston, and a fellow at the liberal Center for American Progress.

After a "five-year window" of employment and wage growth during the late 1990s, Weller says, pressure on the middle class began accelerating in 2001. "There are different explanations, but one is . . . that after the 2001 recession [corporate] profits recovered much faster than in previous recessions, to much higher levels, and corporations were unchecked. They could engage in outsourcing and all these other techniques to boost their short-term profits, but obviously to the detriment of employees. I think what we ended up with was very slow employment growth, flat or declining wages and declining benefit coverage."

The plan has drawn criticism. Paul Schott Stevens, president and CEO of the Investment Company Institute, which represents the mutual-fund industry, called it "a non-starter."[6] Jan Jacobson, senior counsel for retirement policy at the American Benefits Council, said, "We believe the current employer-sponsored system is a good one that should be built on."[7]

But Ghilarducci told the AARP Bulletin Today that "people just want a guaranteed return for their retirement. The essential feature of my proposal is that people and employers would be relieved of being tied to the financial market."[8]

Hacker advocates an approach called "universal 401(k)" plans. The plans would be available to all workers, regardless of whether their employer offered a traditional retirement plan. All benefits would remain in the same account throughout a worker's life, and money could be withdrawn before retirement only at a steep penalty, as is the case with today's 401(k) plans. The plans would be shielded against excessive investments in company stock, and the default investment option would be a low-cost index fund that has a mix of stocks and bonds. Over time, the mix would change automatically to limit risk as a worker aged.

At age 65, government would turn a worker's account into a lifetime annuity that guarantees a flow of retirement income, unless the worker explicitly requested otherwise and showed he or she had enough assets to withstand market turmoil.

Employers would be encouraged to match workers' contributions to the plans, and government could give special tax breaks to companies offering better matches for lower-paid workers.[9]

Teresa Ghilarducci, a professor at the New School for Social Research, says Congress should establish "Guaranteed Retirement Accounts" for workers not enrolled in similar pension plans.

teresaghilarducci.org

Says Hacker, "We have to move toward a system in which there is a second tier of pension plans that is private but which provides key protections that were once provided by defined-benefit pension plans."

[1] "Strengthening Worker Retirement Security," testimony before House Committee on Education and Labor, Feb. 24, 2009, http://edlabor.house.gov/documents/111/pdf/testimony/20090224DeanBakertestimony.pdf.

[2] "The Financial Crisis and Restoring Retirement Security," testimony before House Committee on Education and Labor, Feb. 24, 2009, http://edlabor.house.gov/documents/111/pdf/testimony/20090224AliciaMunnellTestimony.pdf.

[3] Ibid. For background, see Alan Greenblatt, "Pension Crisis," *CQ Researcher*, Feb. 17, 2006, pp. 145-168, and Alan Greenblatt, "Aging Baby Boomers," *CQ Researcher*, Oct. 19, 2007, pp. 865-888.

[4] "The Impact of the Financial Crisis on Workers' Retirement Security," testimony before House Committee on Education and Labor field hearing, San Francisco, Oct. 22, 2008.

[5] For a detailed explanation, see, Teresa Ghilarducci, "Guaranteed Retirement Accounts: Toward retirement income security," Economic Policy Institute, Briefing Paper No. 204, Nov. 20, 2007, www.sharedprosperity.org/bp204/bp204.pdf.

[6] Stevens and Jacobson are quoted in Doug Halonen, "401(k) plans could be facing total revamp," *Financial Week*, Oct. 29, 2008.

[7] Ibid.

[8] Quoted in Carole Fleck, "401(k) Plans: Too Risky for Retirement Security?" AARP Bulletin Today, Dec. 17, 2008, http://bulletin.aarp.org/yourmoney/retirement/articles/401_k_plans_too_risky_for_retirement_security_.html.

[9] See Jacob S. Hacker, The Great Risk Shift (2006), pp. 185-187. See also Testimony before House Committee on Education and Labor, Oct. 22, 2008, op. cit.

And overlaid on all of that, Weller says, was the unprecedented boom in housing.

Even before the housing bubble burst, though, the middle class was on shaky ground, as Weller noted in an article early last year. In 2004, fewer than a third of families had accumulated enough wealth to equal three months of income, he found. And that was counting all financial assets, including retirement savings, minus debt.[50]

"For quite some time," says *Two-Income Trap* co-author Tyagi, "we've had a sizable minority of the middle class under enormous strain and on the verge of crisis, and since the recent meltdown the proportion of middle-class families in crisis increased exponentially.

"Many families teetering on the uncomfortable edge have been pushed over. I really see the [home] foreclosure crisis as front and center in this. We can't overestimate how important home ownership is to the middle class is, and what a crisis losing a home is."

CURRENT SITUATION

Narrowing the Gap

Joel Kotkin, a presidential fellow at Chapman University in Orange, Calif., and author of *The City: A Global History*, wrote recently that "over the coming decades, class will likely constitute the major dividing line in our society — and the greatest threat to America's historic aspirations."[51]

With the gap between rich and poor growing and even a college degree no assurance of upward mobility, Kotkin wrote, President Obama's "greatest challenge . . . will be to change this trajectory for Americans under 30, who supported him by two to one. The promise that 'anyone' can reach the highest levels of society is the basis of both our historic optimism and the stability of our political system. Yet even before the recession, growing income inequality was undermining Americans' optimism about the future."

Obama's legislative agenda, along with his middle-class task force, aims to narrow the class gap. But the deep recession, along with a partisan divide on Capitol Hill, could make some of his key goals difficult and costly to reach.

In announcing his budget, Obama did not hesitate to draw class distinctions between "the wealthiest few" and the "middle class" made up of "responsible men and women who are working harder than ever, worrying about their jobs and struggling to raise their families." He acknowledged that his political opponents are "gearing up for a fight" against his budget plan, which includes tax cuts for all but the richest Americans, universally available health-care coverage and other policies aimed squarely at the middle class. Yet, he said, "The system we have now might work for the powerful and well-connected interests that have run Washington for far too long, but I don't. I work for the American people."[52]

Republicans also are invoking middle-class concerns in expressing their opposition to Obama's budget. Delivering the GOP response to Obama's weekly address, Sen. Richard Burr, R-N.C., said the budget would require the typical American family to pay $52,000 in interest alone over the next decade.[53]

"Like a family that finds itself choking under the weight of credit-card balances and finance charges," said Burr, "the federal government is quickly obligating the American people to a similar fate.

The stimulus package signed by the president in February includes payroll-tax breaks for low- and moderate-income households and an expanded tax credit for higher-education expenses. But costly overhauls of health and retirement policies remain on the table.

Douglas W. Elmendorf, director of the Congressional Budget Office, told a Senate budget panel in February that without changes in health-insurance policy, an estimated 54 million people under age 65 will lack medical insurance by 2019, compared with 45 million this year. The projection "largely reflects the expectation that health-care costs and health-insurance premiums will continue to rise faster than people's income."[54]

Meanwhile, the abrupt collapse of the global financial markets has decimated middle-class retirement accounts. Between June 30 and September 30 of 2008, retirement assets fell 5.9 percent, from $16.9 trillion to $15.9 trillion, according to the latest tally by the Investment Company Institute, which represents the mutual-fund industry.[55]

In announcing his middle-class task force, Obama said his administration would be "absolutely committed to the future of America's middle class and working families. They will be front and center every day in our work in the White House."[56]

The group includes the secretaries of Labor, Health and Human Services, Education and Commerce, plus the heads of the National Economic Council, Office of Management and Budget, Domestic Policy Council and Council of Economic Advisors.[57]

According to the White House, the task force will aim to:

- Expand opportunities for education and lifelong training;
- Improve work and family balance;
- Restore labor standards, including workplace safety;
- Help to protect middle-class and working-family incomes, and
- Protect retirement security.

Has U.S. trade and globalization policy hurt the middle class?

YES
Thea Lee
Policy Director, AFL-CIO

Written for *CQ Researcher*, March 2, 2009

The middle class is not a single entity — nor is trade and globalization policy. The clothes we wear, the food we eat, the air we breathe, the jobs we have, the places we choose to live — all are affected by trade and globalization policy, but in many different ways.

I would argue, nonetheless, that U.S. trade and globalization policy has failed the middle class in numerous ways. It has eroded living standards for a large majority of American workers, undermined our social, environmental, consumer safety and public health protections, exacerbated our unsustainable international indebtedness, weakened our national security and compromised our ability to innovate and prosper in the future.

Most significant, especially during this global downturn, the negative impact of globalization on American wages should be a top concern — both for policy makers and for business. Economists may disagree about the magnitude of the effect, but few would dispute that globalization has contributed to the decades-long stagnation of real wages for American workers.

The Economic Policy Institute's L. Josh Bivens finds that the costs of globalization to a full-time median-wage earner in 2006 totaled approximately $1,400, and about $2,500 for a two-earner household. It only makes intuitive sense that if the point of globalization is to increase U.S. access to vast pools of less-skilled, less-protected labor, wages at home will be reduced — particularly for those workers without a college degree. And this impact will only grow in future years, as trade in services expands. We won't be able to rebuild our real economy and the middle class if we can't figure out how to use trade, tax, currency and national investment policies to reward efficient production at home — not send it offshore.

That is not to say, however, that trade and globalization in themselves are inherently pernicious. U.S. globalization policies in recent decades prioritized the interests of mobile, multinational corporations over domestic manufacturers, workers, farmers and communities. At the same time, they undermined prospects for equitable, sustainable and democratic development in our trading partners.

If we are going to move forward together in the future, we need to acknowledge that our current policies have not always delivered on their potential or their promise — particularly for middle-class workers. If new trade and globalization initiatives are to gain any political momentum, we will need deep reform in current policies.

NO
C. Fred Bergsten
Director, Peterson Institute for International Economics

Written for *CQ Researcher*, March 2, 2009

The backlash in the United States against globalization is understandable but misplaced. Despite widespread and legitimate concerns about worsening income distribution, wage stagnation and job insecurity, all serious economics studies show that globalization is only a modest cause of these problems. In the aggregate, globalization is a major plus for the U.S. economy and especially for the middle class.

An in-depth study by our nonpartisan institute demonstrates that the U.S. economy is $1 trillion per year richer as a result of global trade integration over the last half-century, or almost $10,000 per household. These gains accrue from cheaper imports, more high-paying export jobs and faster productivity growth. The American economy could gain another $500 billion annually if we could lift the remaining barriers to the international flow of goods and services.

Of course, any dynamic economic change, like technology advances and better corporate management, affects some people adversely. The negative impact of globalization totals about $50 billion a year due to job displacement and long-term income reductions. This is not an insignificant number, but the benefit-to-cost ratio from globalization is still a healthy 20-to-1.

The United States could not stop globalization even if it wanted to. But it must expand the social safety net for those displaced while making sure that our workers and firms can compete in a globalized world.

The Obama administration and the new Congress have already begun to shore up these safety nets through the fiscal stimulus package. Unemployment insurance has been substantially liberalized. Sweeping reform of the health care system has begun. Most important, Trade Adjustment Assistance has been dramatically expanded to cover all trade-impacted workers and communities.

We must also remember that globalization has lifted billions of the poorest citizens out of poverty. No country has ever achieved sustained modernization without integrating into the world economy, with China and India only the latest examples. The flip side is that products and services from these countries greatly improve the purchasing power and an array of consumer choices for the American middle class.

Fears of globalization have expanded during the current worldwide downturn. But strong export performance kept our economy growing through most of last year, and global cooperation is now necessary to ignite the needed recovery.

Soaring home foreclosures and job losses are battering middle class families. Home prices doubled between the mid-1990s and 2007, prompting many families to borrow against the higher values and take out cash for vacations and other expenditures. When values began plummeting, families with job losses and limited or no savings found themselves underwater.

The group's first meeting, on Feb. 27, focused on so-called green jobs.

Jared Bernstein, Vice President Biden's chief economist and a task force member, told *The Christian Science Monitor* that the group "has a different target" than the recently enacted $787 billion economic-stimulus plan, which includes huge government outlays with a goal of creating millions of jobs. "It's less about job quantity than job quality," Bernstein told the *Monitor* in an e-mail. "Its goal is to make sure that once the economy begins to expand again, middle-class families will reap their fair share of the growth, something that hasn't happened in recent years."[58]

Biden expressed a similar sentiment in an op-ed piece in *USA Today.* "Once this economy starts growing again, we need to make sure the benefits of that growth reach the people responsible for it. We can't stand by and watch as that narrow sliver of the top of the income scale wins a bigger piece of the pie — while everyone else gets a smaller and smaller slice," he wrote.[59]

In late January, as he pushed Congress to pass the stimulus plan, Obama said that not only would the task force focus on the middle class but that "we're not forgetting the poor. They are going to be front and center because they, too, share our American Dream."

Cash-Strapped States

Cash-strapped state governments are on the front lines of dealing with the swelling ranks of the nation's poor. States are struggling to handle a rising number of Americans in need of welfare assistance as the economy weakens — some of them middle-class households pushed over the financial edge by job losses and home foreclosures.

Despite the economic collapse, 18 states reduced their welfare rolls last year, and the number of people nationally receiving cash assistance was at or near the lowest point in more than four decades, a *New York Times* analysis of state data found.[60]

Michigan, with one of the nation's highest unemployment rates, reduced its welfare rolls 13 percent, and Rhode Island cut its by 17 percent, the *Times* said.

"Of the 12 states where joblessness grew most rapidly," the *Times* said, "eight reduced or kept constant the number of people receiving Temporary Assistance for Needy Families, the main cash welfare program for families with children. Nationally, for the 12 months ending October 2008, the rolls inched up a fraction of 1 percent."

While the recession has devastated households across the demographic spectrum, it has been especially hard on minorities. The overall unemployment rate in January stood at 7.6 percent, but it was 12.6 percent for African-Americans and 9.7 percent for Hispanics. The rate for whites was 6.9 percent. What's more, unemployment among minorities has been rising faster than for whites.[61]

The crash of the auto industry, among the most spectacular aspects of the past year's economic crisis, has devastated African-Americans.

About 118,000 African-Americans worked in the auto industry in November 2008, down from 137,000 in December 2007, the start of the recession, according to researchers at the Economic Policy Institute, a liberal think tank.[62]

"One of the engines of the black middle class has been the auto sector," Schmitt, told *USA Today* in January. In the late 1970s, "one of every 50 African-Americans in the U.S. was working in the auto sector. These jobs were the best jobs. Particularly for African-Americans who had migrated from the South, these were the culmination of a long, upward trajectory of economic mobility."[63]

For those living in high-cost urban areas — whether black, Hispanic or white — the strain of maintaining a middle-class standard of living is especially acute. According to 2008 survey data by the Pew research organization, more than a fourth of those who defined themselves as middle class who lived in high-cost areas said they had just enough money for basic expenses, or not even that much, compared with 16 percent living in low-cost metropolitan areas.[64]

In New York City, the nation's biggest urban area, people earning the median area income in the third quarter of 2008 could afford only about 11 percent of the homes in the metro area — the lowest proportion in the country — according to the Center for an Urban Future, a Manhattan think tank. To be in the middle class in Manhattan, according to the center's analysis, a person would need to make $123,322 a year, compared with $72,772 in Boston, $63,421 in Chicago and $50,000 in Houston.[65]

"New York has long been a city that has groomed a middle class, but that's a more arduous job today," said Jonathan Bowles, the center's director and a co-author of the report. "There's a tremendous amount of positives about the city, yet so many middle-class families seem to be stretched to their limits."[66]

OUTLOOK

Silver Lining?

No cloud is darker over the middle class than the deepening recession. "Everything points to this being at least three years of a weak economy," Nobel economist Krugman told a conference in February sponsored by several liberal groups.[67]

The economic crisis, he said, is "out of control," and "there's no reason to think there's any spontaneous mechanism for recovery. . . . My deep concern is not simply that it will be a very deep slide but that it will become entrenched."

Still, Krugman said, "If there's any silver lining to [the crisis], it's reopening the debate about the role of public policy in the economy."

Many liberals argue that policy changes in such areas as health-care coverage and higher-education benefits offer avenues for lifting middle-class families out of the economic mire and that getting medical costs under control is a key to the nation's long-term fiscal health. But many conservatives oppose more government spending. Advancing major reforms amid partisan bickering and a budget deficit inflated by bailouts, recession and war will be difficult.

University of Arizona political scientist Kenworthy says focusing policy changes on people living below the poverty level could be "easier to sell politically" and would still benefit those in higher income brackets.

"For example, think about the minimum wage," he says. Raising it "has an effect further up the wage distribution. The same with the earned-income tax credit," a refundable credit for low and moderate working people and families. "If it's made more generous, it has effects a bit further up. The same with health care."

As Washington grapples with potential policy changes, the plunging economy is forcing many middle-class consumers to live within their means. Many see that as a good thing.

"I certainly think some of the entitlements we have come to expect, like two homes, a brand-new car every couple of years, college education for all the kids, a yacht or two, expensive vacations — some of this will need to be reoriented," says Georgetown University's Viksnins. "Some reallocation of people's priorities is really necessary."

Yet, long-term optimism hasn't vanished amid the current economic gloom. "We will rebuild, we will recover and the United States of America will emerge stronger than before," Obama declared in an address on Feb. 24 to a joint session of Congress.

Viksnins says he is "utterly hopeful" about the future of the middle class.

And Sherk, the Heritage Foundation labor-policy fellow, says that "as long as your skills are valuable, you're going to find a job that pays you roughly at your productivity.

"For people in jobs disappearing from the economy, it's going to mean a substantial downward adjustment in standard of living," Sherk says. But "those in the middle class who have some college education, or have gone to a community college or have skills, broadly speaking, most will wind up on their feet again."

NOTES

1. Julie Bosman, "Newly Poor Swell Lines at Food Banks," *The New York Times*, Feb. 20, 2009, www.nytimes .com/2009/02/20/nyregion/20food.html?scp=1&sq= newly%20poor&st=cse.

2. For background, see the following *CQ Researcher* reports: Marcia Clemmitt, "Public Works Projects," Feb. 20, 2009, pp. 153-176; Kenneth Jost, "Financial Crisis," May 9, 2008, pp. 409-432; Thomas J. Billitteri, "Financial Bailout," Oct. 24, 2008, pp. 865-888; Marcia Clemmitt, "Mortgage Crisis," Nov. 2, 2007, pp. 913-936, and Barbara Mantel, "Consumer Debt," March 2, 2007, pp. 193-216.

3. For background see Kenneth Jost, "The Obama Presidency," *CQ Researcher*, Jan. 30, 2009, pp. 73-104.

4. Jackie Calmes, "Obama, Breaking 'From a Troubled Past,' Seeks a Budget to Reshape U.S. Priorities," *The New York Times*, Feb. 27, 2009, p. A1. For background, see the following *CQ Researcher* reports: Marcia Clemmitt, "Rising Health Costs," April 7, 2006, pp. 289-312, and Marcia Clemmitt, "Universal Coverage," March 30, 2007, pp. 265-288.

5. For background, see the following *CQ Researcher* reports: Thomas J. Billitteri, "Domestic Poverty," Sept. 7, 2007, pp. 721-744; Alan Greenblatt, "Upward Mobility," April 29, 2005, pp. 369-392; and Mary H. Cooper, "Income Equality," April 17, 1998, pp. 337-360.

6. Demos and Institute on Assets & Social Policy at Brandeis University, *From Middle to Shaky Ground: The Economic Decline of America's Middle Class, 2000-2006* (2008).

7. Paul Taylor, *et al.*, "Inside the Middle Class: Bad Times Hit the Good Life," Pew Research Center, April 9, 2008, http://pewsocialtrends.org/assets/pdf/ MC-Middle-class-report.pdf, p. 5.

8. Edmund L. Andrews, "Fed Calls Gain in Family Wealth a Mirage," Feb. 13, 2009, www.nytimes .com/2009/02/13/business/economy/13fed .html?ref=business. The study is by Brian K. Bucks, *et al.*, "Changes in U.S. Family Finances from 2004 to 2007: Evidence from the Survey of Consumer Finances," *Federal Reserve Bulletin*, Vol. 95, February 2009, www.federalreserve.gov/pubs/bulletin/2009/ pdf/scf09.pdf.

9. Jacob S. Hacker, *The Great Risk Shift* (2006), pp. 5-6.

10. Quoted in Ta-Nehisi Coates, "American Girl," *The Atlantic*, January/February 2009.

11. Julia B. Isaacs and Isabel V. Sawhill, "The Frayed American Dream," Brookings Institution, Nov. 28, 2007, www.brookings.edu/opinions/2007/1128_ econgap_isaacs.aspx.

12. *Ibid.*

13. Arloc Sherman, "Income Inequality Hits Record Levels, New CBO Data Show," Center on Budget and Policy Priorities, Dec. 14, 2007, www.cbpp .org/12-14-07inc.htm. The CBO report is "Historical Effective Federal Tax Rates: 1979 to 2005," www.cbo.gov/doc.cfm?index=8885. Figures are inflation adjusted and are in 2005 dollars.

14. Emmanuel Saez, "Striking it Richer: The Evolution of Top Incomes in the United States," University of California, Berkeley, March 15, 2008, http://elsa .berkeley.edu/~saez/saez-UStopincomes-2006prel.pdf.

15. For background, see the following *CQ Researcher* reports: Pamela M. Prah, "Labor Unions' Future," Sept. 2, 2005, pp. 709-732; Brian Hansen, "Global Backlash," Sept. 28, 2001, pp. 761-784; Mary H. Cooper, "World Trade," June 9, 2000, pp. 497-520; Mary H. Cooper, "Exporting Jobs," Feb. 20, 2004, pp. 149-172; and the following *CQ Global Researcher* reports: Samuel Loewenberg, "Anti-Americanism," March 2007, pp. 51-74, and Ken Moritsugu, "India Rising," May 2007, pp. 101-124.

16. John Schmitt, "The Good, the Bad, and the Ugly: Job Quality in the United States over the Three Most Recent Business Cycles," Center for Economic and Policy Research, November 2007, www.cepr.net/ documents/publications/goodjobscycles.pdf.

17. Alicia H. Munnell and Steven A. Sass, "The Decline of Career Employment," Center for Retirement Research, Boston College, September 2008, http:// crr.bc.edu/images/stories/ib_8-14.pdf.

18. Richard Florida, "How the Crash Will Reshape America," *The Atlantic*, March 2009, www.theatlantic .com/doc/200903/meltdown-geography.

19. James Sherk, "A Good Job Is Not So Hard to Find," Heritage Foundation, June 17, 2008 and revised and updated Sept. 2, 2008, www.heritage.org/research/labor/cda08-04.cfm.

20. George Packer, "The Ponzi State," *The New Yorker*, Feb. 9 and 16, 2009.

21. Paul Krugman, "Decade at Bernie's," *The New York Times*, Feb. 16, 2009, www.nytimes.com/2009/02/16/opinion/16krugman.html?scp=1&sq=decade%20at%20bernie's&st=cse.

22. Federal Housing Finance Agency, "U.S. Housing Price Index Estimates 1.8 Percent Price Decline From October to November," Jan. 22, 2009, www.ofheo.gov/media/hpi/MonthlyHPI12209F.pdf.

23. College Board, "Trends in College Pricing 2008," http://professionals.collegeboard.com/profdownload/trends-in-college-pricing-2008.pdf.

24. Department of Health and Human Services, Centers for Medicare and Medicaid Services, www.cms.hhs.gov/NationalHealthExpendData/downloads/tables.pdf.

25. Sara R. Collins, *et al.*, "Losing Ground: How the Loss of Adequate Health Insurance Is Burdening Working Families: Findings from the Commonwealth Fund Biennial Health Insurance Surveys, 2001-2007," Commonwealth Fund, Aug. 20, 2008, www.commonwealthfund.org/Content/Publications/Fund-Reports/2008/Aug/Losing-Ground-How-the-Loss-of-Adequate-Health-Insurance-Is-Burdening-Working-Families-8212-Finding.aspx.

26. Elizabeth Warren and Amelia Warren Tyagi, *The Two-Income Trap* (2003), p. 19.

27. *Ibid*, pp. 51-52.

28. Press release, "'Women on Their Own' in Much Worse Financial Condition Than Other Americans," Consumer Federation of America, Dec. 2, 2008, www.consumerfed.org/pdfs/Women_America_Saves_Tele_PR_12-2-08.pdf.

29. Ernest Istook, "Land of the free and home of the victims," Heritage Foundation, Feb. 29, 2008, www.heritage.org/Press/Commentary/ed022908b.cfm.

30. "Remarks by the President to Caterpillar Employees," Feb. 12, 2009, www.whitehouse.gov.

31. Foon Rhee, "Partisan spat continues on stimulus," Political Intelligence blog, *The Boston Globe*, Feb. 17, 2009, www.boston.com/news/politics/political intelligence/2009/02/partisan_spat_c.html.

32. Fact Sheet, "The Hidden Link: Health Costs and Family Economic Insecurity," Families USA, January 2009, www.familiesusa.org/assets/pdfs/the-hidden-link.pdf. The research cited by Families USA is by Christopher Tarver Robertson, *et al.*, "Get Sick Get Out: The Medical Causes of Home Mortgage Foreclosures," *Health Matrix Vol. 18*, 2008, pp. 65-105.

33. Reuters, "U.S. may need new retirement savings plans: lawmaker," Feb. 24, 2009, www.reuters.com/article/domesticNews/idUSTRE51N5UM20090224.

34. Lynn Sweeton, "Transcript of Obama, McCain at Saddleback Civil Forum with Pastor Rick Warren," *Chicago Sun Times*, Aug. 18, 2008, http://blogs.suntimes.com/sweet/2008/08/transcript_of_obama_mccain_at.html.

35. Quoted in Jeanna Bryner, "American Dream and Middle Class in Jeopardy," www.livescience.com, October 9, 2008, www.livescience.com/culture/081009-middle-class.html.

36. See Jennifer L. Goloboy, "The Early American Middle Class," *Journal of the Early Republic*, Vol. 25, No. 4, winter 2005.

37. Quoted in David Kennedy, *Freedom From Fear* (1999), p. 264.

38. *Ibid.*

39. For historical background, see *CQ Researcher Plus Archive* for a large body of contemporaneous coverage during the 1930s and 1940s in *Editorial Research Reports*, the precursor to the *CQ Researcher*.

40. Paul Krugman, "The Conscience of a Liberal: Introducing This Blog" *The New York Times*, Sept. 18, 2007, http://krugman.blogs.nytimes.com/2007/09/18/introducing-this-blog/.

41. Paul Krugman, "What Obama Must Do: A Letter to the New President," *Rolling Stone*, Jan. 14, 2009, www.rollingstone.com/politics/story/25456948/what_obama_must_do.

42. James T. Patterson, *Grand Expectations* (1996), p. 312.

43. Barry Hirsch, Georgia State University, and David Macpherson, Florida State University, "Union Membership, Coverage, Density, and Employment

Among All Wage and Salary Workers, 1973-2008," www.unionstats.com.

44. "Remarks by the President and the Vice President in Announcement of Labor Executive Orders and Middle-Class Working Families Task Force," Jan. 30, 2009, www.whitehouse.gov/blog_post/Todaysevent/.

45. U.S. Chamber of Commerce, "Is Unionization the Ticket to the Middle Class? The Real Economic Effects of Labor Unions," 2008, www.uschamber.com/assets/labor/unionrhetoric_econeffects.pdf.

46. George J. Viksnins, "Reaganomics after Twenty Years," www9.georgetown.edu/faculty/viksning/papers/Reaganomics.html.

47. Paul Krugman, "Debunking the Reagan Myth," *The New York Times*, Jan. 21, 2008, www.nytimes.com/2008/01/21/opinion/21krugman.html?scp=1&sq=%22Debunking%20the%20Reagan%20Myth%22&st=cse.

48. Lou Dobbs, *War on the Middle Class* (2006), p. 112.

49. Transcript, "In Bad Economy, Countries Contemplate Protectionist Measures," "The NewsHour with Jim Lehrer," Feb. 19, 2009, www.pbs.org/newshour/bb/business/jan-june09/trade_02-19.html.

50. Christian Weller, "The Erosion of Middle-Class Economic Security After 2001," *Challenge*, Vol. 51, No. 1, January/February 2008, pp. 45-68.

51. Joel Kotkin, "The End of Upward Mobility?" *Newsweek*, Jan. 26, 2009, p. 64.

52. "Remarks of President Barack Obama, Weekly Address," Feb. 28, 2009, www.whitehouse.gov/blog/09/02/28/Keeping-Promises/.

53. "Burr delivers GOP challenge to Obama's budget," www.wral.com, Feb. 28, 2009, www.wral.com/news/local/story/4635676/.

54. Statement before the Committee on the Budget, U.S. Senate, "Expanding Health Insurance Coverage and Controlling Costs for Health Care," Feb. 10, 2009, www.cbo.gov/ftpdocs/99xx/doc9982/02-10-HealthVolumes_Testimony.pdf.

55. Investment Company Institute, "Retirement Assets Total $15.9 Trillion in Third Quarter," Feb. 19, 2009, www.ici.org/home/09_news_q3_retmrkt_update.html#TopOfPage.

56. Quoted in Jeff Zeleny, "Obama Announces Task Force to Assist Middle-Class Families," *The New York Times*, Dec. 22, 2008.

57. Cited at www.whitehouse.gov/blog_post/about_the_task_force_1/.

58. Mark Trumbull, "Will Obama's plans help the middle class?" *The Christian Science Monitor*, Dec. 24, 2008.

59. Joe Biden, "Time to put middle class front and center," *USA Today*, Jan. 30, 2009.

60. Jason DeParle, "Welfare Aid Isn't Growing as Economy Drops Off," *The New York Times*, Feb. 2, 2009.

61. See Bureau of Labor Statistics, "The Employment Situation: January 2009," www.bls.gov/news.release/empsit.nr0.htm.

62. Robert E. Scott and Christian Dorsey, "African Americans are especially at risk in the auto crisis," Economic Policy Institute, Snapshot, Dec. 5, 2008, www.epi.org/economic_snapshots/entry/webfeatures_snapshots_20081205/.

63. Quoted in Larry Copeland, "Auto industry's slide cuts a main route to the middle class," *USA Today*, Jan. 20, 2009, www.usatoday.com/money/autos/2009-01-20-blacks-auto-industry-dealers_N.htm.

64. D'Vera Cohn, "Pricey Neighbors, High Stress," Pew Social and Demographic Trends, May 29, 2008, www.pewsocialtrends.org/pubs/711/middle-class-blues.

65. Jonathan Bowles, *et al.*, "Reviving the City of Aspiration: A study of the challenges facing New York City's middle class," Center for an Urban Future, Feb. 2009, www.nycfuture.org/images_pdfs/pdfs/CityOfAspiration.pdf.

66. Quoted in Daniel Massey, "City faces middle-class exodus," *Crain's New York Business*, Feb. 5, 2009, www.crainsnewyork.com/article/20090205/FREE/902059930.

67. Krugman spoke at the "Thinking Big, Thinking Forward" conference in Washington on Feb. 11 sponsored by *The American Prospect*, the Institute for America's Future, Demos and the Economic Policy Institute.

BIBLIOGRAPHY

Books

Dobbs, Lou, *War on the Middle Class*, Viking, 2006.
The CNN broadcaster argues that the American government and economy are dominated by a wealthy and politically powerful elite who have exploited working Americans.

Frank, Robert H., *Falling Behind: How Rising Inequality Harms the Middle Class*, University of California Press, 2007.
The Cornell University economist argues that most income gains in recent decades have gone to people at the top, leading them to build bigger houses, which in turn has led middle-income families to spend a bigger share of their incomes on housing and curtail spending in other important areas.

Hacker, Jacob S., *The Great Risk Shift*, Oxford University Press, 2006.
A professor of political science argues that economic risk has shifted from "broad structures of insurance," including those sponsored by corporations and government, "onto the fragile balance sheets of American families."

Uchitelle, Louis, *The Disposable American*, Alfred A. Knopf, 2006.
A New York Times business journalist, writing before the current economic crises threw millions of workers out of their jobs, calls the layoff trend "a festering national crisis."

Articles

Copeland, Larry, "Auto industry's slide cuts a main route to the middle class," *USA Today*, Jan. 20, 2009, www.usatoday.com/money/autos/2009-01-20-blacks-auto-industry-dealers_N.htm?loc=interstitialskip.
The financial crisis in the auto industry "has been more devastating for African-Americans than any other community," Copeland writes.

Gallagher, John, "Slipping standard of living squeezes middle class," *Detroit Free Press*, Oct. 12, 2008, www.freep.com/article/20081012/BUSINESS07/810120483.
America's middle-class living standard "carried generations from dirt-floor cabins to manicured suburban subdivisions," Gallagher writes, but it "has sputtered and stalled."

Kotkin, Joel, "The End of Upward Mobility?" *Newsweek*, Jan. 26, 2009, www.newsweek.com/id/180041.
A presidential fellow at Chapman University writes that class, not race, "will likely constitute the major dividing line in our society."

Samuelson, Robert J., "A Darker Future For Us," *Newsweek*, Nov. 10, 2008, www.newsweek.com/id/166821/output/print.
An economic journalist argues that the central question confronting the new administration is whether the economy is at an historic inflection point, "when its past behavior is no longer a reliable guide to its future."

Weller, Christian, "The Erosion of Middle-Class Economic Security After 2001," *Challenge*, Vol. 51, No. 1, January/February 2008, pp. 45-68.
An associate professor of public policy at the University of Massachusetts, Boston, and senior fellow at the liberal Center for American Progress concludes that the gains in middle-class security of the late 1990s have been entirely eroded.

Reports and Studies

Bowles, Jonathan, Joel Kotkin and David Giles, "Reviving the City of Aspiration: A study of the challenges facing New York City's middle class," *Center for an Urban Future*, February 2009, www.nycfuture.org/images_pdfs/pdfs/CityOfAspiration.pdf.
Major changes to the nation's largest city have greatly diminished its ability to both create and retain a sizeable middle class, argues this report.

Schmitt, John, "The Good, the Bad, and the Ugly: Job Quality in the United States over the Three Most Recent Business Cycles," *Center for Economic and Policy Research*, November 2007, www.cepr.net/documents/publications/goodjobscycles.pdf.
The share of "good jobs," defined as ones paying at least $17 an hour and offering employer-provided medical insurance and a pension, deteriorated in the 2000-2006 business cycle.

Sherk, James, "A Good Job So Hard to Find," *Heritage Foundation*, June 17, 2008, www.heritage.org/research/labor/cda08-04.cfm.

Job opportunities have expanded the most in occupations with the highest wages, the conservative think tank states.

Taylor, Paul, *et al.,* "Inside the Middle Class: Bad Times Hit the Good Life," *Pew Research Center,* April 2008, http://pewsocialtrends.org/assets/pdf/MC-Middle-class-report.pdf.
The report aims to present a "comprehensive portrait of the middle class" based on a national opinion survey and demographic and economic data.

Wheary, Jennifer, Thomas M. Shapiro and Tamara Draut, "By A Thread: The New Experience of America's Middle Class," *Demos and the Institute on Assets and Social Policy at Brandeis University,* 2007, www.demos.org/pubs/BaT112807.pdf.
The report includes a "Middle Class Security Index" that portrays how well middle-class families are faring in the categories of financial assets, education, income and health care.

For More Information

Brookings Institution, 1775 Massachusetts Ave., N.W., Washington, DC 20036; (202) 797-6000; www.brookings.edu. Independent research and policy institute conducting research in economics, governance, foreign policy and development.

Center on Budget and Policy Priorities, 820 First St., N.E., Suite 510, Washington, DC 20002; (202) 408-1080; www.cbpp.org. Studies fiscal policies and public programs affecting low- and moderate-income families and individuals.

Center for Economic and Policy Research, 1611 Connecticut Ave., N.W., Suite 400, Washington, DC 20009; (202) 293-5380; www.cepr.net. Works to better inform citizens on the economic and social choices they make.

Center for Retirement Research, Boston College, 140 Commonwealth Ave., Chestnut Hill, MA 02467; (617) 552-1762; www.crr.bc.edu. Researches and provides the public and private sectors with information to better understand the issues facing an aging population.

Center for an Urban Future, 120 Wall St., 20th Floor, New York, NY, 10005; (212) 479-3341; www.nycfuture.org. Dedicated to improving New York City by targeting problems facing low-income and working-class neighborhoods.

Consumer Federation of America, 1620 I St., N.W., Suite 200, Washington, DC 20006; (202) 387-6121; www.consumerfed.org. Advocacy and research organization promoting pro-consumer policies before Congress and other levels of government.

Dēmos, 220 Fifth Ave., 5th Floor, New York, NY 10001; (212) 633-1405; www.demos.org. Liberal think tank pursuing an equitable economy with shared prosperity and opportunity.

Heritage Foundation, 214 Massachusetts Ave., N.E., Washington, DC 20002; (202) 546-4400; www.heritage.org. Formulates and promotes public policies based on a conservative agenda.

Middle Class Task Force, 1600 Pennsylvania Ave., N.W., Washington, DC 20500; (202) 456-1414; www.whitehouse.gov/strongmiddleclass. Presidential task force headed by Vice President Joseph R. Biden working to raise the living standards of middle-class families.

Pew Research Center, 1615 L St., N.W., Suite 700, Washington, DC 20036; (202) 419-4300; www.pewresearch.org. Provides nonpartisan research and information on issues, attitudes and trends shaping the United States.

U.S. Chamber of Commerce, 1615 H St., N.W., Washington, DC 20062; (202) 659-6000; www.uschamber.com. Business federation lobbying for free enterprise before all branches of government.

14

Women's Rights

Are Violence and Discrimination
Against Women Declining?

Karen Foerstel

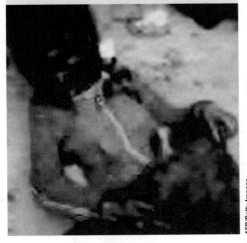

Iraqi teenager Du'a Khalil Aswad lies mortally wounded after her "honor killing" by a mob in the Kurdish region of Iraq. No one has been prosecuted for the April 2007 murder, even though a cell-phone video of the incident was posted on the Internet. Aswad's male relatives are believed to have arranged her ritualistic execution because she had dated a boy from outside her religious sect. The United Nations estimates that 5,000 women and girls are murdered in honor killings around the globe each year.

From *CQ Global Researcher*,
May 2008.

She was 17 years old. The blurry video shows her lying in a dusty road, blood streaming down her face, as several men kick and throw rocks at her. At one point she struggles to sit up, but a man kicks her in the face forcing her back to the ground. Another slams a large, concrete block down onto her head. Scores of onlookers cheer as the blood streams from her battered head.[1]

The April 7, 2007, video was taken in the Kurdish area of northern Iraq on a mobile phone. It shows what appear to be several uniformed police officers standing on the edge of the crowd, watching while others film the violent assault on their phones.

The brutal, public murder of Du'a Khalil Aswad reportedly was organized as an "honor killing" by members of her family — and her uncles and a brother allegedly were among those in the mob who beat her to death. Her crime? She offended her community by falling in love with a man outside her religious sect.[2]

According to the United Nations, an estimated 5,000 women and girls are murdered in honor killings each year, but it was only when the video of Aswad's murder was posted on the Internet that the global media took notice.[3]

Such killings don't only happen in remote villages in developing countries. Police in the United Kingdom estimate that up to 17,000 women are subjected to some kind of "honor"-related violence each year, ranging from forced marriages and physical attacks to murder.[4]

But honor killings are only one type of what the international community calls "gender based violence" (GBV). "It is universal," says Taina Bien-Aimé, executive director of the New York-based

Only Four Countries Offer Total Equality for Women

Costa Rica, Cuba, Sweden and Norway receive the highest score (9 points) in an annual survey of women's economic, political and social rights. Out of the world's 193 countries, only 26 score 7 points or better, while 28 — predominantly Islamic or Pacific Island countries — score 3 or less. The United States rates 7 points: a perfect 3 on economic rights but only 2 each for political and social rights. To receive 3 points for political rights, women must hold at least 30 percent of the seats in the national legislature. Women hold only 16.6 percent of the seats in the U.S. Congress. The U.S. score of 2 on social rights reflects what the report's authors call "high societal discrimination against women's reproductive rights."

Status of Women's Rights Around the Globe

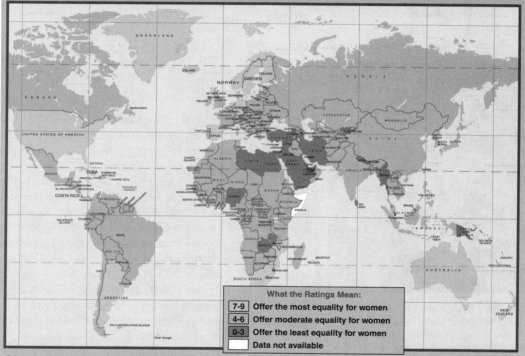

What the Ratings Mean:
- 7-9 Offer the most equality for women
- 4-6 Offer moderate equality for women
- 0-3 Offer the least equality for women
- Data not available

Source: Cingranelli-Richards Human Rights Dataset, http://ciri.binghamton.edu/, based on Amnesty International's annual reports and U.S. State Department annual Country Reports on Human Rights. The database is co-directed by David Louis Cingranelli, a political science professor at Binghamton University, SUNY, and David L. Richards, an assistant political science professor at the University of Memphis.

women's-rights group Equality Now. "There is not one country in the world where violence against women doesn't exist."

Thousands of women are murdered or attacked around the world each day, frequently with impunity. In Guatemala, where an estimated 3,000 women have been killed over the past seven years, most involving some kind of misogynistic violence, only 1 percent of the perpetrators were convicted.[5] In India, the United Nations estimates that five women are burned to death each day by husbands upset that they did not receive sufficient dowries from their brides.[6] In Asia, nearly 163 million females are "missing" from the population — the result of sex-selective abortions, infanticide or neglect.

And since the 1990s some African countries have seen dramatic upsurges in rapes of very young girls by men who believe having sex with a virgin will protect or cure them from HIV-AIDS. After a 70-year-old man allegedly raped a 3-year-old girl in northern Nigeria's commercial hub city of Kano, Deputy Police Chief Suleiman Abba told reporters in January, "Child rape is becoming rampant in Kano." In the last six months of 2007, he said, 54 cases of child rape had been reported. "In some cases the victims are gang-raped."[7]

Epidemics of sexual violence commonly break out in countries torn apart by war, when perpetrators appear to have no fear of prosecution. Today, in Africa, for instance, UNICEF says there is now a "license to rape" in eastern regions of the Democratic Republic of the Congo, where some human-rights experts estimate that up to a quarter of a million women have been raped and often sexually mutilated with knives, branches or machetes.[8] Several of the Congolese rapists remorselessly bragged to an American filmmaker recently about how many women they had gang-raped.[9]

"The sexual violence in Congo is the worst in the world," said John Holmes, the United Nations under secretary general for humanitarian affairs. "The sheer numbers, the wholesale brutality, the culture of impunity — it's appalling."[10]

In some cultures, the female victims themselves are punished. A report by the Human Rights Commission of Pakistan found that a woman is gang-raped every eight hours in that country. Yet, until recently, rape cases could not be prosecuted in Pakistan unless four Muslim men "all of a pious and trustworthy nature" were willing to testify that they witnessed the attack. Without their testimony the victim could be prosecuted for fornication and alleging a false crime, punishable by stoning, lashings or prison.[11] When the law was softened in 2006 to allow judges to decide whether to try rape cases in Islamic courts or criminal courts, where such witnesses are not required, thousands took to the streets to protest the change.[12]

Honor killings are up 400 percent in Pakistan over the last two years, and Pakistani women also live in fear of being blinded or disfigured by "acid attacks" — a common practice in Pakistan and a handful of other countries — in which attackers, usually spurned suitors, throw acid on a woman's face and body.

Women's Suffering Is Widespread

More than two decades after the U.N. Decade for Women and 29 years after the U.N. adopted the Convention on the Elimination of All Forms of Discrimination against Women (CEDAW), gender discrimination remains pervasive throughout the world, with widespread negative consequences for society.

According to recent studies on the status of women today:

- Violence against women is pervasive. It impoverishes women, their families, communities and nations by lowering economic productivity and draining resources. It also harms families across generations and reinforces other violence in societies.

- Domestic violence is the most common form of violence against women, with rates ranging from 8 percent in Albania to 49 percent in Ethiopia and Zambia. Domestic violence and rape account for 5 percent of the disease burden for women ages 15 to 44 in developing countries and 19 percent in developed countries.

- Femicide — the murder of women — often involves sexual violence. From 40 to 70 percent of women murdered in Australia, Canada, Israel, South Africa and the United States are killed by husbands or boyfriends. Hundreds of women were abducted, raped and murdered in and around Juárez, Mexico, over the past 15 years, but the crimes have never been solved.

- At least 160 million females, mostly in India and China, are "missing" from the population — the result of sex-selective abortions.

- Rape is being used as a genocidal tool. Hundreds of thousands of women have been raped and sexually mutilated in the ongoing conflict in Eastern Congo. An estimated 250,000 to 500,000 women were raped during the 1994 genocide in Rwanda; up to 50,000 women were raped during the Bosnian conflict in the 1990s. Victims are often left unable to have children and are deserted by their husbands and shunned by their families, plunging the women and their children into poverty.

- Some 130 million girls have been genitally mutilated, mostly in Africa and Yemen, but also in immigrant communities in the West.

- Child rape has been on the increase in the past decade in some African countries, where some men believe having sex with a virgin will protect or cure them from HIV-AIDS. A study at the Red Cross children's hospital in Cape Town, South Africa, found that 3-year-old girls were more likely to be raped than any other age group.

- Two million girls between the ages of 5 and 15 are forced into the commercial sex market each year, many of them trafficked across international borders.

- Sexual harassment is pervasive. From 40 to 50 percent of women in the European Union reported some form of sexual harassment at work; 50 percent of schoolgirls surveyed in Malawi reported sexual harassment at school.

- Women and girls constitute 70 percent of those living on less than a dollar a day and 64 percent of the world's illiterate.

- Women work two-thirds of the total hours worked by men but earn only 10 percent of the income.

- Half of the world's food is produced by women, but women own only 1 percent of the world's land.

- More than 1,300 women die each day during pregnancy and childbirth — 99 percent of them in developing countries.

Sources: "Ending violence against women: From words to action," United Nations, October, 2006, www.un.org/womenwatch/daw/public/VAW_Study/VAW studyE.pdf; www.womankind.org.uk; www.unfp.org; www.oxfam.org.uk; www.ipu.org; www.unicef.org; www.infant-trust.org.uk; "State of the World Population 2000;" http://npr.org; http://asiapacific.amnesty.org; http://news.bbc.co.uk

Negative Attitudes Toward Women Are Pervasive

Negative attitudes about women are widespread around the globe, among women as well as men. Rural women are more likely than city women to condone domestic abuse if they think it was provoked by a wife's behavior.

Location	Percentage of women in selected countries who agree that a man has good reason to beat his wife if:						Women who agree with:	
	Wife does not complete housework	Wife disobeys her husband	Wife refuses sex	Wife asks about other women	Husband suspects infidelity	Wife is unfaithful	One or more of the reasons mentioned	None of the reasons mentioned
Bangladesh city	13.8	23.3	9.0	6.6	10.6	51.5	53.3	46.7
Bangladesh province	25.1	38.7	23.3	14.9	24.6	77.6	79.3	20.7
Brazil city	0.8	1.4	0.3	0.3	2.0	8.8	9.4	90.6
Brazil province	4.5	10.9	4.7	2.9	14.1	29.1	33.7	66.3
Ethiopia province	65.8	77.7	45.6	32.2	43.8	79.5	91.1	8.9
Japan city	1.3	1.5	0.4	0.9	2.8	18.5	19.0	81.0
Namibia city	9.7	12.5	3.5	4.3	6.1	9.2	20.5	79.5
Peru city	4.9	7.5	1.7	2.3	13.5	29.7	33.7	66.3
Peru province	43.6	46.2	25.8	26.7	37.9	71.3	78.4	21.6
Samoa	12.1	19.6	7.4	10.1	26.0	69.8	73.3	26.7
Serbia and Montenegro city	0.6	0.97	0.6	0.3	0.9	5.7	6.2	93.8
Thailand city	2.0	0.8	2.8	1.8	5.6	42.9	44.7	55.3
Thailand province	11.9	25.3	7.3	4.4	12.5	64.5	69.5	30.5
Tanzania city	24.1	45.6	31.1	13.8	22.9	51.5	62.5	37.5
Tanzania province	29.1	49.7	41.7	19.8	27.2	55.5	68.2	31.8

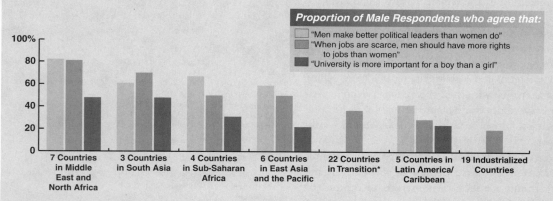

Proportion of Male Respondents who agree that:

- ☐ "Men make better political leaders than women do"
- ☐ "When jobs are scarce, men should have more rights to jobs than women"
- ☐ "University is more important for a boy than a girl"

7 Countries in Middle East and North Africa · 3 Countries in South Asia · 4 Countries in Sub-Saharan Africa · 6 Countries in East Asia and the Pacific · 22 Countries in Transition · 5 Countries in Latin America/Caribbean · 19 Industrialized Countries*

* Countries in transition are generally those that were once part of the Soviet Union.

Sources: World Health Organization, www.who.int/gender/violence/who_multicountry_study/Chapter3-Chapter4.pdf; "World Values Survey," www.worldvaluessruvey.org

But statistics on murder and violence are only a part of the disturbing figures on the status of women around the globe. Others include:

- Some 130 million women have undergone female genital mutilation, and another 2 million are at risk every year, primarily in Africa and Yemen.
- Women and girls make up 70 percent of the world's poor and two-thirds of its illiterate.
- Women work two-thirds of the total hours worked by men but earn only 10 percent of the income.
- Women produce more than half of the world's food but own less than 1 percent of the world's property.
- More than 500,000 women die during pregnancy and childbirth every year — 99 percent of them in developing countries.
- Two million girls between the ages of 5 and 15 are forced into the commercial sex market each year.[13]
- Globally, 10 million more girls than boys do not attend school.[14]

Despite these alarming numbers, women have made historic progress in some areas. The number of girls receiving an education has increased in the past decade. Today 57 percent of children not attending school are girls, compared to two-thirds in the 1990s.[15]

And women have made significant gains in the political arena. As of March, 2008, 14 women are serving as elected heads of state or government, and women now hold 17.8 percent of the world's parliamentary seats — more than ever before.[16] And just three months after the brutal killing of Aswad in Iraq, India swore in its first female president, Pratibha Patil, who vows to eliminate that country's practice of aborting female fetuses because girls are not as valued as boys in India. (*See "At Issue," p. 357.*)[17]

Last October, Argentina elected its first female president, Cristina Fernández de Kirchner,* the second woman in two years to be elected president in South America. Michelle Bachelet, a single mother, won the presidency in Chile in 2006.[18] During her inaugural speech Kirchner

admitted, "Perhaps it'll be harder for me, because I'm a woman. It will always be harder for us."[19]

Indeed, while more women than ever now lead national governments, they hold only 4.4 percent of the world's 342 presidential and prime ministerial positions. And in no country do they hold 50 percent or more of the national legislative seats.[20]

"Women make up half the world's population, but they are not represented" at that level, says Swanee Hunt, former U.S. ambassador to Austria and founding director of the Women and Public Policy Program at Harvard's Kennedy School of Government.

While this is "obviously a fairness issue," she says it also affects the kinds of public policies governments pursue. When women comprise higher percentages of officeholders, studies show "distinct differences in legislative outputs," Hunt explains. "There's less funding of bombs and bullets and more on human security — not just how to defend territory but also on hospitals and general well-being."

Today's historic numbers of women parliamentarians have resulted partly from gender quotas imposed in nearly 100 countries, which require a certain percentage of women candidates or officeholders.[21]

During the U.N.'s historic Fourth World Conference on Women — held in Beijing in 1995 — 189 governments adopted, among other things, a goal of 30 percent female representation in national legislatures around the world.[22] But today, only 20 countries have reached that goal, and quotas are often attacked as limiting voters' choices and giving women unfair advantages.[23]

Along with increasing female political participation, the 5,000 government representatives at the Beijing conference — one of the largest gatherings in U.N. history — called for improved health care for women, an end to violence against women, equal access to education for girls, promotion of economic independence and other steps to improve the condition of women around the world.[24]

"Let Beijing be the platform from which our global crusade will be carried forward," Gertrude Mongella, U.N. secretary general for the conference, said during closing ceremonies. "The world will hold us accountable for the implementation of the good intentions and decisions arrived at in Beijing."[25]

---

* Isabel Martínez Perón assumed the presidency of Argentina on the death of her husband, Juan Perón, in 1974 and served until she was deposed in a coup d'etat in 1976; but she was never elected.

Spain's visibly pregnant new Defense minister, Carme Chacón, reviews troops in Madrid on April 14, 2008. She is the first woman ever to head Spain's armed forces. Women hold nine out of 17 cabinet posts in Spain's socialist government, a reflection of women's entrance into the halls of power around the world.

But more than 10 years later, much of the Beijing Platform still has not been achieved. And many question whether women are any better off today than they were in 1995.

"The picture's mixed," says June Zeitlin, executive director of the Women's Environment & Development Organization (WEDO). "In terms of violence against women, there is far more recognition of what is going on today. There has been some progress with education and girls. But the impact of globalization has exacerbated differences between men and women. The poor have gotten poorer — and they are mostly women."

Liberalized international trade has been a two-edged sword in other ways as well. Corporations have been able to expand their global reach, opening new businesses and factories in developing countries and offering women unprecedented employment and economic opportunities. But the jobs often pay low wages and involve work in dangerous conditions because poor countries anxious to attract foreign investors often are willing to ignore safety and labor protections.[26] And increasingly porous international borders have led to growing numbers of women and girls being forced or sold into prostitution or sexual slavery abroad, often under the pretense that they will be given legitimate jobs overseas.[27]

Numerous international agreements in recent years have pledged to provide women with the same opportunities and protections as men, including the U.N.'s Millennium Development Goals (MDGs) and the Convention on the Elimination of All Forms of Discrimination Against Women (CEDAW). But the MDGs' deadlines for improving the conditions for women have either been missed already or are on track to fail in the coming years.[28] And more than 70 of the 185 countries that ratified CEDAW have filed "reservations," meaning they exempt themselves from certain parts.[29] In fact, there are more reservations against CEDAW than against any other international human-rights treaty in history.[30] The United States remains the only developed country in the world not to have ratified it.[31]

"There has certainly been progress in terms of the rhetoric. But there are still challenges in the disparities in education, disparities in income, disparities in health," says Carla Koppell, director of the Cambridge, Mass.-based Initiative for Inclusive Security, which advocates for greater numbers of women in peace negotiations.

"But women are not just victims," she continues. "They have a very unique and important role to play in solving the problems of the developing world. We need to charge policy makers to match the rhetoric and make it a reality. There is a really wonderful opportunity to use the momentum that does exist. I really think we can."

Amidst the successes and failures surrounding women's issues, here are some of the questions analysts are beginning to ask:

Has globalization been good for women?

Over the last 20 years, trade liberalization has led to a massive increase of goods being produced and exported from developing countries, creating millions of manufacturing jobs and bringing many women into the paid workforce for the first time.

"Women employed in export-oriented manufacturing typically earn more than they would have in traditional sectors," according to a World Bank report. "Further, cash income earned by women may improve their status and bargaining power in the family."[32] The report cited a study of 50 families in Mexico that found "a significant proportion of the women reported an improvement in their 'quality of life,' due mainly to their income from working outside their homes, including in (export-oriented) factory jobs."

But because women in developing nations are generally less educated than men and have little bargaining power, most of these jobs are temporary or part-time, offering no health-care benefits, overtime or sick leave.

Women comprise 85 percent of the factory jobs in the garment industry in Bangladesh and 90 percent in Cambodia. In the cut flower industry, women hold 65 percent of the jobs in Colombia and 87 percent in Zimbabwe. In the fruit industry, women constitute 69 percent of temporary and seasonal workers in South Africa and 52 percent in Chile.[33]

Frequently, women in these jobs have no formal contract with their employers, making them even more vulnerable to poor safety conditions and abuse. One study found that only 46 percent of women garment workers in Bangladesh had an official letter of employment.[34]

"Women are a workforce vital to the global economy, but the jobs women are in often aren't covered by labor protections," says Thalia Kidder, a policy adviser on gender and sustainable livelihoods with U.K.-based Oxfam, a confederation of 12 international aid organizations. Women lack protection because they mostly work as domestics, in home-based businesses and as part-time workers. "In the global economy, many companies look to hire the most powerless people because they cannot demand high wages. There are not a lot of trade treaties that address labor rights."

In addition to recommending that countries embrace free trade, Western institutions like the International Monetary Fund and the World Bank during the 1990s recommended that developing countries adopt so-called structural adjustment economic reforms in order to qualify for certain loans and financial support. Besides opening borders to free trade, the neo-liberal economic regime known as the Washington Consensus advocated privatizing state-owned businesses, balancing budgets and attracting foreign investment.

But according to some studies, those reforms ended up adversely affecting women. For instance, companies in Ecuador were encouraged to make jobs more "flexible" by replacing long-term contracts with temporary, seasonal and hourly positions — while restricting collective bargaining rights.[35] And countries streamlined and privatized government programs such as health care and education, services women depend on most.

Globalization also has led to a shift toward cash crops grown for export, which hurts women farmers, who produce 60 to 80 percent of the food for household consumption in developing countries.[36] Small women farmers are being pushed off their land so crops for exports can be grown, limiting their abilities to produce food for themselves and their families.

While economic globalization has yet to create the economic support needed to help women out of poverty, women's advocates say females have benefited from the broadening of communications between countries prompted by globalization. "It has certainly improved access to communications and helped human-rights campaigns," says Zeitlin of WEDO. "Less can be done in secret. If there is a woman who is condemned to be stoned to death somewhere, you can almost immediately mobilize a global campaign against it."

Homa Hoodfar, a professor of social anthropology at Concordia University in Montreal, Canada, and a founder of the group Women Living Under Muslim Laws, says women in some of the world's most remote towns and villages regularly e-mail her organization. "Globalization has made the world much smaller," she says. "Women are getting information on TV and the Internet. The fact that domestic violence has become a global issue [shows globalization] provides resources for those objecting locally."

But open borders also have enabled the trafficking of millions of women around the world. An estimated 800,000 people are trafficked across international borders each year — 80 percent of them women and girls — and most are forced into the commercial sex trade. Millions more are trafficked within their own countries.[37] Globalization has sparked a massive migration of women in search of better jobs and lives. About 90 million women — half of the world's migrants and more than ever in history — reside outside their home countries. These migrant women — often unable to speak the local language and without any family connections — are especially susceptible to traffickers who lure them with promises of jobs abroad.[38]

And those who do not get trapped in the sex trade often end up in low-paying or abusive jobs in foreign factories or as domestic maids working under slave-like conditions.

Female Peacekeepers Fill Vital Roles

Women bring a different approach to conflict resolution.

The first all-female United Nations peacekeeping force left Liberia in January after a year's mission in the West African country, which is rebuilding itself after 14 years of civil war. Comprised of more than 100 women from India, the force was immediately replaced by a second female team.

"If anyone questioned the ability of women to do tough jobs, then those doubters have been [proven] wrong," said U.N. Special Representative for Liberia Ellen Margrethe Løj, adding that the female peacekeepers inspired many Liberian women to join the national police force.[1]

Women make up half of the world's refugees and have systematically been targeted for rape and sexual abuse during times of war, from the 200,000 "comfort women" who were kept as sex slaves for Japanese soldiers during World War II[2] to the estimated quarter-million women reportedly raped and sexually assaulted during the current conflict in the Democratic Republic of the Congo.[3] But women account for only 5 percent of the world's security-sector jobs, and in many countries they are excluded altogether.[4]

In 2000, the U.N. Security Council unanimously adopted Resolution 1325 calling on governments — and the U.N. itself — to include women in peace building by adopting a variety of measures, including appointing more women as special envoys, involving women in

peace negotiations, integrating gender-based policies in peacekeeping missions and increasing the number of women at all decision-making levels.[5]

But while Resolution 1325 was a critical step in bringing women into the peace process, women's groups say more women should be sent on field missions and more data collected on how conflict affects women around the world.[6]

"Women are often viewed as victims, but another way to view them is as the maintainers of society," says Carla Koppell, director of the Cambridge, Mass.-based Initiative for Inclusive Security, which promotes greater numbers of women in peacekeeping and conflict resolution. "There must be a conscious decision to include women. It's a detriment to promote peace without including women."

Women often comprise the majority of post-conflict survivor populations, especially when large numbers of men have either fled or been killed. In the wake of the 1994 Rwandan genocide, for example, women made up 70 percent of the remaining population.

And female peacekeepers and security forces can fill vital roles men often cannot, such as searching Islamic women wearing burkas or working with rape victims who may be reluctant to report the crimes to male soldiers.

But some experts say the real problem is not migration and globalization but the lack of labor protection. "Nothing is black and white," says Marianne Mollmann, advocacy director for the Women's Rights Division of Human Rights Watch. "Globalization has created different employment opportunities for women. Migration flows have made women vulnerable. But it's a knee-jerk reaction to say that women shouldn't migrate. You can't prevent migration. So where do we need to go?" She suggests including these workers in general labor-law protections that cover all workers.

Mollmann said countries can and should hammer out agreements providing labor and wage protections for domestic workers migrating across borders. With such protections, she said, women could benefit from the jobs

and incomes promised by increased migration and globalization.

Should governments impose electoral quotas for women?

In 2003, as Rwanda struggled to rebuild itself after the genocide that killed at least 800,000 Hutus and Tutsis, the country adopted an historic new constitution that, among other things, required that women hold at least 30 percent of posts "in all decision-making organs."[39]

Today — ironically, just across Lake Kivu from the horrors occurring in Eastern Congo — Rwanda's lower house of parliament now leads the world in female representation, with 48.8 percent of the seats held by women.[40]

"Women bring different experiences and issues to the table," says Koppell. "I've seen it personally in the Darfur and Uganda peace negotiations. Their priorities were quite different. Men were concerned about power- and wealth-sharing. Those are valid, but you get an entirely different dimension from women. Women talked about security on the ground, security of families, security of communities."

The first all-female United Nations peacekeeping force practices martial arts in New Delhi as it prepares to be deployed to Liberia in 2006.

In war-torn countries, women have been found to draw on their experiences as mothers to find nonviolent and flexible ways to solve conflict. [7] During peace negotiations in Northern Ireland, for example, male negotiators repeatedly walked out of sessions, leaving a small number of women at the table. The women, left to their own, found areas of common ground and were able to keep discussions moving forward.[8]

"The most important thing is introducing the definition of security from a woman's perspective," said Orzala Ashraf, founder of Kabul-based Humanitarian Assistance for the Women and Children of Afghanistan. "It is not a man in a uniform standing next to a tank armed with a gun. Women have a broader term — human security — the ability to go to school, receive health care, work and have access to

justice. Only by improving these areas can threats from insurgents, Taliban, drug lords and warlords be countered."[9]

[1] "Liberia: UN envoy welcomes new batch of female Indian police officers," U.N. News Centre, Feb. 8, 2008, www.un.org/apps/news/story.asp?NewsID=25557&Cr=liberia&Cr1=.

[2] "Japan: Comfort Women," European Speaking Tour press release, Amnesty International, Oct. 31, 2007.

[3] "Film Documents Rape of Women in Congo," "All Things Considered," National Public Radio, April 8, 2008, www.npr.org/templates/story/story.php?storyId=89476111.

[4] "Ninth Annual Colloquium and Policy Forum," Hunt Alternatives Fund, Jan. 22, 2008, www.huntalternatives.org/pages/7650_ninth_annual_colloquium_and_policy_forum.cfm. Also see Elizabeth Eldridge, "Women cite utility in peace efforts," *The Washington Times*, Jan. 25, 2008, p. A1.

[5] "Inclusive Security, Sustainable Peace: A Toolkit for Advocacy and Action," International Alert and Women Waging Peace, 2004, p. 15, www.huntalternatives.org/download/35_introduction.pdf.

[6] *Ibid.*, p. 17.

[7] Jolynn Shoemaker and Camille Pampell Conaway, "Conflict Prevention and Transformation: Women's Vital Contributions," Inclusive Security: Women Waging Peace and the United Nations Foundation, Feb. 23, 2005, p. 7.

[8] The Initiative for Inclusive Security, www.huntalternatives.org/pages/460_the_vital_role_of_women_in_peace_building.cfm.

[9] Eldridge, *op. cit.*

Before the civil war, Rwandan women never held more than 18 percent of parliament. But after the genocide, the country's population was 70 percent female. Women immediately stepped in to fill the vacuum, becoming the heads of households, community leaders and business owners. Their increased presence in leadership positions eventually led to the new constitutional quotas.[41]

"We see so many post-conflict countries going from military regimes to democracy that are starting from scratch with new constitutions," says Drude Dahlerup, a professor of political science at Sweden's Stockholm University who studies the use of gender quotas. "Today, starting from scratch means including women. It's seen as a sign of modernization and democratization."

Both Iraq and Afghanistan included electoral quotas for women in their new constitutions, and the number of women in political office in sub-Saharan Africa has increased faster than in any other region of the world, primarily through the use of quotas.[42]

But many point out that simply increasing the numbers of women in elected office will not necessarily expand women's rights. "It depends on which women and which positions they represent," says Wendy Harcourt, chair of Women in Development Europe (WIDE), a feminist network in Europe, and editor of *Development*, the journal of the Society for International Development, a global network of individuals and institutions working on development issues. "It's positive, but I don't see yet what it means [in terms of addressing] broader gender issues."

Few Women Head World Governments

Fourteen women currently serve as elected heads of state or government including five who serve as both. Mary McAleese, elected president of Ireland in 1997, is the world's longest-serving head of state. Helen Clark of New Zealand has served as prime minister since 1999, making her the longest-serving female head of government. The world's first elected female head of state was Sirimavo Bandaranaike of Sri Lanka, in 1960.

Current Female Elected Heads of State and Government

Heads of both state and government:

Gloria Macapagal-Arroyo — President, the Philippines, since 2001; former secretary of Defense (2002) and secretary of Foreign Affairs (2003 and 2006-2007).

Ellen Johnson-Sirleaf — President, Liberia, since 2006; held finance positions with the government and World Bank.

Michelle Bachelet Jeria — President, Chile, since 2006; former minister of Health (2000-2002) and minister of Defense (2002-2004).

Cristina E. Fernández — President, Argentina, since 2007; succeeded her husband, Nestor de Kirchner, as president; former president, Senate Committee on Constitutional Affairs.

Rosa Zafferani — Captain Regent, San Marino, since April 2008; secretary of State of Public Education, University and Cultural Institutions (2004 to 2008); served as captain regent in 1999; San Marino elects two captains regent every six months, who serve as co-heads of both state and government.

Heads of Government:

Helen Clark — Prime Minister, New Zealand, since 1999; held government posts in foreign affairs, defense, housing and labor.

Luísa Días Diogo — Prime Minister, Mozambique, since 2004; held several finance posts in Mozambique and the World Bank.

Angela Merkel — Chancellor, Germany, since 2005; parliamentary leader of Christian Democratic Union Party (2002-2005).

Yuliya Tymoshenko — Prime Minister, Ukraine, since 2007; chief of government (2005) and designate prime minister (2006).

Zinaida Grecianîi — Prime Minister, Moldova, since March 2008; vice prime minister (2005-2008).

Heads of State:

Mary McAleese — President, Ireland, since 1997; former director of a television station and Northern Ireland Electricity.

Tarja Halonen — President, Finland, since 2000; former minister of foreign affairs (1995-2000).

Pratibha Patil — President, India, since 2007; former governor of Rajasthan state (2004-2007).

Borjana Kristo — President, Bosnia and Herzegovina, since 2007; minister of Justice of Bosniak-Croat Federation, an entity in Bosnia and Herzegovina (2003-2007).

Source: www.guide2womenleaders.com

While Afghanistan has mandated that women hold at least 27 percent of the government's lower house seats and at least 17 percent of the upper house, their increased representation appears to have done little to improve women's rights.[43] Earlier this year, a student journalist was condemned to die under Afghanistan's strict Islamic sharia law after he distributed articles from the Internet on women's rights.[44] And nongovernmental groups in Afghanistan report that Afghan women and girls have begun killing themselves in record numbers, burning themselves alive in order to escape widespread domestic abuse or forced marriages.[45]

Having gender quotas alone doesn't necessarily ensure that women's rights will be broadened, says Hoodfar of Concordia University. It depends on the type of quota a government implements, she argues, pointing out that in Jordan, for example, the government has set aside parliamentary seats for the six women who garner the most votes of any other female candidates in their districts — even if they do not win more votes than male candidates.[46] Many small, conservative tribes that cannot garner enough votes for a male in a countrywide victory are now nominating their sisters and wives in the hope that the lower number of votes needed to elect a woman will get them one of the reserved seats. As a result, many of the women moving into the reserved seats are extremely conservative and actively oppose providing women greater rights and freedoms.

And another kind of quota has been used against women in her home country of Iran, Hoodfar points out. Currently, 64 percent of university students in Iran are women. But the government recently mandated that at least 40 percent of university enrollees be male, forcing many female students out of school, Hoodfar said.

"Before, women didn't want to use quotas for politics because of concern the government may try to use it against women," she says. "But women are beginning to look into it and talk about maybe developing a good system."

Quotas can be enacted by constitutional requirements, such as those enacted in Rwanda, by statute or voluntarily by political parties. Quotas also can vary in their requirements: They can mandate the number of women each party must nominate, how many women must appear on the ballot (and the order in which they appear, so women are not relegated to the bottom of the list), or the number of women who must hold government office. About 40 countries now use gender quotas in national parliamentary elections, while another 50 have major political parties that voluntarily use quotas to determine candidates.

Aside from questions about the effectiveness of quotas, others worry about the fairness of establishing quotas based on gender. "That's something feminists have traditionally opposed," says Harcourt.

"It's true, but it's also not fair the way it is now," says former Ambassador Hunt. "We are where we are today through all kinds of social structures that are not fair. Quotas are the lesser of two evils."

Stockholm University's Dahlerup says quotas are not "discrimination against men but compensation for discrimination against women." Yet quotas are not a panacea for women in politics, she contends. "It's a mistake to think this is a kind of tool that will solve all problems. It doesn't solve problems about financing

Women Still Far from Reaching Political Parity

Although they have made strides in the past decade, women hold only a small minority of the world's leadership and legislative posts (right). Nordic parliaments have the highest rates of female representation — 41.4 percent — compared with only 9 percent in Arab countries (below). However, Arab legislatures have nearly tripled their female representation since 1997, and some countries in Africa have dramatically increased theirs as well: Rwanda, at 48.8 percent, now has the world's highest percentage of women in parliament of any country. The U.S. Congress ranks 70th in the world, with 89 women serving in the 535-member body — or 16.6 percent.

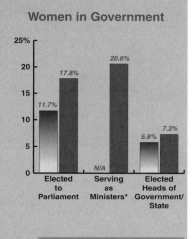

Women in Government

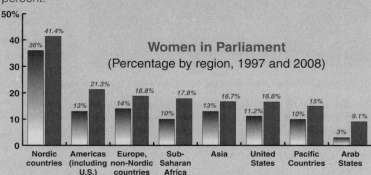

Women in Parliament
(Percentage by region, 1997 and 2008)

* Includes deputy prime ministers, ministers and prime ministers who hold ministerial portfolios.

Sources: Interparliamentarian Union, www.ipu.org/wmn-e/world.htm; State of the World's Children 2007, UNICEF, www.unicef.org/sowc07/; "Worldwide Guide to Women in Leadership" database, www.un.org/womenwatch/daw/csw/41sess.htm.

campaigns, caring for families while being in politics or removing patriarchal attitudes. It would be nice if it wasn't necessary, and hopefully sometime in the future it won't be."

Until that time, however, quotas are a "necessary evil," she says.

AP Photo/Rajesh Kumar Singh

National Geographic/Getty Images/Melvyn Goldstein

Women's Work: From Hauling and Churning . . .

Women's work is often back-breaking and monotonous, such as hauling firewood in the western Indian state of Maharashtra (top) and churning yogurt into butter beside Lake Motsobunnyi in Tibet (bottom). Women labor two-thirds of the total hours worked around the globe each year but earn only 10 percent of the income.

Do international treaties improve women's rights?

In recent decades, a variety of international agreements have been signed by countries pledging to improve women's lives, from the 1979 Convention for the Elimination of All Forms of Discrimination Against Women to the Beijing Platform of 1995 to the Millennium Development Goals (MDGs) adopted in 2000. The agreements aimed to provide women with greater access to health, political representation, economic stability and social status. They also focused attention on some of the biggest obstacles facing women.

But despite the fanfare surrounding the launch of those agreements, many experts on women's issues say on-the-ground action has yet to match the rhetoric. "The report is mixed," says Haleh Afshar, a professor of politics and women's studies at the University of York in the United Kingdom and a nonpartisan, appointed member of the House of Lords, known as a crossbench peer. "The biggest problem with Beijing is all these things were stated, but none were funded. Unfortunately, I don't see any money. You don't get the pay, you don't get the job done."

The Beijing Platform for Action, among other things, called on governments to "adjust budgets to ensure equality of access to public sector expenditures" and even to "reduce, as appropriate, excessive military expenditure" in order to achieve the Platform goals.

But adequate funding has yet to be provided, say women's groups.[47] In a report entitled "Beijing Betrayed," the Women's Environment & Development Organization says female HIV cases outnumber male cases in many parts of the world, gender-related violence remains a pandemic and women still make up the majority of the world's poor — despite pledges in Beijing to reverse these trends.[48]

And funding is not the only obstacle. A 2004 U.N. survey revealed that while many countries have enacted laws in recent years to help protect women from violence and discrimination, long-standing social and cultural traditions block progress. "While constitutions provided for equality between women and men on the one hand, [several countries] recognized and gave precedent to customary law and practice in a number of areas . . . resulting in discrimination against women," the report said. "Several countries noted that statutory, customary and religious law coexist, especially in regard to family, personal status and inheritance and land rights. This perpetuated discrimination against women."[49]

While she worries about the lack of progress on the Beijing Platform, WEDO Executive Director Zeitlin says international agreements are nevertheless critical in raising global awareness on women's issues. "They have a major impact on setting norms and standards," she says. "In many countries, norms and standards are very important in setting goals for women to advocate for. We complain about lack of implementation, but if we didn't have the norms and standards we couldn't complain about a lack of implementation."

Like the Beijing Platform, the MDGs have been criticized for not achieving more. While the U.N. says promoting women's rights is essential to achieving the millennium goals — which aim to improve the lives of all the world's populations by 2015 — only two of the eight specifically address women's issues.[50]

One of the goals calls for countries to "Promote gender equality and empower women." But it sets only one measurable target: "Eliminate gender disparity in primary and secondary education, preferably by 2005, and in all levels of education" by 2015.[51] Some 62 countries failed to reach the 2005 deadline, and many are likely to miss the 2015 deadline as well.[52]

Another MDG calls for a 75 percent reduction in maternal mortality compared to 1990 levels. But according to the human-rights group ActionAid, this goal is the "most off track of all the MDGs." Rates are declining at less than 1 percent a year, and in some countries — such as Sierra Leone, Pakistan and Guatemala — maternal mortality has increased since 1990. If that trend continues, no region in the developing world is expected to reach the goal by 2015.[53]

Activist Peggy Antrobus of Development Alternatives with Women for a New Era (DAWN) — a network of feminists from the Southern Hemisphere, based currently in Calabar, Cross River State, Nigeria — has lambasted the MDGs, quipping that the acronym stands for the "Most Distracting Gimmick."[54] Many feminists argue that the goals are too broad to have any real impact and that the MDGs should have given more attention to women's issues.

But other women say international agreements — and the public debate surrounding them — are vital in promoting gender equality. "It's easy to get disheartened, but Beijing is still the blueprint of where we need to be," says Mollmann of Human Rights Watch. "They are part of a political process, the creation of an international culture. If systematically everyone says [discrimination against women] is a bad thing, states don't want to be hauled out as systematic violators."

In particular, Mollmann said, CEDAW has made real progress in overcoming discrimination against women. Unlike the Beijing Platform and the MDGs, CEDAW legally obliges countries to comply. Each of the 185 ratifying countries must submit regular reports to the U.N. outlining their progress under the convention. Several

AP Photo/Sergei Grits

AFP/Getty Images/Ali Burafi

. . . to Gathering and Herding

While many women have gotten factory jobs thanks to globalization of trade, women still comprise 70 percent of the planet's inhabitants living on less than a dollar a day. Women perform a variety of tasks around the world, ranging from gathering flax in Belarus (top) to shepherding goats in central Argentina (bottom).

countries — including Brazil, Uganda, South Africa and Australia — also have incorporated CEDAW provisions into their constitutions and legal systems.[55]

Still, dozens of ratifying countries have filed official "reservations" against the convention, including Bahrain, Egypt, Kuwait, Morocco and the United Arab Emirates, all of whom say they will comply only within the bounds of Islamic sharia law.[56] And the United States has refused to ratify CEDAW, with or without reservations, largely because of conservatives who say it would, among other things, promote abortion and require the government to pay for such things as child care and maternity leave.

Indian women harvest wheat near Bhopal. Women produce half of the food used domestically worldwide and 60 to 80 percent of the household food grown in developing countries.

BACKGROUND

'Structural Defects'

Numerous prehistoric relics suggest that at one time matriarchal societies existed on Earth in which women were in the upper echelons of power. Because early societies did not understand the connection between sexual relations and conception, they believed women were solely responsible for reproduction — which led to the worship of female goddesses.[57]

In more modern times, however, women have generally faced prejudice and discrimination at the hands of a patriarchal society. In about the eighth century B.C. creation stories emerged describing the fall of man due to the weakness of women. The Greeks recounted the story of Pandora who, through her opening of a sealed jar, unleashed death and pain on all of mankind. Meanwhile, similar tales in Judea eventually were recounted in Genesis, with Eve as the culprit.[58]

In ancient Greece, women were treated as children and denied basic rights. They could not leave their houses unchaperoned, were prohibited from being educated or buying or selling land. A father could sell his unmarried daughter into slavery if she lost her virginity before marriage. If a woman was raped, she was outcast and forbidden from participating in public ceremonies or wearing jewelry.[59]

The status of women in early Rome was not much better, although over time women began to assert their voices and slowly gained greater freedoms. Eventually, they were able to own property and divorce their husbands. But early Christian leaders later denounced the legal and social freedom enjoyed by Roman women as a sign of moral decay. In the view of the early church, women were dependent on and subordinate to men.

In the 13th century, the Catholic priest and theologian St. Thomas Aquinas helped set the tone for the subjugation of women in Western society. He said women were created solely to be "man's helpmate" and advocated that men should make use of "a necessary object, woman, who is needed to preserve the species or to provide food and drink."[60]

From the 14th to 17th centuries, misogyny and oppression of women took a step further. As European societies struggled against the Black Plague, the 100 Years War and turmoil between Catholics and Reformers, religious leaders began to blame tragedies, illnesses and other problems on witches. As witch hysteria spread across Europe — instituted by both the religious and non-religious — an estimated 30,000 to 60,000 people were executed for allegedly practicing witchcraft. About 80 percent were females, some as young as 8 years old.[61]

"All wickedness is but little to the wickedness of a woman," Catholic inquisitors wrote in the 1480s. "What else is woman but a foe to friendship, an unescapable punishment, a necessary evil, a natural temptation, a desirable calamity. . . . Women are . . . instruments of Satan, . . . a structural defect rooted in the original creation."[62]

Push for Protections

The Age of Enlightenment and the Industrial Revolution in the 18th and 19th centuries opened up job opportunities for women, released them from domestic confines and provided them with new social freedoms.

In 1792 Mary Wollstonecraft published *A Vindication of the Rights of Women*, which has been hailed as "the feminist declaration of independence." Although the book had been heavily influenced by the French Revolution's notions of equality and universal brotherhood, French revolutionary leaders, ironically, were not sympathetic to feminist causes.[63] In 1789 they had refused to accept a Declaration of the Rights of Women when it was presented at the National Assembly. And Jean Jacques Rousseau, one of the philosophical founders of the revolution, had written in 1762:

"The whole education of women ought to be relative to men. To please them, to be useful to them, to make themselves loved and honored by them, to educate them when young, to care for them when grown, to counsel them, to make life sweet and agreeable to them — these are the duties of women at all times, and what should be taught them from their infancy."[64]

As more and more women began taking jobs outside the home during the 19th century, governments began to pass laws to "protect" them in the workforce and expand their legal rights. The British Mines Act of 1842, for instance, prohibited women from working underground.[65] In 1867, John Stuart Mill, a supporter of women's rights and author of the book *Subjection of Women*, introduced language in the British House of Commons calling for women to be granted the right to vote. It failed.[66]

But by that time governments around the globe had begun enacting laws giving women rights they had been denied for centuries. As a result of the Married Women's Property Act of 1870 and a series of other measures, wives in Britain were finally allowed to own property. In 1893, New Zealand became the first nation to grant full suffrage rights to women, followed over the next two decades by Finland, Norway, Denmark and Iceland. The United States granted women suffrage in 1920.[67]

One of the first international labor conventions, formulated at Berne, Switzerland, in 1906, applied exclusively to women — prohibiting night work for women in industrial occupations. Twelve nations signed on to it. During the second Berne conference in 1913, language was proposed limiting the number of hours women and children could work in industrial jobs, but the outbreak of World War I prevented it from being enacted.[68] In 1924 the U.S. Supreme Court upheld a night-work law for women.[69]

In 1946, public attention to women's issues received a major boost when the United Nations created the Commission on the Status of Women to address urgent problems facing women around the world.[70] During the 1950s, the U.N. adopted several conventions aimed at improving women's lives, including the Convention on the Political Rights of Women, adopted in 1952 to ensure women the right to vote, which has been ratified by 120 countries, and the Convention on the Nationality of Married Women, approved in 1957 to ensure that marriage to an alien does not automatically affect the nationality of the woman.[71] That convention has been ratified by only 73 countries; the United States is not among them.[72]

In 1951 The International Labor Organization (ILO), an agency of the United Nations, adopted the Convention on Equal Remuneration for Men and Women Workers for Work of Equal Value, to promote equal pay for equal work. It has since been ratified by 164 countries, but again, not by the United States.[73] Seven years later, the ILO adopted the Convention on Discrimination in Employment and Occupation to ensure equal opportunity and treatment in employment. It is currently ratified by 166 countries, but not the United States.[74] U.S. opponents to the conventions claim there is no real pay gap between men and women performing the same jobs and that the conventions would impose "comparable worth" requirements, forcing companies to pay equal wages to men and women even if the jobs they performed were different.[75]

In 1965, the Commission on the Status of Women began drafting international standards articulating equal rights for men and women. Two years later, the panel completed the Declaration on the Elimination of Discrimination Against Women, which was adopted by the General Assembly but carried no enforcement power.

The commission later began to discuss language that would hold countries responsible for enforcing the declaration. At the U.N.'s first World Conference on Women in Mexico City in 1975, women from around the world called for creation of such a treaty, and the commission soon began drafting the text.[76]

Women's 'Bill of Rights'

Finally in 1979, after many years of often rancorous debate, the Convention on the Elimination of All Forms of Discrimination Against Women (CEDAW) was adopted by the General Assembly — 130 to none, with 10 abstentions. After the vote, however, several countries said their "yes" votes did not commit the support of their governments. Brazil's U.N. representative told the assembly, "The signatures and ratifications necessary to make this effective will not come easily."[77]

Despite the prediction, it took less than two years for CEDAW to receive the required number of ratifications to enter it into force — faster than any human-rights convention had ever done before.[78]

CHRONOLOGY

1700s-1800s *Age of Enlightenment and Industrial Revolution lead to greater freedoms for women.*

1792 Mary Wollstonecraft publishes *A Vindication of the Rights of Women,* later hailed as "the feminist declaration of independence."

1893 New Zealand becomes first nation to grant women full suffrage.

1920 Tennessee is the 36th state to ratify the 19th Amendment, giving American women the right to vote.

1940s-1980s *International conventions endorse equal rights for women. Global conferences highlight need to improve women's rights.*

1946 U.N. creates Commission on the Status of Women.

1951 U.N. International Labor Organization adopts convention promoting equal pay for equal work, which has been ratified by 164 countries; the United States is not among them.

1952 U.N. adopts convention calling for full women's suffrage.

1960 Sri Lanka elects the world's first female prime minister.

1974 Maria Estela Martínez de Perón of Argentina becomes the world's first woman president, replacing her ailing husband.

1975 U.N. holds first World Conference on Women, in Mexico City, followed by similar conferences every five years. U.N. launches the Decade for Women.

1979 U.N. adopts Convention on the Elimination of All Forms of Discrimination against Women (CEDAW), dubbed the "international bill of rights for women."

1981 CEDAW is ratified — faster than any other human-rights convention.

1990s *Women's rights win historic legal recognition.*

1993 U.N. World Conference on Human Rights in Vienna, Austria, calls for ending all violence, sexual harassment and trafficking of women.

1995 Fourth World Conference on Women in Beijing draws 30,000 people, making it the largest in U.N. history. Beijing Platform outlining steps to grant women equal rights is signed by 189 governments.

1996 International Criminal Tribunal convicts eight Bosnian Serb police and military officers for rape during the Bosnian conflict — the first time sexual assault is prosecuted as a war crime.

1998 International Criminal Tribunal for Rwanda recognizes rape and other forms of sexual violence as genocide.

2000s *Women make political gains, but sexual violence against women increases.*

2000 U.N. calls on governments to include women in peace negotiations.

2006 Ellen Johnson Sirleaf of Liberia, Michelle Bachelet of Chile and Portia Simpson Miller of Jamaica become their countries' first elected female heads of state. . . . Women in Kuwait are allowed to run for parliament, winning two seats.

2007 A woman in Saudi Arabia who was sentenced to 200 lashes after being gang-raped by seven men is pardoned by King Abdullah. Her rapists received sentences ranging from 10 months to five years in prison, and 80 to 1,000 lashes. . . . After failing to recognize any gender-based crimes in its first case involving the Democratic Republic of the Congo, the International Criminal Court hands down charges of "sexual slavery" in its second case involving war crimes in Congo. More than 250,000 women are estimated to have been raped and sexually abused during the country's war.

2008 Turkey lifts 80-year-old ban on women's headscarves in public universities, signaling a drift toward religious fundamentalism. . . . Former housing minister Carme Chacón — 37 and pregnant — is named defense minister of Spain, bringing to nine the number of female cabinet ministers in the Socialist government. . . . Sen. Hillary Rodham Clinton becomes the first U.S. woman to be in a tight race for a major party's presidential nomination.

Often described as an international bill of rights for women, CEDAW defines discrimination against women as "any distinction, exclusion or restriction made on the basis of sex which has the effect or purpose of impairing or nullifying the recognition, enjoyment or exercise by women, irrespective of their marital status, on a basis of equality of men and women, of human rights and fundamental freedoms in the political, economic, social, cultural, civil or any other field."

Ratifying countries are legally bound to end discrimination against women by incorporating sexual equality into their legal systems, abolishing discriminatory laws against women, taking steps to end trafficking of women and ensuring women equal access to political and public life. Countries must also submit reports at least every four years outlining the steps they have taken to comply with the convention.[79]

CEDAW also grants women reproductive choice — one of the main reasons the United States has not ratified it. The convention requires signatories to guarantee women's rights "to decide freely and responsibly on the number and spacing of their children and to have access to the information, education and means to enable them to exercise these rights."[80]

While CEDAW is seen as a significant tool to stop violence against women, it actually does not directly mention violence. To rectify this, the CEDAW committee charged with monitoring countries' compliance in 1992 specified gender-based violence as a form of discrimination prohibited under the convention.[81]

In 1993 the U.N. took further steps to combat violence against women during the World Conference on Human Rights in Vienna, Austria. The conference called on countries to stop all forms of violence, sexual harassment, exploitation and trafficking of women. It also declared that "violations of the human rights of women in situations of armed conflicts are violations of the fundamental principles of international human rights and humanitarian law."[82]

Shortly afterwards, as fighting broke out in the former Yugoslavia and Rwanda, new legal precedents were set to protect women against violence — and particularly rape — during war. In 1996, the International Criminal Tribunal in the Hague, Netherlands, indicted eight Bosnian Serb police officers in connection with the mass rape of Muslim women during the Bosnian war, marking the first time sexual assault had ever been prosecuted as a war crime.[83]

Two years later, the U.N.'s International Criminal Tribunal for Rwanda convicted a former Rwandan mayor for genocide, crimes against humanity, rape and sexual violence — the first time rape and sexual violence were recognized as acts of genocide.[84]

"Rape is a serious war crime like any other," said Regan Ralph, then executive director of Human Rights Watch's Women's Rights Division, shortly after the conviction. "That's always been true on paper, but now international courts are finally acting on it."[85]

Today, the International Criminal Court has filed charges against several Sudanese officials for rape and other crimes committed in the Darfur region.[86] But others are demanding that the court also prosecute those responsible for the rapes in the Eastern Congo, where women are being targeted as a means of destroying communities in the war-torn country.[87]

Beijing and Beyond

The U.N. World Conference on Women in Mexico City in 1975 produced a 44-page plan of action calling for a decade of special measures to give women equal status and opportunities in law, education, employment, politics and society.[88] The conference also kicked off the U.N.'s Decade for Women and led to creation of the U.N. Development Fund for Women (UNIFEM).[89]

Five years later, the U.N. held its second World Conference on Women in Copenhagen and then celebrated the end of the Decade for Women with the third World Conference in Nairobi in 1985. More than 10,000 representatives from government agencies and NGOs attended the Nairobi event, believed to be the largest gathering on women's issues at the time.[90]

Upon reviewing the progress made on women's issues during the previous 10 years, the U.N. representatives in Nairobi concluded that advances had been extremely limited due to failing economies in developing countries, particularly those in Africa struggling against drought, famine and crippling debt. The conference developed a set of steps needed to improve the status of women during the final 15 years of the 20th century.[91]

Ten years later, women gathered in Beijing in 1995 for the Fourth World Conference, vowing to turn the rhetoric of the earlier women's conferences into action. Delegates from 189 governments and 2,600

Women Suffer Most in Natural Disasters

Climate change will make matters worse.

In natural disasters, women suffer death, disease and hunger at higher rates then men. During the devastating 2004 tsunami in Asia, 70 to 80 percent of the dead were women.[1] During cyclone-triggered flooding in Bangladesh that killed 140,000 people in 1991, nearly five times more women between the ages of 20 and 44 died than men.[2]

Gender discrimination, cultural biases and lack of awareness of women's needs are part of the problem. For instance, during the 1991 cyclone, Bangladeshi women and their children died in higher numbers because they waited at home for their husbands to return and make evacuation decisions.[3] In addition, flood warnings were conveyed by men to men in public spaces but were rarely communicated to women and children at home.[4]

And during the tsunami, many Indonesian women died because they stayed behind to look for children and other family members. Women clinging to children in floodwaters also tired more quickly and drowned, since most women in the region were never taught to swim or climb trees.[5] In Sri Lanka, many women died because the tsunami hit early on a Sunday morning when they were inside preparing breakfast for their families. Men were generally outside where they had earlier warning of the oncoming floods so they were better able to escape.[6]

Experts now predict global climate change — which is expected to increase the number of natural disasters around the world — will put women in far greater danger than men because natural disasters generally have a disproportionate impact on the world's poor. Since women comprise 70 percent of those living on less than $1 a day, they will be hardest hit by climate changes, according to the Intergovernmental Panel on Climate Change.[7]

"Climate change is not gender-neutral," said Gro Harlem Brundtland, former prime minister of Norway and now special envoy to the U.N. secretary-general on climate change. "[Women are] more dependent for their livelihood on natural resources that are threatened by climate change…. With changes in climate, traditional food sources become more unpredictable and scarce. This exposes women to loss of harvests, often their sole sources of food and income."[8]

Women produce 60 to 80 percent of the food for household consumption in developing countries.[9] As drought, flooding and desertification increase, experts say women and their families will be pushed further into poverty and famine.

Women also suffer more hardship in the aftermath of natural disasters, and their needs are often ignored during relief efforts.

In many Third World countries, for instance, women have no property rights, so when a husband dies during a natural disaster his family frequently confiscates the land from his widow, leaving her homeless and destitute.[10] And because men usually dominate emergency relief and response agencies, women's specific needs, such as contraceptives and sanitary napkins, are often overlooked. After floods in Bangladesh in 1998, adolescent girls reported high rates of rashes and urinary tract infections because they had

NGOs attended. More than 30,000 women and men gathered at a parallel forum organized by NGOs, also in Beijing.[92]

The so-called Beijing Platform that emerged from the conference addressed 12 critical areas facing women, from poverty to inequality in education to inadequate health care to violence. It brought unprecedented attention to women's issues and is still considered by many as the blueprint for true gender equality.

The Beijing Conference also came at the center of a decade that produced historic political gains for women around the world — gains that have continued, albeit at a slow pace, into the new century. The 1990s saw more women entering top political positions than ever before. A record 10 countries elected or appointed women as presidents between 1990 and 2000, including Haiti, Nicaragua, Switzerland and Latvia. Another 17 countries chose women prime ministers.[93]

In 2006 Ellen Johnson Sirleaf of Liberia became Africa's first elected woman president.[94] That same year, Chile elected its first female president, Michelle Bachelet, and Jamaica elected Portia Simpson Miller as its first

no clean water, could not wash their menstrual rags properly in private and had no place to hang them to dry.[11]

"In terms of reconstruction, people are not talking about women's needs versus men's needs," says June Zeitlin, executive director of the Women's Environment and Development Organization, a New York City-based international organization that works for women's equality in global policy. "There is a lack of attention to health care after disasters, issues about bearing children, contraception, rape and vulnerability, menstrual needs — things a male programmer is not thinking about. There is broad recognition that disasters have a disproportionate impact on women. But it stops there. They see women as victims, but they don't see women as agents of change."

Women must be brought into discussions on climate change and emergency relief, say Zeitlin and others. Interestingly, she points out, while women are disproportionately affected by environmental changes, they do more than men to protect the environment. Studies show women emit less climate-changing carbon dioxide than men because they recycle more, use resources more efficiently and drive less than men.[12]

"Women's involvement in climate-change decision-making is a human right," said Gerd Johnson-Latham, deputy director of the Swedish Ministry for Foreign Affairs. "If we get more women in decision-making positions, we

The smell of death hangs over Banda Aceh, Indonesia, which was virtually destroyed by a tsunami on Dec. 28, 2004. From 70 to 80 percent of the victims were women.

will have different priorities, and less risk of climate change."[13]

[1] "Tsunami death toll," CNN, Feb. 22, 2005. Also see "Report of High-level Roundtable: How a Changing Climate Impacts Women," Council of Women World Leaders, Women's Environment and Development Organization and Heinrich Boll Foundation, Sept. 21, 2007, p. 21, www.wedo.org/files/Roundtable%20Final%20Report%206%20Nov.pdf.

[2] *Ibid.*

[3] "Cyclone Jelawat bears down on Japan's Okinawa island," CNN.com, Aug. 7, 2000, http://archives.cnn.com/2000/ASIANOW/east/08/07/asia.weather/index.html.

[4] "Gender and Health in Disasters," World Health Organization, July 2002, www.who.int/gender/other_health/en/genderdisasters.pdf.

[5] "The tsunami's impact on women," Oxfam briefing note, March 5, 2005, p. 2, www.oxfam.org/en/files/bn050326_tsunami_women/download.

[6] "Report of High-level Roundtable," *op. cit.*, p. 5.

[7] "Gender Equality" fact sheet, Oxfam, www.oxfam.org.uk/resources/issues/gender/introduction.html. Also see *ibid.*

[8] *Ibid.*, p. 4.

[9] "Five years down the road from Beijing: Assessing progress," *News and Highlights*, Food and Agriculture Organization, June 2, 2000, www.fao.org/News/2000/000602-e.htm.

[10] "Gender and Health in Disasters," *op. cit.*

[11] *Ibid.*

[12] "Women and the Environment," U.N. Environment Program, 2004, p. 17, www.unep.org/Documents.Multilingual/Default.asp?DocumentID=468&ArticleID=4488&l=en. Also see "Report of High-level Roundtable," *op. cit.*, p. 7.

[13] *Ibid.*

female prime minister.[95] Also that year, women ran for election in Kuwait for the first time. In Bahrain, a woman was elected to the lower house of parliament for the first time.[96] And in 2007, Fernández de Kirchner became the first woman to be elected president of Argentina.

Earlier, a World Bank report had found that government corruption declines as more women are elected into office. The report also cited numerous studies that found women are more likely to exhibit "helping" behavior, vote based on social issues, score higher on

"integrity tests," take stronger stances on ethical behavior and behave more generously when faced with economic decisions.[97]

"Increasing the presence of women in government may be valued for its own sake, for reasons of gender equality," the report concluded. "However, our results suggest that there may be extremely important spinoffs stemming from increasing female representation: If women are less likely than men to behave opportunistically, then bringing more women into government may have significant benefits for society in general."[98]

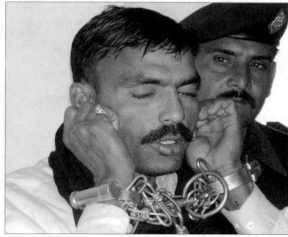

Honor Killings on the Rise

Women in Multan, Pakistan, demonstrate against "honor killings" in 2003 (top). Although Pakistan outlawed such killings years ago, its Human Rights Commission says 1,205 women were killed in the name of family honor in 2007 — a fourfold jump in two years. Nazir Ahmed Sheikh, a Punjabi laborer (bottom), unrepentantly told police in December 2005 how he slit the throats of his four daughters one night as they slept in order to salvage the family's honor. The eldest had married a man of her choice, and Ahmed feared the younger daughters would follow her example.

CURRENT SITUATION

Rise of Fundamentalism

Despite landmark political gains by women since the late 1990s, violence and repression of women continue to be daily occurrences — often linked to the global growth of religious fundamentalism.

In 2007, a 21-year-old woman in Saudi Arabia was sentenced to 200 lashes and ordered jailed for six months after being raped 14 times by a gang of seven men. The Saudi court sentenced the woman — who was 19 at the time of the attack — because she was alone in a car with her former boyfriend when the attack occurred. Under Saudi Arabia's strict Islamic law, it is a crime for a woman to meet in private with a man who is not her husband or relative.[99]

After public outcry from around the world, King Abdullah pardoned the woman in December. A government spokesperson, however, said the king fully supported the verdict but issued the pardon in the "interests of the people."[100]

Another Saudi woman still faces beheading after she was condemned to death for "witchcraft." Among her accusers is a man who claimed she rendered him impotent with her sorcery. Despite international protest, the king has yet to say if he will pardon her.[101]

In Iraq, the rise of religious fundamentalism since the U.S. invasion has led to a jump in the number of women being killed or beaten in so-called honor crimes. Honor killings typically occur when a woman is suspected of unsanctioned sexual behavior — which can range from flirting to "allowing" herself to be raped. Her relatives believe they must murder her to end the family's shame. In the Kurdish region of Iraq, the stoning death of 17-year-old Aswad is not an anomaly. A U.N. mission in October 2007 found that 255 women had been killed in Iraqi Kurdistan in the first six months of 2007 alone — most thought to have been murdered by their communities or families for allegedly committing adultery or entering into a relationship not sanctioned by their families.[102]

The rise of fundamentalism is also sparking a growing debate on the issue of women wearing head scarves, both in Iraq and across the Muslim world. Last August Turkey elected a conservative Muslim president whose wife wears a head scarf, signaling the emergence of a new ruling elite that is more willing to publicly display religious beliefs.[103] Then in February, Turkey's parliament voted to ease an

80-year ban on women wearing head scarves in universities, although a ban on head scarves in other public buildings remains in effect.

"This decision will bring further pressure on women," Nesrin Baytok, a member of parliament, said during debate over the ban. "It will ultimately bring us Hezbollah terror, al Qaeda terror and fundamentalism."[104]

But others said lifting the ban was actually a victory for women. Fatma Benli, a Turkish women's-rights activist and lawyer, said the ban on head scarves in public buildings has forced her to send law partners to argue her cases because she is prohibited from entering court wearing her head scarf. It also discourages religiously conservative women from becoming doctors, lawyers or teachers, she says.[105]

Many women activists are quick to say that it is unfair to condemn Islam for the growing abuse against women. "The problem women have with religion is not the religion but the ways men have interpreted it," says Afshar of the University of York. "What is highly negative is sharia law, which is made by men. Because it's human-made, women can unmake it. The battle now is fighting against unjust laws such as stoning."

She says abuses such as forced marriages and honor killings — usually linked in the Western media to Islamic law — actually go directly against the teachings of the *Koran*. And while the United Nations estimates that some 5,000 women and girls are victims of honor killings each year, millions more are abused and killed in violence unrelated to Islam. Between 10 and 50 percent of all women around the world have been physically abused by an intimate partner in their lifetime, studies show.[106]

"What about the rate of spousal or partner killings in the U.K. or the U.S. that are not called 'honor killings'?" asks Concordia University's Hoodfar. "Then it's only occasional 'crazy people' [committing violence]. But when it's present in Pakistan, Iran or Senegal, these are uncivilized people doing 'honor killings.'"

And Islamic fundamentalism is not the only brand of fundamentalism on the rise. Christian fundamentalism is also growing rapidly. A 2006 Pew Forum on Religion and Public Life poll found that nearly one-third of all Americans feel the Bible should be the basis of law across the United States.[107] Many women's-rights activists say Christian fundamentalism threatens women's rights, particularly with regard to reproductive issues. They also condemn the Vatican's opposition to the use of condoms, pointing

Pakistani acid attack survivors Saira Liaqat, right, and Sabra Sultana are among hundreds, and perhaps thousands, of women who are blinded and disfigured after being attacked with acid each year in Pakistan, Bangladesh, India, Cambodia, Malaysia, Uganda and other areas of Africa. Liaqat was attacked at age 18 during an argument over an arranged marriage. Sabra was 15 when she was burned after being married off to an older man who became unsatisfied with the relationship. Only a small percentage of the attacks — often perpetrated by spurned suitors while the women are asleep in their own beds — are prosecuted.

out that it prevents women from protecting themselves against HIV.

"If you look at all your religions, none will say it's a good thing to beat up or kill someone. They are all based on human dignity," says Mollmann of Human Rights Watch. "[Bad things] are carried out in the name of religion, but the actual belief system is not killing and maiming women."

In response to the growing number of honor-based killings, attacks and forced marriages in the U.K., Britain's Association of Chief Police Officers has created an honor-based violence unit, and the U.K.'s Home Office is drafting an action plan to improve the response of police and other agencies to such violence. Legislation going into effect later this year will also give U.K. courts greater guidance on dealing with forced marriages.[108]

Evolving Gender Policies

This past February, the U.N. Convention on the Elimination of All Forms of Discrimination Against Women issued a report criticizing Saudi Arabia for its repression of women. Among other things, the report attacked Saudi Arabia's ban on women drivers and its

Getty Images/Paula Bronstein

Female farmworkers in Nova Lima, Brazil, protest against the impact of big corporations on the poor in March 2006, reflecting the increasing political activism of women around the globe.

system of male guardianship that denies women equal inheritance, child custody and divorce rights.[109] The criticism came during the panel's regular review of countries that have ratified CEDAW. Each government must submit reports every four years outlining steps taken to comply with the convention.

The United States is one of only eight countries — among them Iran, Sudan and Somalia — that have refused to ratify CEDAW.[110] Last year, 108 members of the U.S. House of Representatives signed on to a resolution calling for the Senate to ratify CEDAW, but it still has not voted on the measure.[111] During a U.N. vote last November on a resolution encouraging governments to meet their obligations under CEDAW, the United States was the lone nay vote against 173 yea votes.[112]

American opponents of CEDAW — largely pro-life Christians and Republicans — say it would enshrine the right to abortion in *Roe v. Wade* and be prohibitively expensive, potentially requiring the U.S. government to provide paid maternity leave and other child-care services to all women.[113] They also oppose requirements that the government modify "social and cultural patterns" to eliminate sexual prejudice and to delete any traces of gender stereotypes in textbooks — such as references to women's lives being primarily in the domestic sector.[114] Many Republicans in Congress also have argued that CEDAW would give too much control over U.S. laws to the United Nations and that it could even require the legalization of prostitution and the abolition of Mother's Day.[115]

The last time the Senate took action on CEDAW was in 2002, when the Senate Foreign Relations Committee, chaired by Democratic Sen. Joseph Biden of Delaware, voted to send the convention to the Senate floor for ratification. The full Senate, however, never took action. A Biden spokesperson says the senator "remains committed" to the treaty and is "looking for an opportune time" to bring it forward again. But Senate ratification requires 67 votes, and there do not appear to be that many votes for approval.

CEDAW proponents say the failure to ratify not only hurts women but also harms the U.S. image abroad. On this issue, "the United States is in the company of Sudan and the Vatican," says Bien-Aimé of Equality Now.

Meanwhile, several countries are enacting laws to comply with CEDAW and improve the status of women. In December, Turkmenistan passed its first national law guaranteeing women equal rights, even though its constitution had addressed women's equality.[116] A royal decree in Saudi Arabia in January ordered an end to a long-time ban on women checking into hotels or renting apartments without male guardians. Hotels can now book rooms to women who show identification, but the hotels must register the women's details with the police.[117] The Saudi government has also said it will lift the ban on women driving by the end of the year.[118]

And in an effort to improve relations with women in Afghanistan, the Canadian military, which has troops stationed in the region, has begun studying the role women play in Afghan society, how they are affected by military operations and how they can assist peacekeeping efforts. "Behind all of these men are women who can help eradicate the problems of the population," said Capt. Michel Larocque, who is working with the study. "Illiteracy, poverty, these things can be improved through women."[119]

In February, during the 52nd session of the Commission on the Status of Women, the United Nations kicked off a new seven-year campaign aimed at ending violence against women. The campaign will work with international agencies, governments and individuals to increase funding for anti-violence campaigns and pressure policy makers around the world to enact legislation to eliminate violence against women.[120]

But women's groups want increased U.N. spending on women's programs and the creation of a single unified

Should sex-selective abortions be outlawed?

YES   Nicholas Eberstadt
Henry Wendt Chair in Political Economy, American Enterprise Institute Member, President's Council on Bioethics

Written for *CQ Global Researcher*, April 2008

The practice of sex-selective abortion to permit parents to destroy unwanted female fetuses has become so widespread in the modern world that it is disfiguring the profile of entire countries — transforming (and indeed deforming) the whole human species.

This abomination is now rampant in China, where the latest census reports six boys for every five girls. But it is also prevalent in the Far East, South Korea, Hong Kong, Taiwan and Vietnam, all of which report biologically impossible "sex ratios at birth" (well above the 103-106 baby boys for every 100 girls ordinarily observed in human populations). In the Caucasus, gruesome imbalances exist now in Armenia, Georgia and Azerbaijan; and in India, the state of Punjab tallies 126 little boys for every 100 girls. Even in the United States, the boy-girl sex ratio at birth for Asian-Americans is now several unnatural percentage points above the national average. So sex-selective abortion is taking place under America's nose.

How can we rid the world of this barbaric form of sexism? Simply outlawing sex-selective abortions will be little more than a symbolic gesture, as South Korea's experience has shown: Its sex ratio at birth continued a steady climb for a full decade after just such a national law was passed. As long as abortion is basically available on demand, any legislation to abolish sex-selective abortion will have no impact.

What about more general restrictions on abortion, then? Poll data consistently demonstrate that most Americans do not favor the post-*Roe* regimen of unconditional abortion. But a return to the pre-*Roe* status quo, where each state made its own abortion laws, would probably have very little effect on sex-selective abortion in our country. After all, the ethnic communities most tempted by it are concentrated in states where abortion rights would likely be strongest, such as California and New York.

In the final analysis, the extirpation of this scourge will require nothing less than a struggle for the conscience of nations. Here again, South Korea may be illustrative: Its gender imbalances began to decline when the public was shocked into facing this stain on their society by a spontaneous, homegrown civil rights movement.

To eradicate sex-selective abortion, we must convince the world that destroying female fetuses is horribly wrong. We need something akin to the abolitionist movement: a moral campaign waged globally, with victories declared one conscience at a time.

NO   Marianne Mollmann
Advocacy Director, Women's Rights Division, Human Rights Watch

Written for *CQ Global Researcher*, April 2008

Medical technology today allows parents to test early in pregnancy for fetal abnormalities, hereditary illnesses and even the sex of the fetus, raising horrifying questions about eugenics and population control. In some countries, a growing number of women apparently are terminating pregnancies when they learn the fetus is female. The resulting sex imbalance in countries like China and India is not only disturbing but also leads to further injustices, such as the abduction of girls for forced marriages.

One response has been to criminalize sex-selective abortions. While it is tempting to hope that this could safeguard the gender balance of future generations, criminalization of abortion for whatever reason has led in the past only to underground and unsafe practices. Thus, the criminalization of sex-selective abortion would put the full burden of righting a fundamental wrong — the devaluing of women's lives — on women.

Many women who choose to abort a female fetus face violence and exclusion if they don't produce a boy. Some see the financial burden of raising a girl as detrimental to the survival of the rest of their family. These considerations will not be lessened by banning sex-selective abortion. Unless one addresses the motivation for the practice, it will continue — underground.

So what is the motivation for aborting female fetuses? At the most basic level, it is a financial decision. In no country in the world does women's earning power equal men's. In marginalized communities in developing countries, this is directly linked to survival: Boys may provide more income than girls.

Severe gaps between women's and men's earning power are generally accompanied by severe forms of gender-based discrimination and rigid gender roles. For example, in China, boys are expected to stay in their parental home as they grow up, adding their manpower (and that of a later wife) to the family home. Girls, on the other hand, are expected to join the husbands' parental home. Thus, raising a girl is a net loss, especially if you are only allowed one child.

The solution is to remove the motivation behind sex-selective abortion by advancing women's rights and their economic and social equality. Choosing the blunt instrument of criminal law over promoting the value of women's lives and rights will only serve to place further burdens on marginalized and often vulnerable women.

agency addressing women's issues, led by an under-secretary general.[121] Currently, four different U.N. agencies address women's issues: the United Nations Development Fund for Women, the International Research and Training Institute for the Advancement of Women (INSTRAW), the Secretary-General's Special Advisor on Gender Issues (OSAGI) and the Division for the Advancement of Women. In 2006, the four agencies received only $65 million — a fraction of the more than $2 billion budget that the U.N.'s children's fund (UNICEF) received that year.[122]

"The four entities that focus on women's rights at the U.N. are greatly under-resourced," says Zeitlin of the Women's Environment & Development Organization. "If the rhetoric everyone is using is true — that investing in women is investing in development — it's a matter of putting your money where your mouth is."

Political Prospects

While the number of women leading world governments is still miniscule compared to their male counterparts, women are achieving political gains that just a few years ago would have been unthinkable.

While for the first time in U.S. history a woman is in a tight race for a major party's nomination as its candidate for president, South America — with two sitting female heads of state — leads the world in woman-led governments. In Brazil, Dilma Rousseff, the female chief of staff to President Luiz Inacio Lula da Silva, is the top contender to take over the presidency when da Silva's term ends in 2010.[123] In Paraguay, Blanca Ovelar was this year's presidential nominee for the country's ruling conservative Colorado Party, but she was defeated on April 20.[124]

And in Europe, Carme Chacón was named defense minister of Spain this past April. She was not only the first woman ever to head the country's armed forces but also was pregnant at the time of her appointment. In all, nine of Spain's 17 cabinet ministers are women.

In March, Pakistan's National Assembly overwhelmingly elected its first female speaker, Fahmida Mirza.[125] And in India, where Patil has become the first woman president, the two major political parties this year pledged to set aside one-third of their parliamentary nominations for women. But many fear the parties will either not keep their pledges or will run women only in contests they are unlikely to win.[126]

There was also disappointment in Iran, where nearly 600 of the 7,000 candidates running for parliament in March were women.[127] Only three won seats in the 290-member house, and they were conservatives who are not expected to promote women's rights. Several of the tallies are being contested. Twelve other women won enough votes to face run-off elections on April 25; five won.[128]

But in some countries, women running for office face more than just tough campaigns. They are specifically targeted for violence. In Kenya, the greatest campaign expense for female candidates is the round-the-clock security required to protect them against rape, according to Phoebe Asiyo, who served in the Kenyan parliament for more than two decades.[129] During the three months before Kenya's elections last December, an emergency helpdesk established by the Education Centre for Women in Democracy, a nongovernmental organization (NGO) in Nairobi, received 258 reports of attacks against female candidates.[130]

The helpdesk reported the attacks to police, worked with the press to ensure the cases were documented and helped victims obtain medical and emotional support. Attacks included rape, stabbings, threats and physical assaults.[131]

"Women are being attacked because they are women and because it is seen as though they are not fit to bear flags of the popular parties," according to the center's Web site. "Women are also viewed as guilty for invading 'the male territory' and without a license to do so!"[132]

"All women candidates feel threatened," said Nazlin Umar, the sole female presidential candidate last year. "When a case of violence against a woman is reported, we women on the ground think we are next. I think if the government assigned all women candidates with guns…we will at least have an item to protect ourselves when we face danger."[133]

Impunity for Violence

Some African feminists blame women themselves, as well as men, for not doing enough to end traditional attitudes that perpetuate violence against women.

"Women are also to blame for the violence because they are the gatekeepers of patriarchy, because whether educated or not they have different standards for their sons and husbands [than for] their daughters," said Njoki Wainaina, founder of the African Women Development

Communication Network (FEMNET). "How do you start telling a boy whose mother trained him only disrespect for girls to honor women in adulthood?"[134]

Indeed, violence against women is widely accepted in many regions of the world and often goes unpunished. A study by the World Health Organization found that 80 percent of women surveyed in rural Egypt believe that a man is justified in beating a woman if she refuses to have sex with him. In Ghana, more women than men — 50 percent compared to 43 percent — felt that a man was justified in beating his wife if she used contraception without his consent.[135] (*See survey results, p. 338.*)

Such attitudes have led to many crimes against women going unpunished, and not just violence committed during wartime. In Guatemala, no one knows why an estimated 3,000 women have been killed over the past seven years — many of them beheaded, sexually mutilated or raped — but theories range from domestic violence to gang activity.[136] Meanwhile, the government in 2006 overturned a law allowing rapists to escape charges if they offered to marry their victims. But Guatemalan law still does not prescribe prison sentences for domestic abuse and prohibits abusers from being charged with assault unless the bruises are still visible after 10 days.[137]

In the Mexican cities of Chihuahua and Juárez, more than 400 women have been murdered over the past 14 years, with many of the bodies mutilated and dumped in the desert. But the crimes are still unsolved, and many human-rights groups, including Amnesty International, blame indifference by Mexican authorities. Now the country's 14-year statute of limitations on murder is forcing prosecutors to close many of the unsolved cases.[138]

Feminists around the world have been working to end dismissive cultural attitudes about domestic violence and other forms of violence against women, such as forced marriage, dowry-related violence, marital rape, sexual harassment and forced abortion, sterilization and prostitution. But it's often an uphill battle.

After a Kenyan police officer beat his wife so badly she was paralyzed and brain damaged — and eventually died — media coverage of the murder spurred a nationwide debate on domestic violence. But it took five years of protests, demonstrations and lobbying by both women's advocates and outraged men to get a family protection bill enacted criminalizing domestic violence. And the bill passed only after legislators removed a provision outlawing

marital rape. Similar laws have languished for decades in other African legislatures.[139]

But in Rwanda, where nearly 49 percent of the elected representatives in the lower house are female, gender desks have been established at local police stations, staffed mostly by women trained to help victims of sexual and other violence. In 2006, as a result of improved reporting, investigation and response to rape cases, police referred 1,777 cases for prosecution and convicted 803 men. "What we need now is to expand this approach to more countries," said UNIFEM's director for Central Africa Josephine Odera.[140]

Besides criticizing governments for failing to prosecute gender-based violence, many women's groups also criticize the International Criminal Court (ICC) for not doing enough to bring abusers to justice.

"We have yet to see the investigative approach needed to ensure the prosecution of gender-based crimes," said Brigid Inder, executive director of Women's Initiatives for Gender Justice, a Hague-based group that promotes and monitors women's rights in the international court.[141] Inder's group released a study last November showing that of the 500 victims seeking to participate in ICC proceedings, only 38 percent were women. When the court handed down its first indictments for war crimes in the Democratic Republic of the Congo last year, no charges involving gender-based crimes were brought despite estimates that more than 250,000 women have been raped and sexually abused in the country. After an outcry from women's groups around the world, the ICC included "sexual slavery" among the charges handed down in its second case involving war crimes in Congo.[142]

The Gender Justice report also criticized the court for failing to reach out to female victims. It said the ICC has held only one consultation with women in the last four years (focusing on the Darfur conflict in Sudan) and has failed to develop any strategies to reach out to women victims in Congo.[143]

OUTLOOK
Economic Integration

Women's organizations do not expect — or want — another international conference on the scale of Beijing. Instead, they say, the resources needed to launch such a

Seaweed farmer Asia Mohammed Makungu in Zanzibar, Tanzania, grows the sea plants for export to European companies that produce food and cosmetics. Globalized trade has helped women entrepreneurs in many developing countries improve their lives, but critics say it also has created many low-wage, dangerous jobs for women in poor countries that ignore safety and labor protections in order to attract foreign investors.

conference would be better used to improve U.N. oversight of women's issues and to implement the promises made at Beijing.

They also fear that the growth of religious fundamentalism and neo-liberal economic policies around the globe have created a political atmosphere that could actually set back women's progress.

"If a Beijing conference happened now, we would not get the type of language or the scope we got 10 years ago," says Bien-Aimé of Equity Now. "There is a conservative movement, a growth in fundamentalists governments — and not just in Muslim countries. We would be very concerned about opening up debate on the principles that have already been established."

Dahlerup of Stockholm University agrees. "It was easier in the 1990s. Many people are afraid of having big conferences now, because there may be a backlash because fundamentalism is so strong," she says. "Neo-liberal trends are also moving the discourse about women toward economics — women have to benefit for the sake of the economic good. That could be very good, but it's a more narrow discourse when every issue needs to be adapted into the economic discourse of a cost-benefit analysis."

For women to continue making gains, most groups say, gender can no longer be treated separately from broader economic, environmental, health or other political issues. While efforts to improve the status of women have historically been addressed in gender-specific legislation or international treaties, women's groups now say women's well-being must now be considered an integral part of all policies.

Women's groups are working to ensure that gender is incorporated into two major international conferences coming up this fall. In September, the Third High-Level Forum on Aid Effectiveness will be hosted in Accra, Ghana, bringing together governments, financial institutions, civil society organizations and others to assess whether assistance provided to poor nations is being put to good use. World leaders will also gather in November in Doha, Qatar, for the International Conference on Financing for Development to discuss how trade, debt relief and financial aid can promote global development.

"Women's groups are pushing for gender to be on the agenda for both conferences," says Zeitlin of WEDO. "It's important because . . . world leaders need to realize that it really does make a difference to invest in women. When it comes to women's rights it's all micro, but the big decisions are made on the macro level."

Despite decades of economic-development strategies promoted by Western nations and global financial institutions such as the World Bank, women in many regions are getting poorer. In Malawi, for example, the percentage of women living in poverty increased by 5 percent between 1995 and 2003.[144] Women and girls make up 70 percent of the world's poorest people, and their wages rise more slowly than men's. They also have fewer property rights around the world.[145] With the growing global food shortage, women — who are the primary family caregivers and produce the majority of crops for home consumption in developing countries — will be especially hard hit.

To help women escape poverty, gain legal rights and improve their social status, developed nations must rethink their broader strategies of engagement with developing countries. And, conversely, female activists say, any efforts aimed at eradicating poverty around the world must specifically address women's issues.

In Africa, for instance, activists have successfully demanded that women's economic and security concerns be addressed as part of the continent-wide development plan known as the New Partnership for Africa's Development (NEPAD). As a result, countries participating in NEPAD's peer review process must now show they are taking measures to promote and protect women's rights. But, according to Augustin Wambo, an agricultural specialist at the NEPAD secretariat, lawmakers now need to back up their pledges with "resources from national budgets" and the "necessary policies and means to support women."[146]

"We have made a lot of progress and will continue making progress," says Zeitlin. "But women's progress doesn't happen in isolation to what's happening in the rest of the world. The environment, the global economy, war, peace — they will all have a major impact on women. Women all over world will not stop making demands and fighting for their rights."

NOTES

1. http://ballyblog.wordpress.com/2007/05/04/warning-uncensored-video-iraqis-stone-girl-to-death-over-loving-wrong-boy/.

2. Abdulhamid Zebari, "Video of Iraqi girl's stoning shown on Internet," Agence France Presse, May 5, 2007.

3. *State of the World Population 2000*, United Nations Population Fund, Sept. 20, 2000, Chapter 3, "Ending Violence against Women and Girls," www.unfpa.org/swp/2000/english/ch03.html.

4. Brian Brady, "A Question of Honour," *The Independent on Sunday*, Feb. 10, 2008, p. 8, www.independent.co.uk/news/uk/home-news/a-question-of-honour-police-say-17000-women-are-victims-every-year-780522.html.

5. Correspondence with Karen Musalo, Clinical Professor of Law and Director of the Center for Gender & Refugee Studies at the University of California Hastings School of Law, April 11, 2008.

6. "Broken Bodies, Broken Dreams: Violence Against Women Exposed," United Nations, July 2006, http://brokendreams.wordpress.com/2006/12/17/dowry-crimes-and-bride-price-abuse/.

7. Various sources: www.womankind.org.uk, www.unfpa.org/gender/docs/studies/summaries/reg_exe_summary.pdf, www.oxfam.org.uk. Also see "Child rape in Kano on the increase," IRIN Humanitarian News and Analysis, United Nations, www.irinnews.org/report.aspx?ReportId=76087.

8. "UNICEF slams 'licence to rape' in African crisis," Agence France-Press, Feb. 12, 2008.

9. "Film Documents Rape of Women in Congo," "All Things Considered," National Public Radio, April 8, 2008, www.npr.org/templates/story/story.php?storyId=89476111.

10. Jeffrey Gettleman, "Rape Epidemic Raises Trauma Of Congo War," *The New York Times*, Oct. 7, 2007, p. A1.

11. Dan McDougall, "Fareeda's fate: rape, prison and 25 lashes," *The Observer*, Sept. 17, 2006, www.guardian.co.uk/world/2006/sep/17/pakistan.theobserver.

12. Zarar Khan, "Thousands rally in Pakistan to demand government withdraw rape law changes," The Associated Press, Dec. 10, 2006.

13. *State of the World Population 2000*, op. cit.

14. Laura Turquet, Patrick Watt, Tom Sharman, "Hit or Miss?" ActionAid, March 7, 2008, p. 10.

15. *Ibid.*, p. 12.

16. "Women in Politics: 2008" map, International Parliamentary Union and United Nations Division for the Advancement of Women, February 2008, www.ipu.org/pdf/publications/wmnmap08_en.pdf.

17. Gavin Rabinowitz, "India's first female president sworn in, promises to empower women," The Associated Press, July 25, 2007. Note: India's first female prime minister was Indira Ghandi in 1966.

18. Monte Reel, "South America Ushers In The Era of La Presidenta; Women Could Soon Lead a Majority of Continent's Population," *The Washington Post*, Oct. 31, 2007, p. A12. For background, see Roland Flamini, "The New Latin America," *CQ Global Researcher*, March 2008, pp. 57-84.

19. Marcela Valente, "Cristina Fernandes Dons Presidential Sash," Inter Press Service, Dec. 10, 2007.

20. "Women in Politics: 2008" map, *op. cit.*

21. *Ibid.*; Global Database of Quotas for Women, International Institute for Democracy and Electoral Assistance and Stockholm University, www.quotaproject.org/country.cfm?SortOrder=Country.

22. "Beijing Betrayed," Women's Environment and Development Organization, March 2005, p. 10, www.wedo.org/files/gmr_pdfs/gmr2005.pdf.

23. "Women in Politics: 2008" map, *op. cit.*

24. Gertrude Mongella, address by the Secretary-General of the 4th World Conference on Women, Sept. 4, 1995, www.un.org/esa/gopher-data/conf/fwcw/conf/una/950904201423.txt. Also see Steven Mufson, "Women's Forum Sets Accord; Dispute on Sexual Freedom Resolved," *The Washington Post*, Sept. 15, 1995, p. A1.

25. "Closing statement," Gertrude Mongella, U.N. Division for the Advancement of Women, Fourth World Conference on Women, www.un.org/esa/gopher-data/conf/fwcw/conf/una/closing.txt.

26. "Trading Away Our Rights," Oxfam International, 2004, p. 9, www.oxfam.org.uk/resources/policy/trade/downloads/trading_rights.pdf.

27. "Trafficking in Persons Report," U.S. Department of State, June 2007, p. 7, www.state.gov/g/tip/rls/tiprpt/2007/.

28. Turquet, *et al.*, *op. cit.*, p. 4.

29. United Nations Division for the Advancement of Women, www.un.org/womenwatch/daw/cedaw/.

30. Geraldine Terry, *Women's Rights* (2007), p. 30.

31. United Nations Division for the Advancement of Women, www.un.org/womenwatch/daw/cedaw/.

32. "The impact of international trade on gender equality," The World Bank PREM notes, May 2004, http://siteresources.worldbank.org/INTGENDER/Resources/premnote86.pdf.

33. Thalia Kidder and Kate Raworth, " 'Good Jobs' and hidden costs: women workers documenting the price of precarious employment," *Gender and Development*, July 2004, p. 13.

34. "Trading Away Our Rights," *op. cit.*

35. Martha Chen, *et al.*, "Progress of the World's Women 2005: Women, Work and Poverty," UNIFEM, p. 17, www.unifem.org/attachments/products/PoWW2005_eng.pdf.

36. Eric Neumayer and Indra de Soys, "Globalization, Women's Economic Rights and Forced Labor," London School of Economics and Norwegian University of Science and Technology, February 2007, p. 8, http://papers.ssrn.com/sol3/papers.cfm?abstract_id=813831. Also see "Five years down the road from Beijing — assessing progress," *News and Highlights*, Food and Agriculture Organization, June 2, 2000, www.fao.org/News/2000/000602-e.htm.

37. "Trafficking in Persons Report," *op. cit.*, p. 13.

38. "World Survey on the Role of Women in Development," United Nations, 2006, p. 1, www.un.org/womenwatch/daw/public/WorldSurvey2004-Women&Migration.pdf.

39. Julie Ballington and Azza Karam, eds., "Women in Parliament: Beyond the Numbers," International Institute for Democracy and Electoral Assistance, 2005, p. 155, www.idea.int/publications/wip2/upload/WiP_inlay.pdf.

40. "Women in Politics: 2008," *op. cit.*

41. Ballington and Karam, *op. cit.*, p. 158.

42. *Ibid.*, p. 161.

43. Global Database of Quotas for Women, *op. cit.*

44. Jerome Starkey, "Afghan government official says that student will not be executed," *The Independent*, Feb. 6, 2008, www.independent.co.uk/news/world/asia/afghan-government-official-says-that-student-will-not-be-executed-778686.html?r=RSS.

45. "Afghan women seek death by fire," BBC, Nov. 15, 2006, http://news.bbc.co.uk/1/hi/world/south_asia/6149144.stm.

46. Global Database for Quotas for Women, *op. cit.*

47. "Beijing Declaration," Fourth World Conference on Women, www.un.org/womenwatch/daw/beijing/beijingdeclaration.html.

48. "Beijing Betrayed," *op. cit.*, pp. 28, 15, 18.

49. "Review of the implementation of the Beijing Platform for Action and the outcome documents of the special session of the General Assembly entitled 'Women 2000: gender equality, development and peace for the twenty-first century,' " United Nations, Dec. 6, 2004, p. 74.

50. "Gender Equality and the Millennium Development Goals," fact sheet, www.mdgender.net/upload/tools/MDGender_leaflet.pdf.

51. *Ibid.*

52. Turquet, *et al.*, *op. cit.*, p. 16.

53. *Ibid.*, pp. 22-24.

54. Terry, *op. cit.*, p. 6.

55. "Inclusive Security, Sustainable Peace: A Toolkit for Advocacy and Action," International Alert and Women Waging Peace, 2004, p. 12, www.huntalternatives .org/download/35_introduction.pdf.

56. "Declarations, Reservations and Objections to CEDAW," www.un.org/womenwatch/daw/cedaw/ reservations-country.htm.

57. Merlin Stone, *When God Was a Woman* (1976), pp. 18, 11.

58. Jack Holland, *Misogyny* (2006), p. 12.

59. *Ibid.*, pp. 21-23.

60. Holland, *op. cit.*, p. 112.

61. "Dispelling the myths about so-called witches" press release, Johns Hopkins University, Oct. 7, 2002, www.jhu.edu/news_info/news/home02/ oct02/witch.html.

62. The quote is from the *Malleus maleficarum* (*The Hammer of Witches*), and was cited in "Case Study: The European Witch Hunts, c. 1450-1750," *Gendercide Watch*, www.gendercide.org/case_witch-hunts.html.

63. Holland, *op. cit.*, p. 179.

64. Cathy J. Cohen, Kathleen B. Jones and Joan C. Tronto, *Women Transforming Politics: An Alternative Reader* (1997), p. 530.

65. *Ibid.*

66. Holland, *op. cit*, p. 201.

67. "Men and Women in Politics: Democracy Still in the Making," IPU Study No. 28, 1997, http:// archive.idea.int/women/parl/ch6_table8.htm.

68. "Sex, Equality and Protective Laws," *CQ Researcher*, July 13, 1926.

69. The case was *Radice v. People of State of New York*, 264 U. S. 292. For background, see F. Brewer, "Equal Rights Amendment," *Editorial Research Reports*, April 4, 1946, available at *CQ Researcher Plus Archive*, www.cqpress.com.

70. "Short History of the CEDAW Convention," U.N. Division for the Advancement of Women, www .un.org/womenwatch/daw/cedaw/history.htm.

71. U.N. Women's Watch, www.un.org/womenwatch/ asp/user/list.asp-ParentID=11047.htm.

72. United Nations, http://untreaty.un.org/ENGLISH/ bible/englishinternetbible/partI/chapterXVI/ treaty2.asp.

73. International Labor Organization, www.ilo.org/ public/english/support/lib/resource/subject/ gender.htm.

74. *Ibid.*

75. For background, see "Gender Pay Gap," *CQ Researcher*, March 14, 2008, pp. 241-264.

76. "Short History of the CEDAW Convention" *op. cit.*

77. "International News," The Associated Press, Dec. 19, 1979.

78. "Short History of the CEDAW Convention" *op. cit.*

79. "Text of the Convention," U.N. Division for the Advancement of Women, www.un.org/women-watch/daw/cedaw/cedaw.htm.

80. Convention on the Elimination of All Forms of Discrimination against Women, Article 16, www .un.org/womenwatch/daw/cedaw/text/econvention .htm.

81. General Recommendation made by the Committee on the Elimination of Discrimination against Women No. 19, 11th session, 1992, www.un.org/women watch/daw/cedaw/recommendations/recomm .htm#recom19.

82. See www.unhchr.ch/huridocda/huridoca.nsf/ (Symbol)/A.CONF.157.23.En.

83. Marlise Simons, "For First Time, Court Defines Rape as War Crime," *The New York Times*, June 28, 1996, www.nytimes.com/specials/bosnia/ context/0628warcrimes-tribunal.html.

84. Ann Simmons, "U.N. Tribunal Convicts Rwandan Ex-Mayor of Genocide in Slaughter," *Los Angeles Times*, Sept. 3, 1998, p. 20.

85. "Human Rights Watch Applauds Rwanda Rape Verdict," press release, Human Rights Watch, Sept. 2, 1998, http://hrw.org/english/ docs/1998/09/02/ rwanda1311.htm.

86. Frederic Bichon, "ICC vows to bring Darfur war criminals to justice," Agence France-Presse, Feb. 24, 2008.

87. Rebecca Feeley and Colin Thomas-Jensen, "Getting Serious about Ending Conflict and Sexual Violence in Congo," Enough Project, www.enoughproject .org/reports/congoserious.

88. "Women; Deceived Again?" *The Economist*, July 5, 1975.

89. "International Women's Day — March 8: Points of Interest and Links with UNIFEM," UNIFEM New Zealand Web site, www.unifem.org.nz/ IWDPointsofinterest.htm.

90. Joseph Gambardello, "Reporter's Notebook: Women's Conference in Kenya," United Press International, July 13, 1985.

91. "Report of the World Conference to Review and Appraise the Achievements of the United Nations Decade for Women: Equality Development and Peace," United Nations, 1986, paragraph 8, www .un.org/womenwatch/confer/nfls/Nairobi1985report.txt.

92. U.N. Division for the Advancement of Women, www.un.org/womenwatch/daw/followup/back-ground.htm.

93. "Women in Politics," Inter-Parliamentary Union, 2005, pp. 16-17, www.ipu.org/PDF/publications/ wmn45-05_en.pdf.

94. "Liberian becomes Africa's first female president," Associated Press, Jan. 16, 2006, www.msnbc.msn .com/id/10865705/.

95. "Women in the Americas: Paths to Political Power," *op. cit.*, p. 2.

96. "The Millennium Development Goals Report 2007," United Nations, 2007, p. 12, www.un.org/ millenniumgoals/pdf/mdg2007.pdf.

97. David Dollar, Raymond Fisman, Roberta Gatti, "Are Women Really the 'Fairer' Sex? Corruption and Women in Government," The World Bank, October 1999, p. 1, http://siteresources.world-bank.org/INTGENDER/Resources/wp4.pdf.

98. *Ibid.*

99. Vicky Baker, "Rape victim sentenced to 200 lashes and six months in jail; Saudi woman punished for being alone with a man," *The Guardian*, Nov. 17, 2007, www.guardian.co.uk/world/2007/nov/17/ saudiarabia.international.

100. Katherine Zoepf, "Saudi King Pardons Rape Victim Sentenced to Be Lashed, Saudi Paper Reports," *The New York Times*, Dec. 18, 2007, www.nytimes .com/2007/12/18/world/middleeast/18saudi.html.

101. Sonia Verma, "King Abdullah urged to spare Saudi 'witchcraft' woman's life," *The Times* (Of London), Feb. 16, 2008.

102. Mark Lattimer, "Freedom lost," *The Guardian*, Dec. 13, 2007, p. 6.

103. For background, see Brian Beary, "Future of Turkey," *CQ Global Researcher*, December, 2007, pp. 295-322.

104. Tracy Clark-Flory, "Does freedom to veil hurt women?" *Salon.com*, Feb. 11, 2008.

105. Sabrina Tavernise, "Under a Scarf, a Turkish Lawyer Fighting to Wear It," *The New York Times*, Feb. 9, 2008, www.nytimes.com/2008/02/09/world/ europe/09benli.html?pagewanted=1&sq=women& st=nyt&scp=96.

106. Terry, *op. cit.*, p. 122.

107. "Many Americans Uneasy with Mix of Religion and Politics," The Pew Forum on Religion and Public Life, Aug. 24, 2006, http://pewforum.org/ docs/index.php?DocID=153.

108. Brady, *op. cit.*

109. "Concluding Observations of the Committee on the Elimination of Discrimination against Women: Saudi Arabia," Committee on the Elimination of Discrimination against Women, 40th Session, Jan. 14-Feb. 1, 2008, p. 3, www2.ohchr.org/english/ bodies/cedaw/docs/co/CEDAW.C.SAU.CO.2.pdf.

110. Kambiz Fattahi, "Women's bill 'unites' Iran and US," BBC, July 31, 2007, http://news.bbc.co .uk/2/hi/middle_east/6922749.stm.

111. H. Res. 101, Rep. Lynn Woolsey, http://thomas. loc.gov/cgi-bin/bdquery/z?d110:h.res.00101.

112. "General Assembly Adopts Landmark Text Calling for Moratorium on Death Penalty," States News Service, Dec. 18, 2007, www.un.org/News/Press/ docs//2007/ga10678.doc.htm.

113. Mary H. Cooper, "Women and Human Rights," *CQ Researcher*, April 30, 1999, p. 356.

114. Christina Hoff Sommers, "The Case against Ratifying the United Nations Convention on the Elimination of All Forms of Discrimination against Women," testimony before the Senate Foreign Relations Committee, June 13, 2002, www.aei.org/publications/filter.all,pubID.15557/pub_detail.asp.

115. "CEDAW: Pro-United Nations, Not Pro-Woman" press release, U.S. Senate Republican Policy Committee, Sept. 16, 2002, http://rpc.senate.gov/_files/FOREIGNje091602.pdf.

116. "Turkmenistan adopts gender equality law," BBC Worldwide Monitoring, Dec. 19, 2007.

117. Faiza Saleh Ambah, "Saudi Women See a Brighter Road on Rights," *The Washington Post*, Jan. 31, 2008, p. A15, www.washingtonpost.com/wp-dyn/content/article/2008/01/30/AR2008013003805.html.

118. Damien McElroy, "Saudi Arabia to lift ban on women drivers," *The Telegraph*, Jan. 1, 2008.

119. Stephanie Levitz, "Lifting the veils of Afghan women," *The Hamilton Spectator* (Ontario, Canada), Feb. 28, 2008, p. A11.

120. "U.N. Secretary-General Ban Ki-moon Launches Campaign to End Violence against Women," U.N. press release, Feb. 25, 2008, http://endviolence.un.org/press.shtml.

121. "Gender Equality Architecture and U.N. Reforms," the Center for Women's Global Leadership and the Women's Environment and Development Organization, July 17, 2006, www.wedo.org/files/Gender%20Equality%20Architecture%20and%20UN%20Reform0606.pdf.

122. Bojana Stoparic, "New-Improved Women's Agency Vies for U.N. Priority," Women's eNews, March 6, 2008, www.womensenews.org/article.cfm?aid=3517.

123. Reel, *op. cit.*

124. Eliana Raszewski and Bill Faries, "Lugo, Ex Bishop, Wins Paraguay Presidential Election," Bloomberg, April 20, 2008.

125. Zahid Hussain, "Pakistan gets its first woman Speaker," *The Times* (of London), March 20, p. 52.

126. Bhaskar Roy, "Finally, women set to get 33% quota," *Times of India*, Jan. 29, 2008.

127. Massoumeh Torfeh, "Iranian women crucial in Majlis election," BBC, Jan. 30, 2008, http://news.bbc.co.uk/1/hi/world/middle_east/7215272.stm.

128. "Iran women win few seats in parliament," Agence-France Presse, March 18, 2008.

129. Swanee Hunt, "Let Women Rule," *Foreign Affairs*, May-June 2007, p. 109.

130. Kwamboka Oyaro, "A Call to Arm Women Candidates With More Than Speeches," Inter Press Service, Dec. 21, 2007, http://ipsnews.net/news.asp?idnews=40569.

131. Education Centre for Women in Democracy, www.ecwd.org.

132. *Ibid.*

133. Oyaro, *op. cit.*

134. *Ibid.*

135. Mary Kimani, "Taking on violence against women in Africa," *AfricaRenewal*, U.N. Dept. of Public Information, July 2007, p. 4, www.un.org/ecosocdev/geninfo/afrec/vol21no2/212-violence-aganist-women.html.

136. Correspondence with Karen Musalo, Clinical Professor of Law and Director of the Center for Gender & Refugee Studies, University of California Hastings School of Law, April 11, 2008.

137. "Mexico and Guatemala: Stop the Killings of Women," Amnesty International USA Issue Brief, January 2007, www.amnestyusa.org/document.php?lang=e&id=engusa20070130001.

138. Manuel Roig-Franzia, "Waning Hopes in Juarez," *The Washington Post*, May 14, 2007, p. A10.

139. Kimani, *op. cit.*

140. *Ibid.*

141. "Justice slow for female war victims," *The Toronto Star*, March 3, 2008, www.thestar.com/News/GlobalVoices/article/308784p.

142. Speech by Brigid Inder on the Launch of the "Gender Report Card on the International Criminal Court," Dec. 12, 2007, www.iccwomen.org/news/docs/Launch_GRC_2007.pdf

143. "Gender Report Card on the International Criminal Court," Women's Initiatives for Gender Justice,

November 2007, p. 32, www.iccwomen.org/publications/resources/docs/GENDER_04-01-2008_FINAL_TO_PRINT.pdf.

144. Turquet, *et al.*, *op. cit.*, p. 8.

145. Oxfam Gender Equality Fact Sheet, www.oxfam.org.uk/resources/issues/gender/introduction.html.

146. Itai Madamombe, "Women push onto Africa's agenda," *AfricaRenewal*, U.N. Dept. of Public Information, July 2007, pp. 8-9.

BIBLIOGRAPHY

Books

Holland, Jack, *Misogyny: The World's Oldest Prejudice, Constable & Robinson*, 2006.
The late Irish journalist provides vivid details and anecdotes about women's oppression throughout history.

Stone, Merlin, *When God Was a Woman, Harcourt Brace Jovanovich*, 1976.
The book contends that before the rise of Judeo-Christian patriarchies women headed the first societies and religions.

Terry, Geraldine, *Women's Rights, Pluto Press*, 2007.
A feminist who has worked for Oxfam and other non-governmental organizations outlines major issues facing women today — from violence to globalization to AIDS.

***Women and the Environment, UNEP*, 2004.**
The United Nations Environment Programme shows the integral link between women in the developing world and the changing environment.

Articles

Brady, Brian, "A Question of Honour," *The Independent on Sunday*, Feb. 10, 2008, p. 8.
"Honor killings" and related violence against women are on the rise in the United Kingdom.

Kidder, Thalia, and Kate Raworth, " 'Good Jobs' and hidden costs: women workers documenting the price of precarious employment," *Gender and Development*, Vol. 12, No. 2, p. 12, July 2004.
Two trade and gender experts describe the precarious working conditions and job security experienced by food and garment workers.

Reports and Studies

"Beijing Betrayed," *Women's Environment and Development Organization*, March 2005, www.wedo.org/files/gmr_pdfs/gmr2005.pdf.
A women's-rights organization reviews the progress and shortcomings of governments in implementing the commitments made during the Fifth World Congress on Women in Beijing in 1995.

"The Millennium Development Goals Report 2007," *United Nations*, 2007, www.un.org/millenniumgoals/pdf/mdg2007.pdf.
International organizations demonstrate the progress governments have made — or not — in reaching the Millennium Development Goals.

"Trafficking in Persons Report," *U.S. Department of State*, June 2007, www.state.gov/documents/organization/82902.pdf.
This seventh annual report discusses the growing problems of human trafficking around the world.

"The tsunami's impact on women," *Oxfam briefing note*, March 5, 2005, www.oxfam.org/en/files/bn050326_tsunami_women/download.
Looking at how the 2004 tsunami affected women in Indonesia, India and Sri Lanka, Oxfam International suggests how governments can better address women's issues during future natural disasters.

"Women in Politics," *Inter-Parliamentary Union*, 2005, www.ipu.org/PDF/publications/wmn45-05_en.pdf.
The report provides detailed databases of the history of female political representation in governments around the world.

Ballington, Julie, and Azza Karam, "Women in Parliament: Beyond the Numbers," *International Institute for Democracy and Electoral Assistance*, 2005, www.idea.int/publications/wip2/upload/WiP_inlay.pdf.
The handbook provides female politicians and candidates information and case studies on how women have overcome obstacles to elected office.

Chen, Martha, Joann Vanek, Francie Lund, James Heintz, Renana Jhabvala and Christine Bonner, "Women, Work and Poverty," *UNIFEM*, 2005, www.unifem.org/attachments/products/PoWW2005_eng.pdf.
The report argues that greater work protection and security is needed to promote women's rights and reduce global poverty.

Larserud, Stina, and Rita Taphorn, "Designing for Equality," *International Institute for Democracy and Electoral Assistance*, 2007, www.idea.int/publications/designing_for_equality/upload/Idea_Design_low.pdf.

The report describes the impact that gender quota systems have on women's representation in elected office.

Raworth, Kate, and Claire Harvey, "Trading Away Our Rights," *Oxfam International*, 2004, www.oxfam.org.uk/resources/policy/trade/downloads/trading_rights.pdf.
Through exhaustive statistics, case studies and interviews, the report paints a grim picture of how trade globalization is affecting women.

Turquet, Laura, Patrick Watt and Tom Sharman, "Hit or Miss?" *ActionAid*, March 7, 2008.
The report reviews how governments are doing in achieving the U.N.'s Millennium Development Goals.

For More Information

Equality Now, P.O. Box 20646, Columbus Circle Station, New York, NY 10023; www.equalitynow.org. An international organization working to protect women against violence and promote women's human rights.

Global Database of Quotas for Women; www.quotaproject.org. A joint project of the International Institute for Democracy and Electoral Assistance and Stockholm University providing country-by-country data on electoral quotas for women.

Human Rights Watch, 350 Fifth Ave., 34th floor, New York, NY 10118-3299; (212) 290-4700; www.hrw.org. Investigates and exposes human-rights abuses around the world.

Hunt Alternatives Fund, 625 Mount Auburn St., Cambridge, MA 02138; (617) 995-1900; www.huntalternatives.org. A private foundation that provides grants and technical assistance to promote positive social change; its Initiative for Inclusive Security promotes women in peacekeeping.

Inter-Parliamentary Union, 5, Chemin du Pommier, Case Postale 330, CH-1218 Le Grand-Saconnex, Geneva, Switzerland; +(4122) 919 41 50; www.ipu.org. An organization of parliaments of sovereign states that

maintains an extensive database on women serving in parliaments.

Oxfam International, 1100 15th St., N.W., Suite 600, Washington, DC 20005; (202) 496-1170; www.oxfam.org. Confederation of 13 independent nongovernmental organizations working to fight poverty and related social injustice.

U.N. Development Fund for Women (UNIFEM), 304 East 45th St., 15th Floor, New York, NY 10017; (212) 906-6400; www.unifem.org. Provides financial aid and technical support for empowering women and promoting gender equality.

U.N. Division for the Advancement of Women (DAW), 2 UN Plaza, DC2-12th Floor, New York, NY 10017; www.un.org/womenwatch/daw. Formulates policy on gender equality, implements international agreements on women's issues and promotes gender mainstreaming in government activities.

Women's Environment & Development Organization (WEDO), 355 Lexington Ave., 3rd Floor, New York, NY 10017; (212) 973-0325; www.wedo.org. An international organization that works to promote women's equality in global policy.

15

Gay Marriage Showdowns

Will Voters Bar Marriage for Same-Sex Couples?

Kenneth Jost

Kate Sheppard and Kory O'Rourke celebrate with their children after obtaining a marriage license at San Francisco City Hall on June 17, 2008. A California Supreme Court ruling in May made California the second state, after Massachusetts, to legalize same-sex marriage. Opponents quickly gained approval to put a state constitutional amendment on the Nov. 4 ballot that would allow marriage in California only "between a man and a woman."

Credit: Getty Images/Justin Sullivan

From *CQ Researcher*, September 26, 2008.

Jennifer Pizer and Doreena Wong met on their first day at New York University Law School in 1984. They graduated in 1987 and moved to California together three years later.

Jenny and Doreena were still together on May 15, 2008, when the California Supreme Court issued its stunning, 4-3 decision establishing a constitutional right to marriage for same-sex couples in the state. As one of the Lambda Legal Defense and Education Fund lawyers in the case, Pizer spoke at a press conference in San Francisco after the decision was released and then flew home to Los Angeles for a rally in the heart of gay West Hollywood.

"You're not going to do anything funny, are you?" Doreena asked Jenny in the car as they drove to the rally. Pizer feigned ignorance even as she was thinking that the event was the perfect time to pop "the question."

So, as she finished her remarks, Pizer looked down toward her partner's face in the crowd and said, "Now, I'd like to ask a question I've waited 24 years to ask: Doreena Wong, will you marry me?"

"Yes, of course," Wong replied. Standing at the microphone, Pizer relayed the answer to the cheering crowd: "She said yes!"

Television cameras recorded the moment, but Pizer admits months later that she has yet to see the full video clip. For even as gay rights advocates are celebrating the victory — and Jenny and Doreena are planning their Oct. 5 wedding in Marin County — opponents of gay marriage are working hard to reverse the state court's decision.

Less than three weeks after the decision, opponents won legal approval to put a state constitutional amendment on the Nov. 4

Most States Ban Gay Marriage

Voters in 26 states have approved constitutional amendments banning marriage for same-sex couples.* Most of the measures may also ban other forms of recognition, such as domestic partnership or civil unions; some may ban legal recognition for unmarried opposite-sex couples as well. Arizona, California and Florida will be voting on Nov. 4 on constitutional amendments to define marriage as the union of one man and one woman.

Seventeen other states have enacted statutory bans on same-sex marriage since 1995. Iowa's ban was ruled unconstitutional by a state trial court; the state's appeal is pending. In addition, pre-existing laws in Maryland, New York, Wyoming and the District of Columbia have been interpreted to limit marriage to opposite-sex couples.

California and Massachusetts are the only states recognizing same-sex marriage. Some states with gay-marriage bans recognize civil unions or domestic partnerships. Two states — New Mexico and Rhode Island — appear not to have addressed the issue.

Broad constitutional ban
Narrow constitutional ban
Statutory ban
No anti-gay marriage measure

*CQ Researcher follows the National Gay and Lesbian Task Force in not counting Hawaii as a constitutional ban state, unlike Stateline.org and the Williams Institute. Hawaii adopted a constitutional amendment in 1998 authorizing the legislature to define marriage in opposite-sex terms, and the legislature did so. However, the point of the constitutional bans is to preclude change, and Hawaii's amendment does not.

Sources: National Gay and Lesbian Task Force; Williams Institute, UCLA School of Law; Stateline.org

recognition of same-sex marriages from other states as well.

"Marriage has always been understood as the union of one man and one woman by California citizens and by other people in the country," says Mathew Staver, founder and chairman of Liberty Counsel, a Christian public-interest law firm, and one of the lawyers who argued against gay marriage before the California Supreme Court. "That provides the best environment for society."

"We absolutely agree that marriage is a special word for a special institution," Pizer responds. "We disagree that the social institution should be available only in a discriminatory manner and that it serves any social purpose to exclude gay and lesbian couples."

The debate over the ballot measure has not deterred but in fact has encouraged gay and lesbian couples in California to get to the altar — or to city hall. By one estimate, some 5,000 same-sex couples got married in California within the first week after the court ruling became effective on June 17. The first-week spike receded, but the weddings are continuing — spurred by the widespread assumption that marriages performed before Nov. 4 will remain valid even if Proposition 8 is approved.

Hollywood celebrities have been among those tying the knot, including TV talk show host Ellen de Generes and ex-"Star Trek" actor George Takei. De Generes wed Portia

ballot that would allow marriage in California only "between a man and a woman." If accepted by a simple majority of the state's voters, Proposition 8 would prohibit marriage for gay and lesbian couples in California and bar

de Rossi, her girlfriend of the past four years, in an intimate, picture-book ceremony at their Beverly Hills home on Aug. 16. Takei and his longtime partner Brad Altman exchanged self-written vows in a more lavish ceremony at the Japanese American National Museum in downtown Los Angeles on Sept. 14. "May equality long live and prosper," Takei said as he left the ceremony amid a horde of photographers and well-wishers.[1]

Most of the newlyweds, however, are non-celebrities, many of them in long-term relationships that had already been registered under a 2003 California law as domestic partnerships with nearly complete marriage-like rights and responsibilities. "There's almost no change" over domestic partnership status, explains David Steinberg, news desk copy chief at the *San Francisco Chronicle*, who married his longtime partner Gregory Foley in July. Steinberg says he and Foley, a nurse at Kaiser Permanente, decided to get married anyway "because they might take it away."

The state high court decision made California the second state, after Massachusetts, to allow marriage for same-sex couples. The Supreme Judicial Court of Massachusetts issued a 4-3 decision in November 2003, holding that the state had "no constitutionally adequate reason" for denying same-sex couples the legal benefits of marriage. The court gave the legislature 180 days to respond but later issued an advisory opinion saying that civil union status would not be an adequate substitute for marriage. When the legislature failed to act by the deadline, the high court decision took effect, and same-sex marriages began in Massachusetts on May 17, 2004.[2]

The California Supreme Court ruled similarly but more directly that the state's constitution guarantees a "fundamental right to marry" to "all Californians, whether gay or heterosexual, and to same-sex couples as well as opposite-sex couples." The majority opinion — written by the Republican-appointed chief justice, Ronald George — specifically rejected civil union or domestic partnership status.[3]

Ten States, D.C. Recognize Same-Sex Unions

Ten states and the District of Columbia grant some legal recognition to same-sex couples, ranging from limited spousal rights in Hawaii to fully recognized marriages in California and Massachusetts. Hawaii was the first to recognize same-sex couples' rights in 1997. An estimated 85,000 same-sex couples have gained legal recognition under the various laws.

State	Date	Provisions
California	2008	Marriage approved by California Supreme Court; Proposition 8 on Nov. 4 ballot would overturn ruling
Connecticut	2005	Civil unions approved by legislature; marriage suit pending before Connecticut Supreme Court
District of Columbia	2002	Limited domestic partnership law enacted by D.C. Council in 1992; delayed by Congress until 2002
Hawaii	1997	"Reciprocal beneficiaries" (limited spousal rights)
Maine	2004	Limited domestic partnership law approved by legislature
Massachusetts	2004	Marriage legalized as required by November 2003 ruling by Supreme Judicial Court; constitutional amendment to overturn ruling failed to qualify for ballot
New Hampshire	2007	Civil unions approved by legislature
New Jersey	2006	Civil unions approved by legislature to comply with October 2006 ruling by New Jersey Supreme Court
Oregon	2007	Domestic partnership law approved by legislature
Vermont	2000	Civil unions approved by legislature following ruling by Vermont Supreme Court in December 1999
Washington	2007	Limited domestic partnership law approved by legislature; marriage suit rejected by state Supreme Court, July 2006

Sources: National Gay and Lesbian Task Force; Williams Institute, UCLA Law School

An anti-gay protester demonstrates against same-sex marriage during the 38th annual LA Pride Parade on June 8, 2008, in West Hollywood, Calif. Constitutional amendments that would deny marriage rights to same-sex couples are on the ballot in Arizona and Florida, as well as California.

The ruling invalidated a statutory initiative to define marriage as between one man and one woman approved by slightly over 61 percent of the state's voters as Proposition 22 in March 2000. Gay marriage opponents had already begun circulating an initiative to write the "one-man, one-woman" definition of marriage into the state constitution. By June 2, they had submitted petitions with approximately 1.1 million signatures — sufficient for the secretary of state to certify the proposed constitutional amendment for the Nov. 4 ballot.

The state Supreme Court added to the urgency of the opposition by declining to stay its decision pending the Nov. 4 vote. Same-sex marriages began in California on June 17. The first marriage license in San Francisco went to two longtime lesbian activists, Del Martin and Phyllis Lyons, who had been together for more than 50 years. San Francisco Mayor Gavin Newsom officiated at the ceremony. Martin died 10 weeks later — at age 87.

Besides Massachusetts and California, eight other states and the District of Columbia permit some legal recognition for same-sex couples, including four that permit civil unions with virtually the same rights and responsibilities as marriage. (*See chart, p. 371.*) On the opposite side, 26 states have constitutional amendments that prohibit marriage for same-sex couples, and another 17 have similar statutory bans. In addition, the federal Defense of Marriage Act — known as DOMA — prohibits federal recognition for same-sex marriages. The 1996 law also provides that states need not recognize same-sex marriages from other states. (*See map, p. 370.*)

Massachusetts recorded approximately 11,000 same-sex marriages in the three years after the state high court ruling, according to demographer Gary Gates, a senior research fellow at the Williams Institute, UCLA School of Law. He says an exact count is not possible in California because marriage licenses are no longer recording the parties' sex, but a projection based on the increased number of marriages in the months after the state high court ruling indicates more than 5,000 same-sex couples married in the first week after the decision.

All told, Gates and his colleagues at the institute — which studies sexual-orientation policy and law, primarily funded by a gay philanthropist — estimate that 85,000 same-sex couples have taken advantage of recognition provisions in those states permitting that status. But a higher percentage of same-sex couples are opting to marry than are registering for civil union or domestic partnership.[4]

Supporters of marriage equality say the growing number of same-sex couples in legally protected relationships is eroding opposition to gay marriage. "We're seeing a growing public understanding that ending gay couples' exclusion from marriage helps families and harms no one," says Evan Wolfson, executive director of Freedom to Marry, self-described as a gay and non-gay partnership advocating marriage rights for same-sex couples.

Opponents disagree. They point to the gay marriage bans already enacted as the better gauge of public attitudes on the issue. "Supporters of same-sex marriage have a real uphill climb if they hope to undo what has been accomplished in the past 10 years by supporters of traditional marriage," says Peter Sprigg, vice president for policy at the Family Research Council, a Christian organization based in Washington, D.C., promoting traditional marriage.

An initial poll in California indicated the ballot measure was ahead, but statewide surveys in August and September showed the proposition trailing by at least 14 percentage points.[5] Two other states — Arizona and Florida — will be voting on similar constitutional amendments on Nov. 4. Arizona's measure needs a majority vote; Florida requires a 60 percent vote for a state constitutional amendment (*see p. 386*).

In addition to those three ballot measures, Arkansans will be voting on a statutory initiative to prohibit unmarried couples — whether same-sex or opposite-sex — to adopt or take foster children. The initiative was proposed after a regulation barring adoption or placement with same-sex couples was overturned in court.[6]

As the debates over same-sex marriage continue, here are some of the major questions being discussed:

Should same-sex couples be allowed to marry?

George Gates and Brian Albert met in 1991 when they both worked at the Human Rights Campaign, a gay rights advocacy organization. They held a big commitment ceremony at the posh Jefferson Hotel in Washington, D.C., in 1996 and, five years later, a small wedding on Cape Cod in Massachusetts.

With both of them still in Washington — now working for other nonprofit groups — Gates and Albert get no tangible benefits from their Massachusetts marriage license. But Gates says he and Albert viewed it as a matter of equal rights to take advantage of the Bay State's welcoming attitude toward gay couples. "We did feel that our relationship was no different from an opposite-sex couple," Gates says, "and we felt we were entitled to the same benefits and responsibilities as they are."

Opponents counter that gay marriage amounts to a redefinition of an institution created by God and universally understood in opposite-sex terms until the recent gay marriage movement. "Never before have we had such a serious effort to make such a profound change to the institution of marriage," says Lynn Wardle, a professor at Brigham Young University Law School, which is

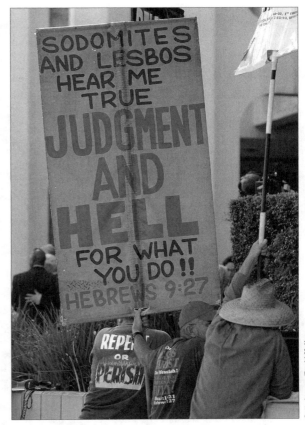

Anti-gay religious protesters picket at the marriage ceremony of Robin Tyler and Diane Olson, in Beverly Hills, Calif., on June 17, 2008. The two women were plaintiffs in one of the lawsuits that led to the overturning of California's gay marriage ban in May.

operated by the Church of Jesus Christ of Latter-day Saints — the Mormons.

The opposing sides disagree more concretely about the effects that legal recognition of same-sex relationships has or would have on heterosexual marriage, on children and on gay men and lesbians themselves. Opponents say gay marriage will harm the institution of marriage, hurt children and have no significant effect for same-sex couples. Supporters of gay marriage say legal recognition will promote stable relationships for same-sex couples, benefit children in same-sex families and have no effect whatsoever on opposite-sex marriages.

Liberty Counsel's Staver, who is also dean of the School of Law at Liberty University, the Lynchburg, Va., school

Census Won't Recognize Same-Sex Marriages

"It really is something out of Orwell," a critic says.

Even though Massachusetts and California recognize same-sex marriages, the U.S. Census Bureau will not count gay or lesbian spouses as married in the 2010 census.

Census Bureau officials say the policy of treating married same-sex couples as unmarried partners is dictated by the federal Defense of Marriage Act, which bars the federal government from recognizing same-sex marriages for any purpose under federal law. The law "requires all federal agencies to recognize only opposite-sex marriages for the purpose of administering federal programs," Census spokesman Stephen Bruckner explained shortly after the policy was disclosed in July.[1]

The policy has drawn criticism from same-sex couples in both states and from gay rights advocacy groups. "To have the federal government disappear your marriage I'm sure will be painful and upsetting," Shannon Minter, legal director for the San Francisco-based National Center for Lesbian Rights, told the *San Jose Mercury News*, which first disclosed the policy. "It really is something out of [*1984* author George] Orwell."[2]

Demographer Gary Gates at the pro-gay marriage Williams Institute, UCLA School of Law, says the decision amounts to deliberately producing inaccurate population data. "Bureau officials should acknowledge the reality that same-sex couples can legally marry in this country," he says, "and stop altering the accurate responses of same-sex couples who describe themselves as married."[3]

Anti-gay marriage groups, however, defend the bureau's decision. "We're dealing with a government entity that is given certain charters and mandates, and they have to subscribe to public law," says Kris Mineau, president of the Massachusetts Family Institute.[4]

The bureau's decision will not affect the overall population count, which the Constitution requires every 10 years in order to apportion seats in the House of Representatives among the 50 states. But detailed information from the household questionnaires is used by the bureau and by independent researchers to provide demographic analyses in such areas as family structure and size, income and education.

The bureau says the questionnaires used in the 2010 census will not be destroyed, so the data will theoretically be available to independent researchers later. But the bureau's decision will slow a count of married same-sex couples in California, where marriage licenses now identify spouses only as "Party A" and "Party B."

---

[1] Quoted in Eric Moskowitz, "Federal rules mean thousands of same-sex marriages in Massachusetts will be ignored in the U.S. 2010 Census," *The Boston Globe*, July 27, 2008, p. B1.

[2] See Mike Swift, "U.S. Census Bureau won't count same-sex marriages," *San Jose Mercury News*, July 12, 2008.

[3] See Gary J. Gates, "Making same-sex marriages count," *Los Angeles Times*, July 18, 2008, p. A25.

[4] Quoted in Moskowitz, *op. cit.*

founded by the late televangelist Jerry Falwell, calls same-sex marriage "a huge, unknown sociological experiment done . . . with no understanding of the implications on our children and our society." Wardle and other opponents say recognition of same-sex marriages will contribute to a further decrease in the percentage of people who are married.

Wolfson of Freedom to Marry bluntly disagrees. Same-sex marriage "is not going to change anything" for heterosexual marriages, he says. Gay author Jonathan Rauch goes further to argue that recognizing gay marriage would strengthen the institution overall. "America needs more marriages, not fewer," Rauch wrote in a recent op-ed article, "and the best way to encourage marriage is to

encourage marriage, which is what society does by bringing gay couples inside the tent."[7]

Opponents also argue that heterosexual marriages are the best environment for raising children. "Same-sex marriage says as a matter of policy moms and dads are irrelevant to the raising of children," Staver says. In like vein, the pro-Proposition 8 Campaign for Families and Children says on its Web site, "From the commitment of a man and woman in marriage comes the best opportunity for children to thrive."

Gay and lesbian advocacy groups cite studies by, among others, the American Academy of Pediatrics to argue that children raised in families with gay or lesbian parents fare as well overall as children raised in opposite-sex households.[8] "All the evidence and common sense arguments indicate that this will help children who are being raised by gay families without hurting other children at all," says Wolfson.

Opponents also say, some more bluntly than others, that same-sex couples are not entitled to marriage because so many couples — particularly gay men — have short-lived, sometimes non-monogamous relationships. "Whether we like it or not, a big part of the gay agenda for decades has been to repudiate what are regarded as overly restrictive expectations of monogamy and sexual fidelity," University of Pennsylvania Law School Professor Amy Wax wrote in an online debate sponsored by the Washington-based Federalist Society, a prominent conservative organization for lawyers.[9]

Gay marriage advocates counter that allowing marriage for same-sex couples would actually help stabilize their relationships. "Marriage advocates argue that marriage provides a mechanism and incentive to form more stable unions," Williams Institute researcher Gates says. "If that's true, then you would expect the same effect among gays and lesbians."

Apart from the individual points of disagreement, Wardle insists that supporters of traditional marriage should not be forced to prove the case against gay marriage. "When you have a proposal to redefine a basic social institution, the burden of proof is on those who advocate a change," Wardle says.

"Both sides agree that marriage is a powerful institution," Gates rejoins. "Opponents make the argument that we have to be so cautious. Proponents say that's exactly why this is important. This is an important social institution, and you're leaving gay people out of it."

Should state constitutions prohibit marriage for same-sex couples?

The anti-gay organization Focus on the Family dispatched its vice president for public affairs, Ron Prentice, to California in 2003 to launch and become executive director of the affiliated California Family Council. Now, as chairman of the Protect Marriage/Yes on Proposition 8 campaign, Prentice is helping lead the effort to overturn the California Supreme Court's gay marriage ruling by amending the state constitution to define marriage as only "the union of one man and one woman." "We are going to change the constitution and say on Nov. 4, 'Judges, you can't touch this,' " Prentice says.[10]

Gay marriage opponents have enjoyed great success with the strategy. Constitutional amendments limiting marriage to opposite-sex couples have been approved by voters in 26 states, which together represent about 43 percent of the U.S. population. Hawaii voters approved an amendment in 1998 authorizing the legislature to limit marriage to opposite-sex couples. Only once — in Arizona in 2006 — have voters rejected an anti-gay marriage amendment.

Supporters say Proposition 22 represents a legitimate political response to the state high court ruling. "A victory in California will not only protect marriage," the Alliance for Marriage, in Merrifield, Va., says on its Web site, "but will send a strong democratic rebuke by voters to radical, activist groups who've used the courts" to try to gain recognition for same-sex couples.

Gay marriage supporters, however, say the tactic is antithetical to American democracy. "The whole idea of amending constitutions to fence out groups of people is yet another debasement of American fundamentals," says Freedom to Marry's Wolfson. "That is a radical idea: the idea that you amend constitutions to carve out a group of people, shove them outside, and say they can't go to the legislature, that they are permanently treated as second class by the constitution where they live."

Overall, state courts have been responsible for the most dramatic gains realized so far by advocates of legal recognition of same-sex relationships. The Vermont Supreme Court in 1999 became the first state high court to require marriage-like rights for same-sex couples; the state legislature enacted a civil union law five months later. The Supreme Judicial Court of Massachusetts effectively required recognition of gay marriage with a November 2003 ruling that took effect six months later. Opponents of the Massachusetts ruling have tried but failed to get the state legislature to put a constitutional amendment before the voters to overturn the decision.

Gay marriage opponents say the California Supreme Court invited retaliation with a decision that not only nullified the 2000 ballot measure but also used the state constitution's equal-protection clause to require the highest level of scrutiny for any laws discriminating on the basis of sexual orientation. Wardle calls the ruling "a very clear example" of judges "openly using their position to promote their political preference."

Gay marriage supporters had failed to match their victory in Massachusetts until the California ruling — suffering defeats in closely watched cases in New York and Washington. "To their credit, a number of state supreme courts are behaving more judiciously," Wardle says. But gay marriage supporters are hoping the California ruling may influence supreme court justices in two other states — Connecticut and Iowa — with pending marriage cases. "The California Supreme Court is recognized as by far the most influential state high court in the country," says Lambda Legal's Pizer.

In California, opponents of Proposition 8 won a significant tactical victory with the decision by Attorney General Jerry Brown to list the measure's title on the ballot as, "Eliminates Right of Same-sex Couples to Marry." Prop. 8 supporters tried but failed to get a state court judge to order a change in what they called "an inherently argumentative" title.

Prop. 8 opponents are using the title to frame their campaign message. "We think it's always wrong to be voting on taking away people's rights," says Dale Kelly Bankhead, statewide campaign manager for Equality California/No on Proposition 8.

In a later skirmish, Prop. 8 opponents tried but failed to block the initiative from the ballot. In a petition to the state Supreme Court, they argued that the measure amounted to a "revision" of the state constitution that — under the constitution — could not be put on the ballot without a two-thirds vote of the legislature. Prop. 8 supporters called the lawsuit a "desperate" effort to avoid a vote. The court unanimously declined to hear the request, but the issue could be revived if the measure passes in November.

Should states recognize same-sex marriages from other states?

A one-page legal memorandum that New York Gov. David A. Paterson's legal counsel David Nocenti sent to state agency directors on May 14 quietly handed gay marriage supporters a major victory. Following up a ruling by a state appellate court in February, Nocenti directed state agencies to recognize same-sex marriages from other jurisdictions — a list that then included Massachusetts and five countries: Belgium, Canada, the Netherlands, South Africa and Spain.*

---

*The Norwegian Parliament completed approval of a gay marriage law on June 17; the law will take effect on Jan. 1, 2009.

Nocenti made no announcement of the directive — issued, by coincidence one day before the California Supreme Court's ruling. But three days later Paterson disclosed the move in a videotaped message to the annual dinner of the Empire State Pride Agenda, a gay rights advocacy group. Paterson, who had supported unsuccessful bills in the state legislature to legalize same-sex marriage, called the directive "a strong step to marriage equality."[11]

The possibility that states would either choose or be required to recognize same-sex marriages from other states has been a major concern of gay marriage opponents ever since a Hawaii court's preliminary approval of an ultimately unsuccessful gay marriage suit in 1993. Gay marriage opponents included a provision in the federal Defense of Marriage Act (DOMA) in 1996 strengthening states' discretion to refuse to recognize same-sex marriages. At the same time, they began building a firewall against same-sex marriage by pushing for gay marriage bans in individual states.

The United States' federal system leaves marriage laws generally to states — with the inevitable consequence of differences from state to state. For example, some states permit and others prohibit marriages between first cousins.

Northwestern University law Professor Andrew Koppelman, an expert in an area known as "conflict of laws," says state courts over time have developed some general rules for when to recognize out-of-state marriages that would not be valid within their own state. In general, Koppelman says, states recognize marriages for people who travel through or move to a state with laws otherwise precluding legal status for the union. But states will not recognize a marriage for residents who go to another state to circumvent the state's law — especially if the law reflects a strong public policy.

Gay marriage opponents say the gay marriage bans fit that situation. "You don't have to recognize that status," Brigham Young Professor Wardle says, referring to a same-sex marriage from another state. "It's up to the state to choose for itself what domestic status it will recognize."

Koppelman — who supports same-sex marriage — says, however, that the state bans are "badly drafted" and ignore the real-world situations that will inevitably arise as same-sex couples travel or move from the state where their marriage was performed. "A blanket non-recognition rule is absolutely loony," Koppelman says.

Courts in two non-gay marriage states have already bowed to states that grant legal recognition to same-sex couples. In June, the Virginia Supreme Court ruled that Vermont rather than Virginia courts have jurisdiction over a custody dispute between two former lesbian partners following the dissolution of their Vermont civil union. Lisa Miller, who gave birth to a daughter during the civil union and moved to Virginia after the dissolution, had sought to block visitation rights that a Vermont court had granted to her former partner, Janet Jenkins. In an earlier decision, the federal appeals court for Oklahoma invalidated a state law refusing to recognize an out-of-state, court-approved adoption by a same-sex couple.[12]

Both courts said that the Constitution's "Full Faith and Credit Clause" required the state court to recognize court judgments from other states. Koppelman notes that despite widespread misunderstanding, the constitutional provision does not apply to the more common instances that do not involve litigation already in progress.

The California gay marriage ruling heightened the stakes for both sides because the state has no residency requirement to be married. Massachusetts had been enforcing a 1913 law that barred marriages for out-of-state residents if the union would not be recognized in their home states. But the state repealed the law in August. As a result, businesses in Massachusetts and California are now actively encouraging same-sex couples to come to their states to be wed. (*See sidebar, p. 382.*)

Gay marriage opponents still maintain that states can enforce bans against recognizing same-sex unions from other states. "It's contrary to the strong public policy in those states," says the Family Research Council's Sprigg.

Koppelman disagrees. "Same-sex marriage ought to be, as a general matter, recognized," he says. But gay marriage supporters are sufficiently concerned about their prospects that they are urging same-sex couples not to initiate legal challenges to the state bans at this time.

BACKGROUND

Coming Out

The history of same-sex relationships is long, but the issue of legally recognizing those relationships is of recent origin.

Up until the mid-20th century, gay and lesbian couples in the United States generally kept a low profile politically and even socially. An outbreak of repressive laws and policies dating from the 1920s helped give rise to a gay rights movement and by the 1970s to a self-identified gay and lesbian community. Marriage, however, was not a priority or even a widely agreed on goal until the AIDS epidemic and the so-called lesbian baby boom of the 1980s prompted many gay men and lesbians to view legal recognition of their relationships as a practical necessity.[13]

Male couples and female couples can be found in history and literature from ancient times to the present. In the United States, same-sex couples formed part of the gay subcultures present but only somewhat visible in many major cities from the turn of the 20th century. Gay and lesbian couples generally drew as little attention to themselves as possible. As one example, the 1993 book *Jeb and Dash* recounts through posthumously published diaries the secret love affair between two government employees in Washington from 1918 to 1945.[14]

The federal government and many state and local governments began cracking down on homosexuals during the period between the two world wars. "Sexual perverts" were barred from entering the country and were made subject to exclusion from the military. Disorderly conduct and anti-sodomy laws were used to break up gay organizations and arrest individuals looking for or engaging in gay sex.

After the repeal of Prohibition in 1933, gay bars could still be shut down through license suspensions or revocations. The repressive atmosphere increased after World War II as homosexuals came to face the same kind of persecution as suspected communists. The historian David K. Johnson suggests that more federal employees lost jobs because of suspected homosexuality during what he terms "the lavender scare" than were dismissed because of suspected communist leanings.[15]

Threatened in their workplaces and gathering places, gay men and lesbians in the 1950s formed the forerunners of the present-day gay rights movement. The gay Mattachine Society and the Daughters of Bilitis both adopted assimilationist stances: no garish costumes, no lavish parades. In 1965, however, a fired government astronomer, Franklin Kameny, staged the first "gay rights" picketing outside the White House, aimed at reversing policies generally barring homosexual from federal employment. Then in

Before 1970 *Gay rights movement begins to form; same-sex marriage low on agenda.*

1968, 1969 Metropolitan Community Church in Los Angeles performs first public weddings for same-sex couples.

1970s-1980s *Gay rights measures enacted in some states, localities; AIDS epidemic, "lesbian baby boom" spur interest in legal recognition for relationships.*

1971 Marriage rights suits filed by gay Minnesota couple and lesbian couple in Kentucky are rejected; over next six years, 15 states pass laws defining marriage as opposite-sex union.

1984 Berkeley, Calif., becomes first city to provide domestic-partner benefits to employees.

1986 U.S. Supreme Court upholds state anti-sodomy laws.

1990s *Gay marriage rulings spur backlash in Congress, states; Vermont court is first to require state to give legal recognition for same-sex couples.*

1993 Hawaii Supreme Court requires state to justify ban on same-sex marriage; trial court rules ban unconstitutional in 1996, but ruling is nullified by state constitutional amendment approved in 1998.

1996 Congress passes and President Bill Clinton signs Defense of Marriage Act, which bars federal benefits for same-sex couples and buttresses states' authority not to recognize same-sex marriages from other states.

1998 Alaska trial court rules ban on same-sex marriage unconstitutional; ruling nullified by constitutional amendment approved by voters in November.

1999 California passes limited domestic-partnership law for same-sex couples; rights under law expanded in 2001, 2003. . . . Vermont Supreme Court rules state must allow same-sex couples to enjoy legal benefits accorded to

heterosexuals; state legislature implements ruling by passing civil-unions law in April 2000.

2000-Present *Massachusetts recognizes marriage for same-sex couples; after setbacks in several states, gay rights supporters win second pro-marriage ruling in California; opponents qualify ballot measure to overturn decision.*

2003 U.S. Supreme Court rules anti-sodomy laws unconstitutional; majority opinion does not address gay marriage. . . . Supreme Judicial Court of Massachusetts rules same-sex couples entitled to same rights as opposite-sex couples; gives legislature 180 days to act.

2004 Voters in 13 states pass gay marriage bans, all by substantial margins. . . . Federal Marriage Amendment fails in Senate (and again in 2006).

2005 Connecticut legislature passes civil-union law — first state to act without court mandate.

2006 State high courts in New York and Washington uphold laws limiting marriage to opposite-sex couples. . . . New Jersey Supreme Court rules same-sex couples entitled to same benefits, protections as opposite-sex couples, with legislature to choose between "marriage" or "civil unions"; legislature approves civil-union bill two months later.

2007 Connecticut Supreme Court hears arguments in gay-marriage case; decision still pending in fall 2008. . . . Judge in Iowa rules gay-marriage ban unconstitutional; same-sex couple weds before decision is stayed pending appeal to state Supreme Court.

2008 California Supreme Court says same-sex couples entitled to marriage, anti-gay laws presumptively unconstitutional (May 15); ruling goes into effect one month later after justices decline request for stay. . . . Gay-marriage opponents qualify Proposition 8 for Nov. 4 ballot; measure would define marriage as union of one man, one woman; bar recognition of same-sex marriages from other states. . . . Same-sex marriage bans also on ballot in Arizona, Florida; Arkansas to vote on banning adoptions, foster-child placements with unmarried couples.

1969 the gay patrons of the Stonewall Inn in New York City rose up in protest after a police raid on the Greenwich Village bar. The disturbance attracted little attention in the straight world but quickly became a rallying point for a newly assertive gay and lesbian community.

Marriage was not high on the community's agenda, however.[16] Many other issues were more pressing: pushing for gay rights ordinances, fighting employment bans and seeking to repeal anti-sodomy laws. In any event, many gay and lesbian activists actively opposed marriage, as Yale University historian George Chauncey recounts. Gay liberation celebrated sexual freedom, not committed relationships. And many lesbians viewed marriage as an inherently patriarchal institution to be reformed (or even abolished), but certainly not to be imitated.

The activists' views should not be overemphasized, Chauncey cautions. "Most lesbians and gay men across the country looked for a steady relationship," he writes. Indeed, the Metropolitan Community Church, a gay congregation formed in 1968 in Los Angeles, began blessing same-sex unions at its creation and performed 150 marriages in its first four years. In addition, same-sex couples in Minneapolis and Louisville, Ky., filed lawsuits in 1971 seeking to win the right to marry. Courts in both cases said marriage was only for opposite-sex couples, even though the state laws did not say so. To fill in the gap, 15 states passed laws from 1973 to 1977 limiting marriage to heterosexual couples.

The AIDS epidemic brought gay men face to face with the consequences of legally unrecognized relationships. The illness or death of a "longtime companion" became even more painful when hospitals, funeral homes or government agencies refused to give any regard to the relationship. Medical costs and medical decision-making were difficult issues as long as the patient lived; at death, many survivors had bitter conflicts with their deceased lover's "real" family over funeral arrangements and disposition of property.[17]

Meanwhile, the growing interest in childrearing also focused attention on the disadvantages of legally unrecognized relationships. Gay men and lesbians who had children from previous opposite-sex marriages typically faced difficulties in winning custody or sometimes even visitation rights. As historian Chauncey explains, the lesbian baby boom of the 1980s "represented something new: a generation of women who . . . no longer felt obliged

to marry a man in order to have a child." A biological mother's relationship to her child was not legally difficult, but her partner could gain a legal relationship only through a cumbersome second-parent adoption. Moreover, couples who split up had no assurance that courts would respect or enforce agreed-on custody and visitation rights.

Debating Marriage

Marriage gradually moved toward the top of the gay rights agenda in the 1990s as dissenting views within the GLBT (gay, lesbian, bisexual, transgender) community were either transformed or suppressed. An initial victory in Hawaii, however, resulted in a major setback with congressional passage of the federal Defense of Marriage Act in 1996. DOMA limited federal status to opposite-sex couples and buttressed states' prerogatives to refuse to recognize same-sex marriages from other states. Gay rights advocates' later successes in winning civil unions in Vermont in 1999 and marriage in Massachusetts in 2003 were offset by losses in other state courts and a new flurry of so-called mini-DOMAs approved by voters in the 2004 election cycle.[18]

For gay rights advocates, Hawaii ended as a ballot-box defeat after a potential judicial victory. In 1993, the Hawaii Supreme Court held the state's ban on same-sex marriage presumptively unconstitutional and ordered a trial for the state to try to show a compelling interest to justify the restriction. The trial opened in Honolulu just as the Senate was about to complete action on DOMA in Washington. The judge ruled for the gay couples who brought the suit, but the state high court kept the appeal under advisement long enough for voters to approve a state constitutional amendment in 1998 that authorized the legislature to limit marriage to opposite-sex couples. The next year, the state Supreme Court dismissed the suit.

In Washington, Republican lawmakers cited the Hawaii Supreme Court's 1993 ruling as the motivation for the bills introduced in May 1996 that led to DOMA's enactment four months later. The bills provided that no state was obligated to recognize a same-sex marriage from another state. In a second section, the measures defined "marriage" and "spouse" in opposite-sex terms for federal law, thus precluding same-sex couples from filing joint tax returns or qualifying for any federal marital or spousal benefits. Opponents said the federal provision was discriminatory, the state law provision either unconstitutional or unnecessary. But the Republican-controlled

McCain and Obama Diverge Over Legal Recognition

But both oppose same-sex marriage.

Democrat Barack Obama and Republican John McCain both oppose marriage for same-sex couples. But the two presidential nominees diverge significantly on a secondary question about gay and lesbian relationships: Should they receive legal recognition?

Obama favors civil unions that would give same-sex couples all of the legal rights of marriage. The Illinois senator also wants to repeal the federal Defense of Marriage Act (DOMA), which defines marriage as the union of a man and a woman. And he displays both positions along with other gay-rights stances on a full page devoted to GLBT (gay, lesbian, bisexual and transgender) issues on his campaign Web site (www.obama.com).

McCain says same-sex couples should be allowed to establish some rights through "legal agreements," but he appears to oppose civil unions. The Arizona senator voted for DOMA in 1996; the Republican Party platform opposes repealing it. McCain's campaign Web site has no GLBT page; the only tacit references to GLBT issues endorse the one-man, one-woman definition of marriage and oppose "activist" judges (www.mccain.com).

The two candidates also differ on the Nov. 4 ballot proposition in California to overturn the state Supreme Court's decision granting full marriage rights to same-sex couples. McCain favors the measure; Obama opposes it. Both candidates called little attention to statements

Sen. John McCain voted for the Defense of Marriage Act in 1996.

AFP/Getty Images/Gerardo Mora

announcing their positions in late June.[1]

Unsurprisingly, major GLBT advocacy organizations are supporting Obama in the Nov. 4 presidential balloting. "Sen. Obama has consistently shown that he understands, as we do, that, GLBT rights are civil rights and human rights," Human Rights Campaign President Joe Solmonese said in formally endorsing the Democratic ticket on June 6.

But the Log Cabin Republicans, a gay GOP group, is backing McCain — four years after withholding its endorsement from President Bush. In announcing the endorsement on Sept. 2, President Patrick Sammon pointed to McCain's two Senate votes in 2004 and 2006 opposing the proposed constitutional amendment to bar recognition of same-sex marriages by the federal or state governments.

Obama also voted against the amendment and restates his opposition on his Web site. McCain does not mention the amendment on his site.

McCain says on his Web site that only the definition of marriage as the union of one man and one woman "sufficiently recognizes the vital and unique role played by mothers and fathers in the raising of children, and the role of the family in shaping, stabilizing and strengthening communities and our nation." He has been less clear in his position on civil unions.

Congress approved the measure by wide margins: 342-67 in the House, 85-14 in the Senate. President Bill Clinton endorsed the bill as it moved through Congress and then quietly signed it on Sept. 21.[19]

State legislatures followed suit by approving statutes or submitting for voter approval constitutional amendments similarly aimed at precluding legal recognition for same-sex couples. As in Hawaii, a state constitutional amendment

Campaigning in New Hampshire in March 2007, McCain said he opposed the civil union legislation recently enacted in the state. "Anything that impinges or impacts the sanctity of the marriage between men and women, I'm opposed to it," McCain was quoted as saying in a conference call with several political bloggers.[2] Appearing on the "Ellen de Generes Show" in May 2008, however, McCain said "people should be able to enter into legal agreements" and should be encouraged to do so.[3]

Obama professes strong support for civil unions for same-sex couples. "Barack Obama supports full civil unions that give same-sex couples equal legal rights and privileges as married

Sen. Barack Obama wants to repeal the Defense of Marriage Act.

couples," the campaign Web site states. The entry goes on to call for repealing DOMA and providing federal rights and benefits to same-sex couples in civil unions or other legally recognized unions.

Obama has been somewhat reticent, however, on same-sex marriage. "My religious beliefs say that marriage is something sanctified between a man and a woman," Obama was quoted as saying during his 2004 Senate campaign in Illinois.[4] In the presidential campaign, however, he has generally answered questions about gay marriage only indirectly by explaining his support for civil unions — as can be seen in an undated CNN video clip from a campaign town hall meeting in Durham, N.H.[5]

On his Web site, Obama also calls for adoption rights for "all couples and individuals, regardless of sexual orientation." On his site, McCain — father of an adoptive child — calls for promoting adoption as "a first option" for crisis pregnancies. But the site makes no reference to McCain's statement in a newspaper interview opposing adoption by gay couples or individuals. Under criticism, McCain modified the statement the next day to say that adoption is a state issue.[6]

Longtime gay-rights advocate Winnie Stachelberg says the contrast between the two candidates on GLBT issues "could not be more clear." Stachelberg, a senior vice president at the Center for American Progress, a Democratic think tank, says Obama would promote gay and lesbian equality if elected president. She complains that McCain has "studiously" avoided reaching out to the GLBT community.

From the opposite side, Family Research Council policy Vice President Peter Sprigg voices satisfaction with the Republican platform's support for "traditional marriage," while acknowledging ambivalence about McCain's votes against the Federal Marriage Amendment, a proposed constitutional amendment that would define marriage as a union of one man and one woman. But he complains that Obama "is unwilling to support any kind of actions that would defend the traditional definition of marriage. I kind of think he's playing word games in saying that he does not support same-sex marriage."

---

[1] See Michael Finnegan and Cathleen Decker, "Quiet stands on gay marriage," *Los Angeles Times,* July 2, 2008, p. A12.

[2] Ryan Sanger, "Exclusive: John McCain Comes Out Against NH Civil Unions," *New York Sun,* April 27, 2007, www.nysun.com/blogs.

[3] Quoted in Jim Brown, "Is McCain for civil unions?" *OneNewsNow,* May 28, 2008, www.onenewsnow.com/elections. OneNewsNow is a service of the American Family News Network, a Christian news service.

[4] Quoted in Eric Zorn, "Change of subject," *Chicago Tribune,* March 25, 2007, p. C2.

[5] CNN, "Election 2008: GLBT Issues," www.cnn.com/ELECTION/2008/issues/issues.samesexmarriage.html.

[6] See Michael Cooper, "Facing Criticism, McCain Clarifies His Statement on Gay Adoption," *The New York Times,* July 16, 2008, p. A15.

---

approved by Alaska voters in 1998 wiped out a trial court's ruling tentatively backing gay marriage. Gay rights lawyers, however, scored significant victories with cases in two New England states: Vermont and Massachusetts.

The Vermont Supreme Court's ruling in December 1999 held the denial of marital benefits to same-sex couples to violate the state constitution's equal protection provisions and ordered the state legislature to remedy the

Will Gay Weddings Bring Economic Boom?

California and Massachusetts are not cashing in yet.

Same-sex couples from other states who travel to California and Massachusetts to get marriage licenses may spark a modest economic boom in the two states.

The pro-gay marriage Williams Institute at UCLA School of Law forecasts $64 million in added revenue for state and local governments in California from out-of-state couples coming to wed. A similar study for Massachusetts — prepared this summer as the state was about to repeal a law limiting marriage for out-of-state couples — projects a $5 million revenue gain over three years.[1]

Gay-marriage opponents discount the studies. "Those claims are highly suspect, particularly since the only study was done by a blatantly pro-homosexual think tank," says Kris Menau, president of the Massachusetts Family Institute, the major advocacy group working against gay marriage in the Bay State. "We see no evidence of a great migration by out-of-state homosexual couples to come here to marry."

Anecdotal evidence is ambiguous. A justice of the peace in the gay mecca of Provincetown, Mass., told *The Washington Post* she had to use scheduled vacation days in August to perform weddings for out-of-state couples. "I have a full-time job, and this has become a full-time job," Rachel Peters said.[2]

In California, however, the head of a nationwide trade association for wedding professionals says the predicted boomlet has yet to materialize. "The goal was to pull several hundred thousand from other states to come here and get married," says Richard Markel, president of the Sacramento-based Association for Wedding Professionals International. "I haven't seen it totally yet."

Five months after Massachusetts became the first state to extend marriage to same-sex couples, the respected business magazine *Forbes* forecast that gay weddings could mean an additional $16.8 billion for the nation's $70-billion-a-year wedding industry. A wedding industry newsletter cited in the Williams Institute studies puts the average cost of a wedding in the United States today at $30,000.[3]

For its calculations, the Williams Institute used a more conservative figure of about $3,000 per wedding — assuming that out-of-state couples would be somewhat budget-strapped on their celebrations. But after adding in anticipated tourist spending, the institute predicted $111 million in added spending in Massachusetts from more than 30,000 out-of-state couples over the next three years. In California, the institute predicted that 51,000 California couples and 67,000 out-of-staters would spend $638.6 million.

Whatever the exact figure proves to be, gay marriage has been a definite boon for the lesbian couple who founded the Rainbow Wedding Network in 2002. Co-founder Cindy Sproul says she returned to her home state of North Carolina in August with a good-sized boost for the $4.5-million-a-year business after hosting

inequality. The legislature responded in April 2000 with a law creating the marriage-like "civil union" status for same-sex couples. The law took effect July 1, 2000, and by 2008 an estimated 1,485 same-sex civil unions had been registered in the state.

In Massachusetts, lawyers from the Boston-based Gay and Lesbian Advocates and Defenders filed suit in April 2001 on behalf of seven same-sex couples who had been together for periods ranging from three to 30 years. The trial judge rejected the suit the next year, but in November 2003 the Supreme Judicial Court of Massachusetts issued its epochal, 4-3 decision mandating legal recognition for same-sex couples. The ruling gave the state legislature

a 180-day deadline to comply. The first marriages were performed on May 17, 2004.

The victory in Massachusetts, however, proved costly for gay rights advocates by re-energizing opponents of gay marriage, who qualified ballot measures in 13 states in 2004 aimed at banning marriage for same-sex couples. Voters approved all 13: two in early voting in September and 11 more in November. With more than 20 million voters casting ballots, the measures triumphed overall by a better than 2-1 margin. Gay rights advocates had looked to Oregon as their only realistic chance of stemming the tide, but the gay marriage ban prevailed there with 57 percent of the vote.

four wedding expos in California in July.

Sproul and Markel both say gay weddings are similar to opposite-sex weddings. Most gay weddings are performed in places of worship and officiated by clergy, Sproul says, though same-sex couples are somewhat more likely to write their own vows than opposite-sex couples. Same-sex couples — typically older than opposite-sex couples — are also more likely to be paying for weddings themselves rather than their parents.

Sproul says most of the companies that advertise through the network are straight-owned, and the owners have no problems with serving gay ceremonies. Markel agrees. "A majority of the people in the business got into the business because they enjoy celebrations, and they enjoy helping people," he says.

Both Sproul and Markel point to some exceptions, however. "We've had some very hostile e-mails and death threats," says Sproul. Markel quotes one photographer as saying he would shoot a lesbian wedding but — using an epithet — questioned whether he would photograph two men getting married.[4]

The Williams Institute predicted that New York would be the major source of out-of-state couples for Massachusetts.

Same-sex wedding cake figurines will be in demand if the gay-wedding business grows as expected in California.

For California, the institute forecast influxes from New York, Texas, North Carolina and the nearby Pacific Coast and South western states. But among those who already traveled to California to tie the knot was Sproul and her partner Marianne Puechl, who got married on July 22 on a Malibu beach.

The newlyweds flew home the next day to North Carolina. The state enacted a statutory ban on recognizing same-sex marriages in 1996. "We hope [the marriage] will be recognized some day," Sproul says.

[1] See Brad Sears and M.V. Lee Badgett, "The Impact of Extending Marriage to Same-Sex Couples on the California Budget," Williams Institute, June 2008, www.law.ucla.edu/WilliamsInstitute/publications/EconImpactCAMarriage.pdf. The Massachusetts study is referenced in Keith B. Richburg, "A Milestone for Gays, A Boon for Massachusetts," *The Washington Post*, Sept. 3, 2008, p. A3. The Charles R. Williams Project on Sexual Orientation and the Law was established at UCLA in 2001 after a $2.5 million contribution from Williams, a gay businessman and philanthropist.

[2] Quoted in Richburg, *op. cit.*

[3] Aude Lagorce, "The Gay-Marriage Windfall: $16.8 Million," *Forbes*, April 5, 2004. See Sears and Badgett, *op. cit.*, p. 7.

[4] See My Thuan Tran, "Gay Weddings Not Quite a Piece of Cake," *Los Angeles Times*, June 21, 2008, p. B1.

The battles continued. Gay marriage advocates suffered two big disappointments in July 2006 when the highest state courts in New York and Washington both narrowly rejected suits seeking to require marriage equality for same-sex couples. The 4-2 ruling in New York and the 4-3 decision in Washington both said the issue was for state legislatures to decide. In the same month, the Georgia Supreme Court and the federal appeals court for Nebraska reinstated constitutional amendments banning same-sex marriages that lower courts had ruled invalid.

Meanwhile, however, gay rights supporters had scored legislative victories in some states. The California legislature passed a domestic partnership law in 2003 giving same-sex couples virtually all the rights of marriage. Connecticut passed a civil union law in 2005 — the first state to do so without a court mandate. By the end of 2007, same-sex couples had marriage-like status available in three other states: civil unions in New Jersey and New Hampshire and domestic partnerships in Oregon.

California Showdown

Supporters and opponents of legal recognition for same-sex couples have waged virtually nonstop battles against each other in California for nearly a decade. Opponents won the first round in 2000 with the voter-approved Proposition 22 defining marriage in opposite-sex terms.

Supporters won the next round in 2003 with enactment of a domestic partnership law granting all marriage rights allowed under state law. Two gay marriage bills were passed by the legislature but vetoed by Republican Gov. Arnold Schwarzenegger, while the landmark gay marriage case moved toward the state Supreme Court. Instead of settling the issue, the court's May 15 ruling only set the stage for another ballot-box showdown.

California voters' approval of the state Defense of Marriage Act in the March 7, 2000, election followed a fractious campaign that cost both sides together more than $16 million. The late state Sen. William "Pete" Knight, a Republican from Los Angeles County's high desert and father of an estranged gay son, drafted the 14-word initiative. Roman Catholic and Mormon churches did much of the legwork supporting the initiative, which carried with 61.4 percent of the vote. "California is not ready for a marriage between a man and a man," Knight told supporters on election night. Gay rights advocates vowed to regroup. "We're stronger and more galvanized than ever before," said Gwen Baldwin, executive director of the Los Angeles Gay & Lesbian Center.[20]

The setback came six months after California had become the first state to provide domestic partner status for same-sex couples without court intervention. The bill that Democratic Gov. Gray Davis signed into law in September 1999 was limited; it provided hospital visitation rights and, for public employees, health insurance coverage for partners. With Davis in office, the Democratic-controlled legislature significantly expanded the rights of domestic partners in 2001 and again two years later. The California Domestic Partner Rights and Responsibilities Act of 2003 essentially gave state-registered domestic partners all of the rights, benefits and duties of marital spouses recognized by state law. Davis signed the bill on Sept. 22, 2003, before a huge and appreciative crowd at San Francisco's GLBT center in the Castro district. Knight said the law circumvented Proposition 22.

Barely six weeks after signing the bill, Davis was recalled by California voters — who blamed him for a variety of economic problems — and replaced by Republican Schwarzenegger. The change left gay rights groups with a gay-friendly governor from a gay-unfriendly party. Twice — in 2005 and again in 2007 — the Democratic-controlled legislature passed same-sex marriage bills, each time by bare majorities on party-line votes. Schwarzenegger vetoed both bills, saying they amounted to end-runs around the 2000 ballot initiative. "The governor believes the matter should be determined not by legislative action — which would be unconstitutional — but by court decision or another vote of the people of our state," Schwarzenegger's press secretary, Margita Thompson, explained after the first veto in September 2005.[21]

In the meantime, Democratic San Francisco Mayor Newsom had tried to take matters into his own hands in February 2004 by directing the county clerk's office to issue marriage licenses to same-sex couples on request. About 4,000 such licenses were issued over the next month before the California Supreme Court ordered a halt. On Aug. 12, the court voided the same-sex marriages that had been performed. The city-county government then joined with half a dozen same-sex couples in seeking to invalidate Proposition 22 and win a court ruling to permit gay marriage.

The gay marriage plaintiffs won an initial ruling from a San Francisco Superior Court judge in March 2005, but a state appeals court reversed the decision by a split 2-1 vote in July 2006. The seven-justice California Supreme Court scheduled an extraordinary four hours of arguments in the case for March 4, 2008. Attorneys on the plaintiffs' side took some encouragement from some of the questions that Chief Justice George posed.

Still, neither side was completely prepared for the strongly written opinion that George authored for the 4-3 majority on May 15. Shannon Minter, legal director for the National Center for Lesbian Rights, who argued the case for the plaintiffs, called the decision "a powerful affirmation of love, family and commitment."

Liberty Counsel's Staver, one of the lawyers on the other side, said the court had "abandoned the rule of law and common sense."

CURRENT SITUATION
Gay Marriage Ban Trailing

Californians appear to be closely divided on whether to permit gay marriage, but a ballot measure to overturn the state Supreme Court decision granting marriage rights to same-sex couples is trailing in the most recent public opinion surveys. Both sides in the statewide contest, however, expect the election to be close and are planning to

Should the Defense of Marriage Act (DOMA) be repealed?

YES
Evan Wolfson
*Executive Director, Freedom to Marry;
author,* Why Marriage Matters:
America, Equality, and Gay People's
Right to Marry

Written for *CQ Researcher*, September 2008

Congress should repeal the federal anti-marriage law. Couples who are legally married by a state such as Massachusetts or California should not be treated as legal strangers or denied rights by the federal government.

DOMA says that no matter what the need or purpose for any given program, the government will categorically deny all federal protections and responsibilities to married couples it doesn't like, i.e., those who are gay. This is an intrusive departure from more than 200 years in which couples properly married under state law then qualified for the more than 1,138 federal benefits of marriage such as Social Security, tax treatment as a family unit, family unification under immigration law and access to a spouse's health coverage. Through DOMA, Congress for the first time ever gave itself the power to say who is married, a power that under the Constitution belongs to the states.

Even worse, by denying rights such as family leave, child support and survivor benefits to one set of married couples, DOMA penalizes not only the couples themselves but their children. If the government wants to promote strong families, it should treat all married couples, and their children, equally.

There are far better reasons to treat marriages with respect than there are for destabilizing them — for all couples, gay and non-gay alike. And there are many constitutional and legal reasons why DOMA should be repealed: It denies one group of families an important and meaningful safety net; it violates the right of equal protection; it upends the traditional ways in which our country has treated married couples; and it's a power-grab by the federal government at the expense of the states.

Most important, however, Congress should reverse DOMA's radical wrong turn because it leaves no one better off, but it harms some people severely.

When DOMA was stampeded into law back in 1996, no gay couples were married anywhere in the world; Congress was voting on a hypothetical. But today real-life married couples are cruelly affected by DOMA's double standard, and Americans better understand the unfairness of depriving these families of the federal rights and responsibilities that will help them protect their loved ones. Even conservative former Georgia Republican Rep. Bob Barr, the original sponsor, has acknowledged DOMA to be abusive and now calls for its repeal.

In the United States, we don't have second-class citizens, and we shouldn't have second-class marriages. Couples who have made a personal commitment in life deserve an equal commitment under the law.

NO
Peter Sprigg
*Vice President for Policy, Family
Research Council; author,* Outrage: How Gay
Activists and Liberal Judges Are Trashing
Democracy to Redefine Marriage

Written for *CQ Researcher*, September 2008

Cases asserting a "right" to same-sex marriage were heard in both Hawaii and Alaska in the early 1990s. Both states responded with constitutional amendments to forestall such judicial activism, but the cases triggered a national response as well. Fearing that if even one state legalized homosexual marriages, those marriages might then have to be recognized in every state and by the federal government, a bill was introduced in Congress to accomplish two things. First, it declared that for every purpose under federal law (such as taxation, Social Security, immigration and federal employee benefits), marriage would be defined only as the union of one man and one woman.

Second, it declared that no state would be required to recognize a same-sex marriage or other same-sex union that was legally contracted in another state. The Defense of Marriage Act (DOMA) passed both houses of Congress by large, bipartisan majorities and was signed into law by President Bill Clinton in 1996.

Many states followed with statewide DOMAs declaring homosexual marriage contrary to the public policy of that state. The 45 state DOMAs show a strong national consensus in favor of defining marriage as the union of one man and one woman.

Two state courts (Massachusetts and California) have succeeded in forcing homosexual marriage upon their unwilling populations. But the federal DOMA has been effective in preventing the imposition of this radical social experiment on the rest of the country. Unfortunately, some members of Congress (including Sen. Barack Obama, D-Ill.) are now proposing to repeal DOMA. This would open the door for federal taxpayers to subsidize homosexual relationships through domestic partner benefits and pave the way for lawsuits demanding recognition of same-sex unions from Massachusetts and California in every state.

Family Research Council opposes giving formal recognition or benefits to homosexual relationships under any circumstances, for numerous reasons. Even those who support same-sex marriage, however, should acknowledge that such a radical redefinition of our most fundamental social institution should not be imposed by the federal government in the face of a strong consensus among the states against it. Still less should we allow unelected judges from one or two states to force such a policy upon every other state.

The federal Defense of Marriage Act has served us well in the 12 years since its enactment, and it should not be tampered with.

spend about $20 million each on advertising and voter mobilization before the Nov. 4 balloting.

The two most recent polls find Proposition 8 trailing by 17 or 14 percentage points: 40 percent to 54 percent in a late August poll by the Public Policy Institute of California (PPIC); 38 percent to 55 percent in a September survey by the long-established Field Poll. The margins approximate the gap for Prop. 8 supporters recorded by the Field Poll in late May, shortly after the California Supreme Court's gay marriage ruling.[22]

A poll by the *Los Angeles Times* and the Los Angeles TV station KTLA one week earlier in May found 54 percent in favor of and 35 percent opposed to the ballot measure. At the time, Prop. 8 campaign officials described the Field Poll as "an outlier" and called the *Times*/KTLA poll a more accurate gauge of public opinion.[23]

After the most recent surveys, Prop. 8 campaign spokeswoman Jennifer Kerns blamed the gap on the ballot title that Attorney General Brown gave to the measure. Still, Kerns is predicting a "close" race that will turn on the level of enthusiasm among voters on both sides.

"There's a great deal of passion in support of this, which bodes well for Election Day," Kerns said. "People who feel most passionate are the people who go to the polls."[24]

The PPIC poll, in fact, found greater interest in the ballot measure among supporters than among opponents. More than half of those in favor of the measure — 57 percent — called the outcome "very important," compared to 44 percent of those opposed.

For their part, gay marriage supporters are also describing the race as close. "It's a dead heat," says Equality California Campaign Director Bankhead.

The PPIC poll found Californians evenly divided — 47 percent to 47 percent — on letting gay and lesbian couples marry. The earlier Field Poll had found a majority in favor: 54 percent to 39 percent. That was the first time in more than a decade of polling that a survey had found a majority in favor of same-sex marriage in the state.

With more than a month before the election, both campaigns are still in low gear. Political observers in the state report few visible signs of the campaign. The Yes on Prop. 8 campaign is reporting having raised around $17.8 million — much of it from religious or socially conservative groups from outside the state. Equality California has raised $12.4 million, also much of it from out of state.[25]

Despite the current edge in fund-raising, Prop. 8 supporters face some daunting obstacles in winning approval for the measure. In a state where Democrats hold an 11-percentage-point edge over Republicans in voter registration, the PPIC poll found Democrats opposing the measure by better than a 2-to-1 margin (66 percent to 29 percent). Republicans favor the measure — 60 percent to 34 percent. But the state's leading Republican, Schwarzenegger, opposes it.

Prop. 8 supporters also cannot rely on the kind of conservative religious constituencies that helped win passage of same-sex marriage bans in other states. "You don't have nearly the same presence of religious conservatives in California as you do in other states," says Jack Pitney, a political science professor at Claremont-McKenna College in Pomona. The Field Poll found Prop. 8 trailing — 44 percent to 48 percent — in inland counties, where religious conservatives are strongest.

To offset the disadvantages, Prop. 8 supporters are making special efforts to target Latino voters — the state's biggest ethnic minority and thought to be socially conservative. But the Public Policy Institute found Latinos opposed to the measure — 54 percent to 41 percent — by only a slightly smaller margin than whites (55 percent to 39 percent). PPIC President Mark Baldassare said the poll did not have a sufficient number of African- or Asian-American respondents for a valid measure of those groups.

Despite the wide margin, Baldassare says the campaign is "early" and the vote "hard to predict." Pitney, however, says Prop. 8 supporters are unlikely to overcome the gap. "It loses," he says. "The pattern in California ballot initiatives is that once a measure starts losing by a large margin in the polls, it almost never passes."

Gay marriage opponents are also lagging in one of the two other states with ballot measures to forestall recognition of same-sex unions. The measures — Amendment 2 in Florida and Proposition 102 in Arizona — would amend the states' constitutions to define marriage as a union of one man and one woman.

In Florida, the most recent poll shows 55 percent in favor of and 41 percent opposed to Amendment 2 — short of the 60 percent majority required for a constitutional amendment.[26]

In Arizona, Proposition 102, a measure submitted by the Republican leaders of the state Senate and House, would fortify a statutory gay marriage ban adopted in

1996. A broader measure that would have blocked any legal recognition for same-sex or unmarried straight couples failed, 48 percent to 52 percent, in 2006.[27]

Marriage Cases Waiting

Gay rights advocates hope — and gay marriage opponents worry — that the California Supreme Court's decision recognizing same-sex marriages could influence justices considering similar suits already pending in two other states: Connecticut and Iowa.

The California ruling is legally significant because it is the only state high court ruling to date holding that gays are a constitutionally protected class and that laws discriminating against gays are subject to "strict scrutiny" — the highest level of constitutional review. "It was just a matter of time before courts would acknowledge that," says Lambda Legal attorney Pizer.

Judges in the Connecticut and Iowa marriage cases had already signaled their interest in reconsidering the legal standard for judging laws adversely affecting gay men and lesbians. Three of the Connecticut Supreme Court's seven justices asked about treating gays as a specially protected class when the gay marriage case was argued in May 2007.[28] In Iowa, Polk County District Court Judge Robert Hanson applied strict scrutiny in striking down the state's gay marriage ban in a 63-page decision in August 2007.[29]

Gay marriage opponents acknowledge the California Supreme Court to be one of the most influential of state tribunals. "What happens in California is noticed not only around the country but around the world," says Brigham Young law Professor Wardle.

Lawyers and advocates on both sides are waiting impatiently for the Connecticut high court to rule on the case, *Kerrigan v. Department of Health*, after deliberating for well over a year. The plaintiffs — eight same-sex couples — filed their suit in state court in New Haven in September 2004. Connecticut enacted a civil union statute the following year.

In July 2006, Superior Court Judge Patty Jenkins Pittman ruled in a 25-page decision that in light of the legislature's "courageous and historic step," the plaintiffs had "failed to prove that they have suffered any legal harm that rises to constitutional magnitude." The couples appealed the ruling, represented by lawyers from the Boston-based Gay & Lesbian Advocates & Defenders.

The first marriage license in San Francisco went to lesbian activists Del Martin, left, and Phyllis Lyons, who had been together for more than 50 years. Martin, 87, died 10 weeks after San Francisco Mayor Gavin Newsom performed the ceremony on June 17.

The Connecticut Supreme Court includes four Republican-appointed justices and three appointed by Gov. Lowell P. Weicker Jr., a one-time Republican elected to the statehouse under auspices of his self-styled Connecticut Party. The Republican-appointed chief justice, Chase Rogers, recused herself from the marriage case because her husband's law firm filed a brief on behalf of a gay rights organization. A retired Democratic-appointed justice, David Borden, sat on the case in her place. Borden was one of the three justices to question lawyers during arguments about applying strict scrutiny to laws discriminating against homosexuals.

The Iowa case, *Varnum v. Brien*, began with a suit filed by six same-sex couples in 2005 after they were denied marriage licenses by the office of the then-Polk County recorder, Tim Brien, in Des Moines. Lawyers from Lambda Legal's regional office in Chicago represented the plaintiffs.

In his decision, Judge Hanson applied strict scrutiny in ruling that the gay marriage ban violated the state constitution's due process and equal-protection clauses. Hanson found that the county attorney's office had failed to prove that the state's ban would "promote procreation," "encourage child rearing by mothers and fathers," "promote stability for opposite-sex marriages," "conserve resources" or "promote heterosexual marriage."

Lawyers completed filing briefs with the Iowa Supreme Court in June; the court has yet to schedule arguments.

The seven justices on the court include two Republican and five Democratic appointees.

In a unique twist, one gay couple managed to get married the day after the ruling before Hanson agreed to the county attorney's motion to stay the decision pending appeal. Sean Fritz and Tim McQuillan, both in their early 20s, heard of the ruling on Aug. 30 and drove to Des Moines the next day to be wed. They found a judge who was willing to waive the normal three-day waiting period and got their marriage license at 10:45 a.m. Hanson issued his stay 45 minutes later.[30]

OUTLOOK

'It's About Marriage'

The Massachusetts Supreme Court's decision in 2003 granting marriage rights to same-sex couples produced a strong backlash. Public opinion polls registered a sharp drop in support for same-sex marriage, and gay marriage opponents won enactment of gay marriage bans in 13 states in the 2004 election cycle.

Five years later, no comparable backlash has emerged in the wake of the California Supreme Court's decision in favor of marriage equality — either nationally or in California itself. Nationwide surveys generally indicate a majority of Americans continue to oppose same-sex marriage, but surveys registered only a slight increase in opposition after the May 15 decision. And in August a poll by *Time* magazine actually found an even split between supporters and opponents: 47 percent to 47 percent.[31]

In addition, polls over the past five years indicate a stable majority of between 55 percent and 60 percent in favor of allowing either marriage or civil union status for same-sex couples. As one indication of the popular acceptance of some legal recognition of same-sex couples, supporters of California's Proposition 8 to overturn the state high court decision are arguing that the ruling was unnecessary. The state's domestic partnership law, they say, already gives same-sex couples all the rights of marriage.

With Prop. 8 trailing in the polls, gay marriage opponents are still professing optimism about the outcomes in California and the two other states — Arizona and Florida — with proposed constitutional amendments to ban marriage for same-sex couples. Liberty Counsel's Staver, who is helping to organize support for the measures

in Florida and California, envisions three victories to bring the total number of constitutional gay marriage bans to 30. That number, Staver says, is "getting very close to enough to ratify a federal constitutional amendment" to ban same-sex marriages nationwide.

However, the Federal Marriage Amendment, a proposed constitutional amendment that would redefine marriage as a union of one man and one woman, appears to face all but insurmountable obstacles at present. After failing in the Senate twice in 2004 and 2006, the amendment now seems all the more unlikely to win approval in a Democratic-controlled Congress. Public opinion polls over the past several years also show a majority of Americans opposed.

Gay marriage opponents may actually find themselves on the defensive in Congress if Democratic Sen. Barack Obama is elected president. Both Obama and the Democratic Party platform call for repealing the federal Defense of Marriage Act. Repeal would not be a foregone conclusion, however, since Congress passed the law in 1996 with overwhelming bipartisan majorities.

Whether or not DOMA is repealed, states will remain free to decide whether to allow marriage for same-sex couples for their own residents. The existing state constitutional bans mean that for the foreseeable future there will be a patchwork of state laws on the issue — barring the currently remote likelihood of a U.S. Supreme Court decision on the subject.

"We're going to be getting increasingly disparate treatment of same-sex unions," says Mark Strasser, a professor at Capital University Law School in Columbus, Ohio.

Gay marriage proponents think that time is on their side as more Americans come to see or know legally recognized same-sex couples in their communities or workplaces. "Most Americans don't have to fully love the idea of ending discrimination," Freedom to Marry's Wolfson adds. "They just have to realize that they can live with it. And, overall, it benefits the country."

Some opponents also expect eventual recognition for same-sex marriage. "I actually think that it will come within a generation," University of Pennsylvania Professor Wax said in the Federalist Society online debate.

Opponents continue, however, to mount their arguments against recognizing same-sex marriage. In a newly published volume, *What's the Harm?*, Brigham Young's Wardle organizes opposing essays around four perceived harms from legalizing same-sex marriage: to families and child rearing, to responsible sexual behavior and procreation, to the meaning of marriage and to "basic human freedoms," including religious liberty.[32]

"The issue is about marriage," says Wardle. "It's about protecting a basic social institution."

"It's about marriage," echoes Wolfson. "We're not looking to create something new. We're talking about allowing every American to exercise the same freedom to marry, to have the same responsibilities, the same respect as every other American."

NOTES

1. For photo coverage, see "George Takei Beams Up Marriage," *E News*, Sept. 15, 2008; "Ellen & Portia Share the Wedding-Day Love," *ibid.*, Sept. 10, 2008, www.eonline.com.

2. The decision is *Goodridge v. Massachusetts*, 798 N.E.2d 941 (Mass. 2003). For background, see Kenneth Jost, "Gay Marriage," *CQ Researcher*, Sept. 5, 2003, pp. 721-748.

3. The decision is *In re Marriage Cases*, 43 Cal. 4th 757 (2008). For next-day coverage, see Maura Dolan, "Gay Marriage Ban Overturned," *Los Angeles Times*, May 16, 2008, p. A1; Bob Egelko, "California Supreme Court, in 4-3 decision, strikes down law that bans marriage of same-sex couples," *San Francisco Chronicle*, May 16, 2008, p. A1.

4. See Gary J. Gates, M.V. Lee Badgett and Deborah Ho, "Marriage, Recognition and Dissolution by Same-Sex Couples in the U.S.," Williams Institute, July 2008, www.law.ucla.edu/williamsinstitute/publications/Couples%20 Marr%20Regis%20Diss.pdf.

5. Mark Baldassare, *et al.*, "Californians and Their Government: Statewide Survey," Public Policy Institute of California, August 2008, www.ppic.org/content/pubs/survey/S_808MBS.pdf; Field Poll, September 2008, www.field.com/fieldpoll.

6. See Charlie Frago, "Petitions to restrict adoption hit mark," *Arkansas Democrat-Gazette*, Aug. 26, 2008.

7. Jonathan Rauch, "Gay Marriage Is Good for America," *The Wall Street Journal*, June 21, 2008, p. A9. Rauch is a senior writer at *National Journal*, a guest scholar at the Brookings Institution and author of *Gay Marriage: Why It Is Good for Gays, Good for Straights, and Good for America* (2004).

8. See Jost, "Disputed Studies Give Gay Parents Good Marks," *op. cit.*, pp. 732-733.

9. "Same-Sex Marriage," Aug. 6, 2008, www.fed-soc.org/debates/dbtid.24/default.asp.

10. Quoted in Tracie Cone and Lisa Leff, "Gay marriage foes mobilize for ban in California," The Associated Press, Aug. 24, 2008.

11. The memo is posted on the Web site of the New York County Bar Association, www.nycbar.org/pdf/memo.pdf. For coverage, see Jeremy W. Peters, "New York Backs Same-Sex Unions From Elsewhere," *The New York Times*, May 29, 2008, p. A1.

12. The cases are *Miller-Jenkins v. Miller-Jenkins*, Virginia Supreme Court (June 6, 2008); *Finstuen v. Crutcher*, 496 F.3d 1139 (10th Cir. 2007). For coverage, see Frank Green, "Ruling comes in same-sex custody case," *Richmond Times-Dispatch*, June 7, 2008, p. A1; Robert E. Boczkiewicz, "Victory for gay adoptive parents," *The Oklahoman*, Aug. 8, 2008, p. 1A.

13. Background relies heavily on George Chauncey, *Why Marriage? The History Shaping Today's Debate Over Gay Equality* (paperback ed. 2005). See also William N. Eskridge Jr., *The Case for Same-Sex Marriage: From Sexual Liberty to Civilized Commitment* (1996); Allene Phy-Olsen, *Same-Sex Marriage* (2006), pp. 63-72.

14. Ina Russell (ed.), *Jeb and Dash: A Diary of Gay Life 1918-1945* (1993).

15. See David K. Johnson, *The Lavender Scare: The Cold War Persecution of Gays and Lesbians in the Federal Government* (2004).

16. See Chauncey, *op. cit.*, pp. 89-96.

17. *Ibid.*, pp. 96-104.

18. See *ibid.*, pp. 123-136; Jost, *op. cit.* (2003).

19. See "New Law Discourages Gay Marriages," *CQ Almanac 1996*.

20. See these stories by Jennifer Warren in the *Los Angeles Times*: "Ban on Gay Marriages Wins in All Regions but Bay Area," March 8, 2000, p. A23; "Gays Differ Sharply on Their Next Steps," March 9, 2000,

p. A3. The vote on the measure was 4,618,673 yes (61.4 percent) to 2,909,370 no (38.6 percent).

21. Quoted in Nancy Vogel and Jordan Rau, "Gov. Vetoes Same-Sex Marriage Bill," *Los Angeles Times*, Sept. 30, 2005, p. B3. The second veto was on Oct. 12, 2007.

22. See Denis C. Theriault, "Opposition growing to Prop. 8," *San Jose Mercury News*, Sept. 18, 2008; Jessica Garrison, "Bid to ban gay marriage trailing," *Los Angeles Times*, Aug. 28, 2008, p. B1.

23. See "California Poll: Same-Sex Marriage Is OK," The Associated Press, May 28, 2008.

24. Quoted in "Weak support for gay marriage ban," *Monterey County Herald*, Aug. 28, 2008.

25. See Dan Morain and Jessica Garrison, "Backers of California same-sex marriage ban are out-fundraising opponents," *Los Angeles Times*, Sept. 23, 2008; Aurelio Rojas, "Pitt's just another big giver in gay marriage showdown," *Sacramento Bee*, Sept. 23, 2008. Campaign finance filings can be found on the California secretary of state's Web site: http://cal-access.sos.ca.gov/Campaign/Measures/Detail.aspx?id=1302602&session=2007.

26. Mary Ellen Klas, "Same-sex marriage ban falling short," *The Miami Herald*, Sept. 9, 2008, p. B5.

27. See Amanda J. Crawford, "Consistent Message Doomed Prop. 107," *The Arizona Republic,* Nov. 9, 2006, p. 21.

28. The Connecticut case is *Kerrigan v. Department of Health*; for documents, see the Web site of Gay & Lesbian Advocates & Defenders: www.glad.org/marriage/Kerrigan-Mock/kerrigan_documents.html. For coverage, see Lynne Tuohy, "Supreme Court Justices Hear Arguments on Whether State Must Allow Marriage for Same-Sex Couples, Not Just Civil Unions," *Hartford Courant*, May 15, 2007, p. A1; Thomas B. Scheffey, "Following In California's Footsteps?" *Connecticut Law Tribune*, June 30, 2008, p. 1.

29. The Iowa case is *Varnum v. Brien*; for the lower court decision, see Freedom to Marry Web site: www.freedomtomarry.org/pdfs/iowa_ruling.pdf. For coverage, see Jeff Eckhoff and Jason Clayworth, "Judge: ban on gay marriage invalid," *Des Moines Register*, Aug. 31, 2007, p. 1A.

30. See Cara Hall, "Gay couple eyes court rulings," *Des Moines Register*, June 12, 2008, p. 1E.

31. For a compilation, see PollingReport.com, www.pollingreport.com/civil.htm, visited Sept. 19, 2008.

32. Lynn D. Wardle (ed.), *What's the Harm? Does Legalizing Same-Sex Marriage Really Harm, Individuals, Families or Society?* (2008).

BIBLIOGRAPHY

Books

Chauncey, George, *Why Marriage? The History Shaping Today's Debate Over Gay Equality, Basic Books,* **2004.**
A Yale University historian compactly links the increased visibility of the gay and lesbian community and changes in the institution of marriage to the gay rights movement's effort to attain marriage equality. Includes chapter notes.

Koppelman, Andrew, *Same Sex, Different States: When Same-Sex Marriages Cross State Lines, Yale University Press,* **2006.**
A professor at Northwestern University Law School argues that, based on established legal principles, courts should recognize marriages between same-sex couples that are recognized in their home state. Includes detailed notes.

Phy-Olsen, Allene, *Same-Sex Marriage, Greenwood Press,* **2006.**
A professor emeritus of English at Austin Peay State University provides a thorough and balanced account of the background and current debate over same-sex marriage. Includes chapter notes, 24-page annotated bibliography.

Rauch, Jonathan, *Gay Marriage: Why It Is Good for Gays, Good for Straights, and Good for America, Times Books,* **2004.**
A writer for *The Atlantic* and *National Journal* and guest scholar at the Brookings Institution argues that gay marriage would be beneficial by establishing marriage as the norm for gay men and lesbians, reversing the trend toward alternatives to marriage and making the country "better unified and truer to its ideals." The book bears this dedication: "For Michael. Marry me when we can."

Rimmerman, Craig A., and Clyde Wilcox, *The Politics of Same-Sex Marriage, University of Chicago Press,* **2007.**
Fourteen essays examine various aspects of the politics of same-sex marriage, including litigation and public opinion on the issue. Notes with each essay. Rimmerman is a professor of public policy studies and political science at Hobart and William Smith Colleges; Wilcox, a professor of government at Georgetown University.

Savage, Dan, *The Commitment: Love, Sex, Marriage, and My Family, Dutton,* **2005.**
An author and sex-advice columnist relates with humor and poignancy how his mother goaded him into marrying his boyfriend of 10 years — and how their young son picked out skull rings to symbolize the union.

Stanton, Glenn, and Dr. Bill Maier, *Marriage on Trial: The Case Against Same-Sex Marriage and Parenting, InterVarsity Press,* **2004.**
The authors, both with the anti-gay organization Focus on the Family, use a question-and-answer format to argue against recognizing same-sex marriage or encouraging child-rearing in same-sex households.

Wardle, Lynn D. (ed.), *What's the Harm? Does Legalizing Same-Sex Marriage Really Harm Individuals, Families or Society? University Press of America,* **2008.**
Twenty contributors on both sides of the issue debate the potential impact of further legalizing same-sex marriage. Each essay includes notes. Wardle is a professor at Brigham Young University School of Law.

Articles

Denizet-Lewis, Benoit, "Young Gay Rites," *The New York Times Magazine,* **April 8, 2008.**

The writer examines the impact of the Massachusetts ruling legalizing gay marriage through the lives of several same-sex couples in the state.

Reports and Studies

Gates, Gary J., M. V. Lee Badgett and Deborah Ho, "Marriage, Registration and Dissolution by Same-Sex Couples in the U.S.," *Williams Institute, UCLA School of Law,* **July 2008, www.law.ucla.edu/WilliamsInstitute/ publications/Couples%20Marr%20Regis%20Diss.pdf.**
The study provides data on same-sex couples who have taken advantage of legal recognition — marriage, civil union or domestic partnership — allowed in 10 states and the District of Columbia. Gates is the co-author with Jason Ost of *The Gay and Lesbian Atlas* (Urban Institute, 2004).

On the Web

Federalist Society, **"Same Sex Marriage," Aug. 6, 2008, www.fed-soc.org/debates/dbtid.24/default.asp.**
Four law professors — two on each side — debate marriage rights for same-sex couples in an online forum sponsored by the conservative lawyers' organization.

Vestal, Christine, "Calif. gay marriage ruling sparks new debate," *Stateline.org,* **June 12, 2008, www .stateline.org/live/printable/story?contentId=310206.**
The online state news service provides an overview of the same-sex marriage debate following the California Supreme Court ruling, along with a national map and state-by-state chart.

Note: For additional earlier titles, see bibliography in Kenneth Jost, "Gay Marriage," CQ Researcher, Sept. 5, 2003, p. 746.

For More Information

Alliance Defense Fund, 5100 N. 90th St., Scottsdale, AZ 85260; (800) 835-5233; www.alliancedefensefund.org. Legal alliance defending the right to speak and hear biblical beliefs.

Alliance for Marriage, P.O. Box 2490, Merrifield, VA 22116; (703) 934-1212; www.allianceformarriage.org. Research and education organization promoting traditional marriage.

Equality California, 2370 Market St., Suite 200, San Francisco, CA 94114; (415) 581-0005; www.eqca.org. Supports GLBT civil rights protections in California.

Family Research Council, 801 G St., N.W., Washington, DC 20001; (202) 393-2100; www.frc.org. Promotes traditional marriage in national policy debates.

Freedom to Marry, 116 W. 23rd St., Suite 500, New York, NY 10011; (212) 851-8418; www.freedomtomarry.org. Gay and non-gay partnership working to win marriage equality.

Gay and Lesbian Advocates and Defenders, 30 Winter St., Suite 800, Boston, MA 02108; (617) 426-1350; www.glad.org. Opposes discrimination based on sexual orientation, gender identity and HIV status.

Human Rights Campaign, 1640 Rhode Island Ave., N.W., Washington, DC 20036; (202) 628-4160; www.hrc.org. America's largest civil rights organization supporting GLBT equality.

Lambda Legal Defense and Education Fund, 3325 Wilshire Blvd., Suite 1300, Los Angeles, CA 90010; (213) 382-7600; www.lambdalegal.org. GLBT civil rights litigation group.

Liberty Counsel, P.O. Box 540774, Orlando, FL 32854; (800) 671-1776; www.lc.org. Nonprofit litigation group supporting traditional family values.

National Gay and Lesbian Task Force, 1325 Massachusetts Ave., N.W., Suite 600, Washington, DC 20005; (202) 393-5177; www.thetaskforce.org. Promotes equality for gays and lesbians.

Protect Marriage; www.protectmarriage.com. California group opposed to gay marriage initiatives in upcoming ballot.

Supporting researchers for more than 40 years

Research methods have always been at the core of SAGE's publishing program. Founder Sara Miller McCune published SAGE's first methods book, *Public Policy Evaluation*, in 1970. Soon after, she launched the *Quantitative Applications in the Social Sciences* series—affectionately known as the "little green books."

Always at the forefront of developing and supporting new approaches in methods, SAGE published early groundbreaking texts and journals in the fields of qualitative methods and evaluation.

Today, more than 40 years and two million little green books later, SAGE continues to push the boundaries with a growing list of more than 1,200 research methods books, journals, and reference works across the social, behavioral, and health sciences. Its imprints—Pine Forge Press, home of innovative textbooks in sociology, and Corwin, publisher of PreK–12 resources for teachers and administrators—broaden SAGE's range of offerings in methods. SAGE further extended its impact in 2008 when it acquired CQ Press and its best-selling and highly respected political science research methods list.

From qualitative, quantitative, and mixed methods to evaluation, SAGE is the essential resource for academics and practitioners looking for the latest methods by leading scholars.

For more information, visit **www.sagepub.com**.